The Which?
Wine Guide
2003

WHICH? BOOKS

Which? Books is the book publishing arm of Consumers' Association, which was set up in 1957 to improve the standards of goods and services available to the public. Everything Which? publishes aims to help consumers, by giving them the independent information they need to make informed decisions. These publications, known throughout Britain for their quality, integrity and impartiality, have been held in high regard for over four decades.

Independence does not come cheap; the guides carry no advertising; no wine merchant or producer can buy an entry in our wine guide; we also pay for the wine used in our tastings. This policy, and our practice of rigorously re-researching our guides for each edition, helps us to provide our readers with information of a standard and quality that cannot be surpassed.

ABOUT THE AUTHORS

Susan Keevil swapped her desk job, as editor of *Decanter* magazine, for a writing career roving the world's wine regions in 2000, and has since been exploring far and wide in the pursuit of new flavours and interesting wine estates. From a failed attempt to tour the vineyards of Uruguay on horseback (learning more about Montevideo hospitals than she intended) to a more successful vintage making Australian Shiraz in the Barossa Valley, a north-to-south tour of Argentina and an enlightening foray to the ancient wine lands of Greece, the last few years have seen plenty of vinous adventure. Back home, she writes about these excursions (and more) for *WINE*, *Decanter* and *Food & Travel* magazines, and has a column in the American magazine, the *Wine News*.

Susy Atkins is a freelance wine writer and broadcaster. Formerly the Deputy Editor of *WINE* magazine, she is now a regular contributor to *Eve*, *Which?* and *WINE* magazines and numerous other publications. She is the author of several wine books, including, with Dave Broom, the beginner's guide *Drink! Never Mind the Peanuts*, which won the Glenfiddich Drink Book of the Year 2002. Susy broadcasts regularly on TV and radio and was co-editor of *The Which? Wine Guide* from 1997 to 2000.

The Which? Wine Guide 2003

SUSAN KEEVIL with SUSY ATKINS

CONSUMERS' ASSOCIATION

The Which? Wine Guide voucher scheme

The Which? Wine Guide 2003 includes three £5 vouchers that readers can redeem against a £50 wine purchase. (Look for the **£5** symbol after the Tastings and talks information in the Top 100 section, and at the end of the entry in the Also Recommended section, to identify the participating merchants.) Only one voucher may be used against a wine purchase of £50 or more. Remember that your intention to use a voucher MUST be mentioned at the time of buying. The vouchers may not be used in conjunction with any other discount, offer or promotional scheme. Actual vouchers (not photocopies) must be presented. The vouchers will be valid from 1 October 2002 to 30 September 2003.

The Which? Wine Guide online

Internet users can find *The Which? Wine Guide* online at the Which? Online website www.which.net. To access the *Wine Guide* you need to be a member of Which? Online, but you can visit the website for details of how to take out a 30-day free trial to the service.

Which? Books are commissioned and researched by
Consumers' Association and published by
Which? Ltd, 2 Marylebone Road, London NW1 4DF
Email address: books@which.net

Distributed by The Penguin Group:
Penguin Books Ltd, 80 Strand, London WC2R 0RL

Copyright © 2002 Which? Ltd
This edition October 2002
First edition of *The Which? Wine Guide* published in 1981

Designer: Paul Saunders
Cover photograph: Price Watkins Design
Illustrations: Gill Buttons

British Library Cataloguing in Publication Data
A catalogue record for this book is available from the British Library

ISBN 0 85202 911 X

No part of this publication may be reproduced or transmitted in any form or by any means, electronically or mechanically, including photocopying, recording or any information storage or retrieval system without prior permission in writing from the publisher nor be otherwise circulated in any form of binding or cover other than that in which it is published and without a similar condition being imposed. This publication is not included under licences issued by the Copyright Agency.

For a full list of Which? books, please write to:
Which? Books, Castlemead, Gascoyne Way, Hertford X, SG14 1LH
or access our website at www.which.net

Editorial: Lynn Bresler, Alethea Doran, Vicky Fisher, Matt Godfrey,
Charlie Hardy, Barbara Toft
Production: Joanna Bregosz
Typeset by Saxon Graphics Ltd, Derby
Printed and bound in Great Britain by Biddles Ltd, Guildford and King's Lynn

CONTENTS

	Introduction	7
	The Which? Wine Guide Awards for 2003	12
Part I	**Features**	
	Welcome to the new New World	19
	The UK – wine-buying heaven?	25
Part II	**A–Z of wine-producing countries**	
	Argentina	33
	Australia	40
	Austria	58
	Bolivia	65
	Brazil	66
	Bulgaria	66
	Canada	67
	Chile	72
	China	81
	Croatia	81
	Cyprus	81
	Czech Republic	82
	England	83
	France	
	Alsace	87
	Bordeaux	94
	Burgundy	115
	Champagne	135
	Corsica	144
	Jura, Savoie, Bugey	145
	Languedoc-Roussillon	146
	The Loire	155
	Provence	162
	The Rhône Valley	164
	South-western France	176
	Georgia	180
	Germany	180
	Greece	194
	Hungary	197
	India	199

	Israel	200
	Italy	201
	Lebanon	221
	Mexico	222
	Moldova	222
	Morocco	223
	New Zealand	223
	Portugal	235
	Romania	250
	Slovakia	251
	Slovenia	251
	South Africa	252
	Spain	264
	Switzerland	282
	Tunisia	283
	Turkey	283
	United States of America	284
	Uruguay	306
	Zimbabwe	307
Part III	**Where to buy wine**	
	Explanation of symbols	310
	Criteria for inclusion	311
	A–Z of merchants	
	The Top 100	312
	Also recommended	424
Part IV	**More about wine**	
	Grape varieties	473
	The look, smell and taste of wine	490
	Storing wine	498
	Serving wine	500
	Food and wine matching	503
	Magazines and books	505
	Websites	508
	Glossary	515
	Index of merchants	521
	Index	524

INTRODUCTION

It's official – wine is more popular in the UK than it's ever been: in fact it is now an everyday event. It seems consumers no longer have any qualms about picking up a bottle for a Tuesday evening's quaffing. According to recent figures (World Drink Trends 2002), wine drinking has increased by 8.3 per cent (gaining on beer consumption, which has fallen by 3.6 per cent). Put another way, as of 2000, we now drink a mighty 16.9 litres of wine a head each year – an increase from 15.6 litres in 1999 and 14.7 litres in 1998. We're still some way off reaping the full benefits of the French Paradox, as across the Channel they drink a massive annual 56 litres a head to keep themselves healthy, but as the UK's steady increase amounts to approximately a litre more each year, something out there must be tempting us . . .

FRANCE VS 'THE BARBARIANS'

While we Brits are busy sampling their (and others') wares, French wine growers are being rapped over the knuckles. Their millennium might have started with a couple of good vintages (depending on the region) but Jacques Berthomeau, formerly of the French Ministry of Agriculture, has given them one or two more things to think about.

In the face of competition from Australia, California, Chile and South Africa (whom he referred to collectively as the 'Barbarian tribes'), French wine is seeing a drastic decline in its global market share. Berthomeau's view was that the French *vignerons* have been far too complacent, with the result that too much mediocre wine has been produced, particularly at basic level (a point raised in a past edition of this *Guide*). He consequently demanded that France not only produces new, strong brands to take on those of the New World, but also enforces its appellation (AC) system with more rigour (submitted vines will now be subject to inspection).

Working on the lowest-quality wines first, the real shock has come with the instruction that 13 million bottles of Beaujolais and four million hectolitres of *vin de table* from the Languedoc – wine that simply was not selling – be distilled to spirit and vinegar in order to drain excess wine from the market. This has caused both embarrassment and uproar among the affected growers (see Languedoc-Roussillon introduction, page 148). But the bottom line is with Berthomeau; as he said of the competition: 'the most successful Barbarian tribes were not necessarily the largest or the fiercest, but the most organised'. In short, it's time for the French to get their act together.

TOO MUCH OF THE SAME OLD THING?

Our conversations with UK wine merchants over the last year indicate that there's a swing away from New World wines back towards France, Spain and the rest of the Old World. ('Welcome to the new New World', page 19, explains why.) However, they also suggest there's an increasing demand from their customers for 'something different'. If you too are finding the ubiquity of Cabernet and Chardonnay a bit much, we would recommend trying out the Tempranillos, Bonardas and Tannats of Argentina. (Please do, because if you don't, they'll think you don't want them and plant Merlot instead.) The Italians have a much older wine industry, but are only just beginning to reassert the rights of Sagrantino, Vermentino, Verdicchio and a host of others. These grapes have been used in bulk-blended wines for years, their individual characters all but forgotten. A new group of insightful growers, however, is pulling them out of anonymity and revealing their true colours: if you see 'em, try 'em.

The most intrepid wine lovers of all will give Greece a chance, too. Greek grape varieties are even more venerable than Italian ones, but the growers seem to be less confident. However, some canny producers are blending, say, a little Aghiorghitiko with a little Merlot, for the feel of both in one mouthful – the familiarity of one; the spicy wildness of the other. Look out for Xinomavro, Limnio, Assyrtico and Moscophilero.

TREASURE THE BRITISH WINE MERCHANT

This year the wine merchants on the high street revealed themselves to be more treasured assets than many might suppose. After a decade or more of steadily increasing châteaux prices in Bordeaux, a group of stalwarts (Farr Vintners, Morris & Verdin, Berry Brothers and The Wine Society among them) grouped together and put their collective foot down. Enough was enough. They would pay no more money – and what's more, allow their customers to pay no more money – than the wines of the next vintage, 2001, deserved. Amazingly, the châteaux owners took heed, and, perhaps grudgingly, reduced their prices to a level commensurate with the quality of the year.

So don't underestimate the skill, knowledge and buying power of a good merchant. (As our feature ('The UK – Wine-buying heaven?') on page 25 highlights), the small independent merchant is crucially important. Nearly every one of the panel of experts we consulted about wine buying in the UK praised the breadth and individuality of the smaller merchants' ranges. A reliable, helpful merchant can broaden your vinous horizons beyond imagination, and many of them will charge you no more than the supermarkets for doing so.

THE TOP 100 AND A NEW AWARD

This year we've chosen our Top 100 wine merchants. Given the high number of quality retailers, deciding who to include in this listing has been very difficult (for details of our criteria see page 311). We urge you to take serious account also of the merchants in the 'Also recommended' section. These too have been through a stringent selection process – be assured that many have not made it into the *Guide* at all. Some of the 'Also recommended' merchants miss out on a Top 100 listing only for such a reason as focusing on the restaurant trade rather than the public.

Our new Specialist Award this year is for the Most Innovative Wine Merchant. Adventurousness in wine should always be encouraged – the wine-drinking public depends on merchants to bring the cutting-edge events in the vineyard home to the high street. We applaud the efforts and enthusiasm of those who strive to keep challenging our palates.

BUSINESS IN THE WINERY

This year it seems people have been complaining about the high level of alcohol in their wine, and winemakers have been listening. In America, Californian producers now regularly strip the alcohol out of their big Napa Cabernets by centrifuging them (if you ever hear about 'spinning cones', this refers to the device they use). On the other side of the Pacific, the Australians are on the verge of introducing special yeasts which produce less alcohol after fermentation. Which is the best method? Do we want our wines spun around, or made by artificial yeasts? Coping with the higher alcohol level might be preferable to the results of either of these.

But we'll have to wait and see how the wines react and what they taste like.

On the whole, there's been an improvement in the way wines are made. For a start, we can now 'see the grapes for the trees': use of oak barrels and oak staves to give that edge of vanilla has become a lot more subtle thanks to public dissatisfaction. The same goes for wines from regions such as the Rhône: immeasurable improvements have been made in the past few years and, as a result, the quality of the wines has shot up. This all goes to prove that if you don't like something you should say so.

PULL VERSUS TWIST

Nobody likes the taste of a corked wine, and hardly a year goes by without our recounting the latest battles to clean up the cork act. This year the news is not of corks but of metal screw-caps. In April 2002 Tesco launched 26 screw-capped wines (both red and white) in their stores, at prices ranging from £3.99 to £8.99. Screw-caps have proved not only to be airtight, but to keep the wine fresh over a number of years too – they're also easy to re-seal and easily recycle, and are no threat to the Iberian cork forests. Quite which aspect appeals to Tesco consumers most we can't say yet, but ten weeks after the launch, reported sales were of 1.5 million bottles across all categories, which would seem to suggest there'll be more such bottles in the future.

A NEW ERA

With the death earlier this year of Edmund Penning-Rowsell, who wrote the introduction to the very first *Which? Wine Guide* (1981) and was the wine correspondent for the *Financial Times*; and the passing of the esteemed wine critic Harry Waugh, we mourn the loss of two great men of claret (aged 88 and 97 respectively, their venerable age rather proving the point that wine is indeed good for you). Have we ceased to demand the complexity these men asked for in their wine? Are we content to drink wine today without asking for cellarability (the potential to mature with age)? Are we now led more by the marketing people than our own palates?

Fortunately we think the answer to the last three questions is no. While there are certainly those out there who are content to sip an unchallenging everyday wine, others are asking: Where does this Cabernet come from? What is Arneis? Why does this Sauvignon taste different from that one? The more questions the better – questions such as these keep the wine world on its toes as it has to come up with the answers.

On a lighter note, one story we quite like in this year's winemaking news is the arrival of diet Riesling. In conjunction with Weight Watchers, Reh Kendermann of Germany has launched a Mosel Riesling with a mere 80 calories a glass, as opposed to over 100 in most other dry whites. (In Weight Watcher terms, that's the equivalent of one point, as against 1.5.) We haven't tried this wine yet but hope it isn't too much of a lightweight!

Perhaps Weight Watchers Riesling will appeal to that apparently newly exciting category of wine consumers, young(ish) females. Our postbag has been full of reports this year on 'Chardonnay girl' and you can see for yourself the efforts of the industry to appeal to this sector. One new wine, in a bright pink bottle, no less, is actually called Babe Chardonnay. It's good to see new interest from a section of the population hitherto keener on alco-pops, but let's hope things don't get too naff here . . .

THE WHICH? WINE GUIDE AWARDS FOR 2003

In the last edition of *The Which? Wine Guide* we said that UK wine merchants were being more intrepid in sourcing their wines than ever before. This year, wine-lovers are being rewarded by the merchants' intrepidity, and can now discover new areas of the wine world to explore. We're particularly pleased to see an increasing number of New World wines being listed by region rather than country, for example – how refreshing it is to see Margaret River, Pemberton and Clare Valley singled out for their individual Australian flavours. Long may this continue! And better still to see the new-wave regions of the Mediterranean (France's Languedoc-Roussillon, Italy's Mezzogiorno) being included: here there really is new quality to be discovered. It's a pleasure to write about these quirkier wines and just as much a pleasure to drink them. Uniformity in wine should never be encouraged, but innovation (see our new award on page 15) should be. The award winners below clearly take these principles to heart, and their enthusiasm is immediately obvious in their lists and on their shelves.

Best Supermarket Award
Waitrose
For its adventurous and high-quality range Waitrose is a deserving winner, showing what can be achieved when buyers don't automatically resort to bringing in bulk-made brands.
Runners-up: Booths, Safeway, Tesco

Best High-Street Chain Award
Oddbins
We're delighted to see Oddbins being as innovative and off-beat as ever and still supporting the world's smaller, more interesting growers. No other high-street store comes close, although Majestic (more off than on the high street) is another chain whose range and consistent good service we admire.
Runner-up: Majestic Wine Warehouses

Best Mail-Order Merchant
Noel Young Wines
With 'several thousand' new lines per year, a stunning selection of New World wines, and many Old World wines to tempt too, we highly recommend getting hold of Noel Young's take-no-prisoners mail-order list.
Runners-up: John Armit Wines, Lay & Wheeler, Tanners Wines

Specialist Awards

Bordeaux Specialist Award
Corney & Barrow
Stockists of Bordeaux in every style, and every vintage (back to 1900), Corney & Barrow also offers a personal brokering service second to none.
Runners-up: Farr Vintners, Justerini & Brooks, Le Pont de la Tour

Burgundy Specialist Award
Haynes Hanson & Clark
A resourceful and uncompromising list, from a merchant who adheres to the most traditional of values. This is an impeccable range of growers covering all the finest *communes* and top vintages.
Runners-up: Domaine Direct, Lea & Sandeman, Howard Ripley

Rhône Specialist Award
Yapp Brothers
Robin Yapp has always had a passion for the Rhône and at no other time has this been more justified – quality in the region is so high. Years of experience still help in getting hold of the precious best.
Runners-up: Bibendum Fine Wine, Farr Vintners

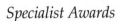

German Specialist Award
Justerini & Brooks
Justerini's German sales have increased by 50 per cent this year, and quality has rarely, if ever, been better. Unfortunately, few merchants appear to be showing as much confidence with these delicious wines.
Runners-up: Howard Ripley, Tanners Wines

Italian Specialist Award
Bennetts Fine Wines
Bennetts has a highly tempting, broadly sourced list, but it seems it cannot help but be more passionate about Italy than any other area. We in turn cannot help but admire merchants who follow their hearts.
Runners-up: D Byrne & Co, Valvona & Crolla

Spanish Specialist Award
D Byrne & Co
This spectacular Spanish range takes in both the classics and the new-wave choices from the exciting smaller regions such as Cigales, Toledo and Tarragona. As with everything at Byrne, quality is top-notch.
Runners-up: Direct Wine Shipments, Moreno Wine Merchants

New World Specialist Award
The Nobody Inn
The Which? Wine Guide picked this range not only for its fabulous allocations of top-quality Australian Shiraz and California Cabernet, but also for the carefully chosen smaller-estate wines that are so fascinating – and which so many other merchants miss. A worthy winner.
Runners-up: Oddbins, Philglas & Swiggot, Noel Young Wines

Fine Wine Specialist Award
Farr Vintners
Supplier of more of the world's most fabulous wines than any other merchant we know, but still retaining affordable, unusual options and its familiar, friendly approachability.
Runners-up: Berry Bros & Rudd, Bibendum Fine Wine, Justerini & Brooks

Organic Wine Specialist Award
Vintage Roots
An energetic, outgoing, colourful approach to organic wine that cannot be faulted – for range or for flavour. We were particularly impressed with the determined way in which Vintage Roots has sold organic wines into the supermarkets this year; this way consumers will see more of them than ever.
Runners-up: Lay & Wheeler, Vinceremos Wines & Spirits

New award

Most Innovative Merchant Award
The Winery
The Winery's determination to source the unusual
rather than the conventional – to expand vinous
horizons rather than settle with the same old bunch
of growers – makes it a deserving recipient of this
award. In this case it is the resourceful collection
of singular burgundies that particularly takes our
fancy, but the quality and individuality of the rest
of the range shows a compelling confidence and
'daring to be different'.
Runners-up: Philglas & Swiggot, Sommelier Wine
Company, Noel Young Wines

Regional Awards

LONDON
Berry Bros & Rudd
This merchant, in a perfect mix of the traditional
and the modern, betters the rest in the capital for
providing diversity, novelty and high class. And
it has a genuinely good website.
Runners-up: Justerini & Brooks, Lea & Sandeman,
Philglas & Swiggot

CENTRAL ENGLAND
Tanners Wines
One of the most widely sourced, high-quality
selections we know of: could be a winner in any part
of the country. In addition, the list is one of the best
presented and easy to use.
Runners-up: Bennetts, Nickolls & Perks

NORTH OF ENGLAND
D Byrne & Co
The rest of the north still hasn't caught up with
Byrne's marvellously extensive, eclectic range of
wines. And the value for money on offer here surely
cannot be bettered.
Runners-up: Martinez Fine Wine, Portland Wine
Company, Wright Wine Company

EAST OF ENGLAND
Lay & Wheeler
Combining a modern, yet at the same time highly traditional, approach to wine, with quality 'right to your door' service, Lay & Wheeler has successfully fended off the rest of East Anglia's fine wine merchants this year.
Runners-up: Adnams, T & W Wines, Noel Young Wines

SOUTH WEST OF ENGLAND
Great Western Wine Company
Going from strength to strength, this Bath-based merchant makes a point of sourcing directly from small suppliers and comes up with appealing bottles time after time.
Runners-up: The Nobody Inn, Christopher Piper Wines

NORTHERN IRELAND
Direct Wine Shipments
James Nicholson and Direct Wine always fight a hard battle to win this award, but again, it's the determination to make wine approachable and fun that really impresses us about DWS.
Runner-up: James Nicholson Wine Merchant

SCOTLAND
Villeneuve Wines
Scotland has several excellent merchants, but this year it was Villeneuve's dynamic range, both from the Old and New Worlds, that proved the most inspiring.
Runners-up: Raeburn Fine Wines, Valvona & Crolla

WALES
Ballantynes of Cowbridge
A high-class list, especially from France, Italy and the New World – Ballantynes wins again.
Runner-up: Terry Platt Wine Merchant

Part I
Features

WELCOME TO THE NEW NEW WORLD

A vinous revolution has been fermenting in the Mediterranean for quite a while now. Old, indigenous grape varieties, long taken for granted, are being recognised once again for the complex flavours they can give. We at the *Guide* have long suspected it was only a matter of time before some new and fascinating wines would start speaking up for themselves, on merchant and supermarket shelves in the UK – and that time has come.

For once we aren't talking about an up-and-coming region making direct copies of the New World gluggers either, say Chardonnay for Chardonnay – a wine from the same grape that just happens to be from somewhere else. These new-wave wine styles aren't necessarily going to be cheap and cheerful, but they have a quality and individuality not seen before from this part of the world – or from any other. In fact, the Mediterranean is now offering the new dimension in wine character that the southern hemisphere has been promising, but hasn't yet delivered.

OLD WORLD, NEW OUTLOOK

The change began with the latest generation of Mediterranean winemakers. These are the sons and daughters, nephews and nieces, who flew off to oenology college – at Roseworthy in Australia, Davis in California, or closer to home in Montpellier or Bordeaux – and came back brimming with modern ideas – about temperature-controlled fermentation, lees-stirring, micro-oxygenation, partial destemming and low-yield fruit. We shudder to think of the conversations that must have gone on ('are you seriously going to crush those Carignan grapes with your *feet*, Papa?'), but fortunately, whether they made their point through attrition or incredulity, the youngsters have been able to put their ideas into practice.

It also has to do with career-changers – publishers from Paris, perhaps, or (our favourite example) brothers-in-law Rémy Duchemin and Michel Jorcin, a video dealer and local goat-herd, who made their dream come true and set up a successful new vineyard business. There are also reformed *coopérateurs* who are fed up with the inexacting task of growing grapes for a co-operative and are now going it alone.

The wines made by these pioneers combine new-wave concentration (as found in the New World: remember, parts of the Med are just as warm) with classic Old World complexity and charm, plus all the individuality of their appellation. These are wines that catch the imagination every bit as much as Australian Chardonnays first did 20 years ago. This new generation of growers also have a strong awareness of their market: the young guns know what they're up against in the supermarkets, and they're learning to play the system to their advantage.

IT STARTED WITH SYRAH

Taking a long, hard look at their own wines *vis-à-vis* those from the Barossa Valley, Australia, or Casablanca, Chile, can't have been easy for the Old World winemakers. But a deciding factor in the Med-versus-New-World tussle must have been the Syrah/Shiraz story. If Syrah was treated with resignation in France, then, during the 1970s in Australia, Shiraz (same grape, different name) was actively criticised. Grown for flagon wines, pasted with the name 'Red Burgundy', it was responsible for little more than thirst-quenching gut-rot, and the Australians were on the brink of grubbing it all up. (Maybe some Gallic heads nodded knowingly at this stage.) But the 1980s saw a complete transformation Down Under: Shiraz (as we now know), with a little more care and attention in the vineyard and winery, turned out to be rich, spicy and marvellous – the darling of the wine world.

Perhaps this discovery struck a chord with the French, causing many to wonder if they could do better with Syrah as well. Having tasted the wines of the southern Rhône in 2002, it's evident that the answer was most definitely yes. Reformed ways in the winery and vineyard mean that Châteauneuf-du-Pape *et al* are now more concentrated than they have ever been, and the Syrah-based Côtes du Rhône Villages are the not-undeserving recipients of a steady stream of awards and constant praise.

In a natural continuation of what was happening in the Rhône, growers in the Languedoc must then have thought: 'Do we have grape stars in our midst too?' In the form of Carignan, Mourvèdre, Grenache and Cinsault, the answer, again, was yes. It's with these grapes that the real threat to the conventional New World lies.

FLAVOURS OF THE LANGUEDOC

We may think of Languedoc-Roussillon as a large 'plonk factory' skirting the shores of the Mediterranean – and, on the plains right next to the Med, that's exactly what it is. Further up in the foothills of the Cévennes and at the edge of the Massif Central, however, the picture is different. The wines from the higher ground tend to be beefy yet well-balanced, while those from the heathland below, known as the *garrigue*, are inclined to borrow its aromas and flavours (wild thyme, bay, rosemary, fennel, dill and olives).

Ever heard of L'En Lel, Lladoner Pelut, Bourboulenc, Picquepoul or Terret? No? Well, add these grape varieties to the picture, alongside Carignan and its chums, for their unconventional flavours such as fennel, aniseed, pear, roasted vegetables, smoky tar, mushrooms, game, hot-earth and salt-edged herbs.

There's much that is ancient about this landscape – vineyards dating from Roman times; estates the legacy of monasteries – but there's also a lot that's new. Carignan and Mourvèdre are two grapes (potential followers of Syrah) that have been plucked from obscurity and singled out for future fame. Judging from today's wines that fame would be justified. Rémy Duchemin and Michel Jorcin decided to take up some abandoned land near the Pic St-Loup a few years ago, brought in modern winemaking techniques and made a speciality out of Carignan to spectacular effect. Ditto Jean-Claude and Christophe Bousquet. Once members of the local *coopérative*, they escaped and struck out on their own, setting up new vineyards in the foothills, at Château Pech Redon. They now pursue wine styles that they long felt to be exciting but, when beholden to the co-op, never got the chance to explore. The Bousquets blend Carignan with the equally unfashionable Grenache and Cinsault. The wine that results, Les Cades, is full of savoury tar and mineral Carignan character plus juniper from the surrounding *garrigue*. These wines prove that, instead of brushing aside the local grapes to plant 'glamorous' Cabernet and Syrah, the varieties that have grown and evolved with the landscape over centuries have more to offer.

THE NEXT APPELLATIONS TO WATCH

Within the broad band called 'Coteaux du Languedoc', three small appellations to watch are Pic St-Loup, La Clape and Picpoul de Pinet. The 'Pic' in St-Loup is a sharp, tooth-like hill that juts out of the surrounding flat landscape. Its higher elevations offer vines a more temperate climate than the vineyards around it. Look out for bold, scented wines, based on big varieties Syrah and Mourvèdre.

La Clape is another hill, this time rising out of the Languedoc plains. Dry and craggy, its vines thrive on sea mists rather than rain, enough for white grapes to survive as well as red – floral Bourboulenc grapes as well as gutsy Grenache. These wines were fashionable in Roman times and are returning to vogue today.

Picpoul de Pinet is the appellation in which the white Piquepoul grape dominates (same flavour, different spelling). Again, highly fashionable with the Romans: expect from these wines a grapefruity bitterness and great acidity.

Into big appellation territory, wilder flavours are more defined. The wines of Faugères come from a geologically separate band of soil: they're rich, red, fleshy and rounded, characterised by blackberries and raspberries; Carignan dominates. Neighbouring St-Chinian's wines are steelier and more tannic – still with a layer of attractive rusticity; here Syrah, Mourvèdre and Grenache dominate. La Livinière, the new name for the top wines of the Minervois appellation, has distinctive *garrigue* and black-olive scents. Other appellation names to watch for are: Limoux, for softly sparkling wine; Corbières, for boisterous reds; and Costières de Nîmes, for chunky Rhône-like wines.

REDISCOVERING SOUTH-WEST FRANCE

A pace or two behind the Languedoc in terms of marketing it may be, but south-west France lays equal claim to the title 'New New World'. It has its own plethora of revived grape varieties and wilder flavours restored to grandeur. (Try the wines of Madiran, Jurançon, Cahors, Gaillac and Fronton, and you'll see what we mean.) But suffering the indignity of being called 'the other Bordeaux' (some of its wines are made from the same grapes) means that the region's efforts are being doubled and redoubled.

Where the south-west kicks in with greatest modernity is in the winery. For a while now the Australians and Californians have led the way with winemaking technology, but one of the latest techniques to hit the vats comes from local winemaker Patrick Ducournu. In order to tame his Madirans (made from the Tannat grape, and you'll know about this brute-in-a-glass if you've ever tasted the big reds from Uruguay) he's introduced a technique called micro-oxygenation. By carefully injecting a steady stream of oxygen into his vats or barrels, Patrick allows his wines to aerate and thus soften and mature a little earlier. This is a method now being used the world over (in the New World in particular, as it happens) to soften aggressive young reds. Makes a change for the Old World to teach the New; in terms of innovation, could this be the first sign of a change of leader?

DISCOVERING THE MEZZOGIORNO

If any Mediterranean region is truly acknowledged by the Californians *et al* as a serious threat to their 'New' status, it might very well be southern Italy – the Mezzogiorno, the heel and toe. After all, it was the Campanian wine Montevetrano which, out of nowhere, first gained 96 points from the American critic Robert Parker a few years back, and caused the wine world to turn its attention to the area.

In this case the grape involved was richly structured Aglianico (blended with Cabernet Sauvignon and Merlot), but there are plenty more claimants to fame. Reds Primitivo (similar to, and possibly the same grape as, California's fruity Zinfandel) and tangy Nero d'Avola from Sicily. The whites: appley Fiano, fulsome Greco di Tufo, historical Falanghina (thought to be related to Roman Falernian) and rounded, yet lemony Vermentino from Sicily.

But Italy highlights the problem of which way the Mediterranean should be heading. Right now there are many (too many) international wine consultants in the region helping these wines into the limelight, but they are also planting, alongside them, a great number of international varieties (Cabernet, Merlot, Chardonnay, etc.). Should the south capitalise on its generous climate and cheap land by producing wines from familiar varietals? Or should it instead focus on its own naturally diverse grape resources? We think the latter. This region isn't going to establish itself in the new New World by copying the old New World.

To pacify the 'give me something I feel comfortable with' crowd, one possible solution (advocated by 'flying' winemaker Kym Milne MW) would be to blend native and international varieties, so the wines benefit from the novelty of one, the familiarity of the other.

OTHER NEW SHORES

Such transformations are not restricted to Italy and France. Spain, focusing on its new-wave regions Toro, Somontano and Tarragona, has equally important new ventures to report – with new winemaking energy and 'refurbished' quality. Greece is in the same predicament as Italy: should it bombard the markets with its own (virtually unpronounceable) grape varieties, full-on, at 100 per cent of the blend? Or should it rein them in with a bit of Merlot, Cabernet, Sauvignon or Chardonnay, bringing familiarity on the palate and on the label? North Africa (Tunisia and Morocco mainly) is hitting the shelves with warm, spicy Carignan and Grenache wines. And Israel and Lebanon have similar stories to tell: again, new-energy winemaking is producing a fascinatingly concentrated set of wines,

23

stealing the thunder from Argentina and Uruguay and all the other southern hemisphere wine regions trying to make a start.

BUT CAN THEY REALLY TAKE ON AUSTRALIA?

We've been waiting patiently for some time now for the Australians to stop going on about the success of their big brands. Because they are the result of cross-regional blending and dumbing down to the lowest price possible, branded wines stifle individuality. What we really want to hear about instead are Australia's smaller regions and oddball grape varieties. So doesn't it make sense for Europe to keep one step ahead and stay true to its own natural diversity? The good news (perhaps) is that, according to the French ministry of agriculture, France (for a start) is ill-equipped to create strong brands – for four reasons. It has too restrictive an appellation system; it has a less scientific winemaking culture (less able to counter the affects of bad vintages); it's a co-operative-dominated industry; and the French wine trade is (restrictingly) dictated by social as much as business goals.

But there's no doubt that the Old World does need to acquire a bit more marketing savvy. Not so long ago, a southern French wine called Wild Pig Shiraz was launched, which sold like hot cakes. But when, for legal reasons, the name had to be changed to Wild Pig Syrah, there followed a disastrous slump. It appears that the wacky New World names are critical for supermarket sales at least. This is bad news for New France (*et al*), which has its own nomenclature to draw from, and another reason why we should break out of the narrow-minded supermarket culture.

AND SO ...

As the marketing people say, 'Premium and super-premium wine is what the Old World does best'. In which case the revolutionary new wines of the Mediterranean, many of which fall into these categories, are set to be winners. The New World might have brought us excitement with a flood of ripe single-grape wines over the last 20 years, but Mediterranean France and its neighbours – now that they have begun to parallel the dramatic quality improvements of the Rhône Valley – have bettered this game with a flourish. They're offering not only an amazing spectrum of new grapes (or rather, old grapes), but a barrow-load of new flavours too. It might be as old as the Romans but, figuratively, we think that makes the Mediterranean the New New World.

SUSAN KEEVIL

THE UK – WINE-BUYING HEAVEN?

It has become something of a cliché to bang on about how extensive the selection of wines is in the UK. To say, smugly, that we are lucky enough to live in the 'shop window' of the wine world. To proclaim that, because of our long mercantile history, we still have a wonderful marriage with the great wine-producing regions of Europe, while enjoying a passionate new affair with the best from Australia, California, Chile and so on.

But do we have a right to boast any more? Do wine lovers around the world still envy those of us living in the UK? Perhaps we are not critical enough – many believe that the choice available in our high-street shops, supermarkets and through our independents has actually become more narrow, more bland, packed with dull big brands and short on interesting, characterful fare.

The Which? Wine Guide asked a group of experts, some based in the UK, others overseas, for their views. As you will see, we stirred up some passions and elicited a wide range of responses. From these a few notable points emerge. First, how often our experts criticise the big brands and urge consumers to look beyond them to the more exciting wines of smaller producers; second, they digressed more than once to lament the high mark-ups in the restaurant sector that they feel are blighting wine buying in the UK; and finally, how almost all of them direct you towards the dynamic, smaller independent wine merchant to find the most interesting wines for sale in the UK. This is a point on which our experts and the *Guide*'s authors wholeheartedly agree. Our small independent merchants are something the UK can (and must) cherish. We list the very best of them in *Where to buy wine*. As another cliché goes: use them or lose them.

We put the question to our panel: is the UK still the most exciting place in the world to buy wine? This is what they told us.

Andrew Jefford is a regular broadcaster on food and drink for Radio 4. A former editor of The Which? Wine Guide, *his latest book* The New France *(Mitchell Beazley) is published in October 2002.*

'I'm sceptical. Everywhere I went when researching the book – but particularly in the south of France – I would discover inspiring smaller producers, people making genuinely brilliant wines at £6 or £7 which were twice as good as all the aspiring £19 New World wines in which our market is swimming. And then I'd discover the French producers were selling those wines to Switzerland, Belgium, Japan and the US – but not to Britain. No one from the UK had sought them out. Enterprising US importers are doing all the hard spade work and often provide financial help in the wine production.

'The UK wine trade has grown rather lazy and fat because New World wine brands are much easier to import and sell than wines from lots of small French grower-producers, with the endless headaches they present. Our new younger wine trade workers, therefore, are primarily brand managers and marketers. Perhaps they are excellent at those jobs but they aren't classic pith-helmeted, foraging wine merchants in the old sense. A few genuine explorers still exist but they are now small-scale independents such as Lea & Sandeman, La Vigneronne, Noel Young, Vine Trail, A & B Vintners. (See *Where to buy wine*.)

'Then there's the demise of the high street. Ten years ago we had both the Thresher group and Victoria Wine as separate companies, trying to outdo each other in buying excellence; we had Fuller's; we had JT Davies and other regional chains; Oddbins was going full throttle. Now? Fewer shops, fewer buyers, fewer alternatives. Those ranges which do exist are unerringly monopolised by brands, deals, multi-buys and discounts. The rise of "silly" wines (the Bastards, Tarts and so on), part of the prodigious "Stupid Britain" movement, privileges style over content. All the interesting and authentic stuff is squeezed off to the margins, small-scale mail-order merchants and surviving large regionals. It's there, but you have to hunt it down.'

Max Allen is a British-born wine writer who moved to Australia ten years ago after a stint in the UK wine trade. He writes a column for The Weekend Australian *newspaper. His latest book is* Sniff, Swirl and Slurp *(Mitchell Beazley, 2002).*

'Yes, the UK is still regarded as the shop window of the wine world but it no longer has the monopoly on that position. Which, in my opinion, is great – just as I see a proliferation of new domestic brands exploding on to the local shelves here in Australia, so I also see and welcome an increase in the variety of imported wines.

'I'm envious of the range available in the UK, but not of its prices. The selection in Britain is not noticeably better or worse since I left ten years ago but with obvious differences in price. If I brought a few bottles home from the UK, it would have to be: Spanish wine – both the traditional wines such as great Rioja, and the up-and-comers like reds from the Toro region; Portugal (new reds, virtually unavailable here); southern French; American (both north and south); and some carefully chosen South Africans.

'I struggle to find great Australian wines from smaller producers when I'm in the UK. I've found a small treasure trove (Oddbins Fine Wine in Notting Hill Gate) but it isn't easy. Perhaps I'm spoiled in Melbourne. Overall there's an increasingly boring selection in the UK, especially in supermarkets and restaurants. With some notable exceptions (and those had huge mark-ups), I am appalled by the pathetic, generic, middle-of-the-road offerings among Aussie wines in most of the UK restaurants at the moment. It's a different culture – in Australia the on-trade is often considered more important than retail as it's seen as the best promotion you can get.'

Tim Atkin MW is editorial director of Harpers Wine & Spirit Weekly *and wine correspondent of* The Observer. *He is based in London but has spent some time living in both France and Spain.*

'You only have to live in France and attempt to buy decent wine in the supermarkets there to realise how lucky we are in the UK. At the lower- and middle-price brackets, we are still the best. In Paris, if you are seriously interested in wine, you tend to ignore the shops and drive off to, say, Chablis at the weekend.

'When it comes to premium wines, the UK is less impressive. While I was in Manhattan recently I came across a great wine shop which appeared to stock every single top wine from around the world, plus other, less famous labels which the owners had sourced themselves. So no, we are not the only shop window of the wine world any more. We do have places like that, fine independent merchants such as La Vigneronne, Lea & Sandeman, Valvona & Crolla (see *Where to buy wine*), but we can be far too smug and self-congratulatory about our wine trade. In France, Italy and Austria you'll find some of the best producers saying they don't like selling to this market because of the way we drive the prices down.

'While our supermarkets are generally good – the overall quality of cheap wine has improved a lot – they have ranges driven by big brands, supplied by companies which put a lot of money in their pockets. I'm not entirely anti-big brands – we need decent entry-level wine – but there does seem to be an unholy alliance between the chains (supermarkets and on the high street) and the brands and it is worrying to think that smaller producers will be priced out of the market. Very few buyers for these chains can afford to take a punt on unusual wines these days – the only exceptions are Waitrose and Oddbins, though since the latter's purchase by a French company, I wonder if the more unusual wines will survive. With global consolidation in every area of the trade, the glorious diversity of the UK retailers is under threat.'

Michael Paul is managing director of Western Wines, a wine importer based in Telford. He has worked in the UK trade for over 25 years selling major brands from Germany, Australia, South Africa and Chile among others.

'If someone from Mars landed and compared the UK wine shops with those from other countries, we would stand up pretty well. Because we are not a major wine producer and because as a nation we are happy to import, we have no axe to grind. We still have a much broader range than anywhere else, although Scandinavia and Holland can compete too. Our large outlets are very competitive, which is why you see supermarket chains selling wines from Uruguay, Moldova or wherever. They want the points of difference.

'But neither the UK consumer nor the UK trade likes spending much on wine. The US and the Far East do. As a result, we have decent cheap wines and we tend to think they are fools overseas if they are prepared to spend a lot of money on cult wines. But then again we sometimes miss out ourselves.

'Retailers' ranges are less broad than they were but it's not as bad as it seems. The wines on promotion are always the same ones and often the big brands. But chances are that if the customer wants to find something esoteric, he or she will still find it in there. The perception is that the range has been reduced but it hasn't by much. And if it ever reduces too much, it is likely to move back in the opposite direction – the retailers want those points of difference and would hate to think they are just stocking the same as everyone else. So they work to adjust the balance.'

Lucy Warner is a sales and marketing consultant to the South African wine industry and lives in Cape Town. She moved there from the UK four years ago after working as a buyer with the Thresher chain.

'Yes, Britain is still the shop window of the wine world. Nowhere else offers such diverse prices/grape varieties/countries. The best thing about the UK wine trade is the people – there are still old-fashioned, pin-striped guys having four-hour lunches, then there are hungry, young marketers driving innovation and trends, and lots of simply great buyers who love their jobs and invest their time talking to winemakers, making new blends and selling boatloads of wine.

'On the negative side, the high taxes are criminal. What is also so sad is to see UK retailers constantly driving down the prices. This so often cripples a wine producer and ruins a country's ability to raise its profile and invest in better wines. It sometimes seems to be "take, take, take" and only the most conscientious retailers and wine buyers take the time to give back to the industry.

'Naturally I love the choice of South African wine I have on my doorstep but I can't buy wine on a Sunday. Moreover, there are not enough good retailers here in the Cape. To get the great stuff you really have to go to the individual farms. There the prices have to be the best thing about the wine purchases I make. Also, imagine visiting a producer and tasting through the range before you buy – heaven on earth!'

Richard Ehrlich is the wine correspondent for the Independent on Sunday. *Now based in London, he was born and bred in New York, and he visits the USA regularly.*

'I know that much is made of the decline of the UK wine market, but I don't see it that way. Offerings from the supermarkets (apart from Waitrose and Booths) are indeed dominated by brands and low-voltage examples of the appellations, but they make it easier than ever to find respectable wine at low price points. This is in marked contrast to the USA, where it is exceedingly difficult to find anything interesting for less than $10 (around £6). If you spend £6 on a bottle here, you can drink pretty damned well – especially if you do your buying from the independent merchants. From these, the choice is extravagantly rich. And it's easy to buy by mail order, which effectively makes the whole country your stamping ground.

'The problems in the UK wine trade lie largely in consumers' expectations. They want to buy wine at the same place they buy washing powder. They want it to be cheap. They want to recognise the name on the label. And, they want it to be Chardonnay or Merlot. If they don't give themselves the chance to discover new things, their enjoyment of wine will lack the element of excitement and adventure. And that would be a terrible shame.'

Philip Reedman sources the Australian and New Zealand wines for Tesco. He worked in the UK wine trade before heading Down Under four years ago. He now lives near Adelaide.

'The UK is still a very exciting place to buy wine – certainly compared with Australia and New Zealand. UK specialists, high streets and supermarkets offer their customers a diverse and stimulating range. Australia in this respect virtually defines the word "parochial" – you have to go to a specialist fine wine merchant to get anything out of the ordinary. Getting "imports" which don't taste cooked [spoiled in transit] can be a challenge too. New Zealand is a little better (interestingly, a great place to buy vintage port) but for sheer range and quality it's hard to beat the UK. Want to buy your wine along with your food? Not possible in Australia, and only recently has New Zealand started stocking wine in supermarkets. UK consumers are very open to new wines, new places, new grape varieties, even new packaging and presentation, so it's a very vibrant, competitive market.

'We do have some advantages here. I love the fact that a new winery opens every day in Oz, so you turn your back and another label appears on the shelves. That can be very stimulating, especially if you go to a bottle shop [off-licence] where they take a bit of interest in what they're buying. Similarly, visiting a wine region is a voyage of discovery – buying at the cellar door isn't always the cheapest option, but for new small wineries it is usually the best way. And I usually duck into Penfolds' cellar door when I'm visiting, because it's amazing what you find that doesn't make it to retail or export.

'I suspect it is now important for some winemakers to be seen to be making it in the USA rather than the UK, at least at the "romantic" end of the market. The remaining 99 per cent of the market certainly looks to the UK which they recognise leads the way in sales.

'The worst thing about buying in Britain is the mark-up in restaurants. I can live with paying over a quid in tax on wine I buy to drink at home, but the mark-ups in some restaurants exceed what is reasonable. But overall, I do miss the range you get back home. I've drunk most of the European wines I brought over when we moved, and replacing them is difficult and expensive. I always bring a few bottles back when I visit the UK.'

SUSY ATKINS

Part II
A–Z of wine-producing countries

ARGENTINA

As we write, Argentina is on the brink of financial calamity: the banks are shut; the country has reached an impasse with the IMF. It needs to come up with a plan, quickly, to restore its economy and pay off its debt – a plan that will suit its banks, its people, its politicians and the IMF itself. Until a suitable solution is found, and implemented, the system of bargaining chitties and bartering will remain, and the livelihood of its people will be threatened.

This, of course, affects the wine industry. Precious little domestic money is now being spent either on general consumption or on the half-finished wineries we optimistically hoped to report on this year. The latter now look unlikely candidates for completion. To generate capital, Argentina will have to rely more heavily on outside funding, and on its export market, than ever before.

The culture of nurturing export markets is one thing that *is* thriving in Argentina, but not in a good way. Almost every grower we have spoken to recently has been orientating his or her range to the British supermarkets (or similar US outlets). Their £3.99 and £4.99 wines were the pride of their portfolio: 'Do you think the UK market will like them?' was a constant refrain. Last year we were worried about the supply of decent Argentinian wine drying up, and of all the possible routes for Argentinian wine to take, that of following the bland, neutral, Chilean style was the most dangerous. Well, if the Argentinians pursue their supermarket goals with any more fervour than they are doing now, they will find themselves so far down the blandness path, they won't be able to turn back.

But we do actually like the wines: Argentina – above almost any other New World country – has the most admirable, different and intriguing red grape varieties. There are weird and wonderful treasures, in the form of forgotten vines such as Primitivo, Bonarda and Corvina from Italy; Mourvèdre from France; Touriga Nacional from Portugal; all inherited from this country's long-established European connections. All these vines, with enough time in this ground, give wines of immense character and complexity, with that addition of enticing ripeness gained from sunny New World soils. Many of these could, and should, make it to our supermarket shelves if growers would give up their preoccupation with the 'Australian model', and desist from churning out yet more Cabernet and Chardonnay. In short, Argentinian wine growers do still have options – they should be asking less 'What do they want?', and more 'What can we do well?', and show a little more confidence in the above-mentioned varieties, plus Malbec, Merlot and some of the very fine Syrahs that are emerging from the top vineyard sites in Mendoza's sub-regions Tupungato and Lujan de Cujo, and in Cafayate and Rio Negro.

Less, on the other hand, should be made of Argentinian Cabernet. Almost every grower has an example, and, due to the global prestige of this grape, it is almost always placed at the top of the range. The samples we've tasted recently, however, have nearly all been dusty, fatigued, brown-looking wines lacking in any varietal richness, even lacking concentration. So beware: this otherwise reliable grape is proving little short of disastrous on this side of the Andes (Uruguay excepted), probably because it doesn't like 'getting its feet wet'. Over-irrigation is likely the problem. As we mentioned last year, in Argentina's predominantly desert-like climes water is a very precious commoditiy, and therefore the flooding of Andean snow-melt into the vineyards is being done with more enthusiasm than it should be. The best growers are using more controlled drip-irrigation systems.

More energy should also be put into Argentina's white wines. At the moment they make up around 15–20 per cent of production and have definite 'also-ran' status. To be fair, regions such as Mendoza are literally too hot to grow fine white grapes, but consumers should be aware of this, and look out for Torrontés, Sauvignon and Chardonnay from up in the Andean foothills (Salta, Tupungato) instead. The only trouble is there aren't many of them. Winemakers need to shake their ideas up where whites are concerned and start thinking 'altitude' – temperatures are cooler in the hills and grapes planted there have far better white-wine flavours.

The one good thing that has come out of the economic troubles is Argentina's increased competitiveness on export markets. Devaluation has reduced wine prices considerably and there should now be more and more wines to choose from in the UK. If, and we stress if, the Argentinians do break out of their 'sheep' mentality and learn to develop their own talents and their own grapes, then they have the potential to leave the Chileans and Australians way behind. They would (and ought to be) laughing.

Red wines – grape varieties

Malbec
This variety, which struggles to excite in south-west France, is the one the Argentinians, rightly, rate the highest. Malbec comes in all guises from simple and juicy to full-bodied, complex and ageworthy – the price usually tells you which to expect. A slightly perfumed blackberry flavour pervades the wines, with the best,

often with French oak in attendance, adding characteristics of damson, black cherry, liquorice and chocolate. Mature Malbec is the ideal foil to a plate-swamping Argentinian steak.

Syrah and Merlot
Over the last few years we've pegged Cabernet Sauvignon as Argentina's second-best red grape. But after some doubts we've now all but given up hope of this variety achieving anything great in this country (see above). Syrah is doing a far better job, as is Merlot. Argentina makes Syrahs that hint at the Australian style but which are invariably a little more serious, with added complexity. Mendoza is the perfect region for this grape and, as Syrah hasn't yet become a supermarket money-spinner, there's no sign yet of over-excited, over-stretched winemaking; yields are still kept low, and the output concentrated and firm. Merlot appears to be performing equally well, with smooth, intense, black-fruited results: these wines are well made, well concentrated and certainly more interesting than those from Chile.

Others
Thanks to the legacy of settlers from Europe, Argentina has a broad range of red grape varieties. Among these are Cabernet, Malbec, Merlot and Syrah from France; Tempranillo and Garnacha from Spain; and Nebbiolo, Refosco, Sangiovese, Bonarda and Barbera from Italy. Mature vineyards of all these grapes exist, but – Cabernet, Malbec and Merlot apart – growers have yet to fully realise what potentially fascinating resources they have at their fingertips. We've tasted some delicious berryish Bonarda, chunky Tempranillo and some tangy Sangiovese, and feel that many people would gladly exchange an everyday Cabernet for something more interesting such as these. The wines certainly prove these grapes are well-suited to this 'pre-Andean' mountain *terroir*. If you're a New World fan but bored with Chilean Merlot or ubiquitous Australian Shiraz, we highly recommend seeking out some of these less usual 'European' grapes.

White wines – grape varieties

Chardonnay
Several good examples exist, but great wines are thin on the ground. Even the finest speak of winemaking processes (usually oak and lees related) rather than of anything uniquely Argentinian. Chardonnay (sometimes with Pinot Noir) appears in some sparklers, but with the exception of Bodegas Chandon's soft creamy wines, few of these are exported.

Torrontés

This peachy, aromatic grape is a little like a spicy Viognier. It's capable of producing some of Argentina's most distinctive wines, but sadly, many producers overcrop it and make something which is perky but seldom compelling. Head up to high-altitude Salta for the crisp, refreshing best. Drink when it's young.

Others

Experimentation continues apace, throughout the country, so you'll find Viognier, Semillon, Sauvignon Blanc, Pinot Gris, Chenin Blanc, Riesling and several other varieties. The greatest potential for any of these is in cooler regions such as Salta, Tupungato or San Rafael but, as yet, only Salta yields anything of true quality.

The regions

More than 70 per cent of Argentina's wine comes from Mendoza – Mendoza province that is, not Mendoza City, which is its capital. Within the province there is a wide variety of climates: as you travel towards the ever-present Andes, the higher and cooler it becomes – although all districts are basically desert, and depend on irrigation water in the form of snow-melt from the Andes for their survival.

Tupungato is the highest, coolest area of Mendoza, and is gaining a reputation for Chardonnay, Viognier and well-balanced reds. Most of the highly rated districts for Malbec lie to the west of Mendoza City, among them Luján de Cuyo, Maipú and Guaymallén. If the lower-altitude vineyards to the east are sometimes considered inferior, this is perhaps more a reflection of the poor standard of the vineyards there than of the region itself. Three hours' drive to the north of Mendoza City, but still within the same province, is San Rafael. Despite being rather hail-prone, this area is turning out wines in a mid-way style, with a little more texture and richness than Tupungato's, yet with more elegance than is found in the rest of Mendoza – reds receiving somewhat more acclaim than whites in this *Guide*.

The regions of Salta and La Rioja lie to the north of Mendoza. North generally means warmer in South America, but the higher altitude, especially in Salta, means that reds and whites with good, tangy, natural acidity can be produced. In fact, Salta is generating so much excitement that suitable flat areas of the Andean foothills are being dynamited to make way for new vineyards. Cafayate is a Salta sub-region at a lofty 1,700m with a growing reputation for fine Torrontés, but by no means concentrating exclusively on this grape. La Rioja, on the other hand, is a land of snakes and scorpions, but its desert environs turn out surprisingly fine wines, both red and white, some of which are produced under strict organic guidelines.

To the south of Mendoza is the cool Rio Negro region of Patagonia, which is competing with Cafayate to cause the biggest stir. Its chalky soils (as in Champagne) are even attracting the attentions of fizz producers. This is apple-orchard territory, prone to high winds and devastating hail, its tiny vineyards surrounded by poplar trees for protection, but fashionable growers are all investing here to produce decent wines against the odds. With intuitive winemaking and less-zealous flood irrigation, as with Argentina's other regions, there is potential here for fine wines.

Pick of the producers

La Agricola Large, cannily export-minded and constantly experimenting winery (now testing Primitivo, Corvina, Pinot Blanc and other grapes to good effect) owned by the Zuccardi family, turning out good-value, tasty wines under the Santa Julia and Pacajuan Peak labels. The Familia Zuccardi Q range, including excellent Malbec and Tempranillo, is a step up; the Syrah is also delicious. The newer Terra Organica range is satisfyingly ripe and smooth.

Alta Vista Traditional old winery revamped with the benefit of Michel Rolland's Bordeaux expertise. Watch for mouth-filling Malbecs and black-strap, monster wine Alto.

Bodegas Balbi Allied Domecq-owned operation based in San Rafael, but sourcing fruit from throughout Mendoza. Syrah rosé is delightful, whites are improving, but reds, topped by fine blend Barbaro, ageworthy Syrah and fruity Malbec, are the pick.

Susanna Balbo Roving consultant winemaker now with her own range of superbly made reds. Modern in style, hefty, but deliciously complex too.

Bianchi The basic Elsa range is acceptable, but the high-end reds, especially the Familia Bianchi Cabernet/Merlot/Malbec blend, are first class. Although excellent work in the vineyards, needs more focus in the winery.

Luigi Bosca From the 1998 vintage, the slightly tired wines of the past have given way to a much more impressive range of both reds and whites. Look out for the stunning Viña Alicia reds (especially good Petit Verdot and Nebbiolo) plus delicious Malbec, Merlot and Syrah, made by a member of the same family.

Humberto Canale Rio Negro pioneer, one-time biscuit-producer, now showing well with Malbec, Merlot, Semillon and Sauvignon in trendy northern Patagonia. New-generation energy sometimes marred by less-than-exciting winemaking efforts.

Catena Dynamic producer showing quality with its top- and bottom-end wines. Has recently launched a joint venture with the Bordeaux Rothschilds, and created a suitably stylish 'Mayan temple' winery to match. The range runs in ascending order from good-value Alamos Ridge and Argento, through Catena, to high-class (and high-price) Catena Alta, then top-of-the-tree Nicolas Catena Zapata (if you taste some, tell us, because we weren't allowed to try any). The usual criticism that these are perhaps international rather than Argentinian wines still holds true, and we don't like the 'soupy' boiled feel of some of the mid-range reds. Catena also owns a variety of other labels, and vineyards in northern Patagonia.

Bodegas Colomé The spicy Cabernet/Malbec blend is one of the best Salta reds we know – more like a Châteauneuf than a Bordeaux wine.

Etchart Owned by Pernod-Ricard, with vineyards in both Mendoza and Salta, its wines all come highly recommended for their individuality and regional expression. Cafayate Torrontés is perhaps the most superior example around, Tannat, Merlot and Syrah are all excellent, and Arnaldo B Etchart Malbec/Cabernet blend outstanding.

Fabre Montmayou/Domaine Vistalba French-owned winery using the expertise of the famed Bordeaux consultant Michel Rolland to make high-quality, good-value reds and whites (Malbec and Chardonnay). Also produces the excellent Infinitus wines from cool Rio Negro (look out for the Patagonia duck on the label of the Chardonnay/Sauvignon white blend and luscious Merlot).

Finca El Retiro Mendoza estate, which until recently benefited from the expertise of Alberto Antonini. Lovely rich reds, especially the Tempranillo, and possibly the best of all the Argentinian Chardonnays – but will quality last?

Finca Flichman Spicy Syrah, ripe Malbec Reserve and big, red blend Dedicado are the most admirable of a large set of wines.

Finca La Anita Move over Australia. This Mendoza *bodega* makes superb Syrah, both straight and in a blend with Malbec. Fine, if expensive, Merlot too.

Bodegas Lurton Best of the flying winemaker projects in Argentina, with a spanking new winery making consistently smashing reds, especially the Gran Lurton Cabernet and Piedra Negra ('black storm') Malbec, and tangy Tupungato whites. Also responsible for the Corazón label.

Navarro Correas Much improved with more sensitive use of oak; good reds, with the stars being spicy Correas Malbec and Colección Privada Cabernet/Merlot. Avoid the Cabernets.

Nieto y Senetiner Mostly known for its Valle de Vistalba range, but chunky, chocolaty, hedonistic top reds, called Cadus, are the pick.

Norton Superbly consistent whites (refreshing Sauvignon and Torrontés) and reds, especially Reserve Malbec and Privada (Cabernet/Merlot/Malbec), which are first rate and (unusually) ageworthy.

La Riojana On the face of it, a 1940s dinosaur co-operative, but new viticultural and winemaking teams are making the most glorious 'silk purses' from long-established vineyards. Watch out for the very good organic duo: Torrontés and Malbec, with more to follow.

Salentin New Tupungato winery, with huge investment from its Dutch owners. Merlot and Chardonnay already impress, though Cabernet and Malbec lag behind – perhaps it's too cool here for them? Portillo range is good.

Terrazas New, non-sparkling wine arm of Bodegas Chandon. Chardonnay, Cabernet and Malbec since 1999, made with heavy investment; vineyards chosen for altitude-to-grape suitability. Basic range is Alto (value), Reserva (confected, over-oaked – avoid) and Gran Terrazas. The last-mentioned is good news: concentrated, complex, well-integrated oak.

Trapiche Best winery of the giant Peñaflor, which also owns Santa Ana and northern star Michel Torino in Cafayate (admirable Don David Malbec, excellent Colección Torrontés, Syrah and Tannat). Top-of-the-range Merlot/Malbec Iscay is classy and now available in the UK; Medalla ranges also good.

Viña Patagonia Based in Mendoza, sister company of Chile's Viña Cono Sur; but not as impressive. Fruit lacks concentration and winemaking lacks flair. Perhaps recent big investments will turn things around.

Viniterra Young winery established by Flavio Senetiner (of Nieto y Senetiner origin). Strong Italian influence makes for impressive Sangiovese; also modern, first-class range of good Malbec, Syrah and Merlot. Whites less of a strong point.

Weinert The wines can occasionally be spoiled by extensive oak ageing, but otherwise they are among the most satisfying in Argentina, densely fruity and more Old World than New in structure and flavour. Pick of an excellent range is the wonderfully perfumed Malbec.

Argentinian vintage guide

Perhaps one of the only wine regions in the world to be able to congratulate itself on a fresh fall of (mountain) snow on the same day as basking in glorious summer heat (40°C). The Andes do have their downside though, in that their presence generates not only heavy relief (that is, cooled) rainfall but deeply damaging hailstorms and high winds. It pays, therefore, to watch your vintages more closely than you would from, say, Australia: the terrible flooding caused by El Niño in 1998 proved the point. The 2001 vintage had similar problems, with rain and hail setting in towards the end of the ripening season. Fortunately, there's enough regional variation in Argentina for disastrous conditions in, for example, Mendoza not to affect, say, Cafayate or Salta. For the record, 2002 was a very good year, 2000 was acceptable and 1999 outstanding.

Most white wines should be drunk on release. Torrontés needs to be enjoyed as young and vibrant as possible. Top Chardonnays can be kept for up to five years from vintage, but even these are probably at their best when younger. Cheaper reds are mostly made for early consumption too. However, some of the more expensive Syrah, Malbec and Cabernet-based wines often need a couple of years in bottle to settle down, and the best (especially from years such as 1999) will often last for a decade or more.

AUSTRALIA

For Australia, this is the 'Marketing Decade' – it's all part of their big, 25-year improvement plan. The 1990s saw an era of vineyard planting; in 2001 a new winery was opened every 72 hours. As a result, a 51 per cent increase in the supply of Australian wine can be expected by 2010; all that's necessary now is for these new wines to be marketed and sold. What the Australians may not have bargained for, however, is that other countries might be doing exactly the same thing. Chile, too, needs to double its export sales over the next three years if it is to sell the fruit of its sweeping new plantings. So can we drink all this wine, or are we rapidly heading for a New World wine glut?

The Australian marketing men and women are typically bullish about this situation. With their brands as strong as they are on the UK market at the moment, they're in little doubt that the extra wines will either go into the big names (the likes of Jacob's Creek, Oxford Landing and Lindemans) or alongside them. 'The supermarkets are wholeheartedly behind Australian wine and the brands are becoming stronger and stronger,' we're told. All that's needed is to 'push out the fringe-dwellers' and Australian brands will increase their power . . .

It's at this stage that we start gasping. Push out the fringe-dwellers? Push out the smaller producers? Is this supposed to be *good*?

From another perspective, the weaker Australian dollar means that their exports are attractively priced, but it also makes it expensive for the Australians to spend money abroad on importing new winemaking technology, not to mention marketing overseas – and the latter is just what that game plan requires right now. How much easier and cheaper it will be then to market two or three big brands rather than all those wines with fiddly grape names and odd regions . . .

Here's what we think. Brands might be great for those who are less secure in their wine choices, but they impose uniformity and reflect a lack of passion – and we know that Australian winemakers are nothing if not passionate. They're technophiles, yes, but they love making wine. A lot of the wine they make today, however, is the result of the marketing men dictating the style – the brand style. Brands might be an accessible entry point for people to branch out from, to then explore the wines that the makers get so excited about, but they have become so strong that they are obscuring the real options. Wine lovers are losing the awareness of the choice available.

Because there are a lot of wines on the shelves, supermarkets may appear to be helping out, displaying the whole gamut. But they aren't. How often do you see a supermarket promoting unusual Australian grape varieties, or the distinctively different wines from the far-flung wine regions? (There are 65 of them, so they ought to be a point of interest.) The answer is, you don't. And if supermarkets don't start leading the way and showing the kind of colour and variation Australia can produce, consumers will give up and reach out to other countries instead. We almost hope they do, to prove the point. Until this changes, you're far better off going to smaller merchants, such as Philglas & Swiggot and Noel Young (see *Where to buy wine*), for the interesting bottles.

The other problem (as in California) is Generation X. Yes, today's 20–35-year-olds might be difficult to market to, but which generation ever wanted to copy its parents? Of course they're going to want to think differently and find their own way. And if it's true that they need quirkier, smaller, more off-beat styles 'to call their own', then surely this is the ideal opportunity to introduce wines from those new, oddly named regions?

In our own way, we've been promoting the bolder, riper Shiraz from the Barossa, sterner stuff from the Hunter, and more elegant spicy versions from Western Australia for quite a while now (see below). Similarly with Semillon, and even Chardonnay when well made, flavours vary from region to region, according to the climate and the *terroir* (yes, there is *terroir* in Australia too). But the worrying thing is, we are seeing fewer and fewer wines that back up our argument. In a tasting room full of Australian white wines in Spring 2002 there was a perplexing lack of discernible regional differences. Only the cooler regions seemed to give full-throttle expression to their character. Why was this? Is it that the winemakers are blocking things? No, it's those multi-region brands blurring the issue again.

The marketing people are to blame. They don't yet think the world is ready to handle Australian wine regions. 'Too complicated,' they say. Well, as we mentioned last year, we think they are wrong – and suspect they are turning our friends the winemakers into puppets.

From smaller wineries, where the winemaker is allowed to innovate, and the land to speak, we recommend the following hotspots. First: Margaret River, with firm, structured, true-to-the-*terroir* reds (taste them and see). Second: Bendigo, Heathcote and the whole plethora of up-and-coming small regions from Central Victoria, for dry, textured reds suddenly emerging as wines with great potential. Third: Frankland River, Pemberton and Manjimup in Western Australia, regions cooled by coastal breezes and with fresher fruit flavours as a result.

Oh, and finishing with more marketing-speak. There is a barrage of new producers in Australia (it's good to see them) launching hefty campaigns with zippy new names to match. Here are the best: Stella Bella and Suckfizzle (Margaret River); Cockfighter's Ghost (Hunter Valley); Whispering Hills (Yarra); and (our favourite) Ten Minutes by Tractor, named for the time it takes to get between the three vineyards (Mornington Peninsula). Let's hope they're putting as much effort into keeping yields down and producing concentrated, characterful wines as they are into making their wineries trendy enough for Generation X.

Red wines – grape varieties

Shiraz

Shiraz is Australia's most widely planted red grape, and is also responsible for many of the country's greatest wines. An amazing diversity of styles is produced in the different regions, from the Rhône-like wines of the Yarra and Lower Great Southern, through the fragrant peppery reds of Central Victoria, and on to the heady berry and chocolate concoctions of McLaren Vale, the opulent, ripe blueberry-spice wines of the Barossa Valley and the strong, some say leathery, wines from the Hunter Valley. In warmer regions, the ripe fruit and alcohol levels of some wines can overwhelm, but the best examples retain balance, and age extremely well. Some producers nowadays are blending Rhône-style and adding a tiny percentage of white Viognier, or even Chardonnay, to add complexity. There are also more new styles emerging from Western Australia – keep an eye out for Shiraz from Pemberton and Margaret River.

Cabernet Sauvignon

Cabernet Sauvignon can be almost as impressive. Again, the wines differ markedly from district to district. For elegance, go to Coonawarra, Yarra Valley and Margaret River, while for honest power, look at Clare and McLaren Vale. Cabernet/Shiraz blends are slipping out of vogue, but can be delicious. Malbec, Merlot and

Cabernet Franc are also used as blending partners with Cabernet Sauvignon, and Petit Verdot and Malbec are creeping into more and more blends from the Bordeaux-centric Margaret River. Merlot plantings are increasing, but good varietal versions are still rare. Stand-alone Cabernet Francs can be pleasantly chunky yet perfumed.

Others

A growing number of producers are making use of the knobbly old vines of Grenache and Mourvèdre (known here as Mataro) that are found especially in the Barossa and McLaren Vale. These two varieties have traditionally been confined to the role of bulk provider, but they are now being treated with greater respect. The best wines tend to be blends, usually with a dollop of Shiraz, but there are some successful 100 per cent Grenaches from producers who manage to provide the depth of flavour to balance the often high alcohol levels.

The Australians continue to make steady progress with Pinot Noir. The Yarra Valley, Mornington Peninsula, Geelong, Adelaide Hills and Tasmania are the regions with the highest concentration of good Pinot although, as in Burgundy, the best are expensive and in short supply. Cheaper ones are better avoided. Plantings of Italian varieties such as Sangiovese and Nebbiolo are increasing, but few wines have been released so far.

White wines – grape varieties

Chardonnay

Australia's most poised, elegant Chardonnays undoubtedly come from cooler-climate regions – including Clare Valley, Adelaide Hills, Margaret River – where they can gain in concentration without losing structure and becoming buttery, flabby monsters. We have high hopes that the latter will soon become a thing of the past as wines become more subtle with each vintage, especially as producers begin to take more care in their vineyards and cut their yields. Oak can still be excessive on occasions, but we're also in two minds about the vogue for unoaked Chardonnay. Many cheaper wines need the woody vanilla flavour, otherwise they can be very bland. However, the best unoaked wines (Chapel Hill, Nepenthe, Pipers Brook's Ninth Island) have the substance to survive – nay, flourish – in a wood-free form.

Semillon

Semillon is one of the best grapes for showing Australia's regional differences, but it's not as immediately luscious as Chardonnay and as a result hasn't been as commercially successful. The best-known

Semillon region is the Hunter Valley, where they pick it very early to make a minerally, low-alcohol wine – 10 per cent is not unheard of – with no use of oak, which needs five years at least to show at its toasty best. In South Australia, it is harvested riper and often treated like Chardonnay, with barrel fermentation and ageing. The result is more forward, more appealing when young, but again ages very well. Margaret River versions tend to this latter style, but often have a grassy edge. Fans of sweet wines should try the opulent *botrytis*-affected Semillons of Griffith in New South Wales.

Semillon also plays a part in some regions in blends with Sauvignon Blanc. Much of Australia is too warm to make Sauvignon, but parts of central Victoria, Coonawarra, the Adelaide Hills and Margaret River have all shown that the variety can thrive in the right conditions. The best are like chubbier New Zealand versions, but the worst, harvested early so they retain lots of 'green' characteristics, are tooth-numbingly hard and bitter.

Riesling
A grape that has shown its mettle in several parts of Australia is Riesling. The Clare and Eden valleys are the traditional strongholds, but many other regions make successful versions. The best start off tight and limey, but develop honeyed petrol and lanolin notes with time. Sweet *botrytised* versions are rare but can be superb.

Others
Verdelho, one of the grapes used in the making of madeira, used to be confined mainly to Western Australia but is starting to appear elsewhere, making wines with aromatic peachy fruit and a nutty/savoury character. Marsanne, mainly found in the Goulburn Valley, provides more peaches, this time with hints of honeysuckle. Apart from at Houghton and a couple of other estates in Western Australia, Chenin Blanc seldom achieves anything of note (its innately cheesy character seems somewhat accentuated, especially in warmer regions). Many Australian producers are currently more excited about the potential of Pinot Gris, and we've been favourably impressed with the tangy, grapefruity wines from Pipers Brook, Henschke, T'Gallant and Brown Bros. Viognier is proving just as much of a challenge in Australia as anywhere else, but after 20 years of experimentation Yalumba has cracked it, with a rich, peachy wine; d'Arenberg's is even better.

Sparkling wines

Australia may be bettering neighbouring New Zealand in the fizz stakes. In terms of complexity and depth of flavour (no, we don't just mean big, ripe, sunny fruit), a lot of the wines are beginning to show real class. But most of them seem to be going on sale too early for our liking. In Spring 2002 we tasted predominantly 1999s or younger, which had had nowhere near enough time to develop any of the classic yeasty characteristics. It's very expensive to keep a wine on its yeast lees for long enough (seven years is good) but it's a shame more growers aren't doing it. The best we've found were from the 1998 vintage: Bethany's wine from the Barossa Valley (yes, we thought Barossa was too hot too); Chandon and Yellowglen. Older wines seemed rather bitter or rubbery; there was also a tendency to over-filter, making some wines taste flat. On the whole, we like the richness of the wines with a higher Pinot Noir content – this awkward grape looks as if it is being particularly well managed these days, especially in the Yarra Valley.

The key to Australian sparkling wine is to source fruit from cool regions, and (amazingly) just about every state can lay claim to some of those. In Victoria, the Yarra Valley leads the way with Domaine Chandon's Green Point and Yarra Bank, and the Strathbogie Hills are showing promising signs. Tasmania is up there too, with Pirie from Pipers Brook and (relatively new on the scene) brut non-vintage from Stefano Lubiana. Brian Croser's Petaluma fizz from the Adelaide Hills is impressive, as is the multi-regional Yalumba D. Western Australia has cool spots; Orange (and a handful of other new areas) in New South Wales have potential; and even Queensland's Granite Belt isn't out of the question.

However, sparkling wine doesn't have to be made by the classic champagne method or with the classic grapes. Everyday, cheap-and-cheerful, summer-drinking wines, such as Yalumba's Angas Brut and Seppelt's Great Western, are fruity and lively but simple, with upfront flavour and lots of froth.

Then there are the sparkling reds – real 'love 'em or hate 'em' wines. Sparkling Merlot is fruity and ripe, but has no real texture: it's just fizzy Merlot. Cabernet's tannic edge balances the sweetness and makes life a bit more interesting. But the sweet spiciness of Shiraz works with the bubbles best of all: lively fruit, spice and tannin, without heaviness. Quirky, but great fun, sparkling Shiraz is fast becoming a classic; it ages magnificently, and is a favoured partner for the Christmas turkey. Charles Melton's and Seppelt's are particularly good. Others (from growers not mentioned below) include: Hollick, Balnaves, Bleasdale and Primo Estate.

Australian 'sticky' wines

Stickies (sweet Australian dessert wines) fall into three groups – late-harvest wines; fortified, fruity 'port' styles; and Rutherglen Muscats. The good thing about all of them is that they're ripe, sweet, rich and fruity but they tend to have enough vibrant acidity to finish cleanly without getting sickly or cloying. Late-harvest and *botrytised* Semillons are the most visible on the market and tend to come from warmer regions – Noble One from De Bortoli is the classic example (and the most expensive); hot on its heels are Penfolds, Yalumba, Elderton and Fern Hill. Muscat and even Sauvignon grapes (from Windowrie) also make intense late-harvest styles, but the prize has to go to the Rieslings – who can resist that mouth-tingling lemony acidity? Mount Horrocks' Cordon Cut, Primo Estate La Magia and d'Arenberg's The Noble are the ones to watch. Oh, and all of them age well – so try to resist guzzling them straight away. Try the lighter sweeties from Gewurz or Sauvignon with blue cheeses or goats' cheese – up the blue content if you're going to pair with sweet Semillon or Riesling.

Fortified styles, called 'ports' and 'tawnies', don't tend to make it to UK shores in great abundance and have a much bolder, fruitier style than the genuine articles – Penfolds Magill and d'Arenberg's Shiraz versions are good. The real classics though are the Rutherglen Muscats. These come from intensely ripe grapes fermented to a mere five per cent alcohol, fortified, then aged in barrels in a sherry-type *solera* (at one time this was in old tin sheds, so there was a lot of heating involved too). There are four grades – Rutherglen Muscat, Classic RM, Grand RM and (most hedonistic of the lot) Rare RM – which depend on the vineyards in question and the ripeness of the year. If you want a match for chocolate or Christmas (or even sticky toffee) pudding, it's these sumptuous monsters you should look to – particularly from Campbells, Chambers and Stanton & Killeen.

The regions

New South Wales

Proximity to Sydney rather than viticultural attributes led to the development of the Hunter Valley, New South Wales's most famous wine region. Australia's first commercial Chardonnay came from the Hunter in the early 1970s; the Upper Hunter, home of Rosemount, in particular can still produce some great examples. However, it is another white grape, Semillon, which is behind many of the best wines. Hunter Semillon can seem rather 'so-what?' in its youth, with the same sort of steely austerity as a young Chablis, but ten years in bottle sees a rich, custard-on-toast character emerge to join the pithy, limey fruit. Cleaned-up winemaking now means that the 'sweaty saddle' Hunter reds are a thing of the past, and the top wines such as Brokenwood Shiraz are magnificent.

Elsewhere in the state, Mudgee has been up and coming for several years, but quality remains erratic. Even so, wines such as Rosemount's Mountain Blue Shiraz/Cabernet show what the region is capable of. To the south, fine Chardonnay and Verdelho are coming out of Cowra, while Orange – the illustrious Rosemount estate once again acting as ambassador – is developing elegant Chardonnays and rich but graceful Cabernet and Shiraz. The bulk region of the state is Riverina, also known variously as the Murrumbidgee Irrigation Area (M.I.A.) or Griffith. Amid simple varietals, here are some of the world's most unctuous dessert wines in the shape of *botrytis*-affected Semillon. Two more new areas to watch are the cool-climate Hilltops and Tumbarumba – even cool enough, they say, for making sparkling wine and Sangiovese.

Queensland

It should be too hot to grow grapes here, but the high altitude in the Granite Belt to the west of Brisbane means that temperatures are low enough for even fizz not to be out of the question. Ballandean Estate is the best-known winery, making decent rather than exciting Shiraz and Sauvignon/Semillon, plus surprisingly good, late-harvest Sylvaner.

South Australia

Victoria has more wineries, but South Australia makes a larger volume of wine, as well as being home to virtually all of the country's major producers. While most of the output comes from the irrigated Riverland region, there are also a number of smaller, higher-quality districts. Clare Valley to the north of Adelaide is the source of rumbustious Shiraz and Cabernet as well as some of Australia's finest Rieslings. Wines from the Barossa Valley vary from rather bland whites from hot valley-floor vineyards to outstanding old-vine Shiraz and Rhône varietals, often from hillside vineyards. The Eden Valley is a cooler sub-region of the Barossa, and vies with Clare to produce the state's most elegant Riesling. Again, Shiraz excels, especially in Henschke's Hill of Grace. The Adelaide Hills is also a cooler-climate region, already making crisp, flavoursome Chardonnays and Sauvignons, and showing promise with Pinot Noir. Wines from the Lenswood sub-region are worth seeking out.

South of Adelaide are McLaren Vale and Langhorne Creek, sources of the type of open-faced, honest reds that we most readily associate with Australia, the best of which are among the country's finest. Further south still brings you to a stretch of regions known collectively as the Limestone Coast. Most famous of these is Coonawarra – with its *terra rossa* soil – home of elegant Cabernet, great Shiraz and a couple of refined Sauvignons. The heated dispute about the precise definition of Coonawarra, with some vineyards, most notably one belonging to Petaluma, falling outside newly drawn-up official boundaries, has at long last been resolved –

with Petaluma ending up in, not out. Padthaway to the north is just as cool but with slightly heavier soils in which Chardonnay thrives. Other Limestone Coast regions you may see on labels in the near future include Wrattonbully, which is making a name for red wines, and cooler, coastal Robe and Mount Benson.

Tasmania

Tasmania contributes less than one per cent to Australia's total grape crush, and the number of wineries on the island is small, with only Dr Andrew Pirie's Pipers Brook and Stefano Lubiana achieving good sales in the UK. However, the cool climate is ideal for grapes for sparkling wines, and several mainland companies now source Pinot Noir and Chardonnay from here to pep up their blends. Pirie and Lubiana's successes with a variety of still and sparkling wines show that, in time, the rest of the island's winemakers could teach those across the Bass Strait a thing or two about elegance and complexity. Look out for the aromatic whites from 'Tassie'.

Victoria

Whatever style of wine you're looking for, chances are you'll find it somewhere in Victoria. The cheap and cheerful bottles come from vineyards along the Murray River in the north-west of the state. Travel eastwards along the border with New South Wales and you hit Rutherglen, home of luscious Liqueur Muscat and 'Tokay', and decent port lookalikes, as well as burly reds made from Cabernet, Shiraz and Durif. Across the centre of Victoria are several small regions, namely (from west to east) Great Western/The Grampians, the Pyrenees, Bendigo, Heathcote and Goulburn Valley. Each is home to only a handful of wineries, but a number of notable ones excel with increasingly fashionable reds, especially Shiraz. Goulburn Valley also has extensive plantings of Marsanne. The other main regions, Geelong, Macedon, the Yarra Valley and the Mornington Peninsula, are clustered around Port Philip Bay. Shiraz can be found here, but Pinot Noir and Chardonnay are the specialities, with both being used for still and sparkling wines (as is Shiraz for that matter). Further east, East Gippsland boasts few wineries but is the source of the outstanding Pinot Noir from Bass Phillip.

Western Australia (WA)

Western Australia produces only two per cent of all Australian wine, but it's a remarkably good two per cent. While many of the large companies have vineyards in WA, none is based here, and most of the producers are medium-sized or smaller. The Swan Valley was the first region to be developed, in the mid-1800s, and it still produces reasonable commercial styles, but the last 30 years

have seen the establishment of wineries in cooler regions further to
the south. Margaret River, at the south-western tip of the country,
ranks as perhaps the most consistent fine wine region in Australia,
with elegant Cabernets, refined Chardonnays, pithy Semillons and
earthy Shirazes. The sprawling Lower Great Southern region along
the south coast, encompassing areas we're hearing more and more
about – Frankland and Mount Barker – is home to top-class
Riesling and can also impress with Cabernet and Shiraz. Between
here and Margaret River lies Pemberton, which is beginning to
make a name with Pinot Noir and Chardonnay. Other new regions
to look out for are Mandurah, Geographe and the Blackwood
Valley.

Pick of the producers

Tim Adams Clare Valley producer of powerful reds, especially The
Fergus (Grenache) and Aberfeldy Shiraz. The creamy fat Semillon
and limey Riesling are also delicious – and long-lived.

Alkoomi Lower Great Southern producer (WA) for beautifully
defined Cabernet, Shiraz, Merlot, Sauvignon and Chardonnay.

Amberley Small, quality winery in Margaret River for superb
ageworthy Semillons; unusual Chenin Blanc is the mainstream
wine, and reds are getting better and better.

d'Arenberg Most dynamic winery in McLaren Vale, offering a wide
range of ever-improving reds at down-to-earth prices – and, of late,
some impressive and carefully made Rhône-blend whites (Hermit-
Crab Marsanne-Viognier and Moneyspider Roussanne).

Bannockburn Fiercely independent Geelong winery turning out
'Burgundian' Pinot Noir and Chardonnay, plus an underrated
peppery Shiraz.

Jim Barry Small Clare Valley winery with fine red range topped by
the intense Armagh Shiraz.

Basedow Good-value varietals, especially Chardonnay and
Semillon, from this Barossa and Adelaide Hills concern.

Beringer Blass see under *Mildara-Beringer Blass*.

Bests Family-run winery in the Grampians, Victoria, making understated Shiraz, Riesling, Cabernet and a Dolcetto – plus interesting Pinot Meunier from vines original to the homestead.

De Bortoli Opulent dessert wines including the intriguing Black Noble from Griffith; also elegant reds and whites from the Yarra Valley.

BRL Hardy Huge conglomerate whose brands include Houghton, Moondah Brook, Chateau Reynella, Yarra Burn, Stanley, Leasingham and Berri Estates, as well as Hardy's. The wines run the gamut from everyday ranges such as Banrock Station, Nottage Hill and Stamp Series to the very classy. Contenders for top wines include a trio of fine Shirazes, namely Eileen Hardy, Leasingham Classic Clare and Chateau Reynella Basket-Pressed. Plummy sparkling Shiraz is made under the Banrock Station, Sir James and, best of all, Leasingham labels.

Brokenwood Candidate for the finest winery in the Hunter Valley, with superb Graveyard Shiraz, substantial ageworthy Semillon and very acceptable second label Cricket Pitch. Also excellent Rayner Shiraz from McLaren Vale.

Brown Brothers Instrumental in bringing Australian wines to many Brits, and still showing a very reliable and wide range. New Nebbiolo and Barbera are good, as are Rieslings of all sweetnesses, Liqueur Muscat and sparkling Pinot/Chardonnay. Pinot Gris is latest impressive development in ever-expanding range of varietals.

Grant Burge A Barossa institution, Burge makes good commercial wines, at the lower end of the price spectrum, and satisfying reds, especially the new Holy Trinity (Grenache/Shiraz/Mourvèdre), for a dollar or two more. Kraft Sauvignon Blanc is also very attractive.

Campbells Rutherglen stalwart making great Liqueur Muscat and chunky reds – Bobby Burns Shiraz and The Barkly Durif.

Cape Mentelle Inspired reds (including a top-notch Zinfandel) and whites from Cloudy Bay's sister winery in Margaret River (now owned by LVMH). Second label Ironstone uses fruit from other Western Australian regions.

Chambers Liqueur Muscats from Rutherglen with extraordinary depth and complexity.

Domaine Chandon Yarra Valley-based offshoot of Moët, making refined fizz. Well-made wines right across the range (which includes buttery NV and Green Point, honeyed sweet Cuvée Riche and delicious savoury Brut Rosé and Blanc de Noirs. Brambley sparkling Pinot-Shiraz is one of Australia's more textured fizzy reds). Also impresses with still Pinot Noir and Chardonnay.

Chapel Hill Distinctly classy wines from McLaren Vale fruit, with The Vicar, a Cabernet/Shiraz blend, being the pick. Crisp, appley Verdelho also good. Winemaker Pam Dunsford, having achieved great things, has now moved on, so will quality be maintained?

Coldstream Hills Chardonnay and Pinot Noir specialist in the Yarra Valley, founded by wine writer James Halliday, who still runs winemaking operations, but now owned by Southcorp (see *Penfolds* and *Rosemount*, below).

Cullens Award-winning mother and daughter team Di and Vanya Cullen make majestic Cabernet blends, rich powerful Chardonnay and pungent Sauvignon at their esteemed Margaret River winery.

Dalwhinnie Pyrenees winery making fine, elegant Shiraz, Cabernet and Chardonnay, which all need time in bottle to show their class.

Devil's Lair Concentrated, stylish Chardonnay and Cabernet/ Merlot from the wacky Margaret River outpost of Southcorp. Second label Fifth Leg is trendy and tasty.

Fox Creek The Reserve Shiraz and Cabernet make this McLaren Vale red specialist one of Australia's most admirable small wineries.

Frankland Estate One of the finest producers in the Lower Great Southern, with tight limey Riesling, fragrant Shiraz and classy Bordeaux blend Olmo's Reward.

Grosset Clare Valley-based but also sourcing fruit from the Adelaide Hills; trump cards are tight, minerally Riesling and powerful, pungent Chardonnay. (See also *Mount Horrocks*, below.)

Henschke Stephen Henschke's winemaking skill combined with his wife Prue's viticultural talents have made this arguably Australia's best small winery. Hill of Grace Shiraz is the star, but if you can't find/afford it, any of the other wines, red or white, from Eden Valley or the Adelaide Hills, makes a lovely alternative.

Houghton Swan Valley-based winery, now owned by BRL Hardy. Best known in Australia for Houghton's White Burgundy (sold in the UK as HWB); also has good-value Wildflower Ridge range, classic WA Verdelho and top red Jack Mann. Reds are often underestimated at this property: the blends are cracking!

Howard Park Based in the Lower Great Southern region of Western Australia, but now with a new winery in Margaret River. Riesling can be good, and Cabernet ranks among the most satisfying in the state. Entry-level brand Madfish Bay trades on trendy origins (WA) but can be underwhelming.

Jasper Hill Stellar Bendigo Shiraz specialist, currently engaged in joint venture with Chapoutier of the Rhône. Fabulously concentrated, tightly woven wines that demand ageing. Also lovely limey Riesling.

Katnook Estate Coonawarra winery with an impressive range topped by the Bordeaux blend Odyssey, Prodigy Shiraz and including one of Australia's most acceptable Sauvignons. Parent company Wingara also produces two other Coonawarra ranges, Riddoch and Woolshed, plus Deakin Estate from the Riverland.

Leeuwin Estate Margaret River showcase winery: the Art Series (including Riesling and Cabernet) are all very classy wines but the Chardonnay is arguably the best in Australia. The second-label Prelude range also puts many others to shame.

Peter Lehmann No-nonsense wines from the Baron of the Barossa. Look out for good-value Vine Vale range, sappy Semillon with a touch of oak and sumptuous Stonewell Shiraz.

Lenswood The Adelaide Hills venture of Tim Knappstein, with (usually) first-rate Semillon, Sauvignon and Chardonnay and making strides with Pinot Noir. Also keep an eye out for Palatine red blend and rare Gewurztraminer.

Lindemans (see *Southcorp*, below).

McWilliams Large company making a broad selection of wines from various regions, but excels as the 'King' of Hunter Valley Semillon. Stick with the very traditional HV wines, which include top Shiraz.

Charles Melton Barossa maverick renowned for an original range – Nine Popes (Grenache/Shiraz), Rose of Virginia Grenache rosé and excellent Shiraz, sparkling as well as still.

Mildara-Beringer Blass Was Mildara-Blass, now merged with mighty Beringer from the USA: huge winemaking resources mean it should achieve almost anything, but the focus on generic 'churning out' is strong. Parent company of several wineries including Wolf Blass (ripe, oaky commercial wines, impressive Black Label Cabernet/Shiraz and lovely Rieslings), Maglieri (classy McLaren Vale Shiraz), Quelltaler Estate (superb Rieslings) and Rothbury Estate (good Hunter Valley Semillon, Chardonnay, Verdelho and Shiraz). Yellowglen sparkling is also worth following. This is a tough outfit so let's hope these estates survive.

Mitchelton Fat, peachy and remarkably ageworthy Marsanne is the best-known wine from this Goulburn Valley winery, but all the wines, including those under the Preece label, are good.

Morris The reds are big and rustic, but the class act is the Liqueur Muscat, bolstered by reserve wines dating back over 100 years.

Mountadam Now owned by LVMH, along with Cape Mentelle. Adam Wynn's enterprising winery in the Eden Valley, coming up with rich but subtle Chardonnay, fine-tuned Pinot Noir and complex fizz. Second labels are David Wynn and the organic Eden Ridge. If Wynn stays, all will be well.

Mount Horrocks Fabulous Riesling (dry, and sumptuous Cordon Cut sweet) plus Chardonnay and Shiraz made by Stephanie Toole. Shares a winery (a converted dairy) in the Clare Valley with husband, Jeffrey Grosset (see above).

Mount Langi Ghiran Wines of great integrity. Trevor Mast crafts one of the most distinctive Shirazes in central Victoria, and his Riesling and Pinot Gris also merit attention. He makes the Four Sisters wines too, but using McLaren Vale fruit. Mast is now involved in a joint venture with Chapoutier of the Rhône.

Nepenthe Enjoyable Riesling, Chardonnay and Semillon from new innovative Adelaide Hills producer. Surprisingly good (if heavily alcoholic) Zinfandel and tangy Charleston Pinot Gris. Also new Tempranillo.

Noon With very little fuss, Master of Wine Drew Noon has transformed his family winery into one of the stars of McLaren Vale, with stunning Shiraz, Cabernet and Grenache (called Eclipse).

Orlando Mammoth, slightly lumbering Barossa operation owned by Pernod-Ricard, best known for Jacob's Creek, but also bolstering its reputation with finer wines such as Steingarten Riesling, Lawson's Shiraz, Jacaranda Ridge Cabernet and the Saints range. JC Chardonnay-Pinot Noir NV fizz is a fun, and cheap, sparkler worth trying.

Penfolds Main brand of Southcorp (see below), still with firm grip on high-quality range of traditional reds. Production of the illustrious Grange Shiraz has upped in quantity but remains impressive, closely followed by 707 Cabernet and RWT Shiraz. Top white is Yattarna Chardonnay, but new Eden Valley Riesling is just as good – at a third of the price.

Petaluma Innovative winery headed by the forthright Brian Croser with very good wines (especially Clare Valley Riesling) from specially chosen sites throughout South Australia. Second label is Bridgewater Mill. Also owns the Knappstein Winery in Clare (great Cabernet Franc) and now has a stake in Stonier's in Mornington Peninsula. Can produce delicious ageworthy sparkling when the mood suits.

Pipers Brook Largest, most important and best winery on Tasmania, thanks to the efforts of the studious Dr Andrew Pirie. Highlights of an excellent range (and an impressive second label Ninth Island) are the Pirie sparkling, lush, complex Chardonnays and the best Pinot Noir in Australia, but don't ignore the aromatic varieties (Pinot Gris, Sauvignon, very good Gewurztraminer). Recently bought out by a Belgian company but Pirie remains at the helm, combatting the tricky Tasmanian climate.

Rockford Robert 'Rocky' O'Callaghan of the Barossa uses ancient equipment and equally ancient vines to make huge, glowering Basket Press Shiraz, ripe Grenache, rich, petrolly Riesling and Semillon and glorious sparkling Shiraz.

Rosemount Long-popular family estate making history in 2001 for its leading role in the merger with Southcorp (see below), to become the largest wine producer in Australia. Gained its stripes in the UK for the good-value Diamond Label range, but also capable of immensely classy wines such as Balmoral Shiraz (McLaren Vale), Mountain Blue Shiraz/Cabernet (Mudgee), Orange Chardonnay (Orange) and Roxburgh Chardonnay (Upper Hunter). Marks & Spencer's Honeytree range comes from Rosemount. Latest news is a joint venture with similarly dynamic Mondavi in California.

St Hallett Shiraz is the speciality, with Old Block and Blackwell standing out, but everything from the good-value Poacher's Blend and Gamekeeper's Reserve upwards is a welcome, honest, flavour-packed Barossa wine. Recent merger with Tatachilla (see below) presents some unknowns.

Shaw and Smith Adelaide Hills white wine specialists making crisp Sauvignons and fine Chardonnays at best, but possibly overstretching themselves of late, sacrificing quality for greater distribution.

Southcorp One of Australia's 'big four' wine companies – owner of prestige Penfolds estate, plus Coldstream Hills, Devil's Lair, Lindemans, Rouge Homme, Seaview, Seppelt, Wynns and others. As a result of the dramatic merger with Rosemount (see above) it is now the largest producer in Australia – size-wise, eighth in the world! The merger is still sending shock waves through the industry. The *Guide* is watching standards.

Chateau Tahbilk Powerful, tannic and long-lived, if occasionally rustic, Shiraz and Cabernet; lovely honeysuckle-scented old vine Marsanne.

Taltarni Good sparklers, including Clover Hill, partly from Tasmania, and decent Sauvignon Blanc, but the stars are the reds from the Victorian Pyrenees, especially the Cabernet Sauvignon.

Tarrawarra Seriously sexy, beautifully textured Chardonnay and Pinot Noir from top-quality Yarra Valley producer; second label Tunnel Hill also commendable.

Tatachilla Now a sister winery of St Hallett (see above), producing an admirable range topped by rich, chocolaty Foundation Shiraz, and Rhôney reliable rest.

Torbreck Dave Powell's top-of-the-pile Barossa reds are hard to find and not cheap, but their combination of power and balance makes them among the best in the region.

Tyrrells Hunter Valley stalwarts – bypass the rather ordinary Old Winery range and head for the Vat 47 Chardonnay, Vat 1 Semillon, Vat 9 Shiraz and Vat 8 Shiraz/Cabernet. Quality can be erratic.

Veritas Small Barossa winery making its own and contracted Shiraz (plus Grenache and Mataro) from old bush vines. Hefty wines Hanisch, JJ Hahn, Heysen and Draycott are all made by the irrepressible Hungarian, Rolf Binder.

Wirra Wirra Solid Southern Vales winery with good whites and very good reds – Church Block, RSW Shiraz and the Angelus Cabernet being the pick.

Yalumba Barossa-based company best known for Angas Brut and Oxford Landing – the quality of both of which remains decent – but with several more aces up its sleeve. Top reds are The Menzies Coonawarra Cabernet, Signature Cabernet/Shiraz and Octavius Shiraz; top whites are Rieslings from the Pewsey Vale and Heggies vineyards, and Virgilius Viognier. Yalumba D fizz is also recommended. Robert Hill Smith and team deserve all credit for this high-quality, ever-explorative range.

Yarra Yering Quirky Yarra winery owned and run by the bright-eyed Bailey Carrodus. Quality and interest level are both very high across the range, and all the wines benefit from extra bottle age.

Australian vintage guide

Yes, there is variation in Australian vintages, although the technical expertise of the winemakers tends to diminish the effects of the lean years. Most wines taste good from the word go, but it's a mistake to think that, because of this, they don't age well. With whites, top examples of Riesling and Semillon are still in fine fettle after ten years – as are any of the sweeties – if you can resist them. Few Chardonnays are worth keeping for more than a couple of years, although a rest of 12 months after release for the oak to calm down is of benefit to many wines.

With reds, some Pinot Noirs can last for a decade, but don't necessarily improve. It's a different story with Shiraz and Cabernet. Many taste delicious on release, but only those who take the trouble to hold back the odd bottle or two, even of relatively humble wines, will be aware of just how well they age. Sparkling Shiraz is surprisingly good after cellaring too.

2002 A short, cool vintage nationwide, with big vineyards seeking high yields failing to achieve ripeness. Those harvesting with integrity and careful yields will produce quality wines.

2001 A long, hot, growing season – mostly scorching in Barossa and Clare; totally rainless in Western Australia – made for easy vintage conditions and balanced, evenly ripened fruit. New South Wales had a trickier time, with rain arriving at harvest, but grapes brought in beforehand had the same long-ripened quality.

2000 A reduced crop, especially in South Australia, thanks to a poor spring and rain around harvest time. Even so, producers were bullish about quality, and those in New South Wales and Tasmania are especially pleased with results.

1999 Frost in spring and autumn; drought and thunderstorms. To hear the Australians talk of 1999, it's a surprise there's any wine at all. 'Patchy' is the word they're using, although we haven't been disappointed with what we've tasted.

1998 Superb vintage, with producers throughout the country saying it was the best red harvest they'd ever seen. Buy up any top Shiraz you can find and enjoy it for the next 15 years. Whites are good, but not in the same class, although some Semillons are delicious.

1997 Rain at harvest time in Margaret River and Hunter Valley caused a few problems with rot, while frost in the Riverland reduced crop levels there, but otherwise this was a good year, especially in South Australia.

1996 A large harvest, from a year when temperatures were on the low side in the Yarra Valley and other cooler parts of Victoria, but more favourable in other parts of the country.

Respectable earlier vintages – Better Shiraz and Cabernet from 1990, 1991, 1992 and 1994 should all still be in good condition.

AUSTRIA

There have been one or two quiet revolutions going on in Austria over the last year or so, and now that we are sure enough of the results – we can spread the news. To start with, the 2000 vintage in this country marked not just a new millennium and a fabulous harvest, but the start of a modern era in terms of red wines. Their quality has turned a corner, and the new wines are hitting the UK right now. Not only has the winemaking improved, but the way the wines are blended together has been enhanced beyond all measure. There has been a move away from the planting of Cabernet Sauvignon and Merlot and all the other international varieties, and the red wines are increasingly based on Austria's own, individual, more traditional grapes – grapes with local character. In the blends, what was 40 or 50 per cent Merlot is now 80 per cent Zweigelt or, better still, 90 per cent Blaufränkisch.

This trend back towards authentic Austrian varieties doesn't only cover reds, there's also been the dawning realisation among growers that they have better things to do with their time than follow the Chardonnay star. The grape variety Grüner Veltliner is at last acknowledged for having more than enough flavour of its own, without needing Chardonnay and Sauvignon Blanc to 'make it modern'. Not that we have any complaints to make about the latter grape, especially from Styria, where there are more than a few spanking new wineries popping up that are testimony to its considerable success on the markets. Austrian Sauvignon has finally achieved the right balance of oak. (It's the same with Grüner Veltliner and the other white varietals: almost everyone has dropped the use of small oak *barriques* and gone back to using large, neutral casks because they don't want to smother the natural crispness of the fruit.) Better still, these wines are also being made to a high enough standard that they will develop complexity with age.

And where can we find them? Well, we've seen a few more scattered through the merchant pages than usual and several dealers are now making a speciality of these wines, though the supermarkets (unsurprisingly given the perhaps off-putting tricky pronunciations of some of the wine names) still don't seem to have taken up the mantle. And here we repeat our plea for the major multiples to experiment more: Austrian wines manage to be different without being *too* different. The flavours may not always echo those found in other countries, but they are unique, a blessing in today's world of 'recipe' wines. And while Austria doesn't dabble in the cheap and cheerful, there's plenty available for under £10, though you may have to do a little searching to find the wines in the first place. But when you do find them (Bacchus Fine Wines, Ben Ellis, Morris & Verdin, Raeburn Fine Wines, T & W Wines and Noel Young are good places to start; see *Where to buy wine*), you're in for a treat, especially with the high quality of the 1997, 1999, 2000 and 2001 vintages.

Red wines

If you imagined that Austrian reds would be rather thin and weedy, their high quality will come as a pleasant surprise. Yes, there are a few pale and not very interesting wines around, but there are also some remarkably full-bodied, well-structured wines made from both imported and native grapes, which can age for a decade or more.

Austria has three main domestic red grape varieties. Blaufränkisch is sturdy and juicy, with a structure reminiscent of Cabernet Sauvignon, while St Laurent is a member of the Pinot family, and some versions have the sweet cherry and berry fruit of Pinot Noir. Zweigelt, a cross between these two, has juicy, earthy berry fruit and can bear an uncanny resemblance to Piedmont's Dolcetto. All three are often aged in new oak and can be impressive, either in pure form or in blends, but the clean, fruity and usually unoaked 'classic' styles (as the Austrians term them) deserve just as much attention.

While Cabernet Sauvignon is the most popular of the foreign grapes, several producers are experimenting with Merlot, since it ripens more successfully. But international varieties are taking more of a back-seat role than they have done. Pinot Noir, which has existed here for centuries, has yet to make a strong impression on us, although the occasional wine manages to pack a pleasant cherry-ish punch (Bründlmayer, Paul Achs and Juris make good examples).

Dry white wines

For a world bored with oaky Chardonnay, Austrian whites are like a breath of fresh air, even if the Austrians often drink them too young and too cold for our liking. Chardonnay, sometimes known as Morillon, is grown, and there are some oaked wines that can proudly stand alongside foreign competitors, but (fortunately) there is no longer the mad rush, as seen in other countries, for growers to prove themselves worthy of this grape. Chardonnay also comes in a steely, dry and unoaked form which is like a slightly fruitier Chablis, and Pinot Blanc (Weissburgunder) and Pinot Gris (Grauburgunder) are often made in similar styles.

The most widely planted variety is Grüner Veltliner, a native grape that has flavours of grapefruit, white pepper and lentil (honestly). Lighter versions are perfect summer aperitifs, while richer wines are more serious and, with two or three years in bottle, can begin to display the minerally characters found in some white burgundy. Grüner Veltliner's rival for making top-quality white wine is Riesling. The best versions lie between the Rheingau and Alsace in style, with the slaty, minerally intensity of the former and the weight of the latter. Welschriesling, a speciality of Styria, doesn't rise to the same heights, but can offer pleasant, crisp floral wines.

Styria's other trump card is Sauvignon Blanc. The wines have evolved from the rather startling but ultimately underripe efforts of the early 1990s and subsequent heavy-handed oaky wines developed towards the end of the millennium, into extremely attractive wines that sit halfway between the flinty, earthy style of the Loire and the overt fruitiness of New Zealand. Shame they're so expensive.

Sweet white wines

Austria deserves its reputation as a source of high-class, sweet wines. Most are made from *botrytis*-affected grapes, often grown in the vicinity of the shallow Neusiedlersee lake in Burgenland, but you can also find a few examples of unctuous *Schilfwein*, made from grapes that have been dried on reed mats prior to crushing. Don't expect these to be the same as German sweet wines: the alcohol is invariably higher, the acidity lower, and the wines have bolder, rounder, more complex fruit-compote flavours. Also, because they are made in greater quantities in Burgenland, these wines are usually more kindly priced too.

As in Germany, the wines are graded by the sweetness of the must, so you'll find *Beerenauslese* (BA) and *Trockenbeerenauslese* (TBA) on the label. Austria has an additional category called *Ausbruch*, which sits between BA and TBA on the sweetness scale. *Ausbruch* is the speciality of the town of Rust on the Neusiedlersee, and has traditionally been made by adding fresh grapes to fermented must to reactivate the fermentation. However, much modern *Ausbruch* is simply TBA under a different label, although usually with a higher level of alcohol (and therefore lower residual sugar level) than a typical TBA. *Eiswein* also exists, although many producers look on it as a step down from *Ausbruch* and TBA.

Riesling and Grüner Veltliner are pressed into service for sweet wines, but you're just as likely to find wines made from supposedly inferior varieties such as Neuburger, Bouvier, Welschriesling, or from grapes not normally associated with sweet wines such as Pinot Blanc and Chardonnay. There are even some sweet red wines. All can display pure, clean fruit flavours, backed up by fresh acidity. They're delicious on release, but have the structure to age well.

Sparkling wines

Austrian *Sekt*, often based on Welschriesling, is seldom great, but for uncomplicated drinking in a Viennese café, it's pleasant enough. Bründlmayer makes the finest.

The regions

Austria has four main wine-producing areas. The capital Vienna, where vines reach almost up to the city wall, is the smallest, and most of the wine is consumed in the local inns or *Heurigen*. Styria in the south makes increasingly refined dry whites from Sauvignon Blanc and Welschriesling, with the occasional plumper Chardonnay. The highlight of Burgenland is the plethora of sweet wines produced in villages such as Rust and Illmitz around the Neusiedlersee. However, move not too far away from the lake, and the humidity drops, giving rise to good conditions for other styles, especially full-bodied reds. The fourth district, Lower Austria, is the largest. Its most famous sub-region is the Wachau, where Riesling and Grüner Veltliner thrive on the steep, terraced slopes hugging the northern bank of the Danube. Growers here also have their own classification system for dry wines. *Steinfeder* is for wines with less than 10.7 per cent alcohol, *Federspiel* for those under 12 per cent and *Smaragd* for those with 12 per cent and above. The best wines of neighbouring Kremstal and Kamptal approach Wachau in quality.

Pick of the producers

Paul Achs Silky, full-bodied Burgenland red blends of Cabernet and local varieties. Well-crafted Chardonnay and Pinot Noir too.

Braunstein Powerful Chardonnay and ripe, plummy Blaufränkisch are the best of an impressive range from Neusiedlersee.

Bründlmayer Working with fruit from prime vineyard sites in Langenlois, Willi Bründlmayer is one of Austria's most thoughtful and intellectual winemakers, crafting intense Riesling, long-lived Grüner Veltliner, rich Chardonnay, unusually good Pinot Noir, and the most 'champagne-like' of Austrian *Sekts*.

Feiler-Artinger Burgenland producer with a well-deserved reputation for high-quality, concentrated *Ausbruch*, and very good red wines.

Freie Weingärtner Wachau A huge co-operative of nearly 800 Wachau grape growers which, despite its size, manages to produce some seriously high-quality whites, especially from Grüner Veltliner.

Gernot Heinrich Full-bodied, tannic reds from Neusiedlersee. The Gabarinza is Zweigelt, Blaufränkisch and Syrah. Both are excellent. Not to be confused with up-and-coming Johann Heinrich from Mittel-Burgenland, another source of fine reds.

Schloss Gobelsburg Fairy-tale castle in Kremstal belonging to adjacent monastery, run since 1996 by Michael Moosbrugger and Willi Bründlmayer (see also *Bründlmayer*, above). The Ried Lamm Grüner Veltliner and Riesling Alte Reben (Old Vines) are the pinnacles of a splendid range.

Gross Styria producer with very clean, pure dry whites including superb Sauvignon Blanc and, since 2000, world-class Gewürztraminer.

Hirsch Organic estate in Kamptal excelling with rich, pure Riesling and Grüner Veltliner.

Franz Hirztberger Benchmark Wachau whites, especially the well-focused Riesling and Grüner Veltliner.

Igler Smooth, creamy blends of Blaufränkisch and Cabernet Sauvignon made by Waltraud Reisner-Igler in Mittel-Burgenland.

Jamek Wachau quality pioneer back on form since late 1990s. Sleek, sometimes austere, dry white wines of crystalline clarity.

Juris Axel Stiegelmar excels with modern, New World-style red *cuvées*, especially the powerful red St Georg and Pinot Noir. Whites, in comparison, are rather boring.

Knoll Master winemaker of the Wachau whose slow-developing and extremely long-lived dry Rieslings and Grüner Veltliners are concentrated and intensely minerally.

Alois Kracher Some of the top Austrian *botrytis*-affected dessert wines made from several different varieties grown in Neusiedlersee; Kracher numbers his *cuvées* 1–9. Also has three joint venture projects: *Beerenauslese* jelly; 'Grand Cru' cheese (with *botrytised* wine the extra ingredient); and, with Los Angeles restaurateur Manfred Krankl, sumptuous California wine Mr K.

Krutzler Burgenland brothers Reinhold and Erich produce one of Austria's most exciting reds – Perwolff – from the indigenous Blaufränkisch grape and just a dash of Cabernet.

Lackner-Tinnacher Styrian estate which rejects any use of new oak in order to achieve the maximum purity of fruit flavour in classical Sauvignon Blanc, Weissburgunder, Grauburgunder . . .

Helmut Lang Another dessert-wine wizard producing sweet wines from Chardonnay and Pinot Noir (yes, really) as well as from more traditional grapes.

Malat Wide range of well-made wines from Krems. Perfumed, acidic Riesling, Grüner Veltliner and forceful Chardonnay are highlights.

Lenz Moser A decent set of good-value wines and a fair introduction to Austrian grape varieties. Sappy, peppery Grüner Veltliner is our favourite; soft, lively reds are also worth a try.

Gerhard Nekowitsch Up-and-coming maker of Neusiedlersee dessert wines; range includes first-rate *Schilfwein*.

Nigl Family-owned Kremstal estate producing arguably the finest dry Riesling and Grüner Veltliner in the region – wines that combine power with racy elegance.

Willi Opitz Eccentric winemaker (and canny marketeer) turning out a range of unusual and innovative sweet wines from the

Neusiedlersee. Red TBA, *Eiswein* and *Schilfwein* are among the bottlings.

FX Pichler One of the master-craftsmen of the Wachau excelling with low-yielding Grüner Veltliner, Riesling and Sauvignon Blanc. Very powerful, concentrated wines: not for the fainthearted!

Pöckl Massive, oaky Neusiedlersee reds, especially Zweigelt varietals and the Zweigelt/Cabernet/Merlot blend Admiral.

Polz Large Styrian estate with fresh, sprightly whites including Chablis-like Pinot Blanc, crisp Sauvignon and spicy Pinot Gris.

Prager Winemaker Toni Bodenstein is obsessed with *terroir* and it shows in his single-vineyard Wachau Rieslings and Grüner Veltliners, each of which has a highly distinct personality as well as impressive concentration.

Salomon/Undhof Estate Fine steely Riesling and Traminer from one of Austria's top vineyards, Steiner Hund in the Kremstal region.

Schlumberger Austria's best-known (but not best) *Sekt* producer, fetching up a froth in Vienna for 150 years.

Heidi Schrock Rust winery making superb *Ausbruch* from Furmint and Yellow Muscat; the dry reds and whites are also worth trying.

Sonnhof Jurtschitsch Langenlois wines of distinction, especially the Alte Reben (Old Vines) Rieslings.

Tement Styrian superstar excelling with Sauvignon Blanc (with which its reputation was made), Pinot Gris and Chardonnay. Also involved (with FX Pichler, see above; and Tibor Szemes from Burgenland) in making tight, earthy red-blend Arachon.

Tinhof Modern, bright Burgenland range, including succulent blend of local reds.

Ernst Triebaumer ET, as he is unfortunately known, makes good, dry whites, but it is for his dense, fleshy reds and heady sweet wines that he is deservedly famous. Maker of the best varietal Blaufränkisch on the planet.

Umathum Organic, Burgenland red specialist, with impressive range topped by Ried Hallebuhl, Zweigelt with small amounts of Blaufränkisch and Cabernet, and burgundy-style St Laurent Vom

Stein. Josef Umathum's wines could almost be French, such is their dry elegance and subtlety.

Velich Since 1991 two ex-casino croupier brothers have made headlines in Burgenland with Tiglat, a remarkable Chardonnay, and are now starting to repeat this feat with their dessert wines.

Weingut Dr Unger Fine Riesling, Grüner Veltliner and Pinot Gris from vineyards in the Wachau and Kremstal.

Fritz Wieninger Rich, complex wines from Vienna, especially the multi-layered, *barrique*-aged (and very pricy) Grand Select Chardonnay.

Austrian vintage guide

2001 A cool winter and spring, with temperatures waiting till July to hot up, then a cooler-than-usual harvest period made for elegant balanced whites and less monumentally massive reds than in the preceding vintage. Sweet whites faired well, with the exception of those made from Welschriesling, which experienced a disastrous year. A good vintage, second only to the 1999s for elegance.
2000 Hot, dry vintage producing a smaller-than-usual crop of abundant richness and high quality. The whites are full-bodied but – despite the heat – not lacking in acidity; both dry and sweet wines are very good. Marks the first vintage of a modern era for full-bodied Austrian reds, with some growers saying they picked the best fruit they had ever seen.
1999 The best vintage for many years produced an embarrassment of riches, with intense, full-bodied reds, ripe, well-balanced dry whites and enough *botrytis* to keep sweet wine fans happy. Snap up those still for sale if you can find them.
1998 Average for dry wines, since it rained hard at the beginning of September. Volumes were up, but the quality is only fair. There was more *botrytis* rot, however, so some decent dessert wines emerged.
1997 Billed by the Austrians as one of the greatest vintages for decades. A warm and dry ripening period lasted right through to the harvest and resulted in fine quality dry whites and reds. There was little *botrytis*, however, so don't expect great sweet wines.

BOLIVIA

The Bolivian wines you're most likely to encounter in the UK come from the high-altitude vineyards in the southern area of Tarija,

65

(1,700m and above) where the majority of vineyards are to be found, the climate being the most favourable for viticulture. The best wines are the rather respectable ones from La Concepción, which are imported by Moreno Wine Merchants (see *Where to buy wine*). This is one of the oldest wineries in the country, yet only sold its first wines in 1991 – testimony to quite how much of a novelty wine is in Bolivia. Cabernet is the pick of the bunch, but the Merlot is OK, and the American-style Chardonnay well made. As we hoped, this year we are able to report on not two but three Bolivian wineries – the two new ones being Kohlberg and Campos de Solana.

BRAZIL

Brazilian wines are noticeable by their absence on UK shelves at present, but that's not to say there's nothing to speak of wine-wise in South America's largest country. Production is still on the up, with forecasts that it will continue to increase over the next five years. The main challenge for the wineries is to cope with the heavy rainfall, which causes many producers to pick their grapes before they have attained full ripeness, and while the acidity is still high. However, this is something of a blessing in disguise, as such attributes are exactly what is required for making sparkling wine. Testimony to this is that Moët & Chandon has a winery in Brazil producing palatable dry white fizz, and a red one too; Maison Forestier also produces a decent sparkler. As for other styles, the Miolo and Valduga wineries are reportedly good for still wines, but the Aurora co-operative in Rio Grande do Sul that we talked about last year is struggling since its flying winemaker, John Worontshak, left. Brazil has a very strong domestic market, so don't expect to see any of these wines on UK shores in the short term.

BULGARIA

Bulgaria still seems to be struggling: the only wines we can find today that really match those beloved full-of-fruit cheapies of the 1980s come from Domaine Boyar's Blueridge label – a large handful of Merlots, Cabernets and Chardonnays, American-oaked and French-oaked, almost all priced £3.99. And while these stand out against other Bulgarian offerings for their concentrated fruit flavour, cleanly made and well-presented, they're not actually that exciting. Certainly, they're no more interesting than the flood of similarly priced wines coming out of Australia and Chile – and the latter are almost always more reliable.

So why should we buy Bulgarian? Domaine Boyar actually accounts for around 70 per cent of all Bulgarian wine sold on the UK market at the moment and, while sound, the apex of its achievement appears to be its £4.99 range of 'premium' wines. But can £4.99 truly be described as premium? This is our point. We'd like to see more evidence of what Bulgaria can really achieve in wine terms. Emerging from behind the Communist curtain hasn't been easy, and the return of vineyards to private hands has been beset with problems, not least lack of money. But as the wineries gain more and more control over their grape sources and develop their own vineyards, one or two flagship wines should have turned up by now, waving a proud banner for Bulgarian authenticity.

It's all very well for Blueridge to release a £5.99 Syrah (which may indeed be very good), but Syrah is everybody's darling right now. What difference is it going to make that it's Bulgarian? Instead, it would be encouraging to see more of the interesting indigenous varieties such as Melník, Mavrud and Gamza. Only the Damianitza winery seems to be making any headway here. From the country's hot and heady south-west, near the border with Greece, it turns out powerful Uniqato – 100 per cent Melník, as black and rich as molasses, selling like hot-cakes on the home market, and with years of life ahead of it (in order to be totally Bulgarian, this wine is also matured in 100 per cent Bulgarian oak barrels); port-like ReDark (Merlot made under the tutelage of St-Emilion-trained Mark Vorkin); and No Man's Land (a blend from vineyards that were once fields of barbed wire dividing East from West). With these wines, Damianitza is trying to break out of the cheap-wine rut and into the upper end of the market, and we wish them luck, as they have the quality to succeed. More wineries, however, should be doing the same.

We'd also like to repeat last year's whinge about down-playing the Bulgarian-ness of the names and regions of these wines. There are already enough 'Rocky Valleys' and 'Sapphire Coves' coming out of Australia and California, and the world could cope with some moderate tongue-twisters these days. So how about using some more evocative Bulgarian names instead?

CANADA

With 2001's triumphant finale to the great Icewine Battle, the EU at long last permitting the admission of this ultra-sweet nectar to UK (and European) shores, we ought to be seeing more Icewine taking our shop shelves by storm. Truth is, however, the 2000 and 2001 harvests were rather poor, and did not provide the evidence those of us who travelled to Canada – and had previously bragged about the wine here – hoped to see. But we'd like you to trust us: it *is* good!

And it is, undoubtedly, Canada's flagship wine. After putting the Canadians squarely on the world's wine map by receiving a Prix d'Honneur at Vinexpo in June 1991, it subsequently became the sweetheart of the Pacific Rim and American markets (who pay up to four times the price the Canadians do). Its followers love it less because it's a wine-making freak, than for being a miracle of the vineyards. Icewine grapes undergo a series of freeze-thaw cycles during their final autumn hang-time which, theoretically, creates an array of intricate aromas and unique tastes in the concentrated juice. Temperatures must freeze to -8°C and stay there for the effect to be complete: the grapes must be frozen solid during the crush to ensure none of their water content dilutes the eventual wine (this doesn't happen with Germany's *Eiswein*, for example).

It is possible to produce Icewine every year (though some years are better than others). And also possible to make a fake one. The CCOVI research laboratories (Cool Climate Oenology and Viticulture Institute at Brock University, Niagara), whose efforts are honed towards winemaking in vineyards where temperatures easily reach -15°C, are introducing diagnostic tests to distinguish real wines from fakes. But here we ascend into the realms of the esoteric . . .

Where Icewine leads, others follow. Red and white Canadian table wines also began upping their game in the mid-1970s and 1980s with the banning of odd-tasting native (Labrusca) grape varieties. It isn't too cold here to produce highly palatable Chardonnay, Riesling, Pinot Noir, Cabernet Franc and Merlot. Far from it. After a barrage of vineyard and winery improvements put in place over the last ten years, Canadian red wines are being sold for up to C$125 a bottle (for Vineland Estates' Meritage Reserve 1998). Not so very far removed, then, from the prices fetched by the top California wines. While we don't necessarily approve of these incredibly high prices, the fact that collectors pay them is surely proof enough that the wines are at least good!

Canada's still wines, though, have yet to make any real impact on the world markets. They remain youthful, with plenty of teething problems: many producers prefer the easy route of making wine from inferior grapes, either hybrids such as Vidal and Baco Noir, or crosses such as Ehrenfelser and Kerner. And we think that titling the country's latest global wine conference 'Bacchus to the Future' (May 2002) is perhaps sending out the wrong message as far as enticing grape varieties are concerned.

But with Icewine making up only the tiniest proportion of Canada's total output (in 2000, Icewine production totalled 3,400 litres; still wines 10.3 million litres) we really ought to be seeing more of 'the rest' on our shelves before too long. Now that the EU has lifted its ban on Icewine, the Canadians may be more willing to send them to us.

Red wines

It might seem a gamble to make red wines at all in snowy Canada, and although late developers such as Cabernet Sauvignon run the risk of not ripening fully due to the numbingly quick onset of winter, Cabernet Franc, Merlot, Pinot Noir and Syrah (earlier ripeners) are all going great guns. Each vintage is seeing producers become more experienced with red varieties, and more adept at matching varieties to particular sites. Willing and expert assistance from New World and Old (Australia, Bordeaux) is ensuring that better and more complex wines are beginning to appear, and not only at 'boutique' but at readily available commercial levels too. Hybrid vines such as Baco Noir and Marechal Foch can make full-bodied, rustic wines, but only go for those producers who have success with more mainstream varieties.

White wines

As Canada's wine industry is still in its infancy, it's no surprise to see that the main influence on the flavour of most wines is the winemaker. For example, Chardonnays often display plenty of oak, plus the influence of malolactic fermentation, which gives buttery characteristics. The tight, oatmealy wines of Ontario's Thirty Bench show what can be done when good fruit is sensitively handled.

Sauvignon Blanc is thinner on the ground, and can impress, but Canada's undervalued trump card is Riesling, especially that from the Beamsville Bench overlooking Lake Ontario. Pinot Gris and Pinot Blanc hint at the styles offered by Oregon's delicious versions and they should have a great future too. In the right hands, the wines are rich, minerally, complex and ageworthy. Sadly, lack of popularity means that they are in short supply.

Riesling is one of the favoured grapes for Canada's Icewine. This can be interesting, with a different sort of refinement from that achieved by Germany's *Eiswein* – concentrated, fleshy sweetness, heady citrus and apricot fruit (the warmer, sunnier New World summer climate creates higher alcohol and a weightier mouthfeel), cleansing acidity, and apparently erring towards Tokaji and Sauternes-type tropical complexity with age. Now that Icewine is available in the UK (since May 2001), we'll be able to judge them.

69

Icewine also now exists in sparkling form. Though we've yet to try one of these rare creatures, we're certainly curious to do so.

The regions

A place of frozen tracts and snowy tundra it might be, but Canada has two thriving wine regions where viticulture is possible without recourse to weird and unwonderful hybrid grapes (varieties that fend off the cold, and all too often the punters as well). The states of British Columbia (BC) and Ontario occupy similar latitudes to Washington and Oregon, and New Zealand's South Island: their successful wine regions are the Okanagan Valley and Niagara, respectively.

Southern Okanagan (BC), on the US border (centred on the town of Penticton) even heats up to northern Napa temperatures in its desert south, and produces red wines of similar 'clout'. Northern Okanagan on the other hand has a Champagne-like/Germanic coolness that is tempered by lake influences – territory that lends itself better to whites.

Despite being at the same latitude as Burgundy, Ontario certainly doesn't enjoy the same climate, and it is only the presence of the lakes (Ontario and Erie) that moderates the conditions and makes grape growing possible. But moderate them it does, and this area turns out 75 per cent of Canada's production. Niagara, 2,000 miles to the east of Okanagan, achieves great results with Riesling, and against the odds sees not insignificant wines from red grapes too – see producers listed below.

Vancouver Island also has 15 or so small, first-generation wineries. Despite an alarming number of odd Germanic varieties, we rather like the Pinot Noir and sparkling wines we've seen.

Pick of the producers

Blue Mountain Vineyard One of the first Canadian vineyards to plant *vinifera* varieties, this South Okanagan, BC producer is to be praised for championing Pinots Gris and Blanc that ought to thrive in Canada – also Pinot Noir and traditional-method sparkling.

Cave Spring Cellars Home of particularly good Ontario white wines, from Chardonnay and Riesling to top-of-the-tree Icewines.

Château des Charmes Ontario outfit whose best releases appear under the Paul Bosc and St David's Bench labels. Chardonnay, Cabernet Sauvignon, Cabernet Franc and Riesling (especially Late Harvest) stand out of a very good selection. Savagnin and Viognier are oddities worth watching out for.

Henry of Pelham Ontario red specialist making chewy, perfumed Cabernet Franc, a full-bodied Cabernet/Merlot blend and praiseworthy Chardonnay (oaked and unoaked). However, Late Harvest Riesling is arguably the best wine.

Inniskillin The company that put Canadian wine on the map – with its prize-winning Icewine in 1991 – and now the world's largest single producer. A slight 'blip' in recent years (complacency?) is over. New-broom winemaker Australian Philip Dowell now presides over the Ontario winery with an excellent range of wines, and success with single-vineyard Chardonnay and Montague Vineyard Pinot Noir. Chenin Blanc Icewine is the British Columbia operation's most impressive effort.

Jackson-Triggs Medal-winning, British Columbia winery cultivating its prestigious international connections to good effect. Merlot, Shiraz and Meritage (Bordeaux varieties) head the billing, the latter evocatively called Osoyoos-Larose (from a local Indian name and that of joint-venture partner Château Gruaud-Larose from Bordeaux). Still and sparkling Icewine shouldn't be overlooked either. Owned by Vincor International.

Malivoire Wine Company Expensive but worth it: Chardonnay, Gewurztraminer and old-vine Foch (the red grape Marechal Foch) from talented winemaker Ann Sperling. Rich, concentrated wines from Ontario.

Marynissen Niagara winery with competent whites, but much more impressive reds made from Cabernets Sauvignon and Franc, Pinot Noir and Petite Sirah.

Mission Hill Family Estate British Columbia leader of the 2001 Icewine influx producing a good commercial range from the New Zealand winemaker John Simes, including the 49 North red and white; also Merlot, Syrah, premium red Bordeaux-blend Oculus and Chardonnay. Striking new C$37-million winery should, and does, produce prize-winning wines.

Quail's Gate First-rate British Columbia winery with class across the range, and excelling with Pinot Noir and Chardonnay. Also makes one of the few good wines with the hybrid Marechal Foch grape.

Sumac Ridge Founded in 1979 – and built on an old golf course – this is BC's largest estate. Sparkling and Pinot Blanc Icewine top the white range, while the red Meritage also doesn't lack style.

Thirty Bench Wines Ontario producer of dense, concentrated low-yield wines of prize-winning stature: chunky Chardonnay, Riesling, Bordeaux varieties and ripe, red blends.

Vineland Estates Winery Superb Rieslings (both dry and 'iced') from an estate with first-class German origins – it was set up by Hermann Weis of St Urbans-Hof in the Mosel. The reds aren't bad either.

CHILE

We thought standards were slipping, but the everyday drinkability of Chilean wines is faring rather better than it was last year. There's a rather bland monotony to the whole Merlot/Pinot/Cabernet/Chardonnay show, but, in fairness, there is also a lot of bright purity in those cassis and blackcurrant flavours (in Cabernet, especially) in the kind of direct style that is special to Chile.

But Chile mustn't follow Australia – in terms of price-cutting, bulk blends – any further than it has already. Australia has the infrastructure in place for consumers to trade up and get out of the big-brand mire: Chile, as yet, doesn't. And a glut of cheap wine can damage a country's reputation very quickly.

It's not that things aren't changing. Chile is beginning to rise to the challenge, and is putting an enormous amount of effort into filling out the £6–£10 range. Things are apparently leaping along, with complexity as well as some welcome concentration coming through in the wines. Better still, there have been some attempts to capture the characteristics of the different regions, such as minerally characteristics from Maipo and eucalypt flavours from Colchagua. All the wineries are looking to extend their ranges both upwards and sideways, so adding a new label from a specific region comes naturally, by isolating areas of different expression – a more defined 'this' or a perfume of 'that'.

More work has been done in the vineyards too: the 'noughties' (2000s) are definitely seeing the dawn of an 'earth era' – getting back to the soil and 'listening' to it. The Chileans are becoming better at managing unusual conditions and understanding irrigation, which has allowed them to make forays into the drier, cooler coastal areas (away from the well-watered Andean slopes), where they've been sinking wells, to make things work for them. They've been to Bordeaux (for example) too, and come back thinking: 'Well, we have this soil, and those weather conditions, so why don't we put our Merlot on a slope like that too.' There's certainly a lot of passion to get it right.

The other thing it's good to see happening in Chilean vineyards is an enthusiastic adoption of organic and biodynamic viticulture. Undoubtedly this has its footing in commercial appeal (call us cynics), but this is a country in which these practices can be adopted with relative ease. A combination of low natural humidity, low rainfall and strong sunlight reduces the risk of fungus, mildews and rot – and thus reduces the need for chemical sprays, etc. Also Chile now seems to have a better grasp of drip irrigation and less of that insatiable desire to flood its vineyards with meltwater (as in Argentina, over the Andes), so vineyards today are nothing like as damp and delightful as far as mould and rot are concerned. Organic winemaking could well be a big feature of the future.

Up another level, at the very top end of the market, the jury's still out. The big, powerful, expensive reds being made by boutique wineries are still too young and out of balance for us to really know how they'll develop. There's plenty of tannin still, but is the fruit going to hold up? New 'garage' style wines are still emerging once in a while, such as Antiyal in the Maipo Valley and Almaviva. And bigger companies, not wanting to be outdone, are developing their own *micro-cuvée* wines, equally impressive. A lot of these wines come from grapes planted on the slopes, where it is very expensive to clear the natural dry thorny scrub, and subsequently only produce tiny yields. Growers have to be very confident they will sell such a wine before they embark on this type of project. And if they sell it, can we drink it?

There are three questions Chile has to answer in 2003: should it opt for a more 'green' wine scene at entry level? (This is one of the few countries where such a stance would be possible, without incurring too much extra cost.) Should it adopt Carmenère as its 'unique selling point'? (The equivalent of Australia's Shiraz? Well, maybe . . .) And, how will it tackle the effects of the economic crises next door in Argentina, the price of its entry level wines tumbling to a parity with Chile's own? We think Argentina might have more to offer in terms of its range of grape varieties (if it uses its assets to best advantage), but if Chile were to play the green card, it may well trump them.

Red wines – grape varieties

Cabernet Sauvignon

Those who have never detected blackcurrant in Cabernet Sauvignon should try Chilean versions. Sometimes there's a hint of mint, sometimes tobacco, sometimes a dusty note, but at the core of many wines is that lush cassis/blackcurrant pastille flavour. Blending and more sensitive winemaking are now resulting in more complexity in the wines, especially at higher price levels – but let's hope that Chile never gives up the joyous cheaper versions at which it currently excels.

Merlot

Merlot is the darling of Chile, the variety that made it famous. Usually bright beetroot-purple in colour with a trademark cherry/ cassis nose and blackcurranty soft cherry palate, it has a velvety smooth, irresistible appeal that put this country instantly on the vinous map. It was only in the early 1990s that it became clear that much of what the Chileans understood to be Merlot was actually the obscure variety Carmenère (see below), which hails from Bordeaux but is virtually extinct there. Today, each grape is treated separately, or used in blends with Cabernet Sauvignon and/or Cabernet Franc. Although many wines labelled Merlot still contain a large dollop of Carmenère, we're not going to get too worried about this just yet as the results are typically rather good.

Carmenère

After several years 'in denial', wanting to believe this was the precious Merlot grape, Chile's winemakers are finally beginning to realise that they have something unique in Carmenère. They have learned to cope with its later ripening time and produce wines to take pride in. It's now hard to understand how the two varieties were ever confused. While there are visual similarities, Merlot gives softer wines, and Carmenère has more structure and fragrance, with an occasional overtone of soy sauce or red pepper (which can be fine, as long as they don't disintegrate into anything green and herbaceous); it is in fact more likely to be related to Cabernet Franc than Merlot. Guestimates suggest that plantings are now roughly 60 per cent Carmenère to 40 per cent Merlot, with the best sites being in Colchagua and Maule. Expect to see great improvements in Carmenère's performance as it is taken more seriously.

Pinot Noir

Cono Sur and Valdivieso wooed us initially with Pinot and the trend caught on. A number of producers are now capable of making attractive, juicy wines brimming with silky berry fruit (and Pinot plantings increased by 52 per cent in 2001). It will still be some time before Burgundy, New Zealand, California, and even Australia, need to worry about Chilean competition – Chile is only *just* beginning to start working with different clones – but now that cool regions such as Bío-Bío and Casablanca are learning to control irrigation (to drip irrigate rather than flood the vines), the results are getting better and better.

74

Others

We've encountered good Petite Sirah, Syrah, Sangiovese, Malbec and Zinfandel in recent times, so it's no surprise to see more producers experimenting with these varieties. Carignan too can turn in surprisingly fine wine. Many producers now grow Malbec, either for a single-varietal wine or for blending. Cabernet Franc is also being used to admirable effect for blending, although Valdivieso has shown how successful it can be on its own.

White wines – grape varieties

Chardonnay

As with Cabernet, Chile's Chardonnays at the lower end of the scale delight, with simple fresh tropical and citrus fruit flavours very much to the fore. However, as one spends more and more, complexity seldom appears, although a growing number of wineries – notably Viña Casablanca, Concha y Toro, Errázuriz – do deliver the goods. Look for sharper, lighter fruit with a lift to it from Casablanca, the best region, and warmer, more rounded styles from Rapel and Maipo.

Sauvignon Blanc

While there is now a differentiation between Merlot and Carmenère in Chile, there's no move to distinguish between true Sauvignon and the inferior Sauvignonasse, which tires quickly in bottle. When real Sauvignon, from a cooler area such as Casablanca, has been grown without too much recourse to irrigation and picked at optimum ripeness, the wines are zippy, fresh and very attractive. The Curico and Rapel regions also make Sauvignon with some style.

Others

Gewurztraminer, from either Casablanca or Bío-Bío in the south of the country, can be excellent. However, we urge you to buy some soon, otherwise the vineyard owners will replant with a more commercial variety. Semillon and Riesling can also be very good, both for dry and sweet wines, although again they are being displaced from the vineyards in favour of other grapes. Viognier has a small but growing following, with Cono Sur's rich heady version showing what is possible. Don't hesitate to buy these wines as the Chileans need every encouragement to diversify rather than revert to boring Chardonnay and Sauvignon.

Regions

Chile has three main wine regions: Aconcagua, Central Valley and the Southern Region. Aconcagua is divided into Aconcagua Valley

75

and the Casablanca Valley, which lies between Santiago and the coast. The Central Valley spreads southwards from Santiago and is split into Maipo, Rapel (zones Cachapoal and Colchagua), Curicó (Teno and Lontué) and Maule (Claro, Loncomilla and Tutuven). Further south still, the Southern Region has Itata and the cool, wet Bío-Bío district as its sub-regions.

Within many of these delineated districts there is a wide variety of growing conditions, ranging from well-drained limestone slopes at high altitudes to much lower, flatter alluvial plains. Because the wines produced are often blended together, factors such as the age of the vines, the extent of the irrigation and the skill of the producer cause more flavour variation than the zone of production.

Exceptions are beginning to emerge, however, with regions such as cool Casablanca, whose proximity to the coast (and the Antarctic Humboldt current, which can lower temperatures by as much as 10°C) means that the growing season can be extended by up to a month, making it the source of several of Chile's finest white wines. Two smaller cool regions emerging are Leyda, 'the next Casablanca', which is again coastal, producing whites with fine natural acidity, and, near to Santiago, the Limarí Valley, semi-arid but which also receives coastal breezes and gives aromatics (more delicate flavours) that, so far, look to be very fine.

Rapel is another highly favoured region, particularly for Merlot. And Bío-Bío's cool sub-regions are also said to yield fresher, crisper wines, but this territory is also damp and rot-prone, so the jury's still out on the likes of Negrete, Traiguén and Mulchén. (The success rate of marginal viticultural regions being what it is, these regions may well turn up trumps in the future.)

Pick of the producers

Almaviva This firm, rich, oaky wine, the result of a joint venture between Concha y Toro and Mouton Rothschild, manages to pack the fruit of Chile into the structure of Bordeaux. From the same stable come the more affordable but still impressive red blend, Escudo Rojo and the Mapa varietal range.

Antiyal First solo-venture wine for ex-Viña Carmen winemaker, Alvaro Espinoza, is a delightful blend of Cabernet Sauvignon, Merlot and Syrah, as complex as anything Chile has achieved so far, and biodynamic into the bargain.

Aquitania/Paul Bruno Maipo brainchild of Paul Pontallier (Château Margaux) and Bruno Prats (Château Cos d'Estournel) making Cabernet Sauvignon that, while showing some improvement, should be even better, given its pedigree.

Caliterra Bold, fruit-forward wines from a winery owned jointly by Errázuriz and Robert Mondavi of California. New Arboleda range outclasses most Chileans at the same price, and Carmenère is one of the best in Chile. (See also *Seña*, below.)

Canepa Continuing to offer good-value wines, despite upheavals in the mid-1990s that resulted in the loss of all its vineyards. Oak-Aged Semillon just one highlight of a very competent range.

Viña Carmen Very consistent Maipo producer making decent whites and even better reds, with inky rich Merlot, Winemaker's Reserve (Cabernet Sauvignon/Carmenère/Petite Sirah/Merlot) and Gold Reserve Cabernet the stars. Look out too for the high-quality Nativa range, made from organically grown grapes.

Casa Lapostolle Michel Rolland-inspired winery with good whites and superb reds. Cuvée Alexandre Merlot used to be the shining star, now eclipsed by quite splendid Clos Apalta, a complex blend of Merlot, Carmenère, Cabernet and Malbec, with Petit Verdot a possible partner for the future.

Viña Casablanca Casablanca-based offshoot of Santa Carolina with some of Chile's finest whites and increasingly impressive reds from the Santa Isabel Estate. Also good reds from the Maipo and Rapel regions, including Fundo Special Cuvée.

Concha y Toro Huge company producing wines of exemplary standard, both under its own label and easy-going entry level wines Trio (of which there are now six) and the new Copper range. Elegant, balanced Terrunyo and Explorer are the next level up (£7–£8). Amelia Chardonnay ranks as one of Chile's best, as does Don Melchor Cabernet. (See also *Almaviva*, above.)

Cono Sur Modern Concha y Toro-owned winery offering interest across the board, including quirky varietals such as Zinfandel, Viognier and Gewurztraminer. 20 Barrels range is especially good, with the Pinot still Chile's best. Wines under the Isla Negra label are also first class.

Cousiño Macul Famous for many years for its full-bodied if rather old-fashioned Antiguas Reservas Cabernet. The new flagship Finis Terrae is made in a more modern style from pre-phylloxera vines, but still lacks the complexity to be ranked among Chile's finest.

Dallas Conte Joint venture between Viña Santa Carolina (see below) and international wine group Beringer Blass. Supple juicy Cabernet is the pick so far.

Echeverria Curicó winery run by the scholarly Roberto Echeverria well known for good-quality Cabernet, Chardonnay and Sauvignon.

Luis Felipé Edwards 200-hectare Colchagua estate, source of some of Chile's best Chardonnay and Cabernet Sauvignon, and now with an ex-Penfolds' winemaker in charge of the cellar. Top red Doña Bernada Privada has flavour and finesse.

Errázuriz Sole winery in the Aconcagua Valley, with high quality across the board from Californian winemaker Ed Flaherty. Best wines are the Wild Ferment Chardonnay and new Wild Pinot Noir (from Casablanca), Don Maximiano Cabernet and a fine Syrah and Sangiovese. Viñedo Chadwick (less weighty than Don Max) is a new second label, £35-ish, from the Maipo Valley. (See also *Seña*, below.)

Gillmore Maule winery making classy reds, the best of which are Merlot and Cabernet Franc, but don't ignore the honest, juicy Carignan.

Viña de Larose/Las Casas del Toqui French-owned, and producing fine Bordeaux-style Semillon and well-structured, fruit-packed Cabernet.

Montes The Montes Alpha reds, topped by the densely fruity 'M', are first class, and the Malbec and Syrah are also delicious, but other releases are more erratic. New Montes Folly, a Rhône-style wine from steep, low-yield vineyards, has a passionate following already, with the vines only three years old.

MontGras Colchagua winery impressing with reds, especially Merlot and the top-of-the-range Ninquen releases. Chardonnays less convincing, but the Sauvignon is among Chile's best.

Viña Porta A new owner, a new winery and new vineyards mean that only the Viña Porta name remains from pre-1999. Silky Cabernet Sauvignon is the best so far of the new regime.

Viña Quebreda de Macul Rising Maipo star making serious but succulent Domus Aurea Cabernet Sauvignon from a single hillside vineyard planted in 1970.

Viña La Rosa Good-quality reds and whites under the La Palmeria and Cornellana labels, mainly from Rapel fruit. Also lovely rosé, and unusually crisp, elegant whites.

San Pedro Very large reliable producer benefiting from the consultancy expertise of Jacques Lurton. Gato and 35 South (formerly 35 Sur) are the volume brands, Castillo di Molina Reserva is a step up, while Cabo de Hornos Cabernet is impressive and not-too-pricy standard-bearer at £20 or so.

Viña Santa Carolina Historic *bodega* based in Maipo, but with vineyards in several regions. Admirable Barrica Selection range includes fleshy Syrah and a Chardonnay that is far more subtle – or rather, less oaky than it used to be. Reservado wines are also good, while new Trébol (Cabernet/Merlot/Syrah) is astonishingly complex for £6. (See also *Dallas Conte*, above.)

Santa Inés Maipo winery offering both Merlot and Carmenère for those who want to compare and contrast. Legado de Familia Cabernet and Chardonnay stand out from an already good range.

Viña Santa Rita Large organisation with an extremely talented winemaker, continuing its climb in quality. Entry-level 120 range includes a delightful Cabernet Rosé, then come Reserva and Medalla Real ranges. Best wines are Casa Real, one of Chile's greatest Cabernets, and Triple C, a blend of the Cabernets with Carmenère.

Seña Joint venture between Mondavi and the Chadwick family, owners of Errázuriz and Caliterra, made with grapes from Errázuriz's Don Maximiano estate in Aconcagua. Wonderfully fleshy, complex and ripe, but not cheap, and the youngest bottles still not ready for another five years.

Tarapac Major investment from California's Beringer (now Beringer Blass; see also *Dallas Conte*, above) and new blood in charge of winemaking is transforming this Maipo winery. Has the potential to be among Chile's finest, but not as yet quite there.

TerraMater Using fruit from vineyards that used to belong to the Canepa winery, Englishman David Morrison makes delicious commercial (in the best sense of the word) wines. On present form, stick with these in preference to the more expensive Altum range.

Miguel Torres Leading light in the 1980s for its whites, overtaken by others in the 1990s, but now reasserting itself with red wines. Manso de Velasco Cabernet is chewy and curranty, while Cariñena-heavy blend Cordillera is a full-bodied winter warmer.

Valdivieso Famous in Chile for sparkling wines, but making a name overseas for still wines. Best are the single-vineyard reds, the new

'V' Malbec and the multi-varietal, multi-vintage blend Caballo Loco. Sauvignon now being 'beefed up' by new New Zealand winemaker.

Los Vascos Co-owned by Château Lafite-Rothschild. The wines so far have been rather hard and charmless compared with their compatriots, but the new top-end *cuvée* Le Dix de Los Vascos is a welcome step up in quality.

Veramonte Winery founded by the Californian Franciscan Winery, and now owned by its former boss Agustin Huneeus, who hails from Chile. Based in Casablanca with vineyards there, but also sourcing fruit from elsewhere. Look for the Casablanca Chardonnay and red blend Primus. Taking a new lead with single-varietal Carmenère.

Villard Casablanca operation of Frenchman Thierry Villard, formerly of Orlando in Australia. Local fruit used for fine Pinot Noir, Chardonnay and Sauvignon, with Rapel grapes used for impressive Merlot.

Chilean vintage guide

Whites – with precious few exceptions, drink the youngest available, especially the Sauvignon.

Reds – again, very few of the wines gain from further ageing after release, although the sturdier Cabernets, Carmenères and Merlots will take bottle age – how much bottle age still remains to be seen. Chile's vintages do not vary as much as those in other countries, but as we write, there are worries of another El Niño on the cards for 2003. (In 1998, this phenomenon did affect certain parts of the country but nowhere near as severely as in neighbouring Argentina.) 2002, the forerunner of worse for 2003 if the meteorologists are right, was a cool and rainy year in which *botrytis* (the unwanted kind) struck and yields were down. The 2001 season also started badly, with yields down by as much as 30 per cent, but warm weather up to harvest turned things around and grapes were picked in very good condition; final quality was high. The gentle 2000 growing season produced plenty of wine. Where growers worked to reduce yields, the reds were among the most subtle and complex Chile has made. 1999 was a small but good vintage.

CHINA

While China has a well-established wine industry that produces almost as much wine as Australia, the home market guzzles up all but a tiny fraction of what is made. The potential however is huge and, recognising this, a number of outside companies are involved in projects here. Rémy Martin provided input for the Dynasty range of wines, Pernod-Ricard did the same for Dragon Seal, while Allied Domecq is involved with the Huadong Winery, which makes the Tsingtao Chardonnay, one of China's best wines, and also one of the few to be exported in any quantity. But the big excitement at the moment comes from Spain's Miguel Torres who is involved with his Great Wall Torres Winery Co, which has recently released its Tres Torres brand to the hotels, restaurants and supermarkets of Beijing, Shanghai, Xiamen, Chengdu, Xian and Guangzhou provinces. When we see this wine on UK shores we'll let you know how good it is. So far, Torres has invested over US$1 million in China and it tells us that while Syrah, Merlot, Carignan and Garnacha have struggled against the climate, Cabernet Sauvignon has been particularly successful in Huailai County, its part of the country.

CROATIA

Grk, Dingač and Opol. No, they're not baddies from a fantasy novel, just names that we'll have to come to terms with if Croatian wine ever comes into fashion – though this is unlikely. This part of the former Yugoslavia has some fine vineyard sites, especially along the Adriatic coast, and a palette of interesting indigenous grape varieties led by the robust spicy Plavac Mali, which some think may be related to Zinfandel/Primitivo. California-based Croat Mike Grgich of Grgich Hills in Napa Valley makes a Plavac Mali (and a white from the Pošip variety) on the island of Korčula in the Adriatic, and Andro Tomic also produces a highly rated version. We'd like to see more of these and other Croatian wines on our shelves, but with the political situation being what it is, we fully understand why UK importers are reluctant to do business here.

CYPRUS

Cyprus has moved on since the collapse of its Eastern Bloc sweet wine market, and embraced a new culture of enticing varietal red wines. In fact, with no phylloxera, mountain viticulture on original rootstocks and a host of characterful native grape varieties to draw from, there's still every reason to assume these wines will go from strength to strength. Cyprus's mainstream varieties are its indigenous ones: Mavro (a widely planted, rugged red grape, particularly successful at higher altitudes, 800m and more, where it takes on more cherry finesse), Xynisteri (the aromatic white grape used for Commandaria), Opthalmo (light, acidic red) and rich, dark Cabernet-like Maratheftico. Cabernet Sauvignon exists in small quantities, as do Mourvèdre, Carignan and Grenache, but the island mentality has led to strict quarantining and a reluctance to bring in new, potentially diseased international vines. For authenticity's sake, this has been a good thing.

Wines to look out for come from Keo, SODAP (Mountain and Island Vines brands), Etko and Loel, the main, public wine companies, but things are becoming increasingly decentralised, and smaller wineries to watch are Vouni, Fikardos, Chrysoroyiatissa Monastery, Laona, Olympus and Mallia. Promotion abroad, however, is still in the hands of the government, so don't expect to see anything more imaginative than the occasional supermarket offer on UK shores.

Australian winemakers have lately been a very positive influence in Cyprus – particularly at the larger wineries. Beer and ouzo being everyday local staples, the wine industry relies heavily on export, so an upgrade to international standards over the 1990s was essential. Australians (used to working in similar hot conditions) have, among other things, transformed cellar technology, introduced controlled pruning and updated vineyard practices – and have even seemed content to stay rather than fly in and out for each vintage. Good news indeed.

Cyprus' long-established sweet wine, Commandaria, the wine of the Crusaders, is still hugely important to the island, and its similarity to Australian Liqueur Muscat makes it another reason for the Antipodeans to feel at home.

CZECH REPUBLIC

The only Czech wines that enjoy reasonable distribution in the UK are the Bohemia Sekt sparklers from near Prague, which come in white, pink and red guises. If you see them, give them a go. They won't strike fear into the makers of champagne, but they're really rather pleasant, in a frivolous, frothy way. Otherwise there's not much to report: a fair amount of lovely spicy Irsay Oliver and fresh sappy Frankovka used to be available at around £4 in the supermarkets – but where are they now?

Moravia, a hop across the border from Austria's Weinviertel, is where more than 95 per cent of Czech vineyards are to be found. Many of the same varieties are grown as in Austria: among the whites are Müller-Thurgau, Riesling, Welsch/Laski Rizling, Irsay Oliver, Pinot Blanc, Pinot Gris, Traminer, Grüner Veltliner and Neuburger, while reds include Frankovka (Austria's Blaufränkisch), St-Laurent and Pinot Noir. The wines aren't quite as good as Austria's, but nonetheless, we're disappointed to see so few of them in the UK.

ENGLAND

Last year we said that if England is to be taken seriously as a wine-producing nation, three things needed to happen: England needed to show more confidence in the wines it produces; continue the trend away from odd-sounding Germanic hybrid grapes; and continue making progress with sparkling wine.

Well, the likes of Nyetimber, Ridgeview and Valley Vineyards are still leading the challenge to Champenoise fizz, with their own equally stylish – and often confusable – versions. Their number may not be increasing dramatically, but the skills in the cellar and vineyard are improving gradually year by year. With growers taking time to rest their wine on the lees for a few years before releasing it for sale, some complex, nutty, classic characteristics are emerging, and already the wines are being offered alongside champagne on some of the top merchant and restaurant lists – at not dissimilar prices. It may be the sparklers with which England eventually makes its mark internationally.

We're also cheered to see a new kind of confidence emerging among English growers, embracing rather than shunning the odd hybrid varieties. This is a marketing move that may not work, but the much-publicised re-launch of the Chapel Down group (which incorporated Lamberhurst and Carr Taylor), as New Wave Wines, included the release of a new brand, Curious Grape, a celebration of all that's odd about those weird and wonderful varieties that survive on English soils. While it concerned us at first to see so much time, effort and money being put into lauding grapes such as Bacchus and Optima (the words damp and squib came to mind), we then thought about it. How many times do we hear complaints about not just the Chardonnay name but its predictable flavours? How often do we hear praise for a new variety discovered? Answer to both – 'lots'! Combined with the sense of national pride aroused during Jubilee week, June 2002, when the wines were launched, it seemed New Wave was on to a good thing. There's no doubt that these varieties are the ones that ripen best in the English climate; and decent winemaking and vineyard management make for far finer, more concentrated flavours these days than we've seen in the past. We like the blends best (however tongue-twisting it is to get to grips with the names).

The other thing we're pleased to see happening with English wine is the launch of a new classification. By the time you read this, any English wine not passing a rigorous tasting test will qualify only as 'Table Wine' with unidentified vintage, varietal or vineyard name. Those that pass will be allowed 'Regional Wine' status (the equivalent of *vins de pays* in France). There will also be a third level, 'Quality Wine', for top-echelon produce. By introducing this series of checks, the English Vineyards Association hopes to raise quality levels of English wine by preventing less-serious growers from labelling their wine as anything they like, regardless of bottle contents, and so guarantee quality.

There's no doubt about it, though, the very best way to get to know English wine is to visit the vineyards in person: travel those country lanes of Sussex, Devon or even Cornwall in pursuit of a different grape variety or a new kind of fizz. To find out about opening hours, locations, tours and tastings, visit the English Wine Producers' website: *www.englishwineproducers.com*. Failing that, look around your local Waitrose, Tesco, Majestic, Unwins or Corney & Barrow, Selfridges or Fortnum & Mason (to name a few; see *Where to buy wine*) and pick up a bottle or two to see what we mean.

White wines

England's cool climate means its wines will always be high in acidity, so don't expect everyday-drinking Chardonnays, but do expect to see more in the way of familiar varieties such as Sauvignon, Pinot Blanc and Riesling than ever before. Chardonnay is planted but most of the grapes are used for sparkling winemaking – although the use of barrels nowadays suggests interesting blending possibilities with oak adding character to the basically fragile flavours this grape offers in England. The predominance of lesser-known grapes of Germanic origin, including Reichensteiner, Kerner, Madeleine Angevine and Bacchus, is still with us. Realistically, these are the varieties that ripen consistently well in this country and more and more growers are deciding to embrace their oddball characters rather than be embarrassed by them. The world needs variety after all, and these grapes are less of a risk when 30°C of sunshine can't be guaranteed. Lastly, high acidity is not a problem with sweet wines. The English climate often leads to favourable conditions for *botrytis*, which creates sweetness, and works well when countered by a crisp, acidic tang. We certainly suggest trying any of these sweet wines when you discover them.

Red wines

Achieving sufficient ripeness in black grapes to produce successful red wines has always been a problem in England, due to the lack of warm sunshine. That said, some thoroughly impressive Pinot Noir and Dornfelder have emerged in the last few years from two estates in particular, Valley Vineyards and Denbies. Oak barrels and oak chips are also proving useful to round out some of the flavours. Other red grapes to watch out for are Syrah-like Rondo and tannic Triomphe – both of which make some flavourful blends.

Sparkling wines

The best wines England has to offer. Made traditionally with Chardonnay and Pinot Noir grapes, they can be mistaken for champagne and are delicious. Given that some of England's vineyards are only one degree latitude above Rheims, with similar soil types, this is hardly surprising. There are now over 40 English sparkling wines, more and more of them coming from Chardonnay and Pinot Noir vineyards planted specifically for making fizz, and quality is getting better and better: some wines are even on sale at similar prices to the *grandes marques* over the Channel, but we recommend those at £12–£14, even available in some supermarkets. Those made from non-traditional varieties (local English varieties) aren't quite as good, but we're increasingly impressed with the new wave of rosé sparklers.

Pick of the producers

Bearsted Tiny Kent winery making particularly good sparkling wine and lively Bearsted Pimpernel rosé. (The author of *The Scarlet Pimpernel* once lived in Bearsted.)

Breaky Bottom Interestingly quirky property near Lewes, in Sussex. Anyone who thinks Seyval Blanc is an inferior grape variety should try Peter Hall's rich and ageworthy version. Also good Müller-Thurgau, Pinot Noir and sparkling wine.

Camel Valley Very Cornish wines from the innovative Bob Lindo. Sparkling is the speciality and lucky southerners will find it in Waitrose, Asda and Safeway stores at a thoroughly reasonable £13.95 or so. Traditional winemaking and traditional English grape varieties (Seyval Blanc and Madeleine Angevine).

Chapel Down Relaunched Spring 2002 under the banner New Wave Wines Ltd. Chapel Down will still be the name of the fine range of sparklers but full-bodied red Epoch (made from Dornfelder), the crisp, smoky Bacchus Reserve (it could pass for a New Zealand Sauvignon) plus Schönburger, Ortega and others now go under the quirky Curious Grape brand. Aiming for wider appeal and the million-bottle mark, with hefty new finance.

Denbies Unbelievably beautiful estate in the Mole Valley, near Dorking in Surrey; well worth a visit. Has the potential to rival Germany with its crisp Rieslings and softly elegant Dornfelder reds when vintage and winemaking are on form, but the latter has not been steady in recent years. With 105 hectares, it covers 10 per cent of all UK vineyards (many grapes are sold on).

Hidden Spring Improvements over the last five years have made this Sussex outfit a great place to visit (the wines are mostly sold at the gate), and done nothing to disrupt the quality of its wines. The Sussex Sunset rosé is one of the biggest hits here.

Nyetimber England's first vineyard dedicated solely to sparkling wine made from the traditional champagne grape varieties. The award-winning maiden release, in 1992, was a 100 per cent Chardonnay Blanc de Blancs; Pinot Noir and Pinot Meunier have featured in subsequent wines. Current vintage, 1994, is showing superbly and looks set to age, 1995 will be released in 2003. A shining example, and wines that ought to keep the Champenoise on their toes. Recently sold to an American song-writer, but Chicagoans Stuart and Sandy Moss still make the wine.

Ridge View Pioneers (with Nyetimber) of traditional-method English sparkling wine made using solely Chardonnay, Pinot Noir and Pinot Meunier grapes. Prize-winning, complex sparkling wines (look out for the 1996 and 1998 vintages) are made at the purpose-built winery high on the Sussex Downs. The wines also appear under the South Ridge label.

Sharpham Eccentric Devon producer with good range of whites (particularly from the Madeleine Angevine variety) but best known for the tiny quantities of Beenleigh red (or rosé in lesser years) made from Cabernet Sauvignon and Merlot grown in polytunnels.

Shawsgate Suffolk winery for consistently good Bacchus and a tempting 'vine leasing' scheme whereby customers can rent a row and have their grapes made into wine come harvest time.

Three Choirs The Reserve Schönburger and Madeleine Angevine, the Reserve Brut and the Late Harvest are the best wines in a very good range produced from vineyards surrounding the cathedral cities of Gloucester, Hereford and Worcester. English Nouveau, released around the same time as Beaujolais, is very popular, and a fruity sparkling wine is almost there (too much Seyval Blanc perhaps).

Valley Vineyards The wines remain as reliable as ever from this Berkshire estate, particularly the impressive sparklers (Ascot, Heritage) and Clocktower, a delicious *botrytis* wine. Watch out also for White Fumé, and Ruscombe Red, a juicy raspberryish red from Triomphe, Pinot Noir, Dornfelder and Gamay. Much of this large range is sold from the gate, so we suggest a visit.

English vintage guide

All things considered, with the 2001 vintage having one of the wettest winters on record and the wettest harvests, with a none-too-bright summer in between, the wines are of surprising quality, with good sugar levels and clean fruit flavours – but then (for the most part) England grows grape varieties that can put up with these conditions. Likewise, 2000 proved that even in a rainier-than-average ripening season it's possible to get it right with a professional attitude to vineyard management. Wineries with good equipment and sound practices made creditable wines from decent fruit. 1999 did not have the ripeness of 1998, but there were no significantly adverse conditions either and the wines show delicacy and finesse.

FRANCE

ALSACE

One of the *Guide*'s authors tutored an Alsace tasting for a group of wine enthusiasts recently and was struck, not for the first time, by just how much people love these wines when they finally get round to trying them. The unusual, exotic aromas, the hints of spice, candied peel, sweet cake and zest, the sheer weight and body – some Alsatian whites (and the vast majority *are* whites) are truly striking. Anyone tired of endless Chardonnay and Sauvignon Blanc should give them a whirl.

There are wines that are perfect as aperitifs, yet many that are generously food-friendly: some are delicious when young, and others age magnificently. There are easy-drinking wines (at sensible prices too), and wines that appeal to the intellect; and wines that will strike chords with palates accustomed to both the New World and the Old World. There are sweet wines, medium wines, dry wines, light and refreshing wines, and opulent, rich ones. So why should it take a tutored tasting, or even a trip to this pretty, wooded part of eastern France, to convince people of such virtues?

In part, it's due to the fact that Alsace wines can be difficult to understand. The tall green bottles, Germanic names and grape varieties such as Riesling and Gewurztraminer all mean they are often confused with German wines. The gabble of words on a label makes things worse – terms such as 'cuvée Caroline' or 'spéciale réserve' don't really indicate anything much. And it is annoyingly difficult to work out whether the whites are dry, medium or sweet; we wish there was a clearer indication of what to expect in this respect. Added to this, many producers turn out a vast range of wines, perhaps from different *grand cru* sites (for more on these, see *Appellations and quality levels*, below), and getting acquainted with them all can seem too much of an effort. Sometimes it all can seem easier to stick to Vin de Pays d'Oc Chardonnay or Pinot Gris.

For the would-be Alsace wine drinker the plus-points are: the UK's supermarkets stock generally competent wines from the region, usually at decent prices. And, unusually for France, Alsace's varietals are labelled by grape – Pinot Blanc, Riesling, Gewurztraminer and Pinot Gris are the most commonly seen – which makes choosing a bottle a little easier. Finally, many of the least expensive usually hail from one of the number of quality-conscious co-operatives to be found in the region.

If you like what you taste and are interested in further exploration, you can always plump for more expensive wines. However, as you move up the quality ladder, Alsace gets a little more complicated, and we would make two recommendations: first, put yourself in the hands of merchants who specialise in Alsace; second, stick initially to one or two producers you like – say Trimbach, Zind-Humbrecht or Hugel – and get to know their full range without adding to the confusion.

Alsace's unusual flavours and aromas aren't immediately to everyone's taste, but give them a chance. A few more people seem to be going for it – UK sales in 2001, although still small compared with other classic French regions, were up by 2 per cent in volume and, more interestingly, by 12 per cent in value terms. Just because they come in unfashionable bottles, and taste a little different, doesn't mean you should ignore these often superb, original wines.

Many more modern restaurants are embracing Alsace wines for their food-friendly qualities and giving the region's wines a much-needed boost. Quite right too. Paired with various fish and vegetarian dishes, trendy 'Asian-fusion' cooking and mildly spicy Thai and Chinese cuisine, not to mention rich pâtés and puddings, Alsace's whites really come into their own.

Appellations and quality levels

There are three appellations in Alsace. AC Alsace is the basic appellation for still wine in the region, while AC Alsace Grand Cru, introduced in 1983, is used for wines at a higher level. The *grand cru* idea sounds good in theory. A *grand cru* wine can come only from the best sites and be made from the best varieties, namely Gewurztraminer, Riesling, Pinot Gris and Muscat. In practice, however, there are too many *grands crus*. Not all of the 50 sites merit the higher designation, while others deserve it for certain grapes (including some outside the four listed above) but not others. Some famous monopole (single-proprietor) vineyards, such as Trimbach's Clos Ste-Hune and Zind-Humbrecht's Clos Windsbuhl, don't even qualify for *grand cru* status, despite producing some of Alsace's finest wines. Moreover, several growers with *grand cru* vineyards don't promote their wines as such, either as an objection to the system or because their yields are too high. So as in Burgundy, while the best wines still come from the best sites, the name of the producer is often a better guarantee of quality than the name of the vineyard. One development that might improve quality is the fact that some (not all) local *syndicats* have recently imposed small maximum yields of 55hl/ha. Indeed, wine growers from 15 *grand cru* vineyards reduced their yields for the 2001 vintage. We can't report on any changes in the glass just yet, as the 2001 *grand cru* wines are yet to come our way, but more on this apparent quality drive next year.

The third AC is Crémant d'Alsace for sparkling wines from the region (see below).

Styles

Vendange tardive Wine made from late-harvested grapes, sometimes medium-sweet and luscious, at other times much drier with high alcohol levels. Potentially confusing. A recent increase (from the 2001 vintage) in the minimum ripeness levels required for *vendange tardive* and *sélection des grains nobles* wines should improve quality somewhat.

Sélection des grains nobles Sweet, rich wines made from grapes affected by noble rot. *Botrytis* does not occur with any regularity in Alsace, and these wines are therefore rare and expensive. They can be absolutely delicious.

White wines – grape varieties

Gewurztraminer

Anyone who has not yet tried Alsace Gewurztraminer should get hold of a glassful, swirl it around and take a good sniff. A strong reaction is guaranteed – one way or the other. Gewurztraminer is Alsace's most distinctive varietal wine, with an extraordinarily exotic perfume propelling rose petals, powdered ginger, lychee and Turkish Delight up from the glass. If there is enough fresh acidity and a fruity citric core of flavour, the wine will taste as good as it smells, and be a great match for Thai cuisine (if dry), or rich pâtés and desserts (if sweet). Poor examples are clumsy and flabby, with a scent horribly reminiscent of floral air freshener.

Muscat

The rarest of Alsace's four noble grapes (the other three being Gewurztraminer, Pinot Gris and Riesling), and often underrated, Muscat produces fresh, dry wines with the mouth-watering character of crunchy, green grapes. Alsace Muscat makes an ideal aperitif and, in the region, is traditionally matched with asparagus.

Riesling

Riesling is considered by Alsace producers to be their greatest grape, probably because with it they can best express the subtleties of *terroir*. Fruity and bracing when young, Alsace Riesling is slightly less steely than its German equivalent, although it can still display the same minerally notes and take on a rich, honeyed and sometime petrolly quality with age. Consummately food-friendly; try it with white fish.

Tokay-Pinot Gris

No relation to the Furmint or Hárslevelű grapes used to make Tokaji in Hungary, Alsace's Pinot Gris (aka Pinot Grigio, Grauburgunder . . .) epitomises the region's opulent style of white wine – rich and fruity with spicy, smoky, slightly peachy depths. Despite an apparent lack of acidity it matches food well and ages brilliantly. Choose with care, however, as there are plenty of one-dimensional, flabby examples around. Drink top wines with creamy savoury courses, or with smooth, decadently rich pâtés.

Pinot Blanc

Pinot Blanc isn't deemed worthy of producing *grand cru* wines, but while it may lack the extrovert personality of other Alsace varieties this doesn't mean the wines are always second-rate. Fine examples have fresh, tangy apple and melon fruit, plus a friendly creamy texture. It's a versatile partner for food, so if you find yourself in a restaurant looking for a wine to accompany four very different dishes, Pinot Blanc is a safe bet.

Others
Auxerrois can be musky and red berry-flavoured in the hands of the right producer. **Sylvaner** is usually uninspiring, but a few wines made in the lean and racy style appeal. **Chasselas**, an Alsace old-timer, is now rarely encountered outside the region.

Blends
Blends of white grapes are traditionally bottled under the generic names Edelzwicker or Vin d'Alsace. Over the years these labels have become associated with cheap, boring wine, and quality producers increasingly choose their own names for specific blended *cuvées*. Some blends remain dull, but others are inspired. Indeed, a few growers, notably Deiss, produce their top wines using a blend of grapes, since they feel that in certain sites it is the *terroir* rather than the grape variety that has the greatest impact on the flavour of the wines. One tip: look out for wines labelled *gentil*. This is an old Alsace name for a blend made from noble varieties only, which has recently been resurrected by Hugel and others who follow strict production rules for their blends.

Red wines

The only black grape cultivated in Alsace is Pinot Noir, which here makes a soft, perfumed, strawberryish red. A few enthusiasts are trying to beef it up into a richer wine, sometimes using oak, with some impressive results. Chilled lightly and paired with fresh salmon it makes an easy-drinking summer red; but even so, its delights are too simple to justify a price tag of £10 a bottle.

Sparkling wine

AC Crémant d'Alsace is not the world's most characterful sparkling wine but don't turn it down at a party. It is made by the champagne method, often from Pinot Blanc, sometimes from Riesling or Pinot Gris. The result is a zippy, fresh sparkling wine with high acidity and hints of lemon and yeast. Again, the price tag can seem a bit steep when compared with, say, Spanish Cava.

Pick of the producers (Alsace)

Beblenheim Good-value, fruity co-operative wines, responsible for some appealing own-label wine in the UK.

Beyer Ancient house, with a relatively dry winemaking style and high-quality range. Long-lived, food-friendly Riesling stands out.

Paul Blanck et fils Increasingly impressive producer with an extensive range including reliable *crémant* and topped by superb Rieslings from the Fürstentum and Schlossberg *grands crus*.

Bott-Geyl Excellent wines from young Jean-Christophe Bott, particularly the Tokay-Pinot Gris.

Deiss Complex, intricately worked whites, with outstanding wines from the *grands crus* of Altenberg de Bergheim, Mambourg and Schoenenbourg.

Dopff au Moulin *Négociant* maintaining high standards and doing well with fresh *crémant*.

Hugel One of the region's most famous producers. Lower-end wines could be better, but the more expensive *cuvées*, especially the superb late-harvest wines, have bags of character yet great finesse.

Charles Koehly et fils Good-value range, especially a limey Pinot Blanc, fresh grapey Muscat and spicy Gewurztraminer.

Marc Kreydenweiss Talented biodynamic producer from the northern part of the region.

Kuentz-Bas One of Alsace's best *négociant* houses, with 12 hectares of prime vineyard site. Especially good for Gewurztraminer, Tokay-Pinot Gris and *vendange tardive*.

Gustave Lorentz Best known for Gewurztraminer, although the Pinot Blanc is worth a whirl too.

Albert Mann Rich wines, including a highly rated Pinot Noir.

JosMeyer Very well-crafted range, but most interesting for Jean Meyer's successful interpretations of minor Alsace grape varieties Chasselas and Auxerrois. The Pinot Blanc Mise du Printemps is an excellent entry-level wine.

Muré Serious Pinot Noir, fine *grand cru* Riesling (Clos St-Landelin), delicious Crémant d'Alsace and sumptuous *sélection des grains nobles*.

Ostertag André Ostertag is an exciting, maverick winemaker creating offbeat wines using low-yielding vines and, sometimes, new oak barrels for richer styles of white.

Ribeauvillé One of Alsace's better co-operatives. Look out for uncommonly fine blends, such as Clos de Zahnacker, made from Riesling, Pinot Gris and Gewurztraminer.

Rieflé Excellent late-harvest wines, elegant Tokay-Pinot Gris and intricately worked Gewurztraminer.

Rolly-Gassmann Dedicated and unpretentious husband-and-wife team making expressive, rich wines, including a spicy Auxerrois and uncommonly tasty Sylvaner.

Schlumberger Extensive vineyard holdings in highly rated *grand cru* sites. Famous for mouth-filling, complex, Gewurztraminer Grand Cru Kitterlé.

Schoffit Finely crafted range from a serious young producer who reads *terroir* well and believes in keeping yields right down. The Rieslings from the Rangen *grand cru* are superb.

Trimbach Arguably the most impressive house of all, producing wine in a distinctive style – elegant, fresh, yet deeply complex. Trimbach's range of Riesling is a benchmark for the region, especially the long-lived, intensely fruity Clos Ste-Hune, with full-bodied Cuvée Frederic Emile a more affordable alternative.

Turckheim Dynamic co-operative providing assured entry-level wines at decent prices. Especially good Tokay-Pinot Gris and highly affordable, tasty Gewurztraminer.

Weinbach The most mind-bogglingly extended family of wines on the shelves but nonetheless a serious set of Rieslings, Tokays and Gewurztraminers in particular. Worth a foray.

Wolfberger Large co-operative responsible for a variable range. Its *crémant* and wines under the linked *négociant* subsidiary Willm label are respectable.

Zind-Humbrecht Master of Wine Olivier Humbrecht offers high quality across the range, from the far-from-basic Pinot Blanc up to the splendid array of *grand cru* Pinot Gris and Riesling. Our only criticism is that the wines give no indication on their labels of the often high residual sugar levels.

Alsace vintage guide

2001 Rainy and cool patches in May and June, then a wet September all put paid to chances of a great vintage. October saw a

fine Indian summer, however, and patient growers who waited
have reaped their rewards. The volume was the same as in 2000 but
quality varies. So, a producer-sensitive vintage – tread with care
and stick to reliable names.

2000 The vintage followed the pattern in much of France, with a
cold July the interruption to warm, sunny weather. A few showers
during the last stages of picking, but quality is generally high.
Plump, fruity wines with sufficient balancing acidity, plus a few
succulent *sélection des grains nobles* wines.

1999 A good spring and warm, dry summer led to a large crop.
Quality, however, varied, thanks to harvest-time rain. Those who
reduced yields have made some lovely wines; others were less
successful.

1998 A hot summer augured well, but rain in September meant a
problematic vintage. Some superb *sélection des grains nobles* wines
made but this wasn't a classic year.

1997 Record hours of sunshine during September meant natural
sugars beyond those of the previous record year, 1989. An excellent
vintage with hot, dry days and cool nights right through the
ripening and harvesting period. Top-quality dry wines all round.

1996 A late harvest due to cold weather in May and August. But a
dry and sunny October brought grapes to a very good level of
ripeness, and those who delayed picking until the warm late
autumn found it paid off. First-class Pinot Gris and Blanc but
Gewurztraminer not as impressive.

1995 A producers' vintage – only the most meticulous were
rewarded. Hot summer followed by a rainy harvest, but late
autumn sunshine. Some high-quality wines.

BORDEAUX

Every year we do it. We complain tirelessly about the price of
Bordeaux, yet 'we' still buy it. There's something about this area of
top-end, luxury goods that seems to say 'pay whatever, you're
lucky to have us!'. Properties just metres apart can differ
enormously in price (£200 and £8,800 per case), and still the sporting
consumer looks at the label and pays the cash. It appears, however,
that the 2001 vintage is about to change all that. Or that's what this
Guide hopes.

  Here's the history: 2000 was a corker of a year in Bordeaux, and
that nobody denies. It came to the rescue of a stream of OK or so-so
vintages, restored some faith in the quality of lesser-rank wines, and
boosted traditional reverence for the top-end versions. Prior to this,
throughout the 1990s, only 1995 stands out as being worthy of real
acclaim, and only 1990 as a first-class stunner. So why, despite the

mediocrity, had prices gradually escalated? We (the wine-writing press) and probably you (the consumer) had been grumbling about this until 1997 when one or two of us made a stand. A dip in quality following the 1996s simply didn't justify another annual price hike, and we wouldn't pay for these wines. But, many people still did . . .

2001 was yet another mediocre year. Its erratic weather conditions started cool and ended stormy with bouts of fine sunshine in between. It was good enough to bring in ripe Merlot, but the Cabernet Sauvignon grapes struggled to reach anywhere near the ripeness they'd achieved in 2000 – those who took less care with their harvest discovered some rather unwieldy green tannins. Straight from the 'horse's mouth', of course, the vintage is talked up: 'a little less powerful than 2000 but more generous than 1999,' they say. But they would, wouldn't they; they want you to pay their prices.

Now to the crux. If prices for the 2000s went up by anything from 35 to 72 per cent – sometimes as much as 400 per cent – should we really accept the usual inflationary increase for the 2001s? 2000 being such a startlingly good vintage in contrast, the obvious answer is no. Case prices should be reduced to somewhere alongside the 1999s.

In the Spring of 2002, the buyers from Farr Vintners (Stephen Browett), Berry Bros & Rudd (Alun Griffiths MW), The Wine Society (Sebastian Payne MW) and other equally mighty merchants penned an open letter requesting just this, that 1999 be used as a reference point, not 2000, adding '[the UK trade] will not buy overpriced wines that it is unable to sell'. The British wine trade then held its collective breath. A price reduction from Bordeaux was virtually unprecedented, so would the châteaux-owners and *négociants* bow to this group pressure? Gradually, in response, a steady trickle of prices came in at between 5 and 20 per cent below the 2000 prices (for the Médoc first growths, the top wines, they were 50 per cent lower). Making a stand did, indeed, stop the greed!

Another matter brought to a head by the 2001s is closely related. The over-extracted, super-fruity wines we complained about last year have been shown up for the confected shams they are. This cooler vintage yielded leaner, greener tannins which modern extractive winemaking methods (long, hot fermentations, vigorous extraction of colour from the skins and so on), only served to emphasise: the resulting wines turned out harsh and bitter at the finish. Either this, or the wines were so fiddled-with that they mostly resembled jam. This is yet another factor giving confidence to the châteaux that have hung-in there and stuck with the traditional winemaking approach. They have ended up with elegant, charming wines that made the best of a tricky year. (For evidence of polarising wine preferences you only have to look to the St-Emilion château Bellevue-Mondotte. The UK trade hated the 2001, Farr Vintners calling it '. . . stewed fruit and high alcohol – more like vintage port than St-Emilion . . . Completely over-blown. A freak . . . A wine made to score big points from American wine critics.' (Said American critic called it, independently: 'A tour de force in winemaking; there's no questioning its quality.')

We're pleased to name a few more names here, and three more châteaux heading back to the traditional style with the 2001 vintage. We mentioned Angélus and Cos d'Estournel last year, this year we add Clinet (Pomerol), Ducru-Beaucaillou (St-Julien) and Smith-Haut-Lafitte (Pessac-Léognan). There are also a few that, against the odds, turned out better wines in 2001 than the marvellous 2000s; these are the exceptions to the rule, for whom higher prices could be tolerated: Eglise-Clinet (Pomerol), Cos d'Estournel (St-Estèphe), Gruaud-Larose (St-Julien), Haut-Brion (Pessac-Léognan), Pape-Clément (Pessac-Léognan) and Le Pin (Pomerol).

Down in the middle and lower echelons, while all this back-slapping and finger-pointing has been going on, a lot of *petits châteaux* will still be trying to sell their 1997s and 1999s. The 2001s may just add to the load. Where the quality of 2000 meant that taking a punt on a *cru bourgeois* was well worth it, in years like 2001 the quality is so variable that, unless you know your property, it simply isn't worthwhile.

However, all this might be about to change, with a move to reinstate the tri-layer Cru Bourgeois classification by early January 2003 (the three divisions being Cru Bourgeois Exceptionnel at the top, Cru Bourgeois Supérieur in the middle, and straight Cru Bourgeois the lowest; see also *The Médoc*, below). This should see further weeding out of bad rubbish from this group – almost a quarter of the existing 419 properties is the rumour. Also, Jacques Berthomeau's ministry of agriculture report calling for the building of wine brands equal to those from the New World has reinforced the message that quality at base level has to improve. We're seeing individual results now, and hope that wholesale reliability will be with us in five years or so once the region has had a chance to change its ways. Steps like this will make Bordeaux less of a confusing mass and we heartily approve!

Bordeaux classification

Bordeaux works on a unique pyramid structure of wine quality classification, with five tiers of *crus classés* – classed growths. There are a number of classification lists, but the most enduring and important is still that of 1855, when the best wines of Bordeaux were ranked according to the price they could command. (In 1855,

Bordeaux was just the Médoc: the 'right-bank' wines of St-Emilion and Pomerol weren't of much importance.)

'Claret' is the term coined by the British to mean any red wine from the whole region; classed growth claret refers to the 60 or so Médoc wines from the 1855 classification. It's a bit like understanding the cast of a play, with major roles taken by the first growths and the supporting players among the second to fifth growth wines. Continuing the 'dramatic' analogy, with every vintage not only can the quality of performance vary, but individual properties can become rising stars for a while, exceeding their designated status and acquiring a cult following in the process. As in theatre-going, it pays to be an avid enthusiast. If you choose to dip in and dip out, then it is vital to rely on the advice and reviews of trusted wine merchants.

Other regions within Bordeaux that have their own classifications include: Sauternes-Barsac (also 1855), St-Emilion (1955, reclassified 1967, 1985 and 1996) and Graves (1959). Ironically, the wines of Pomerol, which are some of the most expensive and most sought-after in the world, have no classification.

The regions

The vineyards of Bordeaux stretch along the left and right bank of the Gironde estuary and its tributaries, the Garonne and the Dordogne. The large, white wine-producing appellation of Entre-Deux-Mers is so called because it sits between the latter two rivers.

Red wines

The Médoc

The Médoc is closest to the Atlantic coast of all the Bordeaux vineyards and, protected by the forests of Les Landes, produces some of the world's greatest and longest-lasting red wines – and almost no white at all. Within these left-bank appellations lie the four star-quality villages of the Haut-Médoc (Margaux, St-Julien, Pauillac and St-Estèphe), where the most famous châteaux can be found and where the Cabernet Sauvignon grape flourishes on the well-drained, gravelly soil near to the Gironde estuary.

Driving north from Bordeaux along the N215, the first village, or *commune*, is Margaux. Key properties include the eponymous Château Margaux, as well as Palmer and Rauzan-Ségla. Purportedly the most feminine of all the wines of the Médoc, Margaux wines can be distinctively delicate as well as exceedingly powerful.

St-Julien comes next and is famed for its consistent, high-quality wines, although there are no first growths from this *commune*.

However, the performance of Léoville-Las-Cases, Léoville-Barton and Gruaud-Larose recently belies their second growth status.

The awesome vineyards in the *commune* of Pauillac, where nearly 90 per cent of the wines are classed growths, produce the most highly prized bottles of all. The first growths Latour, Lafite, Mouton-Rothschild; the excellent second growths Pichon-Longueville and Comtesse de Lalande; and the reputable fifth growths Grand-Puy-Lacoste and Lynch-Bages – all are here.

Lastly, St-Estèphe, a *commune* with a reputation for producing more tightly knit, tannic wines capable of great ageing. This may be to do with the increased clay content of the soil and poorer drainage – the vine needs to work hard to produce good grapes and intensely dislikes being swamped. No first growths here, but Cos d'Estournel, Montrose and Calon-Ségur are worthy of their following.

Apart from the famous names, the Médoc also produces vast quantities of generic Bordeaux for everyday drinking. For probably the best-value wine experience from this region, we recommend experimenting with the Crus Bourgeois (a large designated group of wines just below classed growth status) from the Haut-Médoc. Among these are well-structured, concentrated wines capable of ageing. Look out for châteaux Cantemerle, Coufran, Lanessan and Sociando-Mallet, or find a property whose style you like and follow it through the decent vintages.

Libournais

The Libournais, which includes the right-bank areas of St-Emilion and Pomerol, is known chiefly as the home of softer, more accessible, Merlot-based wines, compared with the heavily structured Cabernet Sauvignon examples on the opposite bank. Right-bank wines are also capable of ageing, but do not have the same tannin content as their left-bank peers, and come to maturity up to a decade earlier.

The great Pomerol properties of Pétrus and Le Pin command stratospheric prices for these rich and velvety Merlot wines. The limited amounts of wine available from these small estates have enhanced their rarity value and contributed to their reputation as the jewels in the crown of Bordeaux. Other well-known names snapping at the heels of these two, albeit from a fair distance, include Vieux-Château-Certan, Bon Pasteur, Lafleur, La Conseillante and Clinet.

St-Emilion, meanwhile, is one of the most confusing appellations of Bordeaux, as well as the most picturesque. The often uninspiring outlook of the Médoc finds a pleasant counterpart in the undulating vineyards surrounding the historic village of St-Emilion itself. Given the variations in soil types and the grapes grown, there is no such thing as a typical St-Emilion wine. While Merlot predominates,

Cabernet Sauvignon and Cabernet Franc can also feature in a wine (for example, Cheval Blanc). The traditional winemaking infrastructure of smallholdings rather than large estates has led, in recent years, to the rise to prominence of many new and dynamic producers. The St-Emilion classification, revised every ten years or so, is complicated, grouping wine not just as *grands crus* (specific enough, you may think, but in St-Emilion of little definitive meaning), but also as *grands crus classés* and *premiers grands crus classés* (A and B). All in all, as in the Médoc, we are talking about 60 or so *crus classés*. Names to watch out for in St-Emilion include the great châteaux Ausone and Cheval Blanc, Clos Fourtet, Figeac, La Gaffelière and Laniote.

Nowadays it is certainly worth discovering the wines from the villages surrounding St-Emilion, some of which, such as Puisseguin and Lussac, can add their name to the appellation on the label. Côtes de Francs and Côtes de Castillon wines also make for excellent everyday drinking. Watch out for the following good châteaux: Griffe de Cap d'Or (St-Georges St-Emilion), Marsau (Côtes de Francs), Domaine de l'A, Aiguilhe, Brisson and Cap de Faugères (Côtes de Castillon). Other quality improvements, and wines to watch, come from the Fronsac and Canon-Fronsac appellations – what's more, at sensible prices too. The Pétrus-owning Mouiex family have long operated in this area; one of their best properties is La Croix Canon. Others to look out for include La Vieille Cure, Moulin Pey Labrie and Fontenil.

Bourg and Blaye
Both these regions, situated directly opposite the Médoc, have much in common with those lesser appellations already mentioned, in that they are the source of many decent and improving, good-value red wines. Exceptional properties include Roc de Cambes in the Côtes de Bourg, and Ségonzac, Grands Maréchaux and Gigault in the Premières Côtes de Blaye.

Graves
Uniquely for Bordeaux, there are several châteaux in the Graves making acceptable white wines as well as red, although the majority of production is red. At the very top, the first growth Pessac-Léognan wine, Haut-Brion, is a historic reminder that the Graves (closer to the town of Bordeaux than the Médoc) has made wine longer than its more illustrious rival areas. Pessac-Léognan itself has five *communes* and, since the 1959 classification, it is generally acknowledged that the best wines of the region, both red and white, come from these. Examples are Haut-Bailly (Léognan), Smith-Haut-Lafitte (Martillac), La Mission-Haut-Brion (Talence), Pape-Clément (Pessac) and Bouscaut (Cadaujac). Below

these famous names are many lesser-known properties that have improved in recent years and provide less-refined but concentrated and flavoursome alternatives to the wines of the Médoc.

Other reds
Classed growth claret and individual appellations, at the top end of the market, belie the fact that the majority of the region's production consists of basic Bordeaux and Bordeaux Supérieur blends – most of them destined for the French supermarkets. In the UK, these are the wines you will usually find with the word 'Claret' or a *petit château* on the label, expressly to give them a more upmarket and traditional feel.

The quality of generic Bordeaux is the battlefield on which the reputation of the region is currently being fought. Things are improving, or beginning to improve, albeit slowly. We feel the best way to identify a decent bottle is to find a name you like and stick to it. It doesn't, unfortunately, pay to be too adventurous; but look to the Côtes de Bourg and Blaye, or the Côtes de Francs, or anything labelled with the 2000 vintage, and you could be off to a reasonable start.

Second wines
These are the unimaginatively dubbed wines made either from the rejected *cuvées* of the top château blends or the fruit of younger vines, as yet not producing enough concentration for inclusion in the top wine. That said, these are often scaled-down versions of the 'real thing' that offer an affordable sneak preview for not much less quality. Exclusion from the top blend can be owed to as meagre a force as a touch too much oak, or the wrong sort of pressings, the result of just a tiny difference in judgement – or a need to cut back on quantity. When as little as 40 per cent of production makes it to the *grand vin*, what you'll get in the 'second' bottle needn't differ much at all. And in lesser vintages second wines will receive even more juice from hallowed *terroir*. The second wines of Latour and Margaux (Les Forts de Latour and Pavillon Rouge), for example, are almost considered classed growths anyway, at a fraction of the price. Seize the day.

Look out for: Clos du Marquis (second wine of Léoville-Las Cases), Bahans-Haut-Brion (Haut-Brion), Les Fiefs de Lagrange (Lagrange) and Sarget de Gruaud-Larose (Gruaud-Larose) among others. Look out for 'third wines' too, for similar reasons.

Bordeaux red wine vintage guide
For more expensive clarets, say over £20 a bottle, our advice is always to check the vintage and the style of the wine. Some

vintages, and nowadays some wines, are ready to drink sooner than others. Drinking young Bordeaux today isn't always like chewing nails, as many, even the most expensive ones, have softer tannins and are made to be ripe and approachable when young. Hefty classed growths will still require (and benefit from) a minimum of ten years' cellaring, but lighter vintages and right-bank Libournais wines may require less time to come round. When purchasing claret, check with your merchant as to when you should start to drink it, and always hold some back to sample at regular intervals, so you can enjoy its development and maturity. Most everyday claret, on the other hand, particularly bottles costing less than £7, is intended to be drunk young and will not benefit from ageing – indeed, the opposite; the freshness and any attractive fruit aromas will quickly fade.

2001 Better than 1999, 1998 and 1997, but not a patch on 2000. A gloomy start – a wet winter and a mild spring – changed into a sunny, warm May and June, but then turned grey and damp again in July and August. An Indian summer in September and October saved the situation and, despite a few thunderstorms, a particularly good Merlot crop was brought in. Cabernet ripened less well, due to the coolness of the vintage. Likely to be a better year for the right bank than for the left.

2000 By all accounts a stunning year – and, with three zeros, one to please the marketing men. Day after day of hot sunshine made for a perfect, rainless ripening season on both banks, and flawless conditions didn't waver during harvest. Merlots were picked, full of opulence and firm structure in mid- to late September; Cabernet Francs in early October were good news in St-Emilion, where this grape features highly; and strong, structured Cabernet Sauvignons were harvested just before the rain set in on 10 October. The best vintage since 1990; not showy but one to last.

1999 September rains and a spectacular hailstorm in St-Emilion resulted in a patchwork performance across the region, after a promisingly bumper crop had materialised during the sweltering month of August. As 1998, this is a year where Merlot benefited from being harvested before the rains, and the later-ripening Cabernet Sauvignon crop, particularly in St-Estèphe, was generally unable to provide its best. Properties from the Médoc with a higher proportion of Merlot in the blend will have produced better wines.

1998 A Merlot year, when September rains arrived after most of the Merlot had been picked but before the harvest of the two Cabernet varieties. Prior to that, August had been hot and dry, producing small berries with intense colour and flavour and no shortage of tannin. Pomerol is the star, closely followed by St-Emilion and other Libournais wines. The Médoc fared worst, and many wines, though deep in colour, are rather attenuated, even at properties which could afford to downgrade inferior batches of wine.

1997 The growing season had been very erratic, with cool spells, hot spells, high humidity and more. By the last half of August, Merlot had high sugar levels and low acid levels, but with unripe flavours and tannins. On 25 August rain came and panicked many growers into picking. Those who waited were rewarded with fine conditions from the end of September which lasted through into October, and most Cabernet Sauvignon was picked fully ripe. The wines are not concentrated, due to the effects of the rain, but they are charming, very accessible and made for early drinking. Pity about the horrendous prices.

1996 A year for Cabernet Sauvignon. The first two-thirds of September were warm and dry, but the last third brought further rain just as the Merlot and Cabernet Franc were being picked. The result was dilution of flavours. The Cabernet Sauvignon harvest took place after the vines had had a chance to dry out, and the resulting raft of wines from the Médoc has plenty of flesh and plenty of tannin. Like the 1986s, they will need lots of patience. A few Libournais châteaux that waited for the Merlot to dry out after the rain and to ripen further have, in many cases, produced some fine wines.

1995 The best and most consistent vintage since 1990, with St-Julien, Pauillac, St-Emilion and Pomerol standing out. The wines fall halfway between 1985 and 1986 in style, with ripe, friendly fruit backed up by good structure.

1994 This was all set to be a great vintage before the cool, rainy September. However, while the lack of autumn sun meant that some châteaux had problems ripening their grapes as much as they would have liked, many decent, if rather sturdy, wines were made, which are reasonable value but still a long way off drinking.

1993 Rain at harvest made for dilute wines, but because the grapes had enjoyed almost perfect ripening conditions up until the rain, the flavours are not underripe. Not a vintage to keep, though some Pomerols have the substance to survive for another few years yet.

1992 There wasn't much sun, and the summer was the wettest for 50 years, so the wines were almost universally condemned. This doesn't explain why we occasionally come across remarkably pleasant and sensibly priced wines.

1991 A small, patchy vintage which, apart from those at the very top properties, is best forgotten.

1990 A brilliant vintage, initially underrated in the wake of the headstrong 1989 but now recognised as at least its equal and very probably its superior. The wines have been delicious since they were released, but those who wish to keep them will not be disappointed. The acids may not be the highest, but the wine has sufficient body of alcohol and ripe tannins to ensure a healthy existence for several years to come. Whether you can afford them is a different matter.

1989 A precocious vintage that prompted some growers to pick their Merlot too early. Cabernet Sauvignon was magnificent, and the best wines of the Médoc and Graves will be going strong for the next 30 years. Prices remain lower than for the 1990s.

1988 When the folk of the wine world refer to 'classic claret', 1988 is the sort of vintage they have in mind. Restrained, elegant wines with a slightly herbaceous, stalky edge, which need plenty of time to show their best, are more the order of the day than the fleshy excesses of 1989 and 1990.

Good older vintages

1986 Powerful vintage producing big, black wines. At less lofty levels, the tannins are often too weighty for the fruit content, and some wines seem destined never to come into balance, but the top Médocs are superb.

1985 Beautifully balanced, utterly captivating vintage – even at *petit château* level – which has been delicious from the word go and is still going strong.

1983 Pick your property well – the Margaux appellation had an excellent vintage – and you could have some of the best mature claret bargains around. However, several wines don't seem to have fulfilled their initial potential.

1982 Spectacular vintage with extraordinary ripeness and now extraordinary prices. The best wines are full of fabulous rich fruit and are destined to join the legendary 1961s in the claret hall of fame.

Pick of the producers (Red Bordeaux)

As well as the reliable, and frequently very expensive, classics listed below (the 'wish list' if you like), the upswing in winemaking standards over the 1990s has meant that a new crop of châteaux names emerges every year – more familiar names, too, are shrugging off mediocrity and making splendid clarets to be proud of, both in modern and traditional styles. The following six good-value properties have performed particularly well in the 2000 and 2001 vintages.

Belgrave Much improved fifth growth Médoc château.
Côte de Baleau Powerful, new-wave St-Emilion, tremendous value and worth cellaring.
Fontenil New cult Fronsac, from cult winemaker Michel Rolland.

Prieuré Lichine A new darling with the UK wine trade, great
Margaux, be quick.
La Tour Carnet Ever-improving Haut-Médoc wine.
La Tour Figeac Biodynamic St-Emilion château: lush ripe wines.

Angélus *1er grand cru classé*, St-Emilion. A string of fine wines
throughout the 1980s and, in particular, in the difficult vintages
of the 1990s has made this large château one of the best of St-
Emilion. A recent style change back to classic elegance is very
welcome.

Ausone *1er grand cru classé 'A'*, St-Emilion. One of St-Emilion's top
two properties, an underperformer through much of the 1980s but
now, with Alain Vauthier at the helm and Michel Rolland as a
consultant, back and doing better than ever – 50:50 Cabernet
Franc and Merlot with 100-per-cent new oak. Wonderful wine.

Beychevelle *4ème cru classé*, St-Julien. This property can produce
wines that are approachable in their youth but which also age well.
Recent vintages have been erratic. Second label: Amiral de
Beychevelle.

Cantemerle *5ème cru classé*, Haut-Médoc. Stylish, elegant wine
which matures relatively early and is usually of exceptionally good
value. Second label: Baron Villeneuve de Cantemerle.

Chasse-Spleen Moulis. Would probably be a fourth growth if the
1855 classification were to be redone. Solid wines with great
concentration of flavour which age well. Was using too much oak,
but now improving. Second label: l'Ermitage de Chasse-Spleen.

Cheval Blanc *1er grand cru classé 'A'*, St-Emilion. Wonderful
property which is unusual in its high proportion – up to two-
thirds – of Cabernet Franc. Wines are remarkably approachable
from a tender age but live as long as any claret. Second label Le
Petit Cheval (very like the *grand vin* but at a quarter of the
price!).

Domaine de Chevalier Pessac-Léognan. Classic elegant claret, as
well balanced as any in Bordeaux. You'll miss the point if you drink
it much before its tenth birthday. Second label: Bâtard-Chevalier.

Clinet Pomerol. The opulent, late-picked wines made in the last ten
years by the late Jean-Michel Arcaute (aided by Michel Rolland) put
this property near the top of the Pomerol tree, and we've recently
detected a welcome tendency towards complexity and elegance.

Cos d'Estournel *2ème cru classé*, St-Estèphe. Top property in its *commune* and one of the most concentrated of all clarets, yet managing to retain more than a vestige of elegance. New rigorous winemaking regime headed by Jean-Guillaume Prats is improving the wines, but there are slightly fewer of them. One of a handful of properties held to have improved on the mighty 2000 vintage with 2001. Second label: Les Pagodes de Cos (Château de Marbuzet now from separate vines).

Ducru Beaucaillou *2ème cru classé*, St-Julien. Back at the head of the St-Julien firmament (stunning 1996 and 2000) after a shaky period in the late 1980s. At its best, expect wonderful sweet cedar and blackcurrant refinement with elegance. Second label: La Croix.

l'Eglise-Clinet Pomerol. Old low-yielding vines and careful winemaking by Denis Durantou result in sumptuous silky wines of the highest class and traditional style. Better every year. Second label, La Petite Eglise, is a bargain!

l'Evangile Pomerol. Powerful, silky, consistently fine Pomerol (up there with Pétrus) rounded out with new oak, from the Lafite-Rothschild stable, whose only negative point is its phenomenal price.

de Fieuzal Pessac-Léognan. The white is the sexier wine, but the delicious concentrated red is improving, and not very far behind. A good buy.

Figeac *1er grand cru classé*, St-Emilion. Property located close to Cheval Blanc and the Pomerol border, with a high proportion of the two Cabernets. The best vintages (1982, 1990, 1998, 1999) are soft and stylish, both accessible young and capable of ageing gloriously. Second label: Grangeneuve de Figeac.

Gazin Pomerol. Large (for Pomerol) estate which maintains quality by rejecting inferior *cuvées* for the *grand vin*. Performed splendidly throughout the difficult 1990s. Making great strides. Good value.

Gruaud-Larose *2ème cru classé*, St-Julien. It's large and flamboyant, it's not too expensive, and the wine is of superlative quality. Very hard to fault. Second label: Sarget de Gruaud-Larose.

Haut-Brion *1er cru classé*, Pessac-Léognan. The top estate of the Graves, which lacks the showiness of some Médoc wines yet ages superbly to a state of pencil-and-cedar refinement and poise that few can match. Second label, Bahans-Haut-Brion, is 40 per cent of production, and very good.

Lafite-Rothschild *1er cru classé*, Pauillac. Easy to misunderstand in its youth but will always emerge to a graceful, perfumed maturity and will keep for decades in the best vintages. High (93 per cent) in Cabernet Sauvignon. Excellent second label is Carruades de Lafite-Rothschild.

Lafleur Pomerol. One of the sturdiest of the Pomerols and one of the few real rivals to Pétrus. Slow to mature: give it lots of time in bottle.

Lafon Rochet *4ème cru classé*, St-Estèphe. Top quality in vintages since 1994 – buy now before prices rise. 2000 is best ever; 2001 deep, dark, powerful and true to form.

Lagrange *3ème cru classé*, St-Julien. Revitalised by the Japanese Suntory group in the 1980s and now producing up to its third growth status at still reasonable prices. Upping its proportions of Cabernet Sauvignon as new vines come on stream. Watch for further change. Second label: Les Fiefs de Lagrange.

Latour *1er cru classé*, Pauillac. Powerful wine – increasingly so under Frédéric Engerer and François Pinault's direction – which lives for decades. The 1990 is the wine of the vintage; the 1995 and 1996 are also superb; 2000 is dense, satin-coated and exceptional; 2001 at least as good as 1995. Second label, Les Forts de Latour, is hardly less grand, from old vines and only a quarter of the *grand vin* price.

Léoville-Barton *2ème cru classé*, St-Julien. Classic, classy claret, firm in its youth but ageing to cedar and blackcurrant perfection. The wines of the 1990s have all been among the best of the vintage; 2000 is tremendous but thanks to media hype broke with its normally reasonable pricing policy. 2001 has power, complexity, great quality and sees a return to a realistic price tag. Second label: La Réserve de Léoville-Barton.

Léoville-Las-Cases *2ème cru classé*, St-Julien. A first growth in all but name, producing powerful, complex and intense claret of superlative quality. Quantities reduced in tricky 2001 vintage, but quality remains on a par with 2000. Second label: Clos du Marquis – big and concentrated, a sneak preview, maturing sooner at a quarter of the price.

Lynch-Bages *5ème cru classé*, Pauillac. Widely acclaimed, and one of the easiest clarets to understand, with an almost Australian wealth of minty, ripe fruit, heaps of oak and the ability to be enjoyed from its fifth birthday onwards. Always modestly priced too. Second label: Haut-Bages-Avérous.

Margaux 1er cru classé, Margaux. Ever since the Mentzelopoulos family bought Margaux in 1977, this has been one of the top ten clarets each vintage; 2000 is no different, fragrantly perfumed, yet backed up by intense fruit and powerful structure. 2001 is full of charm but for the short term. Second label, Pavillon Rouge, of at least fourth growth quality.

La Mission Haut-Brion Pessac-Léognan. Massive oaky wine, just falling short of the standard of its stablemate Haut-Brion but still of superb quality. Second label: La Chapelle Haut-Brion.

Montrose 2ème cru classé, St-Estèphe. Vintages since 1989 have provided a string of powerful, highly extracted and flavour-packed wines, which show a return to form for what was once St-Estèphe's top château. Needs time. When it's good, it's very, very good. Second label: La Dame de Montrose.

Mouton-Rothschild 1er cru classé, Pauillac. A pencil-shavings, oak and cassis brick of a wine with a high proportion – over 80 per cent – of Cabernet Sauvignon. Consistently excellent, although prices, particularly for the 1982, have gone haywire. Shows its best earlier than the other first growths. American collectors will have to buy two different 1993s, since Balthus's original label, depicting a naked young girl of tender age, has been outlawed by US officials. Second label: Le Second Vin de Mouton-Rothschild.

Palmer 3ème cru classé, Margaux. A star in the 1960s and 1970s, producing wines of perfume and class. Recent vintages (1995, 1996, 1998, 2000) show that it is currently second only to Château Margaux in the appellation. Second label was formerly Réserve du Général, now Alter Ego de Palmer: Merlot-dominated and earlier-drinking.

Pape-Clément Pessac-Léognan. Since 1986 one of the classiest wines of the Graves, offering a combination of earth and tar, power and finesse. Superlative effort with the tricky 2001s, deep, concentrated and complex.

Pavie 1er grand cru classé, St-Emilion. Sweet, modern-style, charming wine from one of the largest of the St-Emilion châteaux, which was on form in the late 1980s, slipped up slightly but, under new ownership, is right back in the spotlight – though perhaps a little too modern in style.

Pavie Macquin 1er grand cru classé, St-Emilion. Owned by the Thienpont family of Le Pin and Vieux-Château-Certan and making similarly rich, concentrated wines which need plenty of time to shed their tannic overcoat. Perhaps overpriced in recent vintages.

Pétrus Pomerol. Still king of Pomerol, despite the mob of pretenders led by Le Pin. Not as flashy when young as some of the wannabes, always awesomely powerful and full-flavoured and needing 15 years to show at its best.

Pichon-Longueville *2ème cru classé*, Pauillac, aka Pichon-Baron. Reclaimed its rightful place as one of the chunky, dense Pauillac greats from the 1988 vintage onwards under the guidance of Jean-Michel Cazes and Daniel Llose. Second label: Les Tourelles de Longueville.

Pichon-Longueville-Lalande *2ème cru classé*, Pauillac. Hiccups at this excellent château in the late 1980s were smoothed out by 1994 and it's now one of the sexiest clarets around. More and more Cabernet-based of late and with an unusually high proportion of Petite Verdot: the wines are commensurately powerful. Second label: Réserve de la Comtesse.

Le Pin Pomerol. Pocket-handkerchief estate belonging to the Thienpont family of Vieux-Château-Certan and currently the wine in most demand in the world. Sumptuous, oaky, sleek, Merlot-based, and early-drinking. If you have to ask how much it costs, you can't afford it. (2000 was £6,000/case *en primeur*; £8,250 a year later.)

Poujeaux Moulis. On current form, the best of the Moulis châteaux, making spicy, rich, fruit-packed consistent wines which need plenty of time to evolve.

Rauzan-Ségla *2ème cru classé*, Margaux. Improving with each vintage, thanks to cash from Chanel and inspired winemaking. The 1995 is splendid; 2000 is a top-class blockbuster; 2001 classic, rich and complex. Second label: Château Lamouroux.

Smith-Haut-Lafitte Pessac-Léognan. Up-and-coming property thanks to the efforts of the Cathiard family, making intense yet increasingly elegant claret. 2000 is decadent, seductive; 2001 on a better track with more finesse.

La Tertre Rôteboeuf *grand cru*. A *premier grand cru classé* in any sane classification of St-Emilion; luxurious, silky wine of immense youthful charm – and price.

Trotanoy Pomerol. Classic Pomerol with enough structure to support the lush fruit. Offers relatively good value in the light of demand for Pétrus and Le Pin.

Valandraud *grand cru*, St-Emilion. The Le Pin of St-Emilion (before the arrival of La Mondotte); tiny quantities of an unfined, unfiltered boutique super-wine. Second wine, Virginie de Valandraud, is very similar; third wines: Axelle de Valandraud (from December 2000) and l'Interdit de Valandraud (made outside AC regulations) are priceless.

Vieux-Château-Certan Pomerol. One of the leaner Pomerols, with 20 per cent Cabernet Sauvignon and 25 per cent Franc in the blend. Needs age to show well.

Dry white wines

Bordeaux today is redder than ever – 85 per cent so in fact – and those whites that make it have to be truly excellent. The region is as capable as any nowadays of producing well-made white wines at all levels, and while the classics carry on being classic (see the range of minerally, ageworthy, Sémillon-based Pessac-Léognan whites below), recent effort in the 'everyday' echelons is banishing the tired, over-sulphured underperformers of the 1980s. Straight Sauvignon is the watchword. Intelligent winemaking and careful picking can produce wines that are every bit as crisp and fresh as New Zealand's, with Sémillon taking very much a back-seat role. Some of the best of these Sauvignons (perhaps unsurprisingly) come from the cooler, marginal northern areas of the region, and are thoroughly modern; there's even a touch of American oak being used here and there to round them out. Some whites are still commercial and uninteresting, but – up a level from basic Bordeaux Blanc – Entre-Deux-Mers and Graves are making rich, rounded, oak-aged wines that can rival some of the great Burgundian whites for style and elegance. It's also worth remembering that the best can be excellent to serve with food, whether young and fresh in style, or full, lingering, Sémillon-based classics from Pessac-Léognan. Watch out also for the rare, interest-value whites from the great Médoc châteaux such as Margaux, Lynch-Bages and Mouton-Rothschild.

Pick of the producers (Dry white Bordeaux)
All Pessac-Léognan unless otherwise stated.

Couhins-Lurton The classiest of André Lurton's Bordeaux whites is a spicy, barrel-fermented Sauvignon.

Domaine de Chevalier Very concentrated but tight in its youth and heavenly at ten years old. Not always as expensive as other top Bordeaux whites. 2001 very fine.

de Fieuzal Exciting, spicy 50:50 Sémillon/Sauvignon blend whose price is climbing steeply, despite its not being a classed growth. 2001 is worth watching for.

Haut-Brion Rich, waxy and heady, this is 55 per cent Sémillon and 45 per cent Sauvignon that has been fermented and aged in new oak. Rare and expensive too; good in 2001.

Laville-Haut-Brion The 60-per-cent Sémillon/40-per-cent Sauvignon white of La Mission Haut-Brion is good but should be better given the prices asked. It does age remarkably well though; wait ten years plus for the 2001s.

La Louvière Another André Lurton smoky, spicy success for rather less money than some of the big names.

Margaux The Médoc is not renowned for its whites but Pavillon Blanc de Château Margaux (by far the finest) can take on any of those above or below. 100 per cent Sauvignon Blanc, it reveals the true capabilities of this grape: keep it for five years, or, if you can, for 20. Top notch in 2001.

Pape-Clément Not a classed growth (unlike the red) but making deliciously rich, oaky whites; 2001 is no exception.

Smith-Haut-Lafitte One of the most exciting properties in the whole of Bordeaux at present, making this superlative 100 per cent Sauvignon as well as excellent reds – the white fared as well as the reds here in 2001.

Bordeaux dry white vintage guide
2001 A cooler year, and great, therefore, for aromatics. The warm spells in May and June, and towards harvest, ensured good natural sugars were achieved, and the prolonged nature of the growing season meant that acidities were well balanced in both Sémillon and Sauvignon.

2000 As good a year for the whites as reds. At premium level, some herald this as the best vintage for a decade, while others have more admiration for the vibrance of the 1996s. 2000s are richer and fuller and may do much to abate the gloom cast by previous rainy vintages and past over-production.

1999 Not a spectacular year, with rain – particularly in the Entre-Deux-Mers. However, quality-conscious growers (and there are ever-increasing numbers of them) managed to produce Sauvignon and Sémillon with attractive fruit and concentrated flavours. These wines are worth paying that little bit more for. For the classic Pessac-Léognan whites, which were harvested ahead of the rains, think power rather than finesse.

1998 Hot summer conditions ensured good ripening. The showers at the start of September were generally too light to cause any damage, and the grapes were picked in first-class condition: fully ripe, with near-perfect sugar and acid levels and no signs of rot. The wines are good, some very promising, although not as high quality as they would have been with a slightly less torrid August.

1997 Picking began on 18 August, the earliest start to a vintage since 1893, but humidity and rain at the end of the month caused rot in many vineyards, and a large amount of fruit was picked before it was fully ripe. Grapes that survived through to the sunny September had the chance to finish ripening, resulting in some high-quality Sémillon and aromatic Sauvignon.

Good earlier vintages (now only for the very top properties) 1995, 1994, 1990, 1989, 1988, 1986.

Sweet white wines

For most people, the epitome of sweet white wine remains the enticingly honeyed and intense examples of Sauternes, where *botrytis*, or noble rot, has concentrated the Sauvignon and Sémillon grapes to a degree of seductive sweetness that is unsurpassable in any other climate or with any other grape varieties. Although nowadays there are many unfortified Muscat or Riesling-based sweet wines available, none can really compare with Sauternes for ageing and development potential. Several merchants offer mixed-case, *en primeur* selections, which will provide an interesting experience for enthusiastic amateurs.

Five villages – Sauternes, Barsac, Bommes, Fargues and Preignac – may use the name Sauternes; Barsac is also entitled to its own appellation. These wines are traditionally served to accompany *foie gras* and blue cheeses in south-west France, but equally can be served chilled with simple fruit desserts.

Bordeaux also offers some cheaper alternatives to Sauternes and Barsac, namely neighbouring Cérons (Château de Cérons, in particular), or, on the opposite bank of the Garonne, the good-value wines of Cadillac, Loupiac, Ste-Croix-du-Mont and Monbazillac, near Bergerac.

The tiny appellation of Saussignac, also near Bergerac, is now making waves in the sweet-wine sector and is featuring on the lists of UK wine merchants.

Also worth trying, particularly if you are on a budget, are Clos St-Georges (Graves Supérieures) and Château de Berbec (Premières Côtes de Bordeaux).

Pick of the producers (Sweet white Bordeaux)
All Sauternes unless otherwise indicated.

Bastor-Lamontagne Not the greatest Sauternes but well-made, heady and above all very fairly priced wine.

Climens Barsac. Concentrated, consistent, opulent, yet managing to retain elegance. Textbook Sauternes – sorry, Barsac – which many regard as the finest after Yquem. Outstanding in 2001.

Coutet Barsac. A larger property than neighbouring Climens, to which it is often thought to pay second fiddle. Coutet was on top form throughout the 1990s, however, and at its subtle spicy best in 2001.

Doisy-Daëne Barsac. Go-ahead property whose long-lived sweet wines have been stunning of late, with racy lively acidity. Made by Dennis Dubourdieu.

Doisy-Védrines Barsac. Decent-value wine in a rich, sticky, honeyed vein from former *négociant* Pierre Casteja.

de Fargues Yquem winemaking, Yquem style and not far from Yquem prices, but the wine is very impressive.

Gilette Made only in top vintages and aged in concrete tanks for decades before bottling. The unwooded style can seem out of kilter with more modern Sauternes, but the wine opens up remarkably if given plenty of time to breathe.

Guiraud High-quality estate which has been making top-notch, very ageworthy wines since the early 1980s, albeit at a high price.

Lafaurie-Peyraguey One of the best-balanced Sauternes, matching oak and heady *botrytis* with thick, luscious fruit and acidity.

Rieussec Exotic, aromatic Sauternes under the same ownership as Lafite and l'Evangile, which is one of the best of the region on a good day.

Suduiraut Now owned by AXA Millésimes – which also owns Lynch-Bages, Pichon-Longueville and others – and seeing a return to the form which almost makes it a rival to Yquem. 2001 with its powerful, honeyed presence proves the point.

d'Yquem Expensive but peerless, the greatest sweet wine in the world due to minute yields – a glass of wine per vine – and great care in the cellar. Compare the price to those of the top clarets and Yquem is a relative bargain. Now owned by luxury goods giant LVMH.

Bordeaux sweet white vintage guide
That perfectly poised, apricot sweetness, cut through with a tingling balance of delicate acidity, is the result of a most extraordinary set of climatic circumstances that have been timed to perfection – so precisely that a good vintage seems almost miraculous. And even when that happens, there's often only enough juice for a couple of glasses per vine. Yet still we 'reject' these wines. At the very least, we should be buying them to lay down and drink at their marvellous best – in 20 years' time (50 for the best ones). Maybe then will they be fashionable?
2001 On a par with the great 1988, 1989, 1990 trio; commentators are even calling it 'the best vintage ever'. Cloudy damp weather through the spring and in July, followed by late-summer warmth and a stormy September, made for ideal *botrytis* conditions – the mould developed evenly and the concentration of the berries was not diluted by rain.
2000 While everything else benefited from the heat and good weather, Sauternes had a tougher time. Dry conditions meant *botrytis* took longer to set in, then rain on 10 October dashed most châteaux' hopes altogether. Tiny quantities of sweet wine were made by those who managed to collect some grapes before the downpours. The rest will have nothing at all.
1999 A reasonably decent vintage brought about by the hot, dry summer and with seemingly no adverse effects of picking in the damp conditions of late September. Healthy levels of *botrytis* have led to wines with good sugar levels, balance and fine quality. On a par with 1996 and 1997.
1998 There was no shortage of noble rot, and those who managed to pick before and after the main batch of rains at the end of September/ beginning of October have made beautifully textured fleshy wines.
1997 The first pickings in early September were more to eliminate grapes with grey rot than to pick the nobly rotten ones. The weather

was dry for the rest of the vintage, and the harvest progressed well, with the final pickings taking place in some cases in mid-November. Lovely pure wines, medium-bodied with fine acidity.

1996 September rain followed by a generally dry October gave grapes with high *botrytis* levels and little or no grey rot. The best vintage since the great years of 1988–1990, although not in the same league.

1995 A vintage that suffered none of the problems of grey rot that had caused havoc in the previous four years. Rich wines with reasonable levels of *botrytis* but lacking the concentration for greatness.

1994, 1993, 1992, 1991 With no *botrytis* in 1994 and 1993, little in 1992 and a tiny crop in 1991, these years are generally best avoided, although a few exceptions include the sumptuous 1991 Climens.

1990, 1989, 1988 A superb trio, with 1988 classic and elegant, 1989 opulent and heady, and 1990 powerful and sweet. If you know of any back-to-back tastings of wines from these three vintages, please send us an invitation.

Good earlier vintages 1986, 1983, 1976, 1975, 1971, 1967.

Other wines

Bordeaux Rosé and Clairet (very light red wines) have enjoyed something of a surge in popularity in recent years, helped by improved vinification techniques, such as the gentle presses and cool fermentation employed for white wines. Château de Sours and

Château Thieuley are fine examples of fresh, fruity and elegant pinks, perfect for alfresco dining.

BURGUNDY

The great thing about red burgundy is that it's much less susceptible to the fickle charms of journalistic acclaim than are the great Bordeaux and Napa Cabernets of this world. OK, so a wine happens to get 99 points out of 100 in a wine competition: *félicitations,* that's a fine achievement. But the important thing on the Côte d'Or is to mirror the special character of the land – the *terroir* – in the wine, and you don't do that by pulverising every ounce of ripeness and sweetness out of a grape, and making a wine to please the show judges. With Pinot Noir, the grape of burgundy, only the gentle approach will work.

However, you still need to decide which style of burgundy you're going to opt for, modern or traditional.

In terms of reds, there are the modernists who want their wine to seem serious and to extract enough colour out of it so it looks, for want of a better description, like Syrah. And there are traditionalists who couldn't give a damn about the colour. The school of Burgundians we like best – and it's a growing group – is the middle group who want the best from both camps: colour, depth and ripeness, but not at the expense of elegance, ageworthiness and acidity.

Acidity lies at the heart of good burgundy, holding the wine together. As the lame, spineless wines of the 1960s and 1970s proved – which suffered after the widespread addition of potassium fertilisers caused the acidity to drop out of the wines altogether – when it's gone, you miss it! But acidity is a concept with which today's young generation of wine drinkers is uncomfortable. Brought up on a wave of New World wines, soft and unchallenging on the palate, they now look for similar characteristics from France. Modern burgundy has evolved to suit them, tending to be later-picked and fruitier, with less of a 'zing' on the palate. Don't get us wrong: these wines aren't blockbusters like the full-on right-bank wines of Bordeaux, they still express their *terroir*, and they still vary in nuance from village to village. They're generally more gorgeous to drink young, too. But there's one problem. They don't age.

The less scrupulous wine merchants out there won't alert you to this, but 'modern' burgundies follow a totally different set of rules. White Puligny-Montrachets and Meursaults need to be drunk at three to four years old rather than five to ten, for example; red Volnays and Chambolle-Musignys at six rather than fifteen. They simply aren't holding up any longer. The people who pay high prices for burgundy so that they can cellar it and wait for it to mature will be in for a disappointment. And we have a lot of sympathy with them. Here's why . . .

Traditional burgundies are very different. We recently confirmed a long-held suspicion that we are fans of the chestnut-and-chocolate farmyardy *old* burgundies, the wines showing at their best after 15 or 20 years in bottle. Drinking burgundy early means you miss out on half the pleasure. The wines that caused this revelation were from Domaine Charles Thomas – up until Spring 2002, an estate unknown to us: 1986 Bonnes Mares – mature, chestnutty, cinnamony fruit; 1985 Corton – chocolate-smooth, with spicy fig and walnut to finish; 1973 Pommard-Rugiens – should be dead-and-buried by now but full of firm fruit, fig, mushroom, chestnut and leather; 1959 Clos Vougeot – liquorice, burnt roast-chestnuts and hot rubber (it was a warm vintage!); 1949 Chambolle-Musigny – sultanas and truffles, fantastically plump and sensuous; 1929 Clos de Vougeot – raisins, sultanas, spiced at the edge and lingering ten minutes on the tongue. All intriguing.

Not everyone likes old wine, but for many, this kind of complexity (and fruit that still takes a firm grip on the palate) is just what Pinot Noir is all about. Without acidity, however, the wines will never get there. With it, they might be 'inconvenient' while young, but the wines stay fruitier for longer and have a far greater future ahead of them.

Because it would be virtually impossible to get the Burgundians to label their wines with earlier drinking dates, we've marked, below, the producers whose current wines we think are fit to last to the 2020s.

On another matter, there's been a definite dip in the price of burgundy, red and white, of late (following a market slump after September 11, 2001). Burgundy has a much more level-headed pricing structure than Bordeaux, increasing at only around 4–8 per cent per annum as against the wild hikes claret tends to take. The best will always be expensive wines, but there will be bargains in the middle ground. And don't despair when you hear the vintage reports either. Pinot Noir, especially, has a canny knack of excelling in difficult weather conditions. The odd storm or snow shower seems to create finer flavours than do the heatwaves in which most other French wines thrive (see our note on the 2001 white Burgundy vintage). The same is often true for Chardonnay. But then again, Burgundy is a wine about which you just can't generalise, and maybe that's another reason it escapes the influence of journalistic bullies.

Organisation of the trade

Burgundy's complex wine industry owes much of its structure to the French inheritance laws. For example, Vineyard X originally had just one owner, but two generations later it has been divided between the 12 grandchildren, some of whom have sold their share to their siblings, while others have married into families which also have vineyards. It's easy to see how, today, a typical Burgundy domaine may be split into perhaps a dozen or more plots spread over several villages, and perhaps ranging from a sizeable chunk of Bourgogne Rouge to just a couple of rows in a *grand cru* vineyard.

In the past, it didn't make economic sense for the grower to vinify and sell each wine separately, and this led to the emergence of *négociants*, merchants who would buy some or all of a grower's different batches of grapes, must or wine and then blend them with other similar batches in order to both guarantee continuity of supply and maintain a particular house style. The *négociant* system was clearly open to abuse, and it certainly was abused. For every honest *négociant* there was at least one other whose wines bore little resemblance to what was claimed on the label. Many a pre-1970 Nuits-St-Georges was bolstered by matter from the Rhône and even Algeria.

Gradually, the growers began to realise that not only were such tactics damaging Burgundy's reputation, but that they could make a better living by selling wines under their own label. With the increase in domaine bottling from the 1950s onwards, the reputation of the *négociants* slumped, to such an extent that, come the early 1980s, no serious burgundy lover would choose their wines in preference to that of a small grower. Many went out of business or were bought up by rivals.

Today, the distinction between grower and *négociant* is rather more blurred. The major firms still buy in large quantities of wine and grapes, but they are also looking to expand their own vineyard holdings in order to guarantee both supply and quality. Winemaking standards have improved too, and the best wines stand comparison with those of the top growers – the *négociant* house Jadot is a good example.

Then there has been the emergence of smaller companies, known as '*micro-négociants*', who are prepared to pay high prices for the best grapes, and who then make, mature and sell the wine themselves, focusing only on quality and individual plots. Not only does this allow talented new winemakers, such as Nicolas Potel, and Jean-Marie Guffens at Verget, to break into a wine environment dominated by historic families without owning any vineyards, it also, in an ironic twist, is a direct 'reflection' of the New World model of winemaking. (Penfolds, for example,

frequently buys its fruit from other top-quality growers in
Australia.)

The other recent phenomenon is the rise of the *éleveur*. These are
the *micro-micro-négociants*, who buy in wine ready-made but not yet
barrel-aged. Their role is purely to mature the wine in their cellars
and coax it into perfect condition for sale.

Does this all sound rather confusing? Well, sorry, it is. But as long
as the growers and *négociants* clearly label whether their wine is
estate-grown or from bought-in fruit, then consumers should know
where they stand. So, while we used to list the *négociants* separately
from the growers, they are now listed together later in this section.

The Burgundian hierarchy

Burgundy has well over 100 appellations, ranging from blanket
generics which cover the whole of the region to tiny *grands crus* of
less than one hectare. At the top of the quality tree – and base of the
quantity tree – come the 39 *grands crus*. The 24 red ones are, with
the exception of Corton, all in the Côte de Nuits. Seven of the 15
white ones are in Chablis; one, Musigny, in the Côte de Nuits; the
rest are in the Côte de Beaune. With the exception of the ones in
Chablis, these will simply bear the vineyard name rather than the
village in which they can be found.

Then come the plethora of *premier cru* vineyards, which can be
hard to keep up with – Beaune alone has 34. These annex their
names to the village name, resulting in wines such as Puligny-
Montrachet Folatières. The wines that bear no vineyard name and
just say Premier Cru will be blends from a number of *premier cru*
vineyards. Montagny used to be able to use the words if it reached a
certain alcohol level, but is now in the process of making the
appellation more vineyard-specific. After this are the village wines:
Meursault, Chambolle-Musigny, Givry. Finally come Bourgogne
Rouge and Blanc, Bourgogne Passetoutgrains (Pinot Noir and
Gamay) and Bourgogne Grand Ordinaire (lowest of the low).
Beaujolais has a slightly different hierarchy, which is dealt with
later, although it too can call itself Bourgogne Rouge.

Red wines

You can find small amounts of strange varieties such as César and
Tréssot in the Chablis district. Then there is the frothy Gamay of
Beaujolais fame. However, the grape responsible for great
burgundy, the most sensuous red wine in the world, is Pinot Noir.
Producers use words such as 'fickle' and 'capricious' to describe the
cultivation of Pinot, but it's not that difficult to grow. What *is*
difficult, however, is to grow it well. The sentiment is that it is

impossible to produce great red burgundy unless yields are low – less than 35 hl/ha. Organic and biodynamic viticulture are becoming more and more widespread as growers realise that the chemical treatments of the last 30 to 40 years have resulted in very unhealthy vineyards. A vine that receives all its nourishment from artificial fertilisers doesn't need to stretch its roots far into the soil to obtain sustenance, and so the influence of *terroir* is reduced.

Having grown sound fruit, the general message in the winemaking is 'hands-off'. Definitions of this vary from cellar to cellar. Some highly rated winemakers let their grapes macerate at low temperatures for a few days before fermentation begins, some control their fermentation temperatures, some chaptalise (add sugar) even in good vintages in order to extend fermentation, some use only new oak, some fine and filter their wines before bottling. Others don't. There's no formula for great burgundy – and in a world of identikit wines, praise be for that.

Côte d'Or red

Côte de Nuits
Heading south from Dijon along the N74, nearly all the vineyards – and certainly all the serious ones – lie to the right in a narrow band, rising from the road up an east-facing marl slope. Marsannay and Fixin are the first villages you come to, and although the wines can be attractive, in a light, perfumed way, they only hint at the pleasures to come. The stretch of vineyards from Gevrey-Chambertin down to Nuits-St-Georges produces wines that can take your breath away with their exotic blend of fruit, spice, undergrowth and more. Much Gevrey-Chambertin is instantly forgettable, but good versions, from village level up to the nine Chambertin *grands crus*, show that wine can be powerful yet perfumed. Chambolle-Musigny, Morey-St-Denis and Vosne-Romanée are less robust, but more perfumed, although the best *grands crus* such as Richebourg, Musigny and Clos de la Roche certainly lack nothing in intensity. Nuits-St-Georges has no *grands crus*, but several great *premiers crus*. The wines need more time than other Côte de Nuits reds to open out. Lesser but rather more affordable wines can be found in the appellations of Côte de Nuits Villages and Hautes-Côtes de Nuits.

Côte de Beaune
The reds of the Côte de Beaune are often said to be more feminine than their Nuits counterparts. There is something in their fruit texture that is silky and soft, although many balance this with startling intensity and no dearth of tannin. The hill-vineyard of Corton is the only *grand cru* in the Côte de Beaune, but there are a

119

number of *premier cru* sites, especially in Pommard and Volnay, which are currently producing better wines. Of the villages around Beaune, Savigny is light and perfumed, Aloxe-Corton potentially powerful and intense but rather unreliable, while Pernand-Vergelesses, Ladoix and Chorey-lès-Beaune all offer fairly simple but good-value wines. Beaune itself can vary from sublime to dreary, but the best have fruit in abundance allied with good structure.

The powerful Pommard is Gevrey-Chambertin to the more elegant Volnay's Chambolle-Musigny, and although neither is the most reliable appellation, the top wines of each rival the best in Burgundy. The underrated Monthelie and St-Aubin give rather cheaper glimpses of the Volnay style. Red Chassagne-Montrachet is somewhat rustic, while the best Santenay is satisfyingly full and fruity. The Hautes-Côtes de Beaune needs a good vintage to ripen the fruit properly but the wines can be excellent value.

Pick of the producers (Côte d'Or red burgundy)
Marquis d'Angerville Elegant ageworthy Volnay, especially from the monopole Clos des Ducs. Not widely available. (Marquis d'Angerville pioneered estate-bottling in Burgundy.)

Domaine de l'Arlot AXA-owned estate making delicious Nuits-St-Georges in a modern style (fruit-based, but never over-oaked). Look for the *premiers crus* Clos de l'Arlot and Clos des Forêts-St-Georges.

Comte Armand The sturdy, fruit-packed and ageworthy Pommard from the organically cultivated Clos des Epeneaux is one of the great reds of Burgundy. Undergoing changes. Let's hope quality is maintained.

Robert Arnoux Robust Vosne-Romanée, Echézeaux and Nuits-St-Georges. Not cheap wines but long-ageing and getting better and better.

Simon Bize One of the best growers in Savigny-lès-Beaune: old vines, low yields and ripe, spicy, succulent cellarable wines.

Boisset Burgundy's largest company also owns Bouchard Aîné, Jaffelin, Edouard Delaunay, Ropiteau, F Chauvenet, Pierre Ponnelle and a number of other brands. Modern-style wines from excellent sites, improving with the recruitment of winemaker Pascal Marchand in 1999. Wines from the company's own vineyards now appear as Domaine de la Vougeraie. The Vougeraie wines are agers, the rest are for early drinking.

Chandon de Briailles Important, quality domaine for both ageworthy Savigny-lès-Beaune and (white) Corton.

Bruno Clair Producer of serious Marsannay, but reaching higher quality with his wines from Gevrey, Morey-St-Denis and, further south, Savigny-lès-Beaune.

Joseph Drouhin Now Japanese-owned, but Drouhin still very much in control. This is a fine source of burgundy. Good, honest wines at all levels exemplified by robust, ageworthy Beaune Clos des Mouches.

Domaine Dujac The top estate of Morey-St-Denis, making elegant perfumed wines, best of which are the three Morey *grands crus* of Clos de la Roche, Clos St-Denis and Bonnes Mares. When it's good, it's very, very good: put it in your cellar if you have one.

René Engel Vosne-Romanée domaine making sturdy, flamboyant wines, built to last many years – showing vast improvements since the early 1980s when Philippe Engel took the helm. Good even in poor vintages.

Michel Esmonin et Fille Father-and-daughter team in Gevrey-Chambertin making silky, elegant wines with immense attention to detail. Classy since the early 1990s.

Faiveley Reliable source of good if slightly chunky reds, ranging from very fine Mercurey up to great Chambertin Clos de Bèze.

Geantet-Pansiot Hedonistic, very stylish Gevrey-Chambertin made with a modern approach, maturing early but with structure to last. Reliable wines.

Jean Grivot Since 1993, Etienne Grivot has been making some of the best full-throttle, powerful wines in the Côte d'Or from vineyards in Vosne-Romanée and Nuits-St-Georges. The Richebourg is superb. Dedication shows in top wines from lesser vintages, for example 1998.

Anne Gros Vosne-Romanée domaine making revered reds of intensity and finesse. Top-class Richebourg, Vosne-Romanée, Chambolle-Musigny and Clos de Vougeot. Anne Gros's reputation grows every year.

Hospices de Beaune Major Côte de Beaune landowner that raises money by auctioning its wine each year on the third Sunday of

November. Brand new winery, but the *élevage* – literally 'bringing up' – of the wines is then the responsibility of the *négociant* or domaine that bought it, so some wines can be great, while others are not.

Louis Jadot Well-respected *négociant*-turned-winemaker, with notably holistic approach and spanking-new winery. Winemaker Jacques Lardière's reds need time to show their undoubted class. The range is topped by the Chambertin Clos de Bèze, but the wines from Beaune – particularly Grèves and Clos des Ursules – are also special.

Michel Lafarge Silky but powerful Volnays that exhibit considerable class when young yet age well. Find them if you can; Lafarge courts no publicity but dominates by reputation.

Comtes Lafon Better known for whites, but Lafon's Volnays get better and better each year – California training shows in rich, distinctive wines.

Dominique Laurent Youngster, and former chef, Laurent produces boldly flavoured, powerful reds. The *grands crus*, often heavily oaked, are rare, pricy and built for the long run, but village wines from appellations such as Monthelie and Chambolle-Musigny are affordable and very tasty.

Domaine Leroy Biodynamic viticulture, extremely low yields and total devotion to quality make this one of the greatest Burgundy domaines at present. Critics say that Lalou Bize-Leroy's astonishingly concentrated wines are atypical of Burgundy. If you can find and afford them, and then have the patience to wait the 20 years that some of the wines need, judge for yourself. You may even forget the enormous price.

Méo-Camuzet Fine estate popular in the USA making ultra-modern, chunky wines with lots of fruit, no shortage of oak and great richness. The Vosne-Romanée Cros Parantoux is of *grand cru* quality, while the Clos Vougeot is one of the best around.

Alain Michelot Ageworthy, reliable Nuit-St-Georges from a small but expanding domaine.

de Montille Aristocratic Volnay producer who advocates minimal chaptalisation and whose wines lack the showiness which would make them attractive when young. However, they age superbly into classic red burgundies without too much alcohol (12 per cent maximum).

Bernard Morey Reliable grower of Chassagne-Montrachet and Santenay; ageworthy wines.

Denis Mortet Classy, long-lived, if occasionally over-oaked, wines from Gevrey-Chambertin.

Jean-Marc Pavelot Top Savigny-lès-Beaune domaine with wines of fruit and complexity, elegance, depth and longevity.

Nicolas Potel Son of the late Gérard Potel who ran Domaine de la Pousse d'Or in Volnay, Nicolas has his own *négociant* business and is developing a strong reputation for splendid wines from Volnay, Gevrey-Chambertin, Corton and other Côte d'Or villages.

Domaine de la Romanée-Conti Is it competition from former co-owner Mme Bize-Leroy at Domaine Leroy which is spurring this exceptional estate to greater heights? Quality from the six *grands crus* is as high as it has ever been, and almost justifies some of the phenomenal prices. La Tâche and Romanée-Conti itself remain for many people the pinnacle of red burgundy.

Domaine Georges Roumier et fils Georges' son, the technically brilliant Christophe, makes the wines today and full and rich they are too. Chambolle-Musigny is the main wine but his Bonnes Mares wines are concentrated and impressive. (Also succulent Corton whites.)

Armand Rousseau Consistency, prices which never seem excessive, and top-rack, long-ageing wines have made this Gevrey domaine with considerable holdings of *premier* and *grand cru* vineyards a favourite with many. Rousseau grandson now at the helm and maintaining classic Burgundian style.

Domaine Charles Thomas Vineyard-owners since before the French Revolution, the Thomas family creates a spectacular array of ageworthy reds, from Corton down to straight Côte de Nuits.

Tollot-Beaut Reliable, fairly priced wines at all levels with plenty of fruit and no shortage of oak make this Chorey-lès-Beaune estate a dependable bet. Highly dedicated to organic health in the vineyards.

De Vogüé Renowned Chambolle-Musigny estate which owns over two-thirds of the Le Musigny *grand cru*, and whose best wine is the Vieilles Vignes *cuvée*. Consistency was not always the order of the day in the 1970s and 1980s, but winemaker François Millet has since then gained himself a reputation as a wine 'poet'. Second only to Domaine de la Romanée-Conti. Pity there's so little about.

Côte Chalonnaise reds

The finest reds of the Côte Chalonnaise can surpass those of the Côte de Beaune, so we're surprised that more producers don't feel challenged to expend a little more effort and make some really impressive wine. Red Rully is rarely seen, but Givry and Mercurey in particular are capable of making solid Pinot which age transforms from a chunky adolescent into something richer and more satisfying. The best estate is that of Michel Juillot in Mercurey, a source of supple reds that can confidently be aged for up to ten years, and of very drinkable whites too. This is a region in a state of flux. As a new generation of growers takes time to settle in, it's difficult to say whether things are on track or not.

Beaujolais

Nouveau can be fun, but drinking it so young, tart and insubstantial means that you miss most of the magic of this wine with its sprightly cherry and plum fruit. Basic Beaujolais and the rather better Beaujolais-Villages should be drunk in the spring and summer following the vintage rather than on the third Thursday in November after harvest. A further step up is found in the ten *crus* villages in the north of the region. They are as follows: St-Amour – attractive when young, watch out for price rises around 14 February; Brouilly – perfumed, fruity and reasonable value; Chénas – rarely seen, underrated; Chiroubles – small quantities of often indifferent wine; Côte de Brouilly – firmer (and pricier) than Brouilly; Fleurie – overpriced although can be full and charming; Juliénas – solid, supple and needing a year or so in bottle; Morgon – quite firm but fruity, ideally needs two years in bottle; Moulin-à-Vent – potentially good, the sturdiest *cru*, and not too expensive; Régnié – yet to convince it should have been promoted to *cru* status.

As with mainstream burgundy, there is a new generation of growers taking hold in Beaujolais, who are far more globally aware than their fathers were. The latter may have turned a blind eye as New World competitors – the cheerful, fruity and cheap wines of Chile, for example – took away their market share, but the new kids are taking up the challenge. As they become more scrupulous in their grape selection and winemaking, better wines should result.

Beaujolais is not the trendiest of wines, so you should find plenty in the shops. *Cru* wines from the best growers are not much cheaper than village burgundies, but the standard is high. The big name is Georges Duboeuf, who makes a remarkably reliable range topped by the very good Morgon Jean Descombes and Fleurie Domaine des Quatre Vents. Other growers to look out for include Domaine Berrod, Nicole Chanrion, Fernand Coudert, Marc Dudet, Paul Janin, Jacky Janodet, André Large, Jean-Charles Pivot, Château Thivin and Château des Tours. The best Beaujolais we've tried recently is the range of full-bodied and ageworthy, single-vineyard wines from Louis Jadot-owned Château des Jacques in Moulin-à-Vent.

Burgundy red vintage guide

The higher up the ladder of generic, village, *premier cru*, *grand cru* you go, the longer the wines should last, although there's certainly nothing to stop you enjoying them in their exuberant youth. Red burgundy today can be charmingly fruity at five years old and younger, and leathery and feral at 15 years and over. In between, the best retain their appeal, although some seem to go into a rather moody phase out of which, as long as they have the stuffing, they should eventually emerge. Don't be afraid to open the odd bottle of even the *grands crus* before their seventh birthday. If they are delicious, whether you drink them now or keep them is purely up to you. However, if they don't open out in the glass over the course of an evening, compare your experience with that of the merchant from whom you bought the wine. It may be that more time in bottle is all that is called for. (If you want to give your burgundy 'a lot' more time – or are just feeling generally altruistic towards the younger members of your family – we've recently tasted some that were over 80 years old and still delicious.)

2001 A changeable harvest following an up-and-down growing season: frosts in April, a fine May, but then cool weather in June and July, then violent storms in the south in August. Quality gets better the further north you go, and on the whole the wines are firm-fruited with good aromatics and well-defined acidity.

2000 It started cool but early buds survived July cold and hail for what turned out to be the hottest vintage for ten years. Storms on 12 September quickly cleared and most growers avoided spoilage. A good, if not abundant, harvest was made in cooler weather. Reds with softer tannins and acidity than the 1999s; good for short-term rather than long-term drinking.

1999 Spectacular, close to perfection on the Côte de Beaune. A welcome combination of quality and quantity. Spring weather was irregular, but a hot summer brought a large crop of healthy fruit to full ripeness. Rain towards the end of the harvest may have affected some Côte de Nuits growers, but most have billed this as their 'vintage of the millennium'.

1998 Sorted the men from the boys. It rained for much of the first fortnight of September, and was then dry for a ten-day spell. Those who managed to pick during the dry period and took pains to exclude rotten fruit have produced some good-to-excellent wines with forward, fleshy flavours.

1997 As in Bordeaux, this is a nice, forward, friendly, low-acid vintage producing wines to be drunk while waiting for the 1996s and 1995s to mature. Cool spring weather resulted in a small crop, and the hot summer ripened the grapes well. Rain in late August and early September may have diluted the wines, but the grapes were brought in ripe and rot-free.

1996 Even flowering promised a good vintage, and although August was rainy, strong winds in September dried the grapes out, preventing rot and dilution. Grapes were harvested in excellent condition, and the wines should be full bodied and long lasting.

1995 The uneven flowering due to spring frosts was something of a mixed blessing. The crop size was reduced, but it also meant that the grapes developed thick skins, which were able to withstand the rain that fell in September after a fine July and August. The wines have turned out to be ripe and fruity and close to 1993 in quality.

1994 Nearly a good vintage spoiled by rain just before harvest. Wines are on the light side, but they are not unripe.

1993 Not quite up to 1990 quality, but for those who favour robust wines which take several years to approach maturity, this was a good vintage. In some lesser wines, where the fruit isn't quite up to that chunky structure, there's not a great deal of joy to be had.

1992 Decentish vintage, but with no real weight. Now tiring.

1991 Hail spoiled the party, but amid a sea of mediocrity there are some incredibly concentrated wines around from those scrupulous producers who were prepared to harvest only top-quality fruit.

1990 Wonderful year, with the abundant ripe fruit of 1989 matched with the structure of 1988. The only problem is when to drink them. Their ripe fruit makes even the top *grands crus* deliciously approachable now, but they will last for decades more. However, bargains are hard to find.

Good earlier vintages 1989, 1988, 1985, 1978, 1976, 1971, 1969.

White wines

Yes, there is some Pinot Blanc, and some Pinot Gris (Beurot as it is known here), as well as that Burgundian oddity Aligoté, which needs a ripe year to shed its veil of acidity. And there's some remarkably good Sauvignons being made in St-Bris near Chablis. But white burgundy is really all about Chardonnay. Despite the profusion of Chardonnays from virtually every winemaking country, nowhere comes close to Burgundy for the sheer number of great wines. There may not be large amounts of them, two barrels of one grower's Le Montrachet, three of another's Meursault-Genevrières – and you'll pay heavily for them, but that's a different matter.

The style of Burgundian Chardonnay varies as you travel throughout the region from Chablis in the north to the Mâconnais in the south, but what underlies all the best wines is the feeling that you are tasting something seamless, rather than a concoction of fruit, oak and winemaking techniques. Where do the flavours of nuts and honey come from? How can it be so rich and buttery yet totally dry? Why does it taste so delicious when young yet still manage to age gracefully for several years?

Of course, such comments apply only to the very top wines. There is still plenty of Burgundian Chardonnay that does no favours either to the grape or to the region. But because it's now possible to pick up decent Chardonnay from other parts of the globe, the UK's wine merchants don't feel compelled to stock boring, underflavoured Mâcon. Encouragingly, the Burgundians themselves are now looking at the competition and adapting their techniques accordingly, picking riper fruit and cleaning up their winemaking. Where yields are high, some of the wines could easily pass for New World versions, but where yields are low, the results are best described as excellent modern burgundy.

Chablis

While many agree that Chablis is the perfect accompaniment to shellfish, no one is precisely sure how it should taste. A number of practices, including reduction in the levels of sulphur dioxide, more widespread use of malolactic fermentation and the use of oak barrels for fermenting and ageing wines, are producing wines which have little in common with the classic image of a steely, flinty, green-gold wine that needs years to reach its peak. Fruit – a warm appley fruit, sometimes with hints of rhubarb – has come to the fore, and the wines can be charming at a very tender age. Purists are outraged by these new wines, saying that they are indistinguishable from other white burgundies, while the modernists say that the characters of the wines of the past were more to do with poor winemaking.

There is also heated debate on the matter of soil. The seven *grands crus* – Blanchots, Bougros, Les Clos, Grenouilles, Preuses, Valmur, Vaudésir – live up to their name, as do the majority of the *premiers crus*. However, it is the incorporation of new areas of land into the basic appellation of Chablis, and the development of *premiers crus* where once there was woodland, which has provoked the biggest debate. The traditionalists maintain that proper Chablis needs to be grown on Kimmeridgian (chalky/clay) soil. The opposition argues that the wines made on other soils are as good; since the yields in both cases are usually too high for the effect of *terroir* to be felt, they are probably right. This one could run and run . . .

Pick of the producers (Chablis)

La Chablisienne Large but good co-operative producing a third of all Chablis. Quality, reliability and value are often higher than the majority of the growers. Wines for early drinking.

René & Vincent Dauvissat/Dauvissat-Camus A combination of good sites and fine winemaking makes this one of the top Chablis producers. The wines from the *grands crus* Les Clos and Les Preuses are as sublime as and ageworthy as Chablis gets.

William Fèvre/Domaine de la Maladière/Ancien Domaine Auffray Fèvre's (modern) style was to use oak for fermenting and ageing his wines, and it will be interesting to see whether that changes under new proprietor Joseph Henriot, who also owns Bouchard Père & Fils. Great vineyard holdings, including 15 per cent of the *grands crus*, which still belong to Fèvre but are being leased to Henriot.

Jean-Hughes Goisot Not Chablis actually, but wines from the neighbouring Auxerrois. If you want to see the other grapes Burgundy has up its sleeve, this is an excellent place to come. Sauvignon de St-Bris, Aligoté and Bourgogne Pinot Noir from the top of the alternative tree in St-Bris-le-Vineux.

Louis Michel Classic unoaked Chablis which can age for 20 years or more, yet retain its minerally core. Can be inconsistent though.

Jean-Marie Raveneau With or without oak, first-rank wines that need a minimum of five years' age to begin to show their true class. Though among the best wines in the region, prices are reasonable.

Also look out for: *Jean-Marc Brocard*, *Jean-Paul Droin*, *Jean Durup*, *Domaines des Malandes* and *Laurent Tribut*.

Côte d'Or white

A few whites are produced in the Côte de Nuits, such as de Vogüé's famous Musigny Blanc and the Nuits-St-Georges from Domaine de l'Arlot. However, the vast majority of the great white burgundies are made in the Côte de Beaune between Aloxe-Corton and

Santenay. The best value can often be found with basic Bourgogne Blanc from top producers, but the villages of Pernand-Vergelesses, Santenay, St-Aubin and Auxey-Duresses are somewhat underrated. St-Romain is less reliable, Beaune can be good though pricy, while the majority of Aloxe-Corton is sold as the *grand cru* Corton-Charlemagne, which ages to sumptuous, buttery perfection, providing the grower isn't too greedy with his yields.

However, the villages of Meursault, Puligny-Montrachet and Chassagne-Montrachet produce the majority of the truly glorious white burgundies. The *grands crus* of Le Montrachet and Bâtard-Montrachet, both shared between Puligny and Chassagne, can be awesome. But wines from other *grands crus* and the top *premiers crus* such as Meursault-Perrières, Puligny Les Referts and Chassagne Morgeot can also be exceptional. Some would say that Puligny is the refined one, and Meursault the rich fat one, while Chassagne sits halfway between. However, don't let such generalisations cloud your appreciation of these wines – though we would say that, considering the prices, make sure you know your grower before splashing out on large quantities.

Pick of the producers (White burgundy)
Guy Amiot & Fils Guy Amiot's father leased out a lot of his Chassagne-Montrachet vineyards but now these agreements are coming to an end, son Guy and his son Thierry have increasing control over their own destiny – and wines. Top quality.

Jean-Marc Boillot Excellent holdings in Puligny and Chassagne, including a small parcel of Bâtard-Montrachet, passed to M Boillot when he married into the Sauzet family, and these have now been joined by other red and white vineyards in the Côte de Beaune. Superb quality across the board, and good wines to drink young, but expensive.

Bonneau du Martray Major landowners in the Corton-Charlemagne vineyard and making first-rate, long-lived wine. Watch for still-available older vintages. This estate is burgeoning under the watchful eye of Jean-Charles le Bault de la Morinière.

Louis Carillon Not the most fashionable Puligny producer – perhaps because his wines are for ageing, not for drinking young? – but one of the better ones. Subtle, often sublime wines from village level up to *grand cru*.

Jean-François Coche-Dury Bourgogne Blanc that tastes like good Meursault, village Meursault that rivals the top *premiers crus*, and Meursault-Perrières and Corton-Charlemagne that are sensational.

Given that demand is so high, the prices asked for what is close to perfect white burgundy are very reasonable – if you can find any. They age magnificently.

Michel Colin-Deléger Not cheap, difficult to find, but very fine, elegant wines including Puligny-Montrachet *premier cru* Les Caillerets and Chassagne-Montrachet Les Vergers. For medium-term drinking.

Didier Darviot-Perrin Delicious, reliable Chassagne-Montrachet and Meursault from old vines.

Joseph Drouhin Famous company with extensive estate throughout the Côte d'Or and Chablis, and marginally better whites than reds. Lesser appellations such as Rully are very good, but the highlight is the glorious Montrachet from the Marquis de Laguiche estate.

Jean-Noël Gagnard Increasingly fashionable producer of Chassagne, and rightly so given the superb quality and longevity.

Vincent Girardin Santenay-based Girardin sources fruit both from his own vineyards and from other growers throughout the Côte d'Or (50 in total) to make lovely silky reds, and twice as many whites. Variable in the mid-1990s but now back on form and refusing to get any bigger.

Louis Jadot Top-level *grands crus* far exceed basic Bourgogne Blanc in quality. It's a toss-up whether the Corton-Charlemagne or the Chevalier-Montrachet Les Demoiselles is the best wine. Both live for years.

François Jobard Meursault that can lack opulence in its youth, but which at ten years old is magnificent, particularly the *premiers crus* of Genevrières, Charmes and Poruzot. The wines live forever.

Comtes Lafon Dominique Lafon is deservedly famous for his rich, oaky and quite splendid Meursaults. Tiny amounts of Le Montrachet are produced as well. California-comes-to-Burgundy, modern-style, big Chardonnay.

Hubert Lamy-Monnot St-Aubin domaine, where son Olivier Lamy – now responsible for winemaking – leads a quality upgrade. Midway between traditional and modern, top-quality Criots-Bâtard-Montrachet and Chassagne-Montrachet are lovely to drink young.

Louis Latour Best known for his Corton-Charlemagne; quality is moderate elsewhere.

Domaine Leflaive Biodynamic viticulture and the winemaking talents of Pierre Morey have re-established the reputation of this famous Puligny estate. The wines are expensive, but ageworthy and now slightly softer. Although Olivier Leflaive is co-owner, the wines bearing his name are from a separate *négociant* business.

Paul Pernot Expanding Puligny domaine, with good wines despite young vines. Mostly sold through *négociants* but own-label Bâtard-Montrachet is excellent. *If* you see it, snap it up.

Ramonet Wonderful, if occasionally erratic, Chassagne grower, perhaps best known for the Montrachet, but also offering complex, long-lived Bâtard and Bienvenues-Bâtard as well as stunning *premiers crus*.

Domaine Roulot Underrated and very reliable producer of rich, tasty, gorgeous Meursault – very ageworthy but attractive young, too. Hard to find.

Etienne Sauzet Well-known Puligny producer, now smaller in size than in previous years but making up quantities by buying in grapes (which makes for some inconsistency in the fruit). Winemaking, under Gérard Boudot, is top quality.

Verget Mâcon-based Belgian Jean-Marie Guffens makes some of the best and purest wines in Burgundy. He excels with Chablis and the *grands crus* of the Côte d'Or, but even his Bourgogne Blanc and Mâcon-Villages are stars, though best drunk in their 'flashy' youth.

Côte Chalonnaise white

There haven't been massive improvements in the Côte Chalonnaise recently. Progress, in fact, has almost been backwards. But give it time. A lot of the very good older growers have retired and it's too early yet to say whether the new generation are 'chips off the old blocks' or maybe have a more modern approach. The village of Bouzeron produces Burgundy's best Aligoté, some of which, in a ripe year, is even too good to be mixed with cassis to make kir. The version from de Villaine is the best. As well as the reliable but not very widely seen Bourgogne Côte Chalonnaise, a number of villages produce white wine under their own names. Givry and Mercurey are better known for reds but can produce buttery, spicy whites; Montagny – in the vast majority of cases with the words Premier Cru – can be good if rather lean; while the rounded fruity Rully offers the best value.

Mâconnais

The Mâconnais has row upon row of mature Chardonnay vines with which someone should be able to make decent, concentrated whites costing under £10 a bottle. A few producers are currently making such wines, but – with co-operatives and merchants who see the region as just a source of cheap white burgundy to sell to supermarkets – progress is still slower than we would wish. The new appellation of Viré-Clessé (from 1999), which covers wines formerly labelled Mâcon Viré and Mâcon Clessé (from the region's top two villages), has a maximum level of residual sugar of 4 grams per litre, and some of the top domaines, most notably Thévenet and Guillemot-Michel, routinely make wines which exceed this. Thévenet's 1998s fall under this level, but quite what he'll call his wines in a riper vintage is still not clear.

Most Mâcon Blanc is made to a price; an inoffensive, underflavoured and unmemorable wine. Anyone looking for more character should step up to Mâcon-Villages or one of the more specific village appellations such as Mâcon-Pierreclos. Pouilly-Loché and Pouilly-Vinzelles are one rung up from Mâcon, while Pouilly-Fuissé is better still – a rich, creamy wine which can be excellent and not as overpriced as was once the case. Perhaps the best-value wine is St-Véran – Pouilly quality at a Mâcon price.

The Burgundian rule of producer first, appellation second applies more if anything in the Mâconnais than anywhere else. The best wines are in fact coming from mainstream Burgundy growers, such as Lafon from Meursault, who are beginning to invest in the region and show how things can, and should, be done.

Pick of the producers (Mâconnais)
Domaine Vincent/Château de Fuissé The St-Véran is good but the Pouilly-Fuissé, particularly the Vieilles Vignes *cuvée*, is the star, and probably the best-known wine of the Mâconnais.

Guffens-Heynen Belgian duo Jean-Marie Guffens and his wife Germaine Heynen produce Pouilly-Fuissé and Mâcon-Pierreclos of astonishing concentration and complexity.

Guillemot-Michel An excellent Mâcon-Clessé Quintaine is joined in suitable years by a *botrytised* wine, Sélection de Grains Cendrés.

Jean Thévenet/Domaine de la Bon Gran Old vines, low yields and ultra-ripe fruit make concentrated, long-lived Viré-Clessé, and others. Noble rot often plays a part, with sometimes a separate *cuvée botrytis*.

Also recommended: *André Bonhomme*, *Cordier*, *Domaine Talmard*. New venture, *Les Héritiers de Comte Lafon* – a recent purchase by the top Meursault estate – is one to watch.

Burgundy white vintage guide

Much better selection of grapes in recent years has led to a series of excellent vintages. No bad thing when you consider, rather perversely perhaps, that white burgundy can be a more suitable candidate for extended cellaring than red. There are some bottles of white burgundy that will set you back considerably more than £100, yet which at anything under five years of age just seem large and oaky. Even at village level, most wines benefit from being drunk at least four years after vintage. And of all white wines, burgundy is the one that needs the longest time to breathe. We're not in the 'open-the-night-before' league, but do let it have some time to develop, so you can fully enjoy the whole bottle rather than just the last glass.

2001 A mild winter followed by April frosts, then a cool flowering period resulted in uneven fruit set. Warm-to-hot weather followed in July and August but so did hail and thunderstorms. Difficult, changeable conditions persisted right up to harvest but white wines fared well nonetheless with concentrated fruit and firm acidity.

2000 Where 1999 looked to be the vintage of the millennium for reds, 2000 may well do the same for white burgundy. A cool start to the season followed by a hot summer, and a protracted, cool harvest, led to concentrated aromatics, good ripeness, gentle acidity and very fine wines indeed.

1999 Not as good for whites as for reds, but there's plenty of ripe, low acid wine which is drinking well at an early age. While the large harvest may mean that some wines are dilute, growers who thinned their crop in the summer have made some rich, concentrated wines.

1998 Rain fell in the first half of September, but the hot August weather meant that the grapes harvested were generally ripe with low acidity, if sometimes affected by rot. Hail earlier in the year led to yields in several top Côte de Beaune vineyards being dramatically reduced, and the extra concentration shows in many wines.

1997 As with the reds, the 1997 whites are ripe, fruity wines with low acidity, making them extremely attractive even at this relatively early stage. In some cases, alcohol levels seem high compared with the depth of flavour, but generally this is as friendly as burgundy gets: an ideal vintage for novices to the region.

1996 A fine vintage, with a large and healthy crop of full, ripe grapes. High acidity bodes well for longevity, while the wines should be more perfumed than the 1995s.

1995 A better vintage for whites than reds, although it's still worth waiting for the wines to show their best. Quantities were small, so don't expect many bargains.

1994 A year when rain diluted the flavours of ripe fruit. At the lower end of the scale there was a healthy supply of decent wines, which should be drunk soon, and even the higher-priced wines have been remarkably forward.

1993 A more restrained vintage after the opulence of 1992. Watch out for high acidity. The top wines will benefit from it and could in many cases eclipse the 1992s with bottle age. However, wines with insufficient fruit to stand up to the acidity are not uncommon.

1992 The only problem with this ripe and concentrated vintage is whether the wines have the acidity to hold them together. They've tasted wonderful from the start, but a few are now beginning to show their age. If you have large stocks and haven't tasted them recently, pull a few corks to check on their progress; they may need to be drunk up.

1991 Rain at vintage resulted in rot, and while, as ever, the best producers made some decent wine, there were few real stars.

1990 Not quite in the same league as the reds of the same vintage, nor the whites of the previous one, but still a generally impressive performance. Lowish acidity means that they've been attractive from the word go, and the best still have lots of life ahead of them.

1989 Plenty of heat throughout the summer, and especially at vintage time, resulted in some wines that are excessively alcoholic and low in acidity; and which are really showing their age. However, the best wines are classics: impressive and weighty and will provide excellent drinking for the next five years.

1988 Wines of structure rather than opulence, which are still going strong. The fruit flavours are generally good, although there are occasional hints of underripeness.

Good older vintages 1986, 1985, 1983, 1982, 1979, 1978, 1976.

Crémant de Bourgogne

With such widespread plantings of Pinot Noir and Chardonnay, it is no surprise that Burgundy also produces sparkling wine – but this ought to be significantly better than it is. Although the Burgundians have recently proposed a new appellation designating vineyards specifically for sparkling wine production – and therefore, one would assume, establishment of the special clones, appropriate sites, and the pruning and training techniques needed to produce fine fizz – it so far appears they've only done it to guarantee supply and not quality. Let's hope we're wrong. The wines are made the traditional way, mainly based on Chardonnay, and prices are attractive for the very few creamy, fresh and appealing examples we've found. Very few of the growers' wines ever appear in Britain, but the co-operatives of Bailly, Viré and Lugny produce goodish versions.

CHAMPAGNE

You have to admire the Champenois. It's taken them longer than they expected to recover from the millennium hangover, with over-estimated stocks of party fizz having only just disappeared from merchant shelves in the UK. And then there was September 11, which took a considerable toll on their important US market, with sales tumbling a massive 30 per cent in 2001. But they're determined to rethink themselves somehow. Find another way to draw attention to their plight.

'Plight' was that? No, we know you don't seriously believe that Champagne producers are struggling – nor do we – given their glitzy advertising campaigns, expensive bottles and general marketing savvy. But after every peak in sales (for example, the millennium) there must be a trough, and nobody wants to be in one of those for too long.

The latest streak of creativity sees producers acknowledging the need to offer variety. There is a new understanding of the importance of segmenting their offer – whether it be blanc de blancs, blanc de noirs, single-variety champagnes, single-grower wines, or the *mono-crus* we talked about last year (wines from a single plot of vineyard), we're seeing a whole new wave of 'hand-crafted' *cuvées*, wines that illustrate the individual parts going to make up the whole champagne blend. These are aimed at only a tiny proportion of the market, of course – at connoisseurs, and consumers of a more than usually obsessive/curious nature – but they are very interesting and we do recommend giving them a go. Examples could be single-grape champagnes from the villages best-suited to each variety: Chardonnay from Chouilly, Pinot Noir from Aÿ, Pinot Meunier from Sillery (look for Feuillatte's good-value examples, or Moët's expensive ones).

These wines will never replace the glossy prestige growths, or the big non-vintage brands, but they help the image and they demonstrate versatility. They show that Champagne can produce a wine with 'traceability' – to the exact vineyard and region it comes from – which is all the fashion at the moment.

What's really hitting the news with Champagne, however, is its big move towards 'organic' production – another fashionable issue. The Champenois have announced their intention to avoid further harm to their environment by reducing the use of chemical fertilisers, pesticides (by as much as 50 per cent), fungicides, and so on, and adopting *viticulture raisonée*. This is not organic farming per se, as, at this rainy northern margin of vine growing, some combative chemicals will still be necessary. But it marks a global first for the region, the only one as yet to adopt these techniques en masse. It's a brave move considering its 15,000 growers, but Champagne is determined to lead, and the governing CIVC (Comité Interprofessional du Vin de Champagne) advises us that, when polled, 90 per cent of producers expressed a wish to adopt new, more caring vineyard practices.

These events are somewhat inevitable, however, given Champagne's rather wicked viticultural past. It is a region on the rebound. Until only recently, Champagne has been frowned upon for using the waste of France's capital city as fertiliser, resulting not only in ugly mounds of blue plastic rubbish sacks, used batteries, cigarette packets, and so on, but possible heavy metal contamination. Though these *bleus de ville* have been outlawed since 1998, and outpriced since the early 1980s (when this Parisian waste actually began to cost too much to buy). It can be easily argued that the region has been slow to take care of its *terroir*.

Today, however, we are seeing the wholesale establishment of natural 'eaters of eaters' to confront Champagne's pests. Typhlodromes to fight off spider mites; moth-hormones to confuse the would-be parents of vine-chewing caterpillars; clever forecasting to prevent unnecessary fungicide application; banning of all genetically modified organisms in the vineyards. A good thing, of course. The next question you're going to ask, we bet, is 'won't all these changes make Champagne even more expensive?'. We're told not. While more money will be spent on 'tending', less will be spent on pesticides, and the two will cancel each other out. The costs will *not* be passed on to the consumer. Apparently. Let's hope that's the case.

It's going to take a while for the Americans to return to the fold, but the UK market is biting steadily, with champagne consumption up over 20 per cent following an abstemious year in 2000. Part of this increase has to do with the substantial and welcome price reductions offered by (among others) the supermarkets, 'to bring prices in line with Europe', but it is a sales increase nonetheless.

And we shouldn't abstain from drinking champagne. Remember, this is just like any other wine: you'll like one house style but not another – they're all different; steer away/escape from the big brand traps and branch out, try some of the above-mentioned smaller *crus*, because there are some excellent flavours to be discovered. And on the subject of *mono-cru* wines, can we put a request to the Champenois to make more of them; please?

Grape varieties

Most champagnes are a judicious blend of three varieties: Pinot Noir, Chardonnay and Pinot Meunier. Of these, the best Pinot Noir comes from the Montagne de Reims and is acknowledged to be the grape that provides body and structure to the wine. The most sought-after Chardonnay flourishes on the Côte des Blancs and gives a light, floral elegance, but has a firmness that softens and adds complexity with age. Pinot Meunier is often referred to as the workhorse grape, and is normally left out of the better blends and vintage champagnes, providing balance and fragrance in the standard wines.

How champagne is made

The traditional method of making champagne is by secondary bottle fermentation. The term '*méthode traditionnelle*' now legally denotes this practice and can be found on bottles of sparkling wine from all over the world. The word 'champagne', however, can apply only to sparkling wines from the region itself and this right is fiercely protected by the Champenois.

Ironically, if the still wines of Champagne had not been made into sparkling wine, this famous region would have remained a quiet backwater producing small quantities of mediocre red wine and some very thin and acidic whites. As it is, producers realised hundreds of years ago that very gentle pressing of black grapes gave a light juice, which could be fermented to dryness and then bottled and sealed with a little yeast and sugar to allow it to re-ferment. The sparkle is created by trapping the fermentation gas within the bottles; these are thick enough to withstand up to six atmospheres of pressure. All this takes months, if not years, to achieve, and at any one time there are millions of bottles lying in serried ranks below the streets of Rheims and Epernay and throughout the region. A quiet evolution of epic proportions.

In time, the yeast sediment – via a painstaking series of gentle twists (traditionally done by hand, but now, more often than not, by machine) – drops to the neck of the upside-down bottle, and is then frozen and removed. A final addition of sweetened wine adjusts the style of the finished wine, and the bottle is re-sealed with the distinctive mushroom cork and wire cage, to settle down again. When ready for sale, the bottle is dressed with its unique foil and label.

Styles

Blanc de blancs Champagne made entirely from white Chardonnay grapes. Typically fresh, elegant and creamy.

Blanc de noirs White champagne made from the juice of the red grapes Pinot Meunier and Pinot Noir. Usually a reliably firm and fruity wine.

Brut The term for dry champagne with less than 15 grams per litre of residual sugar. The vast majority of champagne sold in the UK is Brut.

Demi-sec Confusingly, this means sweet.

Extra-dry Again, potentially confusing – dry, but not as dry as Brut.

Mono-cru Single-vineyard wine, the expression of one particular plot of land. If you want to understand how the components of a great champagne blend together, these wines show just how that happens. Drappier's Grande Sendrée is one example, Salon is another.

Non-vintage The producer's standard blend, a true reflection of the house style. Non-vintage can be as young as one year old, though quality-conscious houses aim for a minimum of three years. Good houses draw on base-wines many years older, the important factor being a consistent reflection of the house style, year after year. Cheap, basic-quality non-vintage does not improve with keeping; the best examples may.

Prestige cuvée/de luxe cuvée The champagne at the top of each house range – the most expensive, and supposedly the highest in quality. Many have glitzy or unusual packaging, such as Roederer's Cristal in its clear glass bottle, or Perrier-Jouët's Belle Epoque with its enamelled flowers. Moët's Dom Pérignon is the most famous *prestige cuvée*. Generally speaking, these wines have a more powerful and complex character than most champagnes, and benefit from some age. They are not always made in such tiny amounts as their producers would have us believe.

Rosé Pink champagne, usually made by adding small amounts of red Pinot Noir wine from the Bouzy or Aÿ areas to the blend.

Vintage A champagne from just one good-quality year (in low-quality years none is released). The best are more complex and have a fuller flavour than non-vintage. They should age extremely well. Look for the oldest possible: usually released around five years after harvest. Beware very young vintage champagne – it can taste raw and unready.

Pick of the producers (Champagne)

Billecart-Salmon Small, family-owned house noted for the elegance of its champagne. Non-vintage has a floral note; vintage Cuvée Nicolas François Billecart is also floral-scented yet powerful; rosé is particularly refined. Latest vintage, 1997, showing well, if youthful.

Bollinger One of the best-known houses, 'Bolly' is typically rich and powerful, and ages well. Grande Année vintage wine, made with two-thirds Pinot Noir, is high-quality champagne in an upfront and ripe style. Snap up the 1995 vintage if you see any.

Canard-Duchêne Very popular in France, less well known in the UK. The *Guide* doesn't rate the non-vintage too highly, but vintage wines (the very good 1990s are still out there) and Blanc de Noirs impress more and offer good value for money.

de Cazenove Wines gaining in finesse for a number of years now. Brut Azure and Stradivarius are top labels based mostly on Chardonnay.

Delamotte Small quality-conscious house, one of the oldest in the region, with superb creamy elegant vintage wines (watch for 1995).

Deutz Roederer-owned house producing reliable, well-balanced wines.

Drappier Small, independent house from the south of the Champagne region, with a good following for its attractive, fleshy wines: smooth-as-silk Blanc de Blancs and interesting *mono-cru* Grande Sendrée (from an Aube vineyard with 70-year-old vines – it was once woodland, but burnt down in 1838; the ash still gives a distinctive character to the wines).

Duval-Leroy Family-owned company with some of the best vineyards in the region. Consistent, likeable wines (most of Sainsbury's decent own-label champagne is from this house). Its Fleur de Champagne vintage champagnes regularly win awards.

Nicolas Feuillatte Not the most consistent of houses of late but the range of mono-varietal/mono-vineyard wines (Chardonnay from Mesnil, etc.), and a very good 1992 vintage wine are fascinating.

Gardet Not terribly well known, but for our money one of the best champagne houses. Meticulously made, high-quality wines, especially the lemony, creamy vintage wines (the 1996 is top notch) and Blanc de Blancs.

Pierre Gimonnet A rare, exclusively Chardonnay domaine, run by a family of growers-turned-*vignerons* fanatical about champagnes that express their origins. Brut Fleuron and Gastronome are labels to watch for.

Gosset Small, often overlooked house with first-class range, especially long-lived, rich Grand Millésime. The Grand Millésime Rosé is also a stunner.

Henri Goutorbe Excellent, full-bodied champagne from a single grower. Good older vintages.

Alfred Gratien Family-owned firm using barrels for long ageing. Quality impresses, especially in vintage wine, but classy non-vintage gains richness from mature old reserve wines in its blend, so isn't far behind.

Charles Heidsieck Dense and aromatic range expertly put together by one of Champagne's most talented winemakers, Daniel Thibault, who unfortunately died in March 2002. Thibault will be greatly missed, but his wines live on. *Mis-en-cave* (non-vintage, but with ageing potential) are terrific value for money. Vintage wines, such as the deliciously rich 1996, while superb when young, offer greater delights in full maturity.

Henriot Elegant range, including especially well-balanced, creamy non-vintage. Older wines are often readily available from this house.

Jacquart Reliable, good-value brand from a major co-operative in Rheims, now being seen more widely in the UK. Vintage Blanc de Blancs on great form.

Jacquesson Underrated house with a consistently fine, fresh-tasting range, including elegant, aromatic Brut Perfection non-vintage and ripe, refined *prestige cuvée* Signature (less delicate than Billecart-Salmon, more so than Mumm).

Krug The most exalted champagne house of them all – and with good reason. Impeccable care is taken over fermentation in wood, blending and ageing. The result is great complexity and depth of flavour. Grande Cuvée is always impressive and powerful enough to stem our desire for the terrifyingly expensive single-vineyard Blanc de Blancs Clos de Mesnil. Even the elegant, narrow-stemmed bottles mark out this *marque* (now owned by LVMH).

Lanson The well-known Black Label is as reliable as ever. We also like vintage wines that age well, and Lanson certainly does. House style tends to crispness due to the policy of withholding malolactic fermentation.

Laurent-Perrier We like these fresh and satisfying wines, although the non-vintage may not be as consistently good as it once was. Ultra Brut is a tight-knit, extra-dry style, and rich Grande Siècle comes from a blend of three years' wine.

Moët & Chandon By far the largest house, underrated for its extraordinary achievements. Vintage wines are excellent and there's an impressive amount of character injected into its huge-selling Brut Impériale. *Prestige cuvée* Dom Pérignon combines power and fragrance, and is magnificent after ten-plus years (beware of drinking it too young). Don't forget, also, the non-vintage rosé and the new *demi-sec* Nectar.

Mumm A well-known house, improved tremendously of late – Cordon Rouge NV tastes a little more complex at last, while vintage Cordon Rouge positively sings with character and flavour. Try also the more sophisticated wines further up the range, such as Cuvée René Lalou or Grand Cordon. Purchased in June 1999 from Seagram by a Texan consortium and again in 2001 by Allied Domecq.

Bruno Paillard Rising star, still rising, and creating consistently fine, typically dry but creamy wines in a high-tech winery. (Has agreeable wines from Provence too.)

Pannier Co-operative-run house showing consistent signs of good quality. Definitely one to watch.

Joseph Perrier One of the most traditional smaller houses maintaining exceptionally high standards, particularly with splendid, honeyed, non-vintage wine. Vintage wines need age: 1995 is taut and citrusy, still youthful.

Perrier-Jouët Produces disappointing non-vintage wine but very good Grand Brut vintage (1996 is rich, nutty and concentrated), plus there is fine and fruity Belle Epoque, the *prestige cuvée* in flower-strewn enamelled bottles.

Piper-Heidsieck Large house, not hitting its most impressive form of late but change is afoot, we're told. We're waiting . . .

Pol Roger Much-loved, family-run house with a refined range, including classy, dry White Foil non-vintage; complex, citrusy Blanc de Blancs; and long-lived *de luxe cuvée* Sir Winston Churchill. Vintage wines are never released too early, and are always worth ageing further.

141

Pommery Crisp, elegant non-vintage is good value; *prestige cuvée* Louise Brut is rich and deep. House style is generally lighter on the palate than most.

R Renaudin Little-known quality producer of aromatic, deeply characterful champagnes. One to look out for.

Louis Roederer Consistently high performer with a fashionable image. Well-judged, classy non-vintage (recent tastings suggest it is better than ever); luxurious *prestige cuvée* Cristal in clear glass bottle.

Ruinart Ancient house (now owned by Moët) with well-crafted range that includes the deeply creamy Blanc de Blancs Dom Ruinart, and vintage 'R' de Ruinart (look for 1995).

Salon Small company based in the Chardonnay-producing village of Mesnil-sur-Oger, making tight-knit, fine, expensive and exclusive Blanc de Blancs. Vintage wines only, released after ten years' age: 1985 just hitting the market.

Jacques Sélosse Champagne for oak-lovers. Not us perhaps, but there might be some of you out there.

Taittinger Fashionable, Chardonnay-rich wines. The non-vintage has shaped up well of late, but Taittinger is rightly lauded for its wonderfully creamy Blanc de Blancs Comtes de Champagne.

Veuve Clicquot One of the greatest houses producing classic wines of grace, stature and breeding, their style recently much more youthful. Satisfying, relatively complex non-vintage Yellow Label (the UK's No. 3 brand after Moët and Lanson's NV), long-lived vintages (1995 has years ahead of it) and powerful *prestige cuvée* La Grande Dame.

Champagne vintage guide

Last year we recommended you snap up the last of the excellent, now mature 1989 and 1990 vintages: well there are still some 1990s around, so keep your eyes peeled. Otherwise, most of the main houses are selling the delicious 1995. A fair smattering of 1996s (destined to be the next all-time greats, so put them in your cellar!) and a few 1997s are on general release, while you might still find the occasional 1992 and 1993 from lesser-known houses, particularly those with a high proportion of Chardonnay in the blend.
2001 A harvest so bad that commentators suggest 'not even non-vintage wines will be made'. A wet winter and spring were

followed by more variable weather and rain in the summer with hailstorms into the bargain; incidence of rot was high. An obscenely large crop with very high yields meant base-wines of only 8 per cent alcohol were the norm. Reliance on reserve wines increased from 20 per cent to around 40 per cent for wines made in this year.

2000 A large harvest, not helped by July rains, nor saved by brief sunshine in August. One of the worst of the last ten years, though many houses will not be able to resist the temptation to put '2000' on the label. Careful selection will make some of these perfectly OK, but hardly riveting. Ideally, there should be few declarations.

1999 With stocks under pressure after the demand for millennium champagne, the abundant 1999 crop was very timely. Overall quality is good, despite early localised hailstorms and the odd late summer downpour. Most houses will declare a vintage.

1998 A cold and humid start to the summer was followed by extreme heat in August and heavy rain at the beginning of September. Good weather during the harvest saved the day for many growers, resulting ultimately in a fine vintage. Expect universal declaration of vintage wines.

1997 Changeable and problematic weather conditions during the year, although a sunny September and perfect conditions during harvest saved this from becoming a terrible vintage. The wines are variable and can lack body and elegance, but many houses have, or will be, declaring a vintage.

1996 Generally considered to be an excellent vintage, a 'turbo-charged 1990'. Many outstanding and powerful wines are being released, and though, as yet, they appear much less generous than the 1995s, their very high acidity and alcohol will see them out-shining these and other releases in ten years' time. The best wines are still under wraps.

1995 A classic vintage, and good for Chardonnay, although Pinot Noir was somewhat affected by rain. Almost universally declared and just coming on to the market now, many of them utterly delicious, with Chardonnay growing out of its youthful boney phase and becoming rich, ripe and sensational.

1994 Again, after a warm, sunny summer, this potentially great harvest was spoilt by light rain and rot a few days before picking in September. Euphemistically a 'difficult' vintage, with very few vintage wines made – among them, Roederer Cristal and Lanson.

1993 The quality of the grapes was extremely promising on the eve of the harvest, though a short but intense rainfall at the beginning of the picking led to a tricky harvest. Pinot Noir did best. Most houses released vintages, some of them good.

1992 Very large crop with, yet again, rain causing some rot. The quality was reasonably good, however, especially for Chardonnay, and many producers released a vintage.

1991 Large quantities despite spring frosts. Pinot Noir fared particularly well, and those houses for whom this grape dominates (for example Veuve Clicquot) declared a vintage.

1990 Like the previous year, a classic vintage for champagne, marked by very warm conditions not seen since 1950. A very high-quality, ripe harvest led to brilliant and powerful wines – some believe the best for decades.

1989 Exceptional quality producing excellent, notably rich vintage wines. Will be remembered as one of the greatest of recent vintages, eclipsed only by 1990 and now matched by 1996.

1988 A year characterised by a changeable climate, but which nonetheless produced high-quality wines – the first of a trio of exceptionally fine vintages in the Champagne region.

Other good vintages The superb 1985 wines provide a relatively mature and rich style; 1982 and 1976 are also outstanding older vintages.

CORSICA

On the face of it, all seems quiet in Corsica, but to say nothing's happening would be untrue – the amount of moving and shaking going on would almost put the Californians to shame. But despite Corsica's 2,500 years of winemaking history, favourable climate and a renewed interest in Mediterranean viticulture, very little of its wine makes it to UK shores. Since the mid-1980s the islanders have recognised that their future lies in using their own distinctive local grape varieties rather than foreign interlopers, and significant replanting has taken place. Southern French bulk-producers such as Carignan, Cinsault and Ugni Blanc are being replaced by spicy Sciacarello and robust, tannic Nielluccio for the reds; smoky, minerally Vermentino for the whites.

The international varieties (Cabernet and Chardonnay, say) are no longer welcomed, with the possible exception only of Syrah – though purists seriously believe this variety should be de-listed too. Twenty-two local grapes are currently undergoing rigorous testing as to potential quality. Most are still waiting in the wings, but one, Bianco Gentile, looks set to make its debut soon. And if this wasn't exciting enough, many of these new oldsters have the added advantage of being grown organically – even biodynamically – too. (The island's hot climate, low humidity and strong winds are perfect for fending off disease, rendering fungicides and sprays virtually unnecessary.)

The bulk of Corsica's wine is *vin de pays*, and yes, there's still a lot of generic rosé around. But skirting the coast of the island there are nine appellations in which decent winemaking equipment, lower yields, use of oak, concerted effort and new grapes are beginning to improve quality. Patrimonio, Ajaccio and Vin de Corse are the most commonly seen, plus a *vin doux naturel*, Muscat du Cap Corse, granted AC status in 1993. (The other ACs in development are Corse, Porto-Vecchio, Calvi, Sartène and Coteaux du Cap Corse.) In the north, Patrimonio's top growers are Domaines Antoine Arena (for delicious, complex Vermentino), Gentile, Leccia and Orenga de Gaffory; from Calvi domaines Culombu and Renucci show well. Good growers from the south are Fiumicicoli in Sartène, Domaine de Torraccia in Porto-Vecchio, and domaines Tanella and Canaralli at the island's southern tip, Figari.

The reason we don't see many of these wines in the UK is that, by law, 70 per cent of production must be sold directly in Corsica (tourists make something of a dent, drinking most of the total output). Christian Imbert of Toraccia is president of Uva Corse, a group clubbing together to improve production processes and promote exports. However, other local growers think we in the UK aren't interested – but then, we won't be interested until we see the wines. There *are* a few on sale at Nicolas, Oddbins, The Wine Society and Direct Wine Shipments (see *Where to buy wine*), but come on guys – send a few more over to start the ball rolling . . .

JURA, SAVOIE AND BUGEY

Given the stunning scenery of this part of France, it will be little disappointment to learn that if you want to taste these wines, the best way is to visit the region itself; though skiers are also likely to find them in the Swiss resorts skirting Lake Geneva. We've spotted a few of the wines on merchants' lists (particularly some of those who specialise in neighbouring Burgundy, such as John Armit Wines and Morris & Verdin, see *Where to buy wine*), but mostly they're not made in sufficient quantity, and the trade perceives them as being 'too unusual' for import to UK shores. A shame. We think they are intriguing.

Jura

Jura lies at similar latitudes to Burgundy, so it comes as no surprise to find Chardonnay and Pinot Noir in the 80-km stretch of the region's vineyards. The area has four main appellations (Arbois, Côtes du Jura, l'Etoile, Château-Chalon). Arbois makes light reds from Pinot plus the local varieties, delicate Poulsard and robust Trousseau. Côtes du Jura covers the entire region and can be red, pink or white. More interesting are the *vins jaunes* – yellow wines –

of l'Etoile and Château-Chalon. This peculiar *flor*-affected wine made from the rasping Savagnin grape is produced in other parts of Jura, but it is in these two appellations that it reaches its remarkable peak. Long-lived, yes; memorable, yes – but certainly not a wine that will appeal to all tastes. More accessible, but still an oddball, is *vin de paille*, a sweet wine made from grapes that have been allowed to dry out traditionally on straw (*paille*), in order to concentrate their sugars and flavours. Names to look out for from the region are Château d'Arlay, Jean Bourdy, Durand-Perron, Château de l'Etoile, Jean Macle, Pignier, Jacques Puffeney, Rolet Père et Fils, André et Mireille Tissot and Labet Père et Fils.

Savoie and Bugey

Pinot Noir and Chardonnay make further appearances in these Alpine regions along the upper stretches of the Rhône to the south of Jura. Bugey also has plantings of Gamay, but the main variety for the red Vin de Savoie is the sturdy, smoky Mondeuse. White varieties include the generally rather boring Chasselas; the tangy, rich Altesse (aka Roussette) and Jacquère; and small amounts of Roussanne, here known as Bergeron. The most interesting wines are the Jacquère-based whites from the villages of Abymes and Apremont; Chignin Bergeron dry whites, which are 100 per cent Roussanne; and the appealing sparkler Seyssel. Chardonnay and Pinot Noir under the Vin du Bugey VDQS (Vin Délimité de Qualité Supérieure) can also be very attractive. Savoie producers to look out for include Pierre Boniface (under the Domaine de Rocailles label), Raymond Quénard, André and Michel Quénard, Château de Ripaille, Philippe & François Tiollier and Varichon et Clerc. From Bugey, Philippe Viallet and Eugène Monin.

LANGUEDOC-ROUSSILLON

Languedoc-Roussillon has certainly been the stuff of headlines this year: on one hand rioting; on the other, rejecting Mondavi's grand Californian interests in the region. If the first of these events was in protest against poor wine prices, the second doesn't make sense, as surely (given its illustrious progress in Italy, Chile and at home) Mondavi couldn't do other than bring profit? So what's going on?

Put simply, growers still feel deeply threatened by wines coming out of the New World. At co-operative level (70 per cent of the region's output), where there is still a surplus of mediocre wine being produced which simply won't sell (it can't compete with the Chilean and Australian wine on the shop shelves), there is a certain amount of desperation. Workers have taken to the streets and demanded further subsidy from the government to help them survive.

At another, higher level, however, this region actually has far more on offer than its competition. We'd even argue that it is, itself, a form of 'New New World' (see feature, page 19). Since the early part of the 1990s a new generation of young winemakers has emerged, prepared to break away from the co-operatives and invest hard-won earnings in producing low-yield, concentrated wines, some of them so carefully made as to be hand-crafted; it is these wines that really tell us what the herby/salty/sunshiny Mediterranean countryside is all about. The fruits of those new beginnings a decade ago are now, in the quality vintages of 2000 and 2001, finally being seen. They are a great deal more exciting than anything Australia currently has to shout about.

Alongside the new blood are a large number of wealthy investors – varying in origin from international interests such as Sella & Mosca from Italy and BRL Hardy from Australia, to Bordeaux châteaux (Lynch Bages, Mouton-Rothschild), to moneyed computer whizz kids and publishing types (would that it were us) – even, we hear, the odd partnership of a goatherd and video salesman setting up in St-Chinian. And while these outsiders have the incentive that land here is cheap, the fact that they keep on coming, and the fact that they stay, has to do with the great results they get.

There's little doubt that the future of Languedoc-Roussillon is in *terroir*-specific wines – not from the flat plains skirting the Mediterranean coast (home of those co-operative wines), but from the rocky *garrigue* hillsides farther inland. We particularly like the powerfully rustic wines of St-Chinian and their fleshier neighbours from Faugères. From the Coteaux du Languedoc (an appellation covering a huge variety of micro-climates) we think the bold, damsony wines of La Clape are particularly worthy of attention, as are the herby whites and reds of another geographical blip (OK, hill), the Pic St-Loup. Then, of course, there is the highly fashionable and good-value Costières de Nîmes, remarkable for its wines with luscious yet gamey characteristics.

The revival of Languedoc grape varieties is also being taken very seriously, particularly by local growers. Not that there aren't stunning *vins de pays* from the likes of Merlot, Cabernet and Chardonnay, but it's the Carignans, Mourvèdres, Piquepouls and Vermentinos that really make the difference. (Yes, you might have heard wine buffs slamming these names in the past, but it's amazing the difference a decent schooling – viticultural techniques and vineyard management – makes to a grape.) Unsurprisingly, when harvested at decent low yields, local varieties seem to thrive in their native herb- and rock-strewn hillsides.

The only, though not insurmountable, problem with these new wines is that they're often sold at prices more expensive than the perceived image of the Languedoc will sustain. The region still – wrongly and rightly – has a 'plonk' image, and there is considerable consumer resistance to handing over £20 for a bottle they feel ought to cost less than £5. To those hanging on to this outdated thought, we again suggest a visit to the London merchant La Vigneronne (see *Where to buy wine*), whose range of these southern wines is superb and more than amply illustrates the high quality available – and who will also let you try before you buy!

Now back to those riots. In early March 2002 the European Commission announced an emergency distillation facility to cover four million hectolitres of *vin de table*. This was demanded by Languedoc representatives as the only way of ridding the region of those co-operative surpluses that simply were not being sold – the idea is to then re-launch the region's wines at a more appropriate price point. And here we add our voice to those demanding more drastic action. It shouldn't, now, be a matter of simply 're-launching' but of re-addressing an important quality issue. There should be no further subsidies to co-ops to turn out more mediocre wine, but subsidies instead towards a vast programme of uprooting, to get rid of the poor-quality vineyards on the plains, to encouraging lower yields, and towards paying growers for quality not quantity. A few of the better co-ops are doing this already, but others need to follow. Only the strongest should survive.

And as for Mondavi: our views on this failure to accept Californian interest parallel those of the estate's would-be neighbours in the area of Aniane: while it seems crazy not to accept enthusiastic investment, we feel happier to see local skills being honed 'organically', using local knowledge without outside influence.

AC wines

Of the two areas – Languedoc and Roussillon – the Languedoc is rapidly becoming the more complex and enterprising, with a variety of appellations and sub-regions, particularly those on rugged slopes at the foothills of the Cévennes as opposed to the flat plains nearer the Mediterranean. The vast majority of production is red, although the amount of Vin de Pays d'Oc Chardonnay available on supermarket shelves in the UK might convince otherwise. Don't let the latter put you off exploring the bigger picture.

The best reds from the Languedoc-Roussillon usually comprise a blend of Mourvèdre, Grenache and Syrah with some of the more ubiquitous Carignan and Cinsault. Carignan, however, is the most widely planted variety in the region and, at its best, can provide some marvellously robust and herby reds, particularly from old vines. These perfectly capture the region's innate style. Corbières and Côtes du Roussillon are particularly noteworthy in this case.

While whites are not the strength of the region, Clairette and Grenache Blanc can sometimes be persuaded to yield plump waxy wines, with the addition of the Rhône grapes Viognier, Marsanne and Roussanne adding depth and fragrance. Maccabéo, Vermentino (or Rolle), Piquepoul Blanc and Bourboulenc, when well-tamed, can add floral, pear-like or herby aromas. The only AC permitting Chardonnay in the blend is Limoux, which has to be barrel-fermented and must include at least 15 per cent Mauzac, although some producers have been known to bend this latter rule. While on the subject of Limoux, the intriguing and rarely found sparkling wines Blanquette de Limoux and Crémant de Limoux, made by the traditional method, may also have a proportion of Chardonnay in them, along with a predominance of Mauzac (Blanquette) and Chenin Blanc.

Of the Languedoc appellations, Fitou was first conferred its status in the 1940s, with Corbières, Minervois and the sprawling Coteaux du Languedoc not achieving the same until 1985. Today's wine map of the region also includes Faugères, St-Chinian, Cabardès and Malepère. A dozen villages are allowed to append their name to the sprawling Coteaux du Languedoc appellation, including Pic St-Loup, Montpeyroux and La Méjanelle. Both Corbières and Fitou have vineyards scattered through the mountainous and semi-remote terrain of the Montagne Noire. Along with Limoux and Cabardès, these are vineyard areas sandwiched between the Mediterranean and the Pyrenees, with myriad individual micro-climates and potential for variety. Minervois and St-Chinian, in the north of the region, produce wines varying from the rich and soft to the full and robust – partly according to how far into the high and arid hills the vineyards are located. Many of the best wines of Minervois hail from the La Livinière enclave, which was recognised as a sub-region from the 1998 vintage.

Costières de Nîmes, formerly Costières du Gard, is another rather bitty appellation, enclosed by the towns of Montpellier, Arles and Nîmes. Whether it is in the Languedoc or the Rhône is debatable both geographically and stylistically, since the wines often have elements of the flavours of both. The best wines are well priced and of high quality, and could pass for something rather more expensive from the Rhône – in some cases, the northern Rhône. As we've mentioned, in what could be the first French venture for an Italian producer, Sella & Mosca of Sardinia now owns a vineyard here.

In Roussillon, mercifully, life is a little simpler: the Côtes du Roussillon appellation predominates, although 25 villages are allowed to append their own names to it. Grenache is the main grape in many cases and the wines are, as a result, warmer and earthier than their herby counterparts further east around the Mediterranean basin, particularly in the tiny individual appellation of Collioure. Grenache is also the base for excellent fortified red *vin doux naturel* as produced in Banyuls, Maury and Rivesaltes. These are fascinating wines and worth discovering. Rivesaltes also produces white *vin doux naturel* from the Muscat variety, although we prefer the more delicate Muscat de St-Jean de Minervois, from the Languedoc.

Vins de pays

Vins de pays are not an exclusivity of the Languedoc-Roussillon, but most of the 150-plus designated regions can be found here. Some of these are very localised, while others, such as Vin de Pays d'Oc, cover a number of *départements*. Trying to familiarise oneself with all of them is difficult, and ultimately a rather pointless exercise. The French authorities had originally (in 1973) intended this to be an intermediary level between *vin de table* and *appellation contrôlée* and a stepping stone to improving quality and acquiring AC status. However, the concept of *vins de pays* was well and truly hijacked by growers and producers on two fronts. On the one hand, there were those feeding the demand for keenly priced varietal wines, while on the other there were those aiming for top quality who realised that they could legally produce blended wines using virtually any variety they chose. Nowadays *vins de pays* can be simple Cinsault-heavy blends, impressive Cabernets, Syrahs, Chardonnays and Viogniers, or excellent wines made from local grapes pepped up by Cabernet and Co. As a consequence, the name of the actual *vin de pays* has become almost irrelevant, while those of both producer and varietal have risen in importance.

Pick of the producers (Languedoc-Roussillon)

Abbotts Australians Nerida Abbott and husband Nigel Sneyd, both previously at Domaine de la Baume, make a range of fine reds in the Roussillon; Cumulo Nimbus Syrah is especially good.

Jean-Michel Alquier The best estate in Faugères, producing Syrah-dominated wines of sterling quality, notably oak-aged Les Bastides.

Domaine d'Aupilhac Sylvain Fadat's old Carignan vines are in Montpeyroux, which he hopes will one day be an appellation in its own right. On the basis of these wines, it ought to be.

Clos Bagatelle Age-old (1623) St-Chinian property producing typically steely, strong Carignan-based wines, and top growth La Gloire de Mon Père, with Syrah, Mourvèdre and Grenache.

Baron'Arques Joint venture between Báron Philippe de Rothschild and Aimery Sieur d'Arques of Limoux, making firm, fleshy, oaky blend of traditional Bordeaux grapes with Syrah and Grenache. Good but pricy.

Domaine Léon Barral Rich, powerful, damsony wines from the up-and-coming appellation of Faugères. The Mourvèdre grape is a particular passion here.

Mas Baruel Organically farmed estate which produces a fine Syrah and a very classy Syrah/Cabernet blend, the Languedoc's answer to Domaine de Trévallon in Provence.

Domaine de la Baume The southern French arm of the Australian BRL Hardy corporation. Surprisingly crisp whites, including one of the south's best Sauvignons, good Viognier, and spicy, fruity reds.

Mas Bruguière Pioneers in Pic St-Loup (Coteaux du Languedoc). Reds of real class, particularly the top *cuvée*, Grenardière, raised in oak. White Roussanne also first rate.

Cazes Frères Perhaps best known for their Muscat de Rivesaltes, but the Grenache-heavy Vieux Rivesaltes is a better wine. The Côte du Roussillon reds aren't bad either.

Chemins de Bassac Inspired Vin de Pays d'Oc reds and a tasty rosé made from Syrah, Cabernet Sauvignon, Grenache and Mourvèdre from former school teachers Rémi and Isabelle Ducellier.

CIRA Wines bearing this acronym are from the stable of *négociant* Caroline de Beaulieu – a dynamic, trained oenologist who represents some excellent and great-value properties from around the Languedoc.

Clos Centeilles, Daniel Domergue Mourvèdre, Syrah and Grenache go into Daniel Domergue's outstanding Minervois, but he also makes an immensely attractive wine called Carignanissime made from – guess what? – the humble Carignan.

Domaine de Clovallon Admirable and slightly quirky range including arguably the finest Pinot Noir of southern France, delicious Mas d'Alezon blended red, and an astonishing, heady,

151

barley-sugary Rancio. Top white is a mysterious blend called Les Aurièges, including Riesling and Petit Manseng; there's also a good Clairette de Languedoc.

Domaine des Creisses Venture run by two ex-Bordeaux winemakers making extremely classy wine, with top *cuvée* Les Brunes combining power with elegance.

Mas de Daumas Gassac Pioneer of high-class *vin de pays* – de l'Hérault in this case – with a full-bodied if rather tannic Bordeaux-inspired red and an exotically fragrant white blend of mainly Chardonnay, Viognier and Petit Manseng. Second label is Terrasses de Landoc. Also, now, high-class, single-varietal wines.

Ermitage de Pic St-Loup Delicious Syrah-based wines from the trendy Pic St-Loup appellation.

Font Caude Rising star Alain Chabanon makes sumptuous modern reds, the finest of which is the 100-per-cent Syrah l'Esprit de Font Caude. Also great success with Chenin Blanc, both dry and sweet, and sometimes with added Rolle, for Languedoc authenticity.

Fortant de France Robert Skalli's Sète-based operation was a *vin de pays* pioneer which lost its way slightly through much of the 1990s. F de Skalli Chardonnay and Cabernet show a welcome return to form.

Domaine de Fourn One of the finest proponents of sparkling Limoux wines from the Mauzac grape, both by the traditional method and the gently rustic *méthode ancestrale*.

Domaine Gauby Probably the best estate in Côtes du Roussillon, thanks to old vines and low yields. Huge ripe reds (superb AC Mourvèdre) and very attractive whites from Grenache Blanc and (surprisingly) Chardonnay. *Vins de pays* from above and beyond AC rules.

Domaine de la Grange des Pères Like Mas de Daumas Gassac, a Vin de Pays de l'Hérault, and currently surpassing that famous estate in the quality of its red wine – a blend of Syrah, Mourvèdre and Cabernet Sauvignon. A Roussanne-based white also competes.

James Herrick Now owned by the Australian giant Southcorp, although the eponymous Australian-trained Brit is still involved in making the chunky reds and quite subtle, buttery Chardonnay.

Domaine de l'Hortus The top (and trendy) wine of Pic St-Loup: sumptuous and rich, with the herby scents of the surrounding *garrigue* countryside.

Domaine de l'Hospitalet Showcase winery in the Coteaux du Languedoc, producing first-class reds and a delicious, lightly oaked white.

Domaine des Jougla Alain Jougla's supple, fruity St-Chinian is one of the best wines of the appellation. Good value too.

Mas Jullien The impassioned Olivier Jullien makes splendid reds, whites and rosés, often using varieties which others eschew. Pick of the range is the dense, structured Depierre-les-Cailloutis red, a Grenache/Mourvèdre/Oeillades blend.

Domaine de Morties Two brothers-in-law, one retired from goat farming, the other from video-dealing in Paris, make stunning Pic St-Loup with a heavy emphasis on the local Carignan grapes.

Château Mourges du Gres Costières-de-Nîmes estate close to the Rhône and aspiring to improve on it. Best red, Les Capitelles (Syrah/Grenache) achieves the aim. Champing at the bit to plant Viognier as soon as new AC law allows.

Château Pech Redon The Bousquets are not scared to embrace local varieties in this corner of La Clape (one of the oldest and driest areas of the Languedoc, very popular in Roman times). Carignan features highly, as does the herby white Bourboulenc.

Domaine de Peyre Rose Muscular Coteaux du Languedoc reds from former estate agent Marlene Soria. The Cuvée Syrah Leoné is classy but pricy.

Domaine Piccinini Superior wines from a superior part of the Minervois appellation, La Livinière, believed to have its own characters of '*garrigue* and black olives'. These examples do.

Le Prieuré de St-Jean de Bébian Top-quality, expensive Languedoc estate, with wines the epitome of Mediterranean style. Powerful reds, a new white (incorporating the whole array of Languedoc white grapes), and delicious ageworthy Clos Angély prove the point. Also superior range of *vins de pays*.

Domaine de la Rectorie Producer of the best Banyuls and also three different Collioure wines, which age brilliantly.

Domaine Rimbert Deliciously complex 100-per-cent Carignan and Marsanne white Le Rimberlou, plus range of complex reds – all true to St-Chinian *terroir*. (Jean-Marie Rimbert is in fact from Provence, but was charmed by the Languedoc while on holiday there, and decided to stay.)

Château La Roque One of the leaders in Pic St-Loup producing elegant wines, particularly from the Mourvèdre grape variety, and whites from Rhône varietals.

Val d'Orbieu You'll find the name (or the initials VVO) of this organisation of co-ops and growers on several wines from throughout southern France. Don't expect great shakes from the cheaper wines, but the range of single-estate Corbières and the gutsy Cuvée Mythique red can be very good.

Maurel Vedeau Widely distributed, wines bearing this name are the work of dynamic young winemaking duo Philippe Maurel and Stéphane Vedeau, who have so far specialised in well-made, single-varietal *vins de pays*. Currently turning their attentions to appellation wines as well.

Wild Pig Englishman Guy Anderson and Frenchman Thierry Boudinaud of the major Rhône producer Gabriel Meffre make one of the best ranges of *vins de pays*, formerly know as Galet. Also the source of Fat Bastard Chardonnay and Utter Bastard Red (usually Syrah).

Languedoc-Roussillon vintage guide

2001 is being lauded as one of the best Languedoc vintages ever – growers are really hitting their stride now, having been 'feeling their way' during the revival of the last ten years – rich, ripe and concentrated wines. 2000 and 1998 were both excellent vintages too, producing substantial red wines that at best will age well for several years. Sandwiched between these is 1999, which was less of a blockbuster, but still yielded some splendid if less ageworthy wines. Most rich, robust reds from earlier vintages last well, but choose your property with care. Overall reliability, and ageworthiness, has improved drastically over the last few years, and it's really only the more recent wines that we'd be looking to cellar.

THE LOIRE

It's true, as we said last year, that virtually everything the Loire Valley does is done better by somebody else ('better', in the sense of bigger, bolder and louder). Sauvignon Blanc, in the form of Sancerre and Pouilly-Fumé, sells like hot-cakes, but it's still the New Zealand version that makes the millions. Chenin Blanc in its dry and medium forms is invariably bested by riper, fruitier versions from old vines in South Africa. Cabernet Franc, the grape responsible for the wines of Chinon and Bourgueil, seldom rises to the heights of Cabernet Sauvignon, while Burgundy need never feel under threat from Pinot Noir as produced in Sancerre. Only the sweet Chenin Blancs of Bonnezeaux, Coteaux du Layon and Vouvray remain unbeaten in the world, with their rich, honeyed sweetness and perfectly poised acidity. But sweet whites, though more attractive than ever, are not everybody's cup of tea, and it is dry wines that attract the attention.

However, our suspicion is that people are seeking a little more subtlety in their wines these days and, if this is true, then the Loire could be set for a rise in fortunes, though not, perhaps, to the elevated status it enjoyed both at home and abroad in the 1970s (there wasn't the competition then that there is now). Here's why.

The Loire Valley is becoming increasingly polarised: the big producers are getting bigger and the small ones are getting smaller.

There's been a general squeezing out of the more 'rustic' domaines – which in the case of those producing chewy, tannic rough red wines, for example, is a good thing; but for some of the smaller, quality family producers (from whom you can buy only at the cellar door) this is much sadder. For red wines there's been a polarisation of the wine styles too. There is a groundswell of producers who cross-pollinate ideas with other regions (for example, Didier Dagueneau), and who are using new winemaking technology, de-stemming their grapes and making fruity, supple wines in a modern style. These only serve to show up the 'dinosaurs' – the producers of the casually made, rough reds we mention above.

There are equal extremes with the white wines. Perhaps following the success of New Zealand's Sauvignons, the demand for Sancerre and Pouilly-Fumé (and to a lesser extent Menetou-Salon) has never been so high – this is the one place in the world where red wines are in decline, as growers grub up their Pinot Noir in favour of Sauvignon Blanc. But only a few miles down the road, an even finer 'classic', Savennières, is proving impossible to shift. Savennières is the tragedy of the Loire Valley at the moment, as these can be utterly delicious wines. The trouble is they take some getting to know, as they're not always terribly approachable when young, and they also turn up in dry, medium and sweet styles which growers tend to make in differing quantities depending on the vintage. Worse still, *sec* (dry), *demi-sec* (semi-dry), *doux* (semi-sweet) and *moelleux* (sweet) won't always be marked on the bottle, so you don't always know what you'll be drinking. Don't let us put you off, however. In very few other wines in the world will you get such a fine reflection of the *terroir* in what you're drinking – nor a white wine that ages so well (50 to 100 years is not unusual) or comes up trumps in every vintage (the Loire's climate means it's possible to make sweet Chenin every year, where Sauternes only succeeds once in a while). This is truly Chenin Blanc at its finest.

Another misapprehension that people have about the Loire is that if they follow the good vintages for Bordeaux, they'll find the winner in middle France too. On the contrary: 1997 in the Loire has been described as 'truly awesome', for example, whereas in the Gironde it was little better than miserable – so, do your homework (see the vintage guide later in this section).

The other nice thing about the Loire is the number of vineyards still in family hands. Visit them yourself (but not at lunchtime) and you're more likely to meet the winemaker and pick up a case of the wine than ever you are in Bordeaux and Burgundy.

The Loire is the longest river in France, rising in the Massif Central and winding north before veering due west to the port of Nantes, and along its 1,000-km length more than 100 different wines can be found. The reds and rosés from the upper reaches of the river, such as Gamay-based wines from the Côtes Roannaises or Côtes du Forez, are unlikely to have come your way unless you've visited the region. Further downstream, the wines fall into three convenient segments:

Central Loire

Before New Zealand got in on the act, this was where everybody turned to for crisp, herbaceous Sauvignon Blanc in the form of Sancerre and Pouilly-Fumé. The wines tend to be less assertively ripe and fruity and more flinty, earthy and elegant than New Zealand versions, and take a little longer to reach their peak. While Sancerre and Pouilly-Fumé can be hard to tell apart, Sancerre is probably the more concentrated and consistent of the two. Cheaper alternatives can be found in Menetou-Salon, Reuilly and Quincy. Pinot Noir is the favoured grape for the reds of the region. Most are rather thin and weedy, although the occasional red Sancerre from a good vintage can have attractive, slightly earthy raspberry fruit.

Pick of the producers (Central Loire)
Cotat Frères Tiny amounts of fine Sancerre built for ageing.

Didier Dagueneau A maverick and rare source of innovation and excellence within the Pouilly-Fumé appellation, especially with the barrel-fermented Silex *cuvée*.

de Ladoucette/Château de Nozet Highly fêted producer of Pouilly-Fumé and Sancerre (under the Comte Lafond label). Good wines, sometimes very good – the prices are less easy to swallow.

Henry Pellé Menetou-Salon's top man, with delicious whites, especially Clos de Blanchais, and reasonable reds. Quality classics.

Vacheron Consistently among the best – if not the best – for benchmark Sancerre, both white and red.

Also worth hunting down: *Henri Bourgeois*, *Pascal Jolivet*, *Masson-Blondelet*, *Alphonse Mellot*, *Silice de Quincy*, *Pascal et Nicolas Reverdy*, *Château de Tracy* and *Vatan*.

Anjou-Saumur and Touraine

While these two areas enjoy separate official status, they share the same grape varieties for their best wines. In the white department, Chenin Blanc reigns, and appears in dry, medium, sumptuously sweet and sparkling guises. In this relatively northerly climate, the late-ripening Chenin needs a good site and plenty of TLC to grow well – otherwise, as with much Saumur and Anjou Blanc, its often searing acidity dominates the wine. Savennières is the classic dry Chenin, bracing in its youth and needing considerable bottle age before the apple and honey fruit begins to rise above the sharpness, but when it does, the wine is seamless and delicious. Savennières also appears in intense, sweet guise. Vouvray and Montlouis come in various stages of sweetness, including the unfashionable but really rather attractively nutty, honeyed *demi-sec*. Again, these medium-dry wines benefit from age and can last for several years. However, the real distance runners are the *botrytis*-affected sweet wines from appellations such as Bonnezeaux and Coteaux du Layon. Thanks to their astonishing richness they can be enjoyed in their youth, but as a result of that Chenin acidity and the high sugar levels, they can age gracefully for 50 years or more.

Cabernet Franc is the favoured grape for reds. Again, it takes a decent grower and a decent vineyard to ripen the grapes fully, otherwise the wines have an unappealing vegetal flavour. Even the best have a slightly earthy, leafy – as in blackcurrant leaf – note to them, combined with rich, almost tar-like flavours. Bourgueil and Chinon are homes to the best reds, although St-Nicolas de Bourgueil and Saumur-Champigny can also point to a few stars. Cabernet Franc is also used for rosé in Cabernet d'Anjou. Alas, the ubiquitous Rosé d'Anjou is made from the very ordinary Grolleau grape variety and is typically insipid, semi-sweet and forgettable.

Pick of the producers (Anjou-Saumur and Touraine)

Marc Angeli Anjou protégé of Nicolas Joly (see below): another passionate biodynamist whose Bonnezeaux, among others, sell out almost before they reach the barrel. Hot property.

Domaine de Bablut Christophe Daviau makes wine under the Domaine de Bablut and Château de Brissac labels; good ranges of red, white and pink Anjou, including ageworthy Cabernet d'Anjou. Also impressive Coteaux de l'Aubance.

Domaine des Baumard Top-notch Chenin, both bone dry, and honeyed and sweet from Savennières (Clos du Papillon), Coteaux du Layon (Clos de Ste-Catherine) and Quarts de Chaume.

Bouvet-Ladubay Decent sparkling Saumur, particularly the oak-aged Trésor, from this subsidiary of champagne house Taittinger.

Pascal Cailleau/Domaine Sauveroy Up with Richou and Daviau at the top of the Anjou league, the dynamic Pascal Cailleau makes a great range of reds, whites and pinks, the best of which is a wonderful Coteaux du Layon.

Couly-Dutheil This *négociant* business operating throughout the Loire has reasonable rather than thrilling wines, but the best are the estate Chinons, especially Clos de l'Echo and Baronnie Madeleine.

Pierre-Jacques Druet Leading grower of Bourgueil and probably the best red wine producer in the Loire, making a number of different and serious *cuvées*, all of which are worth looking out for.

Château de Fesles The best of Bonnezeaux, especially since 1996; luscious when young yet will outlast most of us. The wines are made by Thierry Germain, who is busy stirring up quality in the region (see *Domaine des Roches Neuves*, below).

Domaine Filliatreau Vying with Domaine des Roches Neuves for top dog in Saumur-Champigny. Look out for the deep, concentrated Vieilles Vignes *cuvée*.

Gratien & Meyer Makers of high-quality traditional method Saumur sparkling wine, associated with family Champagne house, Alfred Gratien.

Huet Top talent in Vouvray, with dry, medium, sweet and sparkling wines of the highest order. Gaston Huet himself is in his nineties, and the main winemaking responsibility now lies with his son-in-law, the talented Noël Pinguet. The Cuvée Constance Moelleux produced in the best years is exceptional wine; 1953 is showing well at the moment.

Charles Joguet Chinon producer, now retired (wines are made by Alain de Launay), with a series of single-vineyard bottlings which age almost as well as classed-growth claret.

Nicolas Joly Eccentric and meticulous producer making rich, dry, long-lived and expensive Chenin Blanc in the Savennières sub-appellation of Coulée de Serrant. Joly practises biodynamic winemaking.

Langlois-Château Bollinger-owned house in Saumur making reliable reds and whites as well as snappy, refreshing sparklers.

Château de Ligré Rare in making all three styles of Chinon – red, white and rosé. Fresh, fruity, modern wines, red being particularly fine.

Domaine Ogereau Delicious Anjou wines in all styles, red, white and sweet.

Richou Dynamic domaine in Anjou producing sound whites and reds, and excellent sweet Coteaux de l'Aubance.

Domaine des Roches Neuves A startlingly good range of Saumur-Champigny from Thierry Germain, formerly of Bordeaux. Look out for the Terres Chaudes and oak-aged Marginale (both red), and the white L'Insolite made from 75-year-old vines.

Domaine du Val Brun Exceptionally good Saumur-Champigny reds, and a hillside estate well worth a visit.

Les Vignerons de Oisly et Thesée Not-to-be-maligned co-operative making stunning range of Touraine wines, including clear, bright Cheverny.

Château de Villeneuve Very fine, complex Saumur whites and Saumur-Champigny reds. Both have the structure to last.

Pays Nantais

Or Muscadet country. Muscadet is made from Melon de Bourgogne, a rather ordinary grape that needs careful handling in order to make the most of the little character it possesses. Most wines fall into the CFDN bracket – crisp, fresh, dry, neutral – but the better examples have a refreshing tanginess that makes them well worth cracking open alongside a platter of *fruits de mer* on a hot summer day. Top examples can even age superbly well over 30 or 40 years (but serve these with a more complex fish dish instead). The important things to look out for on the label are one of the sub-regions – Côtes de Grand Lieu, Coteaux de la Loire or Sèvre et Maine – plus the words *sur lie*. This latter term indicates that the wines have been aged on the lees to bring about greater depth of flavour and a slightly spritzy finish. Some oak-aged Muscadet even exists nowadays. Muscadet is better now than it has ever been, especially in the hands of producers such as Guy Bossard, Chéreau Carré, Donatien Bahuaud, Luneau, Louis Métaireau and Sauvion, but we doubt it'll ever return to the glorious status it held in the 1970s. And while we applaud the improvements, we still struggle to get excited about most of the wines. And we usually go out of our way to avoid those made from Gros Plant, a variety which combines the acidity of Chenin Blanc with the neutrality of Melon de Bourgogne.

Other wines

While Vin de Pays du Jardin de la France may not enjoy the popularity of its southern equivalents, a run of recent good vintages has meant that some fresh and crisp, easy-drinking varietals (Sauvignon, Chardonnay and Cabernet Rosé) are gradually appearing on the (mainly supermarket) shelves. The itinerant winemaker Jacques Lurton has produced some pleasing examples in conjunction with the vast *négociant* business Ackerman. The Cave Co-opérative du Haut Poitou is another, mostly reliable, source of varietal VDQS (Vin Délimité de Qualité Supérieure) wines, especially Sauvignon and Gamay.

Loire vintage guide

2001 High summer temperatures boded well, and cooler harvest conditions slowed down the ripening. Sauvignon and Pinot Noir fared well, as did the full range of Chenin Blanc styles. There was some localised hail damage in the Touraine, but overall quality in the Loire should be high.

2000 Humidity and hail were just two of the problems growers had to contend with in the run up to vintage, but with the end of August the weather improved dramatically, turning what could have been a disaster into a reasonable year for Sauvignon Blanc and Cabernet Franc. The fine conditions continued into October, enabling those who waited to harvest their Chenin Blanc to make some very good, full-bodied dry whites, and some sumptuous sweet wines as well.

1999 Heavy rain in mid-September dashed all hopes of a great vintage, but since the grapes were almost fully ripe at the time, this only had the effect of diluting the wines. Growers with well-tended vineyards made wines with good acidity in the whites and appealing softness in the reds. Others struggled.

1998 By no means a disastrous year, but tread carefully. Again, wines from the best *vignerons* stand out after a vintage marked by very hot sun in August (some grapes actually burnt on the vine) and rain in September/October. Canny winemakers managed to come up with a decent set of wines, with the high acidity typical of the region; others came a cropper.

1997 Among the sunniest and hottest in the past 50 years and compared to 1990 in terms of fruit ripeness. Wines are, in general, soft and attractive, opulent and rich. Dry whites, however, lack the crisp acidity to last long-distance: drink up.

1996 A second great year in a row throughout the Loire, with top-class reds, great sweet and dry Chenin Blanc, and Sauvignons which, thanks to slightly higher acidity levels, are better balanced than the occasionally top-heavy 1995s.

1995 Excellent year for wines made from Cabernet Franc and Chenin Blanc, with some stunning *botrytis* wines from the latter. A classic year all round.

Other notable vintages 1990, 1989.

PROVENCE

Provençal wine has improved greatly over the last ten years, with better winemaking techniques bringing about a huge transformation in quality, and growers becoming far more regionally aware – the wines of the impressive 2001 vintage are a particularly good starting point if you're just beginning to find out about them. And, more and more, growers are playing to the red and white strengths of their vineyards rather than resorting to rosé. Yes, there's still a lot of the pink stuff around (and tourists are an easy market for it), but things are moving on.

For whites, look to the coastal Cassis appellation for Marsanne and Clairette wines cooled by sea winds; also the new, semi-Alpine Coteaux de Pierrevert region and Côtes du Lubéron (where the Rhône adjoins Provence) for the nutty Rolle grape. Elsewhere the emphasis is on red. Bandol continues to thrive, its new generation of winemakers speeding the ongoing revolution, and making top-rank herby, blackberry Mourvèdre – the vines have to be eight years old, and the wines need a minimum of 18 months' barrel age and long maturation. Les Baux de Provence follows, its warm, dry vineyards bringing out the best in Syrah, Cabernet and Grenache Noir. Coteaux d'Aix is slightly cooler, with an enormous variation in wine styles produced: sensibly there's a 30-per-cent threshold on usurper varieties Cabernet, Sémillon and Sauvignon Blanc. Côtes de Provence wines, however, gain a positive lift from Syrah and Cabernet that makes all the difference to them. Coteaux Varois is a large appellation in which blended rosés are still the most important wines; Palette and Bellet are each much smaller, the former for serious ageworthy Château Simone, the latter somewhat buried in the suburbs of Nice. Where the varieties don't conform to the local appellation rules, Provence's wines usually appear under the Vin de Pays du Var label (as from first-rank Domaine de Triennes, see below).

We can forgive the tourist rosé – as long as it's well made and gluggable, not just swig-me-quick mouthwash – as cash flow is an important starting point for quality improvement. But neighbouring Languedoc-Roussillon is showing a more vigorous rate of improvement. Is Provence too reliant on its tourists?

Pick of the producers (Provence)

Domaine des Béates Coteaux d'Aix producer now partly owned
by Chapoutier of the Rhône and already close to the top of the
Provence league. Best wine is Cabernet/Syrah blend Terra d'Or; Les
Matines is for everyday drinking; Les Béates is a meaty, steak-ready
mouthful.

Domaines Bunan The elegant Mas de la Rouvière Bandol from
brothers Paul and Pierre Bunan is seriously good red wine made
from a four-hectare plot of 50-year-old Mourvèdre. Also watch for
Moulin des Costes and Vin de Pays du Mont Caume labels.

Clos Sainte Magdeleine François Sack's Cassis is a delicious crisp
blend of Ugni Blanc, Marsanne, Clairette and Sauvignon Blanc,
with a flavour of honey, nuts and lemon and a salty influence from
the sea.

Domaine de la Courtade Rapidly improving estate on the island
of Porquerolles to the south-east of Toulon, making ripe, smoky
Mourvèdre-based red and fleshy white from Rolle. Top wine
La Courtade is seriously ageworthy and guaranteed to warm up
your winter.

Château d'Estoublon Serious new wines (red, white, new oak) from
watchmaker investor with Eloi Dürrbach as consultant. Watch this
space for future developments.

Gros Nore No flashy consultants for this 1997 enterprise. Owner is a
new arrival from the building trade, and now winning all prizes.

Château de Pibarnon Concentrated, strapping Bandol, virtually
pure Mourvèdre, from Henri de Saint Victor. Needs bottle age.

Domaine Rabiega Swedish-owned estate, with a classy white
(Chardonnay/Sauvignon) and a number of lovely reds, best of
which is the 100-per-cent Syrah Clos d'Ière Cuvée 1.

Château Routas Exciting Coteaux Varois estate producing
interesting, good-value whites and bold, herby reds, especially the
Cuvée Luc Sorin. Watch out for Mistral Cabernet-Syrah and pure
Syrah, Cyrano, and 100-per-cent pure Carignan from 45-year-old
vines.

Château Simone Rich, basket-pressed whites, serious rosés and
substantial but elegant reds to age, traditionally made from old

163

vines (average 60 to 100 years). Covers 17 hectares of the 23-hectare Palette AC.

Domaine Tempier This family-owned property is probably the most famous of the Bandol estates, and still one of the very best, with the broad-shouldered Cuvée Tourtine being a high point; highest point of all, Cuvée Cabassaou, from the oldest vines of all, planted in 1952.

Domaine de Trévallon Eloi Dürrbach makes arguably the finest wines in Provence. Trévallon red (a Syrah/Cabernet *vin de pays*) bucks AC regulations by missing out Grenache Noir, and is a splendid, smoky, fruit-packed wine that merits its high price and ages superbly. There's a rare, but great, full, nutty white too.

Domaine de Triennes The sideline activity of two eminent Burgundians, Jacques Seysses of Domaine Dujac and Aubert de Villaine of Domaine de la Romanée-Conti. Impressive Viognier, Chardonnay, 50:50 Cabernet/Syrah Les Auréliens, and even better Cuvée Réserve Cabernet and Syrah from first-rate years only. All these are made outside AC rules, so not Coteaux Varois but Vins du Pays du Var.

Château Vignelaure High, cool vineyards making elegant, structured reds with the assistance of illustrious Bordeaux winemaker Michel Rolland. Cabernet and Merlot are best, and improving.

THE RHÔNE VALLEY

For those cynics out there, who cringe at the sight of a good marketing campaign (yes, we'd agree with you most of the time), now's the time to put aside your prejudices and start believing. As mentioned last year, 'Think Different, Think Côtes du Rhône' is exactly what we'd do with a crisp tenner in our pocket – not because of persuasion to do so by the advertisers (although in the case of the Rhône, they're trying mighty hard), but because the quality improvements in this part of France of late have been outstanding – these wines really do seem to be achieving, as nearly as possible, consistently good standards.

Five years ago, if you were to taste a range of Rhônes from the north of the Valley, you'd unquestionably come across some terrific wines, but the selection would be peppered with 'also rans': wines from growers who could do better. At the end of the day, after these tastings, the comment would always be along the lines of 'great vintage but pick your producer carefully'. But things have changed. Gone are the days of indiscriminate early grape-picking, not bothering to remove the stalks prior to vinification. Now we can expect more supple, fragrant, fruity wines with balanced, integrated (still firm) tannins; wines that age well, but which can also be drunk young. Now, we feel a lot more confident about giving broad-band recommendations: Hermitage is good, Côte Rôtie is good, Cornas is good, etc.

In the southern Rhône the turnaround has been even more dramatic. Ten years ago the operative word on Châteauneuf-du-Pape (none of the other regions were really acknowledged) was 'avoid'. The restaurant-beloved familiarity of this name had led to complacency among the growers, who contented themselves with their ancient equipment, happy to turn out wines that were rustic, alcoholic and volatile. Today, even the co-operatives are shaking up their act, sweeping the south into the new millennium: tests are being carried out to avoid bunch rot in the vineyards; *négociants* are buying grapes, not ready-made wine; growers are being advised on clones, sprays (or no sprays), and picking times; *négociants* are paying commensurately for quality; wineries have been souped up to modern high-tech (OK, New World) standards; pumping is kept to a minimum in order to maintain the freshness of the grapes; filtration is becoming less and less severe.

We're told that the winemakers are also acutely conscious not to over-oak or over-extract their wines (these being the gripes about the Rhône in more recent years), and use of the sinful (as far as we're concerned) *flash détente* (heated vinification) techniques, giving boiled, stewed wines, is also being treated with caution.

The proof is in the pudding: the Rhône's market share has increased from 15.9 per cent of French wine sales (to the UK) to 18.5 per cent in the year to September 2001. Among these sales, Côtes du Rhône has increased by 15 per cent and Côtes du Rhône-Villages by a massive 76 per cent! The northern Rhône classics have decreased their share of all of this by 10 per cent.

The marketing campaign is obviously working, but without the quality to support it the efforts would have been worthless. Well done to the guy in the cellar. And, more importantly, congratulations to the guy in the vineyard. We shouldn't lose sight of *terroir* here. The wines that have given the Rhône that 76 per cent increase come from an area of 16 villages, which are allowed to attach their name to the Côtes du Rhône AC. The marketing men don't think 'the world' is quite ready to know the names of these villages yet, but we're not so sure. They are listed below (see *The southern Rhône, Red wines*), and we'll fill you in with more news next year about the different characters they offer.

One other thing. The *Guide* has decided to mirror the tremendous improvement in quality in the southern Rhône by adding a handful more Côtes du Rhône producers to the listings, below. These are the growers who are driving the transformation occurring in this region. Let's hope none of them will rest on their laurels, however, as their neighbours in the Languedoc are chasing them hard to offer the best-value, new quality wines in France.

The northern Rhône

In wine terms, the valley is split into the northern and southern Rhône. Such titles conveniently forget that the river runs through the region of Savoie along the Swiss border, but no matter. For the wine world, the northern Rhône starts at Vienne with the appellation of Côte Rôtie and runs southwards to St-Péray, just across the river from the town of Valence. This is the home of the Syrah grape, capable of producing dense, smoky wines packed with aromas and flavours of black pepper and spice, ripe berries and orange peel; and with a rich, creamy texture. Although vines are grown on alluvial land next to the river, and a number of recent plantings, particularly in St-Joseph, have been on plateau land overlooking the river, the best vineyards are those clinging to the slopes of the valley, often on hard-to-manage terraces.

Red wines
On the evidence of wines currently being produced, Côte Rôtie is arguably the greatest appellation, a mighty wine packed with black fruit, yet with a perfumed elegance, some but not all of which is derived from the addition of small amounts of the white grape Viognier.

Overlooking the town of Tain l'Hermitage is the famous hill of Hermitage, source of blockbuster Syrahs, uptight and glowering in their youth and requiring a decade or more to open out fully. Crozes-Hermitage has *terroirs* varying from flat alluvial plains to slopes adjoining Hermitage, and the wine, too, varies from powerful, potent mini-Hermitage to fairly easy-drinking. The dark, rich wines of Cornas, one of the most reliable appellations in the Rhône, rival those of Hermitage for strength and longevity, although they lack the same elegance.

St-Joseph covers a very large proportion of the western bank of the river that isn't taken up by other appellations. Such a spread results in a small number of high-quality, complex wines but also plenty of rather ordinary ones. Pick your grower with care.

White wines

The white grapes Marsanne and Roussanne can constitute up
to 15 per cent of the blend for red Hermitage and Crozes, but few
producers use this option. Instead, these varieties are used to make
small quantities of white wine, some of which (in St-Péray) is
sparkling. Avoid the fizz, but approach the still St-Péray with a
more open mind. True, many are dull and flabby, but growers such
as Jaboulet and the Cave de Tain l'Hermitage have newer plantings
and slicker marketing that is beginning to help the appellation
immeasurably – the best are now well-made nutty Marsannes,
which are worth following.

There are also fresher, fruitier whites from good growers in
Crozes, along with quite majestic, richly textured, nutty, peachy
and ageworthy wines from Hermitage and, to a lesser extent, St-
Joseph. A few growers dry their grapes on straw mats to make
stunning *vin de paille*, one of the great unsung sweet wines of the
world.

Hermitage's rival for the title of most interesting white of the
region is the fragrant, opulent, peachskin-and-apricot wine called
Condrieu, made from the capricious Viognier. Burgundians
complain about the difficulties encountered with Pinot Noir.
Viognier can be just as frustrating, being relatively easy to grow, but
difficult to both grow *and* vinify well. The essence of Viognier is a
ripe, creamy, floral, apricot and honeysuckle aroma, but this heady
perfume doesn't develop properly unless the grapes are fully ripe,
by which time the sugar levels are high and the acid levels low.
Viognier picked too early is just another simple dry white wine.
Viognier picked too late can be over-the-top, blowsy and alcoholic.
Some growers choose to make sweet wines from this grape: these
can be appealing but the aromas are all too often swamped in sugar
and alcohol.

Apart from Condrieu, the other world-famous Viognier comes
from Château Grillet. For a number of years the wines have hardly
been the stuff of legend, although they carried a legendary price
tag. There has been a return to form of late, but we recommend you
stick to the more dependable Condrieu.

Pick of the producers (northern Rhône)

Cave de Tain l'Hermitage A reliable, good-value co-operative with
stunning red Hermitage Gambert de Loche and delicious, long-
lived *vin de paille*.

Chapoutier A company with major vineyard holdings in Hermitage
and Châteauneuf-du-Pape, which has been revitalised since the late
1980s by the efforts of the dynamic Michel Chapoutier. Biodynamic
viticulture is now the order of the day, and the top wines from all

appellations are superlative. The St-Joseph Les Granits, both red and white, are the best wines of the appellation. Some labels are printed with Braille characters.

Gérard Chave Arguably the best producer of both red and white Hermitage. Expensive, perhaps, especially the top Cuvée Cathelin, but worth it. The bargain is the St-Joseph, a fraction of the price of the Hermitage yet displaying a lot of the same character.

Auguste Clape Old-fashioned Cornas which is dense yet dumb in its youth but outstanding at the age of ten years and more.

Clusel-Roch Source of fine Côte Rôtie, especially the Les Grandes Places *cuvée*, and tiny amounts of superb Condrieu.

Pierre Coursodon St-Joseph producer. Pierre and his son Jérôme have a sound range, including the excellent oddity Le Paradis de St-Pierre, 100-per-cent Marsanne. Silky smooth reds too.

Colombo Enterprising Jean-Luc Colombo may be too brash for many Rhône *vignerons*, but his influence has been felt in cellars throughout the Rhône Valley in a generally positive way. He has vineyards in Cornas, including a 90-year-old plot from which the superb Les Ruchets *cuvée* is made. He also buys in grapes from other areas including the Côtes du Roussillon. Now a new *négociant* arm to the business. Quality is high – look out for authentic Rhône flavours minus the faults and the excess tannins.

Yves Cuilleron New star making appetising, if rather oaky, Côte Rôtie, but excelling with Condrieu, especially the intensely fruity Les Chaillets Vieilles Vignes *cuvée*.

Château de Curson Exciting, modern Crozes-Hermitage producer Etienne Pochon makes bright, spicy, fruity reds and dry, floral whites in a 400-year-old castle.

Delas Revitalised, Roederer-owned company which, thanks to new management in the cellar in 1997, is now exploiting its extensive domaine of vineyards to the full, and showing consistent improvement year after year. Hermitage Les Bessards is the star.

Pierre Dumazet Solid, traditional Viognier specialist, making *vin de pays*, Côtes du Rhône and two Condrieus. Low yields and ripe fruit ensure plenty of heady perfume.

Jean-Michel Gerin Up-and-coming producer advised by Colombo and producer of impressive Côte Rôtie Les Grandes Places and delectable Condrieu.

Alain Graillot Proof that Crozes need not be Hermitage's poor cousin. Full-flavoured, aromatic wines, which are attractive while young yet develop very well, and a top *cuvée* called La Guiraude, which is complex, brilliant and fairly priced. Fine Hermitage too.

Bernard Gripa Do you like Marsanne? Bernard and his son Fabrice make a good, stylish St-Péray, so if you do, this is a grower to watch. Main wine St-Joseph is also stylish, powerful, oaky; needs five years' ageing.

Guigal Master of Côte Rôtie, with a trio of single-vineyard wines – La Mouline, La Turque and La Landonne – that are the most expensive and probably the best in the appellation. Other stars of an extensive range are the Hermitage, Côtes du Rhône (always great value) and Condrieu. Not content with this, Marcel Guigal also owns Vidal-Fleury, has recently acquired the estates of de Vallouit and Grippat in the northern Rhône, and is said to have his eye on domaines in Châteauneuf-du-Pape.

Paul Jaboulet Aîné Famous for the excellent Hermitage La Chapelle, but also a reliable source of wines from throughout the Rhône. The bargain is the long-lived Domaine de Thalabert Crozes-Hermitage.

Jamet Extremely concentrated, rounded, cassis-laden wines from Côte Rôtie.

Jasmin One of the best Côte Rôtie producers, making bold yet elegant wines of considerable class.

Michel Ogier Michel and his son Stéphane show year-by-year improvements with their wines – leaning now towards a modern fruity style.

André Perret The Condrieu Coteaux du Chery is one of the finest in the appellation, and the red and white St-Josephs are also of note.

Gilles Robin Rising star of Crozes-Hermitage, making fine, fragrant wine, on its way up.

Vernay Famous Condrieu producer whose wines, particularly from the Coteau de Vernon, are wonderfully scented essences of Viognier.

Noël Verset Even though Verset has retired it's still worth looking out for his wines, as he hasn't been able to resist making 'just one more vintage', for a few years now. Traditional dense Cornas which can be stalky when young but which ages wonderfully.

Les Vins de Vienne High-class, new *négociant* venture for a trio of eminent producers, Cuilleron, Gaillard and Villard, making impressive wines from both northern and southern Rhône.

The southern Rhône

After the last part of St-Joseph, there is not much of vinous interest, except for a few little pieces of Côtes du Rhône, before the southern section of the Rhône Valley begins below Montélimar. The valley opens out into a plain, and the vineyards spread out, mainly to the east. This is a scorched, arid region, and the Mistral and Sirocco winds sweep through most days of the year. Yet the southern Rhône is capable of making great red wine and the occasional tasty white and rosé too.

Red wines

No fewer than 13 different grape varieties are allowed in the blend for the best-known and greatest wine of the region, Châteauneuf-du-Pape. This rich, alcoholic cocktail of sun-baked fruit, spices and herbs derives its power from ultra-ripe Grenache grapes, typically 80 per cent of the blend, backed up in varying proportions by the other 12 varieties, with Syrah and Mourvèdre being the most popular partners (Syrah is seldom used in the south as a 100-per-cent varietal since the warmer climate tends to give wines that are just too hefty).

Châteauneufs are currently bigger, better and more powerful than they have ever been, and although some now command rather high prices, most still represent excellent value.

Other wines of the southern Rhône follow similar lines. Quality-wise, Gigondas is closest to Châteauneuf but, depending on the *terroir* and winemaking, can vary from elegant to rather rustic. Then come Lirac, Vacqueyras and wines from the 16 named Côtes du Rhône villages: Cairanne, Chusclan, Laudan, Rasteau, Roaix, Rochegude, Rousset-les-Vignes, Sablet, St-Gervais, St-Maurice, St-Pantaléon-des-Vignes, Séguret, Valréas, Vinsobres, Visan and Beaumes-de-Venise, of which (improvements being what they are) we're going to start seeing more and more: keen Rhône followers should start memorising these names.

Côtes du Rhône itself can vary from declassified Côte Rôtie from a top winemaker to a rather soft and weedy red resembling basic Beaujolais. Similarly styled wines are made in the Côtes du Lubéron and Côtes du Ventoux between the Rhône and Provence.

White wines

Whites, made here from Clairette, Bourboulenc, Roussanne and Grenache Blanc, are very much in the minority. White Châteauneuf is typically a crisp, fresh wine with a nutty edge which is at its best when young, although it can be kept for up to five years, with the top wines such as Beaucastel's Roussanne Vieilles Vignes lasting much longer. Those weaned on a diet of New World Chardonnay may find that the flavour takes some getting used to – it's not particularly fruity, although it is a great partner for rich fish and poultry.

The southern Rhône is also home to one of France's most renowned *vins doux naturels*, the soft, grapey Muscat de Beaumes de Venise, which should be drunk as young as possible. The versions from Jaboulet, Domaine de Coyeux and Domaine de Durban are among the best. There is also a notable red *vin doux naturel*, the rounded, fleshy, almost port-like Rasteau.

Rosé wines

Serious rosé (well, as serious as rosé ever gets) is made in Lirac and Tavel using the same varieties as for the reds. These pink wines can be more concentrated and fruity than other rosés – their strong Syrah component makes them quite masculine, even slightly tannic, but we would recommend you drink them within two years of the vintage, and choose carefully, as from less-attentive growers they can be a little too rustic for our liking.

Pick of the producers (southern Rhône)

Daniel & Denis Alary Conscientious producers of Cairanne and Rasteau (Côtes du Rhône-Villages) – balanced, elegant wines.

Château de Beaucastel First-class estate which uses all 13 permitted varieties for its Châteauneuf. The Mourvèdre-based Cuvée Hommage à Jacques Perrin is a classic, but then so is the regular wine. The star white is the rich and nutty 100-per-cent Roussanne Vieilles Vignes. Other wines to look out for are the red and white Côtes du Rhône Coudoulet de Beaucastel and the Côtes du Ventoux La Vieille Ferme.

Bosquet des Papes Châteauneuf from the shadow of the 'château'. Big, textured Cuvée Grenache has all the red-fruit, soft generosity we love about this grape.

Les Cailloux Ripe, concentrated, good-value Châteauneuf-du-Pape, some from ancient vines.

Domaine du Cayron Smooth but hefty, purple-hued Gigondas packed with cassis. Old vines play a large part here. Very sadly, the owner was recently killed in a car crash.

Cave de Chusclan Excellent range of Côtes du Rhône-Villages (Chusclan and Laudun), full of thick, spicy, ripe Grenache fruit. Also AC Lirac.

Domaine Couroulu Big, alcoholic Vacqueyras and some pure straight Grenache from Guy Ricard's up-and-coming *caves*.

Cave Estezargues Another booming Vin de Pays du Gard co-operative, achieving success with remarkably pure, deliciously fine fruit.

Château des Fines Roches Delicious, smoky-smooth yet elegant Châteauneuf (ageworthy), and also white Châteauneuf (honeyed, spicy, grassy).

Domaine du Grand Tinel Excellent but little-known property owned by Elie Jeune in Châteauneuf, making long-lived, fruity, spicy wines using plenty of old-vine Grenache. Good, solid, mainstream stuff.

Domaine de la Janasse Up-and-coming estate in Châteauneuf with strapping, concentrated, classy reds and slightly spicy, dry whites.

Cave de Lumières Ventoux co-operative for fresh, crisp tangy reds and delicate floral, wild-fruit rosé.

Clos du Mont Olivet Châteauneuf with a high percentage of Grenache; longer, larger-cask maturation (2–3 years) than most makes these extremely elegant wines (the oak flavour having had time to resolve itself in barrel).

Domaine de la Mordorée Based in Lirac, and making the best red, white and rosé in that appellation. Also Côtes du Rhône and Châteauneuf of considerable class.

Domaine de l'Oratorie St-Martin Côtes du Rhône-Villages Cairanne, from Frédéric Alary: elegant, floral, red fruity wines (from the usual blend: Grenache, Syrah, Mourvèdre).

Clos des Papes Consistently good Châteauneuf producer using lots of Mourvèdre; also makes an interesting, long-lived white.

Domaine du Pégaü Big, old-fashioned blockbuster Châteauneuf with loads of extract and huge prices to match. Plan Pégaü is good value but only a *vin de table*, due to the Merlot in the blend. Rest of the range is diverse and rather confusing, but has some good wines.

Luc Pelaquie Very good Côtes du Rhône-Villages (Laudun), red and white, and delicate, spicy Lirac.

Raspail-Ay Rounded, ready-to-drink Gigondas from Dominique Ay, with 80 per cent Grenache adding to its approachability.

Château Rayas Jacques Reynaud died in 1997 but the world-famous Rayas style from Châteauneuf lives on in the hands of his nephew, Emmanuel Rayas. Rayas and second label Pignan are concentrated, sweetly ripe reds made from 100-per-cent Grenache from extremely low-yielding vines. The Rayas Blanc and Fonsalette Côtes du Rhône wines are commendable too.

La Remejeanne Rémy Klein makes typically 'Gard' *vins de pays* with fine-flavoured, stylish fruit, great substance, length and ageworthiness (they need a year or two!).

Domaine Sainte-Anne Côtes du Rhône-Villages (St-Gervais), straight Côtes du Rhône and very good white Viognier from the Steinmaier brothers, who pack in lots of Mourvèdre so these pure, extracted wines need time for their velvety tannins to soften. They're worth the wait.

Domaine Saint-Cosme Rising Gigondas star, whose sumptuous top *cuvée* Valbelle was described by American critic Robert Parker as the 'Château Le Pin of Gigondas'. The Côtes du Rhône Les Deux Albion is as good a wine as you'll find for under £10.

Cave Saint-Didier Co-operative with a good, wide range of Côtes de Ventoux *cuvées* (soft reds; juicy, lively rosés), carefully made and ever-improving.

Domaine Saint-Gayan Eulogies for Jean-Pierre Meffre (don't confuse with the bigger Châteauneuf Meffre) and his tiny quantities of traditional Gigondas are all-too-frequently heard these days, so make sure you buy it if you see it: aromatic, pruny, powerful, long-lived.

Le Sang des Cailloux Serge Férigoule makes strong, supple, black Vacqueyras, typically ageworthy and notoriously good – so grab it if you see it.

Domaine Santa Duc Powerful Gigondas which manages to retain a vestige of elegance. Best *cuvée* is the sweet, sexy Hautes Garrigues.

Tardieu Laurent The 'Laurent' in question is Burgundian Dominique Laurent, but it is Michel Tardieu who is largely responsible for the range of modern, forcefully flavoured, oaky but typically excellent reds from throughout the Rhône valley. (Priced accordingly.)

Domaine de la Vieille Julienne Tannic, ageworthy Châteauneuf and also very good Côtes du Rhône from *vieilles vignes* across the road (80-year-olds) – the latter is softer and less structured than the Châteauneuf but has a pure expression of place, finer than many a more commercial wine.

Domaine du Vieux Chêne Côtes du Rhone from Jean-Claude Bouche tends to be full of character, finesse and – as its subtle interesting tannins evolve – very long-lived. The 1994 (for example) still needs time. Jean-Claude's wine is organic, too.

Domaine du Vieux Télégraphe Juicy, fruity Châteauneuf which is attractive young but ages well. Drink the delightful, peachy white as young as possible. Since the 1998 vintage, the estate has been a part-owner of Domaine Les Pallières in Gigondas.

Other wines

Falling into neither the southern nor northern Rhône are the wines produced around the town of Die on the river Drôme, a tributary of the Rhône. This is a beautiful rural retreat, its hillsides planted with lavender and vines, but if you can find the rare red and white Châtillon-en-Diois, don't expect to be thrilled. Crémant de Die, made from the lacklustre Clairette, is slightly better, while Clairette de Die Tradition, or Clairette de Die Méthode Dioise Ancestrale, as it is now called, is far more interesting. It's made from at least 75 per cent Muscat Blanc à Petits Grains by the *méthode dioise ancestrale*, which involves halting fermentation partway through and bottling a wine with residual sugar, so the fermentation continues in the bottle, producing the bubbles. If you like Asti (and we know you all do), then you'll love this peachy, grapey fizz.

Rhône vintage guide

The wines of the northern and southern Rhône differ in many ways, and it doesn't always follow that a good vintage for one is also good for the other. In general, the Syrah-based wines of the north, especially Hermitage and Cornas, need more age than the southern offerings, being rather forbidding and tight in their youth. Wines from the south are approachable earlier, but better vintages of Châteauneuf (and occasionally Gigondas) from a top producer can age gracefully for 20 years or more. The top whites of the north should (in our view) be drunk either in their perfumed, peachy youth or after many years. Ten-year-old white Hermitage can seem rather flabby and flat, an expensive disappointment.

2001 After a very mild, wet winter, spring arrived sunny and warm and the season got off to a good start. A hot summer upped the sugar levels and phenolics developed nicely in cooler September – cooler in the north than the south, where the Mistral blew savagely, reducing crops by up to 30 per cent. Overall, a very satisfactory ripening period and strong, concentrated wines with fine aromas and firm acidity should be the result all round.

2000 The third great year in a row. Spring and early summer were cool but, with the exception of showers in mid-August, the rest of the growing season brought good weather, meaning that the fruit ripened well and was brought in in a very healthy state. Quality may not be as consistent as in the two previous vintages, but the best reds are of a similar standard, while the whites, especially those of the north, will be the finest for several years.

1999 If the southern reds slightly overshadowed those from the north in 1998, the opposite was true in 1999. Rain in mid-September coincided with harvest time in parts of the south, so there will be wines which, though ripe, are slightly dilute. The rain also panicked some northern growers into picking too early, but those who waited were rewarded with good weather through to mid-October, giving a large crop of high-class wines.

1998 A great vintage in the south and at least a very good one in the north. Frost and hail hit some northern vineyards, but the hot dry summer brought the fruit to full maturity. By the time rains came at the end of September, virtually all the grapes had been picked in the south, and the wines are exceptional. Some northern vineyards were hit by the wet weather, so the wines are not quite so concentrated.

1997 Not an easy vintage because of the very hot spring followed by a dull cloudy summer. Fortunately, the sun came out for an Indian summer, and the conditions during the harvest were hot and dry. The wines are good to very good, and the reds should age well.

1996 The cool summer in the north meant that the Syrah did not ripen as well as in 1995, although sunny weather from late August onwards ensured grapes were by no means unripe. Quality is high, but not of the standard of 1995. The south was slightly more patchy, as grapes struggled to mature fully in the cool weather. However, whites from both regions were excellent.

1995 A classic. The summer was the driest and sunniest since 1990. Rain fell for two weeks at the start of September, but those who waited for it to abate produced some great wines, well-structured but with plenty of ripe fruit. Superb white wines as well, especially Condrieu.

1994 A difficult vintage spoilt in both north and south by rain in the autumn. There were a number of noteworthy wines, but also plenty of indifferent ones.

1993 Not great. Cool summer weather in the north meant that when rain arrived at the end of September, the grapes had not been picked. Scrupulous growers made some light, reasonably attractive wines. In the south the overall quality was higher, if not remarkable.

1992 Not for keeping. Rain at flowering and rain in October meant that survivors in both the north and the south were sound but not for the long term.

1991 A classic example of the north and south enjoying different vintage conditions. Uneven ripening produced wines that ranged from decent to mediocre (and worse) in the south. Meanwhile, the north produced some excellent wines for the fourth year on the trot, with Côte Rôtie excelling.

Good earlier vintages
Northern Rhône: 1990, 1989, 1988, 1985, 1983, 1982, 1979, 1978.
Southern Rhône: 1990, 1989, 1988, 1985, 1981, 1979, 1978.

SOUTH-WESTERN FRANCE

In the past, we've referred to this wine region as a 'satellite of Bordeaux', and in this we stand corrected. The south-west has as strong, if not stronger, a tradition of winemaking than its illustrious neighbour – and, in fact, has been known to 'lend' Bordeaux some of its produce to beef up its less robust vintages (just as Algeria once did for Burgundy). But this, of course, is history. No grower would do such a thing today.

The wines of Buzet, Marmandais, Duras and Bergerac are all made from Bordeaux grapes (that is Cabernets Sauvignon and Franc, plus Merlot); on occasion, south-western growers still utilise them to better effect. But the further you travel from Bordeaux the more the style of wine changes, until, on reaching Madiran and Jurançon in the south, and Cahors, Gaillac and Fronton in the east, the grapes change altogether (Malbec, Tannat, Colombard, the two Mansengs and many others come into play). All these varieties are just as traditional here as Bordeaux' grapes are to Bordeaux; if anything, they have been in place for longer, since before Bordeaux was making any wine at all.

But don't let that put you off this fascinating region. While Abouriou, Courbu, Negrette, Len de l'El, Fer, Servadou and Arrufiac aren't in the top league of grape varieties, they make a pleasant change from a constant diet of the familiar and shouldn't be ignored, especially as they are usually very good value. The only difficulty with some of the more obscure appellations is that you'll find them difficult to track down in the UK. Comptoir Gascon, a speciality food and wine shop in Smithfield in London, offers an excellent selection, otherwise you'd do better to go to the region yourself.

Red wines

The red wines from the areas nearer Bordeaux, such as Bergerac (undergoing something of a quality renaissance at present), the Côtes de Duras and the Côtes du Marmandais, naturally have claret-like characteristics and share the grape varieties. Pécharmant, a sub-appellation within Bergerac, produces slightly heftier wines, such as Château de Tiregand, which benefit from bottle age. The legendary 'black wine' of Cahors in reality varies from deeply coloured, tannic and practically undrinkable (until it's had nearly a decade in bottle) through to light, quaffable, everyday Malbec. It's at its best with a middling depth of flavour without hanging on to the huge tannins – too light and it loses its regional character. (The big old classics still exist of course, usually oaked, usually 100-per-cent Malbec, without tempering add-in varieties.)

Côtes du Frontonnais, made mainly from Negrette, is undergoing a huge revival: lighter and not far removed in flavour from the Dolcetto of northern Italy, a group of younger growers are now exploiting this variety's damsony, slightly bitter fruit (not least as an excellent match for local cassoulets). The wines of Madiran, Béarn and Irouléguy, down in the south-west, are made mainly from the chunky Tannat grape blended with Cabernet of some description, and typically need time in bottle to soften. Alain Brumont has been demonstrating for several years that Tannat can be tamed with good winemaking and new oak barrels, though unoaked Madirans are often softer and quicker to mature than the oaked kind. Don't expect either Madiran (Tannat) or Cahors (Malbec) to resemble anything you might find from Uruguay or Argentina. There are few similarities.

White wines

As a rule, the modern, basic dry whites of the south-west are extremely reliable. Humble Vin de Pays des Côtes de Gascogne, grassy and fresh, was one of the success stories of the 1980s and is still going strong – Domaine du Tariquet (made from Ugni Blanc) and the wines from the co-operative at Plaimont are always worth following. Similar wines may be found from the Côtes de St-Mont appellation (the Plaimont co-op turns its hand to these too). In Gaillac, white wines are made to varying degrees of sweetness from the Mauzac and Len de l'El grape varieties, and are fast improving in quality – particularly those from producers such as Plageoles or the co-operative at Tecou. Mauzac also makes the little-known sparkling wines of Gaillac, which has its own *méthode gaillacoise* appellation. Ugni Blanc (of Cognac fame) and Colombard (floral, aromatic) are used to bolster blends here and there too.

Sweet whites from south-west France are something of a revelation. Monbazillac and Jurançon tend to be the most recognised, although they are completely different. The grape varieties for Monbazillac, and the now extremely upwardly mobile Saussignac appellation not far away, are the same as for Sauternes (Sémillon, Sauvignon Blanc and Muscadelle). Because of the steeper slopes and cooler nights here, *botrytis* rot attacks them with, if anything, more regularity, and careful winemakers are able to produce wines of great distinction and honeyed richness for a fraction of the price. As with Sauternes, however, discriminate when purchasing, as clumsy, short-cut wines are not unknown.

Jurançon wines offer a much more refreshing experience for sweet wine lovers. Here Gros and Petit Manseng and Courbu are harvested ultra-ripe but do not succumb to *botrytis*, remaining lighter and more delicately scented in style. But watch out for some ultra-sweet, *micro-cuvée* wines from the more 'macho' winemakers – they're deliciously different and extremely concentrated, but rather rare. The dry Jurançon Sec is also worth trying, particularly those examples now fermented in oak from Domaine Cauhapé. The last mention must go to the gloriously named Pacherenc de Vic Bilh, a tangy sweet white from Madiran made resolutely from local varieties such as Arrufiac, Courbu, Gros and Petit Manseng. In some cases the grapes are left to dry (*passerillé*) on the vines at the end of a warm vintage to be turned into sweet wines of great longevity.

Pick of the producers (south-western France)

Domaine Berthoumieu Producer of top-quality Pacherenc, and rival in Madiran to Alain Brumont, below. Didier Barré's top *cuvée*, the oak-aged Charles de Batz, is a rich, velvety, prize-winning Madiran.

Alain Brumont Brumont's three properties – Domaine Bouscassé, Château Montus and Domaine Meinjarre – produce some of the best Madiran, using a high proportion of Tannat and a courageous dose of new oak. New in 2000, Montus Cuvée La Tyre is a pure Tannat from the highest vineyards in the appellation. The dry Pacherenc de Vic Bilh from Bouscassé is good, but the Moelleux is excellent. The range of *vin de pays* varietals is less convincing.

Domaine Cauhapé Henri Ramonteu is the mover and shaker in Jurançon, making dry and sweet whites of consistently high quality, particularly the luscious Quintessence.

Domaine des Causses-Marine Patrice Lescarretat is an important new Gaillac specialist, with ultra-sweet wines and also excellent varietals 'Maczau' and 'Rasdu' (Mauzac and Duras respectively, but not allowed to appear as such on the labels, hence the anagrams).

Clos du Cadaret Rising Côtes de Duras property which makes reds comparable with top St-Emilion (especially the Cuvée Raoul Blondin) and astonishingly complex whites.

Château du Cèdre Acclaimed Cahors producer whose wines spend 24 months in barrel but emerge harmonious, ripe and elegant, nearly black to look at.

Château des Eyssards The up-and-coming property of Pascal Cuisset, impassioned producer of astounding sweet Saussignac wines, especially the Cuvée Flavie, from 100-per-cent Sémillon.

Domaines Grassa Yves Grassa was the man who helped establish the reputation of Côtes de Gascogne in the mid-1980s, and is still among the top producers. Of the various labels, Domaines du Rieux, du Tariquet and de Plantérieu are the best. Grassa wines are tasty and excellent value.

Clos Lapeyre At least as good as Domaine Cauhapé (above) for strong, clear, remarkably complex, aromatic Jurançon.

Primo Palatum *Négociant* business producing small quantities of astonishingly concentrated wines from throughout the south-west (including Bordeaux). Critics slate these wines as atypical, over-oaked, over-priced and too 'Californian'. They are, nonetheless, impressive.

Producteurs Plaimont Large but dynamic co-operative organisation that makes reds and whites of good quality in several south-west appellations, but probably best known for white Côtes Saint-Mont and Côtes de Gascogne. Supplies several UK own-labels.

Elian da Ros Fairly new (1997) Côtes du Marmandais estate already on form with powerful chunky reds and a rather fine rosé.

Château Tirecul La Gravière Stunning Monbazillac buoyed up by a large proportion – 50 per cent – of Muscadelle. Most Sauternes struggle to keep up with the regular bottling, while the Cuvée Madame is mind-blowing (as is its price).

Château Tour des Gendres Now the finest estate in Bergerac. Talented winemaker Luc de Conti produces rich but refined reds which repay keeping, as well as a range of lovely whites capped by the brilliant Anthologia, which can hold its own against almost anything from Pessac-Léognan.

Clos Triguedina Old estate reviving the mythical black Cahors to almost spoon-standing proportions. Achieves elegance too, but not before five years old.

Clos d'Yvigne An Englishwoman, Patricia Atkinson, makes among the best and most elegant of Saussignacs – and, fortunately for us, sends them to England too.

GEORGIA

Georgia is the cradle of wine-growing – one of the historic centres of viticulture, and one of the few ex-USSR countries to be visible on UK shop shelves (mostly thanks to Georgian Wines & Spirits, the sole exporter). Most of Georgia's wine comes from the eastern Kakheti region; cheaper, more everyday wines (some sparkling) come from central Kartli. Look out for local white grape varieties Mtsvane and Rkatsiteli for zesty, dry, minerally whites, and reds Matrassa (Merlot-like) and gutsy, blackcurranty Saperavi. Some of the Georgian wines we have seen have been prone to the typically Eastern European high-yield/poor ripeness syndrome (plus accompanied signs of poor storage, poor transportation, and so on), but you may have better luck with your choice.

GERMANY

There are three ways into the German wine maze at the moment. One, via the original *'Prädikat'* system – for which you need 'the knowledge' about ripeness levels (see 'The German wine classification system', below) and a certain grasp of the German language. Two, via the geographical system, which defines 'first growth' (*Erstes Gewächs*) vineyard sites and expects (quite rightly) a certain level of quality in the wine. And three, at a more basic level (more friendly to the £5-note), by the new system of 'Classic' and 'Selection' wines.

We talked about the latter two styles last year, and are pleased to say that they are quietly beginning to make an impact. 'Classic' is the label the Germans have chosen to bring a more global feel to their dry white wine styles. (Note the use of an Anglicised 'C' rather than the hard German 'K'.) It is a designation used for simple, everyday wines, made from single grape varieties that are considered typical of each region.

'Selection' is for wines a notch higher in quality, using the same grape varieties but with further stipulation as to yields (they must be lower), alcohol (which must be higher, at least 12.2 per cent) and individual vineyard sites. The latter also have to gain the approval of a tasting panel – no doubt a tough one, knowing the rigorous Germans!

The one thing that can be guaranteed about Classic and Selection wines is that they will be modern. That is, they will be dry, cleanly made (don't assume temperature-controlled fermentation has been universally adopted for decades now, some Germans are only just beginning to take this technique on board) and there will be a refreshing absence of 'runic' clutter on the label. The designers have been brought in: the bottles are new, the packaging is clear, the images simple without losing the German feel – but the message is readable, and elegant. Over 350 growers are now subscribing to this scheme so, by the time you read this, you'll be able to taste for yourselves.

But if it's those charismatic Mosel vineyard sites you're after then there's little alternative but to get to grips with the tongue-twisting *Erstes Gewächs* names. Then, to fully anticipate the ripeness and sweetness of the wine, you'll need to understand such terms as *Kabinett*, *Spätlese* and *Auslese*. Frankly, though, if you can find your way around the *grands* and *premiers crus* of Burgundy, these terms aren't so very difficult. And, just as with Burgundy, the flavours in your glass will be more than worth the effort.

If you think getting to grips with three different classifications is too confusing, simply look for a producer you like: the best of them are listed under the regions, later in this section. Bear in mind, too, the new generation of winemakers taking their influences from the New World, and from winemaking college, rather than depending on years of father-to-son tradition. These new kids know that the world might be tiring of hot-climate whites, full of alcohol and oak, and they are ready to capitalise with their own fresh, new wines. OK, some of them might be going overboard with the likes of

Chardonnay *Beerenauslese* aged in 100-per-cent new Palatinate oak, or a bit wild with aroma-enhancing enzymes, which produce fragrances more regularly found in the bathroom. But, bizarre as they sound, it's system-breaking wines like these that bring new energy and new life to what has definitely been a flagging wine world – it's an approach the Italians adopted, and just look what happened to the Super-Tuscans.

A word about oak. For those of you who have never understood whether good German wine does or doesn't see an oak barrel, the answer is fewer and fewer do. Oak is never used for the flavour, but more for the slight softening effect of oxygen coming through the staves in the barrel. In a really cool, damp cellar, with minimal evaporation, the following top growers are a few that 'do': JJ Prüm (depending on how it feels about the individual wine), Burklin-Wolf (who has no cellar but simulates these conditions above ground, at great expense), Schloss Saarstein (again, some wines do, some don't) and Dirk Richter (just for a few months). Wines solely made in stainless steel, on the other hand, don't tend to go to sleep mid-term (the 'dumb phase', when the aromas and flavours close up for a while), but are expressive as they age, yet are still built to last because of that famously crisp Riesling acidity.

The German wine classification system

Around 98 per cent of Germany's production qualifies for the title of 'quality wine'. The fraction that doesn't comprises **Deutscher Tafelwein** and **Deutscher Landwein**. These are generally wines to be avoided, apart from some modern experimental ones that are only permitted to be called **Tafelwein** – their high price normally gives them away.

The lower level of quality wine is **Qualitätswein bestimmter Anbaugebiete (QbA)**, meaning quality wine from specific regions. QbA wines vary from the bland, such as Liebfraumilch and friends to quite classy estate wines, which in many cases may have been voluntarily downgraded from a higher quality level.

Süssreserve – unfermented grape juice – may be used after fermentation to alter the sweetness of the wine. Chaptalisation is permitted to increase the alcohol content of QbA wines. Indeed, some producers whose wines would qualify for QmP level (see below) opt for QbA status as they feel that chaptalising gives them a better wine. This is especially true for wines made in the southern reaches of the country from the Pinot grape family.

The higher level is **Qualitätswein mit Prädikat**. The QmP system categorises the wine according to the amount of sugar in the grapes at harvest rather than by the sweetness of the final wine. This means that from the same batch of grapes, a producer could make both a bone-dry wine and a sweeter wine that was lower in alcohol, and both would be labelled as *Spätlese*. The label gives few clues as to which style to expect, although the words **Trocken** (dry) and **Halbtrocken** (semi-dry) may offer some assistance (see also our comments earlier relating to Classic and Selection wines). Chaptalisation is not allowed for QmP wines; *Süssreserve* is, although its use is declining as the demand for drier wines grows.

QmP wines fall into one of six categories. The lowest grade is **Kabinett** (typically dry), then come **Spätlese** (off-dry), **Auslese** (medium), **Beerenauslese** (sweet) and **Trockenbeerenauslese** (very sweet). The sixth category is **Eiswein**, which is made from grapes that have frozen on the vines after winter frosts and been crushed before the ice has a chance to melt, thus concentrating the flavours. *Eiswein* is higher in acidity than the *botrytis*-affected *Auslese*, *Beerenauslese* and *Trockenbeerenauslese* wines.

According to this system, all vineyards and all grapes are created equal, so the finest Rieslings from sites on the slopes overlooking the Mosel and Rhine are thus given the same ranking as mass-produced Müller-Thurgau. This is patently nonsense, so the producers have taken things into their own hands. Founded in 1972, the **Verband Deutscher Prädikatsweingüter e.V. (VDP)** is a group of estates whose members have agreed to a set of regulations concerning preferred varieties, methods of viticulture, lower yields and a commitment to the higher-quality vineyards. Not all wines bearing the VDP symbol, a black eagle, are great, and not all great estates have applied for membership of the organisation. However, the VDP stamp of approval is a more reliable measure of quality than anything in the wine laws.

Since the mid-1990s, some regions have taken this a stage further and come up with their own classification of vineyards, the *Erstes Gewächs* (first growths). In order for a wine to be designated as a first growth, it has to conform to certain requirements, including yields, and must be approved by a tasting panel. The Nahe and Rheingau schemes stipulate that only Riesling is permitted, while the Pfalz system also includes Weissburgunder and Spätburgunder (Pinot Blanc and Pinot Noir).

As yet, these schemes are unofficial and still in their early stages, and are now being joined by a third such system, the Classic and Selection wines, as detailed earlier. Although the aim is for simplification, to make German wines more accessible, it remains to be seen whether these three classifications dovetail as neatly as the authorities hope, or result in more confusion – the last thing this country's wine industry needs.

White wines – grape varieties and wine styles

Riesling

Apart from being unfairly tarred with the Liebfraumilch brush,
Germany's greatest grape has also suffered in recent times from
confusion of identity. Should it be made as a light and slightly
sweet wine (often described as 'fruity'), or a dry (*trocken*) one?
Adherents of both styles use a variety of historical evidence to back
up their arguments as to which was the traditional Riesling wine.

At the heart of the debate is Riesling's acidity, which requires
something to balance it. For quality producers, the alternatives are
residual sweetness for the fruity style, and body – in other words
alcohol and extract – for the dry or *trocken* styles. In cooler regions
such as the Mosel, where the potential alcohol levels of wines
even from good growers may only be 11 per cent, it makes more
sense to make wines in the fruity style with around 8–9 per cent
and some residual sugar. In warmer areas, where good growers
have no problem achieving 13 per cent potential alcohol, there is
a choice as to which style to make and, increasingly, the choice is
to make a *trocken* wine. Even so, the *trocken* category permits up
to 9 g/l of residual sugar, and most producers make full use of this
allowance. (Those making cheaper, dry Rieslings resort to other
means such as malolactic fermentation and occasionally oak
ageing to knock off the gawky edges, but they are seldom
successful.)

Providing they're well made, both the full-bodied dry and the
lighter fruity styles are enjoyable. The dry wines are better with
food, although they need time in the bottle – three to four years at
least – to flesh out. The fruity styles drink well from the word go,
are the perfect summer aperitif, and usually outlast the dry wines. If
you've had bad experiences with *trocken* Riesling in the past but are
willing to give it another go, a good rule of thumb is to look for
wines with at least 12 per cent alcohol.

The above comments apply to grapes that have not been affected
by *botrytis*. Nobly rotted Riesling retains the citrusy, sweet 'n' sour
flavours and fresh acidity, and can vary from fairly delicate *Auslesen*
to rich *Beerenauslesen* and *Trockenbeerenauslesen* – which are not too
far removed from liquid marmalade.

Müller-Thurgau

Or Rivaner, as many now like to call it. Any change of name will do
little to disguise the fact that this is not one of the world's great
grapes. Unfortunately, it is widely grown, popular for its early
ripening rather than for the vaguely flowery character of wines
such as Liebfraumilch.

Silvaner
Solid, stolid even, but capable of producing full-bodied, slightly earthy wines that sit very nicely with traditional German cuisine. Franken and the Rheinhessen regions produce the best examples.

Rülander/Grauburgunder
The Pinot Gris of Alsace also performs similarly in Germany, producing powerful, spicy dry whites and luscious dessert wines, especially in Baden. Sometimes labelled Pinot Grigio.

Weissburgunder
Aka Pinot Blanc, another variety that has leapt over the border from Alsace and is producing some full-bodied wines in the Pfalz and Baden.

Scheurebe
Like it or loathe it, you can't ignore this fresh, ultra-zesty variety. Dry versions from the Pfalz are akin to liquid grapefruit and are falling out of favour. Sweeter versions are less controversial and can be excellent.

Gewürztraminer
Never reaching the heady heights of Alsace, but capable of quite charming scented wines in Baden and the Pfalz.

Chardonnay
Yes, it's there, but with Riesling around, one wonders why.

Red wines

The red wine boom that is sweeping the world has not passed Germany by, and red varieties have increased from an eighth to a quarter of total plantings – they are now more widely planted than Riesling. In particular Spätburgunder – Pinot Noir – is being put to good use. Efforts in the Mosel and Rheingau generally fail to excite, but some of the versions from Baden and the Pfalz are very good, with supple cherry fruit and the occasional touch of Burgundian silk. Shame they're so expensive, as they're now up to the level of New Zealand's and producers have no trouble in selling them on the German market. Names to look out for are Huber, Hans Lang, Künstler, Fritz Keller, Vollmer, Dr Heger and Johner. There is some Cabernet Sauvignon – avoid it; but do try Dornfelder – the best (but only the best) are Germany's answer to Dolcetto. And give the spicy Lemberger a whirl too.

Sparkling wines – Sekt

Some of Germany's *Sekts* can command the same money as *prestige cuvée* champagne on the home market. Even so, we're hard pushed to find many we enjoy. Some of the wines based on Riesling are pleasantly fruity, but the assertive character of the grape sits rather awkwardly with the bubbles. *Winzersekt* is a higher-quality version from smaller yields, just one vintage and just one vineyard – Spätburgunder, Weissburgunder or Riesling grapes. Those made from the Pinot family are more promising, particularly from specialists Andreas & Mugler in the Pfalz – two youngsters (both under 30) proving Germany can make decent fizz – but few wines receive the attention in production that quality sparkling wine demands.

THE REGIONS
Baden-Württemberg

With co-operatives dominating production, Baden is best known for making large quantities of attractive, easy-drinking Weissburgunder. Reds are considered a speciality of the region, although sometimes it's hard to see why. A worrying boom in plantings of heavily cropped red Dornfelder (red wine being so fashionable) has little recourse to quality, but commentators hope that the pendulum will swing back before there is too much to be ashamed of. In the meantime, Spätburgunder is the red grape that's really thriving, and there are also some high-class estates making impressive Grauburgunder. Sadly, though, few of these wines ever leave the region. Co-ops also dominate production in Württemberg but, once again, some quality-minded producers do exist.

Pick of the producers
Weingut Bercher From the Kaiserstuhl (Baden's warm, volcanic district) producing Weisburgunder and top-notch Spätburgunder.

Dr Heger Best of this Baden range are Weissburgunder and oak-aged Spätburgunder reds.

Bernard Huber Grauburgunder, Weissburgunder and Spätburgunder from a rising star grower with eyes on Burgundian styles for the last two varieties.

Franken

Bavaria is not just beer gardens and BMWs. The wines from Franken, often in the traditional *Bocksbeutel* (stumpy bottle), also deserve a try. Dull Müller-Thurgau is the most widely planted variety, although the region is more famous for its rather earthy Silvaner, which can take some getting used to but goes splendidly with the hearty local cuisine. However, the best wines are made from Riesling.

Pick of the producers
Rudolf Fürst Producer of probably the best Spätburgunder reds in Germany; also delicious barrel-fermented 'Pinot Blanc' (Weissburgunder).

Juliusspital Large and famous estate belonging to a hospital with holdings in all five of what are considered to be Franken's best vineyards. Riesling, Rieslaner, Silvaner and Weissburgunder all deserve attention.

Horst Sauer Maker of powerful, modern-style, dry Sylvaners and Rieslings, intensely aromatic, with great length; good with food too.

Hans Wirsching Elegant wines from an estate in the Steigerwald region with fresh but powerful Silvaner and Riesling.

Mosel-Saar-Ruwer

If you've never drunk a chilled Mosel *Kabinett* on a fine summer's day, you've missed out on one of life's greatest pleasures. This north-westerly region is the source of the quintessential German Riesling with a touch of sweetness, seemingly light but packed with flavour. With estate wines from great vineyards such as Wehlener Sonnenuhr and Urziger Würzgarten still available at very reasonable prices, there is no reason to drink the dreary Müller-Thurgau that is still produced in large quantities.

Pick of the producers
Deinhard Focus is on large-volume, cheaper wines from southern regions. D No.1, a Riesling/Pinot Blanc blend, is fleshy, aromatic and remarkably successful.

Robert Eymael/Mönchhof Classic wines from Urziger Würzgarten and Erdener Pralat. Some of the Mosel's more convincing *trocken* styles, but the sweeter wines surpass them.

Friedrich-Wilhelm-Gymnasium Good-value Rieslings from vineyards bequeathed by Karl Marx's old school.

Fritz Haag Top-quality, text-book minerally Mosel Rieslings from Brauneberger Juffer-Sonnenuhr.

Reinhold Haart Theo Haart makes proper Piesporter from the Goldtröpfchen vineyard, with quality and fleshy fruit in abundance.

Heymann-Löwenstein It's hard to find a more vocal supporter of dry German Riesling than Reinhard Löwenstein anywhere in Germany, and his wines have a richness that ensures they are first class (despite being totally atypical of the Mosel). Schieferterrassen – slate terraces – is his (very good) basic *cuvée*, and he also makes some fine *botrytis* wines.

Karlsmühle Dramatic, flashy wines from the Ruwer: small production, made to age and keep.

Karthäuserhof Superb, tangy, steely Rieslings from Christof Tyrrel's estate in the Ruwer.

Reichsgraf von Kesselstatt Large, reliable estate with extensive vineyards in various parts of the region, including Graach and Scharzhofberg. Can be dull, but showing well from 2001.

Carl Loewen Small mid-Mosel estate, not famous, but worth watching for superb quality, long-lasting wines. Look for wines from the Laurentiuslay vineyard site, and *Eiswein*.

Dr Loosen Ernie Loosen is one of the finest ambassadors for quality German wines. Everything, from the tangy Riesling QbA up to the *Auslesen* from Erdener Prälat and Urziger Würzgarten, is of exemplary quality, and the clear labelling also deserves praise.

Egon Müller-Scharzhof Classic, top-of-the-tree wines from the Saar, delicate, pure and long-lived.

Paulinshof Big, flashy Mosel wines from the top Riesling village Brauneberg, in bottles that look like Easter eggs, but we rather like them!

JJ Prüm Excellent wines from Graacher Himmelreich and especially Wehlener Sonnenuhr, which are firm and fleshy in their youth and age brilliantly.

Max Ferd Richter Dirk Richter's vineyards include parcels of Wehlener Sonnenuhr and Brauneberger Juffer. Wines range from dry and spicy to exquisite *Eiswein*.

Schloss Saarstein With fruit to the fore, these wines are accessible when young but also age well.

von Schubert Understated, impeccably balanced and fragrant wines from the Maximin Grünhaus estate overlooking the Ruwer.

Dr H Thanisch, Erben Thanisch The better of the two Dr Thanischs in Bernkastel, producing impeccable, pure Riesling in the Badstube and Doktor vineyards. The latter is labelled Berncasteler Doctor, a tradition stemming from the time when these wines were very popular in England.

Weingut Zilliken Classic racy Saar wines, of reliably good quality and great ageing potential.

Nahe

The forgotten region of Germany, lying between the Mosel-Saar-Ruwer and Rheingau districts, lacking its neighbours' popularity but often competing with both in producing pure, lively Riesling.

Pick of the producers
Schlossgut Diel In a range where oak is often no stranger, Armin Diel's best wines are his Rieslings from the Goldloch, Burgberg and Pittermännchen vineyards in Dorsheim. Diel is also co-author of the *Gault-Millau German Wine Guide*.

Dönnhoff Memorable slaty Rieslings with magnificent fruit flavours from the Niederhäuser Hermannshöhle and Oberhäuser Brücke vineyards.

Emrich Schönleber Rieslings with wonderful cleanness of flavour, both in the modern and traditional moulds.

Staatliche Weinbaudomäne, Niederhausen-Schlossböckelheim The Nahe State Domaine has some of the best vineyard sites in the region, but in recent times has only occasionally realised the full potential of the vineyards.

Rheingau

The sun-kissed northern slopes of the Rheingau are potentially the source of Germany's greatest dry Rieslings, full-bodied, with fairly high alcohol, minerally intensity and ripe fruit flavours. That the many well-sited estates are not fulfilling this potential was shown in the early 1980s when the Charta group of winemakers began to plug its drier wines: many were simply not full-flavoured enough to stand up to such a style. The introduction of *Erstes Gewächs* (see 'The German wine classification system', above) will, we hope, turn growers' attention back to producing better fruit and improving quality in those glorious vineyards.

Pick of the producers

J B Becker Very fine, racy Riesling and surprisingly good Spätburgunder.

Breuer Excellent, full-bodied dry Rieslings from the Rauenthal Nonnenberg and Rüdesheim Berg Schlossberg, as well as exquisite sweet wines and a fine sparkler.

Schloss Johannisberger Historic estate now owned by Henkell & Söhnlein, and showing great progress since 1997. Drier Rieslings are improving to match the quality of its extremely good sweet wines.

August Kesseler Estate on the up-and-up, with red Spätburgunder and white Riesling.

Peter Jacob Kuehn Rich, modern, powerful wines, in wonderfully concentrated dry and sweet styles.

Künstler Up-and-coming estate making finely structured Riesling and one of the region's best Spätburgunders.

Langwerth von Simmern Traditional, carefully made wines from the finest Mosel sites, with a worthy following.

Joseph Leitz Top-quality vineyards, with the smallest yields in Germany: the whole of this tiny range is delicious.

Schloss Schönborn Large but inconsistent estate, capable of magnificent, intense wines but often falling short of its potential.

Robert Weil Power and delicacy are the hallmarks of this splendid range, which excels in all styles from dry to sweet. Kiedricher Wasseros and Gräfenberg are the finest vineyards.

Rheinhessen

On one bank of the Rhine are sprawling vineyards of Müller-Thurgau, destined to become Liebfraumilch and other similar wines. On the other are better-situated slopes, the source of some excellent Riesling and Scheurebe. Silvaner can be good, providing it comes from those south-facing slopes.

Pick of the producers
Gunderloch Classic and simply labelled Rieslings from the Rothenberg (red hill) vineyard in Nackenheim.

Heyl zu Herrnsheim Organically farmed estate based in Nierstein, producing delicious, fragrant wines.

Franz Keller Modern, concentrated, dryish Rheinhessen – atypical, but very fine. Top-end sweet wines really shine.

Weingut St-Antony Dry Riesling of the very highest quality; off-dry also full-bodied and intense.

Weingut Wittmann Young Philip Wittmann is a rising star, producing superior, rich, extra-dry whites.

Pfalz

This is arguably Germany's most dynamic wine region, where newer independent producers such as Lingenfelder, Koehler-Ruprecht and Müller-Catoir, who don't confine their activities to Riesling, rub shoulders with rejuvenated traditional estates such as Bürklin Wolf, von Buhl and Bassermann-Jordan. The 'three Bs', as they're known, are now fully exploiting their first-class sites and have also shown that they too are not averse to a spot of innovation. If/when Germany finally re-establishes itself in overseas markets, the Pfalz could very well lead the way.

Pick of the producers
Bassermann-Jordan Stylish, well-balanced classic Rieslings from vineyards in Deidesheim and Forst – and a surprisingly good Chardonnay.

Bergdolt Amazing Pinot Blanc, mostly unoaked, but also high in alcohol, beautifully balanced and very rich.

Reichsrat von Buhl On form since 1995 after years in the doldrums. The Armand Riesling *Kabinett* manages to combine the best of the ancient and modern aspects of German wines, while the wines (going organic) from vineyards in Deidesheim and Forst are back among the finest in the region.

Bürklin-Wolf There are a few quirky wines, such as a Cabernet Sauvignon and a Riesling/Silvaner blend, named each year after a different operatic character, but the most satisfying wines remain the classic Rieslings from Forst, Deidesheim and Wachenheim. Low yields, and moving to organic production.

Koehler-Ruprecht Maker of the most powerful (13–14 per cent alcohol) dry Rieslings in Germany – muscular, to say the least. Also first-class Spätburgunder.

Lingenfelder Notable fruity Riesling, Scheurebe, Spätburgunder and Dornfelder from the energetic and innovative Rainer Lingenfelder.

Müller-Catoir Despite no vineyard holdings in what are considered the best Pfalz sites, Hans-Günter Schwarz's top-quality Riesling, Scheurebe, Weissburgunder and Rieslaner make him one of the stars of Germany, for both traditional and modern wines.

Rebholz Innovator in Spätburgunder, also makes by far-and-away Germany's best Chardonnay (there is a corner of limestone in the Pfalz on which this grape works well).

J L Wolf Ernest Loosen's Pfalz label for good, rich (13 per cent alcohol), modern wines, since 1998; watch for rich Villa Wolf Pinot Gris.

Other regions

Apart from Toni Jost's lovely Rieslings from the Mittelrhein, it is rare to see wines on sale in the UK from Germany's other regions, the Ahr, Hessische Bergstrasse, Saale-Unstrut and Sachsen. Nonetheless, it is worth noting that the latter two (in the former East Germany), which are not Riesling territory, are moving fast in their return to traditional varieties. Having first thought they'd make a splash with Sauvignon Blanc (yawn), they're now making powerful dry styles from Scheurebe and Gewürztraminer.

German vintage guide

Although 1987 was no great shakes, you have to go back as far as 1984 to find a truly dreadful German vintage. However, tread with caution through German vintage charts. Riesling is a late-ripening grape, and there are usually some growers, worried by the weather conditions, who pick before their fruit has fully developed.

2001 A spectacular vintage in the Nahe and Middle-Mosel (the best since 1959, exceeding even the fabulous 1971, 1976 and 1990 in quality) – with autumn sun coming through at just the right moment – but a cool, wettish September made for an erratic harvest elsewhere. The grapes that survived the rains (e.g. later-ripening Spätburgunder) made elegant, ageworthy wines.

2000 Apart from a wet July and a rather hot August, the weather was favourable throughout the season, and a large healthy harvest was in sight. Then in early September it rained, and didn't stop until most varieties had been picked. Riesling had a chance to dry out after the rain, but even so, problems with rot were not uncommon. Those prepared to go through the vineyard several times and only pick healthy grapes will have made some very good wines.

1999 A very favourable growing season resulted in a large crop, and this was further increased by rainfall in late September, which caused some grapes to swell up. Those who picked at this point will have made ripe if slightly dilute wines. Those who waited were rewarded with a dry October, and late ripening varieties such as Riesling and Spätburgunder were gathered in excellent condition, with high sugar levels and ripe acidity.

1998 With temperatures as high as 41°C, Germany had a summer which if anything was *too* hot. Many vineyards suffered in the excessive heat, with some growers losing as much as a quarter of their crop. Rain came in October, but many grapes had already been picked. The wines are rich in extract and acidity and have a great future. *Beerenauslese* and *Trockenbeerenauslese* wines are rare, but a mid-November frost resulted in the production of some splendid tongue-tingling *Eiswein*.

1997 The frosts and a subsequent summer drought reduced the size of the total crop, but the later-ripening grapes such as Riesling, Silvaner and Scheurebe were harvested in excellent conditions, with some top estates picking through to the second half of November. There was little *botrytis*, but producers have high hopes for their *Eiswein*. The ripe fruit and low acidity make this a very user-friendly vintage.

1996 A cool season saved by good weather in October. Those who had the nerve to hang on harvested their grapes in perfect condition, rich in sugar with concentrated flavours. Few *botrytis* wines were made, but there are some splendid *Eisweins*.

1995 Again late harvesters were rewarded, with a clement October following the rather damp August and September. This encouraged the development of *botrytis* and there are some fine concentrated wines.

Good earlier vintages 1993, 1990, 1989, 1988, 1985, 1983.

GREECE

Greek wine has come a long way in the last five years, and the largely boutique-scale wine industry is even successfully making wines on sale at the precious £4 and £5 levels (having previously charged a lot more): so we now have no excuse not to try them out. They don't even taste like Retsina. But Greek wine producers need the confidence to grow and bottle Greek grapes in their own right – these grapes are certainly good enough.

One of the historic cradles of viticulture, Greece has 250 of its own grape varieties (and counting); not all of them are understood well enough to head up a wine blend, but many of them are worthy of pole position. Unfortunately, however, there's an increasing tendency for them to be hidden away in a blend with Cabernet Sauvignon or Merlot, which, as far as the producers are concerned, will sell more bottles. In marketing terms, it's a good idea to blend with these more familiar varieties, because: (a) they taste good blended with Greek grapes, and (b) they offer an easier understanding of the wine. But the Greek grapes ought to take over at least 60 per cent of the blend, so their flavours shine through and people can really appreciate them for what they are (see grape descriptions below).

The problem is as it's always been: getting people to try the wines in the first place. Step off the boat on to a sunny Greek beach and the mouthwash at the local taverna is unlikely to persuade you to investigate further – even if you've read our rave reviews above and below, you'll trust your own senses and forget our encouragement right away. Be persistent. Venture further inland and you'll find – as many others are now doing – that it's possible to visit the wine regions yourself. Hire a car and follow road trips such as the 'Wine Roads of Macedonia' or the 'Wine Roads of the Peloponnese', or visit the island wineries on Santorini and Cephalonia for starters. The local market is starting to appreciate its own wines so it's about time we did too, or there'll be none left.

The first two vintages of the millennium, 2000 and 2001, have been great years for Greece (2000 hot and dry, making big, ripe wines; 2001 rather cooler, the wines have more elegance). With the wines hitting UK shop shelves now – Oddbins (see *Where to buy wine*) has a respectable supply of these wines, and more and more of the supermarkets are following its lead – what better time to start taking a new look at this country?

White wines – grape varieties

Starting with the white grapes, Greece is producing some stunning Chardonnay, Sauvignon and Viognier, from the Peloponnese in the south (the ragged-shaped mainland below Athens) to the Macedonian highlands in the north. Some of the cooler, coastal vineyards (in Patras, for example) are also producing delicious Riesling. But while these 'international' varieties are thriving (and for some growers they are the whole point these days) we think they're better off playing a supporting role to Greece's more interesting indigenous grapes.

Look to the inland hills of Mantinia (ski-slopes aren't uncommon in this part of the Peloponnese) for wines from the local grape Moscophilero. This variety was thought to be related to Gewurztraminer and has a similar rosewater/Turkish Delight perfume, but on the whole it's crisper, with balancing acidity and is a better partner for red snapper, salmon or seafood. Roditis is the Retsina grape, but don't let that put you off. Although it's powerful enough to support the resin it's even better without it; its own toasty herbaceous qualities (with good concentration) make it stunning. Also on the Peloponnese (coastal again), there's Lagorthi: soft and buttery, delicately fruity and aromatic, like dry herbs. And another white grape you'll start seeing more of is Malagousia, this time from Macedonia in the north – full of herby, lemon-peel characteristics.

Assyrtico is one of Greece's most versatile white grapes (and to our mind its best). It's often used to lend acidity structure to other, fleshier wines, but has enough distinctive honeysuckle and citrus characters of its own to show itself in even the smallest quantities. Grown widely in Macedonia, its lightest, most lemony manifestation (and its finest, crispest, almost saltiest) comes from the Agean island of Santorini, where it's frequently blended with Aïdini and Athiri – the vines need to grow so close to the ground in order to keep out of the strong winds that they curl around themselves in small baskets. Another island vine, Robola, on Cephalonia, makes more rounded, fleshy wines with a hint of limey fruit.

For sweet wines, look to the delicious thyme-scented Vissanto of Santorini (made from those three 'A' grapes again), and Muscats such as the oily, sun-dried Samos Nectar.

Red wines – grape varieties

Starting at the top, Aghiorghitiko is Greece's best red grape. Also known as Saint-George – although Greek wine producers are fairly determined that we get to grips with their difficult grape names, so the latter isn't a name you'll see too often on the bottle.

Aghiorghitiko is like a variation on Cabernet Franc, making anything from juicy, sappy rosés to full-on brambly black monster wines: delicious. 'Ag' comes primarily from the Peloponnese, and the surrounding vineyards are also well suited to strapping Cabernets and Syrahs. Mavrodaphne is another Peloponnese grape, and though usually used to churn out Mavrodaphne de Patras ('poor man's port'), it also makes robust, tannic dry wines.

Further north, in 'Balkan' territory, Macedonia, home of fruit orchards and one or two bears – Xinomavro is the prize red grape in the appellations of Naoussa and Goumenissa. Similiar in structure to Pinot Noir, it has strawberries to Pinot's raspberries; plus an additional (and quite remarkable) tomatoey flavour – it's an equally cantankerous customer in the vineyard, so pick your grower with care. Merlot and Syrah are good grape neighbours. Another grape popular in northern Greece is the beefy sage-and-laurel-scented Limnio variety.

Pick of the producers

Arghyros Santorini producer with the oldest and finest reserves of Vissanto, plus lemony, dry whites.

Gaia Progressive Peloponnese estate for superb Aghiorghitiko (three styles: cherryish rosé; ripe, plummy Notios; rich, spicy, intensely dark-fruited Gaia Estate for ageing), zesty herbaceous Assyrtico from Santorini, and, dare we say it, the finest Retsina.

Gentilini Boutique Chardonnay, Sauvignon Blanc and Robola from Cephalonia, made by British horticulturalist Gabrielle Beamish. New in 2000 vintage is rich, iodine-and-cherry Syrah.

Gerovassilou Esteemed Macedonian producer of delicious new-wave Chardonnay, Sauvignon and Viognier, plus fabulous 2000 vintage Syrah. Also don't miss out on wine from the local, grapefruity Malagousia variety.

Kyr-Yianni One of the most dynamic producers in Greece, making cutting-edge aromatic, flavourful reds from the northern Naoussa region: Merlot, Syrah and (strong suit) Xinomavro. Top wine, Ramnista, has ripe, generous 'raspberry and olive fruit', deliciously unusual.

Constantin Lazaridis One of the Greek estates most visible in the UK. Focus is on a range of international varieties achieving depth as the vineyards gain age. Everyday label is Amethystos; superior wines are made under the Château Julia banner. Crisp Sauvignons, structured Cabernet, herbaceous Assyrtico and rich dark Merlot.

Oenoforos Vibrant, steely Asprolithi whites from the coastal cliffs of Patras. Anghelos Rouvalis brings out the best in Greek grapes.

Papaioannou A mixture of Greek and international grapes. Top is peony-scented red Aghiorghitiko from Nemea, Peloponnese.

Sigalas Charismatic Santorini grower Paris Sigalas makes superb Oia Assyrtiko and tangy, honeyed Vissanto.

Spyropoulos Energetic modern Mantinia producer; also with ripe, rich Cabernet/Merlot/Aghiorghitiko blend.

Strofilia Half and half, Greek and cosmopolitan varieties, from trend-setting winery near Athens.

Tselepos Delicate whites: Gewurztraminer and Mantinia are the main focus.

Other up-and-coming estates to watch for: *Ktima Alpha*, *Ktima Katsaros*, *Skouros*, *Thebes* co-operative, *Ktima Voyatzis*, *Zitsa* co-operative.

HUNGARY

For the last few years we've been crying out for more quality wines from Hungary – a country more than capable of producing them. Consumers in the UK are now prepared to pay more and be a bit more adventurous – in other words, there'd be a market for anything of calibre that could be supplied. But there's still a dearth of characterful produce in the over-£5 bracket (apart from Tokaji/Tokay; more on that later).

The oft-promised premium, dry wines are still in the planning stages. Since 1994, better viticulture and training programmes have ensured lower yields and finer concentration from the top growers – usually the small, private estates. But few of these wines are as yet being exported to the UK. Improvements can often be linked to a foreign influence, as with Tibor G'al, former winemaker at Tenuta dell'Ornellaia in Tuscany, who makes some of the best wines in Eger in the north of the country. (Thummerer is the other star wine producer of the region.) Another name to look out for is Franz Weninger, who has an estate in Austria's Mittelburgenland. Weninger began his Hungarian exploits in the Villány region close to Croatia with a joint venture with Attila Gere, one of the top names in this very promising area, and has since acquired an estate

197

in the Sopron region close to the Austrian border. The reason for his rapid success is simple – he knows how to make wine. Would that more growers followed his lead and sent their wine to the UK as well.

At the cheap-and-cheerful end of the spectrum all is still well, with occasional local surprises such as the almondy, white Zenit grape making a welcome appearance, or tonsil-tingling spice-and-limey Irsai Oliver. Sappy Zweigelt and gutsy Kékfrankos (Blaufränkisch) do the same for the reds. But it's the usual suspects (Chardonnay, Sauvignon, Pinot Gris, Gewurztraminer, Cabernet and Merlot again) that we are bored with. Though they can be enticingly fruity from Hungary, and the price tags remain low, more often than not they're still over-produced, thin and dilute, all churned out in supermarket volumes. A shame, as there's nothing wrong with the conditions they grow in – the vineyards, temperature and climate are perfect.

The efforts of flying winemakers and inspired locals, most notably A'kos Kamocsay of the Hilltop Neszmély winery, are all commendable too, and we especially like the highly individual results they have achieved from making dry wines with the Tokaji grapes – crisp, resiny Furmint and aromatic, limey Hárslevelű. These have the richness of Alsace Riesling or Pinot Gris and a similar tangy acidity – excellent food wines. As with Sauternes, however, the dry wines are not the main event, and they also tend to be relatively expensive. All in all, Hungary could still do better in the middle ground.

Tokay

In the past decade or so, much of the international interest and investment has focused on the fabled sweet wines of Tokaj in north-eastern Hungary. And rightly so – how many other wines are reputed to have revived fading monarchs on their death beds? Currently, Tokaji ('Tokay' in its Anglicised form) is Hungary's most important contribution to the wine world. Today there are two main styles: modern (single-fermented) and traditional (double-fermented). For each, a paste made with Furmint with maybe a third Hárslevelű and a small amount of Yellow Muscat, is blended from ultra-ripe, often nobly rotten, grapes (Aszú). For the 'double-fermented' wines this is then added to a vat of wine, and re-initiates fermentation. For the more modern Tokajis, the paste is added to unfermented must, and then fermented for the first time. The finished wine is graded according to how much of the Aszú paste was added. Wines of 3 to 5 puttonyos – puttonyos are literally 'buckets' – are fairly common, 6 puttonyos is rarer, and Aszú Eszencia, an 8-puttonyos wine, that is rarer still. Tokay Eszencia is made from the treacle-like liquid which oozes out of the Aszú grapes before they are crushed. It takes ages to ferment – we've heard of wines that only reach four per cent alcohol after three years.

Compared with the Tokajis from the Communist era, the modern wines, often made by foreign producers, have the same burnt apricot, marmalade and honey flavours, but are fresher and more concentrated, and fully deserve their place among the sweet wine elite. Traditionalists argue that this pure-fruited style is wrong and that the minerally, oxidised notes from double fermentation are more in keeping with older practices. As only a few tired wines exist from the happier times preceding the last political regime, it is impossible to say who is right.

Estates to look out for are Domaine Disznókö, Château Megyer, Oremus, Château Pajzos, The Royal Tokay Wine Company and István Szepsy. Vintages to watch for (noble rot only thrives in the better ones) are 1993, 1995 and newly released 1996, plus yet-to-be released 1998, 1999 and 2000 – 1993 and 1999 are by far the best.

INDIA

Until May 2002, the attractive Omar Khayyam sparkling wine from Château Indage was the extent of our exposure to Indian wine here in the UK. Grover Vineyards (established in 1988) is about to change all that. Up in the Nandi Hills near Bangalore, the Grover estate is on the same latitude as Barbados and Bangkok, sees two harvests a year (one sold off as table grapes) and yet makes wines worthy of investment from French consultant Michel Rolland and Champagne house Veuve Clicquot (each involved since the mid-1990s). Unsurprisingly, these wines are made to go with spicy foods, and in the UK they're aimed at Indian restaurants. They'll be a welcome addition: there's everything from a toasty, spicy Blanc de Blancs de Clairette sparkling wine, to a smooth-cherry Syrah rosé ('good with tandoors and kebabs') and a full-on Cabernet/Shiraz, black and concentrated, tasting of fruit dried in the sun. There are between 10 and 15 other wineries in India, and, unlike some of them, Grover does not buy in grapes from outside India but uses French grape varieties planted on its own 120 acres of vineyards. Here's new fuel for your Bollywood parties.

ISRAEL

Despite the fact that most of Israel is desert, under irrigation, it is as adept at producing quality wine as is neighbouring Lebanon. Indeed, many of the best wines are made in similar, high-elevation conditions less than 40 miles from the Bekaa Valley in Lebanon. Israeli wines are more 'New World' in style, where Lebanon's are heavily French-influenced. Lebanon has its serious reds, but Israel (its best wineries anyway) has a plethora of fruity Chardonnay, Sauvignon, Sangiovese and Merlot-type varietals (from higher, cooler sites, there are even Riesling and Gewurztraminer too). The best mid-sized wineries are Yarden, in the Golan Heights, Tishbi, Dalton and newcomer Recanati. Boutique-scale specialists to watch for are Margalit, Domaine du Castel near Jerusalem (improving Bordeaux-style wines), Soreq (single-vineyard Cabernet and Merlot) and Amphorae. Other names you might spot are Carmel and Barkan, makers of widely available kosher wines produced by flash-pasteurising (necessary to fulfil religious requirements), which makes them, to our palates anyway, undrinkable.

The top wines today are all made by winemakers who have qualified abroad, in Italy or Australia for example, and the international influence shows in the wines. One of the most exciting new projects, Galil Mountain, a joint venture between Yarden and Kibbutz Yiron in the Upper Galilee, is now bearing good fruit (and good wines) and reflects just the kind of new energy being seen all around the Mediterranean at the moment (not just in Israel, but in Greece, Morocco and Tunisia – none of these countries being associated with wine, but all of them investing heavily and battling the odds). The wines of Galil Mountain, being from a peaks, streams and mountainside area (this is new territory in terms of Israeli vineyards), turn out very differently from those from the Golan plateau or the desert flats of the south, and although it's early days yet (the first wines are just reaching the UK markets), the Merlot in particular is outstanding, with Cabernet hot on its heels. (The added advantage of this site over the Golan Heights is that the vineyards are less likely to revert to Syrian control . . .)

There are, in fact, new vineyards opening up all over Israel. Planting of quality rootstock has doubled over the last few years, firstly because more people are getting into wine and, secondly, because grapes are being seen as more successful than other fruit (dates or oranges, for example). The third factor clinches the deal: grapes need less water than other crops, and water in the Israeli desert is expensive. Ever the optimists, we think these new plantings will eventually go some way towards improving the rather 'tired' kosher brands, and will also inspire other new wineries to follow Yarden, Domaine du Castel and Galil Mountain's footsteps. Let's hope so.

ITALY

Italian wine is a bit of a battle-ground these days. Administrators are busy laying down laws; growers are busy ignoring them. A number of producers are planting as many French varieties as they can lay their hands on; others are busy denouncing them and promoting Italy's own. The new oak versus old chestnut *botti* (casks) debate still rages on in the cellars. In the grape world, underling Barbera is making a challenge to Nebbiolo's throne in the north. Plus, there are threats to shoot down the flying winemakers in the south. There are no definites, it seems. Nothing is settled. But then this is Italy.

There's no doubt about it, this country's wines are still as much a challenge (for beginner and expert alike) as they ever were. But at least the question is no longer 'Can Italy produce a good wine?', as these days there is little doubt on that front. Yes, it can. Whatever your pocket or palate, Italy has a wine for you. For those reared on the classic regions of France, there are structured, ageworthy reds from Piedmont and the Veneto, plus increasingly impressive whites from the north-east. For those more accustomed to the exuberant fruit of the New World, the south of the country and Sicily present rich, juicy offerings. And in between there are the classic, savoury, tangy Chiantis from the Sangiovese grape. There are classy sparklers, reds ranging from delicate to distinctly burly, and whites of all sweetnesses. When it comes to the quality and sheer diversity of wines produced, only France can rival Italy.

The crucial question, this side of the millennium-change, is: 'Is Italy throwing away its heritage?' Two years ago we commented that we were relieved Italy could grow Merlot and Cabernet Sauvignon without letting them take over from the vast array of indigenous grapes. Superstar grape varieties in the making, such as Verdicchio and Negroamaro, seemed well on their way to shining success. But now we're not feeling quite so complacent. From the north – Friuli-Venezia-Giulia and Trentino-Alto Adige – it's almost assumed that white wines will be Sauvignons or Pinot Gris (Pinot Grigios), and not a thought is cast to Cortese, peachy Arneis (even the Australians are growing some of this grape) and Garganega, all of which, given the attention they deserve, can make deliciously characterful concentrated wine. In central Italy – Tuscany – Merlot, Cabernet and even Syrah are snapping at the heels of Sangiovese to such an extent that Chianti has changed its DOC rules (see below), giving more encouragement to keep these grapes out (100-per-cent

Sangiovese is now permitted). This is to say little of those Tuscan outsiders, Brunello and Sagrantino: the one promoted beyond its means, the other not acknowledged at all.

But the real crimes happen in the south. More progressive growers might have latched on to the fact that Primitivo is now widely acknowledged as being, more than likely, the same grape as California's Zinfandel, but too many of them are seizing the opportunity to undercut their American cousins and are churning this wine out at £3.99 rather than showing what's possible in terms of quality. Yes, it might be great news to see diseased old vineyards being grubbed up, but why (as is almost universally happening) replace the old vines with more Merlot? The world doesn't need it. Our advice to the consumer is to look out for the Nero d'Avola, Aglianico and Greco varieties – not to mention the richly perfumed Vermentino whites from Sicily.

There are also two 'in' M-words to watch out for in terms of modern Italy. One, 'Maremma', refers to the coastal region of Tuscany, which includes snazzy appellations such as Bolgheri, Scansano and Val di Cornia. Our money's on this region for producing the country's next great reds – which in fact it is already doing, so keep your eyes peeled for bargains before it gets too

The Leaning Tavola of Pisa

fashionable. (We've included an extra handful of Maremma producers in the listings below.) The other is 'Mezzogiorno', which refers collectively to the southern areas of Puglia, Basilicata, Campania and Calabria (making up the heel and toe of Italy's boot), plus the islands Sicily and Sardinia. The pace of life might be slower here, but don't let anyone pull the wool over your eyes; this is the scene of great things yet to happen.

One last thing. According to a number of merchants who specialise in Italian wine (and as we said last year, there are more and more of them now), Germany, Japan and America are virtually biting Italian arms off to get hold of some of the Maremma and Mezzogiorno wines we've been talking about, but in the UK they don't seem to sell. Why is this? The complaint from the UK trade is that Britons aren't reading enough about Italy; they want easy answers, everything set out for them. We're renowned for being a sophisticated market in the UK, but consumers are turning that into a myth. It's time we got more experimental.

The Italian wine classification system

Italian wines are classified into four categories, the lowest of which is *vino da tavola* (VdT). Prior to 1996, many producers, especially those in Tuscany, chose to bypass the more rigid constraints of DOC and DOCG (see below) and release their top wines as *vini da tavola*. However, since 1996, a VdT can carry neither region of origin, nor grape variety, nor vintage (or at least that's the law – a few producers still choose to ignore it).

Today, most of the Super-Tuscans (as these wines from Tuscany became known) and the other top *vini da tavola* belong to a new category called *indicazione geografica tipica* (IGT), although some now qualify for DOC or DOCG status. IGT is the equivalent of French *vin de pays*, in that certain restrictions about grape varieties and production methods are required. As with *vin de pays*, quality varies from the basic to the sublime. For DOC (*denominazione di origine controllata*) wines, the regulations are more stringent, although this doesn't stop many dull wines receiving such a status. DOCG adds a '*garantita*', and quality is in general higher for these wines. However, with some – Vernaccia di San Gimignano, Albana di Romagna and Asti, for example – the *garantita* is certainly not a guarantee of a high-class wine.

Tuscany and Piedmont vintage guide

Tuscany and Piedmont are the regions where it is most important to follow the vintages. Not that other areas are immune to the effects of the weather, it is just that the likelihood of their wines being kept for any length of time is rather lower. Indeed, we would recommend that you drink up light Italian whites, and all but the best of the soft, fruity reds of the south, soon after purchase.

In Tuscany, 2001 looked to be a troublesome vintage from the start, with frost cutting yields by up to 40 per cent. A hot, dry summer helped the situation, but a cool and rainy autumn made harvest difficult: choose your grower with care. 2000 was another fine vintage, with warm weather throughout the season making for an early harvest. Most grapes were picked before rain came in October, and quality is generally high. 1999 was potentially even better, although work in the vineyards was necessary to reduce yields. The best reds have the structure of 1998 and the plump fruit of 1997. The 1998s are quite firm and lack the opulence of the vintages either side, but the best should age well and could surprise some critics. In 1997 it was very hot and sunny, and several splendidly ripe, fleshy wines with low acidity were produced. 1996 was more patchy, with some fair Chianti but other reds not quite up to scratch. The 1995 vintage was good, although low in quantity. As for older Tuscan vintages, look out for the great wines of 1988 and 1990, followed in rough order of merit by 1993, 1991, 1994, 1989 and 1992.

With frost at the outset, signs were similarly poor for Piedmont's 2001 vintage (not helped by hail and drought through the summer and a damp September), but later-ripening local varieties – particularly Nebbiolo – benefited from the slow ripening bestowed by an Indian summer. Reds will be similar but fruitier than the 2000s. Fine conditions in spring and summer made for an early 2000 vintage; rain fell in early October, but well-tended vineyards had already been picked by then and the reds should be splendid. 1999 yields were as heavy as in Tuscany, and high August humidity in many vineyards may have caused some problems with rot. Even so, there is optimism about the quality. Rain towards the end of harvest caused problems in 1998 but, while some reds are on the light side, the growers who had already picked most of their grapes before the worst of the weather have made excellent wines. 1997 brought very hot weather and very ripe grapes – wines made from fruit grown in cooler sites will keep best as the acidity will be higher. Still, this year was a fine one. 1996 was an excellent year for Barolo, in particular. The older vintages to look out for are 1988, 1989 and 1990. 1993 also produced reasonable wines although it suffered from autumn rain.

THE REGIONS
The north-west – Piedmont, Lombardy

Piedmont is Italy's most mysterious and fascinating wine region.
The softly sloping, fog-cloaked curves of the Langhe hills near Alba
in Piedmont are home to Italy's most majestic and long-lived wines,
Barolo and Barbaresco. Both of these graceful, perfumed giants are
made from the Nebbiolo grape, and have high tannin and acidity
levels, which can jar on palates trained on soft New World wines.
But persevere. These wines evolve from young, treacly brooders to
headily scented and surprisingly delicate, complex concoctions with
a dazzling array of flavours – plums, raspberries, chocolate, tar,
roses, game and more. Styles vary from modern, fruity-oaky wines
to the rather challenging and old-fashioned, with more than a whiff
of volatility. Choose your producer with care, as quality, price and
character of the wine vary enormously.

The Nebbiolo is used for an easier-drinking red from Roero
in Alba, designed to be consumed in its youth, and also for the
Nebbiolo Langhe DOC, which covers everything from light and
friendly to really rather classy. The Nebbiolo-based reds Carema,
Gattinara, Ghemme and Spanna are more easily approached than
their sophisticated cousins in the Langhe, but quality from these
DOC and DOCGs is distinctly unreliable.

When Nebbiolo is blended, its partner is usually the plump,
plummy Barbera, and these wines can be immensely satisfying –
Nebbiolo without the mountaineering. Barbera by itself has
traditionally played second fiddle to Nebbiolo, being used for
simple, fresh, everyday gluggers. However, a number of producers
now award it more respect by planting it on the better sites, cutting
the yields, vinifying it with care and dressing it in a new oak
overcoat. The results can be stunning.

Dolcetto, 'the little sweet one', is the third grape of Piedmont. It
has traditionally behaved as the Gamay of Piedmont, producing
fresh, bracing, cherryish reds for everyday drinking. But, as with
Barbera, a few producers are now giving Dolcetto a makeover and
producing chewy, chocolaty reds of some class.

White varieties play very much a secondary role in Piedmont,
but a few are worth seeking out. Gavi DOCG is a rather neutral,
acidic wine made from Cortese, which commands a price rather
higher than its quality often merits (at best these whites have a
lime-cordial flavour). The nutty, soft whites produced from
Favorita grapes are better value, while the fuller, peachier wines
(not unlike top-class Viognier) made in Roero and Langhe, from
Arneis, are of far better quality. Some modern, fruity Chardonnays
are also made in the region. And then of course there is the fresh,
grapey Asti (the 'Spumante' bit was dropped in 1994). It's one of

the few sparkling wines we'd recommend with wedding cake, but most people are too snobbish to serve it on such occasions. If Asti is just too naff for you, try the more refined, subtle, perfumed Moscato d'Asti.

Lombardy's best wines are also sparklers, namely those of Franciacorta, which are made by the *méthode champenoise*, from the traditional champagne grapes (plus Pinot Bianco), and rank among Italy's finest. Still wines are less successful, although a few producers are making decent reds (from Cabernet Sauvignon and Cabernet Franc) and whites (mainly from Chardonnay) under the Terre de Franciacorta DOC. And finally, Lugana, from along the shores of Lake Garda, is one of the rare wines made from Trebbiano that has a little personality and elegance.

Pick of the producers (Piedmont, Lombardy)
Altare Master winemaker and leading modernist of Barolo, with full, rich Nebbiolo wines.

Araldica/Alasia Large Piedmont co-operative on the up, producing a modern, lively range, widely available in the UK at reasonable prices. Also watch out for top *cuvées* single-vineyard Poderia Alasia and Barbera Rive.

Braida/Giacomo Bologna Barbera specialist with a trio of very good, single-vineyard wines that are able to command Barolo-level prices. Also a partner in the Serra di Fiore winery, source of some of Piedmont's best whites.

Ca' del Bosco Lombardy estate making great Franciacorta fizz and fine still wines, including Bordeaux-style blend Maurizio Zanella and new Carmenero, made from Carmenère.

Domenico Clerico Star producer making well-crafted Barolo, rich, ripe Dolcetto and sweet, spicy Arte (Nebbiolo plus 15-per-cent Barbera and Cabernet Sauvignon).

Aldo Conterno Master of Barolo, with top *cuvée* Gran Bussia being a real winner. The *barrique*-aged Il Favot, a Langhe Nebbiolo, is a fine and affordable introduction to the range.

Giacomo Conterno Powerful, traditional Barolo from Aldo's brother.

Fontanafredda Sleeping giant with excellent vineyard holdings, now back on track thanks to new management. Wines such as the Papagena Barbera d'Alba augur well for the future.

Gaja Influential producer who demonstrates that Nebbiolo can be internationally appealing without sacrificing its character. Highlights of an impeccable (but expensive) range are Sorí San Lorenzo, Sorí Tildin, Costa Russi and Sperss, the first three are single-vineyard wines. Has now dropped use of the names Barbaresco and Barolo, and 'downgraded' wines to DOC Langhe Rosso to accommodate the percentage of 'other varieties' in his blends. (Gaja also has Tuscan ventures – see 'Tuscany', below.)

Bruno Giacosa Quality is high across the range of Barolo, Barbaresco, Dolcetto, Barbera and Arneis from this traditional, top Piedmont producer.

Giuseppe Mascarello Admirable 'old-school' Piedmont reds – intense Barbaresco, Dolcetto and, of course, Barolo. The top Barolo, Monprivato, is deeply complex.

Oberto Highlights of an excellent, if traditional, range are the firm-but-fruity Barolo Vigneto Roche and the supple Nebbiolo/Barbera blend Fabio.

Prunotto Antinori-owned winery making grand Barolo Bussia and fine Barberas, especially Pian Romualdo. Occhetti Nebbiolo d'Alba is a good introduction to the range.

Bruno Rocca Barbaresco maestro, with two first-class but different *cuvées*, Rabaja and Coparossa. Chardonnay, Dolcetto and Barbera are also good.

Paolo Scavino The sumptuous, fragrant Bric del Fiasc and Canobric are among the finest modern Barolos, while the Barbera and Dolcetto also impress.

La Spinetta Superb throaty Barbaresco, equally fine Nebbiolo/Barbera/Cabernet blend Pin, delicious Barbera and Moscato, plus a new Barolo venture to watch out for.

Gianni Voerzio Older brother of Roberto (below), producing outstanding Barolo, etc. in a similar style but lower in price.

Roberto Voerzio Modern Piedmont wines, brimming with fruit and new oak. Barbera, Dolcetto and Chardonnay all excel, but the Barolos, especially Brunate and Cerequio, are the stars.

The north-east – Friuli-Venezia-Giulia, Trentino-Alto Adige, Veneto

Throughout most of Italy's wine regions, reds outshine whites. The north-east, however, bucks this trend, with its fresh, zesty whites being somewhat more serious than its light, quaffable reds. The best whites can be found in Friuli-Venezia-Giulia, at the eastern edge of Italy on the Slovenian border, and in Trentino-Alto Adige, in the mountainous, German-speaking Südtirol. Friuli is the most highly respected region in Italy for single-varietal whites, and its fresh, pure Tocai Friulano, Pinot Grigio, Pinot Bianco and Sauvignon Blanc can be delicious (if sometimes pricy) particularly from the DOCs of Collio, Colli Orientali del Friuli (COF) and Friuli Isonzo. Reds are mainly soft, juicy Bordeaux blends, although there is a resurgence in popularity for the nutty, plummy Refosco grape.

Trentino-Alto Adige produces a wide range of whites, some from the German grape varieties Riesling, Gewürztraminer and Müller-Thurgau. Try Pinot Grigio and Chardonnay from the far north too – the German-influenced style is racy and crisp, lean and lemony. Here, as in Friuli, a small but significant band of producers is beginning to blend varieties to achieve extra complexity. Reds, again, are not terribly serious, but do try the local Teroldego Rotaliano, a deeply coloured, currant-packed and slightly bitter wine. Lagrein, another local grape, makes some excellent red wine and fair *rosato*, but you'll probably have to go there to find them.

Trebbiano vines growing on fertile plains provide the region near Verona with plenty of dull white wines, exemplified by the vast majority of Soave. Don't despair entirely of this wine, as top growers (Pieropan, Anselmi, Inama) make a fresh, salty, appley version that's far from unpleasant – but avoid those that are trying to boost its lack of character with oak. The best wineries bypass the Trebbiano altogether and instead squeeze much more character out of the native Garganega grape to produce a soft, lemon-and-almond-oil-flavoured white. If you are looking for something cheap, the crisp, sherbety Bianco di Custoza is often a better bet. If you're after something sparkling, try the famous Venetian fizz Prosecco, from the hills around Treviso – a light and, again, sherbety wine that is made both sweet and dry. The best are known as Superiore di Cartizze.

The Veneto's most popular red is Valpolicella, which, like Soave, ranges from delicious to dire (the same is true of its close relative, the lighter Bardolino). Good examples are friendly reds with lively, cherry fruit, designed to be drunk in their youth, while better versions – where yields are lower, and the percentage of the region's best grape, Corvina, is higher – have more muscle and don't mind another three to four years in bottle.

More complex are the rich Amarone (dry and bitter) and Recioto (sweet) – late-harvest specialities made from grapes that have been dried before pressing to render them extra-concentrated. Recioto di Soave is the same idea applied to a white grape. All Recioto and Amarone wines are higher in alcohol than ordinary table wines – and they can be expensive too. It's worth trying them as they thoroughly deserve their Italian description, *vini di meditazione* – buy a bottle and work out the translation for yourself. A halfway house between regular Valpolicella and Recioto/Amarone is the *ripasso* style, in which a young wine is passed over the detritus left after a Recioto/Amarone fermentation, and in the process acquires extra character and alcohol.

Pick of the producers (Friuli-Venezia-Giulia, Trentino-Alto Adige, Veneto)

Allegrini The top producer of single-vineyard Valpolicella, or IGT Veneto, as it is now labelled; also fine Amarone and Recioto, plus 100-per-cent oak-aged Corvina La Poja.

Anselmi Fine range of IGT Veneto whites, which came under the Soave Classico classification until Roberto Anselmi withdrew them in protest about abuse of the DOC regulations. Some wines are barrel-fermented; also a toothsome, sweet Recioto called I Capitelli.

Tommaso Bussola Small newcomer grower for top-quality, highly acclaimed Valpolicellas.

Ca' dei Frati Delicious, lemony, nutty Lugana and Il Brolettino, an excellent, oak-aged *cuvée*; both from nearby Lake Garda.

Cesconi Trentino brothers Alessandro, Franco, Roberto and Lorenzo are revolutionising white wine production with top-of-the-league *cuvées* from international varieties. Includes superb barrel-aged Pinot Grigio and, now, new reds too.

Romano Dal Forno Pack leader and ultra-modernist making the very best Valpolicellas with huge attention to detail. Hard-to-find wines.

Livio Felluga Whites that are slow to reveal their true colours, but which are as rich and concentrated as any in Friuli; also spicy, fruity Refosco.

Roberto Felluga Delicious varietal Cabernet Franc from thirteenth-century Friuli estate. Roberto is brother to Livio, above.

Gini Brothers Claudio and Sandro base their reputation on superb unoaked Soave; they produce a refreshing Chardonnay too.

Josko Gravner Maker of superb Friuli Chardonnay.

Franz Haas Elegant, concentrated and fruity wines from Alto Adige.

Inama Superb, single-vineyard Soave and decent, modern Chardonnay.

Silvio Jermann Expensive, often brilliant, but sometimes rather pretentious range. Vintage Tunina is a juicy, white blend of five different grapes, while toasty, barrel-fermented Chardonnay is now labelled 'Were Dreams, now it is just wine'.

Lageder Progressive Alto Adige winery turning out excellent but pricy Cabernet and Chardonnay. The more affordable Lagrein and Pinot Grigio are worth seeking out.

Maculan Superb range from Breganze in the Veneto. Maculan's luscious Acininobili and Torcolato are two of the country's great sweet wines, but the two Cabernets, labelled rather confusingly Fratta and Ferrata, are also great successes.

Masi First-rate Valpolicella Classico, Amarone and Recioto. Specialises in the *ripasso* style.

Pieropan Anyone bored with dull, dilute Soave should take a look at Pieropan's intensely ripe lemony examples, made from low-yielding vines.

Pojer e Sandri Mountainside Trentino range of elegant, international white grape wines and Pinot Noir to watch.

Quintarelli Maverick producer (arch-traditionalist) using old-fashioned methods to craft intense and pricy Recioto, Amarone and Valpolicella. There's also a rare Amarone-style Cabernet.

San Leonardo Alto Adige estate making superb, Sassicaia-like reds from Bordeaux varietals, Cabernets Sauvignon and Franc, and Merlot.

Mario Schiopetto Pure, clean whites from Collio and COF, with Sauvignon and Pinot Bianco being especially successful.

Fratelli Tedeschi Superior range from the Veneto, including Amarone, Recioto and Soave.

Tiefenbrunner Large and versatile Alto Adige producer for excellent Cabernet, Lagrein, Pinots Grigio and Bianco, Riesling and Chardonnay.

Villa Russiz Superb range of powerful aromatic Collio whites, plus a rather good Merlot.

The north-central – Emilia-Romagna

Emilia-Romagna is the broad swathe of land that stretches almost right across Italy, just below the Po river. This is the land of Parma ham, Parmesan cheese, Bolognese sauce and balsamic vinegar, so it sounds as though the region should make a plentiful supply of easy-drinking wine to wash it all down. And it does, in the shape of Lambrusco – typically not the sweet, sickly stuff exported to the UK but a local, dry version, which is frothy, tart and a fitting match for the rich regional food. Co-operatives dominate its production; there are few boutique wineries here.

Otherwise, the rather ordinary white Albana di Romagna is an undeserving recipient of DOCG status, although the sweeter *passito* versions can be delicious. More noteworthy are red wines Sangiovese di Romagna – the best versions of which can stand their ground alongside more expensive Chiantis – and Barbera/Bonarda blends, emerging from the Colli Piacentini DOC in the north-west.

Central Italy – Tuscany

For all Nebbiolo's intensity and complexity, Sangiovese remains the red grape that most outsiders associate with Italian wine. It may be more widely planted in Emilia-Romagna, but most people think of Tuscany as its spiritual home. Some of Italy's finest and most famous reds come from the hilly countryside to the south and east of Florence, and although only two wines have to be 100-per-cent Sangiovese – Brunello di Montalcino and its less serious, younger brother Rosso di Montalcino – this grape lies at the heart of all the finest DOC and DOCG wines.

Chianti is the best-known wine but can be somewhat confusing to the novice. The wines, a blend of Sangiovese with Canaiolo and other grapes (both white and red), range from examples so dilute they could almost pass for rosé, to full-bodied wines similar in structure and ageing potential to claret. What most Chiantis have in common is a distinctive tea-leaf and herb note, plus the juicy cherry-meets-strawberry fruit of Sangiovese. The region has seven sub-zones, the best of which are Classico and Rufina. Since 1996, Sangiovese-only wines can be labelled Chianti Classico – something that less law-abiding producers have been doing for a number of years.

Brunello di Montalcino is also well known outside Italy and commands a higher price than many Chiantis. It can range from one of Tuscany's most memorable experiences to one of the most disappointing, the latter usually a result of excessive oak ageing. Many producers choose to sell their wines as Rosso di Montalcino, which can be sold a year after vintage rather than after four years (five for *riserva*), two of them in barrel, which is the law for Brunello. Vino Nobile di Montepulciano (not connected with the Montepulciano grape of the Marches and Abruzzi) can be a decent halfway house between Chianti and Brunello, although it is not the most reliable of wines. Parrina is similar to a medium-bodied Chianti, with a herbal or minty hint, while the rarely seen Morellino di Scansano is beefier and more rustic.

Cabernet Sauvignon is becoming increasingly important in Tuscany. Sometimes it is blended with Sangiovese, as witnessed in the up-and-coming appellations of Carmignano and Pomino and in numerous IGT (or 'Super-Tuscan') wines made outside the normal DOCG regulations. Sometimes it appears with Bordeaux bedfellows Merlot and Cabernet Franc, again often under an IGT label. Some of the best Cabernet blends are made in the coastal Maremma region, under DOCs Bolgheri (home of Sassicaia and Ornellaia), Montescudaio, Val di Cornia, Scansano, Parrina, Montecucco and Massa Marittima. Merlot by itself is as erratic as it is anywhere in the world, but the best, such as Ornellaia's Masseto, give top Pomerol a run for its money. Syrah is not yet as popular but there are some delicious examples emerging.

As for whites, few exist that can compete with the reds of the region. Vernaccia di San Gimignano DOCG is a pleasant white with lean, limey flavours. Ornellaia makes a decent Sauvignon called Poggio alle Gazze, while several wineries listed below have risen to the challenge of creating successful Chardonnay. Tuscany's most intriguing white is still *vin santo*, the 'holy wine', a *passito* sweetie made from white grapes left to shrivel and dry before being squeezed of their concentrated syrup. The best are sweet (but not as sweet as many dessert wines) and strong, with flavours of nut oil and tart citrus peel.

Pick of the producers (Tuscany)

Altesino Smooth Brunello di Montalcino, pleasant Rosso and a relatively inexpensive Cabernet/Sangiovese blend, Alte d'Altesi.

Antinori Pioneering company, greatly influential in its use of Cabernet Sauvignon to create the Super-Tuscans Tignanello (Sangiovese/Cabernet Sauvignon) and Solaia (Cabernet Sauvignon), but also with fine Chiantis and, from the 1995 vintage, a Brunello from the Pian delle Vigne estate.

Avignonesi Upmarket Vino Nobile di Montepulciano and Super-Tuscan, Cabernet-dominated Grifi, plus admirable Merlot, Chardonnay and *vin santo*.

Badia a Coltibuono Rich, long-lived reds, especially 100-per-cent Sangiovese Sangioveto, made at a historic Chianti Classico abbey estate.

Banfi Huge estate just outside Montalcino, built with money made from exporting Lambrusco to the USA. Wide range of decent wine, especially Brunello and Chardonnay.

Biondi-Santi Original producer of Brunello di Montalcino and responsible for its DOCG status. Traditionally rather old fashioned (and very pricy); more recent vintages, while sturdy, have shown much more fruit. Also good wines from sister estates Poggio Salvi (Brunello) and Castello di Montepo (Morellino).

Capezzana Historic Tuscan estate which almost single-handedly created DOCG Carmignano with its trail-blazing Cabernet and Sangiovese blends.

Castellare Chianti Classico estate best known for its excellent Super-Tuscan I Sodi di San Niccolò – Sangiovese with a touch of Malvasia Nera. Recently announced new joint venture on the Tuscan coast with owners of Château Lafite.

Castello di Ama Having dabbled in Super-Tuscans, Laura Sebasti and viticulturalist husband Marco Pallanti are now shifting their emphasis back to quality Chianti Classicos.

Castello di Brolio Chianti Classico of depth and majesty – the 1997 is a stunner – plus impressive if a little 'international' Sangiovese/ Merlot blend Casalferro. The regular Brolio Chianti Classico is no slouch either.

Castello di Fonterutoli Another fine Chianti Classico estate, which also makes the juicy but powerful Sangiovese/Merlot blend Siepi.

Castello dei Rampolla Now on cracking form after a shaky patch with Tuscan reds, both with the fulsome, easy-drinking Chianti Classico and the stunning Sammarco *vino da tavola*, a Cabernet/Sangiovese blend.

Costanti Historic Montalcino estate owned by Andrea Costanti, now making modern-style, structured Brunellos and a spicy Cabernet/Merlot blend.

Felsina A name to seek out: lovely I Sistri Chardonnay; great, barrel-aged Sangiovese Super-Tuscan Fontalloro; and (the main event) rich Chianti Classico.

Fontodi Delicious 100-per-cent Sangiovese Flaccianello della Pieve and fine Chianti Classico. Look out too for the Syrah.

Frescobaldi Aristocratic family of Chianti producers with an ancient estate in Rufina. Classy wines, especially the Chianti Riservas and Cabernet-based Mormoreto; also a leading producer of red and white Pomino. (See also *Luce* and *Ornellaia*, below, for joint ventures with the Mondavi family.)

Gaja Angelo Gaja has two Tuscan estates, one at Montalcino (Pieve Santa Restituta where he focuses on sumptuous Brunellos Rennina and Sugarille, from Sangiovese grapes), and another at Bolgheri (Cà Marcanda, for purely French grapes – Cabernets Franc and Sauvignon, Syrah and Merlot – which will be blended into top wine Magari and an affordable wine named after the estate).

Isole e Olena Great Tuscan range including top-notch Chianti Classico, Cepparello (Sangiovese) and an excellent, rich Chardonnay. Constantly upgrading: Cabernet and Syrah in the wings.

Luce Joint venture in Montalcino between Frescobaldi and the Robert Mondavi Winery of California to make classy, if pricy, Sangiovese/Merlot blend. Second wine Lucente is also good but still expensive.

Le Macchiole Another of Tuscany's maverick coastal producers (from Bolgheri), with not only striking reds but also by far the best white wine of the region – a blend of Sauvignon, Chardonnay and Vermentino.

Monte Vertine Once revolutionary, now traditional estate, best known for 100-per-cent Sangiovese Pergole Torte, one of the most uncompromising Tuscan reds.

Ornellaia Top-class Bolgheri winery sold by Antinori, and now owned by California's Mondavi and the Frescobaldi family. Ornellaia is a fulsome, classy Bordeaux blend, while Masseto is arguably Italy's best Merlot, with a price to match. New wine (from the 1997 vintage) Serre Nuove is a good, earthy, cheaper substitute, while Le Volte is even more approachable and immediately gluggable. Sauvignon Blanc (Poggio alle Gazze) is crisp and lean.

Poggio Scalette Pure Sangiovese wines sold as IGT ('Super-Tuscans') even though full DOCG Chianti Classico would now be permitted – this way they can charge more!

Poggio di Sotto Producer of excellent Brunello di Montalcino Palmucci.

Poggiopiano Up-and-coming Chianti Classico producer, also with fine Super-Tuscan Rosso di Sera.

Poliziano Arguably the finest producer of Vino Nobile di Montepulciano, also excelling with Sangiovese/Cabernet Sauvignon blend Elegia and 100-per-cent Cabernet Le Stanze.

Le Pupille Star of the southern Maremma (coastal Tuscany), with emphasis on lush Cabernet and Merlot blends.

Querciabella Chianti Classico and *vino da tavola* Camartina in the fruity, modern style.

Riecine Highly structured, long-lived Chianti Classico and Sangiovese Super-Tuscan La Gioia.

San Felice Top Chianti Classico from original author of the Sangiovese-only style; Super-Tuscan blends include 40-per-cent Cabernet Sauvignon.

Sassicaia This remarkable estate, near Bolgheri on the Tuscan coast, is home to probably the most famous of the Super-Tuscans. The blend of Cabernet Sauvignon and Cabernet Franc was first developed by the Marchese Incisa della Rochetta, and Antinori now markets the wine. Deeply sophisticated, world-beating red, which since 1994 has had its own DOC, Bolgheri de Sassicaia.

Selvapiana The leading Chianti Rufina estate, with a particularly impressive *riserva* called Bucerchiale.

Tenuta del Terriccio Fine range of IGT Toscano includes rich, peachy Rondinaia (Chardonnay/Sauvignon), densely structured Lupicaia (Cabernet Sauvignon/Merlot) and fragrant, juicy Tassinaia (Cabernet Sauvignon/Merlot/Sangiovese).

Tenuta de Trinoro A newcomer to the Tuscan 'claret scene', making tasty big Bordeaux blends from Cabernet *et al*.

Tua Rita Enterprising couple Rita Tua and Virgilio Bisti use Cabernet, Merlot and Syrah as well as Sangiovese for their much-admired coastal Super-Tuscan range.

Villa Cafaggio Top Chianti Classico and stunning Super-Tuscan pure Cabernets, from half-Hungarian grower Stefano Farkas. Also interesting experiments with different Sangiovese clones.

Villa di Vetrice Fairly large estate for good and affordable Chianti Classico, easy to find in the UK.

Zerbina Top winery in Emilia-Romagna, making substantial Sangiovese di Romagna, dense, cherryish Marzieno (Sangiovese/ Cabernet) and luscious Albana di Romagna Passito Scacco Matto.

Central Italy – Umbria, Abruzzo, Lazio

Each of these regions is responsible for an ocean of dull white wine. Orvieto comes from Umbria, where it dominates the local wine industry. More adventurous drinkers should instead look out for finer whites from Antinori's Castello della Salla project in the region. Other interesting Umbrian wines include the red Torgiano from Lungarotti, particularly the Rubesco Riserva made from Sangiovese and Cannaiolo, and the Amarone-like Sagrantino di Montefalco from Sagrantino.

   The whites of Abruzzo are made predominantly from the uninspiring Trebbiano grape, so more yawns there. More exciting is the juicy red Montepulciano d'Abruzzo, pizza wine *par excellence* (no mean feat, that). Look out for the following Abruzzo producers, of whom we'll be seeing more and more on our shop shelves over the next few years: Illuminati, Masciarelli and Rocco Pasetti. The neighbouring province of Marches also uses Montepulciano in Rosso Conero, where it can be blended with Sangiovese. And bringing blessed relief after an excess of Trebbiano is Verdicchio, also found in the Marches and improving by leaps and bounds. Verdicchio is currently held responsible for producing Italy's best white wines: the zesty yet creamy wines of Verdicchio dei Castelli di Jesi. The following are producers to watch out for: Garofoli, La Vite and Coroncino.

Lazio's vinous claim to fame is Frascati, made mainly from Trebbiano and Malvasia and, as if you didn't know it already, all too often lacking in character (Castel de Paolis is an honourable exception, as are some others that have added Viognier – a grape which seems to thrive locally). The other notable white – famous for its name rather than its quality, although wines have improved of late – is Est! Est!! Est!!! di Montefiascone. The admirable Falesco shows what can be achieved with a little effort in both the red and white departments.

Pick of the producers (Umbria, Abruzzo, Lazio)
Antinori Whites from Umbria under the Castello della Sala label are excellent, especially the fine Chardonnay called Cervaro.

Bigi A rare Orvieto producer – one managing to inject some character into its wine.

Arnaldo Caprai Hot-shot producer of new-trend Sagrantino di Montefalco (DOCG since 1999). Strong, tannic red wines with richness of mouthfeel; also flavourful Grechetto whites.

Castel de Paolis Super-estate that catapults Frascati into fine wine territory. Top *cuvée* is Vigna Adriana, made from Malvasia and Viognier. Also good reds based on Syrah, including firm-but-fruity Syrah/Merlot blend I Quattro Mori.

Falesco Lazio star owned by famous consultant winemaker Riccardo Cotarella, best known for sexy, spicy Montiano (100-per-cent Merlot). Also the best Est! Est!! Est!!! in the form of the Poggio dei Gelso Vendemmia Tardiva, plus smooth peaches-and-cream Ferentano made from the local Roscetto grape.

Lungarotti Formerly the leading light of Umbria's Torgiano, which put the DOC on the map using Sangiovese and Cabernet for a wide range of high-quality varietals and blends. Now fading slightly.

La Monacesca Marches estate for tasty Verdicchio, Chardonnay and Sauvignon whites – especially Matelica, a blend of all three.

Umani Ronchi Large, reliable range including rounded, nutty Casal di Serra Verdicchio; white, silky 100-per-cent Montepulciano Cumaro; and superb Montepulciano/Cabernet/Merlot blend Pelago.

Valentini Montepulciano and Trebbiano d'Abruzzo of real class, both of which age magnificently.

The South

As is the case in much of southern Europe, the south of Italy is enjoying something of a mini wine boom. Alongside local growers, top producers from the north – the likes of Antinori and Avignonesi – are moving in and changing the shape of things. Wine drinkers all around the world, as a result, are getting to know the fascinating local grape varieties. The best of these are Negroamaro, with its bitter chocolate and cherry flavours, and Primitivo, thought to be genetically the same (although a few disputes linger on) as California's Zinfandel. Tread carefully though, as many cheaper 'international' blends are being made, from the usual Cabernet/Merlot varieties and with a lot less imagination. Puglia is perhaps the best source of good everyday reds, with modern, fruity wines often under the IGT Puglia, together with more leathery, raisiny offerings from the DOCs of Salice Salentino, Copertino and Squinzano.

Campania boasts two whites of interest, the dry, fruity Greco di Tufo and the concentrated, nutty Fiano d'Avellino, which ages well; other varieties to watch for are Falanghina, Coda di Volpe, Biancolella and Forastera. For reds, Taurasi, made from Aglianico, can be very good, but the grape reaches its apogee in Aglianico del Vulture, which, from a top producer such as d'Angelo, is one of Italy's best-kept secrets.

Calabria's only wine of note is Cirò, which comes in red, pink and white and is made on the eastern Ionian coast of the region from the local Gaglioppo grape. Quality is not a strong point, although the reds from Librandi are very respectable.

Pick of the producers (the South)

A Mano Promessa Excellent, modern wines from Mark Shannon, with the Primitivo a dead ringer for a fine Zinfandel from his native California.

Candido Smooth, herbal-scented reds mainly made from Negroamaro in Salice Salentino. Relative bargains; whites are less impressive than reds.

Feudi di San Gregorio The current star of Campania, offering high-class modern Taurasi as well as some of southern Italy's best whites.

Librandi Top exponent of the light red Cirò Rosso, made from the Gaglioppo grape in Calabria.

Masseria Monaci Property of top consultant winemaker Severino Garofano, who oversees production at some of the region's finest estates – Taurino among them.

Mastroberardino The best-known estate of Campania has, since a recent family split, retained the name and the winery but lost the vineyards to Terredora (see below). Now acts as a *négociant*. Quality may take time to restore.

Montevetrano Campania estate now famed for its Cabernet, Merlot and Aglianico blend – acclaimed by Robert Parker and made by top Italian wine consultant Ricardo Cotarella. Tiny quantites; much in demand.

Taurino Delicious, smooth, fruity red from Salice Salentino.

Terredora The new name for the Mastroberardino vineyards (see above): still to be relied on for top-quality Greco di Tufo, Fiano d'Avellino and Taurasi.

Trulli Name used for wines made by the flying winemaker Kym Milne MW in conjunction with the local winemaker Agusto Càntele. All are commendable, with the refreshing, dry Muscat making a perfect aperitif.

The Islands

While progress has not been as rapid as on mainland Italy, Sardinia and Sicily both have their movers and shakers who can turn their hands to local and foreign varieties with aplomb. Sardinia offers the tangy but usually rather bland Nuragus de Cagliari and the rich, perfumed Vermentino, as well as reds made from Cannonau (Grenache), Carignano (Carignan) and Monica, which is believed to be of Spanish origin. Where yields are low, both Carignano del Sulcis and Cannonau di Sardegna can be wonderfully rich, robust wines.

Sicily is more dynamic than it has ever been, with wineries such as Regaleali, Planeta, Settesoli and Terre di Ginestra now leading the way with rich, fruity, modern wines. At Marsala, the local fortified wines are too often over-sweetened, but better versions from producers such as de Bartoli and Pellegrino still delight with their complexity and subtlety. Lastly, the island of Pantelleria, lying halfway between the mainland and Libya, offers a vinous speciality. Here Moscato grapes, known locally as Zibibbo, are used to make a honeyed, sweet *passito* wine. Grape varieties used successfully range from international stars Chardonnay and Syrah to locally produced Nero d'Avola and blends.

Pick of the producers (the Islands)
Accademia dei Racemi Top-quality Primitivo specialist.

Argiolas Fine range of Sardinian reds and whites, both dry and sweet, made from both famous and local grapes – ever heard of Bovaleddu? Top wine is sexy, oaky Turriga, a blend of Cannonau, Carignano, Sangiovese and Malvasia Nera.

Marco de Bartoli The best producer of Marsala; an ever-inventive, colourful local figure. Also makes the lovely Moscato Passito di Pantelleria, an unctuous dessert wine with hints of nut-oil and citrus peel.

Tenuta Capichera Sardinian producer of delicious, perfumed Vermentino wines (not cheap), labelled Vigna 'Ngena, Capichera and Vendemmia Tardiva (late harvest).

Duca di Salaparuta Corvo Rosso isn't terribly exciting, but the Duca Enrico blend is smashing, one of the best in Sicily. Cabernet and Chardonnay are good too.

Salvatore Murana Murana's Moscato and Passito di Pantelleria are world-class dessert wines, with the Martingana Passito being astonishingly complex.

Pellegrino Large-scale Marsala producer, especially for dry styles.

Planeta Sicily's star winery, whose first vintage was 1994. High quality across the range, but the top wine is the red Santa Cecilia, a robust blend of local grape Nero d'Avola with Shiraz.

Regaleali Highly respected Sicilian estate using local grape varieties for richly flavoured reds, the most famous of which is the full-bodied Rosso del Conte, a blend of local varieties. Also fine, if expensive, Chardonnay.

Sella & Mosca Sardinian perfectionist, producing good DOC Vermentino and exciting Marchese di Villamarina red blend. Also makes wine in France's Costières de Nîmes.

Cantina Sociale Santadi If you didn't think Carignan was capable of quality, try the Rocca Rubia *cuvée* from this first-class co-operative.

Cantina Sociale Settesoli Modern Sicilian wines. Look out, in particular, for the red Bonera and white Feudo dei Fiori, made from blends of local grapes. Mandrarossa is new premium range.

Terre di Ginestra Upfront, fresh Sicilian table wines.

LEBANON

We're all in favour of growers holding off the release of their wines until they are ready to drink. Just as with the Spanish laying down their Riojas before sale, we admire the fact that Chateau Musar's wines lie in Serge Hochar's cellars until he considers them *à point* – the 1997 Musar, for example, is still unreleased (and is quickly developing all the aged cedar and mushroom tones of an old claret). This stance is admirable as it 'takes the edge off' young reds which gain no favours by being drunk too early in their bony youth. But, in Chateau Musar's case, we wish the wines were being released *far* earlier, so that their youthful fruitiness could be appreciated, as it is in their first three years they show at their best.

Musar's classic Cabernet blend has long been synonymous with Lebanese winemaking, and has survived against horrific odds, with fruit being trucked across war-torn hills to its cellars north of Beirut. It is still, by far, the most widely available Lebanese wine in the UK, and still highly commendable; however, recent vintages have been a little too oxidised – the wines are beginning to taste old and tired a touch before their time. If Musar isn't careful, its place at the top of the Lebanese tree will be taken by its Bekaa Valley neighbours.

Doing better, in spite of the baking Mediterranean temperatures, are the new-wave producers we talked of last year. Chateau Kefraya's wines run the gamut from thick-textured, nutty, surprisingly good white Cuvée d'Aïda Sauvignon/Chardonnay/Viognier), through delicate rosé, to powerful blueberry-blackcurrant reds that could give Barossa Shiraz or top Chilean Merlot a run for its money. Clos St Thomas, established in 1994, also has impressive, ripe, structured reds. The best of all, Chateau Ksara, makes Cabernet blends that are a fabulous mix of spice, cedar and berries, need a fair bit of cellar time to soften and are a little more classic in style. Lastly there is Massaya, a partnership between a local businessman Sami Ghosn and three Frenchmen, Hubert du Boüard de Laforest (Château Angélus), Dominique Hébrard (ex-Cheval Blanc) and Daniel Brunier (Vieux Télégraphe). The wines (three reds, two whites, one rosé) are good rather than great, but we expect better things in the future.

And just a short word on Lebanese whites. These can be surprisingly good (for such a hot region) in Chardonnay form, but our passion is for the nutty Rhône-like whites from Obeideh and Merwah grapes (Chateau Musar's are excellent). Supple and smooth, but with an unusual salty, tangy flavour, these are some of the only white wines really up to following red – ideal for matching with a cheese course.

MEXICO

As predicted by the *Guide*, we're now seeing more and more
Mexican wine on UK shelves. Much of the country is too hot for
vines, but there are regions where altitude and proximity to the sea
provide good conditions for grape-growing. Most vineyards are on
the Baja California peninsula, which benefits from cooling coastal
currents, and top producers such as Château Camou, L A Cetto,
Casa de Piedra, Monte Xanic and Santo Tomás make wines that
improve with each vintage. Casa Madera from the Parras Valley in
Monterrey is another name to look out for. Cabernet Sauvignon
and Chardonnay are widespread, although other varieties such as
Tempranillo (from Casa de Piedra), Nebbiolo and Petite Sirah (rich,
vibrantly fruity, poised wines from L A Cetto) can be found. The
number of wineries is small, but growing – probably in response to
the success of neighbouring California.

MOLDOVA

In general, Moldovan white wines are good – well, goodish – but
the reds (70 per cent of production) are really something to write
about. An admirable example tasted recently was a 1999 Cabernet
Sauvignon from the enormous Doina winery, which was imperial
purple in colour, smelt like figs and violets, and tasted every bit
like an inky, young port (the sort of concentrated monster that
would certainly have benefited from a few months' softening in
oak). These reds are splendid, if 'raw' wines, made with the
Russian market in mind, but the growers are poised to refine them
and send them to the UK, too. Moldova has perhaps the highest
fine wine potential of any of the Eastern European countries. Not
only are there large plantings of popular grape varieties such as
Cabernet Sauvignon, Merlot, Pinot Noir, Chardonnay, Pinot Gris,
Riesling and Sauvignon Blanc, but there are also a number of local
varieties of note, among them Saperavi, Black Sereskia and Gamay
Fréaux. The climate is favourable and the soils are fine. But, sadly,
it's the same story as elsewhere in this part of the world – the
vineyards need attention, the wineries are poorly equipped,
passable wines are crippled by bad storage conditions before they
see the inside of a bottle, the transport system is inefficient and the
bureaucracy is a nightmare. Improvements are beginning, but very
slowly.

MOROCCO

Once upon a time (about 50 years ago), rich, leathery red wines from Morocco were used for padding out thin French ones, most notably burgundy. Independence from France and tighter appellation laws put a stop to all that in the 1950s and 1960s, and since then Moroccan wine has mainly been sold to tourists. Today it looks as though the French are returning the favours once dealt them, with investors such as Castel working hard to restore Morocco's decaying vineyards. These are mainly in the cooler coastal areas, planted at fairly high altitudes, thus benefiting from lower-than-average temperatures. However, strong winds from the Atlantic can cause difficulties.

The *appellation d'origine garantie* system, modelled on the French AC classification, provides a pointer to quality. And we have tasted some reasonably good Moroccan wines recently, all reds and rosés (steer clear of the whites). The rosés (found mainly in Moroccan restaurants) can be deeply coloured, fruity and slightly sweet, while the reds are typically soft and supple with mocha and spice undertones – the best made from Syrah, although look out for Cabernet Sauvignon and Grenache/Cinsault blends too. Two labels worth seeking out are Celliers de Meknès and Atlas Vineyards, where modern technology, well-maintained vineyards and French experience has resulted in wines we would be happy to pair with our lamb *tagine*. Where can you buy them? Well, Sainsbury's has a trio of palatable reds (especially the own-label Moroccan Syrah and the El Baraka blend), Booths has one or two, and, at the time of writing, Oddbins was expecting the arrival of a new range of Moroccan wines (we'll let you know how they measure up next year). (See *Where to buy wine.*) All in all, wines from Morocco are worth trying, and the country's wine industry is well worth keeping an eye on.

NEW ZEALAND

When we riffle through hundreds of UK merchants' lists each year, it seems that one section which invariably pleases is the New Zealand range. It's not often a wide choice, but merchants rarely go too far wrong with this country's wines, for the simple fact that so few duds are made there. When it comes to consistent, medium-to-highish-quality wine, the New Zealanders get it right more often than most.

Here are some vital statistics that reveal a lot about the wine produced in the Land of the Long White Cloud. Number one: New

Zealand commands the highest average price per bottle of any country exporting to the UK (£5.66, since you ask). So we get little poor wine, then, but not much that's cheap either. Don't expect a £3.49 bargain from New Zealand – in fact, if you see a rare cheapie, we suggest you steer clear as it will almost certainly be a bland white blend.

Interesting figure number two: the number of wineries is rapidly growing – almost trebling since 1991, to 391 at the last count. This is a very young wine industry (it only really sprang into life in the 1980s), peopled by relatively youthful, dynamic winemakers and viticulturists, so it hasn't stopped developing yet. There are plenty more vineyard sites to be discovered; plenty more grapes, clones, blends and styles to be explored. Watch this sunny, fresh and airy space!

And the third fact that contributes to an accurate picture of Kiwi wine: 82 per cent of the wine it exports to UK shores is white. Only 9 per cent is red, with 9 per cent sparkling. New Zealand may have made great strides with its reds of late, but some regions – especially the most famous, Marlborough on the South Island – are still rightly renowned for whites above anything else.

And particularly Sauvignon Blanc, of course. This is the country that gave Sauvignon a new lease of life, producing an extraordinarily expressive blast of fresh gooseberry, grass and white currant. Much has been made of the overt character of Marlborough Sauvignon, with some people complaining that the wines are unsubtle and uniform, but a tasting in Spring 2002 of no less than 44 Sauvignons from around New Zealand found a reasonably diverse bunch, the majority being high quality, and a large number more restrained and complex than we have found in the past.

That said, don't miss New Zealand's other whites, particularly the well-balanced Chardonnays and its Pinot Gris, now emerging as an important style. The fizz is as reliable, joyous and well-priced as ever. Reds have generally improved over the past few years, but Pinot Noir can still be patchy – more so than some over-enthusiastic commentators would have you believe. Tread carefully among the 2000 vintages, perhaps saving your pennies for the Merlots and Bordeaux blends, even the Syrahs, all of which are currently on great form.

This year it has been heartening to see two new initiatives take off. Sustainable Wine Growing New Zealand (SWNZ) should help underline (and authenticate) the 'clean, green' image that the New Zealand wine trade makes so much of. The basic principle is to encourage growers to think hard about their practices they take in the vineyards and to ask themselves whether theirs is the most ecologically friendly path. So far 280 vineyards have signed up to the scheme, which examines, reports on and puts into practice 'a framework for environmentally and economically sustainable viticultural practices'. As yet the criteria for acquiring a SWNZ label logo have yet to be established, but we can expect more wines to be made, if not by strict organic methods, then by something more like it – i.e. much-reduced chemical sprays, artificial fertilisers, and so on. In Marlborough, SWNZ members are shortly to launch a high-tech information base looking at vine-spray programmes in the region and designed to enable growers to make more informed choices.

Then there's the 'screw-cap wine seal' initiative. Thirty-two wineries, many of them big names, are switching to screw-caps for at least some of their wines in the name of eradicating cork taint. Many Rieslings in particular are now appearing with a screw-cap rather than a cork (there is a widely held belief here that unoaked whites show cork taint most clearly), and recently a Sauvignon Blanc from Lawson's Dry Hills became the first wine packaged this way to make it on to the US magazine *Wine Spectator*'s Top 100 list.

Both these new drives show that New Zealand's winemakers collectively a rather serious-minded, proactive lot are pushing forward the boundaries on both quality and environmental concerns. As well as planting furiously, endlessly experimenting with new clones and canopy management, and generally tackling the problems caused by a somewhat cool and unpredictable climate. Come to think of it, they deserve that £5.66.

White wines – grape varieties

Sauvignon Blanc

Sauvignon and New Zealand are synonymous in many wine drinkers' minds. In particular, wines from the ancient stony riverbeds and long, cool, ripening season of Marlborough have grabbed the world's attention – with their bright, upfront scents and flavours, variously described as gooseberry, asparagus, tom cat tomato leaf, freshly cut grass, mixed herbs, blackcurrant leaf, and even sweaty armpits. Today's wines are more restrained and complex than was once the case, and some producers blunt Sauvignon's sometimes gawky edges by using a touch of oak for fermentation and ageing, or by blending in a little plumper Semillon. Poor, dilute vintages send wines veering too far either towards green capsicum and grass, or, in hot years, towards flabbiness.

If you find Marlborough's flavours a little too predictable, try Sauvignons from other regions, particularly nearby Nelson or, for a slightly softer style, Wairarapa (Martinborough) in the North Island.

Chardonnay

For a while it looked as though New Zealand's Chardonnay was being overlooked by British drinkers in favour of its Sauvignon Blanc. But the excellence of Kiwi Chardonnay produced in both islands has now become apparent, and it is selling well in the UK. Chardonnay's malleability in the hands of winemakers makes it hard to pin down regional styles. The further north you travel in New Zealand, the warmer it gets, so the richer and riper the wines should become, but we've found wonderfully fleshy wines from cool Central Otago in the South, and weedy ones from much warmer spots in the North Island. Wines veer from the simple, fresh, tropical fruit-salad-in-a-glass to the toasty/buttery/quasi-Burgundian, in which the fruit flavours have been deliberately underplayed in favour of greater complexity. This is much more a function of winemaker than region.

Riesling

Good to see that Riesling plantings are on the increase (admittedly from a low base), as New Zealand shows great promise with the variety. The style in the 1980s was to make wines with some residual sweetness, but many today are bone dry and can occasionally reach 14 per cent alcohol. Clean, pithy, lime, lemon and apple flavours run through many, and their dryness can make them quite reserved when young. At two years old, however, they blossom, and many are built to drink well for a decade or more. Good and great Riesling can be found in the Wairarapa and any of the South Island regions. Much is now bottled under screw-cap (see introduction, above). *Botrytised* Riesling can also be delicious, but at present it can't be imported legally into the UK – ask your MEP whether this is to protect European producers.

Others

As elsewhere, Pinot Gris is currently very trendy in New Zealand, and an early 2002 tasting of half-a-dozen wines was impressive. A few dull versions exist, but this grape is coming on in leaps and bounds and there are now some fine, mineral- and spice-tinged wines from Central Otago, Marlborough and Wairarapa that hover between the crispness of Italian versions and the honeyed weight of Alsace. Gewurztraminer can also be wonderfully aromatic, and a star choice with 'Asian-fusion' cuisine, which is also deeply fashionable (in New Zealand and elsewhere). A few producers make Chenin Blanc, either in a lemony, often richly oak-tinged, dry guise or as a sumptuous sweet wine. A couple of attractively creamy, lemon-scented Semillons and peachy Viogniers have passed our way recently – both are worth a try. Müller-Thurgau, planted on bad advice in the 1960s, is not. It is, thankfully, disappearing from New Zealand's vineyards but still props up cheap blends.

Red wines – grape varieties

Pinot Noir

Is New Zealand the only country where Pinot Noir is the most widely planted red grape? Much of it goes to sparkling wine production, but there are some wonderfully silky reds, often with nutty, cherry flavours, being made throughout the South Island and in the Wairarapa. Better clones, better sites and better vineyard management mean that the wines have been improving, although at a tasting in Spring 2002, we found several wines from the 2000 vintage in Marlborough disappointingly rough and tart. Still, when they were good they were very, very good, particularly the wines from Central Otago (see 'Pick of the producers', below). While the finest in the future will undoubtedly command Burgundy-level prices, it's nice to see Vidal Estate, Huia and Montana Reserve examples taste just dandy at around £10.

Bordeaux varieties (Cabernet Franc/Cabernet Sauvignon/ Merlot/ Malbec)

If New Zealand has historically had a poor reputation for its red wines, then under-ripe, green bean/grassy Cabernet Sauvignon has largely been to blame. Today, very few spots in the South Island are bothering with the variety, while further north, it takes exceptional sites such as the Gimblett Gravels region of Hawke's Bay and Waiheke Island to ripen it satisfactorily in most vintages (expect high prices for these wines). If Cabernet does appear in today's Bordeaux-inspired blends, it is often as the junior partner in wines where Merlot plays the dominant role, maybe with Cabernet Franc and Malbec in support. Merlot by itself is often extremely successful, giving supple, plummy, well-balanced wines, especially from Hawke's Bay, and Malbec too can be charming and chocolaty. The ripe, concentrated wines of Hawke's Bay in particular have an exciting future.

Others

Last year we tipped the 'remarkably good Syrah' of Hawke's Bay; this is now one of the most exciting red varieties in New Zealand. The best Syrahs have something of a northern Rhône character – dark, spicy and satisfying. A couple of reds made from the Italian grape Montepulciano have not been convincing. However, if you see one of the rare Zinfandels or Pinotages, try it, as some are remarkably tasty.

227

Sparkling wine

New Zealand now produces an admirable range of sparkling wine, mostly *brut* made by the *méthode traditionnelle*. Chardonnay and Pinot Noir from cool Marlborough are especially well suited to sparkling wine production, and these wines are excellent value for money. Indeed, for around £9–£15 a bottle, these are among the best bubblies in the world. Some wineries put the accent on pure, crisp fruit, while others go for a more complex, yeasty, champagne-like style. Recommended are: Hunter's Miru Miru and Deutz Marlborough Cuvée, as the pick of the former style, while Cloudy Bay's Pelorus and Huia Brut head the ranks of the latter.

THE REGIONS

New Zealand's wine-producing regions stretch over a wider spread of latitudes than the vineyards of France, so it's reasonable to expect much variation in wine styles throughout the country. Some regions are a long way down the path to determining which varieties work best, and to discovering which flavours are the result of the *terroir* rather than the winemaking, but others have only just begun.

The North Island

The area around Auckland/Henderson remains the industrial centre of the country's wine trade, and many wineries have their HQ and winery facility there. Waiheke Island, half an hour by ferry from Auckland, is a hot spot in more than one sense. It basks in intense summer sun and has caused a flurry of interest in its impressively rich (and pricy) Cabernet/Merlot blends from small boutique wineries. North of Auckland, in Northland, a number of small estates have also made classed growth Bordeaux lookalikes as well as high-class Chardonnay. Matakana is another warm area north of Auckland, producing fine reds and Pinot Gris.

Gisborne is a decent source of Chardonnay, much of it fairly simple stuff, but with a few stunningly rich examples. Way down at the south-eastern tip is the Wairarapa, or Martinborough, as it is often known. This is home to several of New Zealand's finest Pinot Noirs, as well as some classy white wines. But the most important quality area in the North Island lies between these two regions on the east coast. Hawke's Bay has a wide range of soils at various altitudes, so that the ideal spot can be found for virtually any grape variety from Chenin Blanc to Zinfandel. Bordeaux-style reds, with Merlot now dominating, can be brilliant, with many – but by no means all – of the top wines coming from the Gimblett

Gravels sub-zone. This is an unoffical appellation defined by soil types rather than geographical features or roads. Its 2,000 acres of deep stony soil produces some superb reds, as witnessed at the 2002 annual New Zealand press tasting, when a table of wines from Gimblett Gravels held wine writers in thrall. Look out for Syrah and some fine Chardonnay from Hawke's Bay too.

The South Island

The first vines on this sparsely populated, glacier-strewn island were only planted in the mid-1970s. Since then, sunny, cool, stony-soiled Marlborough in the north-east has grown to become the largest wine region in New Zealand, its Sauvignon Blancs attracting international acclaim. Chardonnay, spicy whites, sparkling wines and, more recently, Pinot Noir are other strong suits, their fresh, vivacious fruit flavours a distinctive stamp on the wine. Nelson lies just one hour's drive west and could best be described as a cooler version of Marlborough, enjoying success with similar varieties, especially Chardonnay from a few boutique wineries, and furiously planting more vineyards. Canterbury, further south around Christchurch, is known for elegant Pinot Noir, Chardonnay and Riesling, with the Waipara sub-region being a particularly promising area, yet to be developed fully. You would think that dramatically beautiful Central Otago, the country's most southerly wine region, was too cold for grapes to ripen properly, but a growing number of producers are making some of the most exciting, complex wines in the country. Pinot Noir, Pinot Gris, Chardonnay and Riesling are all thriving here, and the future looks bright for this most scenic of wine regions – plantings here have more than doubled since 1996.

Pick of the producers
Alpha Domus Hawke's Bay winery with decent whites (including Semillon) and very fine Bordeaux-style reds. Top releases called AD; flagship wine is complex, long-lived Bordeaux blend The Aviator.

Ata Rangi Small Martinborough winery producing one of New Zealand's most worthwhile Pinot Noirs and Chardonnays to date.

Babich High quality from long-established Henderson operation with talented Neil Culley at the winemaking helm. Wide range, of which the Irongate Chardonnay and Cabernet, and Patriarch Chardonnay and Cabernet impress the most. Riesling and Pinotage are also worth tasting.

Chancellor Impressive range of wines, especially Riesling, from the rapidly developing Waipara district near Christchurch.

Cloudy Bay Trail-blazing, now cult Marlborough winery. Sauvignon Blanc is its most famous wine (still fine, but rivalled by many cheaper labels), and others in the range are also excellent (if cultishly expensive), especially rich, mealy Chardonnay and toasty Pelorus fizz. The recently introduced oaked Sauvignon Te Koku, now in the UK, divides opinion. We at the *Guide* prefer the original unoaked version.

Craggy Range Master of Wine Steve Smith's new enterprise really is one to watch. Marlborough Sauvignon Blanc, and Hawke's Bay Merlot and Chardonnay already stand out from the crowd.

Kim Crawford Well-known winemaker using grapes sourced from throughout New Zealand. A little inconsistent. Chardonnay, especially that from the Tietjen vineyard in Gisborne, is the pick of the range.

Delegat's Good-quality Hawke's Bay range from Henderson-based winery – look out for Reserve Chardonnay in particular. Marlborough wines appear as Oyster Bay.

Dry River Top-notch range of premium Pinot Noir, Pinot Gris and others made by Neil McCallum in Martinborough. Low cropping accounts for the concentrated style.

Esk Valley Decent whites from this Hawke's Bay winery, but it is for his outstanding reds that Gordon Russell is rightly known, with The Terraces, a powerful yet elegant Merlot/Malbec/Cabernet Franc blend, among New Zealand's finest wines. Villa Maria-owned.

Felton Road Central Otago star putting out superb Pinot Noir, Chardonnay and Riesling. If you want to try a top New Zealand red, don't miss the Block 3 or Block 5 Pinot from 2000. Now bottling much of range under screw-caps.

Fromm The main focus is on reds, surprisingly for a Marlborough estate. Intense Pinot Noir, plummy perfumed Malbec and rich, peppery Syrah.

Giesen Fine-tuned, elegant range from the three Giesen brothers in Canterbury in the south, where sophisticated Chardonnay and Riesling are produced. Now striking out with additional wines from Marlborough.

Goldwater Pioneering Waiheke Island winery that made its name with intense, cassis-rich Cabernet/Merlot blend, but is now producing plummy Merlot (Esslin vineyard) too. Also Roseland Chardonnay and Dog Point Sauvignon Blanc from Marlborough fruit.

Grove Mill Best known for aromatic, sometimes off-dry whites, notably Pinot Gris, Riesling and Gewurztraminer. Good-value, easy-drinking second label Sanctuary.

Huia Claire and Mike Allen's Pinot Gris, Gewurztraminer and lively sparkler are among the best in Marlborough.

Hunter's Long-established Marlborough winery, producing complex, oaky Chardonnay and rich, creamy Sauvignon. Riesling similarly full-on; also great-value, fruity sparkler Miru Miru.

Isabel Estate Classy estate excelling with some of the most complex and subtly flavoured Riesling, Pinot Noir, Chardonnay and Sauvignon Blanc in Marlborough.

Jackson Estate Pungent Sauvignon, crisp Riesling, complex Chardonnay and top-quality *brut* from John Stichbury's Marlborough estate. A recent convert to screw-cap bottling.

Kumeu River Michael Brajkovich MW is famous for Burgundian-style Chardonnays from his family-run winery north of Auckland.

Lawson's Dry Hills Aromatic wines of some distinction from Marlborough. Elegant Gewurztraminer and classic, flinty Sauvignon.

Martinborough Vineyard Martinborough pioneer, and still among those at the top with complex, silky Pinot Noir and rich, mealy Chardonnay.

Matua Valley Auckland-based winery now owned by Mildara Beringer Blass, making good wines from throughout the North Island. Top releases are Ararimu Cabernet/Merlot and Chardonnay.

Millton Vineyard A rare Gisborne boutique winery producing an interesting range of organic wines – award-winning, barrel-fermented Chenin Blanc is notable.

Montana The giant of the New Zealand wine industry, now owned by Allied Domecq, has a remarkably reliable track record with whites and sparkling wine: Marlborough Sauvignon and Chardonnay, and best-selling fizz Lindauer are all reliable, well-priced wines. At higher levels, the reserve releases of all varieties are commendable, while at the top of the tree, the single-vineyard wines can be superb, as are the Deutz Marlborough Cuvée sparklers.

Morton Estate Morton makes wine in Marlborough and Hawke's Bay and is much admired for its Black Label Chardonnay, although reds are fast catching up. Good-value White Label Marlborough Sauvignon Blanc is on fine form.

Mount Difficulty One of the top Central Otago names, particularly renowned for rich chocolaty Pinot Noir.

Nautilus Owned by Australian company Yalumba and producing fruity yet elegant Chardonnay, Sauvignon, Pinot Noir and fizz in Marlborough.

Neudorf The best winery in Nelson. Tim and Judy Finn craft wines of great depth and complexity, particularly from Chardonnay and Pinot Noir.

Ngatarawa Thoughtful Hawke's Bay producer with elegant citrusy Chardonnay and supple, complex Glazebrook Merlot/Cabernet blend, plus Noble Harvest Rieslings (not allowed in the UK). Top releases named Alwyn.

Nobilo Commercially minded Auckland winery now owned by Australian giant BRL Hardy. Let's hope quality – which seems to have remained static for a few years – improves under the new owners.

Palliser Estate A mainstay of Martinborough, with well-balanced, classy wines, including premium Chardonnay, white-curranty Sauvignon and blackberryish Pinot.

Pegasus Bay Splendid Canterbury (Waipara) winery making much-admired, complex wines, best of which are the Pinot Noir, Chardonnay and Riesling.

Rippon Vineyard Best known for a highly acclaimed Burgundian-style Pinot Noir from Central Otago, but also excelling with Chardonnay and Riesling.

Sacred Hill Good wines across the board from Hawke's Bay winery. The most pleasing are the Graves-style Sauvage Sauvignon and Riflemans Chardonnay. Merlots also fine.

St Clair Reliable, good-quality range from Neal Ibbotson that includes fine *botrytis* Riesling (if you can get hold of it).

Selaks/Drylands Estate One of the quiet performers of Marlborough, making crisp, pithy Sauvignon and tangy Riesling. Has belonged to Nobilo since 1998.

Seresin Ten-year-old Marlborough star, established by film-maker Michael Seresin, with highly experienced Brian Bicknell as manager/winemaker. Already coming up with an accomplished, upmarket range that includes weighty Pinot Gris and juicy Pinot Noir.

Sileni Grant Edmonds is chief winemaker at this newish, state-of-the-art Hawke's Bay winery. Top Chardonnay and Semillon, but best are the exceptional Cabernet/Merlot blends.

Stonecroft Maverick Hawke's Bay producer specialising in Gewurztraminer and Syrah; also impressive Zinfandel.

Stonyridge Stephen White's cultish winery on Waiheke Island is best known for Larose – one of the country's best (and most expensive) reds. It's a Bordeaux blend of considerable concentration and complexity, but UK allocations are tiny.

Te Mata Wine industry spokesman John Buck makes benchmark Elston Chardonnay, consistently fine-tuned, complex Coleraine Cabernet/Merlot and spicy Bullnose Syrah among others, at this long-established, influential Hawke's Bay winery.

Tohu Maori-owned venture producing ripe but fresh Marlborough Chardonnay and well-balanced Gisborne Chardonnay.

Trinity Hill John Hancock will try out Tempranillo and Roussanne as soon as the vines mature at his Hawke's Bay property. In the meantime, his top Gimblett Road wines are excellent.

Unison Hawke's Bay red specialist making just two wines blended from Merlot, Cabernet Sauvignon and Syrah grown in the Gimblett Road area. They both have the finesse found in expensive Bordeaux.

Vavasour Based in Marlborough's deep south, the Awatere Valley, so interesting for sub-regional character. A super-fresh, aromatic range of intense whites and decent Pinot Noir. Second label Dashwood also impresses.

233

Villa Maria High quality across the board, from great-value Private Bin range up to Reserves. The single-vineyard Sauvignons from Marlborough explore the diversity within the region, while the Marlborough Riesling and Hawke's Bay reds deserve attention. Villa also owns Esk Valley (see above) and Vidal wineries in Hawke's Bay. Chief winemaker Michelle Richardson resigned recently; her replacement is Alastair Maling MW.

Waipara West Waipara operation of Paul Tutton of the Waterloo Wine Company (see *Where to buy wine*); fresh, fruity wines, especially Riesling and Pinot Noir.

Wairau River Phil and Chris Rose own some of Marlborough's oldest vineyards, producing a notably rich and pungent Sauvignon which cries out its origins.

Wither Hills Ex-Delegat's winemaker Brent Marris makes some of New Zealand's finest Chardonnay, Sauvignon and Pinot Noir from vineyards established by his father John in 1975.

New Zealand vintage guide

New Zealand Sauvignons are at their best when youthful and crisp, although the best ones age into rich honey- and asparagus-edged maturity. Some Chardonnays gain complexity over two or three years, while the lushest and most complex of the reds will improve over five years and more.

New Zealand's wine-producing regions vary a great deal in terms of both climate and conditions, and the grape varieties that are planted, so a poor vintage for, say, Marlborough whites might be a great one for Hawke's Bay reds.

2002 Whopping great volume – the largest on record and 70 per cent bigger than 2001. It rained at flowering, but a warm Indian summer gave good conditions for ripening. Producers are saying that quality is fine but, given those high yields, one can only expect some disapppointingly dilute wines from lesser producers, especially among the Sauvignons.

2001 A vintage of two halves. Martinborough and the South Island had an excellent year, with hardly any rainfall from early summer to harvest. Some Marlborough whites may be overripe. In Hawke's Bay, rain around harvest caused rot in several white varieties, but reds fared better.

2000 Irregular flowering in many regions meant yields were down in several areas. Marlborough was badly affected, but managed a small crop of intensely flavoured wines. Rain at vintage in the

North means the Hawke's Bay reds and Gisborne Chardonnays
vary in quality.

1999 A good to very good year, producing first-rate, intense whites
but reds that lack the concentration of 1998. Quantity is up.

1998 A hot, dry year led to ripe, full-bodied reds (probably the best
New Zealand has produced to date), especially in Hawke's Bay.
However, Marlborough needed picking early to avoid flabby rather
than herbaceous, crisp whites, and few wineries got it right.

1997 Quality more than satisfactory, but quantities down. An Indian
summer in Marlborough meant fine Riesling, Chardonnay and
Sauvignon Blanc.

1996 A good vintage, with a fair-sized crop produced after plenty of
sunny weather. Reds from Hawke's Bay are excellent.

PORTUGAL

TABLE WINES

In Spring 2002, *Which?* magazine blind-tasted 18 Portuguese red
table wines costing under £7 a bottle, all readily available in UK
supermarkets and large off-licence chains. The labels were covered
up and the panel consisted of six professional wine tasters. The
results? A positive set of marks, higher than average for the *Which?*
quarterly wine reports. 'Portugal has something distinctive to offer,
even at this relatively affordable price,' said one panellist in a
typical conclusion. 'For consumers looking for good value and
prepared for the slightly wild, off-beat character of Portuguese reds,
a good proportion of these wines are worth trying.'

Satisfyingly, this verdict reflects what we have been saying for
several years now. Portugal's table wines, and particularly its reds,
have improved enormously. Where they used to be a dubious way
to part with your money – often turning up tough and fruitless,
even faintly grubby – they are now consistently good quality.

But most important, in our view, is that 'off-beat' nature the
Which? panel picked up on. Although you can get Cabernet and
Chardonnay from Portugal, in the main its winemakers have stuck
cannily to their own grape varieties – fruit that produces different,
idiosyncratic flavours. Grapes such as Baga, Jaen and Touriga
Nacional do indeed provide 'wild', unusual nuances, perhaps of
herbs and black pepper, bristling brambles, dark chocolate and
thick tar. Others (Periquita springs to mind first) simply deliver soft,
easy-going, cherryish fruit. Add the classic fortified wines of the
Upper Douro and you get the picture – Portugal now has a wide
and impressive port-folio (sorry) when it comes to putting anything
red in your glass.

That is partly because many Portuguese winemakers got their act together towards the end of the twentieth century. It's hard to overstate the impact that top boys José Neiva, João Ramos Portugal, David Baverstock and Peter Bright have had on modern Portuguese table wines. This is a (table) winemaking country that was heading downhill rapidly until the new brooms swept out the big co-ops of the central areas (the Estremadura and Ribatejo regions are the most exciting). The old-fashioned, tired styles of Dão and Bairrada further north have been re-thought by the most progressive producers and are consequently softer and more approachable. And now there are even superb unfortified reds made in the Douro by go-ahead winemakers.

We just wish a few more wine drinkers would sit up and take notice. Portuguese table wines remain relatively undiscovered and underrated (hence under-priced, of course). It would help if more UK merchants were taking Portugal more seriously too – there appears to be a wide gap in the market here, although you will find one or two who specialise to an extent in Portugal (for example, Parfrements and Richards & Richards) *Where to buy wine*. Oh, and do try the new red Vida Nova from Sir Cliff Richard (well, from an estate owned by Cliff, but made by David Baverstock). It's ripe and rounded and appealing – and it comes from the Algarve, which might just kick-start the sluggish wine industry there.

Would that we could be so positive about the white wines – they still undoubtedly lag behind the reds, whether it's a tired old Vinho Verde or a passable but dull co-op blend in your glass. There *are* some decent Portuguese whites but you have to work harder to find them. That's partly because Portugal's indigenous white grapes are not nearly as distinctive as its reds, but it still seems clear that there's room for improvement in most quarters. Indeed, if we had to choose a Portuguese white to drink with dinner tonight, we'd probably plump for one of the internationally styled Chardonnays. If we had to choose a red, though, we'd certainly take a walk on the wild side…

The Portuguese wine classification system

The wine classification system in Portugal is less than straightforward. There are, at the last count, around 15 regions designated *denominação de origem controlada* (DOC), followed by some 30 designated *indicação de proveniência regulamentada* (IPR). In practice, DOC and IPR are considered fairly close in Portugal so, short of a crash course in Portuguese geography, the best thing to remember is that these 50 or so regions are neither *vinho regional* (VR), equivalent to *vin de pays*; nor *vinho de mesa*, aka table wine. No, we take that back. It's sensible to remember is a list of the best producers (see 'Pick of the producers', below).

Red wines – grape varieties

For those who remember only the dreary, chewy, fruit-free wines of the past, today's Portuguese reds come as a revelation. Established properties have improved their quality, while many growers who used to deliver their grapes to the local co-operative are now set up in their own brand-new wineries, thanks in no small part to generous EU grants.

Portugal's most consistent DOC for table reds is now the Douro, ironically enough, since it used to be known only for port. Here the same grapes used for port, especially Touriga Nacional and Tinto Roriz (also Tempranillo), are being put to good effect for concentrated, rich red table wines, with flavours of tobacco, leather, plums and berries all vying for attention. Those that blend in foreign grapes such as Cabernet Sauvignon forgo the Douro name and are labelled Tras-os-Montes. Dão, a Touriga Nacional-heavy blend from a hilly, pine-forested region in the central/north zone, and Bairrada, made mostly from the tough little Baga grape and lying between Dão and the west coast, are slowly improving, thanks to the efforts of a number of the producers listed below; but we'd still approach a typical wine with caution – they can be hard and tannic, especially in youth. The venerated red wine of the majestic Buçaco Palace hotel is also largely Baga – shame you can only buy it in the restaurant there. Another variety to look out for in the UK is the fruity, chocolaty Jaen – try the Bela Fonte and Quinta das Maias.

Further south are the central and eastern regions, where the hugely revitalised co-operatives of Ribatejo, Estremadura, Palmela and Alentejo specialise in likeable, cherryish reds made from the local grape Periquita (aka Castelão Frances). If it's inexpensive, palatable red you're after, you could do a lot worse than look out for these co-ops' names in the small print of a label. Watch out, too, for the impressive wines emerging from the region of Alenquer, in the Atlantic-influenced hilly area to the north of Lisbon.

Truly top-notch reds are also appearing, either from revamped co-operatives or single estates. French grape varieties, especially Cabernet Sauvignon, are often used for these, but the majority rely on local grapes. Even the humble Alicante Bouschet is being used to good effect.

White wines – grape varieties

Despite the fact that whites represent 40 per cent of total production, great examples remain rare. To their credit, the Portuguese have resisted the lure of Chardonnay and its ilk and, where winery upgrades have allowed proper temperature-controlled vinification, we are now seeing some fresh and reasonably characterful wines made from indigenous grape varieties.

In the Douro, producers such as Niepoort (the Redoma range) and Quinta de la Rosa make small quantities of very respectable white wine using grapes such as Gouveio (Madeira's Verdelho), Rabigato and Malvasia. The Arinto variety is responsible for the tight, pithy Bucelas made near Lisbon.

As far as single varieties are concerned, in Dão, the Encruzado variety is hitting heights given its fresh, aromatic appley fruit and ability to take oak ageing. Look for the wines from Quinta dos Roques and Quinta dos Carvalhais. Then there is Bical, planted extensively in Bairrada and Dão, and potentially Portugal's answer to Riesling, with its propensity developing from grassy youthfulness to petrolly maturity. The best examples are Casa de Saima, Luis Pato's Vinha Formal (both Bairrada) and Bela Fonte Bical from Beiras. José Neiva also makes exemplary limey and delicious wines in Estremadura from the workhorse, vaguely spicy Fernão Pires grape (also known confusingly as Maria Gomes).

That best-known Portuguese white, Vinho Verde, sadly appears to be falling by the wayside, despite the success of the Alvarinho grape (which together with Loureira makes the best Vinho Verde) just over the border in Spain's Galicia. Many Vinho Verdes you will come across in the UK (or on holiday in Portugal) taste insipid and flat. A major revamp of this potentially fresh, floral, lively young wine would be very welcome.

Rosé, sparkling and sweet

The medium-sweet, spritzy Mateus Rosé has moved way out of fashion (although it now comes in a smarter, new-look bottle), and there is only a handful of drier pink wines available – the best from Bairrada. Try those of the Caves Aliança and Sogrape. Only one or two sparkling wines from Portugal have crossed our paths – those from Luis Pato and J P Vinhos (called Loridos) have impressed. The classic sweet Moscatel de Setúbal from the Setúbal peninsula south of Lisbon can be honeyed and delicious – try J P Vinhos and José Maria da Fonseca's wines. A sweet wine labelled simply 'Setúbal' contains less than 85 per cent Moscatel.

Pick of the producers

As well as the producers listed below, Portugal has a number of co-operatives that turn out large quantities of excellent-value wine (see 'Red wines', above), the best of which is often scooped up by winemakers such as Peter Bright and José Neiva to offer under their own labels. Look out for *Atlantic Wines* (Bright Brothers) and *DFJ Vinhos* (José Neiva) for reliable, fruity, modern-style wines.

Caves Aliança Bairrada-based producer of reliable, modern wines, including a fine, dry white and spicy, peppery reds; also makes soft reds in the Douro and Dão, plus supple Tinta Roriz in Estremadura.

Quinta da Aveleda One of the best Vinho Verde producers. Casal Garcia is commercial but refreshing, while Aveleda is drier and lemony. Also very good varietal Alvarinho.

Quinta do Boavista One of the top Estremadura estates, employing José Neiva as consultant. Quinta da Espiga is an appealing, cheaper quaffer, while higher-quality wines are produced under the Palha Canas, Bon Ventos and (for varietals) Santas Lima labels. Must-try wines.

Bright Brothers Good-value wines from several regions made by the Australian Peter Bright. Chardonnay is strong, as are reds made from Portuguese grapes – spicy Palmela Reserva is deliciously heady. (See also *Fiuza*, below.)

Quinta de Cabriz Up-and-coming Dão estate, with fine range topped by Escolha Virgilio Loureiro *cuvée*.

Casa Cadaval Ribatejo producer offering a wide selection including Pinot Noir and Cabernet 'foreigners' and good, single-varietal Trincadeira.

Quinta do Carmo Single estate in Borba, now owned by Rothschild of Lafite. Produces mellow reds from the Alicante Bouschet grape.

Quinta do Carneiro Small and perfectly formed estate in DOC Alenquer making trusty, great-value wines with a nod to tradition.

Herdade de Cartuxa Large Alentejo estate showcases stunning Per Manca red, and almost as impressive Cartuxa Reserva. The creamy whites are good too.

Quinta da Cismeira Some of the best Douro red table wines – intensely flavoured and lushly fruity. Bordeaux's Michel Rolland is consultant here, so, unsurprisingly, there's excellent Cabernet Sauvignon too.

Cortes de Cima Unabashedly combining New World know-how with Portuguese grapes in the Alentejo, this property was

239

completely revamped by the Danish Jørgenson family in the late 1980s, with the Australian viticultural guru Richard Smart consulting.

Quinta do Côtto Another producer of richly fruity Douro reds, the best of which is the cedarwood-scented Grande Escolha.

Quinta do Crasto Australian David Baverstock of Esporão (see below) works at this Douro property to produce brilliantly rich, concentrated reds, especially the massive but fragrant Touriga Nacional. Small plots of old vines also make great Vinha Dapont, and watch too for the Maria Teresa label.

Herdade do Esporão David Baverstock makes one of Portugal's most consistent, widely distributed ranges at this progressive Alentejo estate. Impressive, soft, peachy whites, but the reds, including varietal Trincadeira, Touriga Nacional and Aragonês, are even better. Other labels: Monte Velho and Alandra.

Ferreira Port shipper, also renowned for soft, generous Barca Velha, one of Portugal's most prestigious (and expensive) wines, although it may be a little old-fashioned for some. It's only produced in the finest years, otherwise a *reserva* is substituted. Other worthwhile wines include Quinta da Leda and Casa Ferreirinha.

Fiuza Ribatejo winery working in conjunction with Peter Bright on New World-ish, oaky Chardonnay, Cabernet and Merlot.

José Maria da Fonseca Not to be confused with Fonseca Internacional, makers of Lancers wine, or with Fonseca port. This is one of Portugal's best table-wine producers, based in the Setúbal peninsula near Lisbon. Reds are wide-reaching and impressive – especially the rich red Tinto Velha (a successful blend of Cabernet Sauvignon and Periquita), full-bodied Quinta da Camarate, single-varietal Periquita and cheap, yet cheerful Terras Altas. Also recommended: fortified Muscat-based Setúbal.

Quinta da Gaivosa Douro table wines with all the richness and concentration of port – but less alcohol. Winemaker Domingos Alves de Sousa is also behind the first-class reds of Quinta Vale da Raposa.

J P Vinhos Palmela-based winery making impressive range, including oaky, berryish Tinta da Anfora and toasty Cova da Ursa, one of Portugal's finest Chardonnays. Also rather tough Cabernet from the historic Quinta da Bacalhôa estate in the Setúbal peninsula, decent fizz called Loridos and appealing fortified Moscatel de Setúbal.

Quinta do Lagoalva Good if slightly too oaky whites, but the reds from this Ribatejo estate are wonderful, especially the Syrah.

Quinta das Maias Exalted, traditional Dão estate.

Herdade de Mouchão Brilliant but hard-to-find red from Alentejo, made using a high proportion of the Alicante Bouschet grape. When it's good, it's very good.

Niepoort Port shipper whose Redoma table wines, a red based on the traditional Douro varieties and a barrel-fermented white produced from a blend of local grapes, are among the finest in Portugal.

Quinta de Pancas The reds from this classy show estate in Estremadura get better and better under the direction of João Ramos Portugal. Special Reserva Cabernet and Touriga Nacional are splendid, ageworthy wines.

Luis Pato Leading Bairrada producer, best known for long-lived reds and now crafting softer, easier styles of wine. The single-vineyard wines Vinha Barrosa and Vinha Pan are firm but very classy, as is the wine from Quinta do Ribeirinho. Pato is also experimenting with Cabernet and makes good fizz.

João Ramos Portugal Talented, motivated winemaker responsible for several ranges (see *Quinta de Pancas*, above), but also with splendid, highly modern selection bottled under his own name.

Ramos-Pinto Another port house, now owned by Champagne house Roederer, making damson and cherryish Duas Quintas Douro red (with a great *reserva*), and also supple Quinta do Bons Ares, which includes some Cabernet, and therefore has to be labelled with the Vinho Regional of Tras-os-Montes.

Quinta dos Roques Textbook modern winery in the Dão at the forefront of the region's renaissance: one to watch for its outstanding premium wines. Single-varietal Encruzado and Alfrocheiro are extremely promising, if scarce.

Quinta de la Rosa Spectacularly sited Douro port *quinta* owned by the Swedish Bergqvist family, whose forebears have been in the port trade since the early nineteenth century. Source of notable and popular red – *reserva* especially – and aiming to increase production.

Quinta de Saes Dão estate coming up with gutsy Touriga Nacional and Tinta Roriz reds, and ripe, full-flavoured whites. Best wines are from Quinta da Pellada.

Casa de Saima Model Bairrada property acquiring cult renown – hand harvesting, grape treading and unfiltered bottling gives you some idea why. Watch for the delicious Garrafeiras.

Caves São João Top-class, traditional Bairradas and Dão from this family winery.

Sogrape Huge, chameleon-like company with countrywide interests, responsible for Mateus Rosé and Gazela Vinho Verde – both highly commercial, off-dry wines. Many exciting wines now emanate from the vast Quinta do Carvalhais winery in the Dão, alongside the Grao Vasco and Duque de Viseu labels. Vinha do Monte red from Alentejo also impressive.

Tapada do Chaves Alentejo estate challenging Mouchão for title of top red in the region. Also rich, full-flavoured white.

PORT

Fans of vintage port will be delighted with the 2000 declaration, which was announced in a flurry of press releases in early 2002. After two rainy, dreary years in 1998 and 1999, it's good to see a classic vintage – wines are generally rich and deeply coloured, with plenty of concentrated, ripe fruit and decent structure. And prices don't seem to have whizzed up too much – an increase of 5–10 per cent on 1997 (the last vintage declaration) can be expected.

Port shippers will be hoping that the 2000s prove as popular as the 1997s and the 1994 especially with the Americans. Given the stock market's rollercoaster ride of late, it's hard to know for sure – but that round figure '2000' will no doubt help and, as we say, the quality is certainly there.

If you buy young vintage port, don't drink it too soon. If you can bear to, cellar it and wait for it to develop the fascinating, softer characteristics of old age. Try 1983s and 1985s but anything more recent shouldn't be opened just yet. Twenty years is about the right time to wait, but sadly much vintage port is the victim of infanticide.

Fortunately, port isn't just about 'vintage' wines. The quality of other styles is increasingly good too, particularly in the cases of *single quinta* and LBV (late bottled vintage): these styles are now widely available. Rarer, but certainly worth a try, are aged Colheita wines. And don't miss tawny port, a brilliant match for chocolate desserts, Christmas puddings and fine cheeses. We prefer our tawny served lightly chilled, but it's up to you.

Winemaking has improved no end in the arid Upper Douro valley in recent years (electricity is now the norm), and twenty-first-century technology is making an impact – literally, since a couple of shippers (Taylor's, Graham) now have high-tech, new crushing machines designed to mimic the effect of – and replace – traditional foot treading in stone *lagares*. It will be interesting to see what else the port houses come up with in the next few years. It's good that investment is being made, but let's hope port never loses its traditional image or, more importantly, its much-loved, classic characteristics.

Styles of port

All red ports begin in the same manner: the grapes are crushed (they are rarely trampled by foot any longer, although the stone *lagares* that contained the grapes can still be seen here and there in the Douro Valley), then brandy is added halfway through the fermentation process. The addition of the brandy halts the fermentation, and any remaining sugar is retained in the wine. After that, the many styles of wines split roughly into two categories. 'Ruby' ports are bottled early and do any maturing they have to in bottle, whereas 'Tawny' ports are aged for long periods in cask and are ready to drink as soon as they have been bottled.

Ruby
A wine labelled 'Ruby' is generally an inexpensive port bottled after two or three years spent maturing in big wooden vats. Drink it unmixed while it is young and fresh, for its fiery, cherryish fruit attack. Vintage character port is nothing more than a premium ruby.

Vintage port
The finest port from the best vineyards (only about two per cent of all that is made) is 'declared' and bottled after just two years in barrel without any treatment or filtration. Only two or three high-quality vintages each decade are deemed good enough by the shippers for a declaration. A question increasingly asked today is: when is vintage port ready to drink? Voracious Americans, can't get enough of it soon enough and will drink vintage port straight after release, preferably with a well-cooked T-bone steak. Others like to drink it when it is still vigorously fruity and exuberant, but is just beginning to release its tannic grip – at about ten years of age. Yet others hang on for decades, although for many, 20 years is just the

time to strike, when the extraordinary bundle of intense berry fruits, brooding tannins and dark hints of tar, herbs and chocolate is beginning to loosen and mellow. Don't forget to decant vintage port carefully (see *Serving wine*) as it throws a heavy sediment from a very young age.

Single quinta port

These are vintage ports, often from an individual estate – *quinta* – that provide the backbone of the company's regular vintage blend. Typically, a *single quinta* from a larger shipper is made in years not universally declared vintage, and is somewhat less tannic and powerful, i.e. ready to drink earlier than vintage ports. They often represent excellent value for money and enable you to drink top vintage port without paying top vintage prices. As a consequence, *single quinta* ports are much loved by genuine fans of delicious port who are not simply after the kudos of a famous vintage.

Late-bottled vintage (LBV)

LBV is wine from a single vintage bottled after spending five or six years ageing in wood. Traditional LBV is bottled without filtration so that it throws a crust and needs decanting just like vintage port. These intense wines can represent good value. Regular, mass-market LBVs, on the other hand, have often been stripped of their character, with some no more interesting than vintage character port (premium ruby). Choose carefully.

Crusted/crusting port

Vintage-style port made from a blend of wines from more than one year. They are rare but can be excellent value.

Tawny port

Proper tawny port, as opposed to the bland blend of white and red port which the French drink in place of vermouth, derives its colour – and hence its name – from long-term cask maturation, acquiring on the way a mellow, nutty quality. Aged tawny comes in 10-, 20-, 30- and 40-year-old styles, and the older wines are well worth the high prices they command. Tawny port is delicious served lightly chilled as an aperitif in the summer, or with chocolate puddings.

Colheita

A tawny from a single vintage, the label of which will state both the year and the date of bottling. The port must be aged for a legal minimum of seven years before bottling. Colheitas are currently enjoying something of a vogue – deservedly so, as they offer easy and pleasurable drinking.

White port
This is made from white grapes and is generally rather a dull drink. The port shippers drink white port as an aperitif, with tonic water and ice, and usually serve it with a bowl of salted almonds. This custom has tended to remain firmly in Portugal, however. In the UK, look out for Dows Extra Dry White or the outstanding Churchill's Dry White Aperitif – too good, when served on a hot day, to mix with anything.

The major port houses

Burmester Fine tawny and Colheita ports from house owned by Amorim cork producers.

Cálem Portuguese house making well-respected Colheitas, a first-class *single quinta* wine – Quinta da Foz – and specialising in wonderful old tawnies. Grapes from Quinta da Foz provide the backbone for the vintage blend.

Churchill Rapidly expanding house founded in 1982. Enjoys a loyal following both in the UK and in America. Vintage wines from Quinta da Agua Alta are the best of a good-quality, full-bodied set, while the excellent Dry White Aperitif is well worth a try.

Cockburn Well known for the best-selling, undemanding Special Reserve (top seller in the UK), Cockburn makes more impressive vintage and tawny ports, though quality can be patchy.

Quinta do Crasto **Single quinta** best known for red Douro wines, also putting out good LBV and upwards.

Croft Light, commercial wines, although vintage ports are good and much-improved since the notable 1994 vintage. Since 2001 part of the Taylor-Fonseca group and being re-thought – look out for portfolio changes

Delaforce Best approached via its fine tawny His Eminence's Choice. Again, very good since 1994. Bought by Taylor's (below) in 2001; expect some streamlining.

Dow A top house owned by the powerful British Symington family (see also entries for Warre, Smith Woodhouse, Quinta do Vesuvio and Graham ports, and the Madeira section, below). The house style is intense and serious, and the *single quinta* wine from Quinta do Bomfim outclasses many true vintage ports. Also nutty, delicious ten-year-old tawny.

Ferreira Leading Portuguese house owned by Sogrape (see Portugal's table wines, above). Produces superior mid-weight vintage wines and rich 20-year-old tawny Duque de Bragança.

Fonseca From the Taylor's stable, Fonseca provides a splendid range, from fine vintage to affordable and full-bodied Bin 27 vintage character.

Graham Superb, sweetly fruity vintage wines, among the best from the Symington group. Six Grapes is recommended, ripe vintage character port, while the LBV is perhaps the best non-traditional version.

Kopke Oldest of all the port houses, bottling small amounts of stunning Colheita ports.

Niepoort The talented and energetic Dirk Niepoort makes powerful, long-lived vintage wines and superb Colheitas at this small, top-notch estate. Quinta do Passadouro is a delicious *single quinta* port.

Quinta do Noval Elegant, fragrant vintage wines and the justly famed, deeply concentrated Nacional (made from the fruit of ungrafted vines) from this French-owned shipper. Wines made from bought-in fruit are labelled Noval. Particularly good since AXA ownership began in 1993.

Offley-Forrester Now part of Sogrape (see Portugal's table wines, above), Offley produces powerful port with fruit from the ancient Quinta da Boa Vista.

Ramos-Pinto Renowned for its complex and classy aged tawnies and now owned by champagne house Louis Roederer.

Quinta de la Rosa Family-owned and producing newly exciting, fine vintage ports.

Royal Oporto Wine Company Port house undergoing a revival. Tawny and vintage port much improved.

Sandeman Port house somewhat adrift between owners, and quality has consequentially slipped a little. However, Vau is a worthwhile *single quinta* port intended for early drinking, and the Sandeman aged tawnies are still stunning.

Smith Woodhouse More Symington-owned port – this time from an underrated house that supplies many UK chains with reliable own-label port. Particularly good at traditional LBV, with vintage port very undervalued too.

Taylor, Fladgate & Yeatman Or Taylor's as most people know it. The grandest port house of them all, and its majestic, concentrated vintage wines are widely considered benchmarks. The *single quinta* wine, Quinta de Vargellas, is excellent and the 20-year-old tawny is simply sublime.

Quinta do Vesuvio Historic *quinta*, Symington-owned and already making its name for powerful, super-concentrated but complex vintage ports.

Warre Venerable brand, another owned by the Symington family, producing traditional, rounded vintage and lovely *single quinta* wine, Quinta da Cavadinha. Warre's Warrior premium ruby also very good, while Otima Ten-Year-Old tawny, appearing in modern, slick labels, is a decent entry-level tawny that might just appeal to younger drinkers.

Port vintage guide

2001 Reasonable, but rain shortages and excessively hot temperatures mid-June meant this was not a classic year by a long way. Expect no declarations, especially in the wake of 2000. The *single quintas* may be decent, middle-of-the-road wines, however.
2000 An outstanding year: for the first time since 1997 there was no rain during vintage, it was a superb ripening season, yields were low and concentration very good. All the major houses have declared. Expect high quality across the board – ripe and concentrated wines.
1999 Not an outstanding year – another one in which it poured with rain – and *single quinta* vintages only have been declared.
1998 A difficult, wet vintage after a warm summer caused volume and quality to drop. Not a declared vintage for the major shippers. The *single quinta* vintaged wines, such as Vargellas, Agua Alta and de la Rosa, show good promise.
1997 A short, high-quality crop, generally declared a fine vintage by all the main houses.
1994 An excellent year, the best vintage ports since 1985, with wines that are full-bodied, dark and rich, the products of a ripe vintage.
1992 Only declared by a handful of shippers, one of whom (coincidentally of course) also celebrated its 300th anniversary in the same year. The best wines are ample and fruity.

1991 A very dry year, declared by most shippers. Fine, perfumed wines to drink from 2010 onwards.

1985 Much-hyped year declared by most shippers. Though priced too high on release, the best wines will be magnificent and approachable from now on.

1983 Powerful, concentrated wines which, while opening up, will still repay keeping. Undervalued.

1982 Not a universal declaration, with wines that are on the light side, but again, fairly priced and drinking well now.

1980 Not a highly praised vintage, but one that produced well-balanced, mature wines, ready for drinking now.

1977 A great vintage – drink lesser wines from now onwards, but the best still need time.

1975 Relatively light wines – drink up.

1970 Outstanding – drink from now onwards.

1966 Very good vintage but drink up wines now.

1963 Classic vintage producing massive wines. Drink from now onwards.

Fine earlier vintages 1960, 1955, 1948, 1945.

MADEIRA

The good news from the island of Madeira is that all bulk shipments of wine were suspended as of the beginning of 2002. Not that we see much of the bulk-made stuff in the UK (the French drink most of it), but it means overall quality should improve and maybe, gradually, people's perception of the wine will change as a result. In theory, that is.

Madeira is designed to hang around; that's how it came into existence in the first place. Barrels of wine were stored in the holds of exploration ships as ballast – to be replaced later by treasures from newly discovered lands – and in transit through the tropics it became baked, burnt and caramelised. Eventually the sailors discovered that their 'ballast' tasted rather good – and so madeira came about. Today those sea journeys are replicated by heating the wine in tanks and warm lofts in a process known as *estufagem*. Because it is cooked, madeira wine is tremendously resilient; not only does it appear to last for ever in bottle, but the wine remains unspoilt for months after opening. And it isn't a heavy, sweet, sickly product, but one with bracing acidity and richness, in a range of styles from raspingly dry to magnificently honeyed.

In a drive to attract new, younger drinkers, a fresh slant on madeira has recently hit UK shores. Blandy's 1994 Harvest (Colheita) Malmsey is a (relatively) young, single-vintage wine and a departure from tradition. It gives a taster of what top-quality madeira is all about, but without the high price – it has about five, rather than 20 to 100 years' barrel age, and costs around £12.

In case the message isn't clear already, beware cheaper madeiras. Those labelled Sweet Rich or Pale Dry are made from the inferior Tinta Negra Mole grape we advise you to confine your drinking instead to the premium madeira varietals – Sercial, Verdelho, Bual and Malmsey. If you buy a cut-price, inferior madeira, make sure it's for cooking purposes. On the other hand, we beg you not to use the best stuff for deglazing the pan – this is an authentic classic, worthy of sipping and savouring at leisure.

Madeira styles and grape varieties

Cheaper madeira, usually made from Tinta Negra Mole, tends to be about three years old. These wines are put through a basic method of *estufagem* in a concrete tank and rapidly cooled. Quality varies – avoid coarse, sickly, inexpensive madeiras, some of them released as own-label supermarket wines.

Older and more expensive wines, however, usually carry the name of the grape used to make them and represent a huge leap in quality. Five-year-old madeira can be appealing, while the 10- and 15-year-old wines are usually complex and fine, more than justifying the price hike. These older madeiras are 'cooked' in the traditional manner – stored in wooden casks and left to develop slowly in specially heated rooms at the *bodega*. Traditionally, vintage or *solera* wines are not subjected to *estufagem* at all. These are the rarest and most precious madeiras and can take over 50 years to reach maturity. Visitors to the island can try to persuade the Madeira Wine Company to offer a few sips of ancient wine at the São Francisco Wine Lodge in Funchal.

Only a few madeira brands, but a fair range of own-label wines, are available in the UK. Blandy's, Cossart Gordon and Leacock's are all owned by the Symington family. Henriques & Henriques, H M Borges and Barbeito are independent marks.

Sercial and Verdelho
The driest and lightest of madeiras are made from the Sercial grape. Fine examples are nutty with a racy acidity. In Madeira, Sercial is often drunk lightly chilled as a refreshing aperitif. Verdelho wines are medium-dry and slightly less acidic, with a nutty, tangy finish, and are traditionally drunk with soups and consommés.

Bual and Malmsey
Bual achieves higher ripeness levels than either Sercial or Verdelho, producing a medium-sweet madeira with a hint of raisin. This is the

madeira to match with cheese. Malmsey, the most famous style of all, is made from the Malvasia grape and is the sweetest, with rich raisin fruit, dates and figs in the flavour. It makes a superb partner for chocolate puddings.

ROMANIA

Privatisation has been more sluggish here than in the rest of Eastern Europe, but although Romania might not yet be snapping at New World heels, it is fast catching up with the likes of Bulgaria. The reason – the new generation of investors (notably from Germany and England) prepared to put in the necessary huge capital to get things going. With them comes a crop of modern designer labels, and a new wave of winemakers gaining in confidence with their Cabernets and Merlots, going from strength to strength with their Pinot Noir, and with a keen eye on Pinot Gris, too. Improvements are slow, and wineries investing the money are still frustrated by the general rusticity of those around them. But there has definitely been a big improvement, the fruits of which are making their way to UK supermarkets as we write. The next stage, which might come as a shock, is that modern Romanian wines won't necessarily cost the bargain £2.99 (or less) we are used to. The best of the 'new wavers' will more likely be £4.99, and deservedly so.

Estates to look out for are Prahova Valley, which produces lighter wines from the high-altitude Dealul Mare ('big hill') region: smoky, smooth Pinot and minerally elegant Fetească Neagră; the Carl Reh winery, with German investment; and the recently privatised Murfatlar estate with Australian Stephen Bennet as winemaker (and smart new Austrian label design for its upbeat Vampire's Taste range). Vinartek, on the warmer Danube Terraces, makes chunky New World-style varietals: 100-per-cent Cabernet Soara ('the sun') from 35-year-old vines is modern but with a Bordeaux-like twist. SERVE (Societé Euro Roumanie des Vins d'Exception) is another winery that shows what Romania can do when it really tries.

And don't forget the local grapes. Spicy reds from Fetească Neagră and Burgund Mare ('big Burgundian', related to Pinot Noir), and the white Tămaîîoasă and Grasă – both capable of making long-lived, sweet wines – are well worth trying. We hope to see more of these as the new investors increase in confidence.

SLOVAKIA

When Czechoslovakia split up in the early 1990s, Slovakia was the part that got the best vineyards, but there is still scope for the influence of neighbours Hungary and Austria to spur things on a bit. In the west of the country, there are plentiful plantings of Frankovka (aka Blaufränkisch), St Laurent and Grüner Veltliner, plus Cabernet Sauvignon and Pinot Noir, but most of the production (65 per cent) is of white wine. It seems that the more noble Irsay Oliver and Pinot Gris varieties are encroaching on insipid Müller-Thurgau and Laski Rizling, but we'll have to wait for the completion of privatisation and a great deal of technical improvement before we can really vouch for any quality. For 'signs of life', we're looking to the Bratislava-Raca, Pezinoka and Nitra wineries and, when we see any progress, we'll let you know. In the east, in Tokájská, sweet wines are made using the same techniques and grape varieties as are employed over the border in Hungary's great sweet wine region, Tokaj (historically, in fact, Tokájská is part of the same region). We confess that we've never tasted any Slovakian sweeties that are as good as Tokay, but then there hasn't been the huge foreign investment which has taken place on the Hungarian side of the border.

SLOVENIA

Rumour has it that some of the top Collio producers from Italy's Friuli region have been buying grapes from over the border in Slovenia for years. There are certainly some similarities in the wines. Good, crisp whites are emerging from wineries such as Simcic and others that are currently busy preparing to make an entry into the UK: the wines should arrive on our shop shelves over the next year or so. Sauvignon, Pinot Gris, Chardonnay, Tocai, and local varieties such as Rebula, are all being crafted the modern way (fermented in stainless steel, aged in *barriques*), though none of them is particularly cheap. The usual Merlot and Cabernet are around too.

Wines of the other regions, best of which is the Kontinentalna Hrvatska in the Sava and Drava valleys, are even trickier to get hold of, and we can't comment further than to mention they exist. The necessary capital is now being injected, so expect to hear more from these regions in future, as the potential quality is apparently (and historically) very high.

SOUTH AFRICA

It's fascinating to look back at recent editions of this *Guide* and marvel at how much has changed in a short time. For example, in 1998 the pronouncement on South Africa was: 'Don't expect too much just yet, but do stick with it, especially the wines from progressive independent estates. South Africa is slowly getting there.' Quite right too, except for that word 'slowly'. Little did we guess just how quickly progress would change the Western Cape. Witness the concentrated, new Merlot and Shiraz, the 'super-premium' Pinotage, the well-balanced Sauvignon Blanc. . .

How has South Africa moved on so quickly after the painfully slow progress in the years that immediately folloewd apartheid? In part it is due to a new generation of winemakers, the majority of whom have spent time overseas, coming home with new ideas and higher standards. They are prepared to push the boundaries back, planting vines in more suitable areas, or sourcing fruit from old workhorse bush vines to make premium wine, or simply trying out new varieties, new blends, better ways to vinify and oak their wine.

Some old-fashioned wineries remain, without a doubt. But in general it's now refreshing to visit the Cape's winelands and talk to its winemakers, in huge contrast to the days of apartheid and for several years afterwards, when most in the wine industry remained narrow-minded and intransigent.

South African wine now accounts for 7.5 per cent of all wine sold in Britain, and the UK market soaks up almost 50 per cent of all South African wine exports. That, too, is a very long way from the days of apartheid, when Cape wine was rightly shunned by many in the UK.

On that subject, it's heartening to see the so-called black empowerment projects in the winelands continue to alter the nature of the industry. Even post-apartheid, opportunities for black winemakers, viticulturists, marketeers and general managers have been shamefully slow in coming, but the gradual success of 'fair trade' projects such as Winds of Change, Thandi, Tukulu and Fair Valley is encouraging. Can we recommend the wines? Yes. Most of them are well-made and fruity, not complex or deeply thrilling perhaps, but highly palatable. Snap them up and help support these projects.

More welcome news: in January 2002 the South African government signed an agreement with the EU which allows South Africa to export 42 million bottles of wine a year free of customs duty. This quota will escalate by three per cent each year. In a show of solidarity, the majority of Cape exporters have agreed to pay the value of the duty-free concession into a fund to ensure these benefits help the wine industry as whole, particularly over ethical labour practices and working conditions, and training schemes for disadvantaged students.

Then there's the Ethical Trading Initiative (ETI), a pilot scheme formed between some British supermarkets, trade unions and South African partners to scrutinise workers' rights, safety and health, and the introduction in 2002 of a legal minimum wage for agricultural workers. Parts of the wine industry are now being carefully monitored under the new ETI body and it is expected to reach a much larger number of employees in the next few years. These are early days, but the ETI sounds promising.

So far, so positive. The success of the Cape's mega-brands is something we are more ambivalent about. The Kumala range, made by Western Wines, is now in the top ten UK brands, and sold an astonishing 1.1 million cases here last year. Other important familiar names, apparently available almost anywhere, are the KWV label, Arniston Bay, Goiya (it's pronounced Hoi-Ya, for all those who have wondered) and bag-in-box Namaqua. Then there are innumerable inexpensive supermarket own-label Cape wines and other bags-in-boxes . . .

Most of these popular, inexpensive wines are reasonably palatable, fresh, soft and fruity. Some of them are also deeply bland. It is these bottles that are driving the sales, of course, not the premium, award-winning wines. It's hard to complain bitterly about them, but restricting your experience of South African wine to these big brands is to miss out – big time! Do try a wide spread from the Cape and move up a notch or two to sample much more interesting fare.

Finally, fans of South African wine (and particularly those lucky enough to be visiting its dramatically beautiful winelands) have recourse to two excellent sources of highly detailed information. First and foremost, try to get hold of John Platter's pocket guide to South African wines (try *www.platterwineguide.co.za* for stockists) and, second, check out the commercial website *www.wine.co.za* for the latest news.

Red wines – grape varieties

In the past, red wines were not a great strength for the Cape's winemakers, but the increase in quality we've seen over recent years means they now have a sure grip. Very sure. Pinotage, the grape with which growers initially chose to lead their charge into the global wine market, was not the ideal choice for showcase wines. Authentic and individual to South Africa, yes, but Pinotage has been less reliably appealing than Shiraz in Australia or even

Zinfandel in California. It's a tricky grape both in the vineyard and winery, allowing only a narrow margin of error before slipping into sour tomato and acetone (nail-varnish) notes. Many estates have taken their time to get it right, but the good news is Pinotage has improved dramatically over the last five years and the best examples are now compelling. Once a grower has mastery over the grape, the results are every bit the rich plum and spice standard-bearers that top South African producers have long wanted.

Shiraz is making a big contribution to South Africa's premium red portfolio at the moment. It's hardly surprising, as this is a grape that likes warmth. We haven't tasted a bad example in months, and the best are wonderfully full-bodied, ripe and peppery. Very promising – perhaps the Australians should watch their backs . . .

Of the other grapes, new virus-free clones of Cabernet Sauvignon are ensuring that austere, gritty examples are a thing of the past; the wines are now full, cassis-laden, almost minty, not unlike some Australian versions. Merlot, too, can be great stuff, packed with rich plum and red-berries and often with well-judged creamy oak. It is popular with growers who are Francophiles – a couple of whom are aiming at Pomerol lookalikes. A few impressive Cabernet Francs exist. Pinot Noir achieves its best in the cooler vineyards of Walker Bay (Hamilton Russell and Bouchard Finlayson are the names to look out for). Cinsault and Ruby Cabernet are more often than not used in everyday generic reds or as part of a blend; these are the more forgettable Cape reds.

White wines – grape varieties

Traditionally, the vast majority of Cape wine was white – most of it made from Chenin Blanc grapes, or 'Steen'. Today Chenin is being grubbed up as if it were an embarrassing weed. While there's little doubt this grape has been responsible for some terribly bland wine, we think this is an over-reaction, and urge South Africa's winemakers to continue trying to make better wines from it. Low-yielding, dry-farmed examples can be ripe, lime-drenched and honeyed, as growers such as Ken Forrester in Stellenbosch and Villiera in Paarl are now proving. There are also sumptuous sweet, sticky wines made – though few, unfortunately, reach the UK – and well-priced, easy-drinking, dryish Chenins that make ideal party wines. Colombard, also widely planted, is more limited to (at best) fresh, simple dry whites or for blending and distilling into spirits.

Now let's extol the virtues of South African Sauvignon Blanc. The last few years have shown that Sauvignon can be as good here as it is almost anywhere else, achieving a fine balance between New Zealand-style lemon-and-lime, racy acidity and tropical, warm-climate ripeness. It needs to grow in cooler regions – those not subject to South Africa's frequent bursts of heat, where it tends to lose its delicate aromatics. A high number of growers are getting it right. And Chardonnay has its pockets of greatness too. Plantings have increased enormously in recent years – thriving in the cooler areas, just as Sauvignon does – and producing, tangy, citrusy wines, but look out for some richer, butter-and-tropical fruit numbers as well. Some examples of Cape Chardonnay are a little too heavily oaked for our tastes. Of the others, the Rieslings are patchy in quality, but the few Semillons and Viogniers are rich, fruity, often oaky, and well worth a try.

Sparkling wines

Méthode cap classique (MCC) is the South African term for sparkling wine made by the French *méthode traditionnelle*. While the method of production mirrors that of champagne, not all the wines are made from the classic champagne grape varieties (Chardonnay, Pinot Noir and Pinot Meunier). There aren't many good MCC sparklers readily available in the UK, but if you see it do try creamy Graham Beck Brut, Blanc de Blancs, made solely from Chardonnay in the hot, flat vineyards of Robertson. New, inexpensive fizz from the big Kumala and Arniston Bay labels has now popped up in the UK – these are acceptable, fresh party sparklers but lack complexity and finesse.

The regions

Generally speaking, the vineyards of the Cape are cooler than their proximity to the equator might suggest. This can be attributed to the climatically moderating influences of the Indian and Atlantic Oceans, and the Benguela current emanating from the Antarctic. Importantly, the varied topography of the Cape offers many different vine-growing conditions and the potential for *terroir* characteristics in the wines (although the latter is still in the process of being realised).

Constantia

This fashionable and affluent suburb of Cape Town is where governor Simon van der Stel established the first Cape vineyards in 1685 and set about making mainly sweet wines. The decision to plant vines here no doubt had much to do with the proximity to Cape Town. Some 315 or so years later Constantia's fortunes are being revived and it has become one of the best areas in South Africa for white wines – particularly Sauvignon Blanc, in our view, which has a lovely fresh acidity combined with passionfruit, guava and lime flavours. It's also worth watching out for the reds; there's a lot of unrealised potential as some ripe, rounded Merlots have proved.

Franschhoek
Franschhoek – or 'French corner' – was named after the French Huguenots who settled there in the seventeenth century. Strictly speaking, this is a sub-region of Paarl (see below), but its verdant valley location and refreshing air of community collaboration mark it out as a separate entity. Since the valley runs east to west, producers can choose where to site vines – north-facing slopes for red grape varieties, south for white grape varieties, with those looking for cooler climates simply planting further up the slopes. There's potential for elegance here, with alcohols invariably 1–1.5 per cent lower than in neighbouring Paarl and Stellenbosch, but as yet it's not often realised. Sauvignon and Semillon currently star as the best of the grapes and some decent fizz has been made here.

Olifantsrivier/Orange River
These two wine regions would be far too hot for wine production if it wasn't for cooling breezes from the Atlantic Ocean in Olifantsrivier, while the Orange River, even further to the north and inland, is another mass of water with a tempering effect on nearby vineyards. Irrigation is widely practised, and yields can be very high. The giant Vredendal co-operative – the single largest winery in South Africa – is to be found here, its overwhelming size not preventing a pioneering drive for quality.

Paarl
Paarl is often thought of as Stellenbosch's (see below) poorer cousin. While that is not strictly fair (some of the wineries are among the country's best), it has a degree of truth. Paarl does not produce as many great wines as Stellenbosch but they tend to be riper and rounder, and it comes a close second. It's generally warmer than Stellenbosch, although the area contains a variety of vineyards from hot valley-floor plots to decidedly chilly mountainside venues. Its wide range of wines, and in particular Chardonnays and Cabernets, can be excellent. Although the KWV once dominated this region, smaller, innovative growers such as Fairview and Glen Carlou are emerging from its shadows.

Robertson
This is a hot, fertile, inland region, known touristically as the 'Valley of Vines and Roses'. Irrigation from the arterial Breede River is essential since the rainfall is only 200mm per year. Despite the high temperatures, Robertson has a name for white wine, with refined, impressive Chardonnay and Sauvignon Blanc particularly

The Which? Wine Guide 2003 voucher scheme

£5

Valid at participating merchants, as listed in *The Which? Wine Guide 2003*, until 30 September 2003

See terms and conditions overleaf

The Which? Wine Guide 2003 voucher scheme

£5

Valid at participating merchants, as listed in *The Which? Wine Guide 2003*, until 30 September 2003

See terms and conditions overleaf

The Which? Wine Guide 2003 voucher scheme

£5

Valid at participating merchants, as listed in *The Which? Wine Guide 2003*, until 30 September 2003

See terms and conditions overleaf

Terms and Conditions

- The vouchers in *The Which? Wine Guide 2003* are valid from 1 October 2002 until 30 September 2003. Each £5 voucher can be used against a wine purchase of £50 or more. No photocopies or any other kind of reproduction of vouchers will be accepted. The vouchers may not be used in conjunction with any other discount, offer or promotional scheme.

- The vouchers are redeemable against a £50 wine purchase. For a voucher to be redeemable, the customer must mention at the time of buying his or her intent to use a *Which? Wine Guide* voucher. The £5 is to be deducted from the bill inclusive of VAT, with the participating merchant bearing the cost of the £5 discount.

- Participating establishments are highlighted in the pages of *The Which? Wine Guide 2003* by the (£5) symbol in the merchant's entry, and an explanation of the symbol and scheme can be found opposite the Contents page of the book.

Terms and Conditions

- The vouchers in *The Which? Wine Guide 2003* are valid from 1 October 2002 until 30 September 2003. Each £5 voucher can be used against a wine purchase of £50 or more. No photocopies or any other kind of reproduction of vouchers will be accepted. The vouchers may not be used in conjunction with any other discount, offer or promotional scheme.

- The vouchers are redeemable against a £50 wine purchase. For a voucher to be redeemable, the customer must mention at the time of buying his or her intent to use a *Which? Wine Guide* voucher. The £5 is to be deducted from the bill inclusive of VAT, with the participating merchant bearing the cost of the £5 discount.

- Participating establishments are highlighted in the pages of *The Which? Wine Guide 2003* by the (£5) symbol in the merchant's entry, and an explanation of the symbol and scheme can be found opposite the Contents page of the book.

Terms and Conditions

- The vouchers in *The Which? Wine Guide 2003* are valid from 1 October 2002 until 30 September 2003. Each £5 voucher can be used against a wine purchase of £50 or more. No photocopies or any other kind of reproduction of vouchers will be accepted. The vouchers may not be used in conjunction with any other discount, offer or promotional scheme.

- The vouchers are redeemable against a £50 wine purchase. For a voucher to be redeemable, the customer must mention at the time of buying his or her intent to use a *Which? Wine Guide* voucher. The £5 is to be deducted from the bill inclusive of VAT, with the participating merchant bearing the cost of the £5 discount.

- Participating establishments are highlighted in the pages of *The Which? Wine Guide 2003* by the (£5) symbol in the merchant's entry, and an explanation of the symbol and scheme can be found opposite the Contents page of the book.

successful on stony, lime-rich sites. Surprisingly enough, there's even good sparkling wine and a passable Riesling from de Wetshof too. Reds are at long last beginning to emerge (Cabernet and Shiraz). An exciting spot.

Stellenbosch

While Stellenbosch is undeniably the source of South Africa's top red wines, white and sparkling stars are increasingly emerging too – thanks to the cool breezes from the ocean at False Bay, which moderate the summer heat. Stellenbosch has excellent vineyard sites, particularly for those winemakers prepared to move off the plains and head for the hills, as it has over 50 different types of soil and terrain – ranging from steep, south-facing slopes to alluvial flats not suited to quality wine production. Some of the most successful new wineries are based in the Bottelary Hills, north-west of Stellenbosch town. The towering Simonsberg Mountain, Jonkershoek Valley, Helderberg and Vlottenberg are also important new districts to watch – for a new younger generation of growers who believe strongly in the individuality of the wines from these sub-regions. In fact, the air of complacency, for which we have criticised Stellenbosch in recent years, has largely given way to the wave of enthusiasm from these new brooms. It may be the increased competition, both within and outside South Africa, that has caused this. Whatever the reason, we feel more confident than ever in suggesting that Stellenbosch has a bright future.

Swartland/Tulbagh/Malmesbury

Since the early 1990s, this hot and previously underrated wheat and tobacco region has been producing some top white wines as well as powerful reds. The cooler, coastal Malmesbury sub-region is now making waves, particularly with concentrated, rounded reds, while inland, scenic Tulbagh is also expanding its range. As the vines are unirrigated, great intensity of flavour is possible. Some excellent value-for-money wines come from the local co-operatives and the few estates.

Walker Bay/Elgin

A cool, damp and humid area south-east of Cape Town, which encompasses the districts of Elgin and Bot River and has been subject to much hype since the 1980s, although there are only a few wineries of note. Stellenbosch-based Neil Ellis has produced splendid Sauvignon Blanc in Elgin, while Bouchard Finlayson and Hamilton Russell make particularly refined Pinot Noir and Chardonnay in Walker Bay. Hip-and-happening Wildekrans at Bot River, six miles further inland, is carving a reputation with a range from a much warmer locality.

Worcester

Worcester is a warm, fertile area which contains nearly one-fifth of the country's vineyards but few producers of note, apart from some decent co-operatives. White wines are generally basic, but Pinotage can be respectable, and a few appealing Ruby Cabernets deserve a much wider audience. Problems with high cropping levels in the past mean it's worth choosing your producer with care.

Pick of the producers

African Terroir This Paarl winery (aka Sonop) has a sound range, notably its soft, ripe and tasty Winds of Change blends – look out for the reds – part of its successful workers' empowerment initiative, and the ecologically sound African Legend range, of which the Shiraz and the Sauvignon are the best examples. Also makes the Out of Africa label and Cape Soleil organics.

L'Avenir Based in the Simonsberg sub-zone of Stellenbosch, this is a smashing range all round, from the dense, ripe Cabernet and Pinotage to the big, toasty Chardonnay.

Graham Beck Convincing MCC sparklers from Robertson. Coastal Range vinified at Bellingham by Charles Hopkins is making waves with impressive Shiraz, Cabernet and Pinotage, plus new Merlot. Also look out for the easy-going, well-made and value-for-money Railroad Red and Waterside White.

Bellingham Rare, superb Cabernet Franc and also decent Shiraz, Chardonnay, Merlot and Cabernet Sauvignon. Stunning Pinotage Spitz in premium range. All from Franschoek.

Beyerskloof (see *Kanonkop*, below).

Boekenhoutskloof Exciting, go-ahead Franschhoek estate where the talented Marc Kent makes superb limey Semillon and a Syrah that uncannily resembes Côte Rôtie. Also great Cabernet and good-value, juicy wines under second label Porcupine Ridge.

Boschendal The Cape's largest, now extensively revamped, estate; these might be old-timer Franschoek wines, but their style is all modern. The rich Chardonnay and Merlot and crisp Sauvignon and MCC traditional sparklers all prove the point.

Bouchard Finlayson Good, crisp Chardonnay, almost like Chablis; very clean, steely Sauvignon; and (consuming passion) the cherryish Pinot Noir from Walker Bay.

Buitenverwachting Hermann Kirschbaum's excellent Sauvignon, Chardonnay, Riesling, and a very decent Bordeaux blend called Christine, are produced in Constantia.

Clos Malverne Exciting Stellenbosch winery dedicated to reds and doing well with Pinotage and Cabernet in particular.

De Toren Famous (and rightly so) for its brilliant, ripe and well-structured Bordeaux blend Fusion V, from Stellenbosch.

De Trafford David Trafford makes excellent Stellenbosch reds, with particularly compelling Shiraz and Cabernet. Do try the astonishingly high-quality, oaked Chenin Blanc.

De Wetshof Larger than life, Danie de Wet is the leading figure in Robertson and best known for his range of fruit-driven, upfront Chardonnays (labelled Bon Vallon, Lesca, Bateleur and d'Honneur); Sauvignon and Riesling are also classy. The fruits of the newly planted Pinot and Cabernet are eagerly anticipated.

Delaire Bruwer Raats notched up vintages around the globe before settling down at Delaire in the Simonsberg area of Stellenbosch. Prices can match European classics but are snapped up anyway. Look out for delicious Chardonnay and Sauvignon too.

Delheim Stellenbosch winery with desirable Vera Cruz range: Pinotage, Merlot, Cabernet and, now, gamey Shiraz.

Neil Ellis Wines The first authentic, roving winemaker in the Cape, with a passion for producing the best wine from a particular locality (or nothing else), Neil Ellis now has a base in Stellenbosch (Jonkershoek Valley). Look out for his Reserve Reds (Cabernet Sauvignon, Shiraz and Pinotage); the elegant whites from Elgin; and the Stellenbosch range.

Fairview Charles Back is a great winemaker and one of the Cape's opinion-formers. Attractive range overall, includes decent Shiraz and stunning Pinotage, as well as excellent Chardonnay and ripe Viognier. Back is heavily into all things Rhône – witness the irreverent, popular Goats do Roam blend, and now premium Goat Roti – but will take on the Californians with his new, impressive Zinfandel. His vision stretches beyond the Paarl estate where he's based to admirably democratic dimensions with the Fair Valley empowerment venture and Spice Route (see below).

Flagstone Motivated team with winery on the docks in Cape Town – selects grapes from all over the Cape to make notably rich, ripe reds, especially the fruitcake-scented Dragon Tree Cabernet/ Pinotage blend, and the smooth, moreish George's Blend Pinot/ Merlot. One to watch.

Glen Carlou Much-admired, award-winning Chardonnay; also seek out Pinot, Shiraz, Bordeaux-blend Grand Classique from a Paarl winery that is making waves.

Grangehurst Small but perfectly formed, Jeremy Walker's Stellenbosch winery turns out some of the Cape's richest Pinotage and Cabernet/Merlot blends. Walker also has a hand in making the superb Hidden Valley Pinotage.

Groot Constantia Great Shiraz plus classic Chardonnay, Sauvignon, Riesling and Bordeaux-blend Gouverneur's Reserve from the original Constantia farm.

Hamilton Russell This much-admired Walker Bay estate now concentrates solely on Chardonnay and Pinot Noir, crafting some outstanding (but expensive) wines as a result. Second label is Southern Right – named after the whales that return annually to nearby Hermanus Bay.

Hartenberg Subtle rather than bold Shiraz (from older vines than most); classic-style Cabernet; and new Zinfandel from progressive young winemakers in the Bottelary Hills (Stellenbosch).

Jordan The California training shows at this Stellenbosch winery. Kathy and Gary Jordan make extremely classy reds and whites with immense attention to detail.

Kanonkop Beyers Truter's influential Stellenbosch Pinotage is still one of the top examples – spicy, brambly, robust. Look out too for the Paul Sauer Bordeaux blend. There's no doubt Truter is one of the Cape's top producers of red wine. He also owns the Beyerskloof winery, noted for exceptional Pinotage and Cabernet, and recently announced he plans to spend more time there, appointing Abrie Bees as Kanonkop's winemaker.

Kanu Newish Stellenbosch winery (1998) making waves with its splendidly rich, aromatic Wooded Chenin Blanc. Check out the pleasant quaffing blend of Ruby Cabernet and Cinsault and the fresh, grassy Sauvignon Blanc too.

Klein Constantia Judging by Ross Gower's Chardonnay and Sauvignon Blanc, his New Zealand training has stood him in good stead. While textbook, beautifully balanced Cape Sauvignon is outstanding, he also makes satisfying Cabernet and Shiraz; the sweet Vin de Constance made from Muscat de Frontignan, re-creating the legendary Constantia wines of centuries past.

KWV International The privatised incarnation of the former, massive co-operative enterprise (with regulatory control to boot) now declares its aim of 'becoming a major international player'. The basic KWV range is better than ever, particularly the Cabernet and Pinotage, while the flagship Cathedral Cellar range is also going great guns (check out the Merlot, or the Chardonnay). Cheaper Robert's Rock label provides good-value, everyday drinking, especially the moreish Cabernet/Merlot blend.

Longridge Probably the best-known label from the large and generally good-quality group gathered under the Winecorp umbrella (other Winecorp productions include the extraordinarily intense Sejana Merlot and decent Bay View range). Longridge puts out superb Cabernet, Merlot, Pinotage and Chardonnay, made by Australian-born Ben Radford based in Stellenbosch.

Meerlust The Pinot Noir and Chardonnay from this Stellenbosch (Helderberg) estate may not be to all tastes, but the Merlot and the Rubicon Bordeaux blend are both stunning wines capable of long, graceful ageing.

La Motte One of the best estates in Franschhoek and one of the most renowned in the whole of South Africa. Jacques Borman makes exemplary Shiraz, Cabernet, Chardonnay and a Bordeaux blend called Millennium, as well as convincing oaked Sauvignon Blanc (all with French role models).

Mulderbosch Top Sauvignon Blanc, oaked, and grassy and crisp. Match that with the splendid Chardonnay and the exuberant Faithful Hound Bordeaux blend and you have a Stellenbosch estate that's hard to beat. Steen-op-Hout (Brick on Wood) Chenin is also justifiably popular.

Nederburg Although the Nederburg range can be rather old-fashioned, the wines have a large fan base and sweet versions are exceptional, especially Edelkeur – Chenin Blanc – and the Weisser Riesling. Based in Paarl, grapes sourced from throughout the Cape.

Overgaauw Over-sized, bold Stellenbosch reds: Cabernet, Merlot, Shiraz and blended Tricorda. There's also new Cabernet/Touriga Nacional (a port grape, here?). Big – but we like them anyway.

Plaisir de Merle Glamorous Paarl estate producing admirable, claret-like Cabernet and other red blends. The Bordeaux influence of Paul Pontallier of Château Margaux no doubt has something to do with the style of the impressive but firm Cabernet and the Graves-like Sauvignon Blanc. The Chardonnay is reasonable, too. Exciting, dark Petit Verdot.

Rustenberg Utterly revamped and loftily ambitious, historic Stellenbosch estate. Excellent flagship wines, Peter Barlow Cabernet Sauvignon and Five Soldiers Chardonnay, sit alongside Rustenberg and Brampton ranges. Unmissable.

Rust-en-Vrede High-flying Stellenbosch red wine specialist. Cabernet, Merlot, Shiraz and Estate Blend all noteworthy.

Simonsig Family-owned, sizeable estate producing consistently appealing dynamic reds (good Pinotage, Shiraz and Bordeaux-blend Tiara) and a notable Chardonnay.

Sonop (see *African Terroir*, above).

Spice Route Two ranges exist from this pioneering Malmesbury venture started by a group of South African wine gurus, but now solely owned by Charles Back of Fairview (see above) its Spice Route 'flagship wines' are thick, concentrated, rounded, but the 'standard' Chenin and Cabernet Sauvignon/Merlot are not to be passed over lightly. Look out, too, for the more broadly appealing Andrew's Hope Merlot-based blend and new Viognier.

Springfield Estate Robertson winery run by the energetic and talented Abrie Bruwer. Chardonnay and Sauvignon in a minerally, elegant style; also fine Cabernet.

Steenberg The new (rich) kid on the old Constantia block, with a remarkable Sauvignon already, and more varieties in the pipeline for future vintages, including Nebbiolo and Shiraz. Merlot currently performing exceptionally.

Stellenzicht Finely crafted Stellenbosch wines across a wide range. Particularly of note are the intensely powerful, iconic Shiraz, the ripe, oaky Pinotage and the serious Founder's Private Release Cabernet; Sauvignon Blanc also a winner.

Thelema Whatever Gyles Webb turns his hand to is world class, whether it be full, fruity, minty Cabernet blends, piercingly flavoured Sauvignon or elegant Chardonnay – or new Pinotage. Good-value second label called Stormy Cape. There's a reasonable supply of this Stellenbosch wine in the UK, yet Thelema's cellar-door sign invariably says 'sold out'. Grab it while you can.

Uiterwyk Historic Stellenbosch estate with excellent Top of the Hill Pinotage, Cabernet-based Cape blend and Shiraz.

Veenwouden Outstanding, cult estate in Paarl, staking a firm claim to the title 'Super-Cape', with reds helped along by the influence of the renowned Michel Rolland from Bordeaux. Merlot dominates. Tiny production, no expense spared and consequent sky-high prices.

Vergelegen The ebullient and outspoken André van Rensberg holds the reins at this state-of-the-art winery in Somerset West (Stellenbosch). Benchmark whites (delicious Semillon, serious Chardonnay and racy Sauvignon) and a bang up-to-date range of reds, particularly Cabernets. Well-distributed and well-priced in the UK. A must-try.

Villiera Solid range all round from Paarl, with particularly noteworthy Chenin Blanc, Sauvignon, Merlot, Gewurztraminer and sparklers. The Grier family has a progressive approach to both its vineyards and its workforce.

Vriesenhof The larger-than-life Jan Boland Coetzee makes hefty reds, although with more easy-drinkability than they once had, with the Kallista Bordeaux blend being the best of the bunch. All Stellenbosch grown.

Warwick Estate Fine Cabernet Sauvignon, Cabernet Franc and Merlot from Stellenbosch, with the blend of all three, Trilogy, one of the Cape's best wines. Look out also for the quite delicious Pinotage and Chardonnay.

Waterford Already making waves, especially with carefully considered Cabernet and Shiraz, this new state-of-the-art Stellenbosch winery, set in a beautiful Mediterranean-style estate, is definitely one to watch.

Wildekrans Precocious Pinotage from happening estate in Walker Bay, now sits alongside some elegant Bordeaux-style wines – particularly the new blend Osiris.

Yonder Hill Another new-wave Stellenbosch boutique winery, making great Merlot influenced by the wines of Pomerol and Australia.

Zandvliet Robertson Shiraz specialists *par excellence*.

South African vintage guide

Cape whites are traditionally not built to last, although the better-structured Chardonnays might easily do so. As winemaking improves and the fruit of virus-free vines begins to take on age, red wines in particular will show more scope for cellaring. Vintage to vintage, weather doesn't vary vastly in South Africa, but the following are some guidelines as to what to expect from the most recent years.

2002 was a difficult year that brought mixed fortunes. Heavy late winter/spring rains replenished dams after four years of drought, but they also brought downy mildew and rot. A long heatwave from February onwards, then cooler autumn weather, badly affected some vines. Cabernets will be patchy; Shiraz has fared much better. Stick to the top producers from 2002.

2001 was less excessively hot than the previous two vintages: wines are good, especially the whites.

The 2000 vintage will be remembered for the massive wildfires that caused heavy damage to some of the Cape's best-known wineries (with the inevitable resulting price hikes) and also tremendous heat. 1999 was similarly hot and favoured early ripening varietals brought in early; reds show concentration and reasonable quality.

SPAIN

It ought to be possible to drink a good-quality Spanish wine on any occasion – this is a country that produces fresh, snappy fizz, fine reds, modern whites, superb fortified wines both dry and sweet, and oceans of cheap-and-cheerful party plonk to boot. Spain's versatility as a wine-producing nation is clearly not in question.

In 1980, high-class Spanish table wine began and ended with Rioja. The rise of premium reds and whites from other regions, and their popularity in the UK, is a relatively new affair. Do explore them – if you are still stuck on Rioja, then venture into Navarra, Priorat, Toro and Ribera del Duero for other reds; if you are bored with cheap, own-label Spanish whites, go for the somewhat better examples being produced in the Somontano, Rueda and Rías Baixas regions.

Like a red wine to a bull.

And even that party plonk seems to have got better of late. Workhorse regions such as Jumilla and Campo de Borja that have turned out cheap *vino* for the UK market for decades are managing to make fresher, more modern wines. The wineries of the vast central plain are at last being revamped and the widespread use of irrigation systems (legal since 1996 and widely used prior to that) means that growers can contemplate planting many more interesting varieties than the drought-resistant but extremely dull Airén.

So, exciting times in Spain. But even now it pays to be cautious: white wines from this country still seem to lag behind reds to a degree. Inexpensive basic Spanish *blanco* is not as good as basic *tinto* and, up a notch, white grape varieties such as Godello and Verdejo are not quite as up-to-the-minute and classy as some would have us believe. The Albariño vine of Rías Baixas can certainly produce appealing fruity white, but some examples are tart and simple, and even the best do not deserve price tags of around £10. In fact, some of Spain's Chardonnays are arguably their best white wines – Torres Milmanda and some top Somontano examples spring to mind – although readers with a hankering for old-fashioned, waxy-yellow, white Rioja will continue to cherish those. Anyway, you get our drift – Spanish reds are a better way to part with your money.

Talking of which, Rioja's prices have fluctuated alarmingly over the past decade. Problems began in the early 1990s when sales increased rapidly. This led to a rise in grape prices, culminating in the small 1999 harvest when the going rate for a kilo of grapes was 440 pesetas, as opposed to 70 just four years previously. Inevitably, these increases were reflected in the prices of the wines, some rising 20 per cent in one year. Just as inevitably, sales began to fall, and a large but fairly mediocre 2000 vintage was just what producers didn't want. Price reductions have followed and lessons may have been learned – it's a little early to say. But one piece of good news for Rioja: the 2001 vintage was high quality but smaller in quantity – just what they *did* want.

Two other positive trends: firstly, wineries now seem willing to pay higher prices for higher-quality fruit, which should encourage growers to produce smaller quantities of better grapes. Secondly, there is a new determination by talented Spanish winemakers to cross DOs (wine-producing areas) and take exciting, progressive winemaking into new regions – something which it is hard to imagine happening in the past. Alvaro Palacios, now producing not only in Rioja, but also in Priorat and Bierzo too, epitomizes this – as does Alejandro Fernandez, famous for his work in Ribera del Duero but now turning out premium reds in La Mancha (El Viniculo) and at Dehesa la Granja, just outside th Toro region.

Spanish wine classification

Spain's equivalent of the French *appellation contrôlée* is *denominación de origen*, or DO for short. DO delimits the boundaries of wine-producing areas and controls matters such as grape varieties, pruning, maximum yields and minimum levels of alcohol. It doesn't however delimit wine quality. In 1991, a further category, *denominación de origen calificada* (DOCa) was introduced. So far, only Rioja has qualified (even if some other DOs achieve a higher average standard), although there is now serious discussion of 'promoting' Priorat and this may well take place soon. Within the DOs, the wines are further subdivided according to length of ageing prior to release. *Joven* ('young') or *sin crianza* ('without oak') wines can be sold as soon as the winemaker feels they are ready, while *crianzas* must spend at least six months in cask (a year in Rioja and Ribera del Duero) and can only be released after two full calendar years, e.g. a 2000 *crianza* cannot be sold before 1 January 2003. *Reservas* require three calendar years of ageing of which at least one must be in cask and another in bottle, while *gran reservas* undergo a minimum of five calendar years ageing, spending at least two of those years in cask and two in bottle.

Below DOCa and DO come the categories of *vino de la tierra* (equivalent to the French *vin de pays*, and potentially just as interesting and maverick – see the above) and *vino de mesa* or table wine.

NORTHERN SPAIN – RIOJA, NAVARRA, RIBERA DEL DUERO

Rioja

For many people, Rioja *is* Spanish wine. It comes from vineyards spread along the River Ebro, and is usually a blend of Tempranillo and Garnacha grapes supported by small amounts of Graciano (for finesse and tannin) and Mazuelo (aka Carignan, for colour and body). Cabernet Sauvignon does feature in certain wines, although it is only supposed to be grown for 'experimental' use.

The region is split into three zones, namely (in rising order of warmth), Rioja Alavesa, Rioja Alta and Rioja Baja, and many producers have traditionally blended fruit from all three to produce their wines. However, there is a slow growth in the popularity of single-vineyard wines, not least because it gives producers far greater control over the quality of their grapes. There is also a move to bypass the traditional *crianza/reserva/gran reserva* system of classification (see above). Many entry-level wines are now made in what the producers call the 'semi-*crianza*' style, to denote wines that have had a few months of oak influence, but not enough to be called *crianza* or *sin crianza*. Semi-*crianza* wines can be pleasant enough, but they lack the mellow, oaky, long-aged character that, for many, is the hallmark of Rioja's reds. It's important to remember that unoaked, cheap (usually sub-£4.99) Rioja doesn't have true Rioja characteristics.

At the opposite end of the scale, several of the finest modern wines qualify for *reserva* rather than *gran reserva* status, by dint of spending less than 24 months in barrel, and here it is the name of a star vineyard or top producer, rather than the *reserva* status, that receives the highest billing. Those barrels, traditionally made from American oak and used for several years, are now often new French oak, which imparts a quite different flavour. Instead of a soft, ready-to-drink red with strawberry and vanilla-cream flavours, high-class modern Rioja is often firmer and chewier, with fresh rather than cooked berry fruit (sounds more New World in style, doesn't it?), and may require several years in bottle before reaching its peak. While some of these modern-style wines are enjoyable, let's hope they are not pursued at the expense of the mellow, traditional style, which is so wonderfully characteristic of the region. At least punters have a wider choice these days – Rioja does not all taste the same. But if you are keen on a particular type, it now pays to both study the label for the ageing category *and* know the *bodega*'s particular house style.

Not all Rioja is red. White Rioja is made predominantly from the rather neutral Viura grape plus Garnacha Blanco and Malvasia Riojana, and comes in a variety of styles. Ten years ago, the fashion was for clean-as-a-whistle wine that had no oak influence, and not much more flavour. At the other extreme, traditional white Rioja, heavy on the Malvasia, deep yellow, almost waxy and heavily oaked, provides a memorable (although not for some people pleasurable) experience. López de Heredia is one of the few *bodegas* persisting with such wines. Arguably the best whites of today lie between these two extremes, with oak- and barrel-fermentation being used with greater sensitivity, but it's really a matter of personal taste.

Pick of the producers (Rioja)

AGE Huge operation, once best known for the insubstantial red Siglo Saco in its distinctive hessian cover. Its replacement, Siglo 1881, is a far better, fruitier wine. The *gran reserva* Marqués del Romeral is also very good.

Allende The prestige *cuvée* Aurus comes in not far short of £100 a bottle. Leave it for the label hunters and head for the excellent regular wine at a fraction of the price, which is one of the best of the new-wave Riojas.

Artadi Main brand of former co-operative Cosecheros Alaveses, making wines using mostly Rioja Alavesa fruit. All the range, from easy-quaffer Orobio up to stunning Grandes Anadas Reserva, comes highly recommended.

Barón de Ley Single-estate wines displaying clever use of French oak and a little Cabernet Sauvignon in some blends.

Beronia Small, good-quality *bodega* owned by González Byass of Jerez, producing juicy but long-lasting *reservas*.

Marqués de Cáceres Successful commercial company making lively, fruity, modern wines plus top-of-the-range wine Gaudium.

Campo Viejo Commendably high standards for such a large concern. *Crianzas* and *reservas* are worth looking out for. Albor is the lighter, less interesting, *sin crianza* style.

Contino Excellent, plummy, single-vineyard wine from Rioja Alavesa made and marketed by CVNE (see below) as *reserva* and *gran reserva* only. The delicious red made from Graciano shows the potential of this fine grape.

El Coto Small Rioja *bodega* making consistently satisfying reds under the El Coto and Coto de Imaz labels.

CVNE (Compañía Vinícola del Norte de España) A fine name from Rioja Alta, producing classy, oak-aged white Monopole, first-rate, accessible Viña Real Reserva; and outstanding Imperial Gran Reserva.

Faustino Martínez Large but reliable *bodega* in Rioja Alavesa, putting out impressive whites, and sound, sweetly fruity reds, the best of which is Faustino I Gran Reserva. The frosted bottles and regal labels are garish, however.

Marqués de Griñón Ripe Cabernet Sauvignon is among the range on offer at this go-ahead winery, which has long been a maverick of the region.

Viña Ijalba Impressive, concentrated red from a new-wave winery that has been organic since 1998. Try the peppery, single-varietal Graciano for a refreshing change.

López de Heredia Venerable *bodega* with a long history of making old-fashioned, ageworthy reds and hugely oaky, waxy-yellow whites. If you like archly traditional Rioja, then try the Viña Bosconia and Viña Tondonia wines; those in search of youthful, fruity flavours should go elsewhere.

Martínez Bujanda Main label Conde de Valdemar is great for both whites and reds in a highly modern style, with plenty of ripe fruit and fine oak to the fore. New single-vineyard wine Finca Valpiedra keeps standards high.

Miguel Merino Impressive recently established *bodega* with stylish, fruit-packed *reserva*.

Montecillo High quality across a wide range at this award-winning *bodega*, which uses French oak for complex, elegant reds.

Muga Historically known for its traditional, finely wrought reds, which have a soft and old-fashioned appeal, especially Prado Enea Gran Reserva. Today reinventing itself with a delicious barrel-fermented white and new-wave Torre Muga Reserva.

Marqués de Murrieta Prestigious *bodega* making traditional, oaky reds and whites. Castillo de Ygay is long-lived and complex; the regular white-label *cuvée* is back on form after a shaky period in the early 1990s. Recent introductions to the range are red Dalmau – big wine, big bottle, big price – and white Capellanía – ancient-meets-modern to good effect.

269

Bodegas Navajas Small producer of straightforward reds and oaky whites.

Palacio A modern operation making supple, concentrated, fruit-packed reds that don't necessarily fit into the rigid system of *crianza*, *reserva* and *gran reserva*. Recommended.

Federico Paternina Large Haro-based *bodega*. We prefer the older, aged reds from its broad, good-value range.

Remelluri One of the best single-estate Rioja *bodegas*, with rich reds well suited to long ageing.

La Rioja Alta Large, admirable *bodega* successfully combining traditional values with modern know-how. Standards are high for the generous, well-constructed *reservas* and *gran reservas*, and citrus-flavoured Viña Ardanza white is attractive.

Bodegas Riojanas Traditional, family-owned winery making powerful, top-quality Monte Real *gran reservas*.

Marqués de Riscal Pioneer of modern Rioja, this house started breaking the rules over a hundred years ago. Long known (but not always liked) for its Cabernet component in the blend. Best wine is Barón de Chirel.

Bodegas Roda Recently built winery in Haro, causing a stir with richly concentrated, well-crafted *reservas*. Roda II Reserva can be superb.

Rioja vintage guide

2001 The Spanish are notorious for issuing hugely positive vintage reports, but it really would appear that 2001 was much better than the previous year, with reduced quantity but higher quality. After a wet winter the spring was dry, the summer relatively free of extreme weather and the harvest slow and well paced. Volume was down 25 per cent on 2000 – just what the producers were hoping for, in order to keep prices stable. Excellent wines with good ageing potential should result.
2000 The growing season had been very good but, as the harvest drew nearer, the weather turned colder and wetter, and the rain didn't stop until all the grapes had been picked. Don't expect anything memorable to result.
1999 The worst frost for 60 years eventually had less than its predicted effect, with only pockets of land being affected, and the

vines caught up with themselves over the summer. Quality should be excellent.

1998 A large harvest spoiled by rain and low temperatures at the final stages of ripening. Given the conditions, the wines are quite satisfactory.

1997 A difficult vintage with a wet summer, saved only by warm, dry weather at harvest time. Quality is erratic, and those who failed to put in the hours in the vineyards are easy to spot.

1996 Officially classified as 'very good', which means less exciting than 1995 and 1994. A sound year with both decent quality and quantity.

1995 An excellent year. Despite heavy spring frosts, the subsequent warm weather meant the vines regenerated and produced high-quality grapes. Reds are rich and generous.

1994 Another great vintage, maybe even better than 1995, producing a smaller-than-average crop of wines with concentration, structure and plenty of fruit.

Good older vintages 1990, 1989, 1988.

Navarra

No longer known primarily for its cheerful *rosados*, Rioja's neighbour Navarra has come up in the world. Its red wines, now the majority of production, continue to win over fans (especially when Rioja's prices are running high . . .) and some of the best deserve their newly fashionable status. An emphasis on modern winemaking leads to juicy, succulent, fruit-driven Tempranillo, often blended with Cabernet Sauvignon or Merlot. Some bright, thoroughly modern Chardonnays are appearing, which easily outdo the local Viura-based whites. Be aware though that the region is still prone to lapses of consistency, so tread carefully. The *rosados*, mouthwatering cherryish Garnacha wines, are still going strong and are often much better than French rosés. Try a chilled glass with a plate of *jamón* for lunch . . .

Interestingly it is Navarra that is home to, and provides local government support for, Spain's most high-tech experimental winery – EVENA – source of inspiration for producers around the country. Partly because of this, Navarra should achieve greater things in the future.

Pick of the producers (Navarra)
Castillo de Monjardín Tangy, unoaked Chardonnay; the best of a lively modern range are the ripe, well-structured Merlot and Merlot Reserve.

Julian Chivite Leading Navarra producer, family-run for three centuries. The range of squeaky clean, elegant wines includes soft reds, crisp *rosado* and richly oaked Chardonnay.

Guelbenzu Serious reds in a fruity, modern style are produced from this stately, family-run boutique winery; try the juicy, everyday-quaffer Jardin before moving on to the more expensive and heftier reds.

Ochoa Modern company producing a quality range, including plummy Cabernet Sauvignon and deeply perfumed Tempranillo, among others.

Palacio de la Vega Rarely putting a foot wrong, this Pernod-Ricard-owned *bodega* turns out consistently impressive, good-value reds and fruit-driven Chardonnay.

Ribera del Duero

Home to the stars, Ribera del Duero only became a DO 20 years ago but is now one of Spain's most sought-after and emulated regions. Here the Tempranillo grape is known as Tinto Fino and is often blended with Bordeaux grapes. The loftiest names to buy are the venerable Vega Sicilia, and comparative upstarts Pesquera and Pingus. In the last two decades the region has boomed, and swanky new estates have sprung up, producing top-notch wine and sparking a fierce debate on the merits of pure Tempranillo versus Tempranillo/Cabernet blends. In fact, both can be excellent. The powerful, intense, black-fruit-laced Ribera del Duero reds represent an often stunning alternative to the more strawberry and vanilla overtones of Rioja. As in Navarra, quality can be a shade patchy; the following producers are the most reliable. There is no DO for Ribera whites, although several wineries make zippy, young wines from the Albillo grape, which also finds its way into some of the reds.

Pick of the producers (Ribero del Duero)
Abadia Retuerta The vineyards fall just outside the official Ribera boundaries – but so what? The wines are brilliant. If you can't afford the extraordinarily good El Palomar (Cabernet/Tempranillo) or El Campanario (Tempranillo), the basic Rivola *cuvée* makes a far-from-disgraceful substitute.

Alion (see *Vega Sicilia*, below).

Hacienda Monasterio Young Dane Peter Sisseck makes superb reds, including the astonishingly concentrated (and priced) Dominio de Pingus.

Pago de Carraovejas Rising star making the most of excellent vineyard sites to produce intense, fruit-driven blends with up to 25 per cent Cabernet Sauvignon.

Pesquera Cult Ribera *bodega* owned by Alejandro Fernandez and famous for concentrated, lengthily aged reds that command high prices, especially top *cuvée* Janus. Sister winery Condado de Haza is a state-of-the-art operation with 300 hectares of vines; wines made here are for earlier release. Standards are high across both ranges.

Bodegas Reyes Teòfilo Reyes has worked at top Ribera *bodegas* all his life and is now creating fine, richly concentrated reds from low-yielding vines at his own winery.

Vega Sicilia Legendary company making Spain's most venerable (and expensive) wine from a blend of Tempranillo, Cabernet, Merlot and Malbec. All wines undergo lengthy wood-ageing, and top-of-the-range Unico spends up to ten years in vat and barrel. Recently acquired and updated the Alion *bodega*, also in the region, and the results are impressive.

Other northern regions

Basque Country
Chacolí de Getaria and Chacolí de Bizcaia are the two DO sources of crisp and lean Basque white wines best suited to the local seafood cuisine, and only really ever found there.

Galicia
Galician whites have taken on 'It' status lately, particularly the Albariño wines of DO Rías Baixas, which at best are peach- and lime-scented, with a tantalisingly fruity and crisp palate. This is probably Spain's best white wine; demand is high in the restaurants of Madrid and Barcelona. As a result, prices in the UK of £8–£12 seem somewhat stretched for a wine that, while undoubtedly delightful, is not hugely complex.

   DO Valdeorras is also worth watching for its light reds from the Mencia grape (akin to Cabernet Franc) and white from Godello, a high-quality, aromatic white grape.

Castilla y León
Although we have found Ribera del Duero, the most famous wine region of the vast province of Castilla y León, worthy of an independent entry of its own, there are also others worth mentioning. One of them, DO Bierzo, is an up-and-coming region now making a name with Spanish enthusiasts for its reds and

whites similar to those in neighbouring Valdeorras (see Galicia, above). Closer to Ribera del Duero is DO Rueda, a source of crisp, fresh, good-value whites from Verdejo or Sauvignon. Lurton is the name to look for – either Hermanos Lurton for crisp, fresh wines, or Bellondrade y Lurton for richer, more ageworthy fare. Nearby DO Toro, not far from the Portuguese border, has made a favourable impression in the UK recently with some intense, gutsy reds made from Tempranillo, known locally as Tinto de Toro. This is a region to watch out for in the future.

Pick of the producers (other northern regions)
Con Class Great-value, zesty whites from Rueda, especially the crisp, grapefruity Sauvignon Blanc.

Bellondrade y Lurton Brigitte Lurton, co-owner of Château Climens in Barsac, makes rich, heady and ageworthy barrel-fermented Verdejo with her husband Didier Bellondrade.

Descendientes de J. Palacios Intense, inky-black wine from 100-per-cent Mencia, made by roving producer Alvaro Palacios in DO Bierzo.

Bodegas Fariña The top producer in Toro. Gran Colegiata, a rich, sweetly ripe red made from Tinto de Toro (aka Tempranillo), is the best wine.

Hermanos Lurton The French Lurton brothers turn out lively, good-quality whites in Rueda from Verdejo, Viura and Sauvignon Blanc varieties.

Lagar de Fornelos Rías Baixas *bodega* relaunched after huge investment by La Rioja Alta. Softly ripe Albariño called Lagar de Cervera has a delightful lime and peach juiciness.

Pazo de Barrantes Snappy, fresh Albariño made at the Barrantes estate in Galicia owned by Marqués de Murrieta.

Pazo de Señorans One of the finest Albariños, a concentrated, rich mouthful of creamy peach flavour.

Marqués de Riscal Historic Rioja *bodega* but here the best bet is white Rueda, made from Sauvignon Blanc.

EASTERN SPAIN – CATALONIA, ARAGON, VALENCIA

Catalonia

The fiercely independent spirit of the Catalans has also pervaded the region's wine industry, which includes some of Spain's most dynamic and innovative producers. The Penedès DO, outside Barcelona, was little known until the energetic and forceful Miguel Torres introduced fashionable Cabernet Sauvignon and Chardonnay to his family *bodega* some 40 years ago. Since then, the area has thrived, although recently it has been replaced as 'hip and happening' by other newly awakened DOs. Still, watch out in the future for Torres wines made using Catalan white grapes such as Vermenti and Rosanna, and red grapes such as Garrut, Monastrell and Cariñena.

Penedès is also home to Cava, Spain's astonishingly successful and value-for-money, *méthode traditionnelle* sparkling wine, made from the local white grapes Parellada, Macabeo (aka Viura) and Xarel-lo, in and around San Sadurní di Noya. As a party fizz, Cava is hard to beat, especially with a humble £5 supermarket price tag – its neutral, slightly earthy base enlivened by apple-peel fruit and a lean, fresh sparkle. The more expensive blends with Chardonnay in them, or vintage Cava, are respectively more creamily rounded and more powerful, but not always worth the price difference. Everyone seems to love Cava (even many wine snobs, who cherish it as an all-purpose party fizz); indeed, last year sales in the UK soared by 14 per cent and Cava now has a whopping 47-per-cent share of the sparkling wine market here.

In the *Guide*'s view, the jewel of Penedès is Priorato (Priorat in Catalan). This wild and picturesque, historic DO, with steeply sloping vineyards above stone villages, is home to a growing number of boutique wineries. Long, very hot summer days, with cold nights and coastal breezes, produce singularly concentrated, alcoholic, long-lived reds based on low-yielding, old-vine Garnacha. The traditional style, in which oxidation and volatility were never far from the surface, has given way to cleaner, more modern wines, in which other varieties such as Cabernet and Syrah are sometimes used. These are some of Spain's finest red wines and in recent years they have commanded prices to match. And, Priorato's top labels, always made in small quantities, are now on strict allocation to the UK.

Impecunious wine lovers should either seek out wines from the local co-op, Vinicola del Priorat (sometimes under the Onix label), or examine what's happening in neighbouring Tarragona, and in the sub-zone around the town of Falset in particular, now with its own new DO of Montsant. Here – for the moment – you'll find Priorat-style wines for a fraction of the price.

Other Catalonian DOs of note are Costers del Segre, home of the huge progressive Raïmat winery; and Conca de Barberà, source of several simple fruity reds but the provenance of two high-class, single-vineyard wines from Torres, the rich Milmanda Chardonnay and the warm, spicy Grans Muralles red blend.

Pick of the producers (Catalonia)

Albet i Noya Family-run estate in Penedès making delicious barrel-fermented Chardonnay and top-notch, oak-aged varietal Cabernet and Tempranillo.

Cellers d'Anguera Tarragona Falset *bodega* making gutsy reds, best of which is the Syrah-heavy Finca l'Argata.

Cellers de Capçanes Tarragona Falset's star estate, making full-bodied reds from local grape varieties, Garnacha in particular, but using modern techniques. Cabrida and Mas Torto are the top *cuvées*, while Mas Collet, which has a little Cabernet Sauvignon in the blend, is a great-value alternative.

Clos Mogador Long-lived Priorato reds from old Garnacha vines, hand-crafted and made in tiny quantities.

Codorníu Giant Cava house based in San Sadurní. Basic wines are unexciting; newer Chardonnay *cuvées* much better.

Costers del Siurana Clos de l'Obac is one of the most concentrated of the new-wave Prioratos, while Dolç de l'Obac is an amazingly concentrated sweet version.

Freixenet Well-known Cava producer making fresh, historically rather characterless Cordon Negro, which has become tastier of late. Segura Viudas sparkling wines are some of the Freixenet group's best.

Juvé y Camps The best Cavas on the market come from this small, family-run operation. The complex Reserva de la Familia wine is well worth its relatively high price tag.

Jean León This ex-Hollywood restaurateur pioneered Cabernet and Chardonnay varietals alongside Torres in Penedès. Pricy, New World-style wines.

Masia Barril Concentrated, thick, inky reds from Priorato. Some new-wave, *joven* wines are made here too, but we prefer the blockbusters.

Alvaro Palacios Massive reds from Priorato made with two particular strains of Garnacha. The top wines, L'Ermita and Finca Dofi, are long-lived, single-vineyard reds and command extremely high prices. Third wine Les Terrasses is made from Garnacha, Cariñena and Cabernet Sauvignon.

Parxet Quality whites from the leading winery in the tiny DO of Alella on the outskirts of Barcelona. Still wines are creamy and floral and there's a crisp, snappy Cava.

Bodegas Pasanau Family-owned *bodega* making excellent, modern-style Priorato reds at almost everyday prices.

Raïmat Huge estate in Costers del Segre that is back on form with a wide range of modern, fruit-driven varietals after a poor patch in the late 1980s. Owned by Codorníu.

Scala Dei Boutique winery in Priorato, with cult status for its intense, alcoholic Cartoixa reds. Whites, both unoaked and barrel-fermented, are appealing too. There's a decent *rosado*, or try the Negre Scala Dei, a lighter red. Now owned by Codorníu.

Torres Catalan family firm, led by the dynamic Miguel Torres, who has created one of Spain's most innovative companies; the single-vineyard range is, in places, world-beating (Mas la Plana Cabernet and Milmanda Chardonnay), while red Coronas, white Gran Viña Sol and aromatic Muscat/Gewurztraminer Viña Esmeralda are the best of the blends.

Aragón

Stretching from the Pyrenees in the north to the edges of Valencia and Castilla-La Mancha further south, Aragón embraces some of the current DOs to watch. Cariñena, Calatayud and Campo de Borja have long made chunky, cheap reds, but now there are signs of distinct upward mobility. Campo de Borja, especially, is moving into better-quality production. Cheerful, everyday reds and value-for-money dry whites, not complex, but tasty, are the result, often bottled for the UK's supermarket own-labels.

A more exciting DO is Somontano, nestled in the relatively cool foothills of the Pyrenees and turning out modern, elegant whites and reds from both local and international grape varieties. Happily, these are now making regular appearances on the shelves of UK merchants.

Pick of the producers (Aragón)
Enate An up-to-the-minute range of familiar varietals behind eclectic labels. All the wines are good, with a dry but spicy Gewurztraminer being one of the best outside Alsace.

Bodegas Pirineos A large and appealing set of reds, whites and *rosados*, some under the Espiral label, from a revamped co-operative in Somontano.

Viñas del Vero Somontano producer making modern varietals, particularly Chardonnay and Pinot Noir, plus more ambitious blends Clarion (white) and Gran Vos (red). Blecua (Cabernet Sauvignon/Merlot/Tempranillo/Garnacha) is a recently introduced flagship red.

Valencia

This region, most famous for its sweet Muscat, also accounts for vast amounts of inexpensive sweet and dry white table wine that appears in the UK. Valencia's wines are, generally speaking, reasonable value and fairly reliable. The small inland DO of Utiel-Requena puts out strapping reds and lurid *rosados* made from the Bobal grape.

Pick of the producers (Valencia)
Vicente Gandia Valencia's slickest modern producer, making the inexpensive and workmanlike Castillo de Liria range. Also responsible for attractive, honeyed Moscatel hiding behind many supermarket own-labels in the UK.

Central and southern Spain

Famous as the land where Don Quixote tilted at windmills, the limitless, baking hot central plain of Castilla-La Mancha has traditionally been the source of vast quantities of cheap plonk, much of it dull and oxidised whites from the downmarket Airén grape. Given the size of the region and improvements in winemaking practices, including cool picking and fermentation, there is much potential to exploit – and certain wineries are beginning to do so, witness the improving La Mancha reds and whites cramming UK supermarket shelves. Indeed, La Mancha now appears to be a region to watch, with several talented producers newly trying their hand there.

A handful of decent producers in the Valdepeñas DO, an enclave within La Mancha, has long made soft, slightly old-fashioned, baked reds of reasonable quality. The wine industry here is dominated by the two producers cited below. Then there are the bargain, robust reds from Jumilla. While in Jumilla, port fans should look for the Dulce Monastrell from Bodegas Olivares – it's actually unfortified, but with its sweetness, ripeness and 16-per-cent alcohol, you wouldn't know. Yecla, where the traditional Murcian full-bodied reds from Monastrell grapes are being toned down to suit the tastes of the export market, is also upping the quality of its wines. These areas are where much experimentation is currently taking place – for example in Yecla, where the exuberant sparkling red La Pamelita is made by Pamela Geddes, an Australian-trained Scot.

Pick of the producers (Central and southern Spain)
Bodegas Agapito Rico Producer of well-made, not over-alcoholic Jumilla reds, working well with international grape varieties.

Bodegas Castano Yecla winery, new to the UK. Source of value-for-money Monastrell blends.

Los Llanos Great value from this reliable Valdepeñas producer – reds are better than whites.

Felix Solis Soft, ripe reds from the largest, and one of the best, producers in Valdepeñas, with Viña Albali Reserva the top of the range.

FORTIFIED WINES
Sherry

Good news from Andalucía: sales of sherry in the UK were up (by nearly seven per cent) in 2001 for the first time in years. The UK remains the major consumer of sweet sherries, but perhaps younger consumers are beginning to discover the drier, lighter styles of fino and manzanilla, as opposed to the sweet concoctions favoured by previous generations. Certainly, when we have suggested to non-drinkers of dry sherry that they sample fresh, chilled fino or manzanilla, it has immediately produced converts. And the producers are aware that a slight shift is taking place; look no further than Gonzalez Byass's famous Tío Pepe, which recently received a multi-million-pound makeover, and now comes in a smart, New World-esque bottle on which the word 'sherry' appears in very small letters.

While such a move doesn't necessarily signal a full-scale sherry revival, it would appear that the rot has been temporarily stopped. Many younger wine drinkers thankfully cannot remember the 'pleasures' of British sherry (neither 'British' nor 'sherry', it was and still is made from imported concentrate and is now labelled 'fortified wine') and are discovering the real thing for the first time. Add in the avid wine enthusiasts, who have never needed much persuasion to drink fine sherry, and you have a drink whose revival *may* be just around the corner. And about time too, we say. Sherry is one of the world's great and classic wines – and certainly its most affordable.

Fino and manzanilla

These types of sherry, made from first pressings of Palomino grapes, are affected by the yeast-like fungus *flor*, which exists naturally in the air of the sherry region and which grows like a creamy blanket on the surface of the ageing wine. *Flor* is the magic ingredient in the sherry-making process – it protects the sherry from oxidation, while giving it a tangy ripeness. When chilled, a crisp, mouth-watering fino or manzanilla is one of the most delectable dry wines in the world. Drink it young and fresh, though – this is one sherry that does not keep for months, but only for a fortnight once opened. Buying half bottles is a good idea.

The three sherry towns – Jerez, El Puerto de Santa María and Sanlúcar – all make fino-style sherry, but the character of their wines varies because the natural *flor* of each town is slightly different. Jerez's finos are the most lemony and taste stronger in alcohol. The finos of El Puerto de Santa María, nearer the sea, are more heavily influenced by *flor* and tend to taste saltier, while their aroma is more olivey and pungent. Manzanilla is the name given to fino-style wines made in the coastal town of Sanlúcar, where the *flor* influence is the strongest of all. At its best, manzanilla is soft and slightly briny but with a well-defined yeasty, bready character.

Amontillado, palo cortado and dry oloroso

Amontillado is a fine, aged, dry sherry that starts out as a fino. It is fortified to about 17 or 18 per cent, thus killing off the *flor* and exposing the wine to the air. This should give the sherry an attractive amber colour and nutty, rich character. Sadly, many amontillados on the market taste like nothing of the sort, but like sweetened young wine of low quality. Caveat emptor.

Palo cortado is a rare treat, the style of which falls between amontillado and dry oloroso. It is pale caramel in colour and tastes delicately nutty.

Dry oloroso is the most noble of dry sherries: a warming, aromatic, sipping wine with layers of fruitcake, spice and nuts. It makes an ideal accompaniment to strong, hard cheeses.

Sweeter styles

The sweeter sherries, medium, pale cream and cream, are sweet styles developed especially for the export market and (we are sorry to say) they still account for four out of every five bottles sold in the UK. The best contain good-quality, aged oloroso wine; the worst are masked by sugary sweetness. The Pedro Ximénez (PX) grape is used for its intense sweetness to make an unctuous wine with the character of black treacle and raisins, which is great with desserts and cakes with a hint of ginger. The Spanish soak raisins in it and pour the lot over vanilla ice-cream for a delicious treat.

Pick of the producers (Sherry)
Barbadillo The largest *bodega* in Sanlúcar, noted for its fine manzanilla, especially the yeasty, mature Solear bottling.

Diez-Merito Producers of the excellent Don Zoilo fino, often seen in bars and on restaurant lists.

Domecq This distinguished Jerez *bodega* is rightly famous for one of the best finos, the elegant La Ina; also dry oloroso Rio Viejo.

González Byass The most famous sherry producer of all maintains admirably high standards across a range that includes the yardstick fino Tío Pepe, now with a slick new modern look; rare and authentic Amontillado del Duque; and opulent, raisined, sweet Matúsalem. The company has released a few precious, vintage-dated dry olorosos for sale.

Harvey's Commercial sherries, now repackaged in modern bottles. The less well-known 1796 range is much better.

Hidalgo Family-owned Sanlúcar *bodega*, best known for soft, fresh manzanilla La Gitana, but look out for the amontillado Viejo Pastrana, a rare but wonderful single-vineyard sherry.

Lustau A wide range of *almacenista* sherries are bought from small family concerns and bottled by this Jerez *bodega*. Some are much better than others, but the top bottlings are fascinating. Well worth a foray.

Osborne Giant, family-owned company in El Puerto, with huge brandy interests, but offering fair-quality sherry. Fino Quinta is a full-flavoured, bone-dry style.

Valdespino Highly respected sherries from this traditional, family-owned Jerez *bodega*. The pungent Inocente fino, dry amontillado Tío Diego, fine palo cortado and dry oloroso all regularly top tastings.

Williams and Humbert Large concern with tangy Pando fino and Dos Cortados oloroso the best in the range.

281

Other fortified wines

Montilla-Moriles
The DO region in the hills south of Cordoba produces sherry-style wines in *solera* systems mostly from Pedro Ximénez (PX). PX attains higher sugar levels here than the Palomino of Jerez, and many of the wines remain unfortified. Most Montilla that reaches the UK is designed to compete with the cheapest sherry and as such is best avoided. Better-quality, aged Montilla in the amontillado and oloroso styles can be very good but is only sold in large quantities in Spain.

Condado de Huelva
Lesser-known source of fortified wines, now drastically declined as the grape crop is replaced with strawberries and wheat.

Málaga
Andalusian DO whose production of nutty, caramelly, madeira-like dessert wines has sadly declined to a dribble in the early twenty-first century. Málaga wine is a rare treat, even more so now that the Scholtz Hermanos *bodega* has ceased production.

SWITZERLAND

Last year we mentioned that we wanted to see more Swiss wines under the magic £5 mark, in order to entice people to try them. We also said that the Swiss weren't defeated by uphill struggles, as their landscape dictates they might be – and they haven't been. Difficult terrain, steep vineyards, expensive labour and an eager-to-drink domestic market aside, today more Swiss wines are available in the UK than ever before. There are now eight importers, twice the number as last year, and over 20 different retail outlets (see Tanner Wines, S H Jones, Love of Wine, and Virgin Wines in *Where to buy wine*).

All this underlines the sure signs that some bottles of interest are emerging – wines that are affordable (averaging around £6), recognisable (made from familiar grape varieties) and 'readable' (with clearer labels). There is also an energetic Switzerland-based promotional body (*www.swisswine.ch*) helping to raise the profile and distribute knowledge. Would that Canada, with a similar vinous output, could say the same.

In our view, those interesting wines start with Pinot Noir and Pinot Blanc. Pinot Noir can turn out to be almost as juicy as its Burgundian neighbours, with a deliciously heady, sour-cherry perfume and berryish, black peppery fruit on the palate. Pinot

Blanc is rounded and supple, with rich melon and toasty fruit. Then come the crowd of local varieties led by reds Gamay (nothing like the bubblegum Beaujolais versions), Cornalin and Humagne Rouge; and whites such as flinty Aligoté, grapefruity Petite Arvine and Amigne. Then there's the unforgettable and much-maligned Chasselas or Fendent, whose bland waxy texture is one of its finest assets as a wonderful placator of fiery Thai and Asian food flavours. In its best manifestations (if vinified carefully), when it's less bland, earthy and honeyed, Chasselas demonstrates the different nuances of Switzerland's individual wine areas very clearly, which is probably why it's grown just about everywhere.

Watch out for the following growers, who are among the best: Luc Massy, Mauler, Caves Orsat, Les Perrières, Jean-Paul Ruedin, J&P Testuz, Frédéric Varone and Zweifel.

As far as consistency goes, Swiss wines are not perfect – a one-in-five hit-rate; we'd like to see a lot better. The labels can still be confusing (whether in German, French or Italian). Some of the wines can still be decidedly 'lean'. But Swiss wines are at the very least intriguing for being the total antithesis of anything the New World has on offer. And on a hot summer day, well-chilled, they have the potential to be light, elegant and delicious.

TUNISIA

Developments in Tunisian wines appear to be few and far between. The Sicilian investor Calatrasi, in conjunction with Tunisian businessmen, is doing a good job of breathing new life into Domaine Nefris: do try the spicy reds (a Carignan and a Syrah) that have resulted. They are stocked by Bibendum (see *Where to buy wine*) under the Accademia del Sole range. Other decent producers we have come across are Château Thibar, Royal Tardi and Mornag, but tracking these down in the UK can be a problem. Other than Carignan and Syrah, grape varieties to look out for include the usual Cabernet Sauvignon, plus Grenache, Cinsault, Clairette and an unusual grape called Beldi.

TURKEY

Turkey has a wealth of different micro-climates and indigenous grape varieties, and *Vitis vinifera* has been grown here for thousands of years. Today it is the world's fourth-largest grower of grapes, but don't get too excited – this is after all a predominantly Muslim country, and around 98 per cent is grown for the table and/or for drying. Even so, Turkey makes as much wine as Canada and New Zealand do, mainly for tourist and home consumption. With winemaking taking a turn for the better, expect to see fresher, cleanly made, surprisingly light whites and robust tangy reds – mainly while on holiday there. A few wines trickle through to the UK, mostly appearing in Turkish grocers or restaurants. You may come across the infamous red Buzbag from eastern Anatolia. It can be palatable, but then again Buzbag can be Scumbag (as one waggish fellow critic recently put it). The Doluca brand of reds is OK, and its whites are relatively fresh and appealing. Kavaklidere is the other exporter, but as yet only in tiny quantities. Turkish wines may benefit from the increased interest in the unusual grapes of Europe (and particularly of Greece), but unless there is a big supermarket or off-licence deal, exports will continue to be on a very small scale.

UNITED STATES OF AMERICA

CALIFORNIA

Three things are causing consternation to the California wine industry at the moment. Firstly, the glassy winged sharpshooter, spreader of the fearsome Pierce's disease that could potentially wipe out all the prize vines of Napa and Sonoma (and eventually everywhere else). Secondly, 'Generation X' – how to sell wine to the next crop of vodka- and beer-drinking, should-be-Chardonnay consumers. Thirdly, cracking the UK trade – do they really need to?

There's an outer layer of calm about the sharpshooter. 'If it hits, we'll just have to raise our tolerance,' said one grower, which would in fact be tricky since the wee winged beastie actually kills the vines. (Once infected, the vine's vascular system is clogged up by Pierce's bacteria and the plant effectively starves to death.) Others are denying it will ever hit: the northward spread of disease-bringing flies is very slow; the hope is that a cure/prevention will have been found before they start thinking they can cross the San Francisco Bay. The reality could be devastating, however, and more cautious growers are quietly buying up land further north, away from the precious Napa *terroir*, in Mendocino and Anderson Valley, in the hopes that these regions can't be reached.

As the sharpshooter lives in water-loving plants, the nicest solution we've witnessed so far has been the introduction of sheep, cattle, ducks and geese to the humid riverbank areas surrounding the vineyards in order to keep plant growth (and likely hiding places) in check. This approach has a sort of naturalness about it – as well as providing a wholesome new nitrogen source . . . But we

somehow think the Australian method will be more effective: great hoardings at intervals along the roadside, banning the transport of garden plants (in Australia's case, they ban fruit transport to prevent the spread of fruit flies), with hefty fines the penalty.

Generation X might prove an even fiercer problem. Savvy, web-surfing and informed, these twenty-somethings don't like being 'marketed to', and they don't want to drink wine. So how to change their minds? A slow trickle of information via the web is the solution of some wineries, but another method might well be to bring the prices down. It is very difficult indeed to pick up a decent (interesting, regional, oddball grape variety) sub-$10 wine on the US supermarket shelves – that's sub-£7 in UK terms.

And that's where we're lucky. Thanks to recent tough campaigns on the part of the California Wine Institute, a plethora of Golden State wines are newly on sale in the UK at around the £4 mark. Here the Californians have very successfully introduced that 'starting point' that was needed to germinate interest in their wines. Statistics indicate that sales of California wine are increasing more rapidly than Chile's, South Africa's or Australia's (and that they're now in fourth position in terms of UK market share). But the trouble is – to tell the truth – these wines are boring. Just one too many corners have been cut in order to keep the prices down and, compared with the new wines coming out of the Rhône, Languedoc, Italy and Spain, what the Californians are turning out is, frankly, bland, and a pretty poor representation of what they can actually do.

The next problem is, there's nothing to trade up to. California wines start getting seriously good at around the £12-a-bottle mark, but there's not too much of interest below this. And at £12, these wines face the traditionalist buyer, who has a habit of sneaking off for a decent Bordeaux or burgundy instead. 'Be less narrow-minded,' say the salesmen, 'then the Californians will send over more wines, and we'll have a better selection to choose from.' But who should move first really? The buyer or the seller? Following the tragic events of September 11, 2001, Californian wineries reportedly lost up to $75 million in sales as a result of reduced on-trade and airline takings – that's a one per cent loss.

Note must also be made of this year's important wine trends: the adoration of Merlot has been replaced by a new mood for Syrah (it's good too). In the winery, the new 'holy grail' is now to make 'fruit-forward wines, with complexity'. The latest winery techniques in use (winemaking is also subject to fashion) involve 'spinning cones', which remove alcohol. (The producers have been listening to consumer complaints about their wines being too alcoholic, and are addressing the issue. We're not convinced, however, that all the spinning this extraction process necessitates is good for the wine – and as long as the alcohol is in balance with the fruit, we're not too bothered about it anyway. It will be interesting to see the long-term effect it has on the flavours.) 'Co-pigmentation', the addition of up to 10-per-cent white grapes to a red wine to stabilise its colour, is another technique in vogue.

The summary report of the rest of this year's California wine trends goes something like this: a move away from American oak barrels towards the use of French (thank goodness – French oak gives more delicate flavours compared to the very obvious vanillary ones given by American oak); a similar move away from the use of sprays towards organic practices, ducks, owls, geese, gophers, etc, roaming the vineyards (again, thank goodness); a move away from bulk-blended cross-regional wines towards reflecting the character of the *terroir* (once again, thank goodness). The strapping 'blockbuster' wines, at great expense, however, are still with us.

Oh yes, and whatever happened to Chardonnay? We're hearing stories of growers giving their Chardonnay grapes away, no charge, to lucky hobbyists and weekend winemakers, because there simply isn't the demand any more for them to be made into wine . . . Grape-growing comes over all Hollywood: when you're in, you're in, and when you're out, you're *really* out.

Red wines – grape varieties

Cabernet Sauvignon

Some of these wines are so massive that we wouldn't know what to do with them. The best, from Napa, Sonoma and a few spots south of San Francisco Bay, are deeply serious, offering a level of complexity second only to Bordeaux. But many of the rest are gigantic, alcoholic 'blockbuster' wines that win prizes and fetch top auction prices, but even a small glassful is difficult to drink – if you do like them, we suggest you try the wines from Napa's hillside vineyards, which provide some of the biggest mouthfuls. Producers have also progressed in making wines with more friendly tannins, and the result is that more Cabernets are now drinkable very young and can also (we're told) age well. But we're not so impressed by other tricks in the winery – leaving a slug of sugar in the wine to make it enticingly sweet tasting and playing with the acidity to the same effect. Many of the wines that result are too simple to merit their £10 (and higher) price tags. Signs are that people aren't prepared to pay as much for these monsters as they have in the past and, as with Chardonnay, there are a few growers attempting to make more elegant wines that go well with food.

We like the best of these. There's something of the cassis note of claret, but the flavours are often more reminiscent of berries and plums, with notes of mint, olives, herbs and sometimes all three. It was Cabernet from the Napa Valley that first established California as a potentially great wine state, so let's hope Napa can put Cabernet back on track again.

Merlot
Merlot has had its day in California; its share of the total vineyard area is declining rapidly as growers regraft and replace it. Although the best can still be as good as almost anything from Pomerol, with a wealth of lush, plummy fruit and the structure to age for ten years or more, unfortunately the majority now prove this grape has become a victim of its own success. Too many growers have tried to cash in, and too many corners have been cut. One-time Merlot lovers are now wise to the mean, green stalky flavours resulting from over-cropped vines, and are turning their affections towards the likes of Syrah and Sangiovese instead. Wise punters aren't fooled by the addition of new oak in an attempt to simulate quality in poor wines either.

Other Bordeaux reds
Many Bordeaux-inspired reds from California are now blends including Cabernet Sauvignon, Merlot, Cabernet Franc and even Petit Verdot and Malbec, some of which go by the ghastly name 'Meritage' (rhymes with heritage). As with 'straight' Cabernet (which, by the rules, can also blend in 25 per cent of these varieties), there are gaping gulfs between the good and the bad and the ugly. Single-varietal Cabernet Franc is rare but can be very tasty – Ironstone makes a cracker. And Petit Verdot is beginning to make

frequent appearances, beloved for its rich intense flavours and deep black colour. The more upmarket Bordeaux blends from Niebaum-Coppola, Sinskey, Schug and Lang & Reed have both intensity of flavour and the all-important perfume.

Pinot Noir

Many of the best California Pinot Noirs don't reach the UK, as they are made in quantities that would seem small even to a Burgundian. However, we see enough – from producers such as Saintsbury, Au Bon Climat or Calera – to know that places such as Carneros, new vineyards on the Sonoma Coast, Russian River Valley and Santa Barbara County are capable of making Pinot Noir with the sensual appeal of great burgundy, even if the fruit flavours are somewhat riper. Unfortunately, too many inferior wines are too jammy, dilute, or too oaky, and poor value at any price. Sterling's Redwood Trail and Ramsey Estate's delicious wines sell at around £10 a bottle, but sadly we can't think of many others over here to recommend.

Syrah

Watch out Australia. Syrah in California has just gone crazy. It's arguably better suited to many existing wine regions than Cabernet, and we've been very impressed by most of what we've tasted so far. The worry, unfortunately, is still that growers have been greedy and planted too much. Over the last few years over 8,000 new hectares have gone in, and if there aren't quite as many takers as they anticipated it could be a disaster for quality. We'd hate to see the same thing happen as to Merlot (see above). But, let's not get too pessimistic. The general style is for full-bodied, fruity wines similar to those of Australia, but which can often veer a little more towards the elegance and perfume of the Rhône, depending on the region and the winemaker. Kudos to Fetzer for a delicious, sensibly priced version.

Zinfandel

Although widely acknowledged as being identical to southern Italy's Primitivo, there are still some doubts as to the truth of this identification. Nonetheless, Zinfandel can fairly be called California's own grape. It comes in all versions from pink (or 'white' as the marketing types would have it) to fortified, but the best are robust, juicy reds with plenty of gutsy berry-fruit. Just a minor complaint, however. We realise that Zinfandel was never meant to be elegant, but with more than a few wines now weighing in at 16-per-cent alcohol or more, it seems that some producers are playing a rather childish game of 'mine's bigger than yours'. The prices for these big wines are getting bigger and bigger too, although some of their thunder is being stolen by the new crop of Syrahs.

Others

Syrah isn't the only Rhône variety enjoying popularity. Thanks to the activities since the 1980s of a band of producers who call themselves the Rhône Rangers, Grenache and Mourvèdre (often sourced from ancient vineyards) have risen in popularity. More fashionable still, however, is the Cal-Ital brigade – producers who have planted Italian grapes such as Sangiovese (delicious from Seghesio, Shafer and Fetzer's Bonterra) and Nebbiolo (look for Il Podere dell'Olivos), and are also beginning to take more of an interest in the many old Barbera vines dotted around the state. Petite Sirah is also decidedly in the ascendant for its rich, black, concentrated qualities (perhaps because of its remote association with Syrah?). This grape variety has long been ignored as just another, if beefier, component of the everyday-glugging 'jug wine' team with a long history in the State, but there are some gnarly old vines around and good growers are newly appreciating their intense, spicy value.

White wines – grape varieties

Chardonnay

We are still concerned that, after a period in the early 1990s when the ideal balance between oak, alcohol and sweet fruit appeared to have been struck, California Chardonnays seem to be getting bigger once again in all three departments – impressive to taste but a challenge to drink. Many of them are also very low in acidity, to the point of tasting like milkshake. A handful of progressive growers realise this, and are aiming to produce wines in a more balanced, minerally (they call it 'Burgundian') style. They are holding back malolactic fermentation, which softens natural grape acids, and taking full advantage of newly planted, cooler vineyards. (Californians now seem to realise that their original Chardonnay vineyards were too warm, and so are seeking out cooler regions with their new plantings – there are good signs from Carneros, Russian River and the Sonoma Coast.) However, such vineyards and better clones are not enough on their own. The winemaking has to be right too. And unfortunately, the progressive growers who are on the right tracks are very much in the minority. At the cheaper end of the market, we find the wines too sweet and under-flavoured, and the more expensive ones are often oaky, clumsy and just plain overweight. Oh yes, and don't be fooled by the wines from the 1998 vintage: they might seem finer-tuned, but this is a sign of uneven ripeness that year, not necessarily of less oak.

Sauvignon Blanc

We're pleased to say that California Sauvignon has evolved in recent years, largely because many producers who were never very enthusiastic about the variety have simply stopped making it. In addition, those who have continued have honed their winemaking to good effect. Wines used to fall into two categories – flabby with oak and flabby without oak – but today, more of Sauvignon's crisp, grassy nature is evident in the wines. The fruit flavours are typically richer, riper and more tropical in nature than in Sauvignons from the Loire and New Zealand. The best oaked wines – the best, mind you, often labelled Fumé Blanc – can be very good, like fleshy, white Graves. The worst generally come from regions that are far too hot for this grape.

Viognier

The prime beneficiary (in the white wine department at least) of interest in Rhône grape varieties is Viognier. It will never be 'the new Chardonnay', but the Californians have quickly learned how to make wines that have plenty of Viognier's heady pearskin and apricot kernel aromas and flavours. As with the Chardonnays, some are just too weighty (and woody) for their own good. However, some delicious wines are made, as many perhaps as in the northern Rhône. While most are expensive, Fetzer's version shows that good, rich Viognier doesn't have to break the bank.

Others

California tries its hand at almost anything, but, unfortunately, we see a lot of normally fragrant white grapes either overpowered by oak or with baked 'exhausted' fruit from being grown in vineyards that are too warm. Riesling is rare, although a few producers (Bonny Doon) make honeyed versions from cooler parts of the Central Coast, and some growers still use it for opulent late-harvest wines. Dry Creek Vineyards still makes a lovely Chenin, although the abundance of Chardonnay means this grape is appearing less and less. Fashionable Pinot Grigio (Pinot Gris), on the other hand, is mirroring the rise in popularity of Italian red varieties with occasional success, although it doesn't do nearly as well as it does over the border in Oregon, and tends to be light and insubstantial. Muscat in its various forms is being put to good use, most notably by Quady and Bonny Doon.

Sparkling wines

The enthusiasm for sparklers in California remains muted – a shame, as the best can be very fine indeed. Each year several new wineries specialise in Bordeaux- or Burgundy-style wines, but there are few newcomers who choose to concentrate on fizz. Indeed, many of those who set up as specialist fizz producers now include still wines in their portfolio, simply because they make more money by doing so. This is a pity, as the best wines, usually based on Pinot Noir and Chardonnay from cool-climate regions such as Carneros or Anderson Valley, are only a whisker away in style from the French originals, and can be easily confused. Look especially, for those made in West Coast offshoots of the Champagne houses – Cuvée Napa Mumm, Domaine Carneros from Taittinger and Roederer Estate.

The regions

Wines labelled 'California' must have been produced from grapes entirely from the state. If 75 per cent of the grapes (85 per cent for wines entering the EU) come from one of the state's 58 counties (Sonoma for example), that county can be named on the label. Approved Viticultural Areas (AVAs) are distinguished by their geographical features alone, not by the quality of the wines.

Napa Valley
California's most famous wine region is only 26 miles long, but it contains a large number of AVAs: Stags Leap, Oakville and Rutherford among them. Napa is known primarily for Cabernet Sauvignon and Bordeaux grapes, but beware over-hyped wines – not everything from Napa merits its high price tag. There are wide variations in climate, depending on whether a vineyard is on a hillside or the valley floor, and also whether it lies at the cool, southern end or the warm, northern end. The hillside vineyards (the Howell Mountain, Mount Veeder, Atlas Peak and Diamond Mountain AVAs) are fast gaining a reputation for producing the brawniest Napa wines of the lot, but a few growers outside these areas are, thankfully, making wines with more elegance. Much hard graft has taken place out in the vineyard since the valley was ravaged by phylloxera in the early 1990s; producers have used the opportunity to replant with the grape varieties most suited to their particular sites, and a large number have moved (or are moving) closer to organic viticulture and/or testing new clonal material.

Sonoma County
Just over a hill from Napa, but often seemingly a world apart, Sonoma has in the past been more laid-back than its over-hyped neighbour, but it's catching up fast. It's a much larger region, boasting everything from ancient Zinfandel vineyards in the Dry Creek Valley, to brand-new plantings of top-grade Pinot Noir and Chardonnay in the cool Russian River; Alexander Valley has something of everything as soil and climate vary so much; but the real region to watch is the new Sonoma Coast AVA – where all the most fashionable Pinot Noirs and Chardonnays are beginning to be

made. Most grapes grow well in Sonoma, and the standards are high – Zinfandel, Chardonnay, Pinot and Shiraz are all better here than in Napa. As a region, it might have nearly as much shoulder-padding as Napa these days, but fortunately it still has more charm.

Carneros
The relatively cool Carneros Valley at the southern end of Napa and Sonoma is shared between them and offers good sparkling wine and complex Pinot Noir, as well as elegant Chardonnay.

Mendocino County and Lake County
These two northernmost California wine counties both provide good-value wines. Mendocino is a cool coastal region where Fetzer and a couple of top sparkling producers are at work; Lake County is making a splash, particularly with Sauvignon Blanc. It's likely we'll see more and more wine from these areas; Syrah from Mendocino is already beginning to make its presence felt. While the glassy winged sharpshooter still threatens to head north, growers from Napa and Sonoma are buying up land here just in case the worst should happen and Pierce's disease reaches their precious quarter of the state – it makes sense not to have all their vines in one basket. It also helps that the land here is considerably cheaper.

Central Coast
A huge AVA which stretches from San Francisco to Los Angeles and incorporates:

Edna Valley A cool valley in San Luis Obispo, making some of the most exquisite Chardonnay around.

Monterey Coolish coastal spot south of San Francisco; generally underrated but becoming better known for Pinot Noir, Pinot Blanc and Chardonnay.

San Joaquin Valley Part of the baking hot Central Valley, where much of the bargain-basement California jug wine is made.

Santa Cruz Mountainous district south of San Francisco, home to a handful of off-beat wineries such as Ridge and Bonny Doon.

Santa Maria and Santa Ynez Valleys Part of the relatively cool-climate Santa Barbara County, these up-and-coming areas make fantastic Chardonnay and Pinot Noir, and increasingly impressive Syrah.

Sierra Foothills
Vineyards were in fact established in the Sierra Foothills (to slake the thirst of local gold miners) long before they were in Napa. All

but the highest, coolest sites are warm and best suited to red varieties: Zinfandel, Syrah and other Rhône grapes are the most at home. There are also good results from Italian varieties – we definitely like the results from juicy, low-tannin Barbera. As yet, this is still a very under-appreciated region, so the wines are cheaper.

Pick of the producers (California)

Au Bon Climat One of the best Santa Barbara wineries, producing Burgundian-style Pinot Noir and classy, ageworthy Chardonnay. Owner Jim Clendenen also makes fine Italian-style wines under the Il Podere dell'Olivos label.

Beaulieu Vineyard Historically important Napa estate, which was overtaken by others in the 1980s but is now showing a welcome return to form with Private Reserve Cabernet, classy red blend Tapestry and an all-Carneros Chardonnay.

Beringer Huge Napa operation producing admirably accomplished wines across a wide range. Reds from the Bancroft Ranch on Howell Mountain are deeply sophisticated, and the Chardonnays are consistently ripe and fruity, rather than over-rich. Recently upped the brand size by joining forces with Mildara-Blass.

Boeger High-elevation Sierra Foothills vineyards producing elegant wines – from 25 varieties including Riesling. Warmer sites produce great reds: signature Zinfandel and Barbera are especially good.

Bonny Doon Splendid, if erratic, collection of eccentricities based on anything that isn't a mainstream variety. Rhône, southern French and Italian varieties feature, as does Riesling. Winemaker/philosopher/ dude Randall Grahm's Rhône-style wines are probably his best.

Bonterra (see *Fetzer*, below).

Cain Chris Howell's complex and subtle Bordeaux blend Cain Five is one of California's most underrated wines. Also delicious Sauvignon Musqué from a perfumed clone of Sauvignon.

Cakebread Napa Valley grower (Rutherford/Oakville) for carefully made Cabernet reds and some of the only whites that thrive on Napa's hot soils (Sauvignon and beefy-but-balanced Chardonnay).

Calera Monterey producer of palatable and ageworthy Pinot Noir, especially the single-vineyard wines. Also fine Chardonnay and Viognier.

Caymus Special Selection has been at the top of the Napa Cabernet tree for many years. Sauvignon Blanc is also produced, as is a sweetish white blend.

Chalone Wine Group Parent company for a number of wineries. These include Chalone itself and Acacia, both sources of lovely Chardonnay and Pinot Noir; Jade Mountain, which specialises in Rhône-style reds; Carmenet, which specialises in Bordeaux-style reds and whites; and Edna Valley Vineyards, which excels with Chardonnay. Quality vastly improved since arrival of new winemaker in 1998. A new top-end Napa Cabernet is a recent launch.

Domaine Chandon Moët-owned sparkling operation in Napa making admirable fizz; we'd like to see more of it.

Cline Cellars Specialists in big, powerful reds based on Rhône varietals from ancient vineyards; densely spicy Mourvèdre is recommended (and reasonably priced), Carneros Syrah has Australian ripeness and Rhône-like restraint.

Clos Pegase Owner, Jan Schrem, is a passionate collector of modern art and built his winery in a suitably flattering form to accommodate both his paintings and his state-of-the-art Napa Valley wines: Bordeaux varieties, plus three styles of Chardonnay (from Carneros).

Clos du Val Pioneering Stags Leap operation run by a Frenchman, Bernard Portet, and now producing delicious reds with none of the harsh tannins of early vintages.

Cuvaison Swiss-owned winery turning out tasty Carneros Chardonnay and improved reds, including juicy Pinot Noir.

Diamond Creek A range of single-vineyard Napa Cabernets, which are tight when young but age splendidly. Quality in 1995, 1996 and 1997 is superb.

Dominus Increasingly impressive Napa wines produced under the guidance of Christian Moueix of Bordeaux' Château Pétrus.

Dry Creek Large, well-made range of Sonoma wines including dense-packed, old-vine Zinfandels, unusual Chenin Blanc and hefty Petite Sirah. Good, long agers.

Duckhorn Big, concentrated Howell Mountain Merlot is the jewel in the crown at this Napa winery. Paraduxx (geddit?) is the separate brand for chunky Zinfandel. Big investments are beginning to pay off.

Far Niente Luxury Napa Valley estate focusing on Bordeaux varieties. The new Nickel & Nickel brand for everything else (Pinot Noir, Zinfandel, Syrah and so on) will, if the quality rubs off, be worth watching out for.

Fetzer Large Mendocino winery with a vast, visible and affordable portfolio, most of it highly commendable. Look out for the rich, fruity organic wines under the Bonterra label (the first major brand to obtain organic status, and proof enough that green is good); off-beat varietals such as Roussanne, Sangiovese and Syrah; and the top-of-the-range Private Collection.

Flora Springs Everything from Wild Boar Cabernet, to truffle-smooth Merlots, to savoury Sangiovese is balanced and thoughtfully made at this Napa estate. They say that no winery can make both Pinot Noir and Cabernet well: Flora Springs proves the exception.

Frog's Leap Organic viticulture produces delicious juicy Zinfandel and Cabernet, among others, at this jolly Napa operation. John Williams' aim is for his wines to be 'less Jennifer Lopez, more Coco Chanel' – they are, indeed, more classy than many.

E & J Gallo Mammoth organisation making more wine than the whole of Australia. Avoid the cheaper labels such as Turning Leaf, Indigo Hills and Garnet Point and head for the Gallo Sonoma wines, especially the complex Chardonnays. Coastal Vineyards Cabernet and Chardonnay is a new label to watch for.

Grgich Hills Beret-clad Mike Grgich arrived in the USA from Croatia in 1958 and has since made consistently fine, structured wines without any concession to modern 'sweetness'. They're unostentatious, but show the best of the Napa Valley.

Hanzell Progressive, neo-Burgundian winery established in the 1950s, and always ahead of its time. Exceptional and long-ageing Chardonnay and Pinot Noir. Snap 'em up if you see them.

Harlan Estate Napa estate producing small amounts of powerful, ageworthy Cabernet. Cult stuff.

Hess Collection Cabernet is the main attraction here, especially the Napa Valley Reserve; the Chardonnays also impress. Not flashy wines, but elegant.

Jordan Sonoma winery; the 'J' sparkler ranks highly.

Kendall-Jackson The Vintners Reserve range is a decent bestseller in the USA, while the single-vineyard wines, especially the Camelot Chardonnay, are top-notch. Also owns other brands such as Cambria, La Crema, Matanzas Creek (a recent purchase) and Stonestreet.

Kistler Sonoma specialist in single-vineyard, very expensive Chardonnay, but also lovely Pinot Noir. Resting on laurels: it needs to be challenged.

Landmark Sonoma grower of supremely good Chardonnay and Pinot Noir: 'all decisions are based on palate, not chemistry' says winemaker Eric Stern.

Marcassin Helen Turley, described by the wine critic Robert Parker as a winemaking 'goddess', is consultant winemaker for some of California's finest (and most expensive) wines. This is her own label, under which she releases small amounts of opulent, virtually unobtainable Sonoma Coast Chardonnay and Pinot Noir.

Marimar Torres Miguel Torres' sister Marimar makes seductive and ever-improving Chardonnay and Pinot Noir in Sonoma.

Peter Michael Chardonnays and a Bordeaux blend of considerable class are the best wines from ex-pat Sir Peter Michael. Wines come from cooler vineyard sites in Knights Valley and Sonoma Coast. Helen Turley (see *Marcassin*, above) was original consultant for first (1987) vintage.

Robert Mondavi Founder of the modern California wine industry, still at the top, and experimenting continuously to find ways to improve. Bypass the so-so Woodbridge range (mostly from the Central Valley) in favour of the wines from Napa and other coastal districts. Cabernet, Chardonnay, Zinfandel and Pinot Noir all impress. Look out also for the Italian varietal range La Famiglia di Robert Mondavi. Has joint ventures in Chile (Seña, with Errázuriz), Tuscany (Luce, with the Frescobaldis), with the Rothschilds (see *Opus One*, below) and Arowood (Sonoma) in California. Ventures in the south of France have not been as successful, but headline-grabbing buy-up of Super-Tuscan Ornellaia and yet-to-be-named venture with Rosemount in Australia look to offer the next sensations.

Mumm Cuvée Napa Reliable, fruity sparklers from Mumm's West Coast operation, with top-of-the-range DVX made in conjunction with Champagne Devaux.

Newton Fruit from coolish mountain vineyards makes complex, well-balanced Cabernet, Merlot and Chardonnay.

Niebaum-Coppola Film magnate Francis Ford Coppola's wine holdings now encompass the Inglenook winery, producing serious reds with high kudos – and price tags. Rubicon is the top, prestige blend, while Coppola Family wines are good and good value. Diamond Series is one of the top new-wave Syrahs to look out for.

Opus One Illustrious joint venture from the Mondavi and Rothschild empires. Style is Napa Valley crossed with Bordeaux, with commensurate price tag. Delicious, ageworthy blends of Cabernet and other Bordeaux varieties, from Oakville vineyards.

Pedroncelli Fourth- and fifth-generation Sonoma growers: specialists with an intriguing range of Zinfandels.

Joseph Phelps Admirable pioneer of single-vineyard Cabernet, classy Bordeaux blend Insignia and Rhône varietals, including Syrah and Viognier. Unsurprisingly, this upmarket winery now has a new venture in the trendy Sonoma Coast.

Quady Eccentric Central Valley producer of quirky but delicious Muscat dessert wines and port-style fortifieds – and Vya Vermouth.

Qupé More Rhône varietals, including Marsanne and Syrah, from this Santa Barbara innovator.

Ravenswood Sonoma winery rightly famed for its rich, fruity Zinfandels.

Renaissance Classy Sierra Foothills estate for steely, crisp Sauvignon, Cabernet and even late-harvest Riesling.

Ridge Working high in the Santa Cruz mountains to make some of the state's most complex and concentrated Zinfandels and Cabernets, Paul Draper is one of California's most dedicated winemakers. Very reasonable prices (in Californian terms). New-wave Petite Sirah is pure black-fruited concentration.

Roederer Estate Mendocino County offshoot of the champagne house Louis Roederer. Top wine Quartet is one of the West Coast's most refined sparklers.

Saintsbury Dynamic duo Dick Ward and David Graves specialise in lovely Pinot Noir and Chardonnay from Carneros.

297

Sanford Top-notch Santa Barbara Pinot Noir, Chardonnay and Sauvignon characterised by intense, pure flavours – the Pinot Noir is almost more Rhône than Burgundy.

Schramsberg Glamorous Napa producer of super, sparkling wines.

Schug Carneros grower of Pinot Noir and Bordeaux blends. Walter Schug has moved on from an illustrious career making high-price Napa heavyweights to producing wines under his own label, with far more elegance and finesse.

Screaming Eagle Sadly, only 6,000 bottles of Jean Phillips' seductively rich and extremely cultish Napa Cabernet are made in a typical vintage. Of the cult wines, this is one of the best – it's not just about new oak. Prices are sky-high.

Seghesio Sonoma estate with Italian origins; its 100-years' experience of growing Sangiovese shows in the wines. Sangiovese-Bordeaux blend Omaggio is meaty, spicy, almost-Shirazy, concentrated, Italianate, delicious. Room to improve with Pinot Grigio, but Zinfandel is 'where it's at' here.

Shafer Stags Leap winery specialising in supple, sweetly ripe reds, best of which is brilliant Hillside Select Cabernet. Also notable Sangiovese/Cabernet blend called Firebreak; strapping Red Shoulder Chardonnay (token white), and violetty-rich Relentless Syrah.

Simi Sonoma producer of excellent Chardonnay and Sauvignon; Cabernet much improved recently.

Sinskey Robert Sinskey's wines are as organic, as elegant and as 'Bordeaux' as he can make them. He's looking for food matchability, not the 'cherry dollops' other Napa growers achieve.

Sobon Estate Dense, concentrated Zinfandel and Sangiovese from old Sierra Foothills vines – also good Barbera and Syrah. Shenandoah is second label for still-impressive reds.

Sonoma-Cutrer Chardonnay specialist – the intricate, single-vineyard Les Pierres Chardonnay is top of the pile.

Stag's Leap Wine Cellars Superb Cask 23 Cabernet, with the SLV and Fay *cuvées* not very far behind. Arcadia is new unoaked Chardonnay label aiming to lead the region in a drive for elegant, fine-tuned whites.

Sterling Vineyards Huge, Seagram-owned Napa winery capable of producing good-value wines – but tread carefully. Soft, easy-drinking Redwood Trail Pinot Noir is a good place to start; build up to strapping Godzilla-like Zinfandels if you dare.

California vintage guide

California wines are drunk young, but the most serious Cabernets require several years – as much as a decade in some cases – to reach ideal maturity. Beyond ten years the jury's still out on how long they'll last. Fine Chardonnays can also benefit from two years' bottle age for the oak influence to calm down, but after that extra age is not necessarily beneficial.

2001 Sharp frosts in April led to a loss of up to 40 per cent of the Merlot crop, but the preceding warm, dry winter made for a good fruit set in other varieties. A hot May, June and July continued the admirable progress and a cooler autumn into harvest led to good ripeness, retained acidities and positive aromatics. Bodes well for a supremely fine red vintage. Tonnage 6 per cent down on 2000.

2000 A mild vintage with two heat peaks and a 5.2-rated earthquake, plus a dash of rain at harvest, could have been tricky – but in fact yielded sound, strong reds of consistent quality and white and sparkling wines that benefited from the initial coolness. Yields were about average but tonnage up by 23 per cent due to increased plantings. Expect to see more California wine than ever.

1999 'Late, small and great', was the verdict from one producer. A long, cool growing season, with vintage as much as six weeks behind schedule in some areas, resulted in a reduced crop of small, intensely flavoured grapes. Rich, powerful reds and well-balanced whites.

1998 The effects of El Niño resulted in record rainfall together with record lows and highs of temperatures, and the harvest was also one of the latest on the books. Fine autumn weather saved the vintage from being a complete write-off, but many wines are not up to their usual standards – so tread with caution.

1997 After two small vintages, this was a record harvest for California. Initial worries that it would make dilute wines have proved groundless, and quality is very good across the board, with the Cabernet vying with 1994, 1991 and 1999 for the best of the decade.

1996 Just like the previous year, this was a short vintage – up to 30 per cent down on average crops. Quality, however, was high, especially for Chardonnay and Merlot.

1995 Heavy rain, cool temperatures and hail all contributed to a small vintage (down 20 per cent) but, owing to a warm, dry harvest, the quality was ideal. Excellent reds.

1994 The prolonged growing season made for intense dark reds, with Cabernet and Pinot Noir being especially fine.
1993 A late, difficult harvest with reduced quantities in many areas, produced first-class Chardonnay and structured Cabernets that appeal more to European palates than American.
1992 Copious winter rain, followed by a hot summer gave a small crop of ripe, forward wines; drink up quickly!
1991 Generally very good-quality reds, with tannins that will preserve the wines for several years to come.
1990 Wonderful year producing extremely rich Chardonnay and ageworthy Cabernet.

OREGON

Oregon's wines still don't seem to have taken off in the UK, possibly because of the huge prices being charged. The very cheapest of them come in at £8 a bottle, and most fall around the £15 mark over here, so newcomers are bound to be put off. Yes, there are some lovely Pinot Noirs on offer, but when asked to pay £25 for the best of them, are people really going to make the effort?

There are three reasons why they should. As we mentioned last year, Pinot Noir is a grape the Oregonians can definitely 'do better' than the Californians – the top wines really do come in second only to the Burgundian versions. And with 80 per cent of Oregon's vine plantings devoted to this grape – particularly in its heartland, the northern Willamette Valley – there are plenty to choose from. There aren't as many good ones as there should be, perhaps, because (unfortunately) many growers are still capitalising on the Burgundy comparison and spending a little less time over these wines than they ought. They need to take care: Pinot Noir is a pernickety variety after all. So if you get hold of a wine that's 'skinny' on the fruit, mean-tasting, even oxidised, don't accept it as true to Oregonian form. Accept, instead, the smooth, sour-cherry and orange layered versions, as full of rich ripeness as only a New World wine can be. These are worth the money. If we're not buying Oregon's wines on price, but on quality, our message is – let's make sure they *are* good.

It's possible to be a lot more upbeat about Oregon's white wines. Pinot Gris is where we'd feel most comfortable in spending our cash, but more needs to be available – much more. It took over from Chardonnay as Oregon's major white in 2000, with the trend strengthening in 2001 (now at 15 per cent of production). In Oregon this has been the standard white grape for around 25 years, well-made by many, but totally under-appreciated. It was initially used as a cash crop, for cheap gluggable wine to fill in the gaps while the

Pinot Noirs matured in cask. This state's cooler climate means that more natural acidity is retained in the grapes. Some Pinot Gris is fermented in stainless steel and bottled when young, giving a sprightly, spicy wine, while others are fermented and aged in oak barrel, which results in a fuller, richer version, like a gingery Chardonnay. Look out for these wines before the Californians get hold of them all, or the Oregonians realise they're on to a good thing and bump the prices up.

Riesling, Semillon, Marsanne, Syrah, Roussanne and Sangiovese are also showing positive signs in Oregon, where they're all likely to do better in the cooler climate than, for example, in California's hotter one. Plus, in other US states a varietal wine only needs 75 per cent of a grape in the blend to take its name, but from Oregon the minimum is 90 per cent. So you get more of what you think you are getting!

Pick of the producers (Oregon)
Adelsheim Growing winery (15 to now 142 acres) in third decade; Pinot Noir is the grape to watch here.

Amity Skilled range of Pinot Noirs, including both ripe, cherry-flavoured and rustic, spicy Burgundian versions. All made by heavily bearded, hippyish Myron Redford: one of Oregon's greatest characters. Organic range due to come on stream soon.

Beaux Frères Exciting producer of pure, rich Pinot Noir. The American wine writer Robert Parker is a shareholder.

Bethel Heights Well-made Pinot Noir from Willamette, since 1977. Chardonnay, Pinots Blanc and Gris all aim at Burgundy style.

Domaine Drouhin French know-how combined with ten years' experience in Oregon makes for very fine Pinot Noir, especially the Laurene *cuvée*. Aim is for an Oregon expression, not a French one. Chardonnay also excellent.

Elk Cove Decent Pinot Gris and relatively rich Pinot Noir from this winery in the north-west corner of the Willamette Valley.

Erath Vineyards Leading producer of consistently well-balanced Oregon Pinot Noir, Pinot Gris and Chardonnay. New winemaker could herald new style.

Eyrie Well known for ground-breaking Pinot Noir back in the 1970s, and today notable for particularly fine whites as well – try the Pinot Gris or Chardonnay if you spot them on a wine list.

301

Firesteed Delicious Alsace-like Pinot Gris and bold, fruity Pinot Noir are highly visible and sound but extremely 'international'.

Henry Estate Based down south in the Umpqua Valley, Henry Estate is notable for its ripe Pinot.

King Estate Strides ahead with Pinot Noir, despite just ten years' experience and despite being Oregon's largest producer, providing the consistency with this grape that others in the state often lack. Reserve bottlings very good, as are those of the tangy, lingering Pinot Gris.

Ponzi Founded by Dick and Nancy Ponzi in 1970, with second generation now champing at the bit. Pinot Noir and Riesling are first rank; plus Pinot Gris, Chardonnay and Italian varietals.

Sokol Blosser Innovative producer of top Pinot Noir, Chardonnay and Riesling. The 'Randall Grahm' of Oregon (see *Bonny Doon*, California, above).

Willamette Valley Vineyards Whites currently lead the range, with ripe, rounded Chardonnay and enticing Tualatin Pinot Blanc. Pinot reds currently rather rustic.

Ken Wright Wright's range of silky Pinot Noirs sets him among the most notable producers in the state. Pinot Gris also amazing, and exciting new Syrah project soon emerging.

WASHINGTON STATE

We sometimes get the impression that Washington and Oregon winemakers can't find their way through the maze of wine styles – they can't settle on anything that particularly suits them. Oregon might have drawn a short (or difficult) straw in finding that the cantankerous Pinot Noir grape was its best partner, but Washington now has no excuse not to start proving what it can do. Last year it seemed that Syrah could amount to greatness in Washington, and this year we can confirm that, here, at last, is a variety in which this state's growers have really found their way.

You might ask what a state further north than Oregon – which excels with cool-climate grapes – would possibly get out of planting a 'big' red variety like Syrah. Surely it's cooler still up there? The truth is, Washington's vineyards (in the Columbia River Valley, Yakima Valley, Walla Walla, and the new Red Mountain AVA) lie on the dry, eastern side of the Cascade Mountain Range; in Oregon, they lie on the coastal west – which is more lush and damp.

This is one of the most arid, empty, sun-bleached spots in north-west America, yet as you fly across it, heading east from Seattle, you suddenly spot enormous green circular vineyards among the pale, scrubby wasteland. On each circle sits a long metal arm, like the hand of a huge clock. This is the irrigation pipe that keeps the vines verdant in this otherwise desert landscape. This is where those marvellous Syrahs grow.

Why Washington should hit its stride with this one particular variety is not clear, but although the other wines can be good (Cabernet in particular), their quality tends to be a direct reflection of either yields or winemaking. And as a rule there seems to be little traceable vineyard character. Just to reinforce the point, we're particularly bored with the woody, lacklustre Chardonnays – the problem might lie with the above-mentioned irrigation pipes. Some of the wines appear to be from high-yielding vines, where over-zealous watering is the norm. What we'd like to see instead is 'concentration'. There's no excuse: Washington is blessed with one of the most reliably dry growing seasons in the viticultural world – rain at harvest time is almost unknown.

Once the growers have found their strength, they need to have the courage of their convictions to stick with a style they know is good. Several UK merchants have found a source of delicious Washington wines, only to discover a year later that the winemaker has gone all 'Californian' on them, opting for bland, fruity crowd-pleasers rather than listening to the individuality their land gives them. Come on: you've got a new chance in Syrah, don't blow it!

There are now 208 wineries in Washington, with 12,000 hectares of vineyard. Syrah is 10 per cent of the total plantings, the third most popular red varietal after Merlot and Cabernet Sauvignon.

Pick of the producers (Washington state)

Cayuse Winery Worth seeking out for strapping Walla Walla Syrah attentively made by the 'Bionic Frog' himself (with an eponymous wine) Christophe Baron. Christophe is from Champagne, but his vineyards are as stony as Châteauneuf's – wines commensurate with the latter.

Chateau Ste Michelle One of the state's pioneers, producing modern-style premium wine in Washington for 35 years. Best known for Merlot and Cabernet, although we think highly of the fruit-packed Chardonnay. New joint venture with Antinori (Italy) has produced impressive Col Solare, while another very successful collaboration is that with Ernst Loosen of the Mosel in Germany, to produce the wonderful limey Eroica Riesling. Parent company Stimson Lane also owns Columbia Crest for entry-level wines.

Columbia Winery English Master of Wine David Lake is the founding father of Syrah in Washington State: when he first planted it in 1985, he was thought to be misguided, but has now been proved right. Sold to American giant Canandaigua in 2001, so wines a bit 'transitional' at present.

Delille Bordeaux blends (red and white both excellent) from Woodinville Francophiles. Ageworthy Chaleur is the top-label Cabernet/Merlot blend; delicious, approachable D2 (named after the main road through the Médoc) is number two. New Doyenne Syrah, from 1999, is big and modern, raspberry-smooth with a spicy element; bodes well.

L'Ecole 41 Beautifully crafted, flavour-packed wines from small producer based in Walla Walla. The creamy, ripe Semillon is still top of this range – there are three different styles, best of which is Bordeaux-blend Apogee. Merlot also splendid in a rich, oaky way.

Hedges Fine, all-round selection topped by full-bodied but supple Three Vineyards Cabernet/Merlot and Merlot-dominated, structured Red Mountain Reserve. (Hedges led the drive to establish the new Red Mountain appellation.)

Hogue Cellars Successful large operation making a modern, affordable 'fruit-forward' (their description) range. Wines pleasant: at best 'sassy', if rather short. Entry-level Syrah and Viognier sell like hot-cakes. Bulk production, high-yield wines.

Leonetti Rare but fabulous Cabernet and Merlot, both of which benefit from ageing. Also successful with Sangiovese. Devoted mission is to produce 100-per-cent Walla Walla Valley wines in near future.

McCrea Puget Sound winery for especially good Syrah, Viognier and Grenache and other Rhône varietals. Complex, elegant wines made within sight of Mt Rainier.

Quilceda Creek Well-made Cabernet Sauvignon with lots of finesse from a tiny Puget Sound winery, where Alex and Jeanette Golitzin, their son Paul and son-in-law Marv, are at the helm.

Andrew Will Rarely available in the UK, but if you come across the classy Cabernet Sauvignons and Merlots made by Chris

Camarda, snap them up. They're all boutique-quality, from individual vineyard sites.

IDAHO

Idaho has been making wine since the 1860s, so is far from being a newcomer. The 14 wineries, which initially started up along the cool Snake River Valley, took a knocking during Prohibition, but – gathering some reflected glory from neighbouring Washington and Oregon – at long last things are beginning to pick up again. With just over 700 acres planted, there's a long way to go before we see many of these wines in the UK; but the aim is high – to make Nampa Idaho as popular as Napa California! Wineries to watch out for are Pend d'Oreille, Camas and Ste-Chapelle, but more are still springing up. We're told Idaho has better Rieslings than almost anywhere and reds that'll soon be on a par with those in Washington. Those who are patient (more patient than we are) should keep watching this space.

OTHER STATES

The most important and prolific state after California, Washington State and Oregon is undoubtedly New York State. Coolish-climate vineyards alongside the Finger Lakes in upstate New York can produce palatable, oaked Chardonnay and some perky, traditional-method sparklers (especially at Lamoreaux Landing, and also at Glenora estate) but, most importantly, there has been a big push lately in Riesling. We're still, perhaps, five years off seeing these wines on UK shores but they're really very good, and capable – even needing – bottle-age. It's just a shame they're all sold out the back door, to thirsty New Yorkers. Michigan is another state producing good Riesling, and it also has a rare and blossoming talent for Pinot Noir . . . We await further signs of this with interest.

Closer to the Big Apple, on Long Island, a few boutique wineries are producing increasingly impressive Chardonnay and Merlot in a rich, fruit-driven style. With a huge wine-quaffing metropolis less than three hours' drive away, the Long Island winemakers are in no rush to export their wines; if you find yourself in New York, we recommend you sample them, especially those from Bridgehampton, Hargrave, Peconic Bay and Pindar.

Of the remaining 46 states in the USA, 36 of them (including Hawaii) produce wine. Our experience of these has ranged from an excellent Zinfandel from Callaghan Vineyards in Arizona and a surprisingly good Texan Gewurztraminer, to a quite dreadful, murky red from Missouri. There are also small players making good Riesling in Colorado and New Mexico. But as far as winemaking on a serious scale is concerned, we're still waiting for news from Virginia and Maryland, where signs are promising. Once there are more wines from these states available in the UK, we'll tell you more about them.

URUGUAY

The main reason to buy Uruguayan wine is still the red grape variety Tannat: lovable for its molasses-rich fruit, mulberry aromas and meaty, smoky, steak-friendly concentration; easy to remember for its main characteristic – 'Tannat has tannin'. This thick-skinned, rot-resistant variety does very well in Uruguay's relatively damp maritime climate – no other country can say the same. Even in its spiritual home, Madiran in south-western France, it makes a more severe wine, sturdy but less generously fruity than these Uruguayan versions.

Of the Tannats currently available, we prefer those without the rough prominent tannins that the locals have become used to, those that have been softened up by adding Merlot or Cabernet Franc. Look out for the wines of Casa Luntro and Casilla Dorada, made by the Frenchman Jacques Lurton, and Juanico's wines (made by the Australian Peter Bright), plus Filgueira, Pisano, Irurtia, Castillo Viejo and Castel Pujol. Plus, particularly successful since the 2000 vintage, Stagnari and Toscanini. On the other hand, if you want to see the monster version – it's a meal in itself – seek out the strapping wine from Vino de El Colorado. Stick to younger vintages though, as, contrary to expectations, in Uruguay Tannat's tannins tend to fall apart very quickly with age.

But Uruguay has a lot more going for it than just one grape – if you ignore its three major problems: firstly, poor image (it's famed for football and Fray Bentos pies); secondly, being sandwiched between Argentina and Brazil, it becomes a dumping ground for cheap goods/wines whenever either of these countries is in financial trouble (such as now); and thirdly, it also suffers from the 'how to please the British supermarkets' syndrome. Leave aside these things and focus instead on Uruguay's geography: its natural rainfall and lack of drenching, flood irrigation or badly employed drip systems (as in Argentina next-door); its long, slow ripening seasons; its rolling hills and well-drained soils. What you're left with is crisp, concentrated, undiluted fruit with fine natural acidity. The worst thing that could happen is for the growers to get bogged down in supermarket contracts – for which they'll be paid good money, but which will end up stretching their wines to suit demand. (We know it's tempting, but please don't do it guys). We've seen it all before. You'll quickly blur that top-Tannat image.

Uruguay is right to play Tannat as its strong suit: its 'unique selling point'. But there are other grapes doing well here too: Merlot, Syrah and Cabernet for starters. And whites also. For some reason Uruguayans are less proud of their blended wines, in spite of the above-mentioned Tannat/Cabernet Franc blends and some of the admirable Chardonnay-Viognier blends – the latter showing gentle use of oak, peachy ripe fruit, and that tangy natural acidity again, which gives a delicious grapefruity twist at the finish.

It's too early to seek out definitive regional characteristics, but from the Rivera region in the north of Uruguay expect more powerful reds from hotter soils; from the south, around Montevideo, where vineyard temperatures are tempered by Atlantic breezes, you'll see fruitier, more supple styles emerge.

ZIMBABWE

A few years ago it looked as though we might see some wines from Zimbabwe becoming readily available in the UK. The Thresher chain thought the country had potential and made some serious enquiries. Its buyers gave up simply because of costs: the off-licence buyers wanted £3.99 wine, and the Zimbabweans couldn't produce the goods at that price point. Today, the possibilities the country has for winemaking are the very least of its concerns. It's to be hoped that the progress that was being made before the current political disarray will be picked up again one day – but don't expect to see Zimbabwe's wines around much for the foreseeable future.

Part III

Where to buy wine

Explanation of symbols

   The merchant operates mixed case sales only.

   The merchant operates unmixed case sales only.

   Mail order only.

   Online sales only.

   This symbol indicates that the merchant has elected to participate in *The Which? Wine Guide*'s £5 voucher scheme. (In 'The Top 100' section the symbol appears after information on tastings and talks; in the 'Also recommended' section it appears at the end of the entry.) For more information on this voucher scheme see the page opposite the Contents page. The terms and conditions of the voucher scheme are outlined on the back of the vouchers.

   Denotes generally low prices and/or a large range of modestly priced wines.

   Indicates that the merchant offers exceptionally good service. We rely on readers' reports in allocating service symbols; this means that there may be merchants offering first-class service who appear here with no symbol because such distinction has gone unreported. Readers, please report!

   Indicates high-quality wines across the range.

   This award is given for a wide range of wines from around the world.

Criteria for inclusion

This year we've been tougher on the merchants – to give you a selection of the absolute best. For the first time ever, we're listing the Top 100 in the UK, using some exacting criteria. Our choice has been a difficult one. The criteria are easily met by the best merchants, but some fail on just a minor point or two, necessitating that they be listed as 'Also recommended' when the quality of all else in their range is impeccable.

The criteria for the Top 100 are as follows.

- Wide-ranging wine choices from the majority of wine regions covered – not just branded wines, or old-fashioned favourites (say, from the 1970s).
- A reasonable quantity of wines to choose from (merchants listing just 30 wines, for example, we felt do not give enough options).
- Quality: not everything listed has to be top rank, but there must be good opportunity to trade up from the basic, everyday level.
- A wide range of price points (wines can err to the cheap, or the very expensive, as long as there are alternative options and reasonable value for money is represented).
- A certain percentage of trade must be with the public. Merchants focusing on wholesale, selling to the wine trade, are frequently less geared up to individual customer requirements, with a heavy emphasis on bulk-buying, and sometimes bias towards trade customers.
- Detailed assistance (whether it be tasting notes, region and vintage descriptions, in-store bottles to try, or helpful over-the-counter advice) must be given to aid customers in their choices.
- Innovation: a merchant must demonstrate that it is moving with the times, evolving with its customers' needs, or constantly striving to replenish its stocks with something new.

We also strongly urge you to take very seriously the merchants in the 'Also recommended' listing. These too have been carefully assessed (the criteria for this section are similar to the above, but with slightly lower thresholds) – and there are many who have not made it into the *Guide* at all. Some of the 'Also recommended' merchants even offer wines of our Specialist or Regional Award quality, meeting most of the more stringent criteria, but missing out on a Top 100 listing for such a reason as focusing on the restaurant trade rather than the public. It is quite possible that next year some of the 'Also recommendeds' will be up for promotion.

Don't underestimate the skill, knowledge and buying power of a good merchant. In the following pages we look at the best of the independents, high-street chains and supermarkets.

The Top 100

Adnams Wine Merchants

Head office
Sole Bay Brewery, East Green, Southwold,
Suffolk IP18 6JW

Tel (01502) 727222
Fax (01502) 727223

The Cellar & Kitchen Store
Victoria Street, Southwold, Suffolk IP18 6JW

Tel (01502) 727222
Fax (01502) 727223

The Wine Shop
Pinkney's Lane, Southwold, Suffolk IP18 6EW

Tel (01502) 722138

Email wines@adnams.co.uk
Website www.adnams.co.uk

Open Mon–Sat 10–6, Sun 11–4, public holidays (times may vary between stores)
Closed Sun, 25 & 26 Dec, 1 Jan, Good Friday   **Cards** Delta, MasterCard, Switch, Visa;
personal and business accounts   **Discount** 5% on 5+ cases   **Delivery** Free nationwide
service (min. 1 case)   **Glass hire** Free with order (must return clean)   **Tastings and
talks** Regular tastings and events, phone for details

Adnams is an establishment of zero-tolerance – no boring wines. There's
something fierce, 'sphingoid' even (to use one of his own terms) about
buyer/chairman Simon Loftus, that means we wouldn't want to be a
member of staff found 'compromising' or a grower intent on supplying a
duff wine – worst of all, a limp, lame New World brand. Not even the
'Classics' get away with mediocrity here, and we get the feeling the team
would have no qualms about replacing a complacent *grand cru* château
(big name, or no big name) with a new wine that fits snugly into the
burgeoning organic selection. But then many of the classic wines here are
organic wines too – from Bordeaux seek out châteaux Bel Air, Le Chec and
Chantelys, for example, and be aware that this is not a region renowned
for its whole-earth approach. Look out for the green leaf organic
recommendations.

Even though you have to be quick off the mark to get hold of some of the
fine wines in stock (loyal customers have a tendency to snap up interesting
properties or vintages as soon as they see them listed), prices range from a
very modest £3.35 a bottle and there's plenty to be found in the sub-£10
arena. Adnams Best Buy Cases (at a choice of £58, £79, £112, £118 or £125) are
put together in a series of fascinating combinations that don't allow for any
'I only drink New World' nonsense, but keep the mind broad, the palate
keen and the wallet tremor-free. These are not, by any means, 'beginner's
wines', but a great way to benefit from the experience of the well-travelled
buying team: let them choose for you.

Similarly, with 'The Adnams Selection', customers can look forward to a
case of four different wines (three bottles of each) arriving on their doorstep
every month, if they so wish. 'The more you order, the more we reduce the
price' is the motto. Those who order regularly also receive a 10 per cent
discount on all Adnams' own-label wines.

As you leaf through the 'Adnams Classics' and 'Adnams Fine Wine' mail-order brochures you can't help but get a sense of place, and a sense of the personalities behind the excellent wine choices. Producer profiles, newly discovered regions, stories of chance wine discoveries and unexpected new introductions colour each page. The Adnams wine lists are updated quarterly and each edition serves to renew acquaintances with old *terroirs*, rediscover forgotten classics and cover new ground too. 'We only sell what we like to drink,' says senior buyer Alistair Marshall at the end of it. We'd like to drink these impeccable wines too.

There is, in fact, no end to the service this company provides. 'If you don't like any wine that you buy from us, for whatever reason, return it within a month of purchase and we shall refund your money without question or delay,' is the guarantee. Not that we imagine many people use it. There is also a new Cellar and Kitchen Store to discover, as well as the numerous hostelries and restaurants that serve these wines (and Adnams beer) locally, plus wine courses, wine weekends and winemaker lunches.

Look out for
- *En primeur* offers of Ridge Monte Bello (California)
- Châteaux Lynch-Bages, Palmer, Haut-Brion and Latour (Bordeaux)
- Top burgundies from Leflaive, Marchand de Gramont and Domaine Anne Gros
- Regional Australian choices, including Cullen from Margaret River and Charles Melton from the Barossa Valley
- Nine different organic wines from the Languedoc, ten from the Rhône and seven from Provence
- Tommasi Amarone, Pervini Primitivo and Cavallotto Barolo from Italy.

John Armit Wines

5 Royalty Studios, 105 Lancaster Road,
London W11 1QF

Tel 020-7908 0600
Fax 020-7908 0601
Email info@armit.co.uk
Website www.armit.co.uk

Open Mon–Fri 9–6 **Closed** Sat, Sun, public holidays **Cards** Amex, Delta, MasterCard, Switch, Visa; personal and business accounts **Discount** Available, phone for details **Delivery** Nationwide service (min. 1 case), charge £15 per order, free for orders of £180+ **Glass hire** Not available **Tastings and talks** Regular tastings and events, phone for details

The 'It' wine merchant has at last gone IT – in other words, it now has a website. This makes sense, given the all-round 'slickness' of everything else about this company (designer wine list, elegant tastings, fashionable Notting Hill address, smart prices, etc.). We're pleased to see, however, that the advent of technology hasn't distanced the customer. There's still the same individually tailored feel about every aspect of the service here – nothing is too much trouble. In fact, one of the services now offered by the team is to send a mixed case of 2000 Bordeaux to a godson or goddaughter in 20 years' time.

In their own words, the company represents: 'Starry châteaux, domaines and wineries from around the world: rare, top-quality Bordeaux, Super-Tuscans, California boutique wines, superb Spanish estates and a wonderful selection of New World wines. Every wine in the portfolio has been selected for its individuality, expression of *terroir*, quality of fruit and value for money'. And alongside all the top-price, glittering stock in each section of the list, there's an even cleverer selection of day-to-day wines, which don't dabble in mediocrity but continue to shine as great examples of their kind. Take Italy, for example, there is a whole range of case options around the (very reasonable) £150 mark, taking in Nebbiolo d'Alba, Dolcetto, Passomaggio Rosso from Sicily and other fascinating choices before things take off to the 'POA' (Price on Application) Super-Tuscan levels. Oh yes, and there are plenty of wines to choose from below and in between these prices too.

Apart from the illustrious wines, we'd always return to Armit for the add-ons. Not only the godchildren service (as mentioned above), but the Armit Selection and the Armit Cellar Service. The former is a collection of own-label wines ranging from modestly priced South African Semillon/Sauvignon, to Armit champagne at an impressive £144 a case. Mixed-case options are available too, so that's variety without the worry of having to choose. Then there's the Cellar Service, by which the Armit team put together a 'Terroir Cellar' (at £10,000) including top burgundies, Rhônes and a few German sweeties, or, perhaps, a more modest £5,000 cellar with Pomerol (modest?), Pouilly-Fuissé and Spanish Pesquera to wait for. If you prefer to choose for yourself, many hours of happy perusal are to be had by sitting down with the main list.

The one negative about this range is that being such an energetic supplier of the restaurant trade (as befits an 'It' merchant, Armit works with London's finest, the likes of Ransome's Dock, The River Café and Lomo) treasures from older vintages aren't that easy to come by: high turnover means they disappear all too quickly. But as we said last year, the trend is to drink wine young these days, and the team at Armit certainly know how to be trendy.

Look out for
- Leflaive, Raveneau and Faiveley burgundies
- Off-beat, upbeat southern French choices from domaines d'Aupilhac, Clavel and Cazeneuve le Roc des Mates
- Tuscan offerings from Brunello di Montalcino to Ornellaia and Sassicaia
- Top Australian bottlings from Hahn to Hare's Chase (both Barossa Valley), Yerringberg and beyond
- Hess Collection, Dominus and Laetitia Winery strapping reds from the USA
- Ready-to-drink Bordeaux choices from Châteaux Mazeyres, La Fleur de Boüard and Faugères.

Asda Stores

Head office

Asda House, Southbank, Great Wilson Street,   *Tel* 0500 100 055
Leeds LS11 5AD   *Fax* 0113-241 7732
(230 branches nationwide)   *Website* www.asda.co.uk

Open Mon–Sat varies between stores, Sun, public holidays 11–5   **Closed** Varies
between stores   **Cards** Delta, MasterCard, Switch, Visa   **Discount** 5% on 5 bottles
Delivery Available within 10–15-mile radius, charge £3.50 per order   **Glass hire** Free
Tastings and talks In-store customer tastings in addition to larger events

Asda informed us last year that its customers had been trading up and that
they were now more open to experimentation. Great, we thought, this is
exactly what supermarket wine buyers should be doing. It was
commendable – not to say unusual in a group of stores this size – that
branching out, getting away from mainstream Chardonnay, was being
encouraged. But this year, we're left wondering what it is – or was – that
customers *were* finding encouraging?

Asda's list draws heavily on the world's major branded wines: Gallo from
California, Jacob's Creek, Wolf Blass and Barramundi from Australia, Blue
Nun and Black Tower from Germany. These are the wines that are available
in all Asda's UK outlets. They are cheap and moderately cheerful, but not at
all the adventurous choices we thought would be appearing in response to
an increasingly wine-conscious public. It appears that the company is happy
not to have the exact-same wine list in every store, so why can't there be
more small-production, hand-crafted wines representing the flavours of the
world's different regions, rather than the same old homogeneous dollops
that come from everywhere?

The answer probably has to do with money. Asda's biggest asset, not just
in the wine department, is its extremely pleasing prices. But keeping things
below the £4 mark (which it frequently does) is inevitably going to take its
toll. Proof that our theory is correct comes in the Australia and France
sections, where a few of the wines on sale for around £6 do begin to show
some character. 'Other grapes' make their way into the Australian collection,
for example: Marsanne, Verdelho and Chenin Blanc for the whites,
Grenache, Malbec, Sangiovese and Chambourcin for the reds. And in
France, each of the major Médoc *communes* (such as St-Julien and Margaux)
gets a mention, as do some of the major *communes* of Burgundy and the
Rhône. (OK, these do get a little more expensive than £6!) So Asda *can* make
things more interesting when it tries. And its customers *can* find out
something about the world's really good wines at most of the stores, as long
as they're prepared to pay a little bit more.

Look out for

- Bigger, better choices at the Supercentres – particularly of New World
  wines
- Tempting collection of Rhône wines from Vacqueyras, Rasteau and
  Gigondas
- Oddities from Greece and Puglia (southern Italy)
- Neil Ellis and Beyerskloof, plus other goodies from South Africa

- Fizz from as little as £10.97 a bottle, to Taittinger, Bollinger and Krug at the top end.
- Free, unconditional glass hire, enticing discount offers, plus evening tasting clubs held in-store

The Australian Wine Club 🖐️ ✉️

Head office
3rd Floor, Regal House, 70 London Road,   *Tel* 020-8843 8450
Twickenham TW1 3QS   *Fax* 020-8843 8444
                                            Email orders@austwine.co.uk
                                            Website www.austwine.co.uk

Open Mon–Fri 8–8, Sat 9–6, Sun 10–4 **Closed** Public holidays **Cards** Amex, Delta, Diners, MasterCard, Switch, Visa; business accounts **Discount** Not available **Delivery** Nationwide service (min. 1 case), charge £4.99 per order **Glass hire** Not available **Tastings and talks** Several tastings and dinners per year, phone for details

Mail order is the name of the game at the Australian Wine Club, but this is still very much 'an exploration of Real Australian wine'. Keith Heddle, head of marketing, explains that this business began life specialising in high-quality, small Australian estates, and sees no reason for that to change: the family-sized wineries are still, predominantly, those that make the best wine. (One big change, however, has been the recent addition of one or two New Zealand estates – De Redcliffe is one.)

Quirky individual wine estates are exactly what we need to see from Australia these days, and AWC is still the safe haven from brands it always was. There are plenty of characterful choices (OK, you have to buy by the case) but prices are still pretty much the same. We do, however, mourn the lack of ultra-quality Australian wines on this list. It's great to see the likes of Steve Hoff (Barossa) and Cornerstone (Clare Valley) making a splash, but what about Veritas, Grosset, Mount Horrocks and Henschke from the same neighbourhood? And what about listing more of the top-notch estates of Western Australia? We get the impression that one or two cheaper choices from the bulk-producing Riverlands region are sneaking in, and while there's nothing wrong with saving a pound or two, it's the mass-supply side of this that makes us twitchy. Surely it's getting away from the whole point of the business?

Look out for
- Customer Club membership at £10 entitles you to a quarterly pre-sale selection and two to three tastings a year
- Bin-end mixed cases: the 'Quiet Night In' mix, 'Give Me More Reds' mix, 'Chardonnays Galore' mix, and more
- Primo Estate sparkling red Joseph and Rare Print Cabernet/Malbec fizz
- Tim Adams' delicious Clare Valley Semillon and Riesling
- Big Barossa Shirazes aplenty.

Averys of Bristol

Head office
Orchard House, Southfield Road,   *Tel* (01275) 811100
Nailsea, Bristol BS48 1JN   *Fax* (01275) 811101

Cellars
9 Culver Street, Bristol BS1 5LD   *Tel* 0117-921 4146
                                                    Fax 0117-922 6318

Shop
8 Park Street, Bristol BS1 5HX   *Tel* 0117-921 4145
                                        Email averycellars@dialstart.net

Open (Shop) Mon–Sat 10–6.30 (cellars) Mon–Sat 10–7 (office) Mon–Fri 9–5.15 **Closed** Sun, public holidays **Cards** Amex, Delta, MasterCard, Switch, Visa; personal accounts **Discount** Not available **Delivery** Nationwide service, charge £4.99 per order **Glass hire** Not available **Tastings and talks** Tastings and masterclasses, phone for details

'There is hardly anything in the World that some man cannot make a little worse and sell a little cheaper, and the people who consider price only, are that man's lawful prey,' says the quote from Ruskin on the back page of the Averys list. This merchant may have been established since 1793 but this is the motto it stands by rather than trading on past glories.

John Avery and Beverley Tabron (both Masters of Wine) fully admit to the traditional side of the business and proudly list around 16 pages of Bordeaux and burgundies – these are the everyday wines from recent vintages, with some classy properties among them – but you have to look to the Fine and Rare list for the full spectrum. Among Italian wines, expect to find all the classics from some of the best and most modern growers, with the Rhône, Loire and Languedoc selections hard on their heels. The New World's not forgotten; we're particularly impressed by the range of wines stocked from South Africa (Spice Route and Hamilton Russell's wines among them).

There's nothing old-fashioned about the way Averys conducts the mail-order side of its business either. If you don't have time to visit the Bristol shop, we thoroughly recommend joining the 'Automatically from Averys' (AfA) scheme, whereby once every three months members receive a mixed case of pre-chosen wines at one of two price levels, £75 or £125.

We still think the Australian, Chilean and Californian sections of this list could use some more diverse choices, and that the Spanish range is somewhat overshadowed by the enticing Italian range – perhaps the team should think about including some of the other up-and-coming Spanish regions? Also, perhaps some regions do rely rather heavily on one or two key producers. But we are pleased to see some adventurous oddities, such as Cafayate Argentinian wines from Michel Torino and Canadian Icewine sneaking in. Averys certainly isn't in the business of sameness.

Look out for

- Tedeschi Amarone and Chiarlo Barolo from northern Italy
- Inniskillin Riesling and Vidal Icewines from Canada
- Crisp, dry white Bordeaux from Châteaux Timberlay, de Haux and Baret

- Médoc classics from Châteaux Montrose, Gruaud-Larose and Pichon Longueville
- Illustrious burgundies such as Mommessin's Clos de Tart and Domaine de la Vougeraie's Bonnes Mares
- Fine Alsace wines from Domaines Trimbach and Léon Beyer.

Bacchus Fine Wines

Warrington House Farm Barn, Warrington, Olney,	*Tel* (01234) 711140
Buckinghamshire MK46 4HN	*Fax* (01234) 711199
	Email wine@bacchus.co.uk
	Website www.bacchus.co.uk

Open Mon–Fri 10.30–6.30, Sat 10.30–2 **Closed** Sun, 25–28 Dec, bank holiday Mondays **Cards** Amex, Delta, Diners, MasterCard, Switch, Visa; business accounts **Discount** Available, phone for details **Delivery** Free within 10-mile radius (min. 1 case); nationwide service (min. 1 case), charge £7.05 for 1 case, negotiable for additional cases **Glass hire** Free with order **Tastings and talks** 5 tutored tastings annually plus frequent in-store tastings, phone for details **(£5)**

Russell Heap, Bacchus' director, says: 'We hope to buck the trend and lead the middle market customer away from dull international brands and towards growers' wines with character and "typicity".' Amen to that. We're none too keen on international brands either.

Russell expects his range to illustrate a selection of classics plus wines from emerging regions; 'funky' is the word he likes to use for some of the latter. With options such as Frog's Leap Zinfandel, Redhead Petite Sirah and Bonny Doon Ca'del Solo from California, and wines from lesser-known Australian regions such as Pemberton and Blackwood Ridge, we'd happily concur that these are unusual and 'funky' choices and have no complaints to make about wines from Uruguay, Lebanon and France's wildest region, the Languedoc, creeping into the equation.

Bacchus claims two speciality areas: individual domaines and Austria. Flicking through this company's wine list, we can see it is illuminated with growers we know to be free-thinkers and passionate proponents of *terroir*, keen to reveal the individual qualities of their vineyards in their wines. Russell highlights the red wines of Paul Achs, Gernot Heinrich and Joseph Pöckl for whom Bacchus acts as UK agent, and which have been taken on board for their feisty, red-berry characters and general food matchability.

There's good value to be had right across the range, with prices in the main between £5 and £10 a bottle, and the choices above this (squeezing up to £20 and £30) remaining steadfastly good value for the money-spinning territory they traverse (Bordeaux, Burgundy, Rhône, Champagne). Our only concern, perhaps, is that alongside all the less-mainstream, cleverly chosen producers from regions such as Bordeaux, it might be comforting (if not cheaper) to see a few more familiar classics, so life wasn't always such a gamble. Nonetheless, we admire Russell's bravery.

Purchase of a minimum of one mixed case will be little problem, with the enticement of 5 per cent discount under Bacchus' Loyalty Account system. Plus there's a bimonthly newsletter, the *Bacchus Gazette*, with special offers,

'Meet the Maker' grower profiles, tastings to attend, new discoveries and food matches.

Look out for

- Tunisian Carignan – this selection is nothing if not adventurous!
- Top-notch Infinitus Malbec from Argentina, plus reds from Finca El Retiro and Santa Rosa
- 'Six-puttonyos' Oremus Tokaji from Hungary
- Superb range from Mediterranean France, including Pic St-Loup, St-Chinian, Faugères
- Chablis classics from l'Eglantière, Tremblay and Durup
- Interesting, lesser-known Pomerol châteaux: Robert, Perron and Clos du Clocher.

Ballantynes of Cowbridge

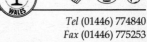

3 Westgate, Cowbridge,
Vale of Glamorgan CF71 7AQ
211–217 Cathedral Road, Cardiff

Tel (01446) 774840
Fax (01446) 775253
Email richard@ballantynes.co.uk
Website www.ballantynes.co.uk

Open Mon–Sat 9–5.30, Sun 12–4 (Cardiff) **Closed** Sun (Cowbridge), public holidays
Cards Delta, MasterCard, Switch, Visa; personal and business accounts **Discount** 8%
on 1 case **Delivery** Free within 10-mile radius (min. 1 case); nationwide service,
charge £7.95 for 1 case, £3.95 for subsequent cases **Glass hire** Free with order
Tastings and talks Regular tastings and talks, phone for details **£5**

Now that the Cowbridge store has been extended, Richard Ballantyne is presiding over the opening of a new branch in central Cardiff. Good to hear it – the company that regularly wins our Regional Award for Wales is going great guns. And that's no surprise when you look at its remarkable range. Ballantynes sticks firmly to quality wines, and sources as much as possible directly from the producer, especially in France. 'We are particularly proud of our Languedoc wines and domaine burgundies and have worked with some producers for over 20 years,' says Richard with justifiable pride. The Italian selection is almost as strong as that from France, and features top makers from around the country's diverse regions. Of the New World countries, Australia continues to be the ace, although the California/Oregon/ Washington State bins from America come close. Vintage ports, sherries and fine malt whiskies feature heavily. A spirited all-rounder working at the quality end of the market – no other Welsh merchant comes close. If you live in Cardiff, get along to that new shop, pronto.

Look out for

- Rhônes from Beaucastel, Chave, Chapoutier and lesser-known domaines
- Off-beat Australians from Bass Phillip, Yarra Yering, Mount Langi Ghiran, Jasper Hill
- Ridge, Saintsbury, Newton, Amity from California/Oregon
- Lovely Southern French wines
- Wither Hills, Kumeu River, Mudhouse from New Zealand
- Fine Spanish wines, modern and traditional, including Abadia Retuerta, López de Heredia, Muga.

Balls Brothers

313 Cambridge Heath Road, Bethnal Green,
London E2 9LQ
(18 wine bars and restaurants)

Tel 020-7739 1642
Fax (0870) 243 9775
Email wine@ballsbrothers.co.uk
Website www.ballsbrothers.co.uk

Open Mon–Fri 9–5.30 **Closed** Sat, Sun, public holidays **Cards** Amex, Delta, Diners, MasterCard, Switch, Visa; personal and business accounts **Discount** Available, phone for details **Delivery** Free within central London (min. 1 case); nationwide service, phone for details of charges **Glass hire** Free with order, charge for breakages **Tastings and talks** Regular tastings and events, phone for details **£5**

For all the image of a trusted and traditional old wine merchant, the modern face of Balls Brothers takes some beating: most contemporary of all are its 18 bars and restaurants spread throughout London's City and West End. While these tempt guests to such traditional British fodder as Cumberland sausage and onion, or roast beef and horseradish sandwiches, they serve alongside these dishes distinctly up-to-date wines – a Puglia Sangiovese from Italy's deep south. Then there's the website: one of the first to be up-and-running and spreading these wares to Generation X and others keen to buy their wines by logging on.

Balls Brothers also have one of the most get-at-able, easy-to-read wine lists we've seen, full of photographs, helpful tasting notes, background information and new offers. This, combined with winemaker events, 'Call My Bluff' tastings, 'Taste to Buy' sessions (if you spend £100 or more on a wine purchase, you get your £15 ticket money back), serves to make wine more accessible and enjoyable to everyone. Quite the reverse of the crusty side of wine merchanting that you expect to see, given this company's long-standing family presence. (As we write, the latest Taste to Buy session is entitled 'Lutte Raisonée', covering a range of organic and biodynamic wines.)

Balls Brothers still ship, age and store their wine themselves, so retain the finer elements of the old-school wine trade. And they also have the thoroughly respectable range of Old World classics you'd expect (Châteaux Gruaud-Larose, Palmer and Pomys from the Médoc, with some fine old vintages). They are also particularly proud of their South African and Australian offerings which are, indeed, extensive. But although there is a good range from around the world, we do feel that the wine choices here mostly reflect a fairly high turnover in stock, i.e. they come from suppliers able to keep up with heavy demand. (That modest medium-sized producer, C J Pask, is responsible for the majority of the wines here from New Zealand, for example.) It would be heartening to see a few more of the special, small-batch wines we used to see on the lists of this popular merchant – just to make things lively and interesting again.

Look out for

- Delicious stocks of old port vintages from Warre, Grahams and Fonseca
- Good-idea Gift Sets, ranging from £13.95 for a couple of Classic South African wines, to £340 for Richard Balls' personally selected 12-bottle Burgundy set

- Top new domaines from Southern France: Pech-Céleyran, Gilbert Alquier, Comte Cathare
- White burgundy from Chablis to Chassagne-Montrachet (J-M Brocard to Domaine Bachelet).

Barrels & Bottles

3 Oak Street, Heeley Bridge, Sheffield S8 9UB

Tel 0114-255 6611
Fax 0114-255 1010
Email sales@barrelsandbottles.co.uk
Website www.barrelsandbottles.co.uk

Open Mon–Fri 9–5.30, Sat 9–5 **Closed** Sun, public holidays **Cards** Amex, Delta, MasterCard, Switch, Visa; personal and business accounts **Discount** 5% on 6 bottles, 10% on 1 mixed case, 15% on 1 unmixed case **Delivery** Free within 30-mile radius (min. 1 case); nationwide service, charge £8.50 for 1 case, £12 for 2 cases, free for 3+ cases **Glass hire** Free with order **Tastings and talks** Monthly themed tastings, daily in-store tastings, phone for details **£5**

Barrels & Bottles has a tidy range selected from growers for which it acts as sole UK agent. Andrew Coghlan, the director, trains his staff well: 'Because we are the only stockists, most of our wines are not widely known, so it is important the team understands them, so that they can sell them.' Andrew broadcasts a weekly wine slot on BBC Radio Sheffield (Thursdays, soon after 11am, if you're interested) so he obviously knows a thing or two about communication.

A new 60-seater tasting room, a monthly newsletter, an active website, and the colourful and (we admit) enticing presentation of this list bear witness to Andrew's skills. We admire this enthusiasm, but we would, however, like to see a little more depth in the range of wines.

Bordeaux and Germany are the specialities, and in these sections there are both first-class 'classic' wines (châteaux Gruaud-Larose, Chasse-Spleen, Mouton-Rothschild; Wehlener Sonnenuhr and Bernkasteler Kurfürstlay wines from the Mosel) and unusual alternatives from nooks and crannies such as Côtes de Bourg and Blaye. But, although there is increased confidence in regions such as New Zealand – B&B is newly the agent for Marlborough's Highfield Estate – there's a limited number of growers, and therefore styles of wine to choose from, in most other areas: three producers from Argentina, only two each from the Loire and Languedoc, for example. But B&B obviously does good service in supplying the rest of the wine trade with these smaller estates, so are to be lauded. It is teams like this that chip away at the monopoly of big, nationally available brands that we see every day on supermarket shelves. 'We work mainly with smaller growers who reflect their personality in their wines,' says Andrew. This we like to see.

Look out for
- Top-notch German choices from the Mosel, Pfalz, Rheinhessen, Franken, Nahe, Ahr Valley and Würtemberg
- Well-known Australian estates, including Cape Mentelle and Ironstone from Western Australia

- Krug champagne
- Developing ranges from Chile and South Africa
- Impressive Burgundy names, including Moillard-Grivot, La Chablisienne and Ramonet
- Tempting Rhône selection, Guigal and Vidal-Fleury's wines included.

Bat & Bottle

Grange Road, Knightley, Stafford,	*Tel* (01785) 284495
Staffordshire ST20 0JU	*Fax* (01785) 284877
	Email ben@batwine.com
	Website www.batwine.com

Open Mon–Thur phone for details, Fri 2–7, Sat 11–4 **Closed** Sun, public holidays
Cards Delta, MasterCard, Switch, Visa **Discount** 5% on 1 unmixed case **Delivery**
Nationwide service, charge £4.99 per order, free for orders of £150+ **Glass hire** Not
available **Tastings and talks** Regular tastings in Knightley, also in London and South-
west; phone or visit website for details

Bat & Bottle has got braver than ever this year. 'We de-list wines that have
provided us with hangovers,' says buyer/partner Ben Robson. 'And we don't
really do New World; we specialise in the "Med".' All of which means that
(Alsace excepted), Ben no longer supplies any French wines from north of
St-Joseph in the Rhône. In the last year, he has ruled out Champagne, the
Loire, Bordeaux and Burgundy altogether.

In doing this, Bat & Bottle has shrugged off all outside expectations and
left itself with a clean slate on which to impress with the wines they know
and like. Above all, their energy goes into uncharted Italy, from which they
source many wines directly from the producer, keeping the prices
attractively low. We agree with Ben that the north-east Italian section of the
list is better than ever this year – with Ca La Bionda from Valpolicella
(makers of everything up to Amarone and *passito* level) and a new Prosecco
(good refreshing summer fizz) from Le Case Bianche.

The Spanish selection is also impressive, and from closer to those French
Mediterranean shores, it's pleasing to see the likes of Château Pech-Haut,
Jerôme Roger and Domaine Fontaine making an appearance, all fashionable,
new-look wines from Languedoc-Roussillon.

'The surviving New World estates that we have decided to keep, do
bring something to the list but we would rather buy from regions we know
and visit regularly,' says Ben. The only Australian wines he trusts are from
Western Australia, 'the only state where quality seems to come before
quantity'. Bonny Doon is one of the few California estates to make it here,
and further exemplifies the kind of integrity and individuality Ben is looking
for in his wines.

Should you be in Staffordshire, you can stop in and browse at this 'very
rural' off-licence for yourself. But Ben also puts a lot of energy into
spreading the news about honestly good wine, with three tastings a year
held in London, two in the south-west and one in the north (and nearly
every week at home in Knightley).

The customer club sounds good to us too: there's a small (£25) joining fee
but you get to be in on the 'Conspirators' wines (10 per cent discount), plus

£68 mixed cases and £72 'Vini Curiosity' packages. We too can't help but be curious about the less-usual offerings in the latter. Congratulations: great list, great outlook!

Look out for

- Frankland and Wignalls estate wines from Western Australia
- Great things, modestly priced, from Tuscany: Isole e Olena, Podere Il Poggiolo
- Plenty of sub-£5 Italian bottles from a variety of grapes and regions
- Cerro Chapeu Tannat from Uruguay
- Fashionable Priorato and Rías Baixas Spanish wines.

Bennetts Fine Wines

High Street, Chipping Campden,
Gloucestershire GL55 6AG

Tel (01386) 840392
Fax (01386) 840974
Email enquiries@bennettsfinewines.com
Website www.bennettsfinewines.com

Open Mon–Fri 10–6, Sat 9–6 **Closed** Sun, public holidays, 5 days over Christmas
Cards Delta, MasterCard, Switch, Visa; business accounts **Discount** Available, phone
for details **Delivery** Free within 10-mile radius (min. 1 case); nationwide service,
charge £6 per case/item (min. order £12) **Glass hire** Free with order **Tastings and
talks** 2 annual tastings (May and Nov) plus regular wine dinners, phone for details

This is a list to browse through either on the sofa at home or on a trip to the Cotswolds to explore the Chipping Campden shop itself. However, don't set out with only a fiver in your pocket, as the quality-first approach here will necessitate one or two pieces of plastic.

As we've said before, at Bennetts there are no hangers-on. 'We are determined never to sell or to continue stocking any wine for the sake of ease or convenience. If quality drops we de-list,' says Charlie Bennett. It's hard to imagine quality dropping in the likes of Allegrini, Gaja, Conterno from Italy, nor for that matter in some of the stunning burgundies available.

Look too to the Australian section for fine quality; California is up to speed; as are Alsace (with six different growers to most merchants' one), Germany and the regional French selections. We were a little worried about the shortage of red Bordeaux choices in the context of the other quality classics, but then we turned to the Fine and Rare listings and found a tempting array of old vintages. Not every region is given the nod, however. As indicated, if Charlie doesn't like it, he doesn't stock it – 'Every bottle has to be one we would personally drink.' So this rules out South African wine, which isn't a big hit here (only one is stocked and that was made by a Frenchman, Jean-Jacques Mouiex), and gives more space for other passions such as a variety of different port and madeira styles, indigenous Portuguese grapes and (he can't resist it) more from Italy.

We recommend getting the full picture by laying your hands on the Fine and Rare supplement and regular Bennetts offers. Also take advantage of the fabulous tasting opportunities in Chipping Campden School Hall (twice a year, in May and November), plus the wine dinners with visiting growers.

Look out for

- One of the country's best Italian ranges, including wines from the South and Islands
- Red Rhônes from Chapoutier, Jean-Luc Colombo and Domaine de la Mordorée
- Top Bordeaux vintages going back to 1955
- Spanish Vega Sicilia and the superb wines of Bodegas y Vinedos
- Ruthless selection of Australian wines, including only the best (Shadowfax, Mount Langi Ghiran, Cullen and Pierro amongst them)
- Classic burgundies through the 1990s from Bonneau du Martray, Leflaive, Lafon and Verget.

Berkmann Wine Cellars/Le Nez Rouge

Head office   *Tel* 020-7609 4711
10–12 Brewery Road, London N7 9NH   *Fax* 020-7607 0018
                                    Email info@berkmann.co.uk
                                    Website www.berkmann.co.uk

Open Mon–Fri 9–5.30 (phone first) **Closed** Sat, Sun, public holidays **Cards** Delta, MasterCard, Switch, Visa; personal and business accounts **Discount** Available, phone for details **Delivery** Nationwide service, charge £8 per order, free for orders of £100+ **Glass hire** Not available **Tastings and talks** Available on request, contact Peter Mair for details **(£5)**

'Our portfolio has a unique collection of family-owned wineries from around the world and a collection of wines more often found in restaurants than retail outlets,' says director Andrew Bewes modestly. But this is no empty brag. A hefty handful of the world's prominent wine producers are represented here and Berkmann has opened two new branches of late so there is now more opportunity than ever for non-wine trade customers to get hold of its wines. So while we're reluctant to recommend a firm that's so heavily wholesale based (65 per cent), we think everyone deserves a chance to get their hands on decently priced Domaine de la Vougeraie Burgundy, or Antinori's Super-Tuscans (e.g. Tignanello) at less than £25 a bottle. (NB these prices include VAT too, which gives a far clearer picture than many wholesale traders offer.) Norton from Argentina, Stag's Leap from California and Yalumba and Jim Barry from Australia are others we're happy to see among this good-quality, comprehensive selection.

Look out for

- Valpolicellas and Amarones from top Italian estates Masi and Serègo Alighieri
- Marqués de Griñón, Bodegas Berberana and Martínez Bujanda, all stylish Riojas
- Half and large-format bottles from many of the stellar estates (Antinori, Norton, Colin-Déléger)
- Great-value, French regional reds from Faugères to Frontonnais.

Berry Bros & Rudd

Head office   *Tel* 020-7396 9600
3 St James's Street, London SW1A 1EG   *Tel* (0870) 900 4300
Orders office   *Fax* (0870) 900 4301

Berrys' Wine & Fine Food Shop
Hamilton Close, Houndmills, Basingstoke,   *Tel* (01256) 323566
Hants RG21 6YB   *Fax* (01256) 340144

Duty-free shops
Terminal 3 Departures Lounge,   *Tel* 020-8564 8361/8363
Heathrow Airport TW6 1JH   *Fax* 020-8564 8379

Terminal 4 Departures Lounge,   *Tel* 020-8754 1961
Heathrow Airport TW6 3XA   *Fax* 020-8754 1984

Cellar Advice   *Tel* (01256) 340123
      Fax (01256) 340149
      Email orders@bbr.com
      Website www.bbr.com

Open (London shops) Mon–Fri 10–6 (Basingstoke Fri 10–8), Sat 10–4 (Heathrow)
Mon–Sun 6am–10pm **Closed** Sun, public holidays (exc. Heathrow) **Cards** Amex,
Delta, Diners, MasterCard, Switch, Visa; business accounts **Discount** 5% on 1
unmixed case **Delivery** Nationwide service, charge £9 per order, free for orders of
£120+ **Glass hire** Not available **Tastings and talks** Dinners and tastings, phone or
visit website for details **£5**

A word of advice: you might find this lengthy range of wines easier to access
via the sort engines of the Berry Bros website rather than by wading
through the densely packed printed list. We'd favour this website over that
of almost any other merchant – it includes offers, news, tastings, even a
pronunciation guide. Not what you'd expect from a traditional wine
merchant established 300 years ago, perhaps. But then, since the arrival of
Alun Griffiths MW as buyer in the early 1990s, nothing's been quite the
same. As you'd expect from a merchant in this part of town, BBR specialises
in French classics for your cellar, but the fine old wine side of things here
has been spruced up and become distinctly modern.

    We'd even say that Berry Bros is several paces ahead of the rest of the
wine-trading game in the UK; for example, it doesn't just view the likes of
California and Australia as a source of everyday gluggers but of wines
genuinely testing the limits of quality. Pierro and Leuwin Chardonnays
from Margaret River, Australia, Montes Alpha and Casa Lapostolle Chilean
wines, and Ridge, Dominus and Quintessa from California all bear witness.
Similarly, as demonstrated with the choice of *en primeur* wines from the
mediocre 2001 vintage in Bordeaux (see introduction to Bordeaux in Part II
'The A–Z of wine-producing countries'), Alun and team don't accept also-
rans on the claret front just because they have grand labels: only 40 specially
selected 2001 clarets were chosen for sale in the summer of 2002.

    The integrity of BBR is to be trusted: from the mixed-case batches (from
£85) and its own-label wines at the start of the selection, through to the
champagnes and sparklers, the Rhône wines, the Hungarian Tokajis and the

Tuscan Chiantis and Vino Nobiles, everything will be a stellar representation of the character of its region.

If you happen to be in St James's Street in London, it's well worth visiting the shop at 'number 3' and letting the team guide you through the 2,000 or so wines – either via the website on the premises or on the shop shelves (there are now three new showrooms in which you can peruse this merchant's wares).

Look out for

- Well-priced and carefully-chosen selections of Bordeaux and burgundy offered *en primeur* each year
- Top estates of Alsace all represented: Trimbach, Hugel, Bruno Sorg and Zind-Humbrecht included
- Vosne Romanée burgundies from domaines Réné Engel, Jacques Cacheux and Sylvain Cathiard
- Magnums and large-format wines including vintage port, Chianti, champagne and red Rhône
- Two shops at Heathrow Airport in which to pick up gifts and tax-free bargains
- Fine and rare spirits in the Still Room at 3 St James's Street.

Bibendum Fine Wine

113 Regents Park Road, London NW1 8UR

Tel 020-7449 4120
Fax 020-7449 4121
Email sales@bibendum-wine.co.uk
Website www.bibendum-wine.co.uk

Open Mon–Fri 8.30–6.30 **Closed** Sat, Sun, public holidays **Cards** Amex, Delta, MasterCard, Switch, Visa; personal and business accounts **Discount** Not available **Delivery** Nationwide service, charge £10 per order, free for orders of £150+ **Glass hire** Not available **Tastings and talks** Regular tastings, phone for details

---

Note the name change. What was straight 'Bibendum' is now 'Bibendum Fine Wine', modified in order to refocus on this merchant's blue-chip stock. Fair enough. Buyers Simon Farr, Katie Macaulay and their team obviously have contacts in all the right places to bring in those top-notch wines. And it seems to have worked, too, as customers trade up all over the shop; business is doing better than ever.

We thought this might serve to make Bibendum a bit remote to those of us wanting a more regular, everyday bottle or two. But then the 'one unmixed case' minimum purchase always has limited customers to those with a real – not a passing – interest in wine. This current stance has probably served to up the average spend a bit.

The mission statement here, after all, has always been 'to make Bibendum a comprehensive access point for all that was good in wine'. And good these wines certainly are. Burgundy and the Rhône are the greatest strengths, with Bordeaux, Champagne and Languedoc-Roussillon hot on their heels. Turn to the New World (a more recent, but no less enthusiastic venture for Bibendum in its first 20 years of life – we write in 2002, its 20th birthday year) and there's a small but impressive collection of quality-conscious estates from Australia, Argentina, California, South Africa and Mexico. Mexico? (Actually, we haven't tried the wine from Casa de Piedra, the Mexican estate, but if it's anything like the rest of the wines on the list, it's probably more than drinkable.)

The full Bibendum list is on the company's website, and much trade is carried out thereon, and via email. But if you don't have time to surf, then the staff in the shop – and at the blue chip desk – are always extremely helpful in guiding any decisions. We're also as keen as ever on the walk-around tastings, often with producers in attendance, and the Fine Wine Events, such as the Cheval Blanc vertical tasting and the annual Burgundy cask sample event of the newest vintage.

Look out for

- Fabulous *en primeur* Burgundy offers – top estates, *grand* and *premier cru* vineyards
- New classic Languedoc estates: Domaine de Lavabre, Le Prieuré de St-Jean de Bébian and Pech Redon
- Top Bordeaux in Salmanazars, Balthazars and Nebuchadnezzars, and from vintages back to 1978
- Lail, Viader and Ridge: makers of big reds from California
- Argentina's classiest wines, from the illustrious Catena Zapata estate.
- 1996 burgundies from Emmanuel Rouget, Domaine Ramonet and Michel Lafarge.

Booths Supermarkets

Head office

4–6 Fishergate, Preston, Lancashire PR1 3LJ	*Tel* (01772) 251701
(Outlets throughout Cheshire, Cumbria,	*Fax* (01772) 255642
Lancashire, Yorkshire)	*Email* admin@booths-supermarkets.co.uk
	Website www.everywine.co.uk

Open Mon–Fri 8.30–8, Sat 9–8, Sun 10–4 (times vary between stores), public holidays 11–4 **Closed** 25 & 26 Dec, Easter Sun **Cards** Delta, MasterCard, Switch, Visa **Discount** 5% on 6+ bottles **Delivery** Nationwide service, online purchases only (min. 1 case), charge £4.95 per order **Glass hire** Free with orders of £25+, £10 deposit **Tastings and talks** Available, phone for details **£5**

Recipients of last year's 'Best Supermarket' award, the team at Booths takes great pride in their wine list and ensure that amidst the world of day-to-day food produce, their vinous choices extend beyond the average. 'Eat, Drink and be Merry' is their maxim, broadcast in lively fashion on their wine list, and buyers Sally Holloway, Dave Smith and Phil Godwin seem merry enough to us . . .

Booths now has 26 stores, up from 25 last year; but this smallish number gives the team greater flexibility for stocking more quirky, interesting wines (most supermarkets have to display their range across many more outlets than this, so can source only from producers who bulk supply). Twelve of the outlets stock the full range. 'Our size means we can offer a range of smaller producers with individuality,' says Sally Holloway, who is particularly pleased with the Southern France entrants to this array.

Working through the range, Booths offers an encouraging smattering of £2.99 and £3.99 to lure the punters in, and while (as everywhere) these aren't particularly scintillating, the next level up, 'around £5', has plenty of novelties to explore – this is where Sally's regional French trophies come in, from Cabardès, Costières de Nîmes and Luberon. The £5 to £10 range is where things, to our mind, begin to get really exciting, including the fabulous Donnhoff and Wehlener Sonnenuhr Rieslings from Germany. From Italy, A Mano Primitivo, Tre Uve Ultima from Abruzzo and Chianti Leonardo all come in nearer £5 than £10 and we'd buy these any day of the week. The offerings from Spain is equally inclusive of modern wines and classics. There's enough of the likes of Fairview, Clos Malverne and Jordan from the New World (South Africa in this case) to keep us fascinated further afield too.

Things get really adventurous in the higher echelon, £10 to £20 range (it doesn't get much higher, this is a supermarket after all) and although we're not sure how quickly these wines sell, we give Booths full credit for stocking such treasures as Castello di Banfi's Brunello di Montalcino and Château Beauséjour-Bécot 1986 (yes, there's still some left!) on offer. Booths encourages its customers to learn and gain in confidence in their wine choices. The wine list is full of helpful savings, 'cooking with wine' tips and tempting serving suggestions. 2002 also marked its first consumer wine fair, in Windermere.

Look out for

- Everything sparkling, from Shiraz (£8.99) to Bollinger RD (£69.99) and upwards.
- Delicious range of rosés for luscious summer drinking
- Modern Hungarian (Hárslevelű), modern Greek white (Kretikos) and and also Retsina should you wish it
- Syrah, Malbec and Bonarda: Argentina's top red grapes
- Moroccan Cinsault/Grenache – spicy and sassy, and only £3.49
- In addition: stunning (and extensive) ranges of local beer and English cheese.

Bottoms Up

see Thresher Wine Shops

(£5) Bottoms Up only

WHERE TO BUY WINE – THE TOP 100

The Butlers Wine Cellar

247 Queens Park Road, Brighton,
East Sussex BN2 9XJ

Tel (01273) 698724
Fax (01273) 622761
Email henry@butlers-winecellar.co.uk
Website www.butlers-winecellar.co.uk

Open Tue–Wed 10–6, Thur–Sat 10–7 **Closed** Sun, Mon, public holidays **Cards** Amex, Delta, MasterCard, Switch, Visa **Discount** Not available **Delivery** Free within 15-mile radius (min. 1 case); nationwide service, charge £10 for 1–3 cases, free for 3+ cases **Glass hire** Free with order **Tastings and talks** Regular shop tastings and tutored tastings, phone for details

Butler's main list is full of modest, middle-rung classic wines and although the Regional French and Italian choices from 'the South and Islands' caught our imagination, the rest constitutes a steady selection, fairly priced, but with little to get excited about. The longer Bin End list, however, is (as we've always said) the real treasure trove here – if you happen to be near Brighton, it's well worth the detour to take a look.

There might be only one or two bottles each of these wines available, but the choices are peppered with Bordeaux *crus classés* (Lafite, Mouton, Talbot) right back to 1960s and 1970s vintages, but none of the weaker years. Burgundy features nearly as strongly, as does Italy – with a series of ready-to-drink 1970s Barolos to tempt Italophiles. As there are no 'case only' regulations at this merchant, it would be pretty easy to pop in and pick up a bottle of Clos Vougeot or Chassagne-Montrachet from an ancient vintage such as 1983 and still come away with change from £30 – OK, some of the most delicious wines exceed this price, but it certainly helps not to have the crippling blow of buying 12. A visit to this merchant is truly as good as a delve into an Edwardian butler's cellar, with mature bottles of anything and everything on hand for whatever supper you choose to serve.

Henry Butler has now taken over the business outright, and in the last year has created the 'Brighton Wine School' for the education of the locals. We wish our vinous education could have been based on such a wide and fascinating range of wines.

Look out for

- Birthday bottles: crusty old ports from the 1960s and 1970s
- Modern classic whites from Australia: Mount Horrocks Riesling and Penfolds Yattarna
- Dom Pérignon 1985 (plus a selection of other mellow, old champagnes)
- Italian classics from Chianti Montalbano to Barolo Monfalletto
- Solid Rhône range, including top 1980s Hermitage
- Modern classic Bordeaux: Cissac, Cos Labory and Cos d'Estournel from 1996.

D Byrne & Co

Victoria Buildings, 12 King Street,
Clitheroe, Lancashire BB7 2EP

Tel (01200) 423152
Fax (01200) 429386

Open Mon–Wed 8.30–6, Thur, Fri 8.30–8, Sat 8–6, public holidays 10–4 **Closed** Sun, 25 & 26 Dec, Good Fri, Easter Sun & Mon **Cards** Delta, MasterCard, Switch, Visa **Discount** Not available **Delivery** Free within 50-mile radius (min. 1 case); nationwide service, phone for details of charges **Glass hire** Free with order **Tastings and talks** Annual week-long in-store tasting; small in-store group tastings **£5**

'Producing an up-to-date list is very difficult. We're forever on the lookout for new and exciting wines. We seem to be trapped in a vicious circle of purchasing, and constantly ringing the changes. We find this a very successful way of maintaining a very loyal and happy customer base,' says partner in the firm, Tim Byrne. And, amid this flurry of buying activity, he and the team waste no time with new-fangled modernisations to organise themselves but revel in the whole unpretentious muddle of it all. This way, as we've said before, the shop presents its customers with more of a treasure hunt than a predictable trip-to-the-supermarket-style outing.

Come the day D Byrne & Co start posting out their wine list, we recommend all wine lovers have their hallway floors reinforced, so heavy is it. They don't do this yet. They do, however, have a telephone and a fax, so if you know the wine you want, you can place your orders this way. Otherwise, we'd highly recommend a visit to the Lancashire shop itself. You'll almost have to be there to believe the prices (a bottle of 1982 Domaine de Chevalier Pessac-Léognan comes in at less than £50, and 1996 Château d'Angludet Margaux at £16.39). Besides, all the original fixtures and fittings in this crammed-in shop make fascinating viewing and we can't imagine things have changed much in this company's 123-year history.

We have a copy of the weighty wine list in front of us so we know that Tim is right when he says his cellar provides customers with a geographical tour of the world's wine-producing countries. Like many a wine foray, it begins with Bordeaux' *crus classés* and continues into the highest realms of burgundy (where among the many great growers' wines, magnums of Bonneau du Martray's delicious Corton can be found for a mere £70). Bargains and the-very-best can also be found from the Loire and Rhône, and just about all the rising stars of the Languedoc are here too (Château des Estanilles, Mas Champart, Jean Orliac and many more).

In 'Part B' (few binders would have a spine strong enough to hold all this in one volume), the New World choices show equal breadth, spanning as they do simple wines such as Wolf Blass Riesling and Rosemount Shiraz from Australia (at nice prices too) and rising stars such as Pierro Estate Chardonnay and Cabernet from Margaret River, costing a little more money. Plus there are famous choices from California, including Saintsbury, Shafer and Seghesio (this section is 'safer' than some of the others). Byrne also has one of the finest selections of South American wines we've seen in a while – particularly good on Argentina, but also taking in Uruguay, Brazil and Peru.

Look out for

- Spectacular Spanish choices taking in smaller regions such as Cigales, Toledo, Priorato, Somontano and Tarragona
- Italian Super-Tuscans at under £30 a bottle (Ornellaia, Cepparello, Campora and Fontalloro)
- Over 100 half-bottle choices from around the world
- Oddities from Austria, Mexico, Côtes de Jura, Jurançon and the Ardèche
- Chambolle-Musigny, Bonnes Mares and Echézeaux burgundies
- Reasonably priced annual *en primeur* offers of burgundy and Bordeaux
- Spirits listings including top brandies and single malt whiskies.

Andrew Chapman Fine Wines

14 Haywards Road, Drayton, Abingdon, Oxfordshire OX14 4LB

Tel (01235) 550707
Fax (0870) 136 6335
Email info@surf4wine.co.uk
Website www.surf4wine.co.uk

Open Mon–Fri 9–5, Sat, public holidays 10.30–1 **Closed** Sun, 25 & 26 Dec **Cards** Delta, MasterCard, Switch, Visa; personal and business accounts **Discount** Available, phone for details **Delivery** Free within 20-mile radius (min. 1 case); nationwide service, charge £7.50 for 1 case, £3.50 for subsequent cases **Glass hire** Free with order **Tastings and talks** Range of tastings available, phone or visit website for details **(£5)**

Andrew C talks at 100 miles-an-hour: he needs to, otherwise he'd never have enough time to say what he has to say. Our questionnaire this year was supplemented by a four-page printout of new happenings at Andrew Chapman Fine Wines, happenings of such magnitude that he couldn't hope to squeeze them into a measly four lines. But to sum up: the website and web-sale facilities are being upgraded and extended (ask for a wine list and you'll get the web version printed: this is Andrew's way of being as up to date as possible). New producers are being added to the list. A wider spread of vintages has been included 'so that customers can taste how wines might turn out if the wine or property is new to them'. And the mail-order business (especially for sending wine as a gift) has been expanded.

Andrew also wants to reassure people that the traditional side of this business is important, too. Quality of stock and efficiency of service, he says, are crucial. 'It seems very obvious that people have got pretty tired of the purely web-based wine retailer. This is why we emphasise that we are first and foremost a bricks-and-mortar wine merchant with stock in hand, where customers can come and visit/taste whenever they wish.' (Look out for the frequent tastings held for local groups, and, for anyone in the Oxford area, bottles are opened on a Saturday morning for sipping and sampling.)

All this is great back-up, and we're pleased to say that the list of wines it supports is ever-improving too. France and Italy both have strong selections – Andrew is keen on developing one-on-one relationships with growers (particularly in the Rhône these days) for whom he acts as UK agent, so expect to see smaller names/estates of which you may not have heard before. Much energy has gone into the Austrian range too. Spain needs work, but there's a (typically) full-on approach to Australia – and we like the

fact that the wines are presented by region. Plus there's thorough coverage
of South Africa and a range of well-chosen Argentinian wines.

Look out for

- Smart burgundies such as Puligny-Montrachet from Etienne Sauzet and
  Domaine Leflaive
- New-wave Languedoc producers: Domaine Roque Sestière, Château de
  Gourgazaud, Château Pech Celeyran, Clos Bagatelle
- Austrian regional wines capturing the characters of the Wachau,
  Kamptal, Neusiedlersee and Thermenregion
- Allegrini Valpolicellas and Amarones from Italy
- Classic Western Australian wines from the Cullen, Vasse Felix and Cape
  Mentelle estates
- Michel Torino and Finca El Retiro: two top Argentinian estates
- Chatty newsletters to keep everyone up to date.

Cockburns

7 Devon Place, Haymarket,
Edinburgh EH12 5HJ

Tel 0131-346 1113
Fax 0131-313 2607
Email sales@winelist.co.uk
Website www.winelist.co.uk

Open Mon–Fri 9–6, Sat 9–1 **Closed** Sun, public holidays **Cards** Amex, Delta,
MasterCard, Switch, Visa; personal and business accounts **Discount** Not available
Delivery Free within 5-mile radius (min. 1 case); nationwide service, charge £6 + VAT,
free for 2+ cases **Glass hire** Free **Tastings and talks** Available, phone for details
£5

This isn't the most adventurous list in the world, but it is full of reliable,
well-priced wines from just about everywhere: in fact, it's as safe as you'd
expect a 200-year-old merchant to be. Things did step up a notch or two last
year, with the introduction of a new customer club (free to join, with tasting
invites and newsletters every three months) and a new website, but as far as
the wines go there's little that'll set your cellar alight. But perhaps that's just
the point: this would be a great place to shop for anyone wishing to stock
their cellar without breaking the bank. Most wines stop at well under the
£10 mark, and that's where, we know, a lot of you like them.

However, anyone wishing for a bit more excitement should read the fine
print. Cockburns has never been known for its hard sell, and we suspect
that deep in those Edinburgh cellars there's many a treasure waiting to be
discovered that either the company is keeping to itself, or is too modest to
talk about. All the list says is: 'We do keep a larger range of wines at Devon
Place, so please ask if you are interested.' (Cockburns also suggests signing
up for the newsletters so that you can read of any special offers and bin-end
sales.) This is Scotland's oldest wine merchant after all, so who knows
what's lurking after the annual *en primeur* campaigns.

Cockburns tells us it's still in hot pursuit of new classics rather than old,
but we'd still come here for the Old World wines. We're even pleased to
report that the team has a new Italian wine supplier – so expect to see the
odd Frescobaldi and Tedeschi wine making an appearance.

Look out for

- Classy Spanish choices from Ribera del Duero (Protos) and Rioja (Bodegas Breton and Muerza)
- Rhône wines from lesser-known estates such as Mathelin, Mousset and Domaine des Ondines
- *Négociant* burgundy from Bouchard and Champy
- Chilean white wines from the Francisco de Aguirre and Echeverria estates (Sauvignon, Viognier and Chardonnay)
- Bargain sub-£15 Bordeaux from all regions.

Corkscrew Wines

Arch No. 5, Viaduct Estate, Carlisle,
Cumbria CA2 5BN

Tel (01228) 543033
Fax (01228) 543033
Email corkscrewwines@aol.com
Website www.corkscrew-wines.com

Open Mon–Sat 10–5.30 **Closed** Sun, public holidays, 2 weeks in Feb **Cards** Amex, Delta, MasterCard, Switch, Visa; business accounts **Discount** Available, phone for details **Delivery** Free within 25-mile radius (min. 2 cases); nationwide service, charged at cost **Glass hire** Free **Tastings and talks** 2 major tastings per year, phone for details **£5**

Last year we reported that Corkscrew customers were putting aside their anti-French sentiment and delving once again into the likes of Alsace, the Rhône, Burgundy and Languedoc. We're not surprised, as the imaginative, well-priced choices from these regions here are nothing if not tempting. This year, buyer Laurie Scott tells us Spain is gaining in the popularity stakes, too. Again, with the careful, quality offerings chosen for this succinct selection (Albariño, Beronia Tempranillo and Guelbenzu) we can see why.

This isn't a large list, but, as we've mentioned before, there are no major gaps in it. The New World fares equally as well as the Old, without recourse to a lazy choice of brands. Emphasis, instead, is placed on 'other white grapes' from Australia such as Riesling and Verdelho, small, quality producers (Mount Langi Ghiran and Charles Melton) and oddities such as delicious old Stanton & Killeen Muscats and Tasmanian Pinot Noir. We're particularly impressed with the confident range of wines chosen from South Africa, too – some favourite Stellenbosch estates, Neil Ellis, Clos Malverne and Hazendal, are more than worth the space they have here.

Laurie says he 'worked in oil, construction, horticulture and as a management consultant, but still wound up in the wine trade'. He obviously has a talent for buying, and his enthusiasm (despite its founding in the 'school of hard knocks') certainly shines through in the wines. It is also visible in a five-times-a-year newsletter – although it could be a little easier on the eye, those two A4 pages are as jammed with text as they possibly could be. It costs £15 a year to belong to the customer club, for which members gain a handy 10 per cent discount per case. Added to the special offers in the newsletter, there are plenty of £5-a-bottle bargains to be had. Free tastings will undoubtedly be conducted with the same kind of passion Laurie shows in everything he does, and we thoroughly recommend attendance.

Look out for

- Alsace wines from the Cave Vinicole de Turckheim
- Reliable Burgundy sources: Gérard Chavy, Chartron et Trébuchet, Lamy-Pillot and Jean-Pierre Mugneret
- Cheerful range of house wines: Marktree Australian blends coming in at a barely believable £1.49 a bottle!
- Wide range of sparklers, including New Zealand's Pelorus, England's own Nyetimber, and Champagne reaching to the heights of Roederer Cristal
- Carefully chosen Chilean and Argentinian wines
- Impressive (and extensive) sideline in malt whisky.

Corney & Barrow

Head office

12 Helmet Row, London EC1V 3TD

Tel 020-7539 3200
Fax 020-7608 1373
Email wine@corbar.co.uk
Website www.corneyandbarrow.com

8 Academy Street, Ayr KA7 1HT

Tel (01292) 267000
Fax (01292) 265903

Oxenfoord Castle, By Pathhead, Midlothian EH37 5UB

Tel (01875) 321921
Fax (01875) 321922

Belvoir House, High Street, Newmarket, Suffolk CB8 8DH

Tel (01638) 600000
Fax (01638) 600860

194 Kensington Park Road, London W11 2ES

Tel 020-7221 5122
Fax 020-7221 9371

Open Times vary between stores, phone for details **Closed** Sun, public holidays
Cards Amex, Delta, MasterCard, Switch, Visa; personal and business accounts
Discount Available, phone for details **Delivery** Nationwide service, free for 3+ cases
or for 2+ cases within M25 or local area, otherwise £9 + VAT **Glass hire** Available,
phone for details **Tastings and talks** Tastings and winemaker dinners, phone for
details

'Young team; old company,' says Laura Taylor, marketing manager at Corney & Barrow, and that just about sums it up. The 13 trendy wine bars in the City and West End of London, the cheery newsletter, the 'introductory' tasting events, the innovative Sampling Cases and the diverse range of wines under £6.99 all reflect the young side. The bundle of elegant literature we received for this review (wine list, *en primeur* offers, details of new agencies) complete with gold blocking and emblazoned royal warrants, however, speak of more sedate times.

Corney & Barrow takes obvious pride, for example, in the kind of blue-chip services it provides. Alongside those top *en primeur* offerings, of first-class Bordeaux and burgundy, are choices from ancient vintages dating back to 1900. What we find impressive is that whether you choose these wines or go for some of the more exciting options from further afield, the broking division will ensure that the same member of staff nurtures you through your enquiry and purchase every time you get in touch. That's old-fashioned service for you, and it's here that this company really excels.

C&B customers are very loyal to traditional Bordeaux and Burgundy but the team aren't content to restrict their dabblings to these smart areas only. In the last year 47 new wines, ranging from Tardieu-Laurent's fabulous Rhônes to the magnificent Rieslings of Schloss Schönborn (Germany) and the wines of New Zealand's Crossroads estate have been introduced. Topping the newcomers is Bonneau du Martray, whose luxurious Corton and Corton-Charlemagne sit nicely alongside the wines of Domaine de la Romanée-Conti in splendid Burgundian state.

The team is also particularly proud of its Spanish listings this year, with the fabulous Dominio de Pingus and Bodegas Alvaro Palacios now on offer – allow £2,000 per case in the event of purchasing the former!

You have to wade around a bit for the good-value offers on this list – which is smart, but not all that clearly presented – but they are there. We just wish the likes of Italy, Australia, California and South America could be taken a bit more seriously. C&B might be very proud of the broad range it offers, but we think that in some of these areas it isn't broad at all. If you're into Burgundy or Bordeaux, however, and have a bit of cash to splash, this is the chance to realise your vinous dreams.

Look out for

- Leflaive, Marquis d'Angerville, Domaine de la Romanée-Conti and Bonneau du Martray from Burgundy
- Sauternes, from Château Briatte to Château d'Yquem
- Top California estates, Cakebread and Dominus
- Modern Bordeaux: Hosanna, Petit Village and Certan de May
- Classic Bordeaux: 1982 Pichon-Lalande, d'Angludet and Ausone
- Maturing Australian wines: 1990 Grange, Eileen Hardy Shiraz and St Hallet Old Block Shiraz.

Croque-en-Bouche

221 Wells Road, Malvern Wells, Worcester WR14 4HF

Tel (01684) 565612
Fax (08707) 066282
Email mail@croque-en-bouche.co.uk
Website www.croque-en-bouche.co.uk

Open Any time by arrangement **Cards** Delta, MasterCard, Switch, Visa **Discount** Available, phone for details **Delivery** Free within 10-mile radius (min. 1 case); nationwide service (min. 3 cases), charge £9.50 per order, free for orders of £400+ **Glass hire** Not available **Tastings and talks** Not available

This year we bring the devastating news that, by the time you read this, the restaurant part of the Croque-en-Bouche will be closed. The good news, however, is that the merchant side of the business is still trading full throttle, and the wines are just as good as they ever were.

Croque-en-Bouche is in a pretty part of Worcestershire; for non-locals the Internet is an easier (if less romantic) way of sourcing what's on offer here (a massive 50 per cent of this merchant's customers now feel the same way).

335

The website is smartly presented and informative, full of current tips, tasting notes and background detail. It's not just the delicious upper-echelon wines that Robin Jones, the buyer-owner, gets his hands on that make the difference here, but the sheer amount of choice available, both off-beat and upbeat – including wines at decent price points too.

Robin currently has an 'In Memoriam' section on his list: not for the restaurant (not yet anyway) but for some of the very wonderful old vintages that have departed his stocks in the last few months. This section pays tribute to the likes of Henschke Hill of Grace 1991, fabulous Bonnes-Mares burgundy from 1959 and a bottle of Moldavian red from 1978. Fortunately, while deserving of respect, this list only serves to highlight the kind of wines that are still available here. Robin not only has a fine line in classic burgundy and Bordeaux from vintages dating back to at least 1920 (Château Brane-Cantenac Margaux, for example), but also has a great love for 'unusual and eclectic stuff' – hence the collection of Swiss, Canadian, Corsican, Mexican and Uruguayan wines we see. These are not just an indulgence but a reflection of a true passion for vinous individuality – and you don't always see that in a wine merchant these days, so log on and find out what we mean!

The minimum of a mixed case will be no chore to choose here as, though you can spend £105 on a bottle of Sassicaia, you could pack the rest of the box with 11 juicy Spanish wines for under £6 a bottle.

Look out for

- Bordeaux right bank 1988s: Châteaux Le Tertre-Rôteboeuf, L'Arrosée and La Fleur Pétrus
- Old Spanish classics: Marqués de Murrieta Rioja Reservas and Vega Sicilia from the 1980s
- Fabulous array of Rhône wines – Guigal, Chave, Chapoutier and Clape, from 1966 to the present day
- Château Chalon 1953 and *vin de paille* half bottles from Henri Marie: strange and wonderful wines from the Jura
- Top Australian estates: Cullen, Henschke, Jim Barry and Penfolds
- Rarely seen California 'cult' wines from Trefethen, Philip Togni and Beringer, plus oldies such as Heitz Napa Cabernet from 1975.

For an explanation of the symbols used at the top of some of the merchant entries, see page 310.

Direct Wine Shipments

5–7 Corporation Square, Belfast,
Northern Ireland BT1 3AJ

Tel 028-9050 8000
Fax 028-9050 8004
Email enquiry@directwine.co.uk
Website www.directwine.co.uk

Open Mon–Wed & Fri 9.30–6.30, Thur 9.30–8, Sat 9.30–5.30 **Closed** Sun (exc. Christmas period), public holidays **Cards** MasterCard, Switch, Visa; personal & business accounts **Discount** Available, phone for details **Delivery** Free within Northern Ireland (min. 1 case); nationwide service, phone for details of charges **Glass hire** Free with bulk order **Tastings and talks** Tastings, dinners and courses, phone for details

As we said last year, the McAlindons are wine communicators extraordinaire who've battled the odds and come out ahead of the paramilitary hold-ups, petrol bombs and devastating fires that on many occasions have looked set to destroy this company. From the relative safety of a nearby garage (to which the wines were once transported by milk float when times got turbulent) to the comfortable security of an extensive docklands warehouse, things have gone from knife edge to cutting edge and at long last look set for the profitable future this company deserves.

'We like to be "vino evangelists"! We like our customers to leave excited by what they have purchased,' says Peter McAlindon, not content with mere survival. Only 30 per cent of trade is carried out with the general public (supplying the Irish on-trade and others makes up the rest of business), but from bottles open in-store for customers to taste every Thursday, Friday and Saturday, a very enticing customer club (free to join, with a free bottle for every case ordered and free delivery), a friendly focus on £5 and £10 wines, 50 to 200 new wines listed per year and regular promotions (£60 case offers, for example), make no mistake about it, the Direct Wine Shipments team knows how to tempt. Added to all this, there are beginners' courses, tasting competitions, food-matching courses, themed tastings ('Wines of Spain', 'The Cool Climate Wines of Australia', 'The Merging of Old and New World', and other such interesting topics) – proving they know how to teach, too.

'We constantly review our portfolio with new samples, comparing them with what we have already got', says Peter. And in doing this his range remains as high quality as ever: an impressive array of Hugel's Alsace wines; Bordeaux choices from £2.99 to a massive £1,000 a bottle (1945 Château Margaux); burgundies from de Vogüé, Tollot-Beaut and Amiot; and, from Italy, Masi. The Spanish list is as strong (and long) as ever, and we're still impressed to see various oddities such as dry Szamorodni from Hungary and Mount Barker Australian Cabernet Franc cropping up – although, haven't we seen more of these weird and wonderful wines on this list in the past?

Look out for

- Cool-climate Australian whites from Margaret River (Cullen), the Mornington Peninsula (Stonier's) and Clare Valley (Annie's Lane)
- Top Bordeaux at decent prices – watch out for 1996, 1997 and 1998 vintage bargains
- Classic Rhône wines from Chapoutier and Château Rayas
- Rioja from Marqués de Cáceres, Toro from Bodegas Farina and Navarra wines from Chivite
- Fonseca port and Cossart Gordon madeira
- Regular wine events with expert hosts.

337

Domaine Direct

6–9 Cynthia Street, London N1 9JF

Tel 020-7837 1142
Fax 020-7837 8605
Email info@domainedirect.co.uk
Website www.domainedirect.co.uk

Open Mon–Fri 8.30–6 **Closed** Sat, Sun, public holidays **Cards** MasterCard, Switch, Visa; business accounts **Discount** Not available **Delivery** Nationwide service (min. 1 mixed case); free within London & environs, otherwise £10.52 for 1 case, £14.04 for 2 cases, free for 3+ cases **Glass hire** Not available **Tastings and talks** Biannual themed tastings, charged at cost; private tastings, free to customers

Burgundy is the speciality here and you'd do well to find a better array of wines from the region. Simon Taylor-Gill and Hilary Gibbs pride themselves on having 'the best and most rigorously selected list of domaine-bottled burgundies', and the fact that they have been acknowledged as specialists right since the company's inception in 1981 goes some way to proving this pride isn't misplaced.

The rules by which Domaine Direct live are: 'No compromise on quality; complete integrity in the buying process; absolute commitment to top-quality service and insightful knowledge.' Judging by the level of detail and the quality of the wines on offer in the price list, it lives closely by these tenets. And judging by the price points, the integrity side of things is particularly active – there's not too much here to make the wallet squeal, with a notable £504 for a case of 2000 vintage *premier cru* Combettes Puligny-Montrachet, but little else squeezing over the £500 mark. (And there are plenty of non-wallet squealers coming in at under £250 per case, along the lines of Michelot Morey-St-Denis, Meursault Les Tillets from Guy Roulot and Chablis *grand cru* Vaudésir from Jean-Paul Droin.) The greatest thing about Domaine Direct is just that: you don't see all the super-size *négociant* houses, who provide terrific luxury at the top end, but far more dubious quality from the everyday ranks. Instead, this list covers the reliable smaller houses, who see through the production of their wines from start to finish, and from whom quality is far more consistent.

Of the other regions on offer, Domaine Direct is particularly proud of its expanding range of wines from Western Australia and a new focus on the Loire Valley. Another highlight is the small but splendid California selection, including some strapping 'blockbuster' wines from Spottswoode and Viader – again, they're not too cripplingly priced.

Our case of wine, mixed or not, would almost certainly be burgundy though. Domaine Direct does a great job of making the complex warren of villages and *premiers crus* on the Côte d'Or seem understandable and quantifiable.

Look out for

- *Grand cru* Echézeaux from Christian Clerget
- Volnay *premier cru*: Ronceret, Les Pitures, Les Brouillards and Les Robardelles
- Selection of 1990s burgundy vintages, including the top-quality 1996s

- Burgundian oddities such as Marsannay Rosé, and red and white Auxerrois
- Leeuwin estate Art Series wines from Western Australia
- Roger Champault, Domaine Ricard and Domaine des Roches Neuves from the Loire Valley.

European Wine Growers Associates

Head office
Challan Hall, Silverdale, Lancashire LA5 0UH
Tel (01524) 701723
Fax (01524) 701189

Shop
WineTime, 37 Beetham Road, Milnthorpe, Cumbria
Tel (015395) 62030
Email winetime@ewga.net
Website www.winetime.ewga.net

Open Mon–Sun, public holidays 9–6 **Cards** Amex, Delta, MasterCard, Switch, Visa; personal and business accounts **Discount** Not available **Delivery** Free within Cumbria/Lancashire (min. 1 case); nationwide service (min. 1 case), charge £7.50 + VAT per case **Glass hire** Free **Tastings and talks** Tastings, lectures, wine trips to Europe; phone for details **£5**

A seriously industrious little company this. We'd be happy to have its cheery presence near to us so that we could pop in and pick up a few of the ancient old bottles on offer – the ones that partner Deryn Moeckell says are too many to list. So we can't actually tell you what these unlisted bottles are, but judging by the rest of what's on offer, they must be pretty good.

EWGA offers an enticing selection from the world over – the aim being to supply the local restaurant trade, plus stock its Milnthorpe shop, WineTime. The list starts with a couple of choices from Mediterranean France, then switches to the Loire, both big names and small, then the full gamut of Alsace grapes makes an appearance from the top-notch Schlumberger estate. Burgundy hits some high notes, as well as some 'get-at-able' ones (in the form of bargain sub-£10 choices from Faiveley and Jaffelin), and the Bordeaux selection seems to have no problem reaching the heights of Talbot, Pétrus and Pichon-Baron. Spain and Italy cover the classics with the same careful comprehensiveness, and when you get to the New World, from Australia, the story's the same: everything from Jarah Ridge Verdelho to Yalumba Octavius (£2.95 to £26.50, respectively). The range from the Americas is a bit less exciting, with only one or two rather unadventurous estates listed, but we don't doubt the Moeckell's ability to dig out something special from this list of old vintages they talk of – particularly when the likes of 1982 Château Pétrus and 1994 Bonneau du Martray get mentioned in the newsletters . . .

We like the shop name better than the cumbersome title of this merchant, but the Moeckells must have their reasons for this arrangement. We like their rationale for everything else: wine courses and an annual wine fair, witty monthly newsletters, plus staff who take time to chat and help out the customers. However, a more descriptive wine list – (may be with a few helpful tasting notes) would be appreciated. Look out for the 'Threefors' (offers of three bottles for £10), which are a good opportunity not to have to fork out for a whole mixed case.

Look out for

- Well-priced champagnes, with the opportunity of ordering large-format bottles from Jeroboams through to Nebuchadnezzars
- Primitivo and other treasures from the Italian south
- 1980s clarets at thoroughly reasonable prices
- Handy selection of half bottles, focusing mainly on burgundy
- Useful selection of websites from which to learn more about your favourite wines.

Farr Vintners

19 Sussex Street, Pimlico, London SW1V 4RR

Tel 020-7821 2000
Fax 020-7821 2020
Email sales@farr-vintners.com
Website www.farr-vintners.com

Open Mon–Fri 9–6 **Closed** Sat, Sun, public holidays **Cards** None accepted; business accounts **Discount** Not available (min. order £500) **Delivery** Nationwide service, charge £12 per order **Glass hire** Not available **Tastings and talks** Occasionally, phone for details

If money is no object and you want the absolute best, Farr is the place to come – this merchant supplies more of the world's most fabulous wines than any other we know. The selection is unrivalled. Only the two major auction houses see parallel treasures, and Farr differs from these in that it actually takes ownership of the stock, rather than acting as a 'middle man'. That's why director Stephen Browett can cheerfully say: 'We have the largest stock holding of fine wines in the UK and usually the lowest prices.'

So, with your necessary £500 in hand (that's the minimum spend here) you can avail yourself of the great and the good without having to resort to a whole case purchase. A bottle of Romanée-Conti here, a bottle of 1961 Palmer there would be no problem – and you'd already be way over your minimum spend! But don't be put off by this. Success and high prices have most assuredly not gone to Farr Vintners' heads. Despite the illustrious stock he deals with, Stephen's relaxed, friendly approach is mirrored throughout the team, and even the lowliest purchases here will be met with unbiased advice and helpful assistance.

Bordeaux makes up 77.5 per cent of business (red Burgundy 4 per cent, white 3 per cent, Italy 3 per cent, and everywhere else less) so don't be surprised to see page after page of 1980s clarets, and nearly 100 wines to choose from the fabulous 1990 vintage. Farr sales increased in 2001, partly thanks to a very active Bordeaux 2000 *en primeur* campaign. But Stephen also lists 'individual domaines' as another house speciality, and these you'll find from all over the world – that's both fine modern wines and old rarities.

If you aren't sure of the merits of a particular property or harvest, there are plenty of notes from world wine luminaries such as Jancis Robinson, Robert Parker and Clive Coates to help you reach a decision. The four or five lists a year make great reading matter – but for more regular delectation, they're updated monthly on the web.

Look out for

- Yquem, Yquem, Yquem! More sightings of this great sweet wine than we've ever seen in one place
- 1982, 1961, 1959 – all the great Bordeaux vintages
- Cult Bordeaux châteaux such as Valandraud, Ausone, Pavie, Le Pin and Pétrus
- Nebuchadnezzars, Balthazars and Salmanazars of top claret – should you wish them
- Fabulous Guigal and Jaboulet-Aîné Rhône wines going back to the 1970s
- Grange, Grosset and Henschke from Australia; Ridge and Harlan wines from California
- Full condition reports and provenance details on any wine offered.

Fine and Rare Wines

Pall Mall Deposit, 124–128 Barlby Road,   *Tel* 020-8960 1995
North Kensington, London W10 6BL   *Fax* 020-8960 1911
Email wine@frw.co.uk
Website www.frw.co.uk

Open Mon–Fri 9–6 **Closed** Sat, Sun, public holidays **Cards** Amex, Diners, MasterCard, Switch, Visa **Discount** Not available **Delivery** Nationwide service, phone for details of charges **Glass hire** Not available **Tastings and talks** Not available

Most Fine & Rare clients know what they're looking for before they come to this list. There is no need, therefore, for the team to clutter it up with unwieldy wine descriptions, no need for newsletters to entice, no in-store tastings, no customer club, no special discounts. The wines speak for themselves, and very loudly: the noisiest from the front cover – Gaja, Sassicaia and Tignanello from Italy; Domaine de la Romanée-Conti, de Vogüé and Comte Lafon's top burgundies; Beaucastel and Guigal from the Rhône. Thereafter, over 30 densely packed pages are full of big names, mature old vintages and high-flying newcomers.

'We are proud of our heritage,' says dapper chairman Mark Bedini, adding: 'We bring our clients a fantastically broad choice, not only concentrating on the Parkerised super-grog, but including these too.' The 'super-grogs' include such efforts as the immortalised 100-pointer 1989 Château Pétrus, plus other lauded beings such as Château Pichon-Lalande 1996, Lafite-Rothschild 1998 and L'Evangile 1990 (the latter priced at a mere £1,575 a case; the Pétrus at £9,600).

The trick with this company is, as we said last year, to school yourself to expect a few more zeros on the case prices, and to realise that any figures under 100 will be for single bottles. Not that these wines are necessarily over-priced, they just happen to be rather illustrious. This is definitely the place to come for the big-name wines, but also to pick up lesser-known stars – we particularly admire the stunning array of 'A'- and 'B'-list wines from Italy. The focus is almost entirely on the Old World, but there's no shortage of choice for all that, and at least there's no minimum purchase.

As Fine & Rare point out, though, the traffic is 'two-way'. The team not only sells (to the trade as well as the general public) but it also buys. So if you have any old wine treasures in your cellar, which you can't see yourself benefitting from, Bedini and his staff undoubtedly will.

Look out for

- Romanée-Conti bottles going back to 1954
- Pre-war port and pre-decimalisation claret
- Antinori, Frescobaldi and Fontodi wines from central Italy
- *En primeur* Bordeaux from châteaux Hosana, l'Eglise-Clinet and Vieux Château Certan
- Illustrious, French second labels: l'Interdit de Valandraud, Clos Margalaine and Alter Ego de Palmer
- Spanish classics from Vega Sicilia and Dominio de Pingus.

Fortnum & Mason

181 Piccadilly, London W1A 1ER

Tel 020-7734 8040
Fax 020-7437 3278
Email info@fortnumandmason.co.uk
Website www.fortnumandmason.com

Open Mon–Sat 10–6.30, Sun 11–5 (Christmas only) **Closed** Sun, public holidays
Cards Amex, Delta, Diners, MasterCard, Switch, Visa; personal and business accounts
Discount 1 bottle free per mixed case **Delivery** Nationwide service, charge £7 per order **Glass hire** Not available **Tastings and talks** 4 winemaker dinners per year, phone for details

It's impossible not to be impressed by the sheer range and class of the Fortnum & Mason wine department. It's not just that this is a glittering collection of some of the most famous and reputable names in wine, but that buyer James Taylor is making a considerable effort to seek out smaller producers that are not readily available elsewhere. So fine clarets, from top châteaux, and big-label champagnes are here in abundance, naturally – but so are: superb but somewhat obscure dessert wines from Austria; dry whites, sparklers and even meads from England; rare top reds from New Zealand; and unusual grape varieties from Australia. In short, we sense Fortnum's range was not simply created with the traditional buff in mind. The own-label wines are sourced from excellent suppliers (Hostomme champagnes, Vacheron Sancerre, Josmeyer from Alsace and La Rioja Alta, to name a few) and in our view make up one of the best own-brand collections around.

Look out for

- Lovely Italian selection from Haas, Isole e Olena, Antinori, Planeta
- Great champagnes, plus jolly good sparklers from Australia, New Zealand and England
- Showcase of the best English wines
- Fine own-label wines at decent prices
- Lustau's *almacenista* sherries
- Wide range of classic French wines from Bordeaux, Burgundy and the Rhône.

Gauntleys of Nottingham

4 High Street, Exchange Arcade,
Nottingham NG1 2ET

Tel 0115-911 0555
Fax 0115-911 0557
Email rhone@gauntleywine.com
Website www.gauntleywine.com

Open Mon–Sat 9–5.30 **Closed** Sun, public holidays **Cards** Delta, MasterCard,
Switch, Visa **Discount** Available, phone for details **Delivery** Local service (min. 1
case), charge £8–10; nationwide service, charge £9.50 + VAT for 1–3 cases, free for 4+
cases **Glass hire** Not available **Tastings and talks** In-store tastings on Saturdays **£5**

A fairly succinct range, but one of high quality. Gauntleys has been
supplying Nottingham and its environs with fine wine since 1880, so it's of
little surprise that it now acts as sole agent for some of the most precious
properties of Alsace, the Rhône and southern France. It has a long enough
track record to inspire even the most sceptical of French growers to part
with their wines. John Gauntley and his partner in buying, Victoria Ross,
still travel the continent on excursions to expand their horizons and take in
many interesting estates from Italy and Spain (not forgetting Jerez of
course), and one or two from Germany. Don't expect to find much else,
however. John only stocks wines that he's truly passionate about – nothing
he's half-hearted about makes the grade. Perhaps this is why, despite his
pride in 'unearthing New Zealand long before anyone else did', he no
longer lists even one of this country's wines. Surely they can't all be *that* bad
John?

One other thing: if the in-store Saturday tastings aren't tempting enough
(for us the thought of dipping into the Alsace selection certainly would be)
then maybe the long list of Havana cigars might be your thing? Prices for
these – as with the wines – are reasonable, if not on the cheap side.

Look out for
- Delicious Alsace Riesling from domaines Clos St Landelin, Josmeyer and
  Schoffit (for starters)
- Fine Blanc de Blancs Salon champagne (1976 and 1985 vintages)
- Brovia Barolo and Fellini Primitivo from Italy
- Sound range of Loire Valley classics from Didier Dagueneau, Pascal
  Reverdy and Charles Joguet.

Specialist and Regional Award Winners are listed on
pages 12–16.

Great Northern Wine Company

The Warehouse, Blossomgate, Ripon,
North Yorkshire HG4 2AJ

Tel (01765) 606767
Fax (01765) 609151
Email info@greatnorthernwine.com
Website www.greatnorthernwine.com

Open Mon–Thur 9–6, Fri 9–6.30, Sat 9–5.30 **Closed** Sun, public holidays **Cards**
Amex, Delta, MasterCard, Switch, Visa; personal and business accounts **Discount** 10%
on 1 mixed case **Delivery** Free within 60-mile radius (min. 1 case); nationwide service,
charge £6.50 per order **Glass hire** Free with order **Tastings and talks** In-store
tastings, gourmet dinners, annual wine fair **£5**

A couple of years ago Mark Ryan's company shed its Leeds outlet and
moved 'lock, stock and barrel' to Ripon – becoming 'leaner and meaner',
according to Mark. We still think the selection is, in fact, anything but mean
– particularly the Australian shelves, which display excellent range and
depth, drawing in wines from many different regions and highlighting lots
of different grape varieties. Spain is another strong point. To see Portugal
taken so seriously is more of a surprise – so few merchants make the most of
these exciting table wines, yet here are plenty of great reds from Bairrada,
Dão, Alentejo and the Douro. The range of prices within many countries is
admirably wide: for example, the South African selection kicks off with basic
£3.99 Chenin Blanc, but rise to the heights of De Toren Fusion V and Sejana
Merlot (£15.75 and £18.95 respectively). It's true that the list carries few
passengers, which is what Mark probably meant by lean and mean, but this
merchant serves Ripon and its surrounds exceedingly well.

Look out for

- Iberian stars from Vega Sicilia, Abadia Retuerta, Viñas del Vero (Spain),
  and Esporão, Casa de Saima and Niepoort (Portugal)
- Fine Australian range that takes account of regionality and varied grapes
- Great Cape selection including De Toren, Clos Malverne, Jordan, Neil
  Ellis
- Small but appealing set of Californians including Marimar Torres, Frog's
  Leap, Clos du Val
- Hugel, Trimbach and Turckheim from Alsace.

Great Western Wine Company

The Wine Warehouse, Wells Road,
Bath BA2 3AP

Tel (01225) 322800
Fax (01225) 442139
Email post@greatwesternwine.co.uk
Website www.greatwesternwine.co.uk

Open Mon–Fri 10–7, Sat 10–6 **Closed** Sun, public holidays **Cards** Amex, Delta, MasterCard, Switch, Visa; personal and business accounts **Discount** Available, phone for details **Delivery** Free within 10-mile radius (min. 1 case); nationwide service, charge £5 per case **Glass hire** Free, deposit required **Tastings and talks** Range available, phone for details **£5**

We've been watching this 20-year-old company with some interest, and continue to be impressed by the way Philip Addis has built the operation up into one of best in the West. In particular it is good to see an independent merchant that doesn't simply pick from UK wholesalers but which makes a huge effort to track down interesting wines of its own and source directly from the vineyard. And when we have tasted Great Western wines, we have been struck by the quality and subtlety of much of its range – Addis and his right-hand man Joel Lauga are clearly not after obvious blockbusters. France receives the most attention – it's hard to single out one region here, but the Loire and Rhône sections certainly deserve your time. There's inspiration in many other parts of the list, too, particularly New Zealand, Australia and Chile. Don't miss the fine Cognacs and Armagnacs too. This merchant has a strong reputation for good service from a relatively young but experienced staff, so do pick their brains. And if you live near Bath (or are visiting this lovely city) why not get along to one of the good-value tasting events with winemakers (£7)? All in all, a company that lives up to its name – great!

Look out for

- Many smaller grower wines from France, sourced directly from the winery
- Viña Alamosa from Chile
- Strong Californian range
- New Zealand wines from Chancellor
- Con Class, Guelbenzu and Pago de Carraovejas from Spain
- Attractive northern Italian range from the Friuli and Alto Adige regions
- Fine Calvados, Cognac and Armagnac.

Alexander Hadleigh Wine Merchants

19 Centre Way, Locksheath Centre,   *Tel* (01489) 564563
Southampton SO31 6DX   *Fax* (01489) 885960
                                    Email info@ahadleigh-wine.com
                                    Website www.ahadleigh-wine.com

Open Mon–Thur 9–6, Fri & Sat 9–7   **Closed** Sun, public holidays   **Cards** Delta,
MasterCard, Switch, Visa   **Discount** 7.5% on 1 case   **Delivery** Nationwide service
(min. 1 case), phone for details of charges   **Glass hire** Not available   **Tastings and
talks** Available, phone for details **£5**

Big bottles are the speciality at this merchant, these and 'one of the most
outstanding lists of fine and rare wines dating from the sixteenth century'.
For the latter, you'll no doubt need access to some inner sanctum of the
Alexander Hadleigh Cellars, as they're not on the main list, but judging by
the roll call of top-class châteaux among the 1990s selection (Tour-Figeac,
Pavie, Trottvieille, Cheval Blanc, Ausone and more) we can well believe they
rank among some of the most illustrious.

But back to those large-format bottles: these run from two-bottle
magnums to 24-bottle (18-litre) melchiors in size and among the list of
benefits named for making such purchases, Alexander Hadleigh suggests
that 'flavours can be more concentrated in a larger format', 'the wine will
mature more fully over a longer period', 'they make glorious presents for
wedding anniversaries or special occasions' and 'they'll be a "show stopper"
at an important party'. You could either fork out £97.76 for an impériale
(eight bottles) of Château Les Charmettes Bordeaux or £4,172.00 for a
Nebuchadnezzar (20 bottles) of Cos d'Estournel 1996 to see what they mean.

As we said last year, this merchant's list oozes quality, and it's not just
Bordeaux that impresses – five different Barolo producers from Italy, a
helping of Super-Tuscans, six different Alsace houses from France and
representations of the top Burgundy estates all testify. There's even a trend-
bucking selection of Rieslings from Germany – this team goes for quality
first, not popularity. In the past, we've criticised the list for its inattention to
large tracts of the New World (California, Australia and South America to be
precise) but things appear to be shaping up on this front and there are now
choices falling within most price brackets. It is particularly pleasing to see
the likes of Montes from Chile and Clos du Val from the Napa Valley,
California, making an appearance. We'd still prefer, however, to see less
emphasis on the bulk-producing estates, if this side of the list is to parallel
the focus on quality of the Old World selection.

Don't be intimidated by the prices charged for the big bottles, there's
plenty here at under a tenner. And this year the shop's got even bigger, so
there's 'more of everything' from which to choose – including, as buyer Del
Taylor points out, wine accessories and gourmet foods.

Look out for
- Magnums and double-magnums of Le Pergole Torte from Italy
- Top burgundies from Domaine de la Romanée-Conti, Henri Gouges and
  René Engel
- Champagne in jeroboams, balthasars and methuselahs (Bollinger and
  Roederer included)

- Delicious Australian Rutherglen Muscats, plus classic Tokaji and Austrian *Beerenauslese* sweeties
- Simonsig, Jordan and Uitkyk wines from South Africa
- A mostly French selection of tempting half bottles.

Handford-Holland Park

12 Portland Road, London W11 4LE

Tel 020-7221 9614
Fax 020-7221 9613
Email james@handford-wine.demon.co.uk
Website www.handford-wine.demon.co.uk

Open Mon–Sat 10–8.30 **Closed** Sun, public holidays **Cards** Amex, Delta, MasterCard, Switch, Visa; personal and business accounts **Discount** Available, phone for details **Delivery** Nationwide service (min. 1 case), charge £7.50 per order, free for orders of £120+ **Glass hire** Free with order **Tastings and talks** Range available, phone for details **£5**

A relatively young independent merchant trading in affluent W11, James Holland (MW)'s company appears to be doing very well, thank you. 'Our customers are trading up,' says retail director David Penny. 'They are searching for more individual wines, not brands, and they are more discerning.' He reports particular interest in wines from South Africa, Spain and Portugal this year.

It's not a surprise to hear such encouraging news from the company, if the wine list is anything to go by (even if we did have to look it up on the website, there being no printed version available). This is an upmarket selection, but not terrifyingly so. It's well-balanced and appealing and, although you can splash out if you wish, as both big names and big price tags are here, there is plenty of excellent drinking to be had at under £10 a bottle.

The French collection features superb burgundy and fine Bordeaux from some top châteaux, and we particularly like the Loire wines, representing some of this *Guide's* favourite producers (Guy Saget, Didier Dagueneau, Pinard, Joguet . . .). The current customer interest in Spain is understandable when a wine merchant highlights such inspiring wines – this is the best and trendiest small set of Spanish whites we have seen this year (from Alella, Rueda, Rías Baixas Dos), followed by a larger slate of reds that reveals a particular attachment to the Ribera del Duero region.

There are rich pickings from all the major New World areas, but those in a rush should focus on the bottles from Western Australia and on the strong South African range. Champagnes are glorious; Niepoort, Fonseca and Noval dominate the ports; and fine French and Scottish spirits bring up the rear. Good taste is evident throughout. Now that Handford-Holland Park is well-established, though, with that newly discerning clientele, we are eager to see some more quirky and truly unusual wines hitting the list in the future.

We've heard that the service is personal and friendly here, and the wine school, tastings and dinners are said to be excellent. Tastings are a reasonable £12.50 and might include Meursault, deluxe champagnes, Rioja or South Africa. If you want to be sure of hearing about them (and the other numerous events that this dynamic company puts on), join the Handford Wine Club, which meets five times every quarter. You'll get discounts on case sales of wine too.

Look out for

- Illustrious burgundies and Bordeaux from Domaine de la Romanée-Conti and châteaux Lafite and Latour, plus more humble fare and *en primeur* offers
- Fashionable Spanish wines from Galicia, Ribera del Duero and Rueda regions
- Excellent set of Loire whites and reds
- Henschke, Cape Mentelle, Vasse Felix and Jim Barry heading a serious Australian list
- Fine South African range from Warwick Estate, Meerlust, Rustenberg . . .
- Highly rated wine events, including tastings, seminars and wine courses.

Haynes Hanson & Clark

25 Eccleston Street, London SW1W 9NP

Tel 020-7259 0102
Fax 020-7259 0103

Sheep Street, Stow-on-the-Wold,
Gloucestershire GL54 1AA

Tel (01451) 870808
Fax (01451) 870508
Email london@hhandc.co.uk

Open (London) Mon–Fri 9–7, (Stow-on-the-Wold) Mon–Fri 9–6, Sat 9–5.30 **Closed** Sat (London), Sun, public holidays **Cards** Amex, Delta, Diners, MasterCard, Switch, Visa; personal and business accounts **Discount** 10% on 1 case **Delivery** Free within Central London (min. 1 case); nationwide service, charges per case: £8 for 1, £5.50 for 2–3, £5 for 4+; free for orders of £500+ **Glass hire** Free with order **Tastings and talks** Available, phone for details

---

Jim Eustace directs operations at Haynes, Hanson & Clark these days – Anthony Hanson's time is now spent conducting proceedings at Christie's wine auctioneers over in St James's. Jim, however, sums up the situation here just as eloquently: 'We have a fantastic range of growers from throughout France, particularly from Burgundy, the Rhône and the Loire Valley. We can handle small parcels of exciting wines, and we love selling less-fashionable appellations such as Quincy, Reuilly and all red Loire wine. Our range is marked by freshness, crisp acidity, finesse and elegance. We hate thick, oaky heavy styles.' In other words, this team has no time for flashy, flamboyant wines but is quite prepared to devote its energy towards anything that's full of genuine regional character, whether it's an 'It' wine or not.

It's really the burgundies we'll come back for, time and time again. There's an impeccable array of producers to choose from, and we highly recommend getting to one of the team's annual burgundy tastings if you can wangle your way on to the invitation list (as regular customers can). From the likes of Champy Père et fils, Maison Faiveley, Blain-Gagnard and Olivier Leflaive a wide range of *communes* are listed, but there are also tempting oddments from the likes of Bonneau du Martray, Anne-Françoise

Gros, Chandon de Briailles and Etienne Sauzet. Plenty of vintage options are still available from the 1990s for those keen on cellaring their own, and be assured that though burgundy (of course) can get a little pricy, these wines aren't coming in at over the odds.

Italy, Alsace, Bordeaux and Champagne also feature highly here and you can expect any of the New World wines on offer to be of parallel elegance and quality – there are one or two smart wines from Australia, New Zealand, California and Chile creeping in.

There's still no sign of an HH&C website hitting our screens, but we don't think there's any hurry for this. More haste, less speed, as the saying goes.

Look out for
- Regular discount offers available to those on the mailing list
- Fifty new wines on the books annually
- Sancerre and Pouilly-Fumé from top growers Château de Tracy, Pascal et Nicolas Reverdy and Serge Dagueneau
- Favourite Burgundy villages represented: Volnay, Chambolle-Musigny, Pommard and Gevrey-Chambertin
- Rostaing, Jaboulet-Aîné, and de Beaucastel Rhône wines
- First-class Italian names: Allegrini, Isole e Olena and Villa Antinori
- Busy shops for friendly advice in Belgravia and Stow-on-the-Wold.

Hoults Wine Merchants

10 Viaduct Street, Huddersfield, West Yorkshire HD1 6AJ	*Tel* (01484) 510700 *Fax* (01484) 510712
5 Cherry Tree Walk, The Calls, Leeds LS2 7EB	*Tel* 0113-245 3393 *Fax* 0113-246 7173 *Email* bob@malvasia.freeserve.co.uk

Open Mon–Sat (inc. Good Fri, May Day) 9–6, Sun 11–3 **Closed** Other public holidays **Cards** Amex, Delta, MasterCard, Switch, Visa; business accounts **Discount** 10% on 1 mixed case **Delivery** Free within 10-mile radius of each store (min. 1 case) **Glass hire** Free with order **Tastings and talks** Not available **£5**

Rob Hoult gets people walking through the door of his shop by providing a better deal, so he says, than the Tesco's supermarket opposite. All the major brands are on display here: Lindemans Bin 65, Gallo Ruby Cabernet and White Zinfandel ('remember, we all start our drinking somewhere,' says Rob). And Rob regularly discounts them to make sure the prices don't top the £4 mark. While all this wouldn't necessarily impress us, it's all part of Rob's big campaign not to become yet another independent merchant squeezed out of business by the major multiples. It's an 'if you can't beat 'em, join 'em' type of approach, and it seems to work.

However, Rob is not a believer in the 'staggering amount of dross that is peddled as good wine', so he doesn't dwell overly on the lower-priced wines. Further up the range, there are all the Old World treasures and New World classics you'd expect from a small, passionate wine merchant. Yalumba, Jim Barry and Ravenswood Shirazes all get a mention, and from California Schug, Bonny Doon and Frog's Leap's wines again prove that Rob knows just what he's looking for in terms of quality. There are also plenty of reliable 'trade up' options from France (Rhône wines from Jaboulet and Guigal; Burgundy from Jadot and Girardin) and snapshot ranges from Italy and Spain. In general, each section builds its way steadily towards the £10, £15 and £20 marks and then throws in a few top-priced classics for good measure – and special occasions.

We like the look of this cheery merchant, nestled under its Huddersfield railway arch with piles of boxes stacked three or four high, tempting you to carry one away laden with a mixture of your choice. You can, of course, pop in for just one bottle should you wish – chances are, too, that you'll have been able to try it first, as Rob makes sure there's always something available to taste.

Look out for
- Sparkling wines from Indian Omar Khayyam to Dom Pérignon vintage rosé
- Riesling, Viognier, Marsanne and Verdelho: Australia's best 'other white grapes'
- Montes, Cousiño Macul and Caliterra Merlot from Chile
- Top Bordeaux châteaux: Talbot, Gruaud-Larose, Pichon Baron and Léoville-Barton
- Château de Tracy from the Loire, and Trimbach from Alsace
- Affordable post-prandials: port, sherry and madeira.

Irma Fingal-Rock

64 Monnow Street, Monmouth NP25 3EN
Tel (01600) 712372
Fax (01600) 712372
Email irmafingalrock@msn.com
Website www.pinotnoir.co.uk

Open Mon & Weds 9–2, Thurs & Fri 9–5.30, Sat 9–5 **Closed** Tues, Sun, public holidays **Cards** Delta, MasterCard, Switch, Visa; business accounts **Discount** Available, phone for details **Delivery** Free locally (min. 1 case); nationwide service, free within mainland Wales & England for orders of £100+; otherwise charged at cost **Glass hire** Free **Tastings and talks** Annual tasting in London, local tastings on request, wine dinners at local venue **£5**

Ex-barrister Tom Innes (his wife is the exotically named Irma) tells us excitedly that business has been terrific over the past year. He has always been passionate about wine – Burgundy especially, and lesser-known growers in particular – but this year he sounds more enthusiastic than ever. He spent the winter discovering 'several new growers' in his favourite part of France, the emphasis being on 'white wines, Meursault and Auxey-Duresses', which has clearly strengthened these parts of the range. Incidentally, Tom issues regular, detailed and lively accounts of his buying trips to Burgundy, which brings to life the domaines and winemakers he visits. Refer to his list for a wide range of fairly priced burgundies, supplemented with claret, champagne and other French wines. A short tour round the rest of the world pulls in an eclectic group, such as Lungarotti's *vin santo*, Quinta de la Rosa Douro reds, the much admired Washington State wines of L'Ecole No 41 and local bottlings from Offa's Vineyard. A relatively short, but characterful and discerning, slate.

Small (but perfectly formed) merchants such as this are an essential part of the UK wine trade. You get truly personal service from someone who really knows his (or her) own wines, and you get to try wines from smaller, but often more interesting producers, rather than being dazzled by rows of big brands on a supermarket shelf. Long may the tiny independent – preferably with an exotic name – live!

Look out for

- Wide range of burgundy from basic Bourgogne upwards, sourced from small growers
- Rhônes from Alain Graillot, Domaine des Romarins, Domaine Rocher
- Iberian stars from Navajas and Marqués de Murrieta (Spain) and Quinta de la Rosa (Portugal)
- Duck Pond wines from Oregon and L'Ecole 41 from Washington State
- Henschke, Tyrrell's, Rolf Binder Australian bins.

Jeroboams

(Incorporating Laytons)
Head office — *Tel* 020-7629 7916
8–12 Brook Street, London W1S 1BH — *Fax* 020-7495 3314
(7 branches in London, 1 in Cirencester) — *Email* sales@jeroboams.co.uk
Website www.jeroboams.co.uk

Open Mon–Sat (times vary between stores), Sun (some stores) **Closed** Sun (most stores), public holidays **Cards** Amex, Diners, MasterCard, Switch, Visa; personal and business accounts **Discount** Available, phone for details **Delivery** Nationwide service (min. 1 case), phone for details of charges **Glass hire** Not available **Tastings and talks** Weekly in-store tastings, specialist tastings, phone for details

The merchant with the split personality, being known as Laytons to its mail-order clients and Jeroboams to those visiting one of the eight shops. As we've said in the past, this is something of a gentleman's establishment, reliant on a largish wallet, and very traditional in its approach. There's plenty of Bordeaux and burgundy, and all the pre- and post-prandials you could wish for as you settle into your Chesterfield sofa – champagne through to port, madeira, liqueurs and fine sherry . . . The only thing that's missing is a decent selection of quality German wine.

We reviewed the Jeroboams' list this year via its website – the office being too busy to send us an actual wine list – so we're not sure how well this failure to deliver bodes for the state of the mail-order business, which (given the wines) ought to be thriving. However, we found the site smartly presented and easy to use, with over 650 wines on offer.

We were more excited about the Bordeaux than the burgundy selection (which tends to be dominated by large estates and *négociants*) and, while the Rhône, Loire and Alsace 'ranges' tend to be provided by one grower apiece, the list of small producers from Mediterranean France and oddball regions such as Arbois and the Jura is impressive indeed. Apart from a solid cross-section of Riojas the Spanish selection tends to be rather predictable, but things hot up again (in other words, buyers Neil Sommerfelt MW and Mike Hall get more inspired) on arrival in Australia, South Africa and (showing improvement this year) North America. Laytons/Jeroboams seems to have a particular penchant for Western Australian wines (which we can entirely sympathise with) but doesn't leave Australian shores without bringing back the wines of one of its finest estates, Henschke, over in the Eden Valley. It also has an unusually impressive range of Pinot Noirs from Oregon.

Look out for

- Burgundy from top-class grower Henri Gouges
- Plentiful Chablis and southern Burgundian wines from the Mâconnais (Montagny, Viré-Clessé, among others)
- Frescobaldi Cabernet from Italy
- Quality Western Australian wines from the Frankland River region (Alkoomi and Old Kent River estates), plus Moss Wood, Ribbon Vale and Pierro from Margaret River
- Jordan estate wines from South Africa
- Mumm, Bollinger, Moët and Pol Roger champagne, plus very respectable own-label fizz.

S H Jones

Head office

27 High Street, Banbury, Oxfordshire OX16 5EW	*Tel* (01295) 251179
	Fax (01295) 272352
121 Regent Street, Leamington Spa,	*Tel* (01926) 315609
Warwickshire CV32 4NU	*Fax* (01926) 315609
9 Market Square, Bicester, Oxfordshire OX26 6AA	*Tel* (01869) 322448
	Fax (01869) 244588
	Email shjonesbanbury@aol.com

Open Mon–Sat 8.30–6 **Closed** Sun, public holidays **Cards** Delta, MasterCard, Switch, Visa; personal and business accounts **Discount** Available, phone for details **Delivery** Free within 40-mile radius (min. 1 case); nationwide service (min. 1 case), charge £7.50 per order **Glass hire** Free with order **Tastings and talks** 2 tutored tastings per year, talks by arrangement, Whisky Club at Leamington Spa shop **£5**

For the most part, S H Jones does business with the wine trade, not the general public, but we wouldn't want that to put you off. There are three shops to visit, plenty of intelligent advice on offer, wine tastings, and enough enticing food and wine evenings to give Banbury customers as well as those from further afield plenty of opportunity to find out what's for sale here. Not everything is of top-notch quality (although the Burgundy section gets pretty close) but this team knows how to find the 'best of the rest', which gain thorough representation and at some very reasonable price points too. Breadth of choice and value for money are the name of the game.

To start with, there's a good selection of 'French Country Wines' from Languedoc, then those Burgundy stars; from Bordeaux there's a handy selection of *petits châteaux* and second wines such as Réserve du Général (from Château Palmer), Les Tourelles de Longueville (Pichon Baron) and Allées de Cantemerle (Château Cantemerle). Spain, Italy and the rest of Europe are well covered without extending to anything particularly earth-shattering (Aldo Conterno's Barbera d'Alba might be the one exception).

And pretty much the same can be said for the New World choices: these are widely sourced, dependable wines.

Maybe next year things will start getting a little more adventurous, with fewer bulk brands and some more single-vineyard wines to make a statement.

Look out for

- The occasional New World classic: Seghesio Zinfandel (California) and Jim Barry Armagh Shiraz (Australia) for starters
- Full range of champagne and sparkling wine, including large-format (jeroboam, salmanazar) bottles
- Second and third growth Bordeaux: châteaux Léoville-Barton, Montrose and Langoa-Barton included
- Popular Whisky Club held at the Leamington Spa shop.

Justerini & Brooks

Head office
61 St James's Street, London SW1A 1LZ

Tel 020-7484 6400
Fax 020-7484 6499

Kinnaird House, 14 Coates Crescent,
Edinburgh EH3 7AF

Tel 0131-226 4202
Fax 0131-225 2351
Email justmarketing@justerinis.com

Open Mon–Fri 9–7 **Closed** Sat, Sun, public holidays **Cards** Amex, MasterCard, Switch, Visa; personal and business accounts **Discount** Available, phone for details **Delivery** Nationwide service, charge £9, free for 2+ cases **Glass hire** Free within London and Edinburgh **Tastings and talks** Available, phone for details

There's no shortage of choice at Justerini & Brooks. 'We offer an extensive range of over 3,000 wines from £4 upwards,' the marketing department tells us. 'We offer a good spread of some of the world's best small production wines.' Indeed, they do. Justerini & Brooks is nothing if not impressive. Founded over 250 years ago (although now not exactly family-owned – it's part of the huge global drinks company Diageo), it's one of the UK's most important traditional-style merchants, with a huge collection of wines, fine wine broking and cellaring service, *en primeur* offers – the lot.

Where do you start with a 3,000-strong range, though? With the big, new 'Fine Wine' brochure, is the easy answer. It's highly readable, you'll be relieved to hear, with excellent tasting notes and extra nuggets on vintages, growers and wines that are particularly good for current drinking. (The groovy maps, however, composed of relevant local wine words, are strange and not particularly helpful, especially for beginners – please replace them, J&B, with something sensible.)

The list kicks off with case selections, then the International Wine Challenge medal-winning wines (bronzes are not always brilliant, but silvers and golds are usually a good bet), and a short slate of around 50 bottles under £10 that J&B thinks is excellent value for everyday drinking. (Call us tight-fisted, but we don't think £9.99 is 'everyday' though you, too, might be pleased to note that around half these bottles actually come in at under £7.)

On to the main range, listed alphabetically by country. Hew Blair and his team have pulled out all the stops – here are top clarets, dazzling German bottles (apparently sales of these doubled last year – again, we're impressed), fine Rhônes and an unusually wide array from Alsace. There are luscious dessert wines galore from Austria, an amazing collection of Piedmontese producers, plenty of gems from California and Australia, and even a serious delve into the wonderful world of madeira.

Only very occasionally does one notice a small gap: what about the table wines from Portugal, for example? There are only two listed here – surely a flight to Lisbon is called for, Hew? And it's fair to say that the Old World wines far outshine the New World ones. It's not that the latter are poor (far from it), but they don't make up such a wide and comprehensive range, and they don't exude the passion that the French, German and Italian collections in particular do. Perhaps J&B is happy with that – there is, after all, plenty on offer from the New World elsewhere these days.

As we have said in the past, J&B isn't content to tread a predictable path, and often presents lesser-known names rather than famous stars. This is good. Prices seem fairer than a few years ago – another plus point. Also admirable is the lack of dead wood in the range. So, send off for the list (it's better than calling in to the shops – or at least phone first, as not everything is stocked in them). Then settle down with a glass of something inspiring and have a jolly good read . . .

Look out for

- Decent house selection at unscary prices
- One of the best burgundy ranges in the UK, with more than 30 growers listed and plenty of wines from the 1990s and 1980s
- Rhône, Loire and Alsace wines dealt with in admirable depth
- Spectacular German wines from around 25 growers
- High-quality gems from the New World, such as Chalk Hill Chardonnay (California), Dalwhinnie Cabernet (Australia), Dry River (New Zealand)
- Old ports, madeiras, Cognacs, Armagnacs and Calvados.

For details of the selection criteria for the Top 100 merchants, see page 311

Laithwaites

Head office (orders)

New Aquitaine House, Exeter Way, Theale,
Reading, Berkshire RG7 4PL

Tel (0870) 444 8383
Fax (0870) 444 8282

3 Holtspur Parade, Holtspur, Beaconsfield HP9 1DA

Tel (01494) 677564
Fax (01494) 678097

121 Arthur Road, Windsor SL4 1RU

Tel (01753) 866192
Fax (01753) 621672

Exeter Way, Theale, Reading RG7 4PL

Tel 0118-903 0600
Email orders@laithwaites.co.uk
Website www.laithwaites.co.uk

Open Mon–Fri (order line) 8.30–9, (shops) 9–5.30, Sat (both) 9–6, Sun (order line) 9–6
Closed Sun (shops), public holidays (both) **Cards** Amex, Delta, Diners, MasterCard,
Switch, Visa **Discount** Available, phone for details **Delivery** Nationwide service,
charge £4.99 per order **Glass hire** Free **Tastings and talks** 45 tastings per year
throughout UK, phone for details

Laithwaites (aka the *Sunday Times Wine Club*) has won more than one award
for its customer service this year. So we were accurate, in the last edition of
this *Guide*, in identifying the high standard of service as one of this
company's fundamental strengths. Despite a vast number of customers for
this, the UK's biggest mail-order wine merchant by far, and (according to
Laithwaites) the UK's leading retailer of fine wines over £10, we still hear
remarkably few stories of poor delivery or incorrect orders.

Whether you buy through the Laithwaites' incarnation (Tony Laithwaite
is the entrepreneurial founder of the company, and still very actively
involved), or from the *STWC* brochure, famously fronted by veteran wine
critic Hugh Johnson, your choice will be from over 1,000 lines. However, you
might have to dig hard to uncover that fact. The mailshots continue to focus
closely on special seasonal offers or themed cases – 'Australian Brilliance',
say, or 'The New Spring Case', or a 'Special 12-for-10 deal'; even Tony
Laithwaite's 'favourite white wine – no debate' (a Bordeaux Sauvignon
called, er, Laithwaite. OK, we tasted it and we admit it's good . . .).

Anyway, you get the picture. The marketing is very strong indeed. But
some of the wines are *not* particularly good value. In fact, of the cheapest
Laithwaites' wines we have tasted recently (quite a few, in fact) we were
disappointed by far too many. It's certainly possible to buy better-value vino
for everyday drinking at the big supermarkets. The bottom rung is not great
here.

On a (much) more positive note, though, we've also tasted a large
number of the company's more pricy wines and have been very favourably
impressed. Of a recent batch, several bottles costing between £6 and £11
each were quite superb (they're listed below). The message, then, is clear.
Try to move up from the basic special case offers and on to a higher tier. The
service is good; the marketing bumpf can be informative and fun. Just make
sure you get the better wines Laithwaites has to offer.

Look out for

- De Bortoli Family Reserve Australian Riesling 2001 (£5.79)
- Domini 2000 Douro red from Portugal (£8.99)
- Château Labat *cru bourgeois* 2000 (£10.99)
- Familia Deicas Chardonnay-Viognier 2001, Juanico (£6.49) from Uruguay
- Tastings and dinners throughout the year
- Excellent service.

Lay & Wheeler

Sales office

Gosbecks Park, 117 Gosbecks Road,	*Tel* (0845) 330 1855
Colchester, Essex CO2 9JT	*Fax* (01206) 560002
The Wine Centre (shop)	*Tel* (01206) 713560
Address as above	*Fax* (01206) 769552
Lay & Wheeler (Scotland)	
MacKeanston House, Doune, Perthshire FK16 6AX	*Tel* (01786) 850414
La Grande Marque (wine bar)	
47 Ludgate Hill, London EC4M 7JU	*Tel* 020-7329 0308
The Wine Bar	*Tel* 020-7626 0044
33 Cornhill, London EC3V 3ND	*Email* sales@laywheeler.com
	Website www.laywheeler.com

Open (Sales office) Mon–Fri 8–6, Sat 8.30–4 (Wine Centre) Mon–Sat 9–6 **Closed** Sun, public holidays **Cards** MasterCard, Switch, Visa; personal and business accounts **Discount** Not available **Delivery** Nationwide service, charge £7.95, free for orders of £150+ **Glass hire** Not available **Tastings and talks** Extensive programme of tastings and dinners, phone for details **£5**

This is the classiest of the East Anglian merchants, oozing tradition, yet perfectly *au fait* with everything that's modern and holistic about winemaking. 'Lay & Wheeler stocks over 1,000 wines from every major wine-producing region, from everyday drinking wines to ultra-premium special occasion bottles,' sums up Laura Marschall, the company's highly qualified PR manager (a graduate of the Californian wine university, UC Davis). After the long list of impressive clarets – L&W has the confidence, and the contacts, to bring in lots of different ones – it's the same with the Rhône: not only are the old faithfuls all present and correct (Crozes-Hermitage from Jaboulet-Aîné, St-Joseph from Chapoutier, Côte Rôtie from Guigal) but there are a host of lesser-known or newcomer growers, who, given the skill and buying power of Hugo Rose and David Roberts (both Masters of Wine), we'd have no reservations in trying out.

At the 'day-to-day' end, the list begins with enticingly priced Languedoc wines – they start at £3.95 – but other sections tend to kick off around the £6–£8 mark. We can highly recommend, though, dipping into the six-bottle sampler packs, at around £30 or £40 – the 'Summer Sun' case and the 'Va! Va! Voom!' Italian case are appropriate snapshots of those wine styles. New Zealand is pretty well represented too, with wines from L&W's own 'Clayvin Vineyard' topping the bill. The team also has impressive access to the big, 'cult status' Napa estates. Our only complaint would be that, from many New World regions, there tend to be fewer producers to choose from: there's only one from Argentina, for example.

Back on a positive note, Lay & Wheeler is also widely credited for its popular cellar-starter plans: 'For wine enthusiasts who require a hands-off service'. Pay a monthly standing order and the team simply chooses the wines for you from its impressive stocks. Or, if you're not into storing your own, let L&W cellar your wines in its bonded warehouse where they can mature in perfect condition. Add-on services are the extensive programme of tastings and dinners – not just in Colchester but in London, Edinburgh and Hong Kong (designed for beginners and enthusiasts); regular monthly discounted offers; L&W on Cornhill, the successful new wine bar in London, and 'BOO' codes, for wines that are made 'biodynamically', 'organically' or following 'organic principles' – of these last there are an increasingly delicious quantity.

Look out for

- Organic and biodynamic wines from top estates Henschke (Australia), Hubert Lamy and Tollot-Beaut (Burgundy) and Mas de la Dame (Provence)
- Off-beat choices such as Australian Pinot Gris, white Rhône and Nyetimber's English sparkling wine
- Top-class St-Emilions from châteaux Pavie, Figeac, Magdelaine and Angélus
- Alsace Riesling from a choice of growers: Albert Mann, Clos St-Landelin, Schlumberger and Meyer-Fonné
- Top Shiraz blockbusters from Australia: Yalumba's Octavius, Jim Barry's Armagh and Veritas' Heysen
- Old Spanish Riojas dating back to 1964.

Laytons ✉

see Jeroboams

Lea & Sandeman

Head office

170 Fulham Road, London SW10 9PR

Tel 020-7244 0522
Fax 020-7244 0533

211 Kensington Church Street, London W8 7LX

Tel 020-7221 1982
Fax 020-7221 1985

51 High Street, Barnes, London SW13 9LN

Tel 020-8878 8643
Fax 020-8878 6522

206 Haverstock Hill, London NW3 2AG

Tel 020-7431 4412
Fax 020-7431 1326

Email sales@leaaandsandeman.co.uk
Website www.londonfinewine.co.uk

Open Mon–Sat 10–8 **Closed** Sun, public holidays **Cards** Amex, Delta, MasterCard,
Switch, Visa; personal and business accounts **Discount** Available, phone for details
Delivery Free within Central London (min. 1 case); nationwide service, charge £11.75
per order, free for orders of £250+ **Glass hire** Free with order **Tastings and talks**
Available, phone for details **£5**

There's more than a little reading matter to delve into when you first make
acquaintance with Lea & Sandeman – such is the plethora of sale offers,
Italian offers, Burgundy *en primeur* options, New Estate listings and vintage
reports that'll fall through your letterbox. If you have a comfy sofa and are
keen to browse, there's easily enough for an hour or two's happy perusal.
Or, failing that, visit one of the four London shops and any of the friendly
and enthusiastic staff will be willing to discuss all the options with you. But
be assured that, however you approach this range, you'll still have some
tough decisions to make. 'We bring the best features of the classical British
wine merchant to the high street in a modern format,' says Charles Lea.
Although the website is not yet as serious as the team would like it to be,
we think these wines are every bit as user-friendly as they should be, with
plenty of descriptive tasting notes.

And the wines themselves? 'We are proud of all of our list, because we
are small enough not to have to buy anything. We are also proud that we
can from time to time say "no" to a supplier if we feel the prices have gone
too high, while bringing on new emerging producers so that the list retains
a balance of good value,' says Charles. The aim, as ever, is to provide as wide
a range as 'all the others' but to undercut on price, listing the same wine at
better prices. L&S can do this by sourcing directly from the countries
concerned, and from different growers. This means that while you won't
always recognise the name of the producer, if you trust Lea & Sandeman's
word (and ours), you'll end up with an eminently reliable representation of
the vineyard in question. Bordeaux, Burgundy, Tuscany, the Rhône, the
Loire and Southern France are all areas treated with equal imagination here
(many of the up-and-coming stars get a mention), and we can report that
Australia, South Africa and California now also have a few decent bottles to
choose from – although beware, the New World is very definitely not the
main event here.

Look out for

- Fabulous burgundies from Guffens-Heynen, Jean Thevenet and Domaine Verget
- Tuscan treasures from San Gimignano, Montalcino and Montepulciano
- The most fantastic sweet wines imaginable, from Spanish Pedro Ximenez to 5-puttonyos Hungarian Tokaji and top-class French Sauternes
- Delicious white Rhône wines from Domaine de la Mordorée, Clos de la Cuminaille and Domaine Clusel-Roch
- Affordable Bordeaux from the Graves, Montagne-St-Emilion and Lalande-de-Pomerol
- Vintage reports and frank tasting notes on all new-release *en primeur* clarets listed.

O W Loeb

82 Southwark Bridge Road, London SE1 0AS

Tel 020-7928 7750
Fax 020-7928 1855
Email finewine@owloeb.com
Website www.owloeb.com

Open Mon–Fri 8.30–5.30 **Closed** Sat, Sun, public holidays **Cards** MasterCard, Switch, Visa; personal and business accounts **Discount** Available on 5+ cases, phone for details **Delivery** Nationwide service (min. 1 case), charge £5 for one case, free for 2+ cases **Glass hire** Not available **Tastings and talks** Available, phone for details

---

As ever with this list, the growers might not all be big stars but the character 'snapshots' and rich detail in the wine list (which is better than ever this year) gives plenty of confidence to try out any unknown names. The team at Loeb makes its buying decisions as a group effort, and in our experience of their list this almost always results in quality. You might not have heard of châteaux Paloumey, Panchille and Armens in Bordeaux, but we bet the wines will be good. You *will* have heard of châteaux Kirwan, Palmer and Rauzan-Ségla, however.

Burgundy and the Rhône are the backbone of the business here, and many Loeb hours are spent travelling up and down Route 74 checking out the state of play at each of the domaines on this list. But the reputation of this firm is as a shipper of very fine German wines. 'The best way to get to grips with German wine is to pull some corks. Forget any preconceptions and prejudices. Just savour what is in the glass,' is the advice given, and with access to this little lot, we'd wholeheartedly encourage doing just that. However, there seem to be fewer German wines here than we remember from previous years, which is a shame.

Loeb prices, despite the high quality, aren't intimidating. The Bin End Sale list, for spring 2002, had some juicy sub-£4 bottles on offer, even some sub-£10 wines from quality estates such as Flora Springs in California and Vincent Girardin in Burgundy. And we like the guidance through the list along the lines of: 'For those searching for high quality without having to consult their bank manager, the nearby village of St-Aubin is a welcome sanctuary . . .'.

There's something about the general feel of this merchant (established since 1874) that suggests high calibre, and we can vouch for it, having tasted many of the wines. We would, however, like to see a little more from Spain, Australia, South Africa and New Zealand: new territories that Loeb seems so proud of but which are represented by only a small handful of domaines. After Burgundy and the Rhône we've got used to expecting more depth.

Look out for

- Enticing array of Bordeaux classics from the sumptuous 2000 vintage
- 38 different Burgundy growers, Gouges, Tollot-Beaut and Confuron-Cotetidot among them
- Quality range of Chassagne-Montrachet from £22 to £222 a bottle
- Château de Fesles and Domaine Coulée de Serrant from the Loire
- Top Mosels from Sybille Kuntz, JJ Prüm, Willi Haag and more
- Paul Osicka's trendy Heathcote from Victoria, Australia.

Majestic Wine Warehouses

Head office

Majestic House, Otterspool Way
Watford, Hertfordshire WD25 8WW
(102 branches in UK, 4 in France)

Tel (01923) 298200
Fax (01923) 819105
Email info@majestic.co.uk
Website www.majestic.co.uk

Open Mon–Fri 10–8, Sat 9–7, Sun, public holidays 10–5 (times vary between stores)
Closed 25–27 Dec, 1 Jan **Cards** Amex, Delta, Diners, MasterCard, Switch, Visa; personal and business accounts **Discount** Available, phone for details **Delivery** Free nationwide (mainland) (min. 1 mixed case) **Glass hire** Free with 1 mixed case
Tastings and talks Available, phone for details **£5**

The cheery image that suits these stores (sources of New World, off-beat, easy-drinking choices) belies the fact that this outlet sources some of the most illustrious wines on the planet: the 2000 Bordeaux selection, for example, is a stunning array of Médoc classics, such as second growths Rauzan-Gassies, Cos d'Estournel and first growths Margaux, Mouton-Rothschild and Cheval Blanc. Even some of the smarter London wine merchants in St James's can't say the same. But these wines aren't why people come to Majestic – they only prove that whatever people want in terms of wine, this set of shops can provide it.

Majestic, this year, is busy helping the Old World fight back against the bargain-brand wines of, say, Australia and Chile. It's working hard to stock some of those wild, new southern French wines that have shown such a leap in quality (though not price) of late – Château Flaugergues, Pech-Redon, Mas des Bressades are names of particular interest, but there are about 60 more. But we're wondering whether this effort has distracted it from its usually impressive mission of finding off-beat Australian varietals (there aren't as many of these as we've seen before), and interesting wines from Chile, Argentina and the like. These latter ranges seemed, to us, surprisingly small this year, although the team tells us it's after 'smaller more interesting growers who put an individual stamp on their wines' – so perhaps this is the answer.

Majestic can buck the trends and stock an interesting and upbeat selection primarily because it doesn't have to supply the same bulk brands in every store. The (in our experience) young, enthusiastic staff will open any wine a customer is interested in – subject to stock levels – and will offer guidance through all the wines if requested.

We're pleased to report that this chain (which is low-key about the fabulous clarets, mentioned above) has as much in-store as ever. Not only is there all the competitively priced champagne we've grown to expect – one of these now comes in below the £10 mark, and yes it is the 'genuine article'.

Unsurprisingly, the website now covers 3 per cent of business here. Majestic's site includes food-matching advice, fine wine offers and 'Your Favourites', a customer survey of preferred wines, which keeps the team in touch with your needs.

Look out for

- Taittinger, Roederer, Pol Roger and Perrier-Jouët champagne for under £20 a bottle
- Vegetarian and organic choices scattered throughout the range
- Affordable burgundy from the luxurious Meursault, Savigny and Chambolle-Musigny appellations
- Tasty South African reds from Kanonkop, Fairview and Yonder Hill
- Very un-mainstream wines from Canada and Tunisia
- Spanish and Italian wines from the everyday to the enormously expensive.

Martinez Fine Wine

Head office

35 The Grove, Ilkley, West Yorkshire LS29 9NJ	*Tel* (01943) 816515
	Fax (01943) 816489
87A Town Street, Horsforth, West Yorkshire LS18 5BP	*Tel* 0113-281 8989
The Ginnel, Harrogate,	*Tel* (01423) 501783
North Yorkshire HG1 2RB	*Email* editor@martinez.co.uk
	Website www.martinez.co.uk

Open Mon–Sat 10–6 Sun (Ilkley) 12–8 **Closed** Sun (exc. Dec), public holidays **Cards** Amex, Delta, MasterCard, Switch, Visa; personal and business accounts **Discount** 5% on 6 bottles, 10% on case sales over £150 **Delivery** Free within 10-mile radius (min. 1 case), nationwide service (min. 1 case), charge £9.95 per case **Glass hire** Free with order **Tastings and talks** Regular in-store tastings, annual wine fair, dinners, events and tutored tastings; phone for details

'Sadly, people have been convinced that brand names are the best way to satisfaction, so customer awareness of wine is diminishing,' says marketing manager Mark Lascelles, reflecting on last year's turnover. Brand names are everything Martinez *doesn't* stand for, as this team is all out to encourage adventurous, interesting wine choices, at whatever price level. Fortunately, there are still enough people out there taking an interest in what they are doing. Martinez dispenses with the need for a supermarket visit by kicking off its list with a cheerful selection of £2.99 and £3.99 bottles, plus a 'three-bottles-for-£10' section. Thereafter, just as last year, there are well over 35 choices at under £5 a bottle. And with these wines there's the added convenience of an online ordering service, launched in summer 2002.

Each of the four Martinez outlets specialises in a different vinous area, but the core of the range is made up, as Mark phrases it, of 'trump cards in the form of small producers who are overlooked by the majors'. His best example is Champagne house Claude Cazals, which continues to outshine many bigger names that cost double the price. Other such small growers include a number of the family-owned Australian estates whom we admire tremendously – Grosset, Langi Ghiran, Charles Melton and Mount Mary – and similarly authentic Argentinian choices from Nieto Senetiner, Michel Torino and Navarro Correas. The enthusiasm spreads to a fine selection of modest (and some downright expensive) classics too, although Bordeaux and burgundy are mostly sourced from affordable domaines, and (because of this) they won't always be properties you have heard of. However, Julian Martinez is a skilled wine buyer, so trust his judgement to provide genuinely interesting wines. 'Quality before turnover' is the motto here, as ever.

We're particularly impressed by the five or six newsletters printed per year. *Noble Rot* offers not only news of the regular tutored tastings, but new releases, bargains, seasonal wine suggestions and wine news from around the world – full of salient information and personal anecdote. The one thing we mourn, however, is the loss of those terrible Yorkshire jokes. We complained about them, but we did enjoy them.

Look out for

- Helpful 'ready' and 'not ready' symbols to guide you to wines that you can drink now and those you should keep
- Cracking South African selection, with Pinotage, Shiraz, Pinot Noir and Sauvignon from the major growers
- Precious allocations of Bonny Doon, Testarossa and Ridge wines from California
- Good handful of New Zealand's top names, including Winslow, Goldwater Estate and Kumeu River
- Burgundy from the odd-one-out Sauvignon de St-Bris to top-notch Chambolle-Musigny
- 1988 Mouton-Rothschild and other classic clarets.

For an explanation of the symbols used at the top of some of the merchant entries, see page 310.

Mayfair Cellars

203 Seagrave Road, London SW6 1ST

Tel 020-7386 7999
Fax 020-7386 0202
Email sales@mayfaircellars.co.uk
Website www.mayfaircellars.co.uk

Open Mon–Fri 9–6 **Closed** Sat, Sun, public holidays **Cards** Delta, MasterCard, Switch, Visa; personal and business accounts **Discount** Available, phone for details **Delivery** Free nationwide service (min. 1 case) **Glass hire** Not available **Tastings and talks** Large annual tasting in autumn, other tastings and talks, phone for details **£5**

'We have freshened up our list and have a more modern, open-minded approach to the wine we sell,' says Alex Hunt, associate director of this relatively small but decidedly upmarket merchant, when asked to comment on the past 12 months. Mayfair Cellars began life in 1989 as a fine wine merchant selling to private clients. A couple of years ago it was taken over by the champagne house Jacquesson and the agency side of the business was expanded. We think it now merits promotion to 'Top 100' in the *Guide*, as its list, while still not the longest in the world, has become more comprehensive of late. The company still specialises to an extent in boutique wine producers who don't often appear on the high street, and it still aims to offer 'a highly personal service – ascertaining a customer's taste and making suggestions based on it'. Unsurprisingly, there is a full range of Jacquesson champagnes, plus excellent Australian fizz Clover Hill. Once past the impressive sets of Bordeaux and burgundy, it's good to see the likes of JosMeyer from Alsace, and superior Austrian co-op Freie Weingartner Wachau. New World gems include Sileni from New Zealand, Matanzas Creek from California, and the elegant (but little-known) wines of Lalla Gully in Tasmania. Perhaps the best moment to sample these is at the annual Autumn tasting at the National Gallery; alternatively the company offers corporate 'entertainment' packages involving tastings (sometimes blind) and talks. We look forward to seeing Mayfair Cellars continue to grow.

Look out for
- Wide range of champagnes from Jacquesson, including rare, late-disgorged bottles
- Plenty of white burgundy, especially *premier cru* Meursault
- Half-a-dozen vintages of dry white Bordeaux from Domaine de Chevalier
- Alsace Gewurztraminer courtesy of JosMeyer
- Fine boutique wines from the New World, especially strong on California.

Mitchell & Son

21 Kildare Street, Dublin 2, Ireland	*Tel* +353 (0)1 676 0766
	Fax +353 (0)1 661 1509
	Email mitchkst@indigo.ie
54 Glasthule Road, Sandycove, Co. Dublin	*Tel* +353 (0)1 230 2301
	Fax +353 (0)1 230 2305
	Email wines@mitchellandson.com
	Website www.mitchellandson.com

Open Mon–Fri 9–5.30, Sat 10.30–5.30 **Closed** Sun, public holidays **Cards** Amex, Delta, Diners, MasterCard, Switch, Visa; personal and business accounts, wine club accounts **Discount** 5% on 1 case **Delivery** Within 10-mile radius, charge £8 for 1 case, free for 2+ cases; nationwide service, charge £12 for 1 case, phone for charges for 2+ cases **Glass hire** 17p per glass (min. 48 glasses) **Tastings and talks** In-store tastings every Saturday, plus regular tastings/winemaker dinners for Wine Guild members, phone for details **£5**

As befits a smart Irish wine merchant (established in 1805), service is of paramount importance here. Peter Dunne, having been at Mitchell's for 32 years, appreciates the value of this. (Peter started life at this business bottling the stock – as was the tradition in the days when wines were shipped in barrel – now he is busy buying it.) Weekly wine tasting evenings, a wine appreciation course and wine region visits (the 7-night stay in Alsace was fully booked, but a trip to Tuscany in October, during harvest, looked jolly enticing) for members of Mitchell's Wine Guild, show an almost unparalleled commitment to the customer. Members of the Wine Guild pay a standing order (£50 minimum) each month to avail themselves of significant discounts and invitations to 'relaxed and informal' winemaker dinners, with such characters as Viv Thompson from Best's in Australia and Carlo Pasqua from Italy.

We criticised the Mitchell's Burgundy selection two years ago, but the improvements since have been dramatic, with everything available from Clos du Tart 1992 (£56.48 a bottle) to Mommessin's Mâcon Rouge (£8.95), taking in Meursault, Pouilly-Fuissé, Clos Vougeot and the odd bottle of Echézeaux along the way. Equally inspiring are the intrepid 'other France' choices from Languedoc and the south-west.

There's also an array from the New World, taking in the illustrious Grange from Australia and more gluggable counterparts such as Yellow Tail Shiraz at £8.99. From California, there's Caymus' top Cabernet, and also (more soothingly priced) Ravenswood Zinfandel. This isn't a place for the budget-conscious, however, as even the cheapest glugging brands from Chile and Argentina hover around the £8 and £9 mark. While we find this slightly perplexing, we suspect the real value for money is to be found in the mid-range, which also tends to be more interesting wines.

Look out for
- Bordeaux favourites such as châteaux Pétrus, Phélan-Ségur, Palmer and Margaux
- Classic older vintages: 1982 and 1990 Bordeaux, 1996 Burgundy
- Katnook and Penfolds from Australia

- Oddities such as L A Cetto Petite Sirah from Mexico and Italian Marsala from Sicily
- A brief, but worthwhile dip into Austria, with Domaine Müller
- Banyuls, Madiran, Limoux and Corbières from Mediterranean France.

Montrachet Fine Wines

59 Kennington Road, Waterloo, London SE1 7PZ

Tel 020-7928 1990
Fax 020-7928 3415
Email admin@montrachetwine.com
Website www.montrachetwine.com

Open Mon–Fri 8.30–5.30 **Closed** Sat, Sun, public holidays **Cards** Delta, MasterCard, Switch, Visa; personal and business accounts **Discount** Not available **Delivery** Nationwide service (min. 1 case), charge £10, free for 3+ cases **Glass hire** Not available **Tastings and talks** Available, phone for details

Charles Taylor MW runs a tight ship, concentrating on buying the classic French wines supplemented by a few fine German bins and vintage port. 'We are the leading supplier to the rich and famous of domaine bottled Burgundy and *cru classé* claret,' his company claims, modestly. 'Most of our wines are sold to serious individuals for laying down.' (We presume they mean serious about wine, not, generally earnest.) There are one or two other companies in the UK that might make a similar claim, but there's no doubt Montrachet is up there with the best of them dealing in fine French wine. And we have heard good things about the depth of knowledge and sound advice provided by the staff here. The result is a group of loyal, long-standing customers, we understand. Burgundy is clearly the main passion here, but the selections from the Rhône and Bordeaux are also high quality, and throughout the list there is an emphasis on excellent wines sourced from small family-run estates. Don't, however, expect anything from the South of France, Italy, Austria or the entire New World – they simply don't crop up on this range. Nothing wrong with that: Charles and his team have just chosen to concentrate on a particular group of wines – and they do it very well.

Look out for
- A wide-reaching and impressive range from Burgundy
- Fine Rhône reds from Bosquet des Papes, La Bouissière
- Alsace from one top producer, Bott-Geyl
- Warre, Dow, Taylor, Fonseca vintage ports
- German beauties from Max Ferd Richter, Lingenfelder, Schloss Saarstein
- Customer advice on *en primeur* purchases.

Moreno Wine Merchants

11 Marylands Road, Maida Vale, London W9 2DU   *Tel* 020-7286 0678
Fax 020-7286 0513
Email morenowi@dialstart.net
Website www.moreno-winedirect.com

Open Mon–Fri 4–9, Sat 12–10   **Closed** Sun, public holidays   **Cards** Amex, Delta,
MasterCard, Switch, Visa; business accounts   **Discount** 5% on 1 case   **Delivery** Free
within Central London (min. 1 case); nationwide service, phone for details of charges
Glass hire Not available   **Tastings and talks** Available, phone for details **(£5)**

Our advice is to visit the Maida Vale shop if you want to get the best from
this first-class Spanish and Latin American selection.

As well as modern Riojas from top estates such as Muga, La Rioja Alta
and Castillo Ygay, there are treasures from past vintages delving back to the
1800s – many of them from the classic Rioja estate Marqués de Murrieta.
Ribera del Duero doesn't go uncharted, nor do more trendy regions such as
Priorato, Penedès, Tarragona and Costers del Segre.

Most of Moreno's business is carried out as middleman, directly with the
wine trade – which accounts for the assumption that people reading the list
will not need explanations. And the chances are that many a Spanish wine
you taste will have been shipped by this company without your knowing it.
But for the remaining 40 per cent of customers – the general public who visit
the shop or, as of summer 2002, log on to the website – we guarantee the
team here has all the knowledge of Spanish wine you could ask for.

Look out for
- Rare wines from the 1930s and 1940s – times of the Spanish Civil War
- Vega Sicilia vintages dating back to the 1920s
- Priorato classics from the Scala Dei, Rottlan and l'Ermita estates.

Morrison Supermarkets

Hilmore House, Thornton Road, Bradford,
West Yorkshire BD8 9AX
(114 branches nationwide)

Tel (01274) 494166
Fax (01274) 494831
Email cornwell.suzie@virgin.net
Website www.morereasons.co.uk

Open Mon–Sat 8–10, Sun, public holidays 10–4 **Closed** 25 Dec, Easter Sun **Cards**
Amex, Delta, Diners, MasterCard, Switch, Visa **Discount** Not available **Delivery** Not
available **Glass hire** Free with order **Tastings and talks** In-store tastings by
arrangement

Wine buyer Suzie Cornwell reports 'huge changes over the past year' to the
Morrison list, including, interestingly, 'increases to South America, Australia
and California; decreases to France and Eastern Europe'. What hasn't
changed on the wine shelves of one of our biggest supermarket chains is an
emphasis on value for money. The current range won't set the world alight
in terms of rare gems and mind-blowing new styles, but it might well excite
consumers for its low prices. Indeed, it's hard to think of a list that offers so
much palatable wine under £5 (most have very little that qualifies!). But here
we could point you towards, well, quite a lot. The Chilean and Argentinian
reds, say, many of the Australian bins, the Portuguese wines from Dom
Ferraz, the Sicilian Inycon bottles . . . and so on. Head honcho Stuart Purdie
and his team are clearly a canny lot. True, they list very few expensive,
'splash-out' wines, but if you're looking to stock up on everyday drinking,
Morrison should be a first port of call. And keep an eye open for the special
offers too, which bring prices even lower.

Look out for

- Jindalee, Oxford Landing and Penfolds from Australia
- Three Choirs English wine
- Decent Portuguese reds under £5
- Montana and Villa Maria from New Zealand
- Appealing Chileans including Valdivieso, Cono Sur, Montes . . .
- Impressive, price-slashing special offers.

James Nicholson Wine Merchant

27A Killyleagh Street, Crossgar,
Co. Down, Northern Ireland BT30 9DQ

Tel 028-4483 0091
Fax 028-4483 0028
Email info@jnwine.com
Website www.jnwine.com

Open Mon–Sat 10–7 **Closed** Sun, 25 & 26 Dec, 1 Jan, Easter Mon **Cards** Amex,
Delta, Diners, MasterCard, Switch, Visa; personal and business accounts **Discount**
10% on 1 mixed case **Delivery** Free throughout Ireland (min. 1 case); UK mainland,
charge £6.95 per case **Glass hire** Free **Tastings and talks** Regular in-store tastings,
tutored tastings, winemaker dinners **(£5)**

As we said last year, James Nicholson collects his wines from the finest
estates in the world, including the best names and rarest *cuvées*. So how has
he done it? 'We managed to secure allocations from many wineries
throughout the world in advance of them becoming famous and so very

sought after,' says James (citing, as his most-treasured examples, Rochioli from Russian River, California, and châteaux de la Negly, La Roque and Domaine de la Vielle Julianne from Châteauneuf-du-Pape). We'd be proud to list the likes of hard-to-get Bordeaux châteaux Le Pin, Vieux Château Certan and Tertre-Rôteboeuf too, if we were James. Not to mention some treasured allocations of Ridge Monte Bello, Saintsbury Pinot Noir and Bonny Doon Old Telegram from California.

What also shows in James's choices, through his emphasis on characterful smaller domaines, is that only quality will do – and he's a good enough wine buyer for this to be easy to spot. 'While I have many outside interests, wine is still fundamentally not a business but a passion.' With such a motivation for seeking out the best wines, James's success over the last 26 years is not surprising.

As well as ardour, there's a fair bit of rigour too. All the staff at this merchant are encouraged to take the Wine and Spirit Education Trust certificate exams to increase their wine knowledge. The handy, pocket-sized list is impeccably thought out, and is full of the kind of informative comment that takes weeks and months to prepare. There are *en primeur* Bordeaux offers; a JN Club to pick up limited-release wines and bargain casefuls; a dynamic programme of weekly tastings, often with a visiting winemaker in attendance; and estate profiles for just about every wine on the list. All the kind of service you'd expect from a traditional merchant, presented with a flourish of modernity.

It's well worth getting on the mailing list, as – even if you don't live in Northern Ireland – there are a number of wines here you won't find in mainland Britain, at some extremely affordable prices. Every country section starts with £5 and £6 wines, and the whole list kicks off with a £4-something range of 'everyday' drinkers. You can also spend up to £262 a bottle if you're so inclined.

Look out for
- Twenty-five small, new wineries added to the list within the last year, among them Shafer and Gary Farrell from the USA
- All manner of Rhône from Cornas and Côte Rôtie to wild Mediterranean wines from the Côtes du Ventoux
- Stunning German wines (don't ignore them!) from Dr Loosen, JL Wolf and Reichsrat von Buhl
- Fabulous dessert wines from France (for example, Sauternes), Hungary (Tokaji), Australia and California (dessert Muscats)
- Unbeatable South African wines from the Thelema estate
- Thorough selection of Bordeaux from modern blockbusters to the 1980s.

Nickolls & Perks

37 Lower High Street, Stourbridge,
West Midlands DY8 1TA

Tel (01384) 394518
Fax (01384) 440786
Email sales@nickollsandperks.co.uk
Website www.nickollsandperks.co.uk

Open Mon–Sat 9.30–6 **Closed** Sun, public holidays **Cards** Amex, MasterCard, Visa
Discount 10% on 1 mixed case **Delivery** Free within 20-mile radius (min. 1 case);
nationwide service available, charge £6.50 + VAT per case **Glass hire** Free with order
Tastings and talks In-store tastings on Saturdays, 6 malt whisky tastings per year **£5**

As we said last year, this list just oozes quality: Burgundy, Bordeaux; old vintages of port; Rhône wines dating back to 1959. You can either take a ready-matured bottle straight home with you for a celebratory dinner, or purchase far newer vintages and leave them in Nickolls & Perks' 15th-century vaulted cellars while they mature in perfect peace and quiet over the years.

Nickolls & Perks has been in the business of trading wines and spirits since 1797 (at which time the company was also a 'druggist and a grocer'), so the team has years of experience from which to draw, and plenty of old wines collected over the years. This isn't the shop for a cheerful £5 or £6 bottle (£8 is about the minimum), but it *is* the place for a classic wine with a bit of age, or maybe a small vertical selection – the same wine from a number of different vintages. And we would only come here for the New World choices if the illustrious likes of Penfolds' Bin 707 from Australia and Ridge Monte Bello from California – at around £80 a bottle – were what we were after.

Buyer David Gardener has obviously found the (high) quality level he is happiest with and is sticking to it, with no compromises. The website service (covering 15 per cent of trade) is efficiently run and, with a minimal charge, you can take up the nationwide delivery offer. We also recommend taking advantage of the regular bin-end sales (for which, again, see the website) and *en primeur* offers; there are the weekly in-store tastings, too. And don't forget the malt whisky tastings – the range has tripled in size over the past year and it's now the largest selection in the Midlands.

Look out for

- War-time Bordeaux from 1945 and 1914 – not to mention happier vintages, 1959 and 1961
- Bordeaux 2000s from Haut-Brion, Margaux, Latour, Lafite and Cheval Blanc
- Delicious, ageworthy burgundy 1996s: from Drouhin, Bonneau du Martray, Girardin and Laurent
- Ancient champagne vintages dating back to the 1940s
- Barolo, Barbaresco, Chianti and the Super-Tuscans – Italy's finest
- 1912 Niepoort port; Taylor, Fonseca and Graham's from more recent declarations.

Noble Rot Wine Warehouses

18 Market Street, Bromsgrove,
Worcestershire B61 8DA

Tel (01527) 575606
Fax (01527) 833133
Email info@nrwinewarehouse.co.uk
Website www.nrwinewarehouse.co.uk

Open Mon–Fri 10–7, Sat 9.30–6.30, Sun 10–4 (Dec only) **Closed** Sun (exc. Dec), public
holidays **Cards** Delta, MasterCard, Switch, Visa; business accounts **Discount**
Available, phone for details **Delivery** Free within 10-mile radius (min. 1 case);
nationwide service (min. 2 bottles), charge £8.50 per order **Glass hire** Free with 1+
cases **Tastings and talks** Range of events including tutored and in-store tastings,
winemaker dinners **(£5)**

Julie Wyres, director/wine buyer, freely admits her core range provides
'plenty of low-risk choices', but this is what her customers want – to be
gently lured away from their supermarket purchases but with lots of
familiar wines to fall back on. We can tell that Julie's far more excited about
the 'ever-changing, eclectic mix for our vinous adventurers' part of her
range, which culminates in wines such as Viognier de Campuget from
Costières de Nîmes, Montepulciano d'Abruzzo from Tenuta di Testarossa
and Shadowfax Chardonnay from the Yarra Valley, Australia. But, above all,
this company has thrived (since it was born, in 1990) because of its aim to
please. The sensible, predominantly £5 to £10, prices reflect this stance too.

Unsurprisingly with this mission in mind, many (one third) of Noble
Rot's wines come from Australia. It doesn't just dawdle about with the usual
brand names, but instead valiantly attempts to keep things lively – neither
Charles Melton nor Fifth Leg are boring choices. Take a look at the main
warehouse list for plenty of 'others' waiting in the wings to tempt customers
away from familiar ground. For those 'others' Noble Rot draws an
interesting range from Italy ('staff favourites!'), plenty of (modestly priced)
French classics and colourful selections from California (for example, Frog's
Leap), South Africa (l'Avenir) and New Zealand (Isabel Estate).

To keep up to the minute, Noble Rot no longer issues a complete wine
list. Instead it prints quarterly updates or 'mini brochures' covering special
offers, new arrivals and case deals, supplemented by a fine wine brochure.
Plus there are in-store tastings, a bimonthly newsletter and biannual wine
fair events to look forward to.

Look out for
- Mixed case deals, for around £65
- Discounted French classics (Chablis, Juliénas, Côtes du Ventoux)
- The 'Noble Rot Seasonal Cellar': a mixed case of wine every quarter
- Clos Malverne, False Bay and Leef op Hoop South African stars
- Sumptuous burgundies: Chambolle-Musigny, Pommard and Savigny-lès-Beaune.

The Nobody Inn

Doddiscombsleigh, nr Exeter, Devon EX6 7PS

Tel (01647) 252394
Fax (01647) 252978
Email info@nobodyinn.co.uk
Website www.nobodyinn.co.uk

Open Mon–Sat 12–2.30, 6–11; Sun, public holidays 12–3, 7–10.30 **Closed** 25 & 26 Dec, 1 Jan **Cards** Amex, Delta, MasterCard, Switch, Visa; personal and business accounts **Discount** 5% on 1 case **Delivery** Free within 25-mile radius (min. 1 case); nationwide service, charge £8 for 1 case, £2 per additional case for 2–5 cases, free for 6+ cases **Glass hire** Free with 1+ cases **Tastings and talks** Monthly lectures (usually winter), phone for details

The Nobody Inn's wine list still holds the same allure it always did. Anyone not living in Devon, however, can benefit equally from these imaginatively sourced wines by taking advantage of the informative wine list and nationwide delivery, or by buying via the website (10 per cent of trade is carried out this way). Needless to say, though, we recommend perusing and testing out the wine list while sampling the food and enjoying the atmosphere of this old country pub. Nick Borst-Smith will open any bottle for you to try with your meal, should you wish it.

And what better start to an eclectic wine list such as this than to pay tribute to our own English produce? Ridgeview Estate Bloomsbury Cuvée Merret and Three Choirs Classic Brut kick things off with a fizz, and thereafter sweet Loire wines (fabulous Quarts de Chaume and Bonnezeaux), sweet Bordeaux, feisty south-western Jurançon and a delicious list of unfashionable (but top-quality) German Rieslings all go to show that Nick is no slave to wine-world vogues but is determined to serve wines that are genuinely good. The 'It's Cava Jim, but not as we know it' section even attempts to gain an audience for this under-rated wine.

Even though the list moves on to Greek and Indian wines before launching into the more familiar likes of Bordeaux and burgundy, then Chilean, Californian and Australian wines by varietal, we wouldn't for a moment suggest that it is wacky beyond recognition – just wacky enough to open up a few horizons on the vinous front. There are plenty of tasting notes to help you get to grips with anything you're less familiar with.

Look out for

- Plenty of wines from older vintages (bottles that extend the range of flavour experiences on this list even further)
- Classic Bordeaux from châteaux Talbot, Lynch-Bages, Léoville-Barton and Pichon Baron
- Many a big red from California: Opus One, Ridge and Dominus
- Fabulous allocations of Australian Shiraz from Mount Horrocks, Henschke (top-notch Hill of Grace) and Yalumba
- Delicious range of post-prandials including top vintage ports, ten-year-old madeira and sumptuous Pedro Ximenez treacle-like sherry
- Almost as many liqueurs, whiskies and *eaux de vie* as there are wines.

Oddbins

Head office
31–33 Weir Road, Wimbledon, London SW19 8UG   *Tel* 020-8944 4400
(237 branches in UK, Calais and Dublin)   *Fax* 020-8944 4411
Email customer.services@oddbinsmail.com
Website www.oddbins.com

Open Varies between stores, phone for details **Closed** 25 Dec, 1 Jan **Cards** Amex,
Delta, MasterCard, Switch, Visa; personal and business accounts **Discount** Available,
phone for details **Delivery** Free within 10-mile radius (min. order £50); nationwide
service, phone for details of charges **Glass hire** Free with order, deposit required
Tastings and talks Regular in-store tastings, 2 wine fairs per year

If there was an award for the 'company that sent us the most bumpf', then
Oddbins would be a hot contender. An enormous pile of colourful literature
landed with a thud through our letterbox, as it does every year. Most of it
has the trademark Oddbins' irreverence and sense of fun ('Stomping
Summer Wines!' is a typical title), but some of it did seem a little more
restrained and tasteful this year, especially the informative malt whisky
leaflets.

Oddbins is not known primarily for its subtle approach, however. The
atmosphere in the shops, as most readers will know, is spit-and-sawdust,
bright wacky shelf descriptions, in-yer-face window displays, groovy young
staff, funky music in the background. If you want the rock 'n' roll approach
to wine, come to Oddbins. And that not only applies to the ambience, but to
the wines themselves. Many of them are cutting-edge, even Generation X
(catch the very stylish Quiltro Chilean labels – tasty stuff, in every sense),
and that may alarm the traditionalists. Until, that is, they look at the shelves
properly and see that there are plenty of classics in there too.

This *Guide*, which has been giving Oddbins awards for, oh, centuries
now, suspects this is precisely the secret of its success. On first approach,
Oddbins undoubtedly looks trendy, casual, even cheap and cheerful, and
that way it pulls in the young, style-conscious punters. But underneath that,
it is also about premium-quality wine, the sort of thing that only fairly
seasoned connoisseurs would go for. So you might start buying bottles here
as an impoverished student, but you have no need to move elsewhere as
you grow into more sophisticated tastes. That's certainly been our
experience, anyway.

Lots of news from the chain this year. After years of speculation (and
anxiety on the part of its many fans), Oddbins was finally sold in early
January 2002 to the huge multinational Castel group, which mainly owns
businesses such as *négociant* concerns and bottling lines in Bordeaux, and
has other interests (beer and soft drinks) in Africa. Castel also owns the
Nicolas chain of off-licences, which is big in France and has over 20 outlets
here.

Is the takeover A Good Thing? A restructure was announced in the early
Summer, which merged the wholesale and retail operations; and the joint
venture with Sainsbury's – Destination Wine Company/Taste for Wine – has
been handed back to the supermarket chain. Add some redundancies at
head office and these are the main events so far. PR manager Karen Wise

tells the guide that the plan is to 'focus back on wine and core business'. Let's hope this is the case. But (and we say this in a stern tone), we are watching Oddbins with a beady eye. Our readers love it as it is, and so does the *Guide*. Mess with it, Castel, at your peril! We'll be back next year to report on any 'Frenchification' or otherwise.

Which leaves us with the current selection of wines to review (somewhat more briefly than usual). The Chilean range has been plumped out this year, and those new wines we have tasted were impressive. Greece continues to benefit from the company's pioneering instincts, and some of these wines are excellent, especially the dry, fresh, almost salty whites and some of the rich reds. Will they stay under Castel, we wonder?

Australia has always been one of Oddbins' ace cards, and it continues to be a particularly strong section, with smaller parcels of wine appearing alongside much-loved famous-name wineries and some major brands. For great, ripe styles of red, it's pretty hard to beat the Oddbins' Oz set. At the Spring 2002 press tasting, despite discovering a few more sub-standard (faulty) wines than on previous occasions, we found some delectable German whites, plus decent champagnes and regional French reds. But this year it was perhaps the South African wines that really stood out – winemaking has come on in leaps and bounds in the Western Cape, and Oddbins is certainly making the most of that fact to put some genuinely exciting wines on its shelves. As we would expect. Long may this company continue to blaze a trail.

Look out for

- Regular in-store tastings and two wine fairs a year, in London and Edinburgh
- Super South Africans, including some exclusive wines from Flagstone, Radford Dale, Klein Constantia and Buitenverwachting
- Less-than-usual Australian varieties – Riesling, Grenache, Marsanne, Pinot Gris . . .
- Upmarket German wines at downmarket prices
- A surprisingly wide range of classics, from top-notch Bordeaux to fine champagne, to tempting Rhônes
- Excellent Californian wines from Beringer, Bonterra, Kent Rasmussen, Bonny Doon
- Greek wines galore – plunder them for new flavours.

Specialist and Regional Award Winners are listed on pages 12–16.

Partridges

Partridges of Sloane Street   *Tel* 020-7730 0651
132–134 Sloane Street, London SW1X 9AT   *Fax* 020-7730 7104

Partridges of Kensington   *Tel* 020-7581 0535
17–23 Gloucester Road, London SW7 4PL   *Fax* 020-7581 3449
                      Email partridges@partridges.co.uk
                      Website www.partridges.co.uk

Open Mon–Sun 8am–10pm   **Closed** 25 & 26 Dec   **Cards** Amex, Delta, MasterCard,
Visa; personal and business accounts   **Discount** 10% on 1 case   **Delivery** Free within
Central London; nationwide service, charge £15 per order (includes gift wrapping)
Glass hire Free with order   **Tastings and talks** Regular in-store tastings,
masterclasses; outside tastings by arrangement

If you're really lucky, you'll get to know Partridges' wines by receiving a
bottle or two in one of its famous luxury hampers – complete with wild
smoked salmon, duck confit, spiced peaches and Islay single malt . . . we live
in hope, especially for the Royale wicker basket (a cool £995).

Hampers aside, Partridges, the well-known upmarket grocer's of Sloane
Street, offers, as you might expect, a sophisticated range of wines. It has been
put together by François Ginther, who has been with the company some
time, and was a French hotelier before that. 'We are very traditional', he tells
us, perhaps unnecessarily. So the selections of claret, burgundy and
champagne are wide and top-notch, and there are some cutting-edge wines
from Alsace. But it seems that famous names rather dominate the French
sections – what about more lesser-known growers? Partridges isn't too
traditional for the New World, though; this year we are particularly
impressed by the top-rate New Zealand whites and some of the Californian
bottles. Back in Europe, Rioja is clearly an area of special interest – there are
literally dozens of wines here. One complaint, however: overall, the prices
are decidedly on the high side.

Look out for
- Glamorous range of top champagnes
- Ports from Ramos-Pinto, Sandeman and Noval
- Trimbach, Schlumberger and JosMeyer – wonderful whites from Alsace
- First-rate New Zealanders, especially Sileni, Alpha Domus, Esk Valley . . .
- Many of the biggest names in Australian wine
- Riojas galore – both traditional and modern in style.

Peter Graham Wines

41 Elm Hill, Norwich NR3 1HG

Tel (01603) 625657
Fax (01603) 666079
Email graham@petergrahamwines.com
Website www.petergrahamwines.com

Open Mon–Sat 8–5 **Closed** Sun, public holidays **Cards** Delta, Diners, MasterCard, Switch, Visa; personal and business accounts **Discount** 10% on 1 mixed case **Delivery** Free within Norfolk & Suffolk (min. 1 case); nationwide service, charged at cost **Glass hire** Free **Tastings and talks** 150–200 talks/tastings per year **(£5)**

Last year, (Peter) Graham Donaldson was almost too busy to send us back his questionnaire, such was the furious expansion of his business. But this year things seem to have settled down a little. Turnover might have increased by another 50 per cent (impressive indeed!), but this time there's been room for it to do so.

What we like about this list is its consistency and dependability: not everything will set the world alight (although there's plenty that will) but there's very little that's boring. Even the sub-£5 Australian wines ring the changes and come from less-usual growers, as Graham and Louisa Turner (fellow buyer and director) feel no pressing need to stock big, cheap brands. Graham maintains strongly that it's not just the quality of the wine that counts: 'What's most important to us is the reliability of the back-up, the knowledge of the staff, and above all, the service'. He feels that Peter Graham Wines is a bit of an industry-outsider that likes doing things its own way; priding his team on its depth of knowledge and honesty of advice, plus 'a healthy degree of eccentricity, which seems to work!'.

Graham focuses hard on burgundy but shows less of a devotion to Bordeaux, although we're pleased to see there's a tempting selection of the latter to draw from if customers so wish. Nor does non-fashionability put the team off supplying a delicious array of sherries, from (to our mind) the very best producers, Lustau and Barbadillo. This is a real reflection of customer confidence as, owing to the UK's entrenched 'great-aunt-only' prejudices, sherry is usually almost impossible to sell. More conventionally, Peter Graham Wines now ships directly from New Zealand, Australia, Chile and South Africa, so is able to offer very good deals on New World wines. More good news.

Look out for

- Choice of quality Chablis from Billaud-Simon, Alain Geoffrey and Thierry Hamelin
- Unforgettable Rieslings from Germany's Max Ferd Richter estate in the Mosel
- Ribera del Duero from Vega Sicilia, Viña Pendrosa and Bodegas Alion in Spain
- Classic Australian Shiraz from Mount Horrocks, Mount Langi Ghiran and Vasse Felix
- Well-selected South African reds from 'estates to watch': L'Avenir, Clos Malverne and Whalehaven
- Argentinian Malbec and Chilean Cabernet: top-class South American wines but also some cheapies.

Philglas & Swiggot

21 Northcote Road, Battersea, London SW11 1NG   *Tel* 020-7924 4494
Fax 020 7924 4736
Email philandswigg@aol.com

Open Mon–Sat 11–7.30, Sun 12–5   **Closed** Public holidays   **Cards** Amex, Delta,
MasterCard, Switch, Visa; business accounts   **Discount** 5% on 1 mixed case   **Delivery**
Free within 2-mile radius (min. 1 case); nationwide service (min. 1 case), charged at cost
Glass hire Free with order   **Tastings and talks** Regular in-store tastings, phone for
details **(£5)**

When Karen Rogers and husband Mike founded Philglas & Swiggot
(geddit?) over ten years ago, it was in order to specialise in their beloved
Australian wines. Now the shop has expanded to more than twice its
original size and takes in wines from all over the world. It's particularly
heartening to see a sparky young independent merchant flourishing in the
midst of South London's big chains and wine warehouses; and we are sure
the secret of P&S's success is the sheer energy that the dynamic duo has
brought to its task. The business doesn't sit still for a moment, as Karen and
Mike ferret out over 100 new, premium-quality labels each year – largely
'exciting new wines, many from small producers who cannot supply the
multiples'. This is not the place to go to for discount Lambrusco, as this
merchant mainly deals in quality, boutique wines at around £10 and
upwards – but if you are looking for something exciting to drink, take a
good look around. Or ask the willing and knowledgeable staff to help.

The list still exudes a huge enthusiasm for Australia and, in particular, for
the sophisticated wines of Margaret River, Western Australia; but make
room for the clutch of fine Australian Rieslings, Verdelhos, Pinot Gris and
Pinot Noirs – just about everything from Down Under looks attractive here.
Other good reasons to pitch up in Battersea are the Super-Tuscans and
Piedmont reds (Italy is clearly another passion), the classy Kiwi whites, the
well-chosen burgundies, the Austrian Rieslings . . . Overall, it's clear the
wines are chosen not only on quality but also for their refreshing, original
credentials. So, hardly a surprise that Philglas & Swiggot has thrived, and
we look forward to seeing it expand further. Another branch, perhaps?

Look out for

- Customer club that includes free delivery of a mixed case on a monthly,
  bi-monthly or quarterly basis – a good way to get to know this
  interesting range
- One of the best Australian selections in the UK, highlights being the
  Margaret River wines and the unusual varietals
- Strong French range
- Italian gems from Piedmont, Tuscany, the South and Islands
- Bonny Doon, Cline and Au Bon Climat from California
- Fine collection of sparklers.

Le Pont de la Tour

36D Shad Thames, Butlers Wharf,	*Tel* 020-7403 2403
London SE1 2YE	*Fax* 020-7403 0267

Email patriceg@conran-restaurant.co.uk

Open Mon–Sat 12–8.30, Sun, public holidays 12–6 **Closed** 25 Dec, 1 Jan **Cards** Amex, Diners, MasterCard, Switch, Visa **Discount** Available, phone for details **Delivery** Free within 5-mile radius; nationwide service, phone for details of charges **Glass hire** Free **Tastings and talks** Monthly tastings, phone for details

Precious allocations of the world's all-time great wines should come as little surprise here, this merchant being part of Terence Conran's restaurant empire. And food being the main issue means that there are plenty of wines that will match a menu perfectly – Bordeaux and burgundies, and Barolo, Barbaresco and Barbera from Italy for starters. Less is made of the big, bold, palate-swamping New World wines that'll block out the flavours of anything Conran's great chefs have to offer – we're pleased to say.

The wines on the merchant list are the same as those served up at the table and, if you don't wish to dine, you'll be relieved to hear that the prices are a little more bearable. (Imagine the restaurant mark-up on a burgundies such as the Ramonet 1993 Montrachet when the merchant price is £365, or an Henri Jayer 1988 Vosne-Romanée at £725!) You can, however, visit the Shad Thames shop with as little as a tenner in your pocket and pick up a bottle here and there: there aren't many options, but there are a few – most likely a New World wine, possibly from a producer you haven't heard of before (nothing wrong with that!). Argentina and Uruguay present some of the bargains, and Australian wines make intermittent sub-£10 appearances too. But these aren't really what people come here for.

If you're working your way up to a big spend – say for your cellar or a special occasion – then we recommend you find your way to one of Le Pont de la Tour's tastings, where informed (highly educated and widely travelled) staff will offer all the assistance you could wish for. Wine manager Patrice Guillon is, in fact, in the process of setting up a customer wine club, with tastings and dinner. Keep alert at the tastings and you might get to hear more about this as soon as it's launched – there is no website here.

Look out for
- Château Cheval Blanc from the 1962, 1966, 1970, 1978 and 1985 vintages
- Top Romanée-Conti burgundy plus treasures from Méo-Camuzet, René Engel, Mongeard-Mugneret and Comtes de Vogüé
- Fabulous Côte Rôtie Rhônes from Marcel Guigal and Châteauneuf-du-Pape from Château de Beaucastel
- Seven different Alsace growers to choose from
- Tangy, unusual Austrian white wines, plus other oddities from Greece and Switzerland
- Italian jaw-droppers along the lines of Antinori's Sassicaia, Tignanello and Ornellaia, plus other Super-Tuscans
- The best of South Africa: Simonsig Shiraz, Kanonkop Pinotage and Thelema Cabernet Sauvignon

- Sumptuous dessert wines from Barsac Sauternes to *Trockenbeerenauslesen* from Germany and Austria, Australian Rutherglen Muscats and Greek Samos Nectar.

Portland Wine Company

Head office

16 North Parade, Sale, Manchester M33 3EF	*Tel* 0161-962 8752
	Fax 0161-905 1291
152A Ashley Road, Hale, Altrincham, Cheshire WA15 9SA	*Tel* 0161-928 0357
82 Chester Road, Macclesfield, Cheshire SK11 8DL	*Tel* (01625) 616147
45–47 Compstall Road, Marplebridge, Stockport, Cheshire SK6 5HG	*Tel* 0161-426 0155
	Email portwineco@aol.com
	Website www.portlandwine.co.uk

Open Mon–Sat 10–10, Sun 12–9.30 **Closed** 25 & 26 Dec, 1 Jan **Cards** Amex, MasterCard, Switch, Visa; personal and business accounts **Discount** 5% on 6 bottles, 10% on 1 case (not online orders) **Delivery** Free within 20-mile radius; nationwide service, charge £10 + VAT per order **Glass hire** Free with order **Tastings and talks** Range of tastings including tutored in-store events at Hale, phone for details **(£5)**

A ship-shape, happy-sounding sort of merchant, the kind of excellent all-rounder that it is a pleasure to write about. Portland, based at a shop in Sale, near Manchester, is run by Geoff Dickinson with the help of manager Judith Gilder, and an effective, efficient team it is too.

This is evident if you log on to the website, a thoroughly user-friendly example, which, after accessing several rather more complex sites, also made reviewing this merchant a doddle. Another major plus is the fact that Geoff is adamant about value for money – he makes a point of running the gamut from the cheap (and almost always cheerful) to the luxurious but fairly priced.

Look up the Spanish or the Italian sections, for example, and you'll see there are plenty of appealing bottles at around £5 or under, and that the wines also scale the heights of great and glorious estates (Vega Sicilia Unico, anyone?). And the overall number of bottles is not overwhelming. All in all, it's tempting to call Geoff sensible, except that such a description doesn't really suit anyone who is passionate about wine. But Portland does exude a sense of being well-ordered and carefully considered – something we can't say about wine merchants in general.

All the major wine-producing areas of the world are covered by a keen range. This year, the Rhônes caught our eye (Chapoutier, Jaboulet, Guigal), as did the Italian wines (from the stars of Piedmont to everyday quaffing reds from Puglia). Spain is another strong suit, and from Chile there is a plethora of fine producers (Cousiño Macul, Montes, Casablanca, Casa Lapostelle . . .). And if you're a Mancunian, don't miss Portland's tutored tastings, wine fairs, wine and dine events, all advertised in the Portland Wine Press newsletter.

Look out for
- Fair prices across the full range
- High-quality Spanish wines from La Rioja Alta, Reyes, Guelbenzu, among others
- Wide sweep of Italy's most appealing wines, both glamorous (Piedmont) and down-to-earth (Puglia)
- Upper Loire taken seriously
- Stunning Bordeaux set, including older wines.

Arthur Rackham Emporia

216 London Road, Guildford,
Surrey GU4 7YS

Tel (0870) 870 1110
Fax (0870) 870 1120
Email info@ar-emporia.com
Website www.ar-emporia.com

Open Mon–Sat 10–9, Sun, public holidays 11–7 **Cards** Amex, Delta, Diners, MasterCard, Switch, Visa; personal and business accounts **Discount** 10% on 1 mixed case **Delivery** Free nationwide (min. order £100) **Glass hire** Available, phone for details **Tastings and talks** Available, phone or visit website for details **£5**

Arthur Rackham has undergone a re-launch since the last edition of the *Guide*: it has added 'Emporia' to its title, the smart new name coinciding with a refit of the shop and the arrival of the website. We haven't seen the results of these new ventures yet (the website is being launched just as we write), but the quality of the wines on the list looks to be as good as ever.

Affordability is the name of the game here – but take a look at the Bordeaux listings and don't be surprised to see a fair smattering of quality options too: not only *cru classé* wines, but some carefully chosen 'second label' wines too – the likes of Amiral de Beychevelle (second wine of Château Beychevelle) and La Croix St-Estèphe (second wine of Le Crock) are almost identical to those of the top label and shouldn't be missed. Burgundy and Rhône choices tend to be sourced from larger *négociants*, which are sound, but not so much to get excited about. We'd be keener instead to dip into the southern French section, where there are a plethora of new-wave family domaines to discover – at half the price of course. It is also heartening to see, a determined selection of quality German Rieslings on offer.

Look out for
- Tannat and Trebbiano from the irrepressible Pisano brothers in Uruguay
- Top South African estates Thelema, Meerlust and Hamilton-Russell
- Broad-ranging fizz selection taking in Ruinart Rosé and Krug 1989 champagne, Pipers Brook Pirie from Tasmania and Cloudy Bay Pelorus from New Zealand
- Organic white wines from Bordeaux (from Château Richard and A Piroux)
- Southern French red blends of 'wild' Mediterranean grapes such as Carignan and Cinsault
- First-class Spanish choices from Vega Sicilia, Santa Eulalia and Rioja Alta.

Raeburn Fine Wines

Head office
21–23 Comely Bank Road, Edinburgh EH4 1DS   *Tel* 0131-343 1159
    Fax 0131-332 5166

Cellars
The Vaults, 4 Giles Street, Leith,   *Tel* 0131-554 2652
Edinburgh EH6 6DJ   *Email* sales@raeburnfinewines.com
    Website www.raeburnfinewines.com

Open (Shop) Mon–Sat 9.30–6, Sun 12.30–5, public holidays 10.30–4; (Cellars open by appointment only) **Closed** 25 & 26 Dec, 1 & 2 Jan **Cards** Amex, Delta, MasterCard, Switch, Visa; personal and business accounts **Discount** 2.5% on 1 mixed case, 5% on 1 mixed case **Delivery** Free within 10-mile radius (min. 1 case); nationwide service, charged at cost **Glass hire** Free with order **Tastings and talks** Available, phone for details **£5**

There are so many comings and goings at Comely Bank Road that it's difficult to keep track of the exact state of the wines in stock, and the list only serves as a momentary snapshot. The website's helpful, a little more up to date. But the best way to get to grips here is to make an appointment and visit the Edinburgh vaults yourself – that, and get on the mailing list. The main aim at Raeburn is not to supply plentiful quantities of everything from anywhere but to focus on small-scale quality. (Here's to that!) 'We are always looking for the best and are prepared to take on younger producers who are "on the way up",' says buyer Zubair Mohamed.

The list launches confidently into Austria, for starters; this country's wines are little seen, often misunderstood but frequently delicious. As with every section, Zubair gives plenty of regional colour before outlining the wines themselves, describing vintage conditions and cellar potential. From Burgundy, choices extend to Méo-Camuzet, Henri Jayer, Clos du Tart, Leflaive and Henri Gouges, while Bordeaux covers the famous likes of châteaux Latour, l'Angélus, Le Pin and Léoville-Barton.

The 'on the way up' producers take in Le Prieuré de St-Jean de Bébian and Domaine Gauby from Languedoc – both seriously good – and Ashton Hills, Galah Wines and Rusden, new from Australia. Given the quality it's of little surprise to see the majority of this list hovering at or above the £20 a bottle mark (and there are some a lot higher), but there's also plenty to be had for under a tenner. So all intrepid wine enthusiasts need not despair, this is certainly the place to come for some vinous adventure.

Look out for
- Shafer, Rochioli and Joseph Swan California wines
- Chapoutier, Gilles Barge and Jean-Louis Chave northern Rhône classics
- Tangy Austrian Grüner Veltliner from Emmerich Knoll, F X Pichler and Willi Bründlmayer
- Châteauneuf-du-Pape from Château de Beaucastel and Clos des Papes
- Top Loire Vouvray, Le Haut Lieu from Huet-Pinguet
- Bodega Infinitus: Argentina's finest from northern Patagonia.

La Réserve

Head office
7 Grant Road, Battersea, London SW11 2NU

Tel 020-7978 5601
Fax 020-7978 4934

Knightsbridge
56 Walton Street, London SW3 1RB

Tel 020-7589 2020
Fax 020-7581 0250

Hampstead
29 Heath Street, London NW3 6TR

Tel 020-7435 6845
Fax 020-7431 9301

Fulham
203 Munster Road, London SW6 6BX

Tel 020-7381 6930
Fax 020-7385 5513
Email realwine@la-reserve.co.uk
Website www.la-reserve.co.uk

Open Varies between stores, phone for times **Cards** Amex, Delta, MasterCard, Switch, Visa; personal accounts **Discount** 5% on 1 case, negotiable on larger orders **Delivery** Free within Central London (min. 1 case); nationwide service, charge £7.50 per case, free for orders of £200+ **Glass hire** Free with order **Tastings and talks** Tastings, wine courses and dinners, phone for details

A well-planned, well-presented list with lashings of confidence about it. Wine buyer Mark Reynier's informative commentary on each of the regions puts you right in the picture, and leaves you in little doubt that he has inside knowledge of how to get hold of the best. In fact, such are the prestigious allocations at La Réserve that it's hard to believe this merchant was only established in 1988. Look out for precious burgundies from de Vogüé, Marquis d'Angerville and Domaine de la Romanée-Conti to see what we mean.

This kind of style doesn't just apply to the classic regions. The motivation behind the French Regional selection is impressive too: 'What is the point of having a glass of French Country red or white, only to have it taste like any other Australian or Chilean fruit bomb?' asks Mark. Quite right too. The team has carefully selected plenty of the original local grape varieties (such as red Lledoner Pelut and white Picpoul) and characterful appellations (Montpeyroux, La Clape and Coteaux Varois) to represent this region – there are many Cabernet and Chardonnay choices too, but all with a local twist. This sort of thorough approach means that when it comes to the old and rare vintages, there just isn't enough space to list them all – for these, La Réserve suggests you contact it directly.

There are now five La Réserve outlets in total, all in typically classy London locations – Milroys of Soho was purchased in 2001 and still keeps up appearances as a world-renowned whisky specialist.

And we can't pass up the chance to mention the excellent programme of tastings imparting 'What you really need to know rather than the peripheral boring stuff'. These are demonstrated with 'proper top quality wines' but shown in a down-to-earth, unstuffy manner, covering everything from how to taste, to Ornellaia and Masseto top acts from Italy. (Incidentally, the tastings come with a warning not to wear perfume or aftershave: good move!) The enthusiastic staff at La Réserve are all employed because they know how to sell, but they're not going to sting you (even though they could, with a 1996 600cl bottle of Château L'Evangil costing £795). Instead, all efforts are made to marry the right wine with the right customer; they have plenty on sale at under a fiver if that's your remit.

Look out for

- Fashionable American Syrah from Mount Veeder, Alban Vineyards and Ridge
- Pudding wines from luscious Sauternes to sumptuous Schloss Vollrads *Eiswein*
- Top Italian Barolos from Conterno, Vietti, Voerzio and Revello
- Get-it-while-you-still-can 1996 red burgundy from Bonnes Mares, de Vogüé, Laurent and Tardy
- Near-perfect snapshot of Alsace: Rieslings from Trimbach, Kientzler, Pinot Gris from Bott-Geyl, and more
- Magnums of Château Pétrus at £665 should you wish them.

Howard Ripley

25 Dingwall Road, London SW18 3AZ

Tel 020-8877 3065
Fax 020-8877 0029
Email info@howardripley.com
Website www.howardripley.com

Open Mon–Sun 8–10 **Cards** None accepted **Discount** Not available **Delivery** Nationwide service (min. 1 case), charge £9.50 per order, free for orders of £500+ **Glass hire** Not available **Tastings and talks** Regular winemaker dinners, tastings by arrangement

---

Not only is this one of the best places to buy fine burgundy but there's now a thoroughly dashing selection of German wines too. And despite the latter being the ultimate in Rieslings – from estates such as JJ Prüm, Willi Schaefer and Selbach-Oster – you can pick up a bottle for less than a tenner (well, you'll need to fill a case of such bottles, but . . .). The brightest and best wines are all here, but also more modest ones from the same reliable growers – plus the maturing wines from a few vintages ago.

It is still the stunning range of burgundies, however, that is the main event here. Approach this subject from whatever angle you will, you won't be disappointed. Like the top growers? They're all here, if you have a healthy wallet to match. Interested in seeking out top vintages? You'll find plenty of 1996s for a start. Keen to try the same village from a variety of growers? Howard has nearly 60 domaines to choose from, and picking up a case of 12 different Chambolle-Musignys (for example) wouldn't be a problem. Want to try out the less prestigious/more affordable estates? Dig around among this lot and you won't leave empty-handed. It's particularly good to see the whole range from each of the growers, illustrating all of their skills – for instance, you can try Vosne-Romanée from Anne Gros, but also her Richebourg and straight Bourgogne too. Very few other merchants have a wide enough range to make this possible. Don't forget the range of German goodies on offer; and keep a lookout too for the regular wine dinners and occasional tastings, as these are more than informative.

As we've said before, your wallet may regret your making an acquaintance with this merchant – and it'll tremble particularly hard when you get to the till, as Howard and fellow buyer Sebastian Thomas still haven't had the decency to add VAT to the list prices – but your palate will certainly forgive you. And you can always do business over the website if you think your knees will give out with the shock.

Look out for

- Two or three new domaines each year from each region
- Leflaive, Leroy and Roumier – for full-on, biodynamic burgundies
- Crisp, clear Corton from Bonneau du Martray, René Lequin-Colin and Domaine Rapet
- Sub-£12 burgundies, even from Vincent Girardin, Geantet-Pansiot and Frédéric Esmonin
- Twelve fabulous Mosel estates showing Riesling in all categories from *Kabinett* to *Auslese* and *Eiswein*
- Stylish new wines from the progressive Keller, Müller-Catoir and Mosbacher estates in Germany.

Roberson

348 Kensington High Street, London W14 8NS

Tel 020-7371 2121
Fax 020-7371 4010
Email wines@roberson.co.uk
Website www.roberson.co.uk

Open Mon–Sat 10–8 **Closed** Sun, public holidays **Cards** Amex, Delta, Diners, MasterCard, Switch, Visa; personal and business accounts **Discount** 5% on 1 mixed case, 10% on 1 unmixed case **Delivery** Free within Central London (min. 1 case); nationwide service, charge £12 for 1 case, £6 for each subsequent case **Glass hire** Free with order **Tastings and talks** Not available **£5**

Laurence Haywood, Hamish McLean and David Ball must have a fascinating time purchasing this tidy selection and, as buyers for Robersons, no doubt they get paid to do it, too. We can't imagine dealing with a more hedonistic selection of wines – the kind that most of us would dream of, and sample only on special birthdays, say. As we've said before, this is the Kensington wine shop of wealthy local film stars – who else could afford such prices?

Not that there's anything elite or unapproachable about the shop. Fashionably designed and smartly presented, yes, but there's plenty of airy space in which to peruse the shelves without feeling crowded or intimidated, and friendly advice on hand to assist in whatever you choose. The Bordeaux selection just about matches any wish-list imaginable, with vintages dating back to 1900 and bottles of first to fifth growth Médoc, Pomerol and St-Emilion. Burgundy choices are fractionally more down-to-earth, with big (but respectable) producers Girardin, Jadot and Drouhin bulking up the selection, but also with the illustrious likes of de Vogüé, Engel and Marquis d'Angerville. Look out for quality growers from the Loire (Dagueneau, de Ladoucette and Huet), a cluster of different Alsace producers and smart names from Italy, South Africa, Australia and

Champagne. But South America, North America and Spain fall into the 'could do better' categories for us.

You'll find that the crux of the matter when you visit Roberson is price. There are no bargains here – not even Italian Friuli makes it in under the £10 mark – but at least you can buy by the bottle; you don't have to buy a case-load. And you can be guaranteed there's no mediocrity, but quality all the way.

Look out for

- Delicious Tuscan choices from Antinori, Montevertine and Tenuta San Guido
- Top-quality dessert wines: Austrian *Trockenbeerenauslesen* and Hungarian Tokaji
- Best Australian white wines: Petaluma Tiers Chardonnay, Henschke Louis Semillon and Leeuwin Art Series Riesling
- Bordeaux' classics Montrose, Margaux and Mouton-Rothschild from 1990; Troplong-Mondot and Clos de l'Oratoire St-Emilions from 1989
- Champagne from Gosset 1993 to Krug 1989, and Nebuchadnezzars of Moët non-vintage
- Barbadillo and Lustau sherries (manzanilla and oloroso).

Safeway Stores

Head office

Safeway House, 6 Millington Road, Hayes,   *Tel* 020-8848 8744
Middlesex UB3 4AY   *Fax* 020-8573 1865
(480 branches nationwide)   *Email* safewaypressoffice@btclick.com
       Website www.safeway.co.uk

Open Mon–Sat 8–8, Sun, public holidays 10–4 (times vary between stores) **Closed** 25 Dec, Easter Sun **Cards** Delta, MasterCard, Switch, Visa **Discount** 5% on 1 case of 6 **Delivery** Not available **Glass hire** Available, deposit required **Tastings and talks** Available, phone local store for details

---

First, a few words of praise for the way Safeway is attempting to tackle a major drawback for most supermarket wine departments – the lack of knowledgeable staff. In 2002, the chain (the fourth largest of the UK supermarkets) has been busily educating its staff in all matters vinous, with 330 potential wine advisers embarking on a 12-week training programme, a scheme developed along similar lines as the WSET (Wine and Spirit Education Trust) Certificate. Around 100 of the top candidates will go on to take the WSET Higher Certificate, and the class swots of this lot will get to do the much more advanced Diploma. Sounds good, and something that could certainly improve the currently rather hollow experience of shopping for supermarket wine – but as yet it's a little early to say how successful the initiative will be. (Do let us know if you get anywhere quizzing Safeway staff about wine over the next 12 months and we'll report back in the next *Guide*!)

However, we have no doubts about praising Safeway's wines for their wide-ranging appeal. Here you'll find around 825 lines, offering something for everyone, from tiny bottles of cheap German Liebfraumilch (£1.49 for 25cl), through legions of own-label quaffers at around £4, to the likes of serious Australian Chardonnay (Penfolds Yattarna, £39.99) and mellow, traditional Spanish red (Murrieta's Ygay 1989 at £19.99, and worth every penny).

The richest pickings are to be had among the comprehensive range of Australian wines (a pretty exciting lot, with over 110 to choose from), the great-value Hungarian selection, and the fizz – Safeway's own-label Albert Etienne is the best supermarket champagne around, we reckon. At a recent tasting the non-vintage was offered from magnums and was quite exquisite (and only £27.49 for 1.5 litres). Party planners, take note.

Other wines that showed particularly well on that occasion included the La Nature Torrontés (a fresh and zesty organic white from Argentina; £4.49), Santa Rita Chilean Chardonnay (£6.49), Annie's Lane Semillon from Clare Valley, Australia (£6.99), Vina Morande Syrah (great value at £4.79), Bela Fonte Jaen (a minty, redcurrant-packed red from Portugal that did well in a recent *Which?* tasting; £4.99), Fairview Malbec from South Africa (£6.29) and – more glorious, this – Tedeschi's Amarone 1998, rich and velvety with dark chocolate depths (£13.99). Just some indication of Safeway's wide sweep of wine styles.

Not everything is inspiring, and one can only hope that in the future Safeway's talented buyers get to take a few more risks – such as weeding out more of the nasties that still crop up here and there in corners of each store. There's still a little too much Niersteiner, Cypriot fortified and own-label Lambrusco, and too many cheapish big brands from California, for our liking.

Particularly interesting to note is Safeway's continued enthusiasm for inexpensive, dry, fresh, spicy whites – from Hungary, England, Austria (Grüner Veltliner features), Italy, Argentina – a particular style of wine that this store has always done very well. All in all, then, a supermarket that continues to impress, and which very nearly wrested our Best Supermarket Award from Waitrose this year.

Look out for

- Fine champagnes, including highly recommended own-label Albert Etienne
- Value-for-money whites from Hungary (try the spicy Woodcutter's White)
- Upmarket Spanish reds including Faustino, Marqués de Murrieta, Cosme Palacio . . .
- Serious Australian selection – the best value being between the £6 and £10 price points
- Tasty, well-priced South American bottles from Cono Sur, Errázuriz, 35 South
- Strong selection of organic wines
- Better-than-average claret at under £10.

Sainsbury's Supermarkets

Head office
33 Holborn,
London EC1N 2HT
(430 stores throughout UK and Northern Ireland)

Tel 020-7695 6000
Fax 020-7695 7610

Website www.sainsburys.co.uk

Open Mon–Fri varies between stores, Sat 8–10, Sun 10–4 **Closed** 25 & 26 Dec **Cards**
Amex, Delta, Diners, MasterCard, Switch, Visa **Discount** 5% on 6 bottles **Delivery**
Not available **Glass hire** Free, deposit required **Tastings and talks** In-store tastings,
talks available on request

The mad-keen buying team of six full-time wine-hunters (two Masters of
Wine among them – Justin Howard-Sneyd and Laura Jewell) is led, as ever,
by veteran Sainsbury's man Allan Cheesman, who lacks no passion for this
game. Thanks to Allan and the team, Sainsbury's has over 700 wines in stock
– and the bigger stores out there (30–40 per cent of the total) carry them all.

Equipped with these facts, we began our 2003 review of this supermarket
with high hopes – but on launching into the wine list, the first few pages
made rather depressing reading. Bordeaux is renowned for being good here,
but regular appearances of bulk-supplier names such as Calvet, Dourthe and
Mouton-Cadet, did rather fill us with gloom . . . maybe things will pep up
next year with the arrival of more from the luscious 2000 vintage. However,
the burgundy listings told a similar story of mass production, and while we
know that, when we try them, some of these wines are perfectly palatable,
we're also very aware that they're singularly unexciting. It was only when
we turned to the Rhône page and saw the name Guigal that we began to
wake up a bit, and although this was the only point of interest in the Rhône
range, what followed was better. As we're beginning to find out, the South
of France is a hot-bed of new quality and Sainsbury's is tapping into it (good
for them) like there's no tomorrow.

From southern Italy, where there's a similar story of rejuvenation, there
are some equally exciting wines listed, and while we'd recommend swiftly
passing the Germany, Bulgaria, Romania, and even Australia and California,
shelves while in the store (again, nothing but bulk brands), we'd still be
more than happy to spend a quiet few minutes or so perusing the Chilean,
New Zealand and South African sections. Now why can't all the other wine
regions be approached with such imagination?

Last year we were looking for more zest in the Sainsbury's range, but
unfortunately this time round it still seems somewhat lacking. But at least
this is somewhere to pick up a reliably flavourful wine at a sound price.
Watch out for astonishingly good reductions, with plenty of everyday wines
under the £5 mark – particularly the cut-price Sainsbury's own-label wines.
Don't miss the in-store tastings (Sainsbury's off-licence managers – there are
50 of them – will also give talks to the public if requested), or the no-fee
Drinks Club, whereby customers receive a quarterly magazine and money-
off coupons.

One other positive thing: according to the team, there's been a significant
drop in the number of people buying Chardonnay, so to accommodate this,
there's now a plethora of other varietal wines from the New World. A warm

welcome to South African Sauvignon, Australian Verdelho and Semillon, and Californian Viognier.

Look out for

- Uruguayan Tannat: big wine at a deliciously low price
- £4.99 sparkling wines, and Sainsbury's own-label champagne (made by Duval-Leroy) for only £7.99
- Delicious Moroccan reds – and other good things from the Mediterranean
- Choice of over 20 globally sourced organic wines.

Selfridges

400 Oxford Street, London W1A 1AB	*Tel* 020-7318 3730
	Fax 020-7318 3730
1 Exchange Square, Manchester M13 1BD	*Tel* (0870) 837 7377
1 The Dome, Trafford Centre, Manchester M17 8DA	*Tel* (0870) 837 7377
	Email wine.club@selfridges.co.uk
	Website www.selfridges.co.uk

Open Mon–Fri 10–8, Sat 9.30–8, Sun 12–6, public holidays 10–6 **Closed** 25 Dec
Cards Amex, Delta, Diners, MasterCard, Switch, Visa; Selfridges Card **Discount** 8.5% on 1 case (10% for Selfridges Card holders) **Delivery** Nationwide service, charge £10 per order (UK mainland only), £5 within M25 **Glass hire** Not available **Tastings and talks** Twice-weekly tastings, tutored tastings every 2 months **(£5)**

Andrew Willy, Selfridges' wine buyer since 1996, has built up 'one of the most comprehensive wine lists we know of', as the *Guide* described it last year. Looking at the range he has assembled most recently, we see no reason to change our mind. A key word to describe the wines must be 'quality': this is a collection that oozes class. Andrew even claims it offers the largest selection of Krug champagne in the land (older vintages available on request), and you don't get much classier than that.

From the wonderful Western Australian wines to the collectable California offerings (Screaming Eagle 1997 is £2,300 a *bottle*, if you're interested); from Super-Tuscans to fine and rare claret galore, this is a very sophisticated range indeed. If you're after a desirable, top-notch wine from a leading producer (think Cloudy Bay, Grange, Pétrus, Domaine de la Romanée-Conti), then there's a high chance that Andrew has got it at Selfridges.

But if it's a cheap bottle of plonk you want, this is probably not the place to come. A (very) few bottles hover around the £5 mark, but that's not a price point that counts for too much here. Not all the tags are terrifying though – it's fair to say you can go to Selfridges with £10 to spend on one bottle and easily find something from most regions. And that includes wines from Lebanon, Greece, Switzerland and England (there are six from the excellent Chapel Down to choose from here). So it appears that Andrew is not just sticking to the straight, narrow and widely acclaimed, but is daring to be different too.

It's good to see a decent choice of quality half bottles, and a seductively long set of port and sherry, madeira and even Marsala. Selfridges' shoppers might also be interested to know that there's a free wine club, which offers invitations to tastings (presumably of upmarket wines) and gives out details of special offers.

Look out for

- Extensive choice of fine Australian wines, particularly from South and Western Australia
- Highly fashionable New Zealand producers Cloudy Bay, Seresin, Isabel, Neudorf
- Valuable California collectors' items
- Worthwhile set of organic wines
- Impressive fine and rare Bordeaux – red and sweet
- Serious sherry from Valdespino, Lustau, Barbadillo.

Somerfield Stores

Head office
Somerfield House, Whitchurch Lane,   *Tel* 0117-935 9359
Bristol BS14 0TJ   *Fax* 0117-978 0629
(590 branches nationwide)   *Email* customer.service@somerfield.co.uk
                                            Website www.somerfield.co.uk

Open Mon–Fri 8–6, Sat 8–8, Sun, public holidays 10–4 (times may vary between stores)
Closed 25 Dec, Easter Sun **Cards** Amex, Delta, Diners, MasterCard, Switch, Visa
Discount 5% on 6 bottles **Delivery** Available within 10-mile radius, phone local stores
for details **Glass hire** Not available **Tastings and talks** Monthly in-store tastings in
some stores

Angela Mount joined Somerfield as wine buying controller in 1991, with a remit to build a credible and strongly focused, quality wine range for the company, and in this she has been tremendously successful.

Last year we were as full of praise for these efforts as we are now, but we wondered if, alongside the cheerfully priced wines in the (main) sub-£5 sector, Somerfield would now start to encourage people to trade up and try out different wine regions that might be a little more expensive. In answer, Angela tells us this year: 'We have increased the average spend per bottle considerably, by focusing on promotions of higher price points. Our focus has been on supplying the very best quality across the range, but particularly in building a broader selection of £5-to-£7 wines. Italy, South Africa and South America are our key strengths.'

2002 saw the launch of Somerfield's 'City Fresh' stores – more upmarket, fresh foods-oriented, small city stores – plus the revamp and relaunch of others, to create 'Premium Stores'. All this requires a wider and better selection of premium wine. To this tune, we've spotted £7.99 Chablis from that smartest of co-ops, La Chablisienne; £5.99 Cave de Turkheim Gewurztraminer d'Alsace; and Errázuriz Chilean Chardonnay at £5.99. Plus smart reds such as Barolo I Firmati (1997 vintage), Spice Route Pinotage from South Africa and Châteauneuf-du-Pape Les Clefs de St-Pierre from the southern Rhône. These are all wines that we wouldn't usually expect to see on a supermarket shelf. Other advances in the range over the last year have included the introduction of more reliable synthetic closures, to avoid the disappointment caused by a tainted cork.

You can still expect to benefit from the down-to-earth, straightforward price-enticement at Somerfield. You can still pick up a £1.49 bottle of Lambrusco or a £1.99 non-vintage Moscato Fizz (good old Italy!).

Look out for

- Cono Sur classic Pinot Noir from Chile (plus Carmenère, Merlot and Cabernet from a good variety of other growers)
- Charles Back's Goats do Roam red and white from South Africa
- Sparkling wine from £1.99 to £29.99 (Moscato to Moët's 1995 vintage champagne)
- LA Cetto's Petite Sirah from Mexico, and other oddities such as Australian *botrytis* Riesling and Spanish Moscatel de Valencia
- Primitivo from Italy's deep south.

Sommelier Wine Company

The Grapevine, 23 St George's Esplanade,   *Tel* (01481) 721677
St Peter Port, Guernsey GY1 2BG   *Fax* (01481) 716818

Open Mon–Thur 10–5.30, Fri 10–6, Sat 9.30–5.30 **Closed** Sun, public holidays **Cards** MasterCard, Switch, Visa; personal and business accounts **Discount** 5% on 1 mixed case **Delivery** Free throughout Guernsey (min. 1 case) **Glass hire** Free **Tastings and talks** Monthly winemaker dinners, talks on request **(£5)**

In our view, Richard Allisette and Richard Mathews have all it takes to succeed in the difficult world of independent wine selling. Pity not everyone feels the same: after 12 years, 'my mother still wishes I would get a proper job,' jokes Richard A, adding modestly that this is 'still a hobby that has snowballed into a commercial business'.

Their 'hobby' now offers a choice of hundreds of wines – the well-written and informative list we received stretched to nearly 150 large pages. It is the sort of list that is hard to put down, packed as it is with seriously good stuff (this merchant won our Fine Wine Specialist Award last year). And prices are particularly keen, partly because there is no duty on wines in the Channel Islands.

Highlights are the Loire (Sancerre is taken seriously, as is Muscadet, for once) and Chablis. We reckon the two Richards buy in lots of dry white to wash down the Guernsey seafood on hot summer days; perhaps that's also why there are over 20 rosés listed. Then there are some great Spanish and Italian reds and whites, a truly enticing range of Australian Rieslings, inspiring burgundies, superb South African reds and an extremely classy California collection. In most sections, the choice is wide but succinct enough not to become unwieldy, and prices range nicely from well under £5 to around £20 and more in some sections. Oh, and there is a welcome number of less-well-known producers – and a distinct lack of the very big brands.

Look out for

- Bossard, Henry Pellé from the Loire
- Burgundies galore – ask to see more than is on display in the shop

- Italian stars from Pieropan and Jermann
- Stunning Australian wines including many unusual grape varieties
- From Australia, St Hallett, Yarra Yering, Primo Estate and Henschke, plus lots of other, lesser-known estates
- More New World gems from South Africa (Fairview, Beyerskloof, Steenberg, Spice Route) and California (Ridge, Saintsbury, Newton).

Sunday Times Wine Club

see Laithwaites

Swig

5 & 6 Roxby Place, London SW6 1RU

Tel 020-7903 8311
Fax 020-7903 8313
Email imbibe@swig.co.uk
Website www.swig.co.uk

Open Mon–Fri 9–6 **Closed** Sat, Sun, public holidays **Cards** Amex, Delta, MasterCard, Switch, Visa; business accounts **Discount** Not available **Delivery** Free within M25 (min. 1 case); nationwide service, charge £10 per order **Glass hire** Not available **Tastings and talks** Range of tastings, phone for details **(£5)**

We still think it's a shame that Robin Davis closed the Swig shop in Haverstock Hill, but – after four years of working weekends, early mornings and evenings to keep it all going – we can quite understand why. From what we see, the mail-order business that's replaced it is equally energetic and far-reaching, so it's not as if there's now a glaring gap on the wine map of London. It's just a pity that there's not quite the freedom there was in the past at this outlet. The minimum purchase is now one case – which you may be able to divide into two batches of six if you select the right wines.

Choose from the Rhône, Italy or South Africa, however, and you won't be disappointed, as these are Swig specialities. We're particularly impressed by the range from the Cape, but then Robin and his partner Damon Quinlan took over the South African Wine Centre not so long ago, due to the owner's retirement, so they got off to a good start. Thelema, Kanonkop, Rust en Vrede, Vergelegen, Rustenberg, Neil Ellis, Meerlust and Veenwouden are all names that a couple of other self-professed Cape specialists mentioned in this *Guide* would do well to include. And what we also like about this range is the detailed tasting notes and property profile that come with each wine – but then this is the case in every section.

We notice that Swig has expanded on its three specialities this year: look out for new choices from Alsace, Burgundy, Australia and California – not enormous ranges, but of undoubted quality. 'We're passionate about finding good wine to sell to good people who enjoy it,' says Damon, and limiting their trade to mail-order only has obviously enabled the wine buying here to become considerably more adventurous.

Look out for

- Website and monthly/bimonthly newsletter updates
- A trio of Super-Tuscans: Brancaia, Casalferro and Flaccianello

- Rhône wines from André Perret, St-Cosme, Roger Sabon and Domaine du Vieux Télégraphe
- Full selection of *premier cru* Nuits St-George red burgundy
- Low-priced, mixed-case offers (two bottles of six different wines).

T & W Wines

51 King Street, Thetford, Norfolk IP24 2AU

Tel (01842) 765646
Fax (01842) 766407
Email contact@tw-wines.com
Website www.tw-wines.com

Open Mon–Fri 9.30–5.30, Sat 9.30–1 **Closed** Sun, public holidays **Cards** Amex, Delta, MasterCard, Switch, Visa; personal and business accounts **Discount** Not available **Delivery** Free within 15-mile radius (min. 1 case); nationwide service, free for 2+ cases, otherwise phone for details of charges **Glass hire** Free with order **Tastings and talks** Available, phone for details **£5**

Another of those quality East Anglian wine merchants, in Thetford this time, with a quirky approach all its own. Here at T&W be prepared to view a staggeringly large array of wines, focusing mostly on France but with imaginative forays into Australia and California (Far Niente, Silver Oak Cellars, Patz & Hall). Don't overlook the Austrian and German selections either. 'People are looking for quality rather than the least expensive wine they can find,' says Trevor Hughes, managing director and wine buyer, and this reflects the accent throughout the list.

The wines are presented in their own rather eccentric order – Alsace, Spain, Italy, Rhône – and prices are scattered, rather than in the usual ascending ranks. But who wants to be 'usual'? Not Trevor, that's for sure. And perhaps his odd order for things means you're more likely to stumble on something you weren't expecting – indeed, we were happy after the Italy section to come across a hefty selection of biodynamic wines (27 in all), made with the greatest possible respect to the surrounding *terroir*. The other odd but brilliant option here is the 'A Taste Of . . .' selections. In 'A Taste of South-west France', for example, you can pick up an £83.05 case of four different red wines (three bottles each) that will give an idea what to expect from Provence, Corbières and the Frontonnais. Look out for similar 'get to know you' options from areas such as Alsace, the Loire and Austria.

You'll also find a lot of older, well-chosen vintages. As Trevor explains: 'The greatest possible care is taken in selecting old wines. I never buy from auction. With younger wines I import wherever possible direct from the producer. Quality, not price, is my purchasing criterion.'

The only thing we would complain about, again, is that all prices are listed ex-VAT, which is terribly inconvient for those of us putting our imaginary caseful together (or even a single bottle purchase) as we know there'll always be a shock when we get to the till. But otherwise, we admire this chunky, original list tremendously and always look forward to its landing on our doormat with the inevitable hefty thud!

Look out for

- Wide-ranging, annual bin-end list, full of half, bottle and magnum end-of-range wines
- 'A Passion for Burgundy', including top domaines Olivier Leflaive and Romanée-Conti, Rossignol-Trapet, Jean Thevenet and more
- Fabulous Italian wines from Bava, Gaja and Giulio Cocchi
- Domaine Huet, Charles Joguet, Didier Dagueneau and Domaine des Baumard from the Loire Valley
- Top Rhône estates Guigal, Gripa, Château Rayas and Jean-Luc Colombo
- Colourful property profiles, full of detail and 'how the wines are made' information for each region.

Tanners Wines

Head office

26 Wyle Cop, Shrewsbury, Shropshire SY1 1XD	*Tel* (01743) 234455
	Fax (01743) 234501
4 St Peter's Square, Hereford HR1 2PG	*Tel* (01432) 272044
	Fax (01432) 263316
36 High Street, Bridgnorth, Shropshire WV16 4DB	*Tel* (01746) 763148
	Fax (01746) 769798

Warehouse Shop — *Tel* (01938) 552542
Severn Farm Enterprise Park, Welshpool, — *Fax* (01938) 556565
Powys SY21 7DF
Email sales@tanners-wines.co.uk
Website www.tanners-wines.co.uk

Open (Shrewsbury) Mon–Sat 9–6, Sun 10–4 (Dec only); (Hereford & Bridgnorth) Mon–Sat 9–5.30 **Closed** Sun (exc. Dec, Shrewsbury), public holidays **Cards** Amex, Delta, MasterCard, Switch, Visa; personal accounts **Discount** Available, phone for details **Delivery** Free within 70-mile radius; nationwide service, charge £5.95, free for orders of £80+ **Glass hire** Free if returned clean **Tastings and talks** Range available including tutored tastings with producers, phone for details (£5)

Tanners has one of the best-presented and most useful wine lists we know of – a neat, pocket-sized booklet crammed with clearly set-out producer profiles, wine tasting notes, 'ready to drink' codes, prices per bottle and per case (inc VAT), symbols to denote 'environmentally friendly wines'; and more besides. It's also packed with one of the widest ranges of wine available.

'The quality of the product is paramount to us,' says James Tanner. 'We are not hidebound to sell wines from any particular areas or producers since we hold no agencies. So we are free to sell what we like.' And we like the wines he likes. From Bordeaux to Bulgaria and from Sancerre to South Africa, the Tanners team aims to dig out choices that are accurate representations of their landscape, however far-flung or unusual the region of origin might be – Douro reds from Portugal, French mountain wines from Savoie, or wines from the Valais in Switzerland and 'Baja California' in Mexico being some of the rarer offerings. 'We travel a lot seeking out new suppliers,' adds James, '. . . preferably smaller, family domaines who operate with an eye to the environment'.

The Tanners team is also highly traditional (having been established in these Dickensian premises since 1872), with *en primeur* Bordeaux and new vintage burgundies, old stocks of fine vintages (clarets from the 1970s, 1980s and 1990s) and newer Rhône wines to lay down. Unsurprisingly, France is something of a speciality, and James and team know where to look to find the best prices. And if it's oddments you're into, then contact Tanners directly for its 'Oddments List' of interesting small-parcel wines – and if the wine you're looking for isn't listed, they'll seek it out for you. That's traditional service.

Also included in the service are seven newsletters per year; spring tasting events spanning two nights (with visiting winemakers), plus other tasting events in November. And, at the time of writing, the Tanners website promises to be up and running for web orders soon. With all this 'ear-to-the-ground' action, Tanners has noticed its customers returning to France, rejecting brands, and even investigating the over-£10 bracket. (Whatever next!) We end as James ends his wine list, with a quote from John Ruskin: 'When you pay too little you sometimes lose everything, because the thing you bought is incapable of doing the thing it was bought to do.' Quite.

Look out for

- Bio-conscious wines from everywhere: Germany's top Mosel sites, Australia's Clare Valley, Coteaux du Languedoc, Burgundy, and many more
- Good-value 'mixed dozens': interesting red and white wine cases priced at £59 and £69
- Quality Bordeaux, from châteaux d'Angludet (Margaux) to Yquem (Sauternes)
- Super-Tuscans and Sicilians: fashionable Italian choices
- Forty different champagne options, and 16 cut-price sparklers from elsewhere
- Sixty-eight 'everyday drinking' wines at under £5 a bottle.

Tesco

Head office
Tesco House, PO Box 18, Delamare Road, *Tel* (0800) 505555
Cheshunt, Hertfordshire EN8 9SL *Email* customer.service@tesco.co.uk
Website www.tesco.com

Open Times vary between stores – many open 24 hours **Closed** 25 & 26 Dec, 1 Jan, Easter Sun **Cards** Amex, Delta, Diners, MasterCard, Switch, Visa **Discount** 5% on 6+ bottles **Delivery** Available within 20-minute journey time of local store, charge £5 per order **Glass hire** Not available **Tastings and talks** Not available

First, a big round of applause from the *Guide* to Tesco for championing screw-capped bottles. In Spring 2002 the supermarket launched 26 new red and white wines sealed with screw-caps, at prices ranging from £3.99 to £8.99. No, they weren't all old-fashioned Liebfraumilch and Lambruscos – most of them were modern, even trendy, styles of wine such as New Zealand Sauvignon Blanc and Australian Shiraz blends.

It was difficult to predict how well these would fare. Although many in the wine trade (the *Guide*'s authors included) strongly believe screw-caps should be used more widely while cork taint remains rampant, it is also true that the wine-buying public associates screw-caps with cheap, low-quality wine. So we watched with interest. Ten weeks later, Tesco announced sales in the region of a whopping 1.5 million bottles across the screw-cap range. It's too much to suggest that everyone buying these wines is making a stand against cork taint – but whatever the reason, the launch has been a big success. This could herald the arrival of many more screw-capped bottles, not only in Tesco but also in other retailers.

At the Spring 2002 Tesco tasting, the *Guide* rated several of the new screw-capped wines highly (the 'Unwind' South African Sauvignon Blanc, the Petit Chablis and the Jacob's Creek Dry Riesling, to name but three). Other notable hits were the strong set of organic wines on show, and, as ever, the Australian wines. Tesco buyer Phil Reedman actually lives in Australia, sourcing Antipodean wines to send back to Blighty. His efforts have paid off – if we were choosing a bottle in Tesco, the Australian and Kiwi sections are where we'd start looking.

If your eye is caught by a lot of silver on Tesco's shelves, you've come across the chain's 'Finest' range. This is a set of 65 wines – 'classics', according to the marketing bumpf – that is, supposedly, a special premium selection. Some of them live up to the description, but we've tasted a great many of them, and we don't think they all justify their high price tags (up to £17.99, though not all are this expensive). Tread carefully, is the message – the New World 'Finest' wines are perhaps the most reliable.

That said, we continue to be impressed by the range of Tesco wines, one from which nearly everyone will easily find something appealing. The cheaper and low-to-medium-priced wines are generally relatively good, and there's something typically soft, ripe and easy-drinking about Tesco's lower-priced reds.

Look out for

- Australian wines, from the easy-going Unwind Shiraz, to fine fare from Pipers Brook, Penfolds, Tim Adams, Chapel Hill
- Excellent champagnes, including Veuve Clicquot, Roederer and Krug, and the good-value tasty Paul Berthelot NV
- New Zealand gems by Lawson's Dry Hills, Millton Estate, Jackson Estate and Giesen
- Among a well-priced Cape selection, Beyers Truter's 'Finest' Pinotage, Fairview Goats do Roam, Winds of Change
- Good range of decent claret in top stores
- Inycon Chardonnay, Promessa Negroamaro, Tre Uve Ultima, examples of the best Italian buys.

Thos Peatling Fine Wines

Head office
Westgate House, Bury St Edmunds, Suffolk IP33 1QS   *Tel* (01284) 755948
Fax (01284) 714483

37–39 Little London, Long Sutton,   *Tel* (01406) 363233
Lincolnshire PE12 9LE   *Fax* (01406) 365654
Email sales@thospeatling.co.uk
Website www.thospeatling.co.uk

Open Mon–Fri 9–6, Sat 9–5   **Closed** Sun, public holidays   **Cards** Amex, Delta,
MasterCard, Switch, Visa; personal and business accounts   **Discount** Available, phone
for details   **Delivery** Local service within 30-mile radius (min. order £50), charge varies
with distance; nationwide service, charge £9.99 per case   **Glass hire** Free with order
Tastings and talks Regular tastings and talks, phone for details

This is a fairly 'sensible' wine list – as befits a traditional, old East Anglian
wine merchant – but behind the scenes there have been a few shake ups of
late. In spring 2000, Peatlings re-established itself as an independent
merchant for the first time since 1930. Since then the new team – led by
Nicholas Corke, who masterminded the buy-out from Greene King – has
worked hard on getting 'better and broader', and reasserting itself in its
traditional role. 'If we see a great wine we buy it straight away,' says
Nicholas. By doing this he has rejuvenated the stocks built up over many
years and, to this tune, we counted over 40 different vintages of fine and
rare wines; over 100 different clarets; and over 70 burgundies – all top notch.
Also such treasures as white Hermitage (including 1980s vintages) from the
Rhône, and Alsace wines from Trimbach, Hugel and Caves de Bennwihr. All
most impressive, and not unreasonably priced either, whether it's forking
out £550 for a bottle of 1961 Lafite or £24.99 for a bottle of Vieux Château
Certan 1992 Pomerol.

In terms of 'gaining life', the list of standard fare here still needs more
work. Last year we put in a call for more everyday wines from the Americas
and Spain, and things seem to be quietly improving. But, in general, we
could wish for a more exciting array of producers and grape varieties, with
some scope in the mid-price ranges for trading up. The Australian selection
is far more extensive, although, again, 'sensible'.

More detail on the wine list is still needed – giving some clues as to style
and to regional characters, perhaps – but it is pleasing to see that Peatlings
updates it every month. We also approve of the general sales attitude: 'If a
customer requests a wine we don't stock already, then we're happy to try
and get hold of it'. And the forthcoming collection of Swiss wines sounds
promising: this shows just the kind of adventurousness we were hoping for.

Look out for
- 1990 vintage champagne (a top year)
- Rare old bottles of vintage port (cellared, aged and ready to drink)
- Burgundies from Bonneau du Martray, Faiveley, Drouhin and Leflaive
- Delicious Australian sticky wines, from Campbells, Stanton & Killeen
  and Brown Brothers
- Rare old Bordeaux dating back to 1952

- Classic Australian Shiraz: Armagh from Jim Barry, Cape Mentelle and Simon Gilbert Wongalare.

Thresher Wine Shops

Head office

Enjoyment Hall, Bessemer Road, Welwyn Garden City,   *Tel* (01707) 387200
Hertfordshire AL7 1BL   *Fax* (01707) 387416
790 branches nationwide

Open Mon–Sat 10–10, Sun 11–10, public holidays 11–10 **Closed** 25 Dec **Cards** Amex,
Delta, MasterCard, Switch, Visa; personal and business accounts **Discount** Available,
phone for details **Delivery** Free within 10-mile radius (min. 1 case) **Glass hire** Free
with order **Tastings and talks** Tastings, lectures and wine fairs; phone for details

We asked the giant First Quench chain (the umbrella group that also incorporates **Victoria Wine**, **Wine Rack** and **Bottoms Up** stores) to tell us what it had been up to over the last 12 months, to which it replied in three words: 'Complete range review'. It added that it was 'revising store layouts and merchandising'. So, some rather big changes then. Last year we commented that the dust had still not settled on the Thresher–Victoria Wine merger, or on the buy-out in late 2000 of the company by Nomura International. This year that dust is still swirling furiously.

So we had a really close look at the current wine list (Summer/Autumn 2002). There aren't nearly as many clarets as there have been in the past at Thresher. It's been rationalised, big time, and that seems a shame. There are, however, still some rich pickings among the Rhône reds and Loire whites, and the regional French shelves are worth a visit for upfront, fruity, modern styles (anyone for Utter Bastard and Fat Bastard from the South of France?). The Spanish reds are an attractive, reliable lot, too, with the likes of Torres Sangredetoro, Faustino Riojas and Campo Viejo coming in at very fair prices.

But, in general, the European sections this year seem a bit scanty and uninspiring – there's certainly a lack of off-beat, quirky wines in here (despite the odd silly Bastard). It was only when we entered the New World section that we felt inspired to any degree. But even there, it's generally the big names that keep coming at you – a bunch of Rosemounts from Australia, plus Nottage Hill, Lindemans, Jacob's Creek, etc.; and Montana and Villa Maria dominate from New Zealand. It's not that these producers are poor (far from it in some cases), just that it would be good to see many more smaller, less well-known producers in there with them. As it is, the *Guide* would plump for The Willows Semillon as one exception to the rule among the big-name Australian wines. (This wine recently topped a *Which?* tasting of Australian whites.)

Chile throws up some more exciting choices, however. The Chilean reds section is a strong one at Thresher, with wines from a wide range of producers. And the chain 'does' California a lot better than many of the other large outlets, stocking bottles from Ironstone, J Lohr, Schug, Beringer, Fetzer and Bonterra, to name but six. It's good to see the West Coast being dealt with more thoroughly – a lot of California sections from major retailers have been very disappointing this year. As for champagne, many of the big names are here, but some smaller growers are desperately needed to give depth and choice to the list. But then, more exciting, off-beat wines, small parcels and maverick producers, are what this huge retailer needs all round.

Look out for

- Impressive California selection, featuring many top names and a wide variety of styles
- Wolf Blass, Pewsey Vale, The Willows, St Hallett from Australia
- Interesting regional French wines, both red and white, particularly from the South
- Well-priced Spanish reds from well-known and reputable producers
- Strong Chilean section – go for Errázuriz, Cono Sur, Valdivieso, Santa Rita.

Uncorked

Exchange Arcade, Broadgate, London EC2M 3WA   *Tel* 020-7638 5998
Fax 020-7638 6028
Email drink@uncorked.co.uk
Website www.uncorked.co.uk

Open Mon–Fri 10–6.30 **Closed** Sat, Sun, public holidays **Cards** Amex, Delta, Diners, MasterCard, Switch, Visa; personal and business accounts **Discount** 5% on 1 mixed case, 10% on 1 unmixed case **Delivery** Free within 1-mile radius; nationwide service, charge £8.50 + VAT for 1 case, £4.25 + VAT for each subsequent case, free for orders of £150+ **Glass hire** Free with order **Tastings and talks** 6 in-store tastings per year, others on request **(£5)**

This City of London set-up offers wine of quality, an impressive selection of vintages and an unstuffy attitude – despite the fact that it obviously deals only in the best. 'We cherry-pick the finest wines from the world's fine wine regions and sell them at competitive prices,' says buyer/assistant manager Andrew Rae (who is still only 30, with an Oddbins training behind him).

Uncorked has been up and running for eight years now, and in that time Jim Griffen, its founder, has let nothing stand still. An average of 350 new wines, not always widely known names, hit the shop shelves each year, and Jim expects his team to be on hand to tell customers all about them. He was pleased to announce the company's first ever *en primeur* Bordeaux campaign in 2001 (what better place to start than with the fabulous 2000 vintage), following which, things appear to have gone from strength to strength.

You can, though, walk into Uncorked with only a tenner in your hand and leave with something that'll match the pasta back home. And for Tuesday-night wines, there are plenty of half bottles – or even magnums. As befits its City location, the average bottle spend here is still high, at £15, but Andrew maintains that customers don't spend this amount indiscriminately; that they still look for value, which keeps the team on its toes. The availability of Burgundian treasures such as Domaine Leroy's Richebourg (£199 a bottle) and Leflaive's Bâtard-Montrachet (£125) is always going to bump up the average spend, too.

We should also mention that the second half of the Uncorked list is ex-VAT and by the case only. Here lie the most illustrious wines of the lot, mostly from recent vintages, and to be bought for laying down – or if you like, investment purposes. Watch out for the six annual, free-of-charge tastings – get on the mailing list and, along with the six new lists printed each year (to cope with the enormous amount of new wines coming in), you'll get to know the dates.

Look out for

- Antinori's Super-Tuscans, Tignanello and Solaia, by the case
- Top-class St-Emilions: La Tertre Rôteboeuf, Monbousquet, Bellisle-Mondot and Grand-Mayne
- Lesser-known Australian stars (Veritas, JJ Hahn, Henry's Drive) plus superstar Grange
- Vintage ports dating back to 1963
- New high-flyers from Languedoc-Roussillon: Château de Negly, Domaine Henry and Prieuré de St-Jean de Bebian
- Quality Austrian wines from Emmerich Knoll, Alois Kracher and F X Pichler.

Unwins

Head office
Birchwood House, Victoria Road, Dartford,   *Tel* (01322) 272711
Kent DA1 5AJ   *Fax* (01322) 294469
(427 branches throughout southern England)

Email admin@unwinswines.co.uk
Website www.unwins.co.uk

Open Times vary between stores, phone or visit website for details   **Cards** Amex, Delta, Diners, MasterCard, Switch, Visa; personal and business accounts   **Discount** 5% on 6 bottles, 10% on 1 mixed case   **Delivery** Free locally   **Glass hire** Free with order   **Tastings and talks** Available, phone local store for details   **(£5)**

Last year the *Guide* was fairly critical of Unwins, saying that the wines were 'safe', 'rather pedestrian' and that this was not 'the most inspiring list around'. We suggested that the buying team at this 427-strong chain 'exercised its considerable buying muscle far more widely'. So it did not bode well when the first thing Unwins told us this year was that it had 'reduced its wine range to make the shopping experience easier for customers'.

Still, the chain is in the top 100 here, so it's evident that we like quite a lot of what is on the list. Let's start with the clarets. They are smashing – a large collection ranging from basic red Bordeaux at £3.99 through plenty of *cru bourgeois*, to a fine set of châteaux bottlings in magnum, some of which are mature, and even five impériales, holding six litres of wine. Then the classed growth clarets come thick and fast – around 50, all from the mid-1990s, feature in the list available at the time of writing.

The Italian wines are another strong suit at Unwins. Last year we may have commented that they were not a deeply quirky lot, but many of them are, nonetheless, good-quality classics, with a decent smattering of modern Sicilian and Southern Italian bins for the modernists.

There are some attractive wines from South Africa and Argentina, but the Australian section is far too safe, featuring as it does Penfolds, Rosemount, Wolf Blass and Oxford Landing, but not the plethora of more unusual names and grape varieties that we have come to expect from quality merchants. The older ports are great, but Portugal's table wines are extremely thin on the ground (two are listed), the Spanish wines are not particularly inspiring, and the New Zealand and Eastern European shelves desperately need bolstering.

That said, we switch again to praising the company as the champagnes hove into view – here is a lovely selection of big names, a decent house fizz (Duchatel), and loads of large bottles – magnums, jeroboams, methuselahs, even nebuchadnezzars (15 litres).

So when Unwins is good (claret, Italy, champagne, port), it is very good. The rest of the time it is truly disappointing. As we said last year, in the slightly different context of poor-followed-by-good press tastings: 'Will the real Unwins stand up?' Please?

Look out for

- Excellent clarets from the 1990s, including bigger bottles
- Wonderful champagnes from Charles Heidsieck, Bollinger, Veuve Clicquot and more; some available in several larger-format bottles
- Spice Route, Clos Malverne, Beyerskloof and Jordan from the Western Cape
- Catena, Norton, Terra Organica from Argentina
- Wide range of different Italian styles from across the country.

Valvona & Crolla

19 Elm Row, Edinburgh EH7 4AA

Tel 0131-556 6066
Fax 0131-556 1668
Email sales@valvonacrolla.co.uk
Website www.valvonacrolla.co.uk

Open Mon–Sat 8–6.30 **Closed** Sun, 25 & 26 Dec, 1 & 2 Jan **Cards** Amex, Delta, MasterCard, Switch, Visa **Discount** Available, phone for details **Delivery** Local service within Edinburgh city, charge £3, free for orders of £100+; nationwide service (mainland UK only), charge £8, free for orders of £125+ **Glass hire** Free with order **Tastings and talks** 6–10 tastings per year, phone for details

---

A famous stop for quality food and wine in Edinburgh, Valvona & Crolla is a lovely place, packed from floor to ceiling with aromatic goodies and presided over by the genial Philip Contini. Benedotto Valvona set up shop in the city in the 1860s; in 1934 the business moved to its current premises and Benedotto's son went into partnership with Alfonso Crolla, Philip's grandfather. But although the place has a lovely old-fashioned air about it, Philip has worked extremely hard to keep V&C at the cutting edge. The fact that the company is endlessly mentioned in glossy magazines and newspapers is just one measure of his success – the lifelong, loyal Edinburgh customers who rub shoulders with passing tourists in the shop is another.

Italian wine is the speciality here, unsurprisingly, and this is an inspiring range, featuring many top producers from all round the country. Fans of

Piedmont's wines will be especially delighted – there were literally scores of wines from top-notch producers on the latest list we saw. Tuscany also receives much attention – again, many of the best and most well-known names feature. There are numerous vintages of Sassicaia in bottle and magnum, plus plenty more of Tignanello. Amarone, sweet Italian wines and sparklers abound, and it's great to see both sweet and dry featuring among the latter.

And it's not all Italy. The list also takes in a decent range from Australia, some fine champagnes, a notably admirable selection from New Zealand and a few worthy South American choices. Of course, there is also a surfeit of great malt whiskies. One word of warning: if you buy your wine at the Edinburgh shop, you will not, repeat *not*, be able to resist raiding the deli for some superb sweetmeats to go with your bottles . . .

Look out for
- Fine Piedmont reds from Gaja, Aldo Conterno, Vajra
- Tuscan wines galore, including an impressivee collection of Super-Tuscans
- Sardinian and Sicilian bottles from Planeta, Sella & Mosca
- Good-value modern wines from Puglia
- Sweet and sparkling Italian wines for feasts and festivities
- Wide range of high-quality Australian wines
- Taittinger, Bollinger, Billecart-Salmon among the champagnes.

Helen Verdcourt Wines

Spring Cottage, Kimbers Lane, Maidenhead,   *Tel* (01628) 625577
Berkshire SL6 2QP

Open Daily all hours, phone first to check **Cards** None accepted; personal accounts **Discount** Available, phone for details **Delivery** Free within 20-mile radius (min. 1 case); nationwide service (min. 1 case), charged at cost **Glass hire** Free **Tastings and talks** Through 3 local wine clubs **(£5)**

As we've said before: truly a small but perfectly formed merchant. Helen supplies thoughtfully chosen wines from just about everywhere, direct from Spring Cottage in Maidenhead. The Rhône, Italy, Spain and Chile sections look particularly strong at the moment (scattered with great names such as Guigal, Allegrini, Muga and Montes), nor are there any holes in the Australia list – with good choices to be had from Margaret River to McLaren Vale and more besides. There are about 400 wines in all, tending towards the £10-a-bottle, quality end of the spectrum (and higher), but there are also one or two sub-£5 gluggers in there if you search. It's more than likely that you'll end up with a wine that scales the very highest heights, as Helen certainly knows how to seek out the prestigious bottles. Filling up a mixed case would be no problem for us, and locals can join one of the three wine clubs that meet to taste every month (in Beaconsfield, Charvil and Maidenhead) to get to know the range, and its new additions, before choosing. Helen started her small company in 1978, just after she'd finished her Wine and Spirit Education Trust diploma course; as far as we can see, she's never looked back.

Look out for

- Classic Californians, Ridge and Renaissance, plus sparkling Mumm Cuvée Napa Brut
- Fine set of German Rieslings from basic Dr Loosen wines to ethereal Urziger Wurzgarten *Auslese* from the Mosel
- Chianti Classico from Isole e Olena, Villa Cafaggio and Querciabella
- A pocket-size selection of affordable Bordeaux, topped by the inimitable Château Angélus
- Treasured allocations of Guigal's superb Rhône wines, from old vintages and new
- Delicious Australian Shiraz from Geoff Merrill, Jim Barry, Charles Melton and Rockford.

Victor Hugo Wines

Head office

Longueville Road, St Saviour, Jersey JE2 7SA	*Tel* (01534) 507977
	Fax (01534) 767770
Cash & Carry, Longueville Road, St Saviour,	*Tel* (01534) 507978
Jersey JE2 7SA	*Fax* (01534) 767770
Wine Saver, 15 Weighbridge Place, St Helier,	*Tel* (01534) 507991
Jersey JE2 3NF	*Fax* (01534) 507991
8B Les Quennevais Precinct, St Brelade, Jersey JE3 8FX	*Tel* (01534) 744519
	Fax (01534) 744519
	Email sales@victor-hugo-wines.com
	Website www.victor-hugo-wines.com

Open Mon–Sat 8.30–6.15, public holidays 8.30–1 **Closed** Sun, 25 & 26 Dec, Good Fri
Cards Amex, Delta, Diners, MasterCard, Switch, Visa; personal and business
accounts **Discount** 5% on 6+ bottles **Delivery** Free within Jersey (min. 1 case)
Glass hire Free with order **Tastings and talks** Regular talks and events, phone for
details **£5**

The list of sole-agency wines here is long and wide-ranging (even as far as Israel and South Africa), but it isn't deep. For depth we'd expect to see a few more of the individual domaines of Burgundy, and a helping or two more of the smaller, more exciting Australian players rather than the big brands. This said, managing director Martin Flageul and his team do a good job of making sure there's something on this list from everywhere.

The 'possibility of achieving perfection' (to quote Victor Hugo himself), is what drives them. They might not have got there quite yet, but give the impression they have a lot of fun with the wines they do have, and this freely transmits from the pages of the lists and the services they offer. Take the customer club, for example. For £80 a year you'll get the benefit of 10 per cent discount on your purchases, two annual dinners (with guest speakers and appropriate wines) and at least four tutored tastings. To our mind, however, it's the gossipy monthly newsletter that we'd most look forward to. Not only are there special offers therein, but the pages are packed with up-to-the-minute wine trade news and there are even regular chef competitions to inspire any food and wine matchers out there. But then

Martin Flageul is also a fully qualified WSET (Wine & Spirit Education Trust) lecturer, so perhaps we shouldn't be surprised by the quality of information.

Victor Hugo Wines was once billed as a New World wine specialist, but things have moved on since those days. Being one of only a few outlets for wine on the Channel Islands means that traders all want to sell to this merchant, and the buying team can get their hands on a case or two of almost anything they wish for. Bordeaux vintages through the 1990s, from the top châteaux, don't surprise us with their presence, and nor do classy Alsace wines from Domaine Trimbach or sumptuous Tokaji from the Royal Tokaji Company. But the average spend here isn't all that high (£6 to £7 a bottle), and although Chilean Merlot and Argentinian reds might be doing particularly well at the moment, we can't help wondering if VHW customers shouldn't be encouraged to trade up and buy something more interesting. If this company, given its rather remote location, really does have access to just about any wine, why aren't there more than the usual Burgundian *négociant* houses to choose from? Why aren't things a little less safe and a little more exciting?

Look out for

- Jersey's own wines, including Cuvée de la Mare sparkling
- Cool South African Chardonnay from the Hamilton Russell estate in Walker Bay
- Vintage port to lay down (from 1980 onwards), plus five- and ten-year-old Malmsey madeira
- Traditional Chianti in straw flasks
- Plenty of reliable burgundy from Louis Jadot and Louis Latour
- Lafite, Mouton-Rothschild and Latour – top Bordeaux.

Victoria Wine

see Thresher Wine Shops

La Vigneronne

105 Old Brompton Road, London SW7 3LE

Tel 020-7589 6113
Fax 020-7581 2983
Email lavig@aol.com
Website www.lavigneronne.co.uk

Open Mon–Fri 10–8, Sat 10–6 **Closed** Sun, public holidays **Cards** Amex, Delta, Diners, MasterCard, Switch, Visa; personal and business accounts **Discount** Available, phone for details **Delivery** Free within 1-mile radius; nationwide service, charge £10 per order, free for orders of £250+ **Glass hire** Not available **Tastings and talks** Twice-weekly tasting programme, phone for details

This is the place to come to get a grip on the many and varied – and increasingly fashionable – wines coming out of the South of France, particularly (to our minds) those from the wild shores of the Mediterranean. Owners Mike and Liz Berry (Liz is a Master of Wine) fell in love with the place and it's been their mission over the past 22 years to import the kind of small-parcel wines that reflect the passion of the local *vignerons* and the general feel of this landscape.

Want to know the appellations to look out for? Costières de Nîmes, Minervois, Bandol, Montpeyroux and Coteaux du Languedoc for a start. The names of the producers? We recommend a visit to La Vigneronne's shop on the Old Brompton Road, London, run by Adrian Heaven (not an inappropriate name for someone working in this kind of free-spirited environment) – particularly on a Saturday morning when there'll be bottles open to try, free of charge – and don't hesitate to ask the friendly staff for their advice on which wines to start off with. Or, look at the detailed wine list or (bi-monthly) newsletter and select a case for delivery.

But La Vigneronne doesn't just spend time off one beaten track. Liz and Mike's attention and well-tuned palates are also turned to other parts of France and the world, to ensure their portfolio has no gaps where wines-of-integrity are concerned. They tend to find the producers they like and stick with them, taking in the whole range of wines from each domaine whatever the variations offered; although quite a few of the names might be unfamiliar, they'll all have been chosen because of their abilities and their 'non-international' approach in the *chais* (winery). There are also a number of New World 'classics' on sale (not big brands, though), which for this shop are on the conventional side, but which are no doubt concessions to daily local demand. Oh, and since quality is the name of the game here, expect to pay a few pounds more than usual.

If you're in London, don't miss out on La Vigneronne's twice-weekly 'comprehensive' tasting programme, which, for a small fee, will illustrate just what the South of France is all about.

Look out for

- 'Love or hate 'em' wines from France's obscure Jura region
- Future stars of the Mediterranean: domaines Font Caude, Terre Mégère, de Barroubio and des Chênes
- Spicy, wild south-western flavours from Madiran, Marmandais and Cahors
- Prestige collections from California and Australia (including Opus One, Ridge Monte Bello and Polish Hills Riesling)
- Fabulous Lustau sherries and madeiras dating back to 1900
- Douro, Dão and Bairrada from Portugal – non-international reds at their finest!

Villeneuve Wines

1 Venlaw Court, Peebles EH45 8AE

Tel (01721) 722500
Fax (01721) 729922

82 High Street, Haddington EH41 3ET

Tel (01620) 822224
Fax (01620) 822279

49A Broughton Street, Edinburgh EH1 3RJ

Tel 0131-558 8441
Fax 0131-558 8442
Email wines@villeneuvewines.com
Website www.villeneuvewines.com

Open (Peebles) Mon–Sat 9–8, Sun 12.30–5.30 (Haddington) Mon–Thur 10–7, Fri 10–8, Sat 9–8 (Edinburgh) Mon–Thur 10–10, Fri & Sat 9–10, Sun 1–8 **Closed** (Haddington) Sun, (all) 25 & 26 Dec, 1 & 2 Jan **Cards** Amex, Delta, MasterCard, Switch, Visa; personal and business accounts **Discount** 5% on 1 mixed case **Delivery** Free within 20-mile radius (min. 1 case); nationwide service, charge £7.50, free for orders of £100+ **Glass hire** Free **Tastings and talks** Large annual tasting, phone for details **£5**

'Customers are becoming more discerning, and therefore more demanding,' reports Villeneuve's director Kenneth Vannan. Pleased to hear it, Ken! We are confident this excellent Scottish operation is rising to the challenge – the wine merchant which has been this *Guide*'s Regional Award winner for Scotland before now continues to shine with a top-notch international selection that should appeal both to fine wine drinkers and those on the look-out for interesting everyday vino.

Villeneuve is that rare thing – a merchant that is comfortable departing from the norm, but whose list is based nonetheless on some of the most consistently good winemaking around. Ken says he buys wines 'regardless of what is considered fashionable – we prefer to set trends rather than follow them'. Despite his best efforts, we must disappoint him and state that this is a highly fashionable range – but only in that there are lots of modern innovative wineries listed here that enjoy much critical acclaim. A splendid Italian range stands out, which contains some great names from the north, centre and south of the country; and the New Zealand collection, which includes several listings from cultish region Central Otago, is also noteworthy.

California is the other area of real strength – familiar names such as Ridge, Quady and Saintsbury abound, but the team has foraged about for some rare gems too. The lengthy lists of glorious sherries, madeiras and ports are outstanding, and there are unusually wide ranges of liqueurs, white spirits and brandies. Less surprisingly, whisky connoisseurs will be in seventh heaven.

Look out for
- One of the UK's best Italian ranges, spanning the country from Alto Adige and Friuli to Sicily
- Southern French wines from Puech-Haut and Clos Guirouilh
- Superb champagnes, reaching the heights of mature Bollinger, Krug, Veuve Clicquot
- California rarities such as Wild Hog and MacRostie
- Great Australian range, pulling in Cullen, Moung Langi Ghiran, Stringy Brae
- Kiwi wines including Felton Road and Mount Difficulty from Central Otago.

Vin du Van Wine Merchants

Colthups, The Street, Appledore, Kent TN26 2BX   *Tel* (01233) 758727
                                                        Fax (01233) 758389

Open Mon–Fri 9–5 **Closed** Sat, Sun, 25 & 26 Dec, 1 Jan **Cards** Delta, MasterCard,
Switch, Visa **Discount** Not available **Delivery** Free within 20-mile radius (min. 1
case); nationwide service (min. 1 case), charge £5.95 per order **Glass hire** Free
Tastings and talks Not available

One of the *Guide's* favourite merchants – as much for its attitude to selling
wine as to the actual bottles it stocks. Vin du Van is the creation of former
designer and art director Ian Brown, who started selling wine in 1991. Ian
says he's 'keen on cats and keen on cheese' but he's certainly mighty keen
on wine too, and he's brought together what we reckon is the best range
from Australia in the UK.

The approach has been to collect together 'unusual, rare, and sometimes
weird wines from all over Australia'. We've complained enough in this (and
every) edition of the *Guide* about big boring brands, particularly from Down
Under, so here's an antidote. Vin du Van stocks wines from superb
independent, often smaller boutique, wineries, introducing a plethora of
styles from myriad grape varieties – witness the Cape Charlotte Dry Muscat
that kicks off the brochure, the De Bortoli Verdelho, the Chenin Blanc and
Marsanne, the Pinot Gris, the Riesling and Viogniers . . . and that's just the
white wines.

In the red corner, find Merlot, Zinfandel, Grenache, Sangiovese, Pinot Noir
and Mourvèdre. There's Cabernet and Shiraz here too – just as in amongst the
whites there are Chardonnays and Semillons, but they are carefully sourced
from premium producers and, as a group, have more character than most.
The sparkling sections feature white, pink and red fizz (eight to choose from
in the last section), and there are 'stickies' galore to go with pud.

One word of warning: Ian's approach to wine writing will amuse some
readers of his brochure, but irritate others. We rather like it, but it *is* deeply
eccentric and involves some very surreal episodes. Quite why a Lehmann
Shiraz is described as a 'highly enjoyable, complex and a £6 note/bawbee in
sporran ongoing interface scenario situation' (sic) or what the Green Potato
Fish of North Malagasy has to do with a particular red blend is quite beyond
us. This is a list with a difference, all right.

Look out for

- One of the most exciting selections of Australian wines in the UK . . .
- . . . featuring (among many others) Plantagenet, Best's Great Western,
  Vasse Felix, Pierro, Grosset and Henschke whites . . .
- Coriole, Tim Knappstein, Mount Langi Ghiran, Jim Barry, Petaluma reds
- plus many lesser-known names
- and Charles Melton rosé
- and Stanton & Killeen, Morris, De Bortoli sweet and fortifieds.

Vinceremos Wines & Spirits

74 Kirkgate, Leeds LS2 7DJ

Tel 0113-244 0002
Fax 0113-288 4566
Email info@vinceremos.co.uk
Website www.vinceremos.co.uk

Open Mon–Fri 9–5.30, Sat 10–4 (Dec only) **Closed** Sat (exc. Dec), Sun, public holidays
Cards Amex, Delta, MasterCard, Switch, Visa; personal accounts (by arrangement),
business accounts **Discount** 5% on 5–9 cases, 10% on 10+ cases **Delivery**
Nationwide service (min. 1 mixed case), charge £5.95 per order, free for 5+ cases **Glass
hire** Free locally with order **Tastings and talks** Available, phone for details **£5**

Jem Gardener, director, and his team have been getting people (us included)
to take organic winemaking seriously for 18 years now. He is a self-professed
'vegetarian chef-turned organic wine enthusiast,' who started out selling
Russian vodkas from a bedroom office and took the name of his company
from the Spanish *venceremos*, 'we shall overcome'. Quite what he was
originally overcoming with those early vodkas we're not sure, but in the
intervening years he's turned this small Leeds company into a burgeoning
and popular business. Every wine on the list is either officially organic,
biodynamic, or made with holistic vineyard management in mind. The theory
is that these practices not only ensure the long-term health of the vineyards
but in the long term engender fresher, cleaner flavours in the grapes. Judging
by the many new additions to this list this year, an increasing number of
winemakers and viticulturalists are beginning to think the same way.

Jem's Jewels (his own term!) stick as near as they can to the £5-a-bottle mark
– many will cost less than £50 for the minimum mixed-case purchase. The
Rhône, the Loire and Mediterranean France are the main strengths, but it is
pleasing to see New Zealand, Australia and California well-represented too,
plus the delicious 'La Nature' wines from Argentina. (We look forward to
seeing this latter range expand beyond Barbera and Torrontés before too long.)

'We are not unique in offering a wide range of organic wines but we feel
we have the strongest range, taking price, quality and service into account,'
says Jem. Quite right, too. We felt it was strong enough to lead the way with
our new Organic Award last year. We would quibble with Jem, however, in
that we think the addition of the big-name biodynamic estates from
Burgundy and the Rhône (Leroy, Leflaive, Chapoutier etc) would serve to
make this list still stronger. These wines might be expensive but they are
undoubtedly splendid examples of how good holistically made wine can be.

Look out for

- Organic champagne from José Ardinat (all styles)
- Moroccan wines from Celliers de Meknès
- Vouvray, Sancerre and Muscadet de Sèvre-et-Maine *sur lie*: all Loire
  Valley classics
- Wide choice of organic Australian producers, among them Penfolds
- Fabulous Bonterra range from California (including unusual Syrah,
  Sangiovese, Roussanne and Viognier)
- New stars from the South of France: watch for the Faugères, St-Chinian
  and Costières de Nîmes regions.

El Vino

Head office

Vintage House, 1–2 Hare Place, Fleet Street, London EC4Y 1BJ	*Tel* 020-7353 5384 *Fax* 020-7936 2367
Alban Gate, 125 London Wall, London EC2Y 5AP	*Tel* 020-7600 6377 *Fax* 020-7600 7147
6 Martin Lane, Cannon Street, London EC4R 0DP	*Tel* 020-7626 6876 *Fax* 020-7621 0361
30 New Bridge Street, London EC4V 6BJ	*Tel* 020-7236 4534 *Fax* 020-7489 0041
47 Fleet Street, London EC4Y 1BJ	*Tel* 020-7353 6786

Email elvino.info@corkexpress.co.uk
Website www.elvino.co.uk

Open Mon–Fri 8.30–10 **Closed** Sat, Sun, public holidays **Cards** Amex, Delta, MasterCard, Switch, Visa; business accounts **Discount** Available on 8+ cases
Delivery Nationwide service, charge £8.90, free for 2+ cases **Glass hire** Free
Tastings and talks Open and tutored tastings, phone for details **(£5)**

El Vino's list seems to have become a little more resourceful in the last year. We commented in the last edition of the *Guide* that, although we were impressed by its record of 123 years of trading (this is the oldest wine merchant in the City of London), its wine list was a little too traditional and seemed to lack modern flair. Now things seem to be different. For a start, the sparkling list has stepped beyond the predictable and now includes two Australian fizzes – one of them a sparkling Shiraz – and very reasonably priced they are too. The New Zealand and South Africa sections have taken on board some interesting choices, and the Australian range has improved beyond all measure. Moreover, although the classic European selections appear to remain based on a rather plodding 'one from each region' approach, there are definite signs of branching out, with new growers lighting up the burgundy section particularly.

So what's been going on? Who's been doing the shaking? It appears that the answer lies with Anthony, Michael and Christopher Mitchell who, since the last review, have bought out the rest of the family and begun to run things on their own. It seems as if 'too many cooks' had been spoiling things somewhat. What's nice to see is that this change has happened without disrupting the long line of Mitchells running the show since El Vino started up in 1879. Best of all, the four El Vino 'Tasting Houses' (where you can sample the wines and traditional British fodder) also remain unaltered, scattered as they are throughout the City and West End, and tapping cosily into London's Dickensian past.

We know that Anthony Mitchell is an avid wine-ferret (whose skills we've often thought were being wasted), so fully expect to see this list burgeoning even more by 2003–2004. One to watch.

Look out for

- Year-round gift cases: 'The Aussie three', 'The Aussie six', 'The Picnic Hamper', and more . . .
- Classic clarets from châteaux Lynch-Bages, Pichon-Lalande and Phélan-Ségur
- Reliably good own-label choices from Burgundy and the Rhône
- Tempting Australian Shiraz from lesser-known estates Hare's Leap, Honeytree and St-Mary's Vineyard
- Fine old ports available from El Vino's vaults.

Vino Vino

Freepost SEA5662, New Malden, Surrey KT3 3BR   *Tel* (07703) 436949
                                             Fax 020-8942 4003
                     Email vinovino@macunlimited.net

Open Mon–Sat 9–6 **Closed** Sun, public holidays **Cards** Delta, MasterCard, Switch, Visa **Discount** Not available **Delivery** Free nationwide service (min. 1 case) **Glass hire** Not available **Tastings and talks** Not available **(£5)**

'After attending a trade tasting of Italian wines,' says Derek Dornan, 'I was unable to find any of them in the shops. To remedy this shocking state of affairs Vino Vino was born.' This mail-order business is now one of the best places to shop and get to know Italy's wines better. It has a list of the most stunning proportions and, in terms of presentation, you couldn't wish for greater detail.

'There's more than enough good Chianti here to satisfy even Hannibal Lecter,' is Derek's modest comment. Even were he to escape Tuscany and visit Piedmont, Puglia or Sicily, we don't doubt that Mr Lecter would be equally sated by the quantity and quality on offer. Not, mind you, that you'll necessarily pick up all the Super-Tuscans you might wish for (Antinori, Frescobaldi and the likes of Angelo Gaja further north fail to make an appearance here) but you *will* find all the 'real' wines. Wines that reflect the true traditional character of the country.

Unsurprisingly, these aren't the cheapest Italian wines you'll set eyes on, but don't let that deter you from your mixed case purchase. It would be easy enough to balance up a few bottles of modestly priced (£6) Salice Salentino against a more illustrious example such as Donnafugata's red Mille una Notte at £40, to make sure the overall price didn't get too heavy . . . Not everything is expensive, but many of the expensive wines are there.

Vino Vino's new dimension (from early 2001) is Spain. And Derek's approach to this country (another that's often misunderstood and poorly represented in the UK) is the same: get to know the producer through his/her whole range, the region through the best producers, and the vintage via the wines and the tasting notes. There are also property profiles aplenty.

May we repeat last year's plea, Derek: stick to Italy and Spain – we couldn't bear to see this tremendously detailed selection diluted!

Look out for

- Top Tuscans from San Felice, Castello di Fonterutoli, Biondi Santi and Col d'Orcia

- Piedmont's finest from Pio Cesare, Roberto Voerzio and Michele Chiarlo
- Great-value, characterful southern Italian reds from Illuminati, Taurino and Leone de Castris
- A dozen different Verdicchios (potentially Italy's finest white wine)
- Exciting new estates such as Feudi di San Gregorio, Malvira, Vignalta
- Rarely seen but delicious reds from the historic Spanish region of Protos.

Vintage Roots

Bridge Farm, Reading Road,
Arborfield, Berkshire RG2 9HT

Tel 0118-976 1999
Fax 0118-976 1998
Email info@vintageroots.co.uk
Website www.vintageroots.co.uk

Open Mon–Fri 8.30–5.30, Sat (Dec only) **Closed** Sat (exc. Dec), Sun, public holidays
Cards Delta, MasterCard, Switch, Visa; personal and business accounts **Discount** 5%
on 5+ cases **Delivery** Free within 30-mile radius (min. 6 bottles); nationwide service,
charge £4.95 for 1 case, £5.95 for 2–5 cases, free for 6+ cases **Glass hire** Not available
Tastings and talks Available on request, phones for details **£5**

When Vintage Roots started out in 1986, not much was known about
organic wine production and it was a struggle for the team to get together a
few decent bottles. Today, business is expanding with increasing ease as
more and more growers opt to produce biodynamic or organic wine, and
more and more consumers demand to drink it. Whether you visit the
Arborfield shop, peruse the informative and colourful mail-order list, or log
on to the dynamic website, you'll find at Vintage Roots one of the best and
most comprehensive organic ranges.

Globally, just about everything's covered, from champagne to Australian
Chenin Blanc, with not a few familiar, big-name producers thrown in there
too (Penfolds from Australia, Fetzer from California, Millton Estate from
New Zealand). We'd like to see the large expensive Rhône and Burgundy
biodynamists in among this selection – but we guess that's just it, they're too
expensive. With most wines here sitting cheerily about the £5 mark (£10 at
most) they would make things too top-heavy.

To go back to the list. Turn to the section entitled 'The living soil' to gen
up on just what it takes to be biodynamic or for a 'a bug's eye view' on
organics. You can also get to grips with GMOs (genetically modified
organisms), and find a trustworthy explanation of what it takes to make
vegetarian and vegan wines – all of which are clearly coded throughout the
list, along with tasting notes.

Director Neil Palmer tells us that his main project these days is to ensure
organic wines enter the mainstream, and that the work Vintage Roots does
'feeding' the supermarkets is playing a major part in this. We applaud their
success in this infiltration (and we don't mean that to sound subversive),
and we feel that they're making a huge contribution to holistic vineyard
management and to promoting organic produce. Added to that, the website
is bigger than ever and now covers 20 per cent of mail-order trade, and one
shouldn't overlook the occasional organic tastings or the four or five
newsletters a year.

Look out for

- Delicious organic reds from Mediterranean France (Château Pech-Latt, Domaine de Brau and Domaine de Bassac included)
- Organic Bordeaux from Château Beauséjour and Domaine Jacques Blanc in St-Emilion
- Ever-increasing options in white Rhône and Burgundy (Meursault, Chablis and Puligny-Montrachet among them)
- Biodynamic whites from the Loire Valley (from domaines Huet and St-Nicolas and Guy Bossard)
- Organic and biodynamic champagne from the centenarian house Fleury (est 1895)
- Wide selection of Australian organic wines sourced from Clare Valley, Mudgee and the Murray Valley.

Virgin Wines

The Loft, St James's Mill, Whitefriars,	*Tel* (0870) 164 2034
Norwich NR3 1TN	*Fax* (01603) 619277
	Email help@virginwines.com
	Website www.virginwines.com

Open Mon–Fri 8–7, Sat, Sun, public holidays 10–5 **Closed** 25 Dec **Cards** Amex, Delta, MasterCard, Switch, Visa; personal accounts **Discount** Available on 10+ cases **Delivery** Nationwide service (min. 1 case), charge £4.99 per order **Glass hire** Not available **Tastings and talks** Available, phone for details

'Our mission is to bring a greater diversity and quality to the wine people drink by helping them discover great wines from regions that might not yet get a look-in on the supermarket shelf,' says Richard Halstead, corporate development manager at Virginwines.com. There's certainly every opportunity, when you log on, to find something new here. To start with, the wines are grouped by style rather than by the usual grape variety/vintage/region categories, so branching out is easier. Go via the 'Kiwi Sauvignon Blanc' route, follow 'Oaky Aussie Chardonnay' styles, or check out 'Soft Juicy Reds', 'Huge Reds' or 'Lunchtime Red' styles – each marked with appropriate symbols ('oaked', 'zing!','soft', 'huge' or 'light'). Huge reds, for example, are sourced as diversely as from Argentina (Neito y Senetiner Bonarda and Syrah) to South Africa (Blue Creek Cabernet, Penfolds Bin 28 Kalimna Shiraz) and Italy ('Wine Buyers Choice' Salice Salentino from Pervini) – all at under £10 a bottle. Alternatively, you can search the website using the Wine Wizard, which gives recommendations tailored to customers' own taste preferences ('if you like this, then you'll love these . . .'). Or, for those in a hurry, there are specially designed mixed cases ('Perfect BBQ', 'Classic Case' and 'Stars of Tomorrow', among others) all costing less than £100, some of them significantly less.

The idea here is that wine should be a light-hearted, non-intimidating subject ('no waffle, no jargon, just plain English' is the motto); unfortunately we think the tasting notes are more often groovy gibberish. The opportunity for next-day and evening delivery within the M25 sounds good to us, as does the customer club (just £50 to join, or spend £350 on wine in a year: the benefits are a free 13th bottle with every case, plus regular exclusive offers).

Just one other niggle: it's not always easy to spot which country or region a wine is from. The world of online retailing is going through a difficult teething stage and Virgin Wines will not be immune to this but we wouldn't be surprised if this merchant came through this unscathed and successful.

Look out for

- Sancerre-style Menetou-Salon and Petit Bourgeois Sauvignon Blanc, and the genuine article from Fournier Père
- Widely sourced dry whites: Michel Torino Torrontés from Argentina, Marsanne from Chateau Tahbilk, Australia, and Greco di Tufo from Italy
- Alsace Riesling from a variety of growers: Caves de Hunawihr, Turckheim and Albert Mann
- 'Exotic' wines, such as Rococo Primitivo from southern Italy and Rosemount's Australian Gewurz/Riesling blend
- A stronger focus on South Africa this year
- Plenty of wallet-friendly red Bordeaux choices
- Very few wines costing over £10.

Waitrose

Head office
Doncaster Road, Southern Industrial Area,   *Tel* (01344) 424680
Bracknell, Berkshire RG12 8YA

Waitrose Wine Direct   *Tel* (0800) 188881
Freepost SW1647, Bracknell RG12 8HX   *Fax* (0800) 188888
(Branches throughout southern England)

Email customer_service@waitrose.co.uk
Website www.waitrose.com

Open Times vary between stores: Mon–Fri 8.30–7/8/9, Sat 8.30–7/8, Sun 10–4/11–5 **Closed** Public holidays **Cards** Amex, Delta, MasterCard, Switch, Visa; business accounts, John Lewis/Waitrose card accounts **Discount** 5% on 6+ bottles **Delivery** Nationwide service (Waitrose Direct), charge £4.95, free for orders of £75+ **Glass hire** Free, deposit taken **Tastings and talks** Available, phone for details

---

Created by a cluster of MWs (Masters of Wine), you wouldn't expect the Waitrose wine list to be anything other than top class, but the fact that it overtakes many a high-street merchant for quality still comes as something of a surprise. For a supermarket supplying over a hundred branches, we think this range is adventurous in the extreme and should stand proud as an example of what can be achieved when buyers don't automatically resort to hauling in bulk-made brands.

'We try to have a balanced, wide range of quality wines which is typical and which offers value throughout the range. We like to stock wine producers from new areas as long as the wines are good and offer value,' says Julian Brind MW, retiring head of the buying team. The range is indeed wide, and even the cheapest wines are interesting: at £4.99, Chapel Hill Hungarian sparkling wine made with Chardonnay and Pinot Noir is a quirky oddity; South American cheapies don't just stick with Chardonnay but take in Semillon and Torrontés too, at £3.99, and Pinot Gris for a few pence more. The Waitrose own-brand wines offer plenty of budget possibilities too.

You can also buy examples of top-class vintage port (Taylor's 1997 is £840 a case), not to mention indulge in the occasional *en primeur* offer, or splash out on ultra-expensive champagne (a 3-litre bottle of vintage Charles Heidsieck Brut, 1982, if you so wish, at £300). But within these two extremes the bulk of the wines ranges from imaginative everyday choices, made from interesting grape varietals – there are a couple of Italian Primitivos from the Puglia region – to slightly pricier special bottles up around the £10 mark. Whatever your price-point you won't be short of options.

Waitrose still stocks an impressive array of organic wines (28 in 2002), with particularly good choices from California, Italy, regional France and the Rhône. And we don't quite mean to mention these in the same breath, but there are also un-boring bag-in-box and low-alcohol options for those that so wish.

Just one gripe, though – we do wish the list was as interesting to read as the Waitrose magazine (more tasting notes, more colour please!), and that it could be as bright and cheery as those of some of its competitors.

Look out for

- Stunning collection of Rhône wines, from Chapoutier Côtes du Rhône to Jaboulet-Aîné Côte Rôtie
- Choice selection of English wines, including, in some stores, Camel Valley sparkling
- A mouthwatering selection of first-rate German Rieslings
- Top-class sweet wines from Sauternes and Barsac – also port, madeira, sherry and Montilla for fans of the classics
- Tempting burgundies and Bordeaux *crus classés* (the envy of many a smaller merchant)
- Wide choice of South African reds, including Spice Route, Fairview and Jordan's wines, plus empowerment project Thandi Cabernet Sauvignon, well worth a sip.

Weavers of Nottingham

1 Castle Gate, Nottingham NG1 7AQ

Tel 0115-958 0922
Fax 0115-950 8076
Email weavers@weaverswines.com
Website www.weaverswines.com

Open Mon–Sat 9–5.45 **Closed** Sun (exc. Dec), public holidays **Cards** Amex, Delta, Diners, MasterCard, Switch, Visa; personal and business accounts **Discount** 5% on 5 cases, 10% on 10+ cases **Delivery** Free within 50-mile radius (min. 6 bottles); nationwide service, charged at cost, free for orders of £90+ **Glass hire** 20p per dozen **Tastings and talks** Range of tastings and events, winemaker evenings, phone for details **(£5)**

Weavers is still the cheery family set-up it's always been, with all the family involved: Alan Trease, who runs the show, is the fourth-generation managing director of the business, with over 40 years' wine trade experience; Mary Trease is sales director; Di and Philip Trease are also on the board, one of their day-to-day concerns being beefing up the active website. At their side is a handful of other staff, equally smiley and equally knowledgeable.

Last year we felt that the team needed to put more of their abundant family energy into wine-buying, as the website, wine list presentation, regular tastings and general profile of the business seemed to be thriving but were backed up by a rather safe and lacklustre range of wines. This year, we're pleased to report, things seem to have got a notch or two more exciting. The wine tastings at the family's smart Georgian town house are as popular as ever, the selection of single malt whiskies is just as impressive, and the white and red wine tasting packs (a good idea these) are as imaginative and enticingly priced as we always thought – try the 'Mid-week drinking reds', a quick round-the-world tour in six bottles for £29.50. But there are now additional wines now that smack of a bit more imagination – Frog's Leap Sauvignon Blanc and Zinfandel from California are good organic choices; Southbrook Icewine from Canada is a real sweet treat (and only newly available in the UK); Wehlener-Sonnenuhr and Berkastel Graben Rieslings from Germany reflect a steely will to embrace genuinely good quality as well as fashionable wines; and the new presence of Allegrini's delicious Amarone from Italy shows that top-notch trendy wines are admissable too. More of this sort of progress, with increased emphasis on individuality rather than brands and big estates, may see Weavers competing for our Regional Award for Central England before too long.

Look out for
- Superb Italian choices from Antinori and Allegrini
- Classic Riojas from Berberana, Faustino and Marqués de Caceres
- Sparkling wines from around the world, including 40 champagnes – and big-format bottles up to methuselah level
- Twenty different tasting packs to choose from, from £23 'Party packs' to the £95 'Directors' Selection'.

Wine Rack

see Thresher Wine Shops
(£5) Wine Rack only

Wine Raks (Scotland)

21 Springfield Road, Aberdeen AB15 7RJ

Tel (01224) 311460
Fax (01224) 312186
Email enq@wineraks.co.uk
Website www.wineraks.co.uk

Open Mon–Sat 10–8, public holidays 12.30–6 **Closed** Sun, 25 & 26 Dec, 1 & 2 Jan **Cards** Delta, MasterCard, Switch, Visa; business accounts **Discount** 5% on 1 mixed case **Delivery** Free within 5-mile radius (min. 1 case); nationwide service, charged at cost **Glass hire** Free with order **Tastings and talks** 2 major tastings per year (May and Nov), group tastings on request

We'd say Australia and Bordeaux are still the grand passions at Wine Raks. Other wine choices skim through the rest of the world, touching on some impressive estates here and there – our favourites being the Ridge range from California, Clos Malverne from South Africa, the sumptuous Tokajis of

Château Pajzos, Hungary, and Quinta de la Rosa, Portugal – but never really get to grips with the country or its regions. However, we do admire these pockets of greatness and give credit for really wading in thigh-high where there is more confidence about the wines.

For their Bordeaux *en primeur* campaigns, wine buyers Tariq Mahmood and Mike Corser manage to get their hands on impressive allocations of Médoc first growths, top Pomerols and more affordable châteaux' second-label wines. Thereafter, the range broadens through to the 1990s vintages, including choices from every decade since the 1930s. (Old vintages are a bit of a 'thing' here, and you'll have no trouble picking up an ancient port or two. Dow's 1896 is the oldest – just ask for the 'Fine and Rare' list.)

Aberdonians are also lucky to have such an adventurous selection of Australian wines to choose from; by our calculation there are over 30 different estates, although Mike says that there are 'too many new wines to describe' on the list, so logging on to the website gives the most accurate picture. Whatever the quantity, it's refreshing indeed to see such a collection of oddities and small-estate wines from this country.

As you read this, Wine Raks will be celebrating its 20th birthday. We wish the team as much success in the next 20 years as it's obviously seen in the last, and hope that the ever-expanding list continues apace.

Look out for
- Stunning collection of well-priced vintage champagne
- 1894 Malmsey madeira – a snip at £109 a bottle
- Fabulous Western Australia collection including Devil's Lair, Amberley Estate and Cape Mentelle
- Fashionable, cool-climate Australian wines from Pipers Brook (Tasmania) and Kangaroo Island (a 30-minute flight from Adelaide)
- In-demand St-Emilions from châteaux Angélus, Troplong-Mondot and Pavie-Decesse
- Taster Cases from 'French Luxury' choices to 'The Americas' and an 'Under £6' cheapie collection.

The Wine Society

Gunnels Wood Road, Stevenage,   *Tel* (01438) 740222
Hertfordshire SG1 2BG   *Fax* (01438) 761167
(1 outlet in Hesdin, France)   *Email* memberservices@thewinesociety.com
                         Website www.thewinesociety.com

Open Mon–Fri 8.30–9, Sat 9–2 **Closed** Sun, public holidays **Cards** Delta, MasterCard, Switch, Visa; personal accounts **Discount** Available on orders of 5+ cases **Delivery** Free nationwide service (min. 1 case or orders of £75+) **Glass hire** Not available **Tastings and talks** 100 tastings per year nationwide for members, phone for details

Supplying wine to 80,000 members and still managing to offer an adventurous list is no mean feat. There aren't many better sources of Bordeaux to be found, for example – from *petits châteaux* to first-growth show-stoppers. Chief wine buyer Sebastian Payne MW has it all covered. Think Australia and the stocks are equally impressive: d'Arenberg, Petaluma, Yalumba and Jeffrey Grosset's wines. Back in the Old World,

Loire choices from Muscadet to Menetou-Salon right up to Château de Fesles' honeyed Bonnezeaux sound out the same tune. Yes, there might be moments of 'solidity' (the Spanish, Italian and Burgundy sections could perhaps be a little more energetic) but keeping this many loyal patrons happy is going to mean supplying easy-priced everyday wines as well and, here, the Wine Society's own-label range fits the bill nicely.

The Wine Society is a co-operative. It 'is owned by its members and operates for their benefit, not to maximise profit.' You have to join it to buy its wine, but for a fixed fee of £40 you'll be a member for life. And what do you get for your money? Newsletters, special offers and advice from the staff (most of whom have either a Wine & Spirit Education Trust higher certificate or Diploma, so they know what they're talking about); 500 new wines a year to choose from; 100 tastings a year for members and guests; over 150 wines at under £5 a bottle – all this and you can order, easily, on the company's website (10 per cent of the members choose to buy their wine this way). Plus, if all this wasn't incentive enough, you can opt to join the company's Vintage Cellar Plan, whereby the team both stocks and stores your wines itself – it will even choose them for you. For a monthly standing order fee, you can develop either your own cache of 'Rising Stars' or a mixture of 'Classics'. (We like the look of the Rising Stars: with instalments of either £45 or £65 per month, you can collect the likes of Maison Jaune's superb Faugères from Languedoc and Domus Aurea from Chile.)

Cellaring wine is very much the way the Wine Society works, and it has acres of warehouse space in which to do this. 'Our range benefits from our policy of buying wines young and storing them in our temperature-controlled cellars,' says the blurb, which means, basically, that it buys the wines cheaper, so you buy them cheaper too.

Look out for

- Super South Africa listings, from Thelema, L'Avenir, Hamilton Russell and Charles Back
- Mature claret vintages dating back to 1982 (Pichon-Baron, Pichon-Longueville and Palmer among them)
- Luxury champagne choices from Krug 1988 to Pol Roger Rosé and Bollinger 1995
- French oddities from the Jura, Savoie and Bugey regions; Hungarian Gewurztraminer; organic Greek wine
- Wide range from South America, including Argentinian Malbec and Bonarda and Chilean Carmenère
- Delicious Australian Riesling from the cool Clare Valley and Western Australia.

The Winery

4 Clifton Road, Maida Vale, London W9 1SS

Tel 020-7286 6475
Fax 020-7286 2733
Email dmotion@globalnet.co.uk

Open Mon–Sat 11–9.30, Sun, public holidays 12–8 **Closed** 25 & 26 Dec, 1 Jan **Cards**
Delta, MasterCard, Switch, Visa; personal and business accounts **Discount** 5% on 1
mixed case **Delivery** Free local service (min. 1 case); nationwide service, charge £8.50
per case for 1–2 cases, free for 3+ cases **Glass hire** Free with order **Tastings and
talks** Weekly in-store tastings, wine courses **(£5)**

David Motion is a musician using his creative talents for more than the
composition of the latest harmonious score. Putting together this imaginative
wine list takes up just as much of his time and energy these days. Since 1996,
his skills as a wine merchant have been going from strength to strength. 'We
continue to do what we enjoy most,' he says, 'searching for excellent new
wines and importing direct from the domaines – building our specialist areas
of France (particularly Burgundy), Italy and California.'

Turn to the Burgundy pages of this list and you find both familiar
(trusted) growers and new ones too. So many merchants just stick with the
devils they know; you find one or two big names (mostly *négociants*)
supplying the whole range of villages from Beaune to Bâtard-Montrachet,
but no real diversity. At The Winery you can choose from a number of
Burgundian perspectives – small growers and large ones, influential or
unheard of. (The unheard-of contributors are fleshed-out with useful
profiles, giving a bit of background to the family and how the wines are
made.) And, given the pedigree of the buying team, those new names will
have been selected with good reason. On the team, Vincent Barat learned
the ropes as a top sommelier (at La Tante Claire, one of the top-rated
restaurants in the *Good Food Guide*), as did wholesale manager Bertrand
Boisleve (different restaurant, different skill set); Guillaume Aubert is a wine
graduate with much practical experience under his belt, and each of them
aids David in the final 'yes/no' decision.

From the Rhône Valley too (particularly the southern Rhône), many of
the wines are exclusives that are seldom seen in the UK. Look to South-west
France, Languedoc, and Piedmont in Italy for exclusivities too, and note that
from Bordeaux there are only unusual, up-and-coming names from the
Côtes and St-Emilion (predominantly). And despite the strong French
influence on the buying team, English Nyetimber is among the newly listed
sparkling wine. You can gauge these buying skills for yourselves at the free
Saturday tastings.

Look out for
- No brands, just quality and individuality from the likes of Green & Red,
  and T-Vine from Napa, California
- Classic Alessandria, Veglio and Grimaldi Barolos from Italy
- Lesser-known Côte de Beaune growers René Lequin-Colin, Paul Pernot
  and Maurice Ecard
- Exciting new champagnes from Pierre Moncuit, Gérard Dubois and
  Forget-Chemin

- Unusual Médoc from châteaux Clos du Marquis, Frank Phelan and Segond de Dufort
- Best white burgundy from villages Meursault, Corton and Chassagne-Montrachet.

Wines of Interest

46 Burlington Road, Ipswich, Suffolk IP1 2HS

Tel (01473) 215752
Fax (01473) 406622
Email woi@fsbdial.co.uk
Website www.winesofinterest.co.uk

Open Mon–Fri 9–6, Sat 9–1 **Closed** Sun, public holidays **Cards** Delta, MasterCard, Switch, Visa; personal and business accounts **Discount** 5% on 1 mixed case **Delivery** Free locally (min. 1 or 2 cases), phone for details; nationwide service (min. 1 case), charge £10 for 1 case, £6 for subsequent cases **Glass hire** Free with order **Tastings and talks** Annual pre-Christmas tasting **£5**

Concentrating on quality and not being wooed by fancy names is the issue here. 'And we don't do "chinless and pinstripe"', says Jonathan Williamson – who wants his list to be genuinely interesting, not just full of 'ivory tower' wines that are difficult to find or afford. So, the Bordeaux section begins with the explanation: 'Traditionalists looking for a huge range of clarets will find our selection thin. It is. We have tasted dozens of wines in the last year and rejected them for their meanness of style, lack of fruit, or, all too often, their unripe, stalky, mouth-puckering unpleasantness.' The team claims it will not stock mediocre wines and, along with their other mission to keep bottles as far below the £10-mark as possible, this means Wines of Interest is a happy hunting ground for quality and affordability.

But the rigours don't stop there. The Jonathans (there are two of them running the show, J Williamson and J Hare) get equally twitchy about anything that's bland and boring – be they under £10 or not. 'We stock NO brands. All our wines come from people who are passionate about what they make,' say Jonathan Williamson. Good for him!

The Jonathans couldn't have had better merchant training, one cutting his teeth as a sommelier (Williamson), the other learning the ropes the East Anglian way with Adnams and Lay & Wheeler (Hare). All this background is reflected in a quirky list. Austrian wines make a big showing, with the enticing Pinot Gris (and others) from the Tscheppe estate; lesser-known Rhône wines from Albert Belle, Jean-Paul Remillier and Domaine de la Mordorée make a splash; and there's a particularly good, and unconventional, look at Australia (get your glass round wines from Charles Cimicky, Margan and Amberley rather than the usual Jacob's-Creek-type suspects).

The Sampling Club is still going strong too. It costs a mere £1.45 a month to pick up 'wines of the month' at half price, plus sealed cases of the same (of any quantity) at 5 per cent discount. We still can't understand why more merchants haven't cottoned on to this good idea.

Look out for

- Bargain mixed cases of 'Everyday' and 'Weekend' wines at £48.30 and £111.85 respectively
- Delicious (and rarely seen) Mexican Barbera from L A Cetto
- White Spanish treasures from traditional Muga Blanco Rioja to trendy Albariño from Martin Codax
- Favourite Burgundy villages: Chambolle-Musigny, Savigny-lès-Beaune and (Beaujolais) St-Amour
- Classic range of Hidalgo sherries, vintage ports and 15-year-old Malmsey madeira
- Unpretentious champagnes from lesser-known, lesser-priced, but still fine houses.

The Wright Wine Company

The Old Smithy, Raikes Road, Skipton,　　　　　*Tel* (01756) 700886
North Yorkshire BD23 1NP　　　　　　　　　　 *Fax* (01756) 798580
　　　　　　　　　　　　　Email bob@wineandwhisky.co.uk
　　　　　　　　　　　　 Website www.wineandwhisky.co.uk

Open Mon–Sat 9–6, Sun (Dec only) & public holidays 10–4　**Closed** Sun (exc. Dec)
Cards MasterCard, Switch, Visa; personal and business accounts　**Discount** 5% on 1
mixed case　**Delivery** Free within 35-mile radius (min. 6 bottles); nationwide service,
phone for details of charges　**Glass hire** Free with order　**Tastings and talks** Not
available ⓔⓢ

The wholesaler pitch of this list is disappointingly apparent in its lack of tasting notes, wine description and nitty-gritty detail. However, we like the fact that the Old World and the New are treated with equal enthusiasm, with a fair balance of superstar wines throughout. Even the less-well-represented regions (Uruguay, Greece) gain a worthy mention.

The other thing we like about the Wright Wine Company is its willingness to try out the new. Not for director/buyer Bob Wright a safe selection of Alsace wines from just one grower, or a Chardonnay-only range of California whites (or Chilean whites, or Australian whites come to that). This is a merchant prepared to source as diversely as possible.

The Wright Wine Company still has the most astonishing array of half bottles we know of – 128 in total – and not just the usual Beaujolais and Loires from France either; the selection is well and truly global. As is the range of sparkling wines: running from £5.75 a bottle for Australian Willowglen Brut from de Bortoli, through fabulous Show Shiraz from Seppelt (the famous Australian sparkling red that'll improve with age for 40 years and more, apparently); England's finest traditional method wine, Nyetimber; Pelorus from New Zealand; and, finally, a choice of over 40 champagnes, culminating in 1995 Roederer Cristal (or a Nebuchadnezzar of White Foil Pol Roger if size is your objective). None of this, of course, would be complete without worshipping on both the right and left banks of Bordeaux – which is done too, to good *cru classé* measure.

'Nothing much has changed in the past year,' says Bob – apart, that is, from the expansion into neighbouring premises, giving this merchant two new rooms to dedicate to whisky and the comfortable perusal of wine shelves. If nothing else has changed, that's fine by us.

Look out for

- South American wines spanning the price range from £4.50 Chilean Cabernet/Carmenère and £9.85 Weinert Argentinian Malbec, to top-notch Chilean Concha y Toro Cabernet at £59.75
- Côte Rôtie from Chapoutier and Vidal-Fleury, Hermitage from Domaine de Vallouit
- A 160-year-old Terrantez madeira (vintage 1842)
- More than Cabernet: California reds from Barbera, Carignan, Petite Sirah and other varieties
- Rosé wines from Portugal, the Rhône and Australia
- Over 200 regional malt whiskies to choose from.

Wrightson & Co Wine Merchants

Manfield Grange, Manfield, Darlington,   *Tel* (01325) 374134
North Yorkshire DL2 2RE   *Fax* (01325) 374135
Email ed.wrightson.wines@onyxnet.co.uk
Website www.thatwineclub.co.uk

Open Mon–Fri 9–5.30 **Closed** Sat, Sun, public holidays **Cards** MasterCard, Switch, Visa; personal and business accounts **Discount** 5% on accounts settled within 7 days **Delivery** Free within 40-mile radius (min. 2 cases); nationwide service available, charge £7.50 for 1 case, £10 for 2 cases, free for 3+ cases **Glass hire** Free with order **Tastings and talks** Available, phone for details

Simon Wrightson says his feet never touch the ground: his search for high-quality wines outside France is a life's mission. And taking a look at the 'wines under £5', 'wines under £6' and 'wines under £10' sections that start off his price list, we think he does a pretty good job of finding them, too. He dips into the New World all over the place and nowhere with more passion than South Africa, where he unearths some real treasures (although he doesn't always list the region they come from, which is a shame). But it's the French wines that we'd come to Wrightson for – or, more accurately, sign up at Wrightson for, as business here is mail-order only.

Bordeaux might kick off with the likes of £695-a-case Ducru-Beaucaillou and £398-a-case La Fleur Pétrus, then continue with second growths, third growths and *premier cru classé* Sauternes, but there are plenty of more modestly priced wines from the Côtes to hunt down too. The Burgundian section is a little less illustrious, mainly concentrating on the wines of Olivier Leflaive, but the wines (we breathe a sigh of relief here) are priced accordingly. Guigal crops up in the Rhône selection, Alsace wines are supplied by the highly respectable Mittnacht Klack, and champagne ranges from the modestly priced to the entirely luxurious (Laurent-Perrier NV Grande Siècle at £48.84 a bottle).

As we said last year, this is indeed a wine lovers' list – not exhaustive, but well thought out, and supplemented by three newsletters a year, four tastings and a bin-end sale. We'd be happy to order a mixed case here at any time, and heartily recommend calling up for a Wrightson's list (or seeking them out online). Simon finishes his wine catalogue with a quote, as follows, from Thomas McKeown, 1912–88: 'Wine experts are of two kinds, gastronomic and intellectual, distinguishable according to whether on sight of the bottle they reach for their glass or their glasses.' We think either would be happy with these wines.

Look out for
- Pavillon Blanc de Château Margaux – arguably Bordeaux's very finest dry white wine
- Choices from top Médoc châteaux: Cos Labory, Langoa-Barton, Ducru-Beaucaillou and Marquis du Terme
- Delicious selection of South African Sauvignon and Shiraz
- Enticing range of dessert wines, including Australian stickies from Campbells and Brown Brothers.

Peter Wylie Fine Wines

Plymtree Manor, Plymtree, Cullompton,	*Tel* (01884) 277555
Devon EX15 2LE	*Fax* (01884) 277557

Email peter@wylie-fine-wines.demon.co.uk
Website www.wyliefinewines.co.uk

Open Mon–Fri 9–6, Sat by appointment **Closed** Sun, public holidays **Cards** None accepted; personal and business accounts **Discount** Available, phone for details **Delivery** Nationwide service, phone for details of charges **Glass hire** Not available **Tastings and talks** By invitation only

If you think the roll-call of ancient claret vintages covering almost every harvest of the last century is impressive, take a look at Peter Wylie's white Bordeaux selection. This covers vintages through the *preceding* century, 1811 to 1900. You need to buy by the bottle, of course, and you'd need to have up to £15,000 in your pocket if you were really serious about the early 1800s, but you could be assured of all the critical details for undertaking such a purchase: neck level, label condition, provenance and fine cellar conditions.

Of course, you can buy today's vintages at Peter Wylie too, but the tradition here is for the unusual and cellarable. So expect the focus to be on Bordeaux (white and red), burgundy, port and madeira. We say 'unusual' in that it's almost as if simply being from the 1990s isn't interesting enough for Peter; he prefers to see his clarets in an outsize format if they're going to err towards the youthful – you can pick up a 2000 Pauillac or a super-status St-Julien (Château Léoville-Barton or Gruaud-Larose) in impériale (8 bottles) or a double-magnum (4 bottles). Or opt for a Jeroboam (6.7 bottles) of 1989 Mouton – you'll actually be £1,225 the poorer for this, but just think what a celebratory trophy you'll have at the end of the day . . .

Even with £50 or £100 in your pocket, you'll easily be able to select a special-occasion wine or birthday gift, as there are plenty of more-modest, mature bottles to choose from. Take a trip down to Plymtree Manor in Devon to see for yourself, or explore the website: either way, like us, you should find this one of the most fascinating speciality ranges in the country.

Look out for
- First-World-War clarets from Mouton-Rothschild and Pichon-Lalande; Second-World-War vintages from Cheval Blanc and Beychevelle
- Bordeaux to store (or drink) yourself, from the 1980s and 1990s

- Almost every declared port vintage since 1910 (top houses Taylor's, Cockburns, Fonseca and more)
- Treasurable vintage madeiras dating back to 1870
- Oddities such as a library of 1990s New Zealand Cloudy Bay; ancient German, Russian and Swiss wines; and 'curiosity' 1960s champagne.

Yapp Brothers

The Old Brewery, Mere, Wiltshire BA12 6DY

Tel (01747) 860423
Fax (01747) 860929
Email sales@yapp.co.uk
Website www.yapp.co.uk

Open Mon–Sat 9–5 **Closed** Sun, public holidays **Cards** Delta, MasterCard, Switch, Visa; personal and business accounts **Discount** Available on 6+ cases, phone for details **Delivery** Nationwide service (min. 1 case), charge £3 for 1 case, free for 2+ cases **Glass hire** Free **Tastings and talks** Available, phone for details

Again, they tell us there's been no change at Yapp. But the smart new wine list is a step up. And we also couldn't help noticing that, in addition to specialities from the Loire, the Rhône and Southern France, there's now not only a new Chablis herein but also a wine from the Savoie, another from Alsace, a champagne house, and even an estate (Jasper Hill) from Australia. The latter might stand out like a sore thumb in this Gallic sea, but it's a good complement to the Syrahs from the Rhône.

There's a sense of serendipity about this merchant. Robin Yapp made a tentative sideways step from his career as a dentist a third of a century ago and stumbled, by chance, on a new talent. It's as if he's never quite believed his luck. With son Jason Yapp and step-son Tom Ashworth now involved too, this has become a 'mini-wine dynasty' almost without the team realising it, and the business looks set to continue its success.

The other piece of luck has to do with their chosen speciality. The Rhône has seen a run of good fortune and good judgement in recent years. Not only has there been a series of spectacularly fine vintages there, but the growers have been shaping up their vineyard and winery practices to the extent that this is now one of France's most reliable wine regions. Hot on the Rhône's heels is Languedoc-Roussillon – and (guess what?) Yapp has an ever-increasing amount of these wines too . . . All this has less to do with chance, perhaps, than it does with canny choices.

'We have never had a formal contract with any of our suppliers, but rely on common sense and friendship, and have never had cause to regret our faith in those men and women, most of whom we count among our closest friends,' says Robin. This almost certainly accounts for the abundance of small but top-quality domaines listed on these pages: nobody marked by mass-production greed, but producers who respect tradition and respect their *terroir*, making their wines accordingly. You can read all about them in the list, which is almost a book – full as it is of short stories and winemaking tales.

Look out for

- March: a good time to visit the Wiltshire shop and pick up a bin-end bottle or case
- Domaines Jean-Yves Multier, Georges Vernay and Neyret-Gachet for the fabulous nutty white Rhône wines Condrieu and Château Grillet
- Hot Mediterranean properties: Domaine de Trévallon, Mas de la Rouvière and Domaine Ferrer Ribière
- Unusual flavours from south-west France from Jurançon and Irouléguy
- Top Northern Rhône growers including Bernard Burgaud, Jasmin (Côte Rôtie), Jean-Louis Chave (Saint-Joseph) and Pascal Frères (Hermitage)
- Fine-quality Loire appellations Savennières, Menetou-Salon, Montlouis and Bourgueil.

Noel Young Wines

56 High Street, Trumpington,
Cambridge CB2 2LS

Tel (01223) 844744
Fax (01223) 844736
Email admin@nywines.co.uk
Website www.nywines.co.uk

Open Mon–Sat 10–8 **Closed** Sun, public holidays **Cards** Amex, Delta, MasterCard, Switch, Visa; business accounts **Discount** Available, phone for details **Delivery** Free within 20-mile radius (min. order £60); nationwide service, charge £7 for 1 case, £4 for subsequent cases, negotiable for larger orders **Glass hire** Free with order **Tastings and talks** Available, phone for details **£5**

A passion for Syrah (now catching on in the rest of the world, we might add) is what struck us first about Noel Young Wines. Such a believer is Noel that he travels annually to Australia to get his hands dirty making 'Shiraz' himself (the resulting wine is sold under his own Magpie Estate label). Throughout the rest of the list the grape also crops up from Italy, Austria, Chile, California, the Rhône (of course) and even New Zealand. To keep tabs on these and everything else that Noel is passionate about, get yourself on to the newsletter mailing list, otherwise you might miss out – turnover is so high at this merchant (understandably, given the quality), that the best wines have to be snapped up as soon as they're spotted. The highly superior newsletter is more like a mini wine list, including pre-release, new release and bin-end offers; this is also the place you'll get first sighting of the 'several thousand' new lines per year.

The stunning selection of New World wines, for example, is so good that it's easy to forget just how tempting the Old World classics are too. Noel's own summary (his 'reasons to be proud') gives the best idea of just how diverse his whole range is. 'Some of the most exciting wines include my own Magpie Estate wines from the Barossa Valley, Australia (I do all the blending). Billecart-Salmon, Gosset and Vilmart Champagne. The super sweet wines from Alois Kracher (Austria). The A–Z selection of top Antipodean wines (particularly Australian). Super dry and sweet wines from Horst Sauer in Franconia . . .' And we'd add *cru classé* Bordeaux dating back to 1952, and top Italian names such as Gaja, Frescobaldi and Conterno to those reasons to be cheerful.

Noel self-confessedly has a good 'punter's palate', and hates journalistic generalisations (those whinges about too much Chardonnay in the world and too much alcohol). And, from his list, he looks to be switched on to what customers actually want. A classic example of this is the mixed-case offers from as little as £49 for 12 bottles. Plus, an average bottle-spend of £8.50 means there are plenty of lower-priced and a fair few quality higher-priced wines available, too. This is another of those classic East Anglian wine merchants for whom the unwritten motto seems to be 'we sell no boring wines'.

Look out for

- Big, boisterous Barossa Shiraz from Turkey Flat, Veritas, Yalumba and Noel's own Magpie Estate
- The best of California, including the prestigious Ridge, Rochioli and Seghesio estates
- Off-beat Italians from Super-Tuscan Solengo to Syrah from Planeta
- Top-notch array of Austrian Rieslings, Grüner Veltliners and other native grapes
- Non-mainstream burgundy from Domaine de la Vougeraie to Henri Gouges and René Engel
- Superb Australian choices including Stefano Lubiano sparkling and Riesling, Mount Horrocks Riesling and Cullen Chardonnay.

Also recommended

A & A Wines

Manfield Park, Guildford Road,
Cranleigh, Surrey GU6 8PT
Tel (01483) 274666
Fax (01483) 268460
Email aawines@aol.com
Website www.spanishwines.co.uk

Andrews Bickerton and Connor
have a very large selection of
Spanish wines for sale – rare and
old bottlings among them – and a
little from France, plus Australia,
South Africa, Chile, Mexico and
Uruguay. But it's really the terrain
south-west of the Pyrenees that
they're smitten with, and where
most of their attention lies. If Spain's
your passion too, we recommend
getting on to the A & A Wines
mailing list to receive the twice-
yearly newsletter and annual wine
list. Having a mixed case delivered
to you won't be a problem, but
you'll have to get in quick as the
Andrews do most of their business
directly with the trade. A & A has
also developed a nice line in
importing Spanish foods over the
last year, so stop off here for your
artichoke hearts, pimentos and
olives too. **(£5)**

A & B Vintners

Little Tawsden, Spout Lane,
Brenchley, Kent TN12 7AS
Tel (01892) 724977
Fax (01892) 722673
Email info@abvintners.co.uk
Website www.abvintners.co.uk

With all the buzz about Languedoc-
Roussillon at the moment, it's a real
pleasure to find a merchant who
actually concentrates on the
exciting new producers we've been
hearing about: Domaines Lavabre
and de l'Hortus from Pic St-Loup,
Mas Champert from St-Chinian and
Domaine Alquier from Faugères, for
example – as we've said before, this
merchant is a study in 'focused
excellence'. Ken Brook and John
Arnold set out to specialise in the
wines of Burgundy, the Rhône and
Languedoc-Roussillon; given that
their chosen specialities are now
such fashionable regions, the
company has achieved 'trendy'
status. (The last year has also seen
the addition of a house champagne
to the list, and Riedel glasses are
still available.) Be warned though:
not all the excellent wines sold at
A&B make it to the annual list. We
advise getting on the mailing list for
all the special offers throughout the
year. **(£5)**

Amey's Wines

83 Melford Road, Sudbury,
Suffolk CO10 1JT
Tel (01787) 377144

Amey's Wines, run and owned by
Peter Amey, came of age this year
with its own newsletter and 18 years
of business behind it. The range of
wines reflects the experience and
Peter's informed eye. It's not a large
selection, but it's of high calibre and
from just about everywhere. Our
favourite sightings are Geoff
Merrill's Grenache Rosé from
Australia, Jade Mountain Carneros
Syrah and Marimar Pinot Noir from
California, plus Cuvée Classique
from Domaine des Jougla in St-
Chinian – one of those new
Languedoc-Roussillon classics.
These wines ably represent exactly

what Peter is trying to do: put
together a list of wines with more
'interest and character' than those of
the chain retailers.

Arriba Kettle & Co

Buckle Street, Honeybourne,
Nr. Evesham,
Worcestershire WR11 5QB
Tel (01386) 833024
Fax (01386) 833541
Email arribakettle@talk21.com

A man of integrity, who won't
supply a wine he doesn't feel is up
to scratch, Barry Kettle is pleased to
announce the return of Menetou-
Salon and Sancerre to his list this
year – their 2000 vintage
outweighing the (he felt) mediocre
1999s which were absent. We
admire this kind of honesty, and we
admire this enticing little list, with
its informative forays into Barry's
favourite wine regions. South Africa
features strongly, with top-notch
estates Simonsig, Neil Ellis and
Kanonkop (plus local recipes,
photographs and a bargain case
selection for a mere £87.50). There's
also a handy choice of Spanish reds
and whites, and (as indicated above)
a carefully chosen range from the
Loire, as well as from the rest of
France. Judging from the list, Barry
doesn't like the average bottle
spend to top a tenner – only in his
beloved Spain does he really allow
this to happen – but this makes the
minimum selection of a mixed case
all the easier. **(£5)**

Benson Fine Wines

96 Ramsden Road, London
SW12 8QZ
Tel 020-8673 4439
Fax 020-8675 5543
Email bensonwines@
connectingbusiness.com
Website
www.bensonfinewines.co.uk

Clare Benson specialises in fine and
rare wines, 'normally pre-1980 back
to the nineteenth century', she says.
We have described this list as a
'treasure trove' in the past, and with
good reason – it is stuffed to the gills
with venerable vintages, especially
of Bordeaux (red, white and sweet),
burgundy and port. Other shorter
sections take in some German,
Italian and Loire oldies among
others; there are a few New World
bins, including Canadian Icewine;
and a light coating of newer
releases. Prices are fair, as they are
for the tickets to Benson's fine wine
and supper evenings. Get along to
one if you like mature wines as
much as Clare clearly does.

Bergerac Wine Cellar

37 Hill Street, St Helier, Jersey
JE2 4UA
Tel (01534) 870756
Fax (01534) 737590
Email marylloyd@jerseymail.co.uk

Mary Lloyd has single-handedly set
up in opposition to Victor Hugo
Wines, Jersey's other main stockist,
and we think she does a rather good
job of filling some of the gaps in
their range. Her selection of
Bordeaux easily matches theirs, for a
start, and the wide choice of
burgundies,while mostly sourced
from the giant Faiveley estate,
covers just about every *commune*
imaginable. The one area she could

easily outshine them in would be Australia, but unfortunately this is a missed opportunity as she lists only three or four bulk-producing estates – we're not going to whinge about the stocks of Penfolds Grange, however! That Jurançon, Israel and Hungary get mentioned we find most impressive, and top allocations from Italy and the Rhône, while not being numerous, are certainly welcome. This isn't a bad port of call for a bottle, magnum or decent vintage of champagne either. **£5**

Bloomsbury Wine & Spirit Co

3 Bloomsbury Street, London WC1B 3QE
Tel 020-7436 4763
Fax 020-7436 4765

As befits a smart area of London, this is a smart little shop from which you can buy just about any of your favourite clarets – and as long as you're after a mature one, you can practically name your vintage. White Bordeaux, vintage port, Alsace, the Rhône, Champagne and Germany also feature here but, this being the traditional haunt it is, you won't find anything else: there's nothing from the new-fangled New World, or anything complicated from Spain or Italy, to clutter this selection. No pretensions, this is about as old-fashioned as a wine merchant can get, but we don't doubt for a minute that there's a market for these wines. They're of good quality and – this being Bloomsbury – price (often sky high) isn't an issue.

Booths of Stockport

62 Heaton Moor Road,
Heaton Moor,
Stockport SK4 4NZ
Tel 0161-432 3309
Fax 0161-432 3309
Email johnbooth@lineone.net
Website www.johnboothwines.co.uk

John Booth's small shop is surrounded by Stockport's supermarkets, so he feels the pressure somewhat, but courageously deals with it head-on by providing a solid list that goes beyond the usual choices. ('If you want Wolf Blass Chardonnay go next door, but we can offer Ninth Island and many cheaper alternatives,' he says.) Those alternative options seem to drum up an increasing loyalty, added to by the fact that Booths doubles up as a delicatessen, so you can avoid shopping 'next door' altogether if you wish. We're impressed by the likes of Montes Alpha Syrah from Chile, Santa Rosa Viognier from Argentina and Pic St-Loup from Foulaquier, France – all of which go some way to proving John's still on track in daring to be different. There are also regular tastings and informative newsletters to watch out for. **£5**

Bordeaux Index

6th Floor, 159–173 St John Street,
London EC1V 4QJ
Tel 020-7253 2110
Fax 020-7490 1955
Email sales@bordeauxindex.com
Website www.bordeauxindex.com

Dealing as he does, at the top end, Dylan Paris is a great believer in French wine, and nothing, he feels, really comes close to matching Bordeaux. 'Only Italy's Piedmont and Tuscany can provide a truly individual and broad-based competition to the greatest of France's appellations,' he says. And this stance pretty much reflects the stocks here. Bordeaux leads, with plenty of its finest – Lafites, Latours and l'Evangiles – dating back to the 1960s, some even earlier; culminating in an amazing array of the illustrious Marojallia, Margaux and Valandraud from the 2000 vintage. Then the top names and vintages of Burgundy (Domaine de la Romanée-Conti included), tip-top Rhônes, the big Italian names (Super-Tuscans included) and, to finish, a couple of those California collectibles, Opus One and Dominus. This is not, then, the place to pick up a bargain, more a place to follow up vinous dreams.

The Bottleneck

7 & 9 Charlotte Street, Broadstairs, Kent CT10 1LR
Tel (01843) 861095
Fax (01843) 861095
Email info@thebottleneck.co.uk
Website www.thebottleneck.co.uk

In the last 15 years Chris and Lin Beckett have turned what was a dingy Kent off-licence into a proper wine shop 'where you can find not just everyday wines but special wines too'. The parting shot from the previous owner was: 'Don't bother with any Australian wines, nobody wants to buy them, and don't run out of Liebfraumilch, it's your best seller.' Needless to say, they ignored this advice and Australia is now top of the bill (delicious dessert wines included). New Zealand, Languedoc and an impressive array of sparklers (vintage Pol Roger among them) follow quickly behind, plus good dip-in, dip-out selections from elsewhere. We like the brimming enthusiasm here, which makes itself felt more than ever in the monthly newsletter (giving the word on latest offers and tastings). **£5**

Budgens

Stonefield Way, Ruislip, Middlesex HA4 0JR
Tel 020-8422 9511
Fax 020-8422 1596
Email info@budgens.co.uk
Website www.budgens.co.uk

(229 branches throughout south-east England)

Sub-£5 is the main rule here, and for real vinous excitement we stick to last year's comments and suggest going elsewhere. But Senior Buyer Christine Sandys is nonetheless doing a good job of balancing the branded wines people expect to see with more 'interesting', lesser-known names of great value. Given the small amount of shelf space she has available per store we're quite impressed to see the likes of Louis Jadot Morgon and Marqués de Griñón Rioja Reserva among the wines on offer, not to mention Cabernet, Syrah and Merlot from the Errázuriz estate in Chile. So it's not all dull news, and with such progress as there has been – much more encouragement to trade up than we've seen in the past, plus weekly special offers and in-store tastings on the cards for the future – things are looking better at Budgens.

The Burgundy Shuttle

168 Ifield Road, London SW10 9AF
Tel 020-7341 4053
Fax 020-7244 0618
Email
peter@theburgundyshuttle.ltd.uk
Website
www.burgundyshuttle.co.uk

'There's an awakening of renewed interest in France,' says Peter Godden of Burgundy Shuttle from his HQ in south-west London. If so, that's good news for his business, based as it is on, er, Burgundy, with plenty of other Gallic offerings. We particularly like the look of the Loire section, which includes wines from the estate of actor Gerard Depardieu as well as Bonnezeaux and Savennières from Château de Fesles. Outside France there is a scattering of New World listings. But Burgundian wines dominate the list – an impressive collection from around 50 growers, some well known, others up and coming. Let Peter talk you through them, or sign up for one of his 'Meet the Growers' dinners, held at local restaurant Chez Max.   **£5**

Anthony Byrne Fine Wines

Ramsey Business Park,
Stocking Fen Road,
Ramsey, Huntingdon,
Cambridgeshire PE26 2UR
Tel (01487) 814555
Fax (01487) 814962
Email info@abfw.co.uk
Website www.abfw.co.uk

Anthony Byrne doesn't do an awful lot of business with the general public – a mere five per cent in fact – but we'd say it's well worth trying to get your foot in the door anyway, as the French wines on offer are some of the best you'll find in Cambridgeshire. Anthony stocks around 2,500 wines (he tells us) and they're sourced from just about everywhere, but nowhere in quite as much depth as France (his Australian and Californian choices, for example, tend to rely on bulk producers such as Lindemans, Rosemount, Gallo and Mondavi). We were particularly taken by the less-than-usual reds from the Loire, Provence and the Rhône, and you can expect to see a stunning array of Bordeaux and burgundies too – but, more refreshing than these, is one of the longest lists of Alsace wines we've ever seen.

Cairns & Hickey Wines

854–856 Leeds Road, Bramhope,
Leeds LS16 9ED
Tel 0113-267 3746
Fax 0113-261 3826
Email pcairns@c-hwines.fsnet.co.uk

'We keep striving for good-value new wines,' reports Ernest Cairns. Indeed, the Cairns & Hickey list will appeal to those who want good drinking at under £6, particularly, in our view, if they turn to the shelves containing the well-chosen Spanish wines and the selections from Chile and Eastern Europe. Australia gets a big look-in, again with plenty of affordable bins, but with some more serious fare from the likes of Cape Mentelle, Mountadam and Evans & Tate. The New Zealand range features a small but impressive set of 16 wines, with firm emphasis on Sauvignon Blanc. It would be nice to see some different aromatic varieties creep in throughout this list, and – talking of different whites – the German section needs plumping out. Still, South America and South

Africa are represented by some reputable names and there are vintage ports, malts and liqueurs to round an evening off nicely. **£5**

Cape Province Wines

77 Laleham Road, Staines, Middlesex TW18 2EA
Tel (01784) 451860
Fax (01784) 469267
Email capewines@msn.com
Website www.capewinestores.co.uk

Peter Loose has been a specialist in Cape wines for 30 years now and his Middlesex merchant business certainly lists some of the finest. We would be keen to drink Plaisir de Merle, Klein Constantia and Thelema, among others, from his range. But it would be good to see some of our favourite South African newcomer wines in amongst the old-timers here, however – the likes of Spice Route, Veenwouden, Warwick and Steenberg are much missed, not to mention Jordan, Kanonkop and Vergelegen. (As a specialist, we'd have thought it wouldn't be too difficult for Cape Province Wines to seek these superstars out . . .) But what is on offer here doesn't resort to championing the cheap brands either. Prices very fairly range from about £5 to £17 a bottle, which should suit most pockets. **£5**

Ceci Paolo

The New Cook's Emporium,
21 High Street, Ledbury,
Herefordshire HR8 1DS
Tel (01531) 632976
Fax (01531) 631011
Email
patriciaharrison@cecipaolo.com
Website www.cecipaolo.com

'Italy is the speciality of Ceci Paolo because so much of the business revolves around food, and we believe that Italian wines are very versatile and match extremely well with a whole range of flavours,' says Australian buyer/director Patricia Harrison – rightly. This, as you might have guessed, is not just a wine merchant (there are in fact only 45 wines on the list we currently have in front of us) but more of a 'lifestyle' emporium – with oils, vinegars, enticing food and wine tastings, wine books, glasses and wine paraphernalia, a deli and a café-bar on offer. That said, the wines are very good indeed. Courtesy of Liberty Wines (*q.v.*), and another Italian specialist supplier, Paul Ceci, they ought to be! Included are Allegrini Amarone and the fascinating Alpha Zeta range made in the Veneto by New Zealand winemakers. **£5**

Cellar 28

William Street, Rastrick, Brighouse, West Yorkshire HD6 1HR
Tel (01484) 710101
Fax (01484) 710222
Email admin@cellar28.com

A burgeoning Yorkshire wholesale business this, but one worth looking to for decently priced wines, as private customers do get a look-in too. We love the handwritten wine list and producer descriptions filling us in on all the information we could need, but particularly warm to the lengthy red and white 'wines under-£5' sections at the back of the booklet, which tend to err towards less-mainstream growers, including Simonsig from South Africa and Michel Torino Torrontés from Argentina. Fill up a mixed case and it'll be delivered to your doorstep for free, too. If anything, there's more strength in the New World half of the list but, for all that, don't rule out top champagnes such as Krug or interesting Italian choices such as classy white Verdicchio. We could browse this list for hours, as among the usual safe-bet choices there are many fascinating oddities . . . ever tried the Golan Heights wines from Israel?

The Cellar D'Or

28 Whiffler Road, Norwich NR3 2AZ
Tel (01603) 424828
Fax (01603) 424829
Email
sara.fizzbuzz@netmatters.co.uk
Website www.cellardor.co.uk

This newish Norwich-based company prides itself on its Australia and Burgundy selections, and also its large stocks of fine and rare wines dating back to the 1890s (the latter are on offer via the Cellar D'Or's association with the Antique Wine Company of Great Britain). We like the serious Rhônes and burgundies on offer and had to tear ourselves away from happy browsing in among the less-usual – intrepid even – Australian choices. As we've said before, we'd like to see more vibrancy from the Argentinian and California wines, but if any energy for sourcing these has been spent instead on running the regular tastings and wine fairs,

we can easily forgive, as with this kind of customer service and overall quality on offer, the Cellar D'Or deserves to do well.

Chandos Deli

6 Princess Victoria Street, Clifton, Bristol BS8 4BP
Tel 0117-974 3275
Fax 0117-973 1020

121 Whiteladies Road, Bristol BS8 2PL
Tel 0117-970 6565

97 Henleaze Road, Henleaze, Bristol BS9 4JP
Tel 0117-907 4391

12 George Street, Bath BA1 2EH
Tel (01225) 314418
Email info@chandosdeli.com
Website www.chandosdeli.com

The three Bristol shops, on a mission to prove Italian wines 'are not ugly ducklings', are still going great guns – and there's now a new shop opened in Bath, too. The fine wine list takes in Dolcettos, Barolos and Barberas from Roberto Voerzio; Jermann, Fonterutoli, Anselmi and Ricasoli also get a look-in; and there's even a sweet Barolo Chinato to look out for on the dessert wine list. There have also been real advances into further parts of the world in the last year. Organic wines step in from southern France; from the States, Stag's Leap Wine Cellars make a welcome appearance, as does ebullient Austrian producer Willi Opitz, with his sumptuous Goldackerl *Trockenbeerenauslese* (another sweetie). This isn't an enormous selection of wines, but it includes everything that could possibly complement the produce on sale in the deli – we wouldn't hesitate to stop in if we were in the vicinity.

Charterhouse Wine Co

82 Goding Street, London SE11 5AW
Tel 020-7587 1302
Fax 020-7587 0982

With all the years this merchant has behind it, it's of no surprise to find the good old-fashioned values of quality, value-for-money and plentiful choice being held dear. It's also unsurprising that there's a strong range of classic clarets and burgundies to choose from – these being the stuff of such a traditional London outlet. All this and there's an honourable next-day delivery service too. But it does come as a surprise to see Australia heading up the wine choices, and with one of the most thoughtful and imaginative selections we've seen. This range is neatly divided into four geographical sections (and thank heavens for that: Australia needs to be understood by the varying flavours its different regions offer). Each spans the field from everyday £5 Cabernets, Chardonnays and blends to small-estate special treats, such as Yarra Yering Pinot Noir and Grange from South Australia, Polish Hill Riesling from Clare Valley, the Pierro Cabernets from Margaret River, and plenty of old-vine Shiraz from the Barossa Valley. Italy, Spain, South America and the Rhône are all covered well too, but with nowhere near the same enthusiasm. It would be for the Australian wines that we'd make our stop at Charterhouse. **(£5)**

Châteaux Wines

Head office
Paddock House,
Upper Tockington Road,
Tockington, Bristol BS32 4LQ
Tel (01454) 613959
Fax (01454) 613959

Châteaux Wines Warehousing & Distribution
c/o Octavian, Eastlays Warehouse, Gastard, Nr Corsham, Wiltshire SN13 9PP
Email enquiries@chateauwines.co.uk
Website www.chateauxwines.co.uk

By-passing the *négociants* and big-time dealers, the mission at Châteaux Wines is to supply just these: wines from smaller single domaines or single châteaux. In doing this, David and Cheryl Miller have put together a compact selection of less-well-known wines (almost all French) that takes in Bordeaux, Burgundy, Beaujolais, the Rhône, Mediterranean France, Champagne – oh yes, and Lebanon. The only downside is that the minimum purchase is one unmixed case; quite restrictive given the many unknowns in this selection: we'd be happier trying a bottle here and there, to see what we thought. Prices, however, are very tempting, so it may be worthwhile attending Châteaux Wines' annual London tasting – or dropping in at the Tockington shop to taste in-house – before you select your case. If not, the wine list and the website are full of enough enthusiastic information to help you in your choice. **(£5)**

Brian Coad Fine Wines

Unit B, 41 Valley Road, Plympton,
Plymouth PL7 1RE
Tel (01752) 896545
Fax (01752) 691160
Email
briancoadfinewines@lineone.net

This glossy list is mainly designed
for Devonshire's wholesale
customers – so no tasting notes to
glean from – but producer profiles
usefully abound and we give top
marks for the quality of what's on
offer. Brian Coad is a Francophile
through and through, and this is
unashamedly reflected in his wines
– right from plentiful regional
Mediterranean choices and a
pageful of rosés to top-class
Burgundian offerings from
Domaine de la Vougeraie and
Mugneret-Gibourg. (We wouldn't
rule out filling our mixed case with
Bordeaux either, when there are
crus bourgeois bargains and classy
châteaux' second-label wines to
choose from.) Brian has expanded
his vinous horizons way beyond his
usual shores this year and is now
sourcing from as far afield as
Australia (with impressive additions
from Yalumba and Vasse Felix),
Chile, Canada and South Africa;
he's also one of the few stockists to
list a decent selection of Greek
wines – and he's discovered
Grover's range of Indian wines too.
With all these new adventures, it's
no wonder he's moved into new
premises.

Cochonnet Wines

Trengilly Wartha Inn, Constantine,
Falmouth, Cornwall TR11 5RP
Tel (01326) 340332
Fax (01326) 340332
Email trengilly@compuserve.com
Website www.wineincornwall.co.uk

'Customers come to us for the weird
and wonderful, and go to the
supermarkets for the "supper"
wines,' says Nigel Logan, who
refuses to sell dull brands just to
cover the overheads. Although the
wines here might be unusual, more
tentative purchasers can feel free to
taste many of them by the glass in
the bar of the Trengilly Wartha Inn
(same address, and part and parcel
of the same company). For a flavour
of Nigel's pursuit of individuality,
take a look at the Australian section
of the list (the usual haven for big
brand names): you'll have heard of
Henschke, Moss Brothers and
Nepenthe, but we like the plethora
of smaller estates such as Mallee
Point, Jane Brook and Tortoiseshell
Bay. There's also an impeccably
chosen selection from Portugal and
California (occasionally climbing
towards the £20 mark, but for Ridge
Lytton Springs entirely worth it).
And things really get unusual with
the Austrian range – a whole page
to indulge us in the 'great
Chardonnay escape'. France
receives no less attention, especially
the nine-strong Alsace section (our
favourites). And countrywide
delivery is available, by the way.

432

Colombier Vins Fins

Colombier House, Cadley Hill
Industrial Estate,
Ryder Close, Swadlincote,
Derbyshire DE11 9EU
Tel (01283) 552552
Fax (01283) 550675
Email jehu@colombierwines.co.uk
Website
www.colombiervinsfins.co.uk

An unusual set-up this: buyer and
owner Jehu Attias is a Bordeaux-
qualified winemaker who also runs
a Beaune-based *négociant* business in
Burgundy. It seems strange to find
such a well-qualified French team
(Jehu and his wife Micheline) based
in the middle of Derbyshire, but
then there's obviously a market for
good wine here, and a keen one at
that. Colombier sticks mainly to
France and Italy, taking in quick
snapshots from the rest of the
world. The collection has an
interesting balance between big
names and total unknowns – mostly
Bordeaux for the former, burgundy
for the latter. 'And there's plenty to
chew through,' says Micheline. 'We
have introduced a new "first line
wines" range which gives the
opportunity at a glance to choose
from 50 wines under £4 a bottle.' We
like the idea of the no-charge
customer club too, whereby
members can purchase at ex-VAT
prices. As they say, you won't find
this sort of package in a
supermarket.

Connolly's Wine Merchants

Arch 13, 220 Livery Street,
Birmingham B3 1EU
Tel 0121-236 9269
Fax 0121-233 2339
Email sales@connollyswine.co.uk
Website www.connollyswine.co.uk

The wine list is entitled 'Book of
Bacchus', with a big B, and once
again it begins with one of Chris
Connolly's friendly poems (as
before, we use the word 'poem'
loosely). This year's involves the
'Ground Force' crew, with
Connolly's coming to the rescue
with celebratory champagne once
all the gardening work is done.
Connolly's has a fine selection of
fizz, so we'd be happy to be rescued
by any of these bottles ourselves,
especially as there's not only good-
value champagne here but sparkling
offerings from Australia, New
Zealand and Argentina, too.

Chris is also proud of his
burgundy and Bordeaux classics, his
vintage ports and his Italian list,
each of which, again, runs the
gamut from beginner's
entertainment to expensive items
for the experts (the latter climbs to
£395 for a bottle of 1989 Château
Haut-Brion). We'd like to see more
poetry in the form of tasting notes
and wine descriptions, so that the
beginner would have a little more
idea of where and what to trade up
to, but as only 20 per cent of
Connolly's business is with the
general public, perhaps this isn't felt
to be necessary. It's good, however,
to see that the website is now, at
long last, up and running.

433

The Co-op

Head office
PO Box 53, New Century House,
Manchester M60 4ES
Tel 0161-834 1212
Fax 0161-834 4507
Website www.co-opdrinks2u.com

(1,100 branches nationwide)

The majority of the Co-operative Group's stores are licensed. The wines on sale are sourced by the central Manchester office, but under the Co-op umbrella a number of separate groups, large and small, may choose to stock different (some quite exhaustive, others more limited or less imaginative) ranges from the whole selection. This tends to make generalisations about the Co-op difficult. One thing we can say, however, is that shopping at the Co-op enables some of the lowest wine-spends possible. The most adventurous ranges tend to be found in the north of the UK, and include such treasured findings as Fairview Chardonnay from South Africa and Brown Brothers' Tarrango from Australia. But we did have to peer pretty closely at the list before we spotted these good things.

However, in the last year we have seen an impressive series of customer-friendly improvements, which, let's hope, will extend to the range of wines in the next 12 months. Fifty-three of the stores now offer a home-delivery service; the on-going labelling programme has begun listings of all wine ingredients and also the inclusion of details in Braille on a range of own-brand spirits (we'd really like to see it extending to wine labels too); and the group rightly prides itself on a strengthening organic own-label selection. And more Australian,

Californian and South African wines have upped the availability of those warm, ripe New World flavours.

Davy & Co

Davy's Wine Shop
161–169 Greenwich High Road,
Greenwich, London SE10 8JA
Tel 020-8858 9147
Email was@davy.co.uk
Website www.davy.co.uk

(40 wine bars in London, 1 in Bristol)

The merchant side of Davy & Co operates on a mostly mail-order basis. We recommend signing yourself up with the company as soon as possible, particularly if you're a Bordeaux fan, as any delivery it makes to you will be free of charge. Clarets range from 1978 Château Pichon-Baron, at a respectable £45 a bottle, to 1997 Gruaud-Larose (£35), with plenty of affordable *crus bourgeois* and appellation wines along the way. Londoners can get an idea of the non-Bordeaux French wines in stock by popping into a Davy's wine bar to sample one of its own-label brands – there's plenty on offer at below £10 a bottle – or, as you'll see from the list, snapshot selections are made from just about everywhere else in the world. Being a long-established traditionalist, it's no surprise to see healthy stocks of port and madeira here too. **(£5)**

deFINE Food & Wine

Chester Road, Sandiway,
Cheshire CW8 2NH
Tel (01606) 882101
Fax (01606) 888407
Email
office@definefoodandwine.com

An unusual source of very good
wine, collected by real wine lovers
John Campbell and Graham
Wharmby, who make no space for
bottles they aren't prepared to drink
themselves. Take Bordeaux for
instance: as we've said before, you'd
have trouble filling a case from the
range here. On the other hand,
Italy, Spain and South Africa are
particular passions, so feature
highly (and imaginatively), but
wines from some parts of the world
are bypassed completely. The
disadvantage with deFINE is that
you have to live in Cheshire to
benefit from it, as there is no
website or wine list to delve into off-
site. We can tell you that if you'd
like a case or two of Soave
delivered, the guys have 13 to
choose from (and more to come – if
this *Guide* offered a Soave Specialist
Award, they would be serious
contenders). But beyond that, it's
the lucky residents of Chester who
get to hear about all the new wines
and tasting events. **£5**

Drinks Etc

36 High Street, Boroughbridge,
North Yorks YO51 9AW
Tel (01423) 323337
Fax (01423) 323353
Email andy@drinks-etc.co.uk
Website www.drinks-etc.co.uk

Purveyors of competitively priced
quality wines to the people of North
Yorkshire, Drinks Etc is still taking
Boroughbridge by storm, with the
same wide range of top-quality
wine as last year. It is heartening to
see the likes of châteaux Larrivet
Haut-Brion, Giscours and Brane-
Cantenac priced around the £30-a-
bottle mark, even if that is pre-tax,
and an even better surprise to see
Fontanafredda Barolo and Antinori
Chianti Classico from Italy coming
in below the £20 mark.

Drinks Etc still has as
adventurous an Australian list as it
always did (good-quality estates such
as Mount Langi Ghiran, d'Arenberg
and Mount Horrocks mix in with
everyday brands and smaller, new
properties, giving a great spectrum
of choice) and this year Andrew
Saxon is particularly pleased with
new additions to his South African
list. We can see why. Nationwide
delivery at a minimal charge means
nobody has to miss out on a good
thing, as we're also tempted by the
other 'drinks etc' on the list (malt
whiskies, imported lagers, pale ales
and many more). **£5**

Eckington Wines

2 Ravencar Road, Eckington,
Sheffield S21 4JZ
Tel (01246) 433213
Fax (01246) 433213
Email
qandrewloughran@supanet.com

We strongly suspect that Andrew
Loughran adores big, powerful,
spicy red wines above all else – his
list gives it away, with so much top-
rank Australian Shiraz, Rhône red
and Spanish classics. Throw in some
Argentinian Malbec, Italian Super-
Tuscans, and vintages of Lebanon's
Chateau Musar back to 1966, and
you've got a fine range of reds
indeed. Other areas covered well
include Uruguay, Champagne and
white Rhône. This is an interesting,
premium set of wines with plenty of
mature vintages – from a friendly
local merchant with 38 years'
experience.   (£5)

Edencroft Fine Wines

8–10 Hospital Street, Nantwich,
Cheshire CW5 5RJ
Tel (01270) 629975
Fax (01270) 625302
Email sales@edencroft.co.uk
Website www.edencroft.co.uk

Wine was originally a mere sideline
at this speciality deli and fresh meat
shop, but Edencroft now sells more
bottles of wine than anything else.
Nice to see such enthusiasm in
Nantwich, inspired no doubt by
serious Australian bins, some fine
Italian reds, old stocks of Tokaji, tip-
top champagnes and Trimbach's fine
Alsace whites. Premium stuff – not
once does the range stray off into the
mundane and sub-standard. That
said, there were no prices on the list
they sent us, so we can't comment
on value for money this year.   (£5)

Ben Ellis Wines

Brockham Wine Cellars,
Wheelers Lane, Brockham,
Surrey RH3 7HJ
Tel (01737) 842160
Fax (01737) 843210
Email sales@benelliswines.com
Website www.benelliswines.com

As we've said before, there's nothing
here we wouldn't be happy to try –
no also-rans, nothing middle-of the
road; everything is drinkable in its
own right, and reasonably priced
too. The shop is run by two Masters
of Wine (Mark Pardoe and Lance
Foyster), so the quality of the wine is
hardly surprising – and the tutored
tastings are well worth attending.
The list features France above all
else, and the Bordeaux, Burgundy
and Rhône sections shine with all
the brilliance you'd expect (though
it's a shame that Mark and Lance
didn't think to send us their 'Fine
Wine Supplement' this year, as we'd
have liked to talk about the full 'Ben
Ellis experience' in terms of the
classics). The team has recently
purchased FWW (UK) Ltd and, in
doing so, greatly expanded the
range of Austrian choices. Only 20
per cent of Ben Ellis' business is with
the general public, so you'll have to
get in quick if you want a glimpse of
the kind of quality we're talking
about.   (£5)

English Wine Centre

Alfriston Roundabout, East Sussex
BN26 5QS
Tel (01323) 870164
Fax (01323) 870005
Email bottles@englishwine.co.uk
Website www.englishwine.co.uk

As the name implies, this is the place to come to taste, buy and enjoy English wine, and the range on sale is a pretty good snapshot of just what this country's top growers and winemakers can achieve. Christopher Ann, at the helm, has an obvious enthusiasm for the industry and is keen that his merchant business offers English producers all the support he can give. All our favourites are here: the exceptional Ridgeview sparkling wine, Chapel Down's Epoch range, Hidden Springs' Dark Fields and Decadence, plus an interesting experimental range from Plumpton Agricultural College. The English Wine Centre has been up and running for 30 years now and we can't think of a better place to spend the day getting to know our home-grown wines. Tastings are accompanied by either a local sausage and regional cheese ploughmans or a cream tea. If you can't make the trip, then a nationwide delivery service will bring the wines to you. **£5**

Evington's Wine Merchants

120 Evington Road,
Leicester LE2 1HH
Tel 0116-254 2702
Fax 0116-254 2702
Email evingtonwine@fsbdial.co.uk
Website www.evingtons-wines.com

Simon March is an experienced wine taster and communicator (with 45 years' experience) and a self-confessed 'generally good bloke' – but he is still on a crusade to get customers to part with more money than they wish to. However, this is all to the good purpose of ensuring that they drink better wine. And Evington's is, indeed, a source of better wine. After the obvious delights of the fizz (Laurent-Perrier, Gosset, Bollinger) the list launches into a delicious selection of Loire wines, from Baumard Savennières to luscious Quarts de Chaume, and thereafter treats each of the world's wine regions to the same kind of upper-class discernment. Even the Australia section doesn't waste time trawling the brands but launches in with Brown Brothers' highly respectable varietal range, then builds up to Petaluma Clare Valley Riesling and a selection of Granges going back to 1989. And we're particularly impressed by Simon's intrepid Portuguese and Spanish choices. Don't expect too many bargains here, but do expect wines which reflect genuine enthusiasm.

Falcon Vintners

74 Warren Street, London W1T 5PF
Tel 020-7388 7055
Fax 020-7388 9546
Email eric@falconvintners.co.uk

Buyer/director Eric Sabourin prides his range for its 'extensive selection of young and old Italian classics'. This is no hollow claim. With the words Ornellaia, Sassicaia, Solaia and Tignanello swimming in profusion in front of your eyes before you're past the first two pages of the list, it doesn't take long to see what he means. We admit we've never seen quite so many Super-Tuscans gathered together in one booklet. This isn't just a gaggle of the flashy newcomers, however – the 'old' Italians are more than adequately represented. We counted over 100 Barolos last year, and this year we reckon there are 200 or so, plus Barbaresco, top Amarone, Barbera and more. Not that quantity is the true measure of a fine wine merchant. Access to the all-but-inaccessible is a better marker, and the Bordeaux, burgundy and developing Rhône and champagne lists are ready to add to the stellar Italian selection. Although a mere 20 per cent of Falcon's business is with the public (the rest wholesale), Eric makes sure his range is thoroughly get-at-able by listing with-VAT prices alongside trade rates, and offering a local and nationwide delivery service as well as regular bin-end offers by email. **£5**

Ferrers le Mesurier and Son

Turnsloe, North Street, Titchmarsh, Kettering, Northamptonshire
NN14 3DH
Tel (01832) 732660
Fax (01832) 732660

The Dower House, Parish Road, Stratton Strawless, Norfolk
NR10 5LP
Tel (01603) 279975
Email blaiselm@aol.com

This is one of those clever sub-£10-a-bottle selections that takes in nothing of the New World but focuses instead on wines that the proprietor, Ferrers le Mesurier, is genuinely fond of (you'll see this as soon as you read the tasting notes). France is the hunting ground; Burgundy, the Rhône, Beaujolais and the Loire the favoured regions. 'Certain classic areas are far too complacent, producing pretty dreary offerings. This means that searching out quality producers has become much harder, but we feel we have found some very attractive newcomers,' says Ferrers. He certainly does know what he's looking for. We particularly like his choice of burgundies from A F Gros (the only wines to creep over that £10-a-bottle mark) but would be happy to select a mixed case from anything in this succinct but excellent range. Ferrers and his son Blaise will give talks or tastings by appointment – and we bet 28 years in the Northamptonshire wine trade has provided them with some interesting things to talk about. **£5**

Le Fleming Wines

19 Spenser Road, Harpenden,
Hertfordshire AL5 5NW
Tel (01582) 760125
Fax (01582) 760125
Email cherry@leflemingwines.co.uk

Cherry Jenkins is a one-woman
band, most of whose focus and
energy goes into her fine collection
of Australian wines (as we've said
before, for value and variety this is
one of the best Down Under
collections in the country), but who
can hardly be faulted for the calibre
of her choices from the rest of the
world: we know many far larger
teams who fail to achieve even half
this much quality. From Australia
watch out for the most delicious
collection of Riesling (Rockford's,
Wynn's, Henschke's and Mount
Horrocks' all included); off-beat
varieties such as Pinot Gris, Arneis,
Verdelho and Nebbiolo; plus a
hearty group of full-on Shiraz. Don't
miss the Alsace, Burgundy and
Loire classics from France (to pick
out the best), take advantage of this
year's new venture into Chile
(wines from Carmen, Montgras and
Alvaro Espinosa), and you won't be
disappointed. Our only problem
would be sticking to one mixed case.
One other thing: a one-woman
team she might be, but Cherry's
answerphone is always alert to any
requests – so, should she be away
on a buying trip (not unlikely), have
no fear; your wishes will still be
granted.

For the Love of Wine

See I Love Wine

Forth Wines

Crawford Place, Milnathort,
Kinross-shire KY13 9XF
Tel (01577) 866001
Fax (01577) 866010
Email enquiries@forthwines.com

Forth Wines is owned by Matthew
Clark plc, where Dr Arabella
Woodrow MW heads up the buying
team, so the general high quality of
what's on offer here is unsurprising.
Business is mostly wholesale, so
don't expect any titillating tasting
notes, bottles open for customers or
tastings to attend – but persistent
shoppers will be able to fill their
mixed case with imaginative
choices, such as Grüner Veltliner
from Austria and Idaho Riesling
from the USA. As we've commented
before, it's these quirky alternatives
that balance out what turns out to
be a rather bland bunch of wines
from the New World. For the
classics, however, we'd thoroughly
recommend Kinross-shire locals pay
a visit, as Forth has one of the best
Bordeaux ranges we've seen from a
Scottish merchant. Oh, and there
are a good few malt whiskies on
offer too.

Four Walls Wine Company

The Old Forge, 1 High Street,
Chilgrove, nr Chichester,
West Sussex PO18 9HX
Tel (01243) 535360
Fax (01243) 535418
Email fourwallswine@cs.com

An attractive and wide-ranging set
of two dozen 'house wines' opens
Barry Phillips' list, offering 'drinking
pleasure at reasonable cost and
suitable for any occasion'. Indeed,
with such reliable names as Louis
Latour, Wairau River, Roederer and

Enate featured here, you could be forgiven for being too lazy to venture further. That would be a mistake, however, as you would miss out on some of the French classics and marvellous old bottles to be found in later pages, and these are the main points of interest at Four Walls. The extensive collections of Puligny-Montrachets and Meursaults are dazzling, as are the wonderful, mature Sauternes and Barsacs, the Loire sweeties, the first growths 'and their siblings' and the vintage ports. Barry reports that business has increased of late, especially with the restaurant trade. We say, don't let the on-trade snaffle up the best stock! Oh, and the bin-end list is worth checking out too. **(£5)**

Rhône vintages going back to 1993, and quality Italian offerings such as Fontanafredda Barolo and Barbi Brunello di Montalcino – not to mention more adventurous choices from the fashionable Mezzogiorno (the Italian south). No less intrepid is the New World selection (always particularly good at this merchant): Western Australian boutique estates feature highly, as do more hard-to-get wines such as Penfolds Grange; and the South African and Chilean choices are especially fine. What's also great about this list is that the wines are competitively priced. All this and there are also tastings to attend, bottles open in the shops, and newsletters sounding out any bargains to be had. Carry on like this, John, and this will be a 'Top 100' entry next year . . .

(£5)

John Frazier

Head office
Stirling Road, Cranmore Industrial Estate, Shirley, Solihull,
West Midlands B90 4NE
Tel 0121-704 3415
Fax 0121-711 2710

New Inn Stores, Stratford Road,
Wooten Wawen, Solihull,
West Midlands B95 6AS
Tel (01564) 794151

2 Old Warwick Road, Lapworth,
Solihull B94 6LU
Tel (01564) 784695

Main Road, Tiddington,
nr Stratford-upon-Avon CV37 7AN
Tel (01789) 262398
Email sales@fraziers.co.uk
Website www.fraziers.co.uk

We have John Frazier's 30th-anniversary wine list in front of us (Summer 2002) and we do think this is one of its best ever. Choices are global and broadly sourced from every wine region. There are bargain wines from the French Midi,

Friarwood

26 New Kings Road, London
SW6 4ST
Tel 020-7736 2628
Fax 020-7731 0411
Email sales@friarwood.com
Website www.friarwood.com

Traditionally the place to come for smart older burgundy and Bordeaux vintages – but the bang-up-to-date range of 2000 Médocs, choice selections of Italian Barolo, Amarone and Chianti, and California classics from Ridge, Clos Pegase and Bonny Doon seem to imply that Friarwood is branching out. It is, indeed, opening up two more shops this year: we wish the team luck. This is an imaginative and high-quality collection that appears to carry no slack and, for the most part, keeps its prices manageable. We admire the brief ventures abroad, but it's still the classics that ooze confidence here and it is for these we would return. **(£5)**

Garrards Wine & Spirit Merchants

49 Main Street, Cockermouth, Cumbria CA13 9JS
Tel (01900) 823592
Fax (01900) 823592
Email admin@garrards-wine.co.uk
Website www.garrards-wine.co.uk

Christopher Garrard has suffered the dual setbacks of a heart attack and a Sainsbury's Local moving into town within the last year, so he is trying to take things easy, while attempting to fend off the challenge from a major multiple next door. We don't think he has too much to worry about, as his range of wines (and beers) is a great deal more interesting than anything the supermarkets have to offer. 'We are situated in a small market town and therefore cannot afford to specialise too much,' he says, but his array of choices, particularly from France – to which he has noticed his customers returning after their infatuation with Australia – includes enough special bottles to ensure that any off-the-street purchaser will want to come back. The range of prices at Garrards is particularly impressive: there's plenty to be had for around a fiver, but for just £20 more you can pick up a bottle of top-class claret (châteaux Kirwan, d'Armailhac and d'Issan among others). Bargains indeed. There's also a nice line in pre- and post-prandials – sherry, port, brandy and liqueurs – not to mention champagne.

J A Glass

11 High Street, Dysart, Kirkcaldy, Fife KY1 2UG
Tel (01592) 651850
Fax (01592) 654240

It's always great to see a merchant with an apt name, and Duncan Glass, buyer and partner at this fine old Scottish wine merchant, certainly has one of those. For our glass, we'd head to the Bordeaux section above all others on this list: it exceeds the rest of the bunch by a good way with its healthy balance of different *communes*, ready and not-ready vintages, big illustrious names and smaller, regional châteaux. For the rest of the range, it would be good to see a few more producers – although most major wine countries are covered, their presence seems sketchy. All, that is, except the sparklers at the end of the list: there's everything here from Cuvée Napa Mumm (California) to Krug, Cava and Canard-Duchêne. Would that every other style was covered so thoroughly.

Gloag Taylor Wines 🎖️

Culdeesland, Methven, Perthshire PH1 3QE
Tel (01738) 840494
Fax (01738) 840100
Email sales@gloag-taylor-wines.co.uk
Website www.gloag-taylor-wines.co.uk

Although it's mostly wholesale based, we like Gloag Taylor's cheery newsletters and three- and six-bottle wine box offers, which make this merchant friendly to purchasers of any pocket (the usual minimum purchase here being a mixed case of 12). Starting with the New World, the list works its way towards the Old, finishing with port and

441

champagne, and taking in just about everything as it goes. The Australian selection is by far the superior, charting every region from Barossa to Pemberton and back to Rutherglen; hefty Cabernet and Shiraz are all present, but nothing for which you'll have to break the bank – maximum spend is about £12 a bottle. Turn to the Rhône and Bordeaux sections and you might feel your wallet quaking a little more, but the quality of what's on offer is nonetheless reassuring. Proprietor/buyer Julie Taylor makes some nice choices. **(£5)**

Goedhuis & Co

6 Rudolf Place, Miles Street, London SW8 1RP
Tel 020-7793 7900
Fax 020-7793 7170
Email enquiries@goedhuis.com
Website www.goedhuis.com

The minimum purchase of one mixed case is hardly going to faze any Bordeaux-lovers out there. Goedhuis has a startlingly good array of top-class châteaux from which to choose, many of them at entirely manageable prices. (We don't count the 1999 Château Le Pin Pomerol among this lot, at £3,500 a case, but then it's astonishing even to be able to get hold of it.) The burgundy range is very much on the ball too, and we recommend taking advantage of any of the *en primeur* offers you see – whether buying by domaine, *commune* or price, there's plenty there. France is the main issue at this establishment, but we find the Italian options rather enticing; Ata Rangi from New Zealand, Casa Lapostolle from Chile and Bernardus from California do nothing to quell our enthusiasm either. Snap up the annual bin-end

and regular case offers to make the most of the quality available here.

Gordon & MacPhail

58–60 South Street, Elgin, Moray IV30 1JY
Tel (01343) 545110
Fax (01343) 540155
Email retail@gordonandmacphail.com
Website www.gordonandmacphail.com

Wine still comes second to whisky at Gordon & MacPhail and it probably always will. But then, as purveyors of the largest range of Scotch whiskies in the world, the team can't be expected to be masters of both disciplines. In terms of a wide range, however, they certainly try. There's everything here from Hungarian Chardonnay to top, red burgundy, via Mexican Cabernet and Lebanese white wine. Name the wine-producing country and it's probably on this list – that even goes for Scotland (OK, it's not real wine, but sloe wine, silver birch wine, plum wine . . .). But this isn't the first place we'd come to for wine in Scotland: there's still a heavy reliance on one main bulk producer per region and, in California, for example, we don't think that the wines of Kendall Jackson are representative of what this area can achieve. The same goes for the KWV in South Africa. Perhaps, instead of ensuring they can tick every box, Gordon & MacPhail should focus a little more adventurously on the wine regions it seems to have an affinity with – Burgundy and Australia, for starters.

The Grape Shop

135 Northcote Road, Battersea,
London SW11 6PX
Tel 020-7924 3638
Fax 020-7924 3670
Email dp@thegrapeshop.com

'A former wholesaler and shipper of Loire wines, turned retailer five years ago, now happily providing wine for the denizens of Battersea and Clapham,' is how Grape Shop owner David Potez describes himself. His emphasis has shifted from the Loire in particular to France in general, and is aimed at 'quality affordable wines for drinking now'. We like his cleverly chosen Bordeaux selection, which sticks to a handy £10–£20 range, and includes tempting châteaux' second wines. There's also a wide variety of Burgundy growers, including the excellent La Chablisienne, and good attention is paid to the Rhône, the Languedoc and, of course, the Loire. This looks like a great place for Londoners to pop in for a reliably good bottle, and although the New World choices aren't quite as imaginative, the rest of the stock is above and beyond what you'll find in your average supermarket. Watch out for the free annual tastings too.

£5

Grapeland

27 Parkfield, Chorleywood,
Hertfordshire WD3 5AZ
Tel (01923) 284436
Fax (01923) 286346
Email info@grapeland.uk.com
Website www.grapeland.uk.com

In 2000, Graham Cork decided to exchange 20 years in insurance for the opportunity of setting up his own mail-order wine business. The company may be still young but it's already impressive. Graham sensibly starts most of his country selections with a 'pivotal' group of £4.99 wines, and it's good to see he's not sticking to the obvious Chardonnays with these, but bringing in Verdelho from Australia, plus Viognier and Cabernet Franc from California. Choices are similarly intrepid from Argentina (Bonarda, Pinot Gris and Torrontés grapes) and South Africa, and there are also quality growers to trade up to beyond the big producers. Classics from France have an important presence on the first few pages of the list (such is the way of most serious wine merchants) and there's no shortage of helpful tasting notes to guide the beginner and enthusiast through each vintage and château. Graham has maintained his passion for customer service: bottles are opened in-shop for tasting; there are healthy discounts if you join the (no-fee) customer club; tasting events are held if requested . . . his enthusiasm is infectious. **£5**

Great Gaddesden Wines

At the Sign of the Flying Corkscrew,
Leighton Buzzard Road,
Water End, nr Hemel Hempstead,
Hertfordshire HP1 3BD
Tel (01442) 412311
Fax (01442) 412313
Email info@flyingcorkscrew.co.uk
Website www.flyingcorkscrew.co.uk

Great Gaddesden Wines is an 'Also recommended' entry this year only because just 5% of its trade is with the public. This may well change next year, as it opened a new retail warehouse in June 2002. Either way, it's a company we strongly recommend for its wide range of inspiring bottles from around the world. The clearly laid-out brochure kicks off with southern France, from which Paul Johnson has sourced an admirably adventurous set of wines, including Picpoul and old vines Mourvèdre and Grenache. There are some pickings to be had from the classic regions of France (the Rhône is particularly strong, with offerings from Seguret and Guigal; while Alsace features the wines of Ostertag), and the champagnes and sparkling wines are impressive. We especially like the Italian, Spanish, Californian and South African entries, too, and welcome the appearance of Greece and Austria. The back of the list presents a host of house wines costing under £5 and plenty of irresistible fortified wines, dessert wines and olive oils. An excellent company – we look forward to checking out its new outlet for next year's edition of the *Guide*. **(£5)**

H & H Bancroft ⓦ

1 China Wharf, Mill Street,
London SE1 2BQ
Tel (0870) 444 1700
Fax (0870) 444 1701
Email sales@handhbancroft.co.uk
Website www.handhbancroft.com

This smart, upmarket merchant has been pushed by sheer volume of business into moving its HQ from Covent Garden to China Wharf, thus swapping the 'waft of rotting vegetables for the peaceful lapping of the Thames'. The new, rather more genteel set-up sounds more in keeping with the company, which concentrates on traditional France and Italy and rarely pulls in the cheap and cheerful. Neither does it aim to cover the winemaking globe. Don't expect anything from, say, Germany or Eastern Europe. But when H & H Bancroft covers a region, it does it exceptionally well,

as we have pointed out in the past. Burgundy, the Rhône and the Loire are good examples of this, and we would dearly love to dive into the exciting-looking Italian section, as we admit we haven't tasted some of the wines from lesser-known producers featured there. Indeed, alongside the more familiar names from France, H&HB makes a point of stocking wines from what it hopes are emerging future stars. Two extra marks go to the company for listing plenty of half bottles and magnums, and for including user-friendly maps of wine regions in its brochure.

The Halifax Wine Company

18 Prescott Street, Halifax,
West Yorkshire HX1 2LG
Tel (01422) 256333
Email
andy@halifaxwinecompany.com
Website
www.halifaxwinecompany.com

Andy Paterson is a self-professed 'anorak', who is blissfully happy making a living by indulging his hobby. After 25 years in the business, he has finally taken the plunge, and in August 2001 set up as an independent wine merchant. His soft spot for all things Riesling (any real wine lover will admit the same) is one of the first things to show itself, even in the youthful throes of this list. There's a delicious array of them: German classics, a couple from New Zealand and Austria and, best of all, a selection from Australia – which includes the star of them all, Polish Hill Riesling from Jeffrey Grosset. But the Halifax Wine Company supplies West Yorkshire with far more than this; even in its early days, this list has something of everything – from 'Oh my goodness!' wines (Château

Margaux 1989) to the more off-beat (Jurançon from south-west France), and from everyday, £5-ish prices to one-off £160-bank-busters. One thing's for sure, we can't fault the enjoyment that oozes from the pages of the bimonthly newsletter *Wine-ing On!* . . .   **£5**

Hall Batson & Co

28 Whiffler Road, Norwich NR3 2AZ
Tel (01603) 415115
Fax (01603) 484096
Email info@hallbatson.co.uk
Website www.hallbatson.co.uk

This Norwich-based company is still busy contending to become one of East Anglia's top wine merchants (there's fierce competition up there!). Although there are none of the friendly tasting notes we liked about last year's list (it appears business is rather more wholesale-based than it was, so perhaps these aren't considered to be necessary?), Hall Batson & Co runs regular tastings and gourmet dinners, and has a carefully chosen, affordable range of wines to select from. Gordon Hall and team go to pains to ensure there is a broad spectrum of growers from each region (nowhere relies too heavily on just one estate); nor do New World wines dwell too long on just one or two grape varieties. We'll be watching with interest where the next year takes this merchant.

Roger Harris Wines

Loke Farm, Weston Longville,
Norfolk NR9 5LG
Tel (01603) 880171
Fax (01603) 880291
Email sales@rogerharriswines.co.uk
Website www.rogerharriswines.co.uk

Roger Harris has come a long way since the first bottle of Beaujolais he had shipped to himself in Nairobi 27 years ago, and fortunately those he brings to Norfolk today are in much better condition. But it says something that, despite the fact this original Fleurie had oxidised by the time it reached African shores (Roger *et al* drank every drop anyway), he stuck with his original passion and is still bringing Beaujolais into the UK. It's not often we see a merchant focus with such dedication on one wine region, and we thoroughly recommend obtaining the smart wine list for getting to know Beaujolais really well (don't expect to find mouthwash Beaujolais Nouveau here). Each of the 10 main *crus* is represented by a collection of growers, plus there are Beaujolais Blanc, Beaujolais rosé (great for summer picnics) and an interesting stock of Mâconnais wine (though not as fascinating as the Beaujolais) to choose from. Many cases cost under £100 so this is bargain territory too. Roger's customers will be in for a shock this year as he is introducing a selection of Australian wines. This is a tentative addition, and he's going to see how they react before embarking on any more forays further afield . . .   **£5**

445

Harrods

Brompton Road, Knightsbridge,
London SW1X 7XL
Tel 020-7730 1234
Fax 020-7225 5823
Email food.halls@harrods.com
Website www.harrods.com

Harrods did not supply the *Guide*
with full details of its range this
year, choosing instead to send us a
pack extolling the virtues of its
'temperature controlled Wine Shop',
with 'specially commissioned grey
marble and granite spittoon and
magnificently sculpted glass map of
key wine regions'. We also got the
fine and rare wines list, which
certainly impresses with its splendid
collections of first-rate clarets, top
burgundies, Alsace from all the very
best producers, Austrian dessert
wines, pick of the most desirable
Australian reds and mature ports.
There was information on typical
special offers and promotions
(Bordeaux, Spain, Ruinart and
Lanson champagnes, 'Exclusive
Premium American Wines' and so
on) – again, notable stuff. It's clear
from all this that Harrods offers an
enticing range of the world's most
sought-after and expensive wines.
We can't, however, comment on
whether the store is able to supply
decent everyday wines without
being privy to the full list. Harrods
stocks over 1,000 wines in-store –
if you want to see the full range
perhaps you might have to call in
to Knightsbridge.

Richard Harvey Wines

Bucknowle House, Wareham,
Dorset BH20 5PQ
Tel (01929) 481437
Fax (01929) 481275
Email harvey@lds.co.uk

Master of Wine and consultant to
Bonhams auctioneers: with these
qualifications you'd expect Richard
Harvey to be dealing in a fine list of
wines, and you'd not be
disappointed. Bordeaux is the main
focus here and we strongly
recommend finding your way on to
this mailing list (or into the Dorset
shop) so as to take advantage of the
inspiring selection – Richard's wines
are very popular with the wine
trade, so you'll need to get in quick.
Vintages stretch back to 1966,
châteaux reach the illustrious
heights of Lafite, Latour and
Margaux, and *en primeur* offers take
in both precious allocations of the
famous greats and the smaller,
carefully chosen properties which
(even if you haven't heard of them)
are eminently to be trusted, as
Richard's buying skills have proven
ever-reliable in our scrutiny over the
years. Although Richard Harvey
dabbles in other wine regions, and
promises future expansion to
Burgundy, the Rhône and Italy,
there's nothing yet to parallel the
claret choices. Maybe the soon-to-
be-launched website will carry more
news of his plans? Until then, enjoy
your 20th anniversary Richard! **£5**

Haslemere Cellar

16 West Street, Haslemere,
Surrey GU27 2AB
Tel (01428) 645081
Fax (01428) 645108
Email info@haslemerecellar.co.uk
Website www.haslemerecellar.co.uk

'Wherever possible we try to buy from growers with a "hands-on" approach, where we know the estate, and have got to understand why the wines taste as they do. This is especially true in Burgundy, the Rhône, Alsace, Germany and Italy,' says buyer/director/owner Richard Royds, and his attitude reflects his four-year training stint at La Vigneronne (*q.v.*), the renowned London merchant where the thinking is along similar lines. The wines here are obviously the choice of someone who knows what he's doing: smaller, less-familiar domaines; a representative selection that describes each major wine region; a conscious eye on stocking the top vintages; and, above all, high quality. So we'd be very happy to attend the wine courses and tasting events Richard is running, as they're sure to be very informative. In fact, it would be fascinating to tuck into any of the French, German and Italian choices here – and those from the rest of the world (there's a token nod to just about everywhere). Then there's the 'Cheesebox' next door: the idea of a cheese-shop-cum-deli next to a wine shop like this is more than enticing.

£5

Charles Hennings (Vintners)

London House, Lower Street,
Pulborough, West Sussex RH20 2BW
Tel (01798) 872485
Fax (01798) 873163

Golden Square, Petworth,
West Sussex GU28 0AP
Tel (01798) 343021
Email sales@chv-wine.co.uk
Website www.chv-wine.co.uk

Matthew Hennings has earned his position of sales director at this family firm by working in Bordeaux and Burgundy and seeing wine made for himself, as well as training with Majestic Wine Warehouses (*q.v.*) for four years and generally getting to know a fine set of wines on the home turf. 'We pride ourselves on sourcing wines that are unusual and hard to acquire,' he says, 'the supermarkets will always stock the rest, after all.' From what we see on the list, there is indeed good recourse to the eclectic (Nyetimber sparkling from England, Vistalba Barbera from Argentina and Charles Melton's Rosé from Australia, for example), but there are plenty of good-quality French classics and familiar New World choices too. This being the predominantly wholesale business it is, tasting notes and nitty-gritty detail aren't on offer, but there's a customer club with newsletters and bin-end offers every six to eight weeks to look out for.

Hicks & Don

4 Old Station Yard, Edington,
Westbury, Wiltshire BA13 4NT
Tel (01380) 831234
Fax (01380) 831010
Email mailbox@hicksanddon.co.uk
Website www.hicksanddon.co.uk

With three Masters of Wine making
the choices (Ronnie Hicks, Robin
Don and Anthony Barne) this
merchant can't help but be a source
of decent wines. Its main focus is
mail order to private clients, and we
definitely recommend joining the
mailing list. The wine list opens
with 'Everyday wines', which turns
up plenty of names we haven't
heard of before, but this is
unsurprising, as herein lie the
talents of an MW – sourcing the
unusual-but-good. We like the
arrangement of wines by style: the
'Clarets, Cabernets and Merlots'
section breaks into more familiar
territory (Château Lacoste Borie
Pauillac alongside Casa Lapostolle
Merlot from Chile and Finca El
Retiro Cabernet from Argentina), as
does the 'Burgundies, Pinots and
Gamays' selection. White wine
groupings are equally apposite,
including 'White Burgundy and
other Chardonnays'. Our comments
of last year still apply: this range is
broad, intelligent and occasionally
unusual, and we suggest watching
out for the regular bin-end offers
too – gems and bargains lie within.

£5

High Breck Vintners

11 Nelson Road, London N8 9RX
Tel 020-8340 1848
Fax 020-8340 5162
Email hbv@richanl.freeserve.co.uk

A small but chirpy little business,
mostly France based, which extends
its range from cheerful everyday
Bordeaux to top 2000 vintage *en
primeur* selections (Bordeaux's finest,
including châteaux Montrose,
Léoville-Barton and Pichon-
Lalande). We'd be happy to fork out
for a mixed case of any of the French
wines at this establishment
(particularly as, from outside
Bordeaux, the fork wouldn't need to
be too large . . .) but also recommend
the newer stock from Spain (a
delicious range of sherries), Portugal
(ditto port) and perhaps a few handy
choices from Italy (just in case you
wanted to ring the changes a little in
that box of 12). It's worth signing up
at this London merchant for two
other reasons: the informative
newsletter (four to six issues a year),
which often has tempting bin-end
offers of wines that you won't see
elsewhere, and the 'even if we don't
stock it, we will help our customers
find it' friendly approach.

George Hill

59 Wards End, Loughborough,
Leicestershire LE11 3HB
Tel (01509) 212717
Fax (01509) 236963
Email info@georgehill.co.uk
Website www.georgehill.co.uk

A company that prides itself on
'sincerity and honest opinions'. 'We
do not pay lip service to big names
and/or brands,' says managing
director Andrew Hill, grandson of
the founder, firmly. This is easy to

believe, looking at parts of his list, which has some lovely, characterful wines from South Africa (Jordan, Boekenhoutskloof, Glen Carlou), California (Bonny Doon, Schug, Jade Mountain) and Australia (Pipers Brook, De Bortoli). In other areas it would be nice to see the company 'go for it' a bit more, perhaps with some unusual offerings from Austria or Canada, or further choice from southern Italy, southern France and Portugal. The malt whiskies, brandies, ports and sherries (featuring Lustau's *almacenista* range from small individual producers) are all worth a serious browse. **£5**

Hopton Wines

Hopton Court, Cleobury Mortimer, Kidderminster, Worcestershire DY14 0EF
Tel (01299) 270734
Fax (01299) 271132
Email chris@hoptoncourt.fsnet.co.uk
Website www.hoptonwines.co.uk

Christopher Woodward's business is founded on classic French wines, especially Bordeaux, but we also like the look of the small but well-chosen lists from other parts of the globe, including the New Zealanders (Hunter's), Chileans (Montes) and Oregonians, if that's the right word (Duck Pond). Back in Europe, check out those red Bordeaux, champagnes and burgundies, often from lesser-known but good-value producers. Do leave some space in the case for Hopton's ports – a superior selection featuring a wide range from Niepoort, Taylor's and Fonseca.

House of Townend

101 York Street, Hull HU2 0QX
Tel (01482) 586582
Fax (01482) 218796
Email sales@houseoftownend.co.uk
Website www.hotwines.co.uk

(9 branches in Yorkshire)

'How often have I heard over the past twelve months that it is difficult to make poor wine these days? . . . Nothing could be further from the truth,' says buyer John Townend. He rightly points out that if the vineyards aren't producing top quality then the winemaker doesn't stand a chance – but no duff wines appear on these shelves. House of Townend makes a speciality of Australian boutique estates, which ups the quality stakes right from the start: Bests, Domana and Mitchell wines are all here, as is Gary Crittenden's fascinating range of Italian varietals. Most wines are sourced from Victoria, though Western Australia's Mount Barker region also makes an appearance. On the rest of the list, there are carefully chosen, well-priced wines from South America, California, Italy and Spain, and an impressively confident (and high-quality) German selection. The French wines, for once taking up the back of the list, are no less cleverly chosen – Domaine Leflaive's illustrious biodynamic wines among them. There are also regular newsletters, and regular offers to watch out for.

449

Ian G Howe

35 Appletongate, Newark,
Nottinghamshire NG24 1JR
Tel (01636) 704366
Fax (01636) 610502
Email howe@chablis-burgundy.co.uk
Website www.chablis-burgundy.co.uk

The Howes have extended their remit, from focusing on Chablis only to being 'Chablis and Burgundy Specialists'. Alongside the 16 Chablis we mentioned last year, there are now an additional 14 or so burgundies (red and white), plus a snapshot of the neighbouring wines nobody pays any attention to, from Auxerrois and Vézelay. (To find out whether this is a wise choice or not, you need to try them!) Plus, there are a few champagnes. This is a fine, quirky selection, and it's good to see a merchant tenacious enough to stick with what he or she knows and likes, and make a life's work of it, without being distracted by the usual cash cows. From Chablis, we'd recommend Billaud-Simon, Long-Depaquit, Château Grenouilles and Domaine Raveneau. Just as wholeheartedly, from the Burgundian selection, come here for Jean Tardy Vosne-Romanée, Girardin Santenay and Perrot-Minot Morey-St-Denis.

I Love Wine

4 Beaver Close, Buckingham
MK18 7EA
Tel (01280) 822500
Fax (01280) 823833
Email mail@i-love-wine.co.uk
Website www.i-love-wine.co.uk

I Love Wine was launched in February 2002, as the online/retail arm of For the Love of Wine, which deals with the wholesale end of the business. It was set up 'with the view to offer the wine public the rich wines of Switzerland and Italy. We have regular offers, on both cases and individual bottles in a case, a discussion forum, all with a bit of fun!,' says Robert Steel (son of the irrepressible Ian, who runs For the Love of Wine). As you'll have guessed, the Steel family are nothing if not passionate about what they're selling. Sourcing as far as possible from small, independent growers, the aim is to supply all the oddities and interesting wine you won't find elsewhere from these two countries. From Switzerland that's not difficult (and we don't know anyone with a larger range than this) – but given Italy's increasing popularity, we're mighty impressed to see such an individual range of new growers from Tuscany. If this kind of energetic buying continues, we predict a long and successful future for this newcomer.

Inspired Wines

West End, High Street,
Cleobury Mortimer,
Shropshire DY14 8DR
Tel (01299) 270064
Fax (01299) 270064
Email info@inspired-wines.co.uk
Website www.inspired-wines.co.uk

Still inspired, and still gathering momentum, Tim and Sue Cowin are now happily installed in new premises and about to invest in a bespoke computer system to keep tabs on their burgeoning stocks of wine – a 25 per cent increase since our report last year. The Cowins cover just about everything, but show particular fondness for the newer regions of Italy and Spain (Puglia, Sicily, Valdepeñas, Cariñena and Calatayud), and similarly 'on-the-cusp' New World wine regions such as Tasmania and Uruguay. The prices for these wines are keen (£5–£6), which is part of their appeal, but there's also inspiration from fully fledged favourites such as Turckheim Alsace, Cigale Châteauneuf and Bollinger champagne – so don't get the impression that this is a list simply for newcomers. The great thing about Inspired is that, in the main, you can be inspired for less than £10 a bottle, making it a good next step beyond those supermarket 'same-olds'.   **£5**

Irvine Robertson Wines

10 & 11 North Leith Sands,
Edinburgh EH6 4ER
Tel 0131-553 3521
Fax 0131-553 5465
Email irviner@nildram.co.uk
Website www.irwines.co.uk

Proudly 'independent and Scottish', Irvine Robertson stocks a strong and rather exciting range from around the world. Highlights include Château de Meursault, Guigal Rhônes, Dagueneau's Loires, and a trio of fine labels from Spain in the shape of Enate, El Coto and Bodegas Muga. General manager Graeme White reports that the New World is 'now very popular' – his customers must be more than happy with the likes of Bonny Doon and Stag's Leap from California, and Esk Valley and Isabel Estate from New Zealand. This merchant is mainly a wholesaler, but does a small percentage of its business with the public.   **£5**

ItsWine

11 Upper Wingbury Courtyard,
Wingrave, Aylesbury,
Buckinghamshire HP22 4LW
Tel (0800) 015 6585
Fax (01296) 682500
Email responses@itswine.com
Website www.itswine.com

This website is due for relaunch as we write (Summer 2002), so when you log on you'll see a different set of images from those we're viewing now, but we can't imagine that any of ItsWine's charm will be lost. Packed with visuals and quick-reacting click points, there are plenty of vinous options to choose right from the start. If you're after a speedy mixed case you can either select your own or go for the preselected ones: among the reds, for example, are the New World Reds Six, Smooth Reds, Mediterranean Reds and Blockbuster Reds. If you're unsure about any of the wines in the pack, just click on the bottle and a thorough estate description and tasting notes will be revealed. That's the advantage of having Master of Wine Jonathan Pedley on the team: extra details are added.

ItsWine doesn't stretch too far into the upper echelons but keeps value for money in mind (almost all wines are under £20; most under £10). Amarone and Barolo are the top Italian wines on offer, and you can pick up plenty of good old Australian Shiraz too. (We were somewhat surprised to see Scotland amongst the country search criteria but unsurprised to find the search produced no results!) The easiest shortcut to a reliable case is the best-selling section: the port, fizz and Merlot 'Celebration Party Pack' is up there among the most popular.

451

Richard Kihl

Slaughden House,
142–144 High Street,
Aldeburgh, Suffolk IP15 5AQ
Tel (01728) 454455
Fax (01728) 454433
Email sales@richardkihl.ltd.uk
Website www.richardkihl.ltd.uk

The *Guide* has heard good things about the service at Richard Kihl. (The shop, we would point out, is called Slaughden Wines.) Director Antony Irvine reports that 'younger people are becoming more interested in classic Bordeaux' – which is hardly surprising, judging by the top-notch list available here. This is a glittering array of famous names from Bordeaux, including older vintages, magnums and Jeroboams. Château d'Yquem is here in abundance: in the latest list we saw, vintages dated back, astonishingly, to 1811. Some fine burgundy, a scattering of top labels from the Rhône and Champagne, and a collection of Super-Tuscans and rare madeiras are among the other treats in store. This is serious wine, as you may have gathered, and much of it comes with a serious price tag. **£5**

Laymont & Shaw

The Old Chapel, Millpool, Truro,
Cornwall TR1 1EX
Tel (01872) 270545
Fax (01872) 223005
Email info@laymont-shaw.co.uk
Website www.laymont-shaw.co.uk

This merchant appears in the 'Also recommended' section only because most of its business is wholesale. On all our other criteria it excels – this is one of the West Country's top merchants. And even if you are not lucky enough to live in or visit Cornwall, you can source its wines by mail order. Spain is the main subject of interest here: indeed, Laymont & Shaw won our Spanish Specialist Award last year, such is the range. Reds from Rioja, Navarra, Ribera abound, of course, but you'll also find here whites from Alella, Somontano and Galicia, unbeatable Cava from Juve y Camps and sweet Spanish wines. The producers are invariably top-notch, and vintages may stretch back quite some way. Once you've revelled in the Spanish sections of the intelligent, helpful brochure, you'll find an impressive set of table wines from Portugal and some South American wines. Back in Spain, expect some delectable sherry, including the Laymont & Shaw house range (made by Hidalgo); also Montilla, *aguardiente*, brandy and liqueurs. Half bottles and Spanish olive oil bring up the rear. A truly quality selection. **£5**

Liberty Wines

Unit A53, The Food Market,
New Covent Garden,
Vauxhall, London SW8 5EE
Tel 020-7720 5350
Fax 020-7720 6158
Email info@libertywine.co.uk

This is a classic case of a super merchant moving into the 'Also recommended' section because of its strong focus on wholesale to the trade rather than on business with the public. The quality here, however, is impeccable. It's now five years since Liberty Wines set up as Italian wine specialists, in the highly capable hands of David Gleave MW, and today you won't find many better selections from that boot-shaped peninsula. Liberty is one of those classy establishments where you can really get to know each producer. You may not have heard of them all, but such is the integrity here that, if a dud wine did sneak in, it certainly wouldn't stay. There are 55 estates represented, all set out in detailed fashion. And the wines themselves? Well we think names such as Aldo Conterno (Barolo) and Allegrini (Amarone) virtually speak for themselves. From Tuscany you'll find classic Chianti from Cantine Leonardo (who also makes fabulous off-beat Syrah), Tenuta Fontodi and Isole e Olena, and Brunello di Montalcino from high-powered estates such as Tenuta di Argiano and Conti Costanti. As we mentioned last year, the California, French and German sections of this list are developing pretty swiftly too, and there are some stunners creeping in from Australia. Although you'll need to buy by the case here, if you're a true follower of Italian wines – or of wine in general – the calibre is such that this won't be a problem.

The London Wine Company

1 Armoury Way, Wandsworth, London SW18 1TH
Tel 020-8875 9393
Fax 020-8875 1925
Email sales@thelondonwine.co.uk
Website www.wine-beer.co.uk

The London Wine Company (formerly known as the Wine and Beer Company) has got brighter, cheerier and even more wallet-friendly than ever this year: rarely have we seen quite so many wines costing under a fiver. By our count there were a startling 90 or so bottles on sale at £1.99 or under – some at as little as 79 pence . . . We suppose it helps having three stores in France to source from, but not every wine here, by any means, is French.

There are also quite healthy contributions from Chile, Australia, California and Italy: all nicely priced. All the major brands from these further-flung countries are on show, as well as plenty of Vin de Pays d'Oc *et al* from France – but you'll also find nuggets of excellence cropping up, in the form of second wines from the top Bordeaux châteaux, Faiveley burgundy and more than a few reasonably priced champagnes (Lanson Black Label for £9.99 if you buy two; that sort of thing). This is still the party-planner paradise we described last year, but prices are good enough to entice anyone.

madaboutwine

3rd Floor, Regal House,
70 London Road,
Twickenham, London TW1 3QS
Tel (0845) 090 8100
Fax 020-8843 8444
Email contactus@madaboutwine.com
Website www.madaboutwine.com

Madaboutwine now trades largely by mail order, although a proportion of its business is still conducted online – but the website is the only way to get a picture of the full range of wines available. The site has a couple of advantages over online competitor Virgin Wines (*q.v.*), in that you can buy by the individual bottle and there's a 2,215-bottle Fine Wine Cellar to dip into. Highlights of the latter include 1937 Château Latour (and other venerable old clarets) and Australian Shiraz classics such as Magill, the Armagh and Hill of Grace. Not bad! One big disadvantage with this site, however, to our minds, is that it isn't always possible to discern either the producer or the region – sometimes even the country – of a wine's origin: wines are identified by the brand name only. You could always find out via the 'ask the expert' tool, which answers any wine queries you might have, but we're not sure consumers should have to resort to this. On the plus side, the site is quick, easy to use, cheerfully presented and full of bargain-priced offers (super-six mixes and imaginatively chosen wines of the month, among others).

Marks & Spencer

Head office
Michael House, 47–67 Baker Street,
London W1V 8EP
Tel 020-7935 4422
Fax 020-7268 2674
Website www.marksandspencer.com

(300 branches in UK and Ireland)

Marks & Spencer definitely has its own individual approach to selling wine. Every bottle it offers is made exclusively for the company for a start, and the team of buyers are well qualified to supervise production – a couple of winemakers and an MW among them. The focus of the range is 'wines for everyday drinking' in the main – and affordable prices (plenty below £5 and even more below £10) are very much the name of the game. So there's nothing wrong with popping in to an M&S for a ready meal and an easy-drinking bottle of wine.

On the whole this is a reasonable range of wines, more exciting than it's been in recent years, and there's more choice from each of the countries on offer. For a start, M&S has now increased its range from 200 to 350 wines in all, and there's a greater focus on smaller domaines than ever before (Quinta dos Frades Vital in Portugal, Vega Riaza in Rioja Spain and Château de Fesles from

France's Loire Valley, to name a few). But in some instances, we really do wonder whether all this wine-buying talent is somewhat wasted.

By sending winemakers out to supervise the production of every wine they sell, M&S is imposing the 'Marks & Spencer taste' on the entire selection. Our gripe with this is that some of the winemakers it works with in situ make perfectly good wines anyway, and surely more individual flavours and a better feel for the surrounding vineyards will come from those who live there the whole year round? In short: M&S make a generic style, and by choosing these wines customers are losing out on all that's authentic from these regions and countries.

Spain, Germany and Italy still offer rather pedestrian selections on this list, and the Australian and New Zealand choices rely a little too heavily on the bulk-blending estates for our liking. But, on a positive note, we're certain that almost any wine you choose from the M&S shelves will be a pleasant if unchallenging drink.

F & E May

Viaduct House, 16 Warner Street,
London EC1R 5HA
Tel 020-7843 1600
Fax 020-7843 1601
Email info@fandemay.com
Website www.fandemay.com

Germany and Bordeaux are the main events at this London merchant – German wines from *Tafelwein* to *Trockenbeerenauslese* are listed, taking in some splendid Rieslings along the way, and the Bordeaux vintage spectrum delves back to the 1970s. From elsewhere there's a little of everything (except, we notice, South America is missing). The Rhône, Alsace,

California (Jeremy Randall, the Director, prides himself on stocking the entire Mondavi range) and Spain all have small, 'cherry-picked' selections that home in on the best. This is the kind of merchant where there's enough of interest to make choosing the odd bottle an enticing option – but unfortunately the minimum purchase is a mixed case (F & E May is predominantly a wholesaler after all). However, you can expect, according to Jeremy, 'old fashioned standards of courtesy and service' when you go in to make your purchase.

Mills Whitcombe

New Lodge Farm, Peterchurch, Hereford HR3 6BJ
Tel (01981) 550028
Fax (01981) 550027
Email info@millswhitcombe.co.uk
Website www.millswhitcombe.co.uk

In the last edition of the *Guide* we tipped this two-year-old company as one with 'a cracking future' – and it certainly seems to be going places. 'The portfolio of wines has expanded four-fold,' reports partner Floyd Mills. Together with Becky Whitcombe he has put together an exciting list of good-value, quality and (dare we say it) rather fashionable wines from around the world. The Australian collection stands out, with top producers such as Charles Melton and Plantagenet, as well as Peter Lehmann providing good value. We like the emphasis on a wide variety of Australian styles – from sparkling Shiraz to *botrytis* Semillon and Pinot Gris. There are some temptations among the French wines too – such as the champagnes, which feature a wide range from Pol Roger; the burgundies; and the JosMeyer whites from Alsace. The South

African, Portuguese and Italian sections also repay a serious browse. Ports are from Niepoort. The informal tastings and dinners with winemakers sound like the best way to get to know new wines and regions here. **£5**

The Moffat Wine Shop

8 Well Street, Moffat, Dumfriesshire DG10 9DP
Tel (01683) 220554
Email moffwine@aol.com

Moffat has suffered a difficult 18 months due to the ravages on local businesses caused by the foot-and-mouth outbreak of 2000, which had a 'devastating effect on business', reports owner Anthony McIlwrick. We can only urge you to support the company and stock up on what is a wide and decent range of good-value, tasty wines. There's the occasional foray into classy stuff – witness Argyle Riesling from Oregon, Cloudy Bay from Marlborough, fine Rhônes from Chapoutier – but Moffat mainly offers reliable drinking from the likes of Torres (Spain), Peter Lehmann (Australia) and Montana (New Zealand). The current Australian selection is particularly attractive, and the spicy whites from Hungary are worthwhile for sheer value. Malt whisky connoisseurs will find their subject is taken very seriously here. **£5**

Morris & Verdin

Unit 2, Bankside Industrial Estate, Sumner Street, London SE1 9JZ
Tel 020-7921 5300
Fax 020-7921 5333
Email info@m-v.co.uk
Website www.morris-verdin.co.uk

Morris & Verdin is very much a wine trade organisation, and Jasper

455

Morris (Master of Wine) is much respected for the quality of growers he chooses and for his loyal promotion of their wines. 'We support winemakers from the start of their careers: some have grown into cult producers and others produce well-made boutique wines. We are very proud of each one of their wines we list and know it has been well made,' he says. France, and especially Burgundy, is the main feature here (we look forward to the Grand Burgundy tasting held once a year), but you'll do well to find better ranges from the Loire, Rhône and California – many of the California wines are made with traditional Old World winemaking skills too. While the specialities are very much the main focus, there are a number of treasures creeping in from elsewhere across the globe, with New Zealand, Australia, Austria, Spain and Portugal all making deserved appearances. Much as we love this list, however, we're going to have to rate this merchant 'Also recommended', as not much of its business is geared to the general public.

Nicolas UK

Head office
c/o Oddbins, 31–33 Weir Road, Wimbledon, London SW19 8UG
Tel 020-8964 5469
Fax 020-8962 9829
Website www.nicolas-wines.com

(25 branches in and around London)

There's always a cheerful greeting from behind the till when you walk into a Nicolas store, and invariably the voice will be French. And it has to be said, there's a definite air of Frenchness about the place too. But we still don't think this company

makes the most of the special atmosphere it has created. In fact, the wines are a bit of a let-down. There's an impression of bulk supply here – with more than 300 Nicolas branches in France and 20-plus in the UK it seems that the team wants to supply each of these stores with the same range. As such, very few of the bottles offer any real individuality or hand-crafted special qualities. Affordable, yes, they certainly are, but the few trade-up options (a smattering of reasonable Bordeaux and burgundies) are rarely of the best vintages. The champagne selection is good – you can pick up a bottle for £8.95 or a magnum for £50.99, depending on the scale of your celebration – but we still think that, in the past, Nicolas has done a lot more to enhance the image of French wine. Where are those shelves of odd but wonderful Jura wines now? Or that full range of 'other Sauvignons' from Quincy, Reuilly and Menetou Salon? (Castel, who own Nicolas, has recently purchased the Oddbins chain – for more on this see Oddbins (*q.v.*).

Parfrements

68 Cecily Road, Cheylesmore, Coventry CV3 5LA
Tel 024-7650 3646
Fax 024-7650 6406
Email sales@parfrements.co.uk
Website www.parfrements.co.uk

Any wine list that kicks off with A for Absinthe is bound to have a pleasing quirkiness, and so it is with Parfrements. This is a rather short but distinctly characterful selection from principal Gerald Gregory, who reports this year that he has noticed a new 'willingness to spend over £7 on a bottle of wine'. He certainly stocks plenty of interesting fare between this price point and up to around £20, without dwelling too long on the classic regions of France, which makes a refreshing change. We particularly like the Portuguese section this year, which offers some exciting, unusual flavours. Parfrements has a customers' club with monthly tastings and web bulletins. **(£5)**

Penistone Court Wine Cellars

The Railway Station, Penistone, Sheffield, South Yorkshire S36 6HP
Tel (01226) 766037
Fax (01226) 767310
Email pcwc@dircon.co.uk
Website www.cellars-direct.com

Penistone Court continues to sell a well-balanced selection of wines from around the world, and the keen pricing continues to impress. Such as? Well, some of the Wunsch et Mann wines from Alsace come in at around a fiver, as do Barbadillo sherries and quite a few bottles from Chile. If you want to splash out, take a look at some of the top names from Champagne and California, or turn to the extensive range from Italy, something of a speciality here. From other parts of the world, owner Chris Ward relies rather heavily on just one or two producers, but to be fair they do tend to be trustworthy names. Spirits, liqueurs and fine glassware are also available. **(£5)**

Christopher Piper Wines

1 Silver Street, Ottery St Mary, Devon EX11 1DB
Tel (01404) 814139
Fax (01404) 812100
Email
sales@christopherpiperwines.co.uk

Chris Piper reports that 'after 23 years . . . we all thoroughly enjoy our jobs – it really is service with a smile'. We can confirm that Christopher Piper Wines has a strong reputation as a friendly and approachable company to deal with and that its team has an infectious enthusiasm about all matters vinous. For a taste of that, before you actually imbibe, make sure you get the regular newsletter *Noble Rot*, or sign up for one of the company's lively winemaker dinners. The emphasis here is on France, especially Burgundy and Beaujolais (Chris is head winemaker at Château des Tours, and dubs that wine 'Chairman's plonk'). But, outside France, it is also great to see just about all our favourite German producers in one list, a superb collection of Italian wines, top names from California, Argentina and Australia, and increasingly popular South African wines are given serious thought.

We still think there is the odd gap here and there (perhaps some more far-flung regions of Spain, New Zealand and Argentina could get a look-in) but overall these are prize wines, chosen with an unerring eye for excellence. This is a pleasant list to browse through – full as it is of salient facts and sensible tasting notes, with 'eco-friendly' wines (not always fully organic, but almost) highlighted with a smiley face. The West Country and beyond is served well by such a company –

and the only reason this merchant appears as an 'Also recommended' entry is that a high proportion of its business is with the trade (wholesale). **£5**

Terry Platt Wine Merchants

Council Street West, Llandudno, Conwy LL30 1ED
Tel (01492) 874099
Fax (01492) 874788
Email plattwines@clara.co.uk
Website www.terryplattwines.co.uk

In 2002 this excellent merchant (one of the UK's best, never mind Wales's), celebrated its fortieth year as an independent operation supplying restaurants, hotels and (a small proportion of its business) private customers. Recently the company has noted a trend among its clients towards New World wines, and in response it has added more from Australia, California, Argentina, Chile and South Africa. Chile looks especially impressive, with several bottles we'd happily drink around the £5 price point. In fact, one of the great appeals of Terry Platt is that it's strong at the cheap end of the market (where so many merchants are dire) as well as further up the ranks. From France, the Champagne and Burgundy ranges caught our eye this year, and it's good to note that a couple of Sicilian wines have crept in (the *Guide* criticised the lack of southern Italian wines here last year). So, a well-rounded, well-balanced list with a couple of surprises too – a few Welsh wines, for example (we haven't tasted them, so can't comment) – and a lovely long slate of half bottles and magnums.

Playford Ros

Middle Park House, Sowerby, Thirsk, North Yorkshire YO7 3AH
Tel (01845) 526777
Fax (01845) 526888
Email sales@playfordros.com
Website www.playfordros.com

If the aphorism is true, that you can spot a 'class' establishment by the quality of the things it throws away, then judging by the wines about to be de-listed as we write this review (Leflaive's Chassagne-Montrachet Morgeot, Château Gruaud-Larose 1996) Playford Ros is a class act indeed. Fortunately, these are just remnants, and there's a plentiful choice of new vintages from the same growers as you turn the pages. This is, if you hadn't already guessed, another of those smart Yorkshire wine merchants. The main portion of Playford's business is in supplying restaurants and local hotels, but for members of the public, putting together the minimum purchase of a mixed case, from this range, wouldn't be too tough a task. Look out for an impressive selection of (41) half bottles, 17 wines in magnum and good choices from Bordeaux, Burgundy and Australia.

Quellyn Roberts

21 Watergate Street, Chester, Cheshire CH1 2LB
Tel (01244) 310455
Fax (01244) 346704
Email qrwines@chesternet.co.uk

'If we don't stock it, we will try to find a source and obtain it,' says Paul Quellyn-Roberts. This is a pleasing offer, but one we wouldn't necessarily need to take advantage of, with this tidy selection at our fingertips. While not being over-ambitious in length, the quality and extent of the Quellyn Roberts list is reassuring, right from the £5 bottles of interesting Australian Chardonnay and South African Sauvignon to the likes of Bollinger and Krug heading up the champagne list – and Château Gruaud-Larose making an appearance from Bordeaux. But then, Quellyn Roberts has been selling wine since 1863 (when Alderman Thomas Quellyn Roberts started the shop), so it should know what it's looking for by now. Paul has noticed that younger customers are paying more for wine these days. Perhaps this is because of the 'helpful but not pushy advice' he offers, or the fact that the wines are described in the simplest, most unpretentious terms ('really nice', 'better'. . .)? We think it's because there's always something new, and always something of good quality here. **(£5)**

R S Wines

Avonleigh, Parklands Road, Bower Ashton, Bristol BS3 2JW
Tel 0117-963 1780
Fax 0117-953 3797
Email rswines@talk21.com

Raj Soni buys 'real wine made by real people', adding: 'There are no virtual wines here.' By this we assume he means no multi-region blends or boring brands are included – turning to the list, that indeed is the case. Stellar Bordeaux and not-so-far-off-stellar burgundies are the first big hits, then come quality Loire producers such as Didier Dagueneau and Domaine Huet. Expect no less from the Rhône or Champagne sections, nor from California, Australia or South Africa. Raj certainly has a good eye (and palate) for the top-quality wines out

there, but the true reflection of his abilities comes in the range of quirky stars on the list – take that oddball wine Petite Sirah from L A Cetto in Mexico, for example. In championing the three Rhône domaines Cuilleron, Gaillard and Villard, he will almost certainly be on to a good thing, and we suggest any Syrah-lovers should snap up a case or two. And by the way, thanks for getting rid of the head-spinning block capitals, Raj, we can actually read your list this year!

Reid Wines

The Mill, Marsh Lane, Hallatrow, Bristol BS39 6EB
Tel (01761) 452645
Fax (01761) 453642
Email reidwines@aol.com

We like the Reid list – partly for its witty cartoons and pithy quotes, from novels, poems and newspapers young and old – and also for its admirably frank tasting notes. 'Dry as dust, for those who like austerity' and 'quite good if still alive' are two helpful ones, although many are far more appetising. Anyway, you get the picture. If you have ever felt that the people selling you vino are not particularly interested in the stuff, then look to Reid Wines. These people are passionate about wine; they taste and drink both with vigour and expertise, and appear to know each one of the bottles as if it were an old friend (warts and all). We recommend that you ring and discuss your requirements, just to get the low-down on the more unusual stock.

What about the wines? Rare gems glitter throughout, whether mature magnums of Jaboulet's 1978 Cornas, Penfolds' Grange back to 1964, Vega Sicilia back to 1950,

Crimean 'ports' from the 1930s, or Malmsey madeira from 1808 . . . or, indeed, youthful Australian whites, South African reds and modern Chablis galore. A must-see list not only for collectors of rare classics but also for those who like top names old and new. The only reason this merchant appears here, rather than in the 'Top 100' section, is that much of its business is wholesale. One complaint – the tiny print size of the list means you might need a magnifying glass to read Reid.

Richards & Richards Fine Wines

6 Hebburn Drive, Brandlesholme, Bury, Lancashire BL8 1ED
Tel 0161-762 0022
Fax 0161-763 4477
Email fine.wines@btconnect.com

Bury is lucky to have this merchant selling a well-balanced, never-boring set of wines with an emphasis on France and Portugal. Check out the Portuguese reds if you are thirsty for different and unusual flavours, or head for Burgundy for some classic whites from big-name producers (Javillier, Louis Latour, Leflaive). Don't skip the Australian section – Cullen, Howard Park, Plantagenet and Evans & Tate provide a particularly convincing team from Western Australia. Champagnes are strong too, from Drappier, Gosset and Veuve Clicquot, as is Cava from Juve y Camps, and there are some unusual styles of wine from Germany including *Sekt* and *Eiswein*. The tastings look interesting, especially the regular Portuguese events (Bairrada is a speciality). **(£5)**

Savage Selection

The Ox House, Market Place, Northleach, Cheltenham, Gloucestershire GL54 3EG
Tel (01451) 860896
Fax (01451) 860996
Email wine@savageselection.co.uk
Website www.savageselection.co.uk

The name here is the aim: 'Savage selection at source results in variety and originality throughout the range,' says Mark Savage. He makes no concessions to fashion, nor is he interested in trophy wines or Parker points. Each wine selected must carve its own individual path and express its own patch of *terroir*. In this way, certain vinous oddities creep into the list, which we like very much: a Pinot Noir from Idaho, a Sauvignon de St-Bris, wines from two Greek estates, and Bloodwood, a 'highly eccentric Australian' producer, being the oddest of the lot. But there are classics too: the glorious 2000 vintage clarets make a showing, as do some reasonably upper-crust Burgundians. There are, in fact, one or two estates from just about all the major European wine destinations – France being the happiest hunting ground of them all. The New World gets a selective covering, but given its propensity for turning out non-individual wines, we're not surprised fewer of them make it through the (savage) selection process. And Mark holds tasting events in London and Gloucestershire every year.

Sebastopol Wines

Sebastopol Barn, London Road,
Blewbury, Oxfordshire OX11 9HB
Tel (01235) 850471
Fax (01235) 850776
Email sebastopolwines@aol.com

It hardly needs the likes of us to
spread the Sebastopol word, as,
from this barn in Blewbury, Barbara
and Caroline Affleck do great
business. The wines here are strictly
upper crust, and are their own
advertisement. Nobody in the
surrounding countryside is likely to
mind the upmarket pitch – this is
Britain's smartest county after all,
and the clientele have the deep
pockets to match. To this tune,
we're drooling over the likes of
châteaux Valandraud, Rausan-Ségla
and Ducru-Beaucaillou (multiple
vintages of Bordeaux' finest); a short
but pithy Burgundy section,
including de Vogüé's Bonnes Mares
and Lafon's Volnay Santenots; and
New World choices that don't sully
themselves with everyday
Chardonnays but bask in the likes of
Henschke Hill of Grace, Wynns
Michael Shiraz from Australia and
Opus One from California. We
weren't allowed to view the prices
of the wines this year: we wonder
why!

Seckford Wines

Dock Lane, Melton, Suffolk IP12 1PE
Tel (01394) 446622
Fax (01394) 446633
Email marcus@seckfordwines.co.uk
Website www.seckfordwines.co.uk

Seckford is a wholesaler rather than
a high-street merchant, so is not
particularly geared up to serving the
general public, but if you're happy
enough to buy by the case there are

plenty of top-class wines on offer.
This is, without doubt, another of
those classy East Anglian wine
establishments that seems to have
access to almost everything. The
Bordeaux section, for a start, is
breathtaking (Ausone, La Mondotte,
Le Pin – they're all there); burgundy
from de Vogüé, Domaine de la
Romanée-Conti and Etienne Sauzet
might also tempt one to break the
bank. But be aware that Julian
Downing and his team are just as
adept at sourcing value-for-money
wines too – although we suspect
they get more of a buzz from
dealing in illustrious cases. A few
stars creep in from Australia,
California, Austria and Spain (Italy's
is a wider, better range), but the
main event here is really France,
particularly Bordeaux. Delve into
the 'oddments' section to pick up a
few back vintages and you'll see
what we mean.

Edward Sheldon

New Street, Shipston on Stour,
Warwickshire CV36 4EN
Tel (01608) 661409
Fax (01608) 663166
Email
finewine@edward-sheldon.co.uk
Website www.edward-sheldon.co.uk

This is a merchant that prides itself
on 'absolute' customer care,
claiming that it carries wine to the
car, opens doors, has a superb shop
and cellars and, simply, 'charm'. We
can't vouch for that (although we
have heard good reports), but we do
like the look of the wines. As we
said last year, a few sections could
do with an injection of new stock –
Germany, Portugal and California,
for example. In other places, the
range really takes off: the admirably
wide and imaginative selection of
Australian wines; the classy growers

461

among the Burgundians; the impressive clarets. The quarterly newsletter *The Corker* details good-value dinners and fine wine tastings as well as special offers. **£5**

Slaughden Wines

See Richard Kihl

Spar UK

Head office
Hygeia Building,
66–68 College Road, Harrow,
Middlesex HA1 1BE
Tel 020-8426 3700
Fax 020-8426 3701/2
Email angela.buckle@spar.co.uk
Website www.spar.co.uk

(2,179 branches nationwide)

Gluggable brand wines are the name of the game here, particularly if they cost under £4 a bottle: this is where Spar's own-brand range comes in handy. It looks to us as if Spar customers are digging a little deeper into their pockets than they have before, and that the range they're paying out for is a little broader and a little more adventurous – globally, there's something on offer from just about everywhere. For this we'd have to thank the wine-buying skills of Liz Aked and Alex Williams. This still isn't our first recommendation for a wine shop, but we suspect changes are afoot – and if there are more positive signs, we'll be reporting on them next year.

Springfield Wines

Springfield Mill, Norman Road,
Denby Dale, Huddersfield HD8 8TH
Tel (01484) 864929
Fax (01484) 864929

This is a family-run business (Richard and Lesley Brook with 'occasional help from four daughters . . .') based in a converted textile mill with a 'homely' atmosphere – all of which sounds appealing in these days of supermarket wine domination. The range of 500-plus wines contains much that is attractive and sensibly priced – customers looking for decent bottles at around £5–£7 will be particularly delighted with Springfield Wines. We recommend starting with the wines from Australia (McGuigan, Peter Lehmann), Chile (Concha y Toro) and North America (Pepperwood, Hogue Cellars). From France there are some classy, expensive bottles alongside more everyday fare, and it's nice to see Austrian whites, Tokaji and a decent range of German wine here too. Single malts, other spirits and bottled beers are also available. Popular tasting evenings cost just £10 per head and have themes such as 'A Taste of Spain' and 'New World Selection'. Book well in advance . . . **£5**

Frank Stainton Wines

3 Berry's Yard, Finkle Street,
Kendal, Cumbria LA9 4AB
Tel (01539) 731886
Fax (01539) 730396
Email admin@stainton-wines.co.uk

The team at Frank Stainton Wines has notched up 88 years in the trade between the four of them. 'No pivotal member has ever left the company: we have thrown away the key!' says director Chris Leather. But then being a wine merchant in the Lake District must be one of life's better professions. This establishment provides classic 'special occasion' wines and there are plenty of heart-warming treasures: the likes of Cos d'Estournel 1990, L'Enclos 1995 from Bordeaux, Bâtard-Montrachet from Latour – plenty of old vintages and imaginatively chosen 'second label' bottlings from the better Médoc châteaux. Not that this is in any way a stuffy, traditional list. Bordeaux, Burgundy, the Rhône, New Zealand and Germany are given as the specialities here, but there are also some good choices from Mediterranean France, Argentina, California and South Africa. And we admire the collection of oddities such as Jurançon and Jura's *vin jaune*, and the innovative 'Cook's Corner' selection. In the past, we've felt that there was too much reliance on one producer per region on this list, but, with the exception of Alsace, this no longer seems to be the case.

It is supplier to the local hotel and restaurant industry, but our advice to holidaymakers is to stop off in Kendal and choose from the whole range rather than waiting to see these wines (with marked-up prices) in a hotel or restaurant.

John Stephenson & Sons (Nelson)

Darwil House, Bradley Hall Road, Nelson, Lancashire BB9 8HF
Tel (01282) 614618
Fax (01282) 601161
Email steve@thewinemill.co.uk
Website www.thewinemill.co.uk

This is the sort of list that repays picking through carefully, unearthing the odd gem and bargain. Last year's criticism that there were still too many bland wines in some of the European sections still stands – Germany could do with a serious revamp; Portugal with a bolstering; less well-known European regions/countries, for example Austria, with a look-in – but there are plenty of solid, reliable producers featured here and, even better, there are some real high points where quality and price both impress. Like where? Well, how about a wide range of Cape Mentelle wines. Or some of the best New Zealand bins we have tasted recently (Craggy Range, Alpha Domus, Jackson Estate). Or some thoroughly modern Spanish reds (Martínez Bujanda, Palacio de la Vega). We wish the whole range was up to this standard, but are impressed by certain sections of it. Happy rummaging!   **£5**

Stevens Garnier Wine Merchants

47 West Way, Botley, Oxford OX2 0JF
Tel (01865) 263300
Fax (01865) 791594
Email shop@stevensgarnier.co.uk

Business is mostly wholesale here, as Stevens Garnier is the go-getter responsible for distributing a number of well-known, particularly French, wines throughout the UK. So, when you tuck into your next bottle of La Chablisienne Chablis, Joseph Perrier champagne or Pierre Sparr Alsace Riesling, there's a fair chance that it will have been sourced by this team. If you want to buy these wines directly yourself, without the high-street middlemen, just walk into the Botley shop where there are some good discounts to be had. The list spans the world, but the highlights for us are still the French regional choices:

obscure but wonderful wines from the Côtes de Malepère, Jurançon and Coteaux du Languedoc.

Stratford's Wine Agencies

High Street, Cookham, Berkshire
SL6 9SQ
Tel (01628) 810606
Fax (01628) 810605
Email nigel@stratfordwine.co.uk
Website www.stratfordwine.co.uk

Stratford's is mainly a wholesaler and does only a very small percentage of its trade with the general public, but those consumers who do seek it out will find an extensive range of Australian wines backed up by others from around the world. The Australians run the gamut from £3.99 everyday quaffers to much more serious fare costing over £20, and come from a wide variety of regions. New Zealand is also worth a foray for the wines of Neudorf, Giesen, Jackson Estate and Isabel, and the Californians include Bonny Doon and Qupé. There is now a French section that should keep most people happy, and some worthy wines among the Spanish and Italian lists. Ports, madeira and cigars feature too.

Trout Wines

The Trout, Nether Wallop,
Stockbridge, Hampshire SO20 8EW
Tel (01264) 781472
Fax (01264) 781472
Email
anthonywhitaker@troutwines.co.uk

Anthony Whitaker is frank in reply to our questions: 'Range and price I cannot really compete on but what we do offer is a selection in which I have complete faith – it may not be wide but every one is a winner.' We haven't tasted absolutely every bottle, but generally we agree – and

actually some of the prices do look pretty competitive to us. This very concise list is packed with goodies including Wild Bay Chardonnay from California, Isabel Estate Sauvignon Blanc from New Zealand and Enate Cabernet/Merlot from Spain. There are some lovely dessert wines (Quady, Château Coutet) and sherries from Valdespino. Anthony is friendly and highly knowledgeable and the shop is based in a big, thatched cottage. If you find that larger purveyors of wine seem to have bewilderingly long lists and lack personal service, this could be the place for you. **£5**

Turville Valley Wines

The Firs, Potter Row,
Great Missenden,
Buckinghamshire HP16 9ET
Tel (01494) 868818
Fax (01494) 868832
Email
chris@turville-valley-wines.com
Website
www.turville-valley-wines.com

Turville Valley Wines is a specialist *par excellence* in wines that are 'difficult to find'. Buyer Michael Rafferty cut his wine-trade teeth in Sotheby's wine department, so he knows exactly how special wine can be and where to seek out the best: you don't have to delve far into the list to reach burgundies from Domaine de la Romanée-Conti and Bordeaux from the fabulous 1959, 1966 and 1982 vintages. And while the French classics are the focal points, Italian Super-Tuscans and rarely seen California blockbusters (Screaming Eagle, Harlan Estate) also prove the point. Two things are a shame: one, these wines cost as much as £1,050 a bottle, and two, you have to buy them by the case. While most of Michael Rafferty's business is with the trade, for whom this wouldn't matter as much, we're a bit disappointed, as we wouldn't have minded the trip to Great Missenden to pick up an extra-special bottle or two. A caseful would be a little too expensive, even at around the (cheap for Turville) £60-a-bottle mark.

Vine Trail 🏠

266 Hotwell Road, Hotwells, Bristol
BS8 4NG
Tel 0117-921 1770
Fax 0117-921 1772
Email enquiries@vinetrail.co.uk
Website www.vinetrail.co.uk

Nick Brookes' company focuses firmly on France – and on smaller family-run domaines, to be more precise. We'll be honest and say there are plenty of names we don't recognise here, but then trying wines from lesser-known winemakers, especially French ones, is an essential vinous thrill. What's more, Nick lists wines from relatively undiscovered areas such as Savoie, Jurançon, Gaillac and Madiran. The brochure offers plenty of information on what we will assume are gems of regional France. If you try them, let us know what you think. Vine Trail supplies some highly reputable restaurants, which is usually a good sign. Its list finishes with champagnes, sparkling wines and armagnacs. **£5**

Waterloo Wine Company

61 Lant Street, London SE1 1QN
Tel 020-7403 7967
Fax 020-7357 6976
Email sales@waterloowine.co.uk
Website www.waterloowine.co.uk

Most of Paul Tutton's business is wholesale, but it's well worth tracking down his shop in Lant Street

for its neat and appealing collection of wines, mainly sourced from small independent producers. We suggest you check out the wines from Waipara West in New Zealand's Canterbury region, because they are elegant and delicious (and also to be polite – Paul co-owns the winery!). Pick up the Mark Rattray Canterbury label if you want to explore the region further. Other strong points are the mature German wines, the Loire range, some fine Calvados and (for those who are keen on it) Pineau de Charentes. A merchant that will certainly appeal to those who dislike huge warehouses piled high with big brands.

Wessex Wines 🏠

88 St Michael's Estate, Bridport,
Dorset DT6 3RR
Tel (01308) 427177
Fax (01308) 424383
Email wessexwines@btinternet.com
Website www.wessexwines.co.uk

Michael Farmer knows his French wines. His is an imaginative range of them, particularly intrepid in the Languedoc and south-west, and rooting out some unusual choices from Bordeaux too. 'As a general wine merchant it is our aim that every bottle on the list should have earned its place there through its quality and value,' says Michael, which means that prices keep as far as possible below the £10 mark – not an easy task, but with more than 25 years' wine-trading experience behind him, Michael knows where to look. Spain and Australia also put in respectable appearances, and there are smaller selections from Italy, the USA and South America too. To be depended on throughout at Wessex Wines is the quest for individuality; you won't find boring brands here. **£5**

Whitebridge Wines

Unit 21, Whitebridge Estate, Stone,
Staffordshire ST15 8LQ
Tel (01785) 817229
Fax (01785) 811181
Email
sales@whitebridgewines.co.uk
Website
www.whitebridgewines.co.uk

Francis Peel is one of the few wine
merchants we know who doesn't
love Riesling – it is always a matter
of taste as to which wines any of us
prefer, but we still find this difficult
to understand, particularly as,
judging from the rest of the list
(excluding Germany), Francis
obviously knows his stuff. Choices
from New Zealand, for example, are
peppered with treats such as Ata
Rangi Martinborough Pinot Noir
and Te Motu Cabernet/Merlot from
Waiheke Island. South Africa
includes the delicious wines of
Jordan estate; from California we're
impressed by the presence of
dynamic winemakers Randall
Grahm, Paul Draper and Jim
Clendenen. And, back in Europe,
there's plenty to delight from every
major wine region, even climbing to
the heights of the illustrious
Château Palmer in Bordeaux
(accompanied by second and third
label wines from equally prestigious
estates Beychevelle and Margaux).
There's no one speciality here, but
Francis has cleverly brought in
something from everywhere – the
world's more unusual wine regions,
Mexico, Uruguay and Morocco,
included. (Although where's that
wine from Bolivia? It's still in the
index but we can't spot it on the list;
as this is the only place we've seen
such a wine on offer, we wanted to
try it!)   **£5**

Wimbledon Wine Cellar

1 Gladstone Road, Wimbledon,
London SW19 1QU
Tel 020-8540 9979
Fax 020-8540 9399

84 Chiswick High Road, London
W4 2LW
Tel 020-8994 7989
Fax 020-8994 3683
Email
enquiries@wimbledonwinecellar.com
Website
www.wimbledonwinecellar.com

Andrew Pavli's Wimbledon and
Chiswick stores have come in for a
lot of praise of late – (Pavli won Best
Small Independent Merchant of the
Year at the prestigious International
Wine Challenge awards in
September 2001 – no mean feat).
However, we found it impossible to
prise a full list of his wines out of
him this year so, with the best will in
the world, cannot give the business a
full review (the website didn't help
enormously either). What we do
know about this company, though,
has impressed – the service is
reckoned to be excellent, and the
Guide has heard good things about
the wine ranges too, especially those
from Bordeaux, Burgundy and (best
of all) Italy. 'We offer mature
Bordeaux and burgundy, and
Super-Tuscans,' says Andrew, 'We
ship several wines ourselves,
thereby getting exclusivity, and we
always try to purchase any wine
required by customers even if we
don't usually stock it.' Last year he
told the *Guide* that the range
changes almost daily, so you'll see
why we can't give details of specific
wines. All the signs are promising,
however – so we don't hesitate in
recommending that you check out
the stores yourself.

Windermere Wine Stores

Windermere Wine Store
11 Crescent Road, Windermere,
Cumbria LA23 1EA
Tel (015394) 46891
Fax (015394) 88001

Ambleside Wine Store
Compston Road, Ambleside,
Cumbria LA22 9DJ
Tel (015394) 33001
Fax (015394) 31776
Email sales@windermerewine.co.uk
Website
www.windermere-wine.co.uk

Supply of both 'branded and boutique' wines is the mission here. Most of what's on offer is everyday stuff from the former camp – big-output sources such as the KWV in South Africa, Sutter Home in the USA or Wyndham Estate in Australia – all useful in its cut-priced place. But it's worth scanning the list carefully, as in among all the brands will be the occasional blow-your-mind bottle. Bordeaux has its fair share of surprises – châteaux La Commanderie St-Emilion, Cantemerle, Meyney and Beaumont, all at under £20 a bottle, then Mouton-Rothschild (1988) and Latour (1989) at considerably more than this. Plus there are one or two stars from Burgundy (from the Jadot and Faiveley stables). Our return trip to Windermere (out of season, to avoid the tourists) would mainly be for the sparkling wines, however: a broad selection from Angas Brut Australian fizz to top-class 1990 vintage Bollinger is most tempting.
(£5)

The Wine and Beer Company

See The London Wine Company

The Wine Bureau

58 Tower Street, Harrogate,
North Yorkshire HG1 1HS
Tel (01423) 527772
Fax (01423) 566330
Email thewinebureau@aol.com

French wine lovers based near Harrogate can source at The Wine Bureau such delights as Hugel, Schlumberger and Kuentz Bas from Alsace; Marc Bredif's Vouvray; Pol Roger and Gosset champagnes; and Rhône favourites Chave, Jaboulet and Seguret – as well as rummage around a fairly wide selection of burgundies. You'll also find Martínez Bujanda and Conde de Valdemar Riojas, Redoma and Quinta dos Roques Portuguese table wines, and Itay's majestic Sassicaia. Australia is something of a speciality – look out for Simon Hackett, McWilliams, Tyrrell's and Ironstone. Still in the New World, we welcome the appearance of Hamilton Russell, Jordan and Moreson from South Africa, Echeverria and Terrazas from South America and Hogue Cellars from Washington State (although where are the Californian wines?). The fortified section of the list contains some interesting *eaux de vie* and madeiras, and some older fine wines are available. Some areas of this range could be plumped out a little more, but overall the quality is admirably high. The company hosts regular winemaker dinners and holds classes for the public as well as private tastings for corporate trade and local businesses.

Wine Cellar

Head office
The Cellar 5 Group, PO Box 476,
Loushers Lane, Warrington,
Cheshire WA4 6RQ
Tel (01925) 454545
Fax (01925) 454546
Email david.vaughan@cellar5.com
Website www.winecellar.co.uk

(62 branches nationwide)

Wine Cellar is now owned by the
Cellar 5 Group Ltd, buying manager
David Vaughan tells us. This covers
62 Wine Cellar stores, 320 Booze
Busters and 70 Right Choice Food
Stores, for all of which he is the wine
buyer. As we said last year, this list is
competent, if rarely thrilling. But
given that David has rather a lot on
his plate, selecting wines for the
whole empire (in many other
companies of comparable size he'd
have a team of helpers), we think the
lack of 'zest' in the range is hardly
surprising. Wine Cellar started with
more imaginative intentions back in
1994, but right from the first it was
the everyday wines that actually
moved off the shelves. So most of the
original choices have gone by the
wayside. There are pockets of
greatness, however – with a tidy
selection of 1998 *cru classé* clarets to
look out for and an impressive array
of Argentinian reds. And the
commendable aim of keeping bottles
below the £7 mark is firmly adhered
to – this does at least allow for escape
from the bland and boring £3 and £4
areas. We like the cheery, expensive-
looking (dare we say Oddbins-style)
wine magazine/list (published three
times a year), although we'd prefer
to see its contents offering a little
more inspiration.

The Wine Shop

7 Sinclair Street, Thurso, Caithness
KW14 7AJ
Tel (01847) 895657

Martine Hughes runs this shop as
her hobby, and her husband and
family help out if necessary. She
bought it in order to keep a small
business running, and we think
Thurso should be glad that she did.
This isn't an astonishingly large
collection of wines, but it is
extremely carefully chosen and
there are some fine growers to select
from, plus some nice old Bordeaux
vintages too. We'd stop by for
Tedeschi's delicious Amarones from
Italy, Penfolds and Cape Mentelle
wines from Australia, and Dr
Loosen's fabulous Mosel wines from
Germany – all fairly priced. Martine
also stocks beers and whiskies, so
there's no shortage of reasons to
pop in. That said, customers are
apparently not willing to trade up
these days as quality is so good at
everyday level. We'd recommend
spending a little more lavishly –
you'll discover some interesting and
exciting wines here.

The Wine Treasury

69–71 Bondway, London SW8 1SQ
Tel 020-7793 9999
Fax 020-7793 8080
Email quality@winetreasury.com
Website www.winetreasury.com

Founder Neville Blech has retired
but The Wine Treasury lives on,
now owned by former staff and
with Neville himself still involved as
'Chairman Emeritus'. Only a small
proportion of its business is with the
public, but we reckon those
customers must be pleased with the
Californian wines in particular:
around 20 top wineries are

represented here, including Cline Cellars, Foppiano, Joseph Phelps, Sanford and Sequoia Grove. Some fine Oregon and Washington State wines add depth and range to the West Coast collection. Australia is another point of interest – Penley Estate, Nepenthe and Charles Cimicky provide tempting labels indeed. France and Italy are the twin focal points when it comes to European wines: Rieflé's Alsace whites, some very attractive Rhône Valley reds and Roberto Voerzio's Piedmont wines would be our first stops here. And although we haven't tasted them yet, the newly listed Sicilian wines from Cusumano look well worth a try.

Wines of Westhorpe

Marchington, Staffordshire ST14 8NX
Tel (01283) 820285
Fax (01283) 820631
Email wines@westhorpe.co.uk
Website www.westhorpe.co.uk

The aim at Wines of Westhorpe is to offer a competitive, wide-ranging, non-French mail-order supply service, with good quantity discounts and pre-mixed tasting cases covering the range. There can't be many merchants, however, that would choose to base their non-French range in Eastern Europe. Price is the optimum concern here (£18 per case is not uncommon) and we're pretty sure we've spotted some 'quality' too – check out the Tokajis from Jozsef Monyok and Château Messzelato, for example. Picking up a mixed case or two from this outlet would be one sure way of getting a feel for the real Bulgaria, or the real Hungary – better by far than getting your good/bad impressions from the odd cheapie at the supermarket. Oh yes, and

Argentina, Australia and Chile feature too: we don't recognise the names of the growers but your wallet's not going to suffer too much from trying them out.

Woffenden Wines

103 Chapeltown Road,
Bromley Cross, Bolton,
Lancashire BL7 9LZ
Tel (01204) 308081
Fax (01204) 308081
Email norman@woffendenwines. fsnet.co.uk
Website www.capewines-bolton.co.uk

Dr Norman Woffenden has been a keen supplier of South African wine since Nelson Mandela was released from prison ten years ago. Since then, just as he knew it would, customer enthusiasm has steadily increased for this country's wines – many of which are pretty much mid-way in style between the Old World and the New. A lot of our favourite growers are here (Thelema, Neil Ellis, Whalehaven and Kanonkop) but there are plenty of others we haven't tried yet. It's not often we see a merchant delving so deeply into this part of the world, even focusing on individual vineyards, and we wouldn't hesitate to order up a mixed case, as it looks as though Woffenden would be the next best thing to getting on the plane and going to the Cape ourselves. Bolton locals might also like to keep an eye out for one of Norman's regularly held tastings – there are often winemakers in attendance. **£5**

Young's Wine Direct 🖰

Cockpen House,
20–30 Buckhold Road,
Wandsworth, London SW18 4AP
Tel 020-8875 7008
Fax 020-8875 7009
Email wine_direct@youngs.co.uk
Website
www.youngswinedirect.co.uk

Young's sells mostly beer of course, but the 15 or so wines available by the glass in its drinking establishments put most other brewers to shame. If these tempt you, then Young's have 100 or more further options that can be delivered (by the case or bottle) to your door – by next-day delivery if you happen to live near the brewery. Don't be surprised if the name on the van has changed to Cockburn & Campbell these days, as this is now Young's principal holding company, which has taken over as suppliers of Young's Wine Direct. Choices here take in a very smart selection of Bordeaux and otherwise cover the world in splendidly liberal fashion – if not that much depth. Highlights for us are the northern Rhône wines, Fifth Leg Merlot/Cabernet/Shiraz from Western Australia and 5-puttonyos Tokaji from the Royal Tokaji Wine Company. But don't miss the ports, sherries, madeiras and Marsalas either.

Part IV
More about wine

GRAPE VARIETIES

PREMIER LEAGUE

The following grapes have probably given more pleasure to wine
drinkers over the centuries than any others. Whether currently in
vogue or not, these are the classic grape varieties that most
consistently provide the best wine.

Red

Cabernet Sauvignon
Could this be the most uniformly successful grape variety of all time
– the class swot who excels at everything? Certainly, we cannot
think of anyone who dislikes the deep colour and blackcurrant,
mint and cedar character of fine Cabernet Sauvignon. Winemakers
adore it, so much so that any estate in the Iberian peninsula,
southern France or the New World that turns its attention to
Cabernet seems suddenly to have arrived. And Old World Cabernet
has been clasped to the bosom of British wine drinkers for many
years, as it is a major component in one of the UK's favourite wines
– claret.

In Bordeaux, while hardly ever giving an entirely solo
performance (the 1994 Lafite was an exception, apparently),
Cabernet plays the starring role in the great wines of the Médoc and
Graves. The wines it creates here range from the rustic *petits
châteaux* to elegant *crus classés*, the latter beautifully poised and
dusty dry, with plenty of Cabernet's cassis character held rigid
when young by a magnificent structure of tannins.

A reasonably hardy grape, Cabernet has travelled well, and now
appears in many shapes and forms. Californian, South African and
Australian Cabernets can be first rate in a hefty, rich style, with lush,
ripe fruit to the fore. More recently, Washington State has
impressed us with the best of its Cabernets. And Chile seems to
have an effortless ability to turn out affordable examples that sing
with pure blackcurranty varietal character. Argentina's wines have
looked highly promising in the past, and will be again in the future
we trust, but for now they appear to be losing their way.

Back in Europe, the south of France has proved it can turn out
juicy, ripe Cabernet at fair prices, while Italy creates some of the
most sophisticated, multi-layered Cabernet blends. In Australia,
Cabernet is successfully blended with Shiraz, in Tuscany with

Sangiovese and in Spain with Tempranillo. But Cabernet's most regular bedfellow is Merlot, favoured in Bordeaux because its lush, plummy character softens up Cabernet's toughness. Most of the world's best Cabernet is aged in French oak *barriques*, but American oak has produced some excellent examples in California and in Rioja.

Merlot
High-class grape or fashion victim? Merlot plays both roles convincingly. In its home of Bordeaux, it's traditionally been an understudy to the more serious Cabernet Sauvignon, fleshing out Cabernet's rather austere nature. However, the last 20 years have seen a surge in quality of the wonderfully plummy, Merlot-heavy wines of St-Emilion and Pomerol, and with it a huge upturn in demand. The result is that the world's wine regions have jumped on the Merlot bandwagon, eager to produce Château Pétrus lookalikes. Some, especially in California, Washington State and Hawke's Bay, have enjoyed great success. Others have only made large quantities of rather anonymous, simple, jammy wines. The problem is that given the right conditions, Merlot goes wild in the vineyard, and produces plump but largely flavourless grapes. The result is that much cheap Merlot tastes just that – cheap. Exceptions exist, especially in southern France, parts of Eastern Europe and Chile. Be warned about Chilean Merlot though. As we explain earlier in the book, much of it is made from an unrelated variety called Carmenère. This can be terrific – but Merlot it ain't.

Pinot Noir
Pinot gets a bad press for being one of the most difficult varieties in the world. This is indeed a fickle and exasperating grape, especially in comparison with the accommodating Cabernet. It suffers partly from being thin-skinned and sensitive to poor conditions, and also because expectations of it are so high. On a good day, Pinot Noir can be truly beguiling. As a fine young red, it is gorgeous, raspberry-scented, silky and winsome. When it ages, it takes on a voluptuous, earthy character, turning more pungent and animal-scented all the time. And as a component in champagne and premium sparkling wine, it adds red-berry fruitiness and perfume.

Shame then that it so often refuses to be seduced. The winemakers of Oregon, once heralded as Pinot's home from home, are familiar with the quixotic nature of the grape, and its inability to withstand less-than-perfect weather conditions. The Australians have managed to make elegant Pinot Noir only in relatively cool spots, such as Victoria's Yarra Valley or Tasmania, while in South Africa and Chile just a few good examples exist to prove that it may have a future there.

New Zealand provides more exciting Pinots – indeed, it is the most widely planted red variety. Several plots on the South Island plus Martinborough at the foot of the North Island are already enjoying considerable success with the grape, and the best may be yet to come. Parts of California where the warm sun is tempered by cool Pacific breezes have also proved ideal for Pinot. Regions such as Carneros, Russian River and Santa Barbara County are able to coax it into consistently lush, concentrated wines.

However, it is in Burgundy, if the weather is right and the winemaking shrewd (pretty big 'ifs'), that Pinot Noir is at its best, with a smooth, lush, red-berry youth and a farmyard-rich maturity.

Sensitive in all things, Pinot yields need to be kept low, and oaking should be relatively light. And it is almost always expensive – at the lower end of the price spectrum look out for a few pleasant Romanian wines from the region of Dealul Mare and a few examples from Chile.

Syrah/Shiraz

Syrah scores a double whammy – it is both a star variety in a classic European region (the Rhône Valley), and in Australia, where it goes by the name of Shiraz. After years of kowtowing to Cabernet and Pinot, it is finally receiving the recognition it deserves, and more and more countries are planting Syrah in their vineyards. Good Syrah combines the structure of Cabernet with the wild perfume of Pinot. It ages to herby, spicy, leathery complexity, and is a brilliant partner for red meat, roast poultry and cheese.

In the northern Rhône, Syrah is worshipped, producing great wines such as Côte Rôtie and Hermitage. In the southern Rhône, Syrah makes a small but invaluable contribution to most of the great wines of Châteauneuf-du-Pape and Gigondas. Plantings in the south of France have increased significantly over the past 15 years or so. Some wines produced from these have been ripe and satisfying, and are often successfully blended with Cabernet, Merlot, Grenache and Mourvèdre. The Languedoc region of southern France has impressed in recent years with its concentrated, rich *vin de pays* Syrahs.

The Australians, on the other hand, despite the success of Penfolds Grange (which typically is 90 per cent Shiraz), only recognised it as their greatest traditional red grape towards the end of the twentieth century. Shiraz from ancient, gnarled Australian vines is inky black, hugely concentrated and rich (too rich, in some instances), while the fun, red sparkling Shiraz is an Australian speciality worth trying. These are the two extremes and there are plenty more juicy, concentrated, exuberant wines in between.

Where once Australia and France had a virtual monopoly on quality Syrah, good versions can now be found in Chile, Argentina,

Spain, Italy, Greece, New Zealand and even Morocco. And while
the Australians may currently be the New World Syrah champions,
the quality of wines being made now in California and Washington
State poses a serious threat to their crown.

White

Chardonnay

Well, it's still overload time as far as Chardonnay is concerned. The
grape is everywhere – from Corton to Conca de Barberá in the Old
World – and, we reckon, just about every New World grower either
has some, or is within a stone's throw of some vines. But that's no
reason to turn our backs on it – even if we could. We really don't
think that, however much there is, Chardonnay will ever be as bad
as Müller-Thurgau. To begin with, it not only thrives in almost any
environment, but at almost any yield (high or low), any
winemaking style (still or sparkling), with or without oak, it makes
a cheerful, palatable wine. And when it lifts its game beyond the
cheap, bulk-made offerings, the results can be superb.

Wine buyers and growers alike are really waking up to the ABC
(Anything But Chardonnay) movement. Sauvignon, Viognier,
Sémillon and Pinot Gris are all being planted, even in Chardonnay
strongholds such as Australia (where, for a while, we were worried
the message wasn't going to sink in). And that's great. That gives us
more variety, more options. But we still think that people who say
they're bored with Chardonnay don't fully realise the range of
flavours and styles this grape offers. We heartily recommend that
detractors trade up or trade across rather than give up.

Chardonnay is such a chameleon that it makes an excellent
display piece for *terroir*: in other words, it reflects exactly the
vineyards in which it was grown. So for understanding the
different flavours that come from different parts of France,
California or Australia, choose a Chardonnay from each and
compare the effects of this or that valley, hillside or village. (Just
to complicate matters, however, it also makes an excellent display
piece for different winemaking techniques – see below – so there'll
be many variables at play in each glass of wine you taste.)

The Côte d'Or, as Burgundy is known, is Chardonnay's real
home territory. Within that region there are the steely, flinty
wines of Chablis (although some fruitier, more rounded examples
now exist); the toasty hazelnut Chardonnays from Meursault; and,
somewhere between these two styles, the minerally, buttery ones
of Puligny-Montrachet – vastly different wines, but all from the
same grape. The New World wines tend to be fuller on the palate
and more powerful, but the same diversity shows through. In
Australia, for example, Barossa Valley Chardonnays are rich,

toasty and fat; from Clare they are leaner, creamier with crisper acidity; and from Margaret River they're minerally and elegant, different again.

We're impressed with cooler-climate Chardonnays from New Zealand, South Africa and the Pacific North-west (Washington State and Oregon). There are also ripe, modern styles emerging from South America and Spain; Italian and southern French examples tend to be lighter and more structured. In all cases, cheaper versions can be dull, but, particularly from the New World, deciding on a specified region will increase your chances tenfold of making a good choice.

We're also pleased to report that the global trend for over-oaking is still subsiding. Winemakers are still tinkering and experimenting, and as well as a few more delicate, unoaked Chardonnays coming on to the market, tricks such as lees-stirring and natural yeast fermentation are giving richer, nuttier, more textured, complex wines. We're hearing more and more complaints such as 'I like Chardonnay but I don't like oak!' – so these new techniques and new flavours are certainly to be applauded.

All in all, we'd like to see: both winemakers and consumers taking Chardonnay less for granted; fewer 'churned out', bland wines (generic blends, sourced from anywhere and everywhere); fewer-still of the oaky options; and many more regional choices. But otherwise, we still think Chardonnay is a good thing.

Riesling

We have no hesitation in listing Riesling up among the grape royalty. It is a versatile vine, easy to grow, produces distinctively racy, honeyed wines – and, if it really has been grown on the banks of the Mosel since Roman times, it's been around long enough to deserve a little respect!

Liebfraumilch and Niersteiner have, without doubt, spoiled the Riesling show for a great many would-be consumers, but we now hope the stage is set for change. On the other side of the world, there is a new generation of Australians who have no reason to doubt Riesling. Many weren't even born in the 1970s (the peak of the German wine flood), so, as well as being a long way away, they're children of the Chardonnay boom, who may never have seen or tasted unlovely Liebfraumilch.

Today, Germany produces fantastic Rieslings, ranging from steely and very dry (the version currently very fashionable locally), to delicate, floral wines with a touch of residual sugar sweetness, to delicious, intricately sweet examples. All of them have a firm, nervy acidity that balances any sugar and frequently leads to great ageing potential. You'll have to look further than your high street to track the best of these down: the image of German wine has been so tarnished that most merchants tuck these wines away until they're asked for. But it's heartening that we're seeing more and more fine ones on restaurant and even supermarket wine lists, proving that a return to Riesling is finally taking place – and that people are realising just how good it is with food.

Austria and Alsace produce finely tuned Rieslings which can demonstrate fascinating differences in soils and micro-climates (for those interested in the esoteric). The best New World examples, such as those from Australia's Clare and Eden valleys, are riper, rounded, with a little more alcohol than their German counterparts, but have the same racy acidity and delicate petrolly, floral notes. The best can be outstanding. Cheaper examples can offer attractively ripe, lemon/lime characteristics.

Some of the world's greatest sweet wines are *botrytis*-affected Rieslings, such as the *Beeren-* and *Trockenbeerenauslesen* of Germany. The rare *Eisweins* from Germany and their Canadian equivalent (Icewines) can be sublime.

Sauvignon Blanc
One of the most distinctive (if not always distinguished) grapes in the white firmament; that steely thread of lemony acidity crops up in almost every wine, whether from Sancerre or Central Otago. The same goes for the straightforward, simple, appley green fruit. You can spot a Sauvignon (we normally drop the Blanc) a mile off. This was the grape that the ABC brigade first turned to in their flight to escape Chardonnay. We admit that it's not as outrightly 'acceptable' as Chardonnay, not as versatile or varied. It can be 'grubby' if poorly made, harsh and green if unripe, and doesn't have the same easy relationship with sweet, toasty oak. The gooseberry and nettle fruit – cat's pee to its detractors – is also something you either like or you don't. So as second-in-line to Chardonnay it can be disappointing. But if you were totally disappointed you'd be wrong.

Classic Loire Sauvignons (the best examples) are elegant and stunning. Look out not only for Sancerre and Pouilly-Fumé, but Quincy, Reuilly and Menetou-Salon – the latter are Sauvignons from smaller, lesser-known appellations where growers try harder and the wines are frequently better made. New Zealand is the other Sauvignon stronghold. Flavours are more vibrant, grassy and powerful, but go together to make balanced, long, invariably great food wines. We also like the new wave of Sauvignons emerging from South Africa: they seem to fall halfway between the Loire and New Zealand in weight, but add in a creamy, honeyed dimension, where others can seem simple and linear (boring?). Where California and South America are concerned, however, we do have some doubts. This grape needs a cool climate to thrive – too much heat and it loses its poise and becomes hard and clumsy. Chile's Casablanca Valley is the one possible exception. The continuing vogue for oaked Sauvignon called Fumé Blanc in the States is not something with which we've been particularly impressed.

Without doubt, the wine that proves this grape's class is Pavillon Blanc de Château Margaux. A hundred per cent Sauvignon that can age 20 years and develop the most fabulous minerally, spicy complexity. And while this wine isn't easy to get hold of, it goes some way to proving how good white Bordeaux can be. Though Sauvignon is traditionally blended with Sémillon here, there are more and more pure Sauvignon Blancs emerging from this region – it will be interesting to see how they develop.

FIRST DIVISION

These grape varieties are capable of producing fine wine, either alone or in blends. They do not, however, achieve top quality consistently, or are virtually unique to certain regions.

Red

Cabernet Franc

While it is unfair to think of Merlot as Cabernet Sauvignon's poor cousin, it is a description which we are happy to apply to Cabernet Franc. Except, that is, in France's cool Loire Valley, where it can produce serious reds. This is not a particularly rich grape but its combination of fresh raspberry fragrance, crunchy, red-fruit flavour and hints of green bell pepper and leaf is most appealing. Northern Italian Cabernet Franc is also grassy and light. These perfumed wines benefit from a light chill. Otherwise, Cabernet Franc's main role is as the third most important red grape in Bordeaux (after Cabernet Sauvignon and Merlot).

New World producers have been slow to take up the challenge, and so far only a handful of decent wines has emerged from Australia, California and New Zealand. A grape whose day is yet to come? Perhaps, especially since the general trend is moving away from blockbuster wines.

Grenache/Garnacha

Time was when Grenache was merely the red workhorse of Spain and France. It is the world's second most widely planted grape variety (Airén being the first), and many of us will have quaffed a good deal of Grenache without knowing it, either as cheap and cheerful French carafe wine, as holiday *rosado* in Spain, or even as basic Australian red. Now the grape is gaining more respect. In

Australia, you'll find seriously rich if occasionally jammy varietals or gutsy GSM – Grenache/Shiraz/Mourvèdre – blends, while in California the 'Rhône Ranger' crew also produces enjoyable Grenache. And about time too – the grape which makes up much of the blend in southern Rhône reds (including Châteauneuf-du-Pape) was always going to be good news given a bit of tender loving care. When its yields are kept low, and it is handled skilfully in the winery, raspberry and cherry fruit and a twist of black pepper emerge in the wine. This is a versatile variety, and one need look no further than Spain to witness a wide range of styles, from the hefty, thick-set reds of Priorato and Tarragona in Catalonia and Collioure in southern France, to the fresh, crisp *rosados* of Navarra, to the *vins doux naturels* of Banyuls. Grenache also blends well with grapes with more natural backbone, most famously with Syrah and Mourvèdre in the Rhône.

Malbec

If it were down to the French, Malbec wouldn't merit a great deal of attention. One of the lesser grapes of Bordeaux, where it is known as Cot, Malbec only comes into its own in Cahors, where it forms a minimum of 70 per cent of the blend of the robust local wines. But it is Argentina which has raised the profile of this grape in recent times, and which is responsible for our elevating it to First Division status. Argentina has more plantings of Malbec than the rest of the world put together, and here it can produce anything from attractive, fruity wines easy to mistake for Merlot, to serious, full-bodied, oak-aged reds with delicious black-cherry flavour and a rich, velvety texture.

Malbec is widely planted in neighbouring Chile, although few wineries as yet take it very seriously. In Australia's Clare Valley, some producers have preferred it to Shiraz as a blending partner for Cabernet, while across the Tasman Sea in New Zealand, several Hawke's Bay *vignerons* use it to add seasoning and structure to their red blends.

Nebbiolo

Italy's great red grape is rightly famous for producing the heavyweight and splendid Barolos and Barbarescos of Piedmont. It takes its name from the *nebbia*, the fog that engulfs the vineyards of Alba in north-west Italy. Nebbiolo is extremely tannic and tough when young, and its wines can be slow to mature. When (and, in some instances, if) they finally soften, they are fascinating, complex and perfumed, inspiring the classic tasting note of tar and roses. Some people even claim to detect truffles in the wine, but then in Piedmont they may just have truffles on the mind.

Nebbiolo is also grown in Lombardy and further south near Brescia. Little is planted outside Italy, perhaps because winemakers find it hard to get to grips with such a darkly brooding variety. Nonetheless, it's enjoying a small but significant surge in popularity around the world. We've seen plantings in New Zealand and South Africa, and even Greece and Mexico, although few wines have appeared on the market so far. California is further along the Nebbiolo track, and has a band of producers who call themselves the Cal-Ital brigade. Already several very tasty wines have appeared, most notably from Il Podere dell'Olivos. The Australians are in on the act too – we recommend the wines from Brown Brothers and Garry Crittenden. And finally Argentina, which has quite extensive plantings, is beginning to make better use of this fine resource.

Sangiovese

The classic red grape of Tuscany, Sangiovese combines strawberry and red-cherry fruit with tobacco and tea-leaf to create distinctively Italianate reds. That great Tuscan wine Brunello di Montalcino is made from one specific clone, while in Chianti and Vino Nobile di Montepulciano Sangiovese is the principal grape in a blend of several different varieties. The grape is increasingly used in Super-Tuscan *vini da tavola*, either on its own or in combination with Cabernet.

It exists under various synonyms all over Italy (including Morellino, Prugnolo, Calabrese), but is rarely encountered elsewhere. As with Nebbiolo, however, this is changing. California now boasts several fine versions, and can also point to its own Super-Tuscan-style blends with Cabernet. Argentinian Sangiovese tends to be a little simple, but over the Andes in Chile, the debut wine from Errázuriz is remarkably good.

Tempranillo

Spain's most famous black grape and the mainstay of Rioja, Tempranillo ages well in American (and sometimes French) oak to produce lightly coloured, strawberry-scented, vanilla-packed red wine. It is usually blended with Garnacha (and perhaps some Graciano and Mazuelo) for Rioja, and is widely used elsewhere in Spain under local names such as Tinto Fino in Ribera del Duero, Cencibel in La Mancha and Tinto de Toro in Toro.

Tempranillo is also grown extensively in two regions of Portugal, the central Alentejo, where it is known as Aragonez and used in red table-wine blends of variable quality, and the Douro, where it is known as Tinta Roriz and mainly used, again in blends, to make port. The only other place you are likely to come across it is in Argentina; the quality here can be good, but tread carefully.

Touriga Nacional

One of the red grapes of Portugal's Douro Valley and widely agreed to be the best grape for making port, Touriga is naturally low yielding and produces small, tough-skinned berries. Its young wine is packed with tannin and intense red-fruit flavour – and it has been compared closely with Cabernet Sauvignon. It ages brilliantly as a table wine, and is an important component in red Dão from northern Portugal. In Australia it is sometimes used for fortified wines.

Zinfandel/Primitivo

Zinfandel, at its most concentrated and inky red, should be on prescription for anyone bored with the classic red varieties; its exuberant bramble and strawberry fruit and spicy, leathery depths will soon revive a flagging interest. Zin produces some of California's most idiosyncratic and fascinating wine, often from ancient vines in Sonoma County and the Sierra Foothills. Unfortunately, it is still used to make oodles of insipid, sweet 'blush' wine labelled White Zinfandel. While California is Zinfandel's current home, DNA testing has confirmed that it is actually the same variety as the Primitivo of Puglia. Some Puglian Primitivos, especially A Mano made by Californian Mark Shannon, would seem to provide confirmation of this, but there are still doubts as to the accuracy of those DNA test results. Zinfandel outside California and Italy is rare but not uncommon. Cape Mentelle and Nepenthe make fine versions in Australia, and we've also enjoyed the wine from Chile's Cono Sur.

White

Chenin Blanc

Within the Loire Valley, Chenin Blanc produces an astonishing breadth of wine styles, from humble Anjou Blanc to long-lived, dry Savennières, from sparkling Saumur to honeyed dessert wines such as Coteaux du Layon, Bonnezeaux and Quarts de Chaume. Would that we could say, equally admiringly, that all Chenin Blancs were great. Sadly, they're not. Indeed, mediocre Chenin is one of our pet hates. The best *vignerons*, often benefiting from generations of experience, know exactly how to exploit the naturally high acidity of Chenin – but beware carelessly made, mass-produced examples. There are no real distinguishing features of dry Chenin wines, apart from wet wool and some light floral overtones; if they are over-sulphured and badly handled too, almost no wine is worse!

Our advice therefore is to pick and choose, particularly in off vintages. In good Loire years, Chenin can come into its own, creating unique honeyed wines with the ability to age for years.

Outside France, South Africa has the major plantings of Chenin and the bulk wines it has produced in the past from this grape have gone some way to forming its poor reputation. In warmer climates,

Chenin's high-yielding and high-acid tendencies make it perfect for neutral base wines for sparkling (Argentina) and, very often, wine for distillation into spirits. Today, however, a handful of South African growers is offering it a new lease of life. Pockets of greatness occur where some of them take more care in the vineyards and cellars. From older, low-yielding vines, we are pleased to say that we have tasted honeyed, rich, crisp wines showing exactly the way this grape should be. Serious results are coming from other New World regions too – California and Western Australia, for starters.

Gewürztraminer
If it's exoticism you're after, this is the grape for you. The best Alsace Gewürztraminer will assail your senses with pure aromas of lychees, roses or even ginger – sheer bliss! Rarely do other wines match up to the hedonistic 'Gewürz'. If, however, a nice crisp Chablis is your thing, be prepared to loathe it. One thing is for certain, there is no sitting on the fence. Often Gewürz is the first grape that wine lovers learn to recognise blind – try it if you haven't done so already. Ardent fans swear by Gewürz as the accompaniment for the delicate Eastern flavours of Thai food; we also love it chilled on a summer's evening.

The natural home of Gewürztraminer is Alsace, where its pinkish skin and capacity to ripen easily produce deep-coloured, powerful dry whites with a distinctive oiliness and sometimes a slight sweetness. The late-harvest *vendange tardive* wines of Alsace are naturally sweet, and the exceptional *sélection de grains nobles* can be outstandingly delicious. Elsewhere in Europe, Gewürz is generally lighter in style and can be found in Germany, Italy's Alto Adige, Hungary and Spain, where Torres makes a popular Gewürz and Muscat blend called Viña Esmeralda. The aromatic qualities of Gewürz (German for 'spice', incidentally) can often turn cheap-and-easy white wines into something a little more special. In the New World, Gewürz does better in cooler sub-regions, such as the Casablanca Valley in Chile or New Zealand's Marlborough. Henschke make a good one in Australia's Eden Valley.

Marsanne
In the northern Rhône, Marsanne, blended with a little Roussanne, is responsible for the enigmatic white wines of the staunchly red appellations of St-Joseph, Hermitage, Crozes-Hermitage and St-Péray. These are weighty, rich wines with an intriguing peach or marzipan aroma. Marsanne is also a permitted varietal in the Languedoc and producers there are increasingly coming up with good-value, inexpensive examples. The most interesting Marsanne enclave, however, is the Goulburn Valley in Victoria, Australia, where wines from Chateau Tahbilk and Mitchelton are sturdy with

full-flavoured fruit. The likelihood is that there will be yet more from Australia, as the current Rhône trend really takes hold. There are already plantings in the Barossa Valley and Western Australia – together, of course, with traditional blend partner Roussanne. You may also find the odd Marsanne hailing from California.

Muscat
Truly the grapiest of grapes, aromatic Muscat is responsible, amongst others, for the light and frothy Asti and Moscato d'Asti in northern Italy; dry, scented Alsace Muscats; richly sweet Muscat *vins doux naturels* in the south of France; and the dark and raisiny fortified Muscats in Australia. In fact Muscat is not just one grape but a whole family of them with Muscat à Petits Grains generally accepted as being the best of the lot and behind the wines just mentioned. The next-most-popular Muscat, Muscat of Alexandria, gives us the sweet wines of Spain and Portugal (Moscatel de Valencia, Malaga and Set£bal) and crops up as Hanepoot in South Africa and Zibibbo in Sicily. Useful stuff for a wine quiz!

Pinot Blanc
Definitely a grape without vices, Pinot Blanc is easy to grow and makes easy-drinking, undemanding wines that rarely achieve great heights. In Alsace, the wines have an unusual intensity of flavour and we would argue that this is where Pinot Blanc performs best. In Germany, Pinot Blanc is known as Weissburgunder and does particularly well in southern areas such as Baden, where its adaptability and suitability for oak treatment allows growers to experiment with styles of wine which are not possible in the north. It thrives in Austria and is all over the place in northern Italy, where its neutrality also makes it suitable as a base for sparkling wines. We have occasionally come across the odd, and perfectly acceptable, Californian oaked Pinot Blanc.

Pinot Gris
Following closely along on the spice route after Gewürztraminer, Pinot Gris makes dusky, smoky, dry Alsace wines (known as Tokay-Pinot Gris), sought after mainly as food wines. With extra ripening, it can also produce delicious *vendange tardive* examples.

In Germany, Pinot Gris is known as Rülander and occurs as a rounded, medium-bodied white wine mainly in Baden and the Pfalz. Rülander is also the name of Pinot Gris in Austria, whereas in Italy we find the more appealing-sounding Pinot Grigio, still neutral, but with a crisp, citrus palate. Winemakers have recently turned their attentions to Pinot Gris in the New World, especially in areas cool enough for it to retain its delicate acidity. Some seriously good wines are emerging from Oregon, where this grape has now completely stolen Chardonnay's show. And we've also tried out an excellent example from Australia's Clare Valley – deliciously complex and mellow and eight years old.

Sémillon

Sémillon's (the accent is only required in France) greatest haunt is Australia, where it can occur just as easily in everyday quaffing Semillon/Chardonnay as it can in outrageously, full-bodied and flavour-packed, oaked Barossa Valley wines. The classic examples, however, come from the Hunter Valley. When young, they're nothing to write home about: thin, neutral, low in alcohol and not unlike grassy Sauvignon Blanc. But with time they develop into minerally, powerful wines with a creamy texture and a hint of honeyed beeswax, capable of great age, and well worth waiting for. From Margaret River in Western Australia, the style falls somewhere between these two: honeyed and ripe but with an elegant, spicy crispness.

Sémillon in its classic role, in France, is mostly found as the co-varietal, with Sauvignon Blanc, in the whites of Bordeaux – both humble and classic, dry and sweet. In the Graves, Sémillon provides a soft, rounded counterpart to the crisp and zingy Sauvignon adding depth and intensity, as well as making the wines more suited to oak. The grape's susceptibility to *botrytis* is key to its greatest success in Sauternes and as part of the illustrious and expensive Château d'Yquem. In Barsac and neighbouring Monbazillac, it makes an equally sweet contribution.

Viognier

For a while there, in the late 1990s, Viognier was mooted as the 'new' Chardonnay but these claims were drastically premature. Attractive, fleshy and reliably peachy flavours make it fashionable and very appealing to wine producers and consumers alike, but, truth be told, it's a capricious beast and not as easy to pin down in the winery (or vineyard) as winemakers would like. Viognier's claim to fame lies with the full-bodied, fragrant, and highly sought-after, wines of Château Grillet and Condrieu in the northern Rhône. Light, easy-drinking facsimiles from the Languedoc are peachy, but mostly rather dilute when compared to the real thing. The best we have tasted lately came from Argentina, in fact. California and Australia are the other main sources but here there is a tendency for things to get overblown – over-oaked, and just too much of a peach-parcel. We think many winemakers just haven't worked Viognier out yet. But sufficient effort is being made, and the time will come when they do work it out – with lower yields, less oak and cooler-climate vineyards. We certainly advise giving any that you see a whirl – be prepared for zesty, honeyed, apricoty wines at the cheap end and intensely lush and muskily developed wines for a few pennies more.

SECOND DIVISION

The grape varieties listed below have the potential to make good-quality wines, but they seldom create great ones.

Red

Barbera

Italy's most widely planted red grape typically produces easy-drinking, fruity wines. In Piedmont, Barbera plays second fiddle to Nebbiolo and as such is not usually planted on the best sites. In the right hands, however, it can make more serious, longer-lived reds, either on its own or in blends with Nebbiolo. New World versions are competent rather than outstanding, although Argentina is getting to grips with this variety, and some California offerings have been good.

Carignan

One of the workhorses of southern France, in the past producing largely forgettable wine. However, low-yielding old vines from the better growers are beginning to produce rather good, spicy reds. It is Spanish in origin but its use in Spain, where it goes under the names of Cariñena or Mazuelo, is limited. One of the best examples elsewhere is the Carignano del Sulcis of Sardinia. It is widely planted in North Africa and although not yet producing wines of great distinction it is showing some promising signs.

Dolcetto

The 'little sweet one' produces some of Italy's most gluggable wines, refreshing, fruity and smooth, with a slightly sour cherryish twist on the finish. It is seldom seen outside Piedmont, although Best's in Australia produces a full-flavoured version.

Gamay

The jester to King Pinot Noir in Burgundy, Gamay is the ruby-hued, fruity grape responsible for Beaujolais, typically producing vibrant, strawberry-fresh wines for early consumption, although richer versions from *cru* villages can age well. Most Bourgogne Ordinaire is made from Gamay, while Passetoutgrains is a more attractive blend of Gamay with at least one-third Pinot Noir. A light version appears in Touraine, and a few Californian producers make reasonably decent versions.

Mourvèdre

A red grape used in blends for its firm structure and spiciness, Mourvèdre originated in Spain where, as Monastrell, it is the second most planted red variety after Garnacha and is used in pink Cava. However, it is now more famous in southern France, where it is used in blends and occasionally alone as in the strapping and long-lived wines of Bandol. It appears in a few Californian bottlings and pops up in Australia where a little is grown as Mataro. Gaining in popularity: expect to see more and more of this grape.

Pinot Meunier

The 'other' Pinot of Champagne, where it is the most widely planted variety, contributing fruitiness to the blend but lacking the finesse of Pinot Noir and Chardonnay. Sparkling wine producers in other parts of the world have plantings too.

Pinotage

The Cinsault/Pinot Noir cross developed in South Africa in the 1920s has yet to set the rest of the world on fire, but Cape versions get better and better. Styles range from simple, fruity Beaujolais lookalikes to hefty blockbusters such as the benchmark wine from Kanonkop Estate. The rough, tomatoey flavours of the past are slowly being phased out, but don't be surprised to detect a whiff of banana in many wines. The rare New Zealand Pinotages, especially those from Babich, are worth trying.

Tannat

Southern French varietal found in the deep, dark, powerful wines of Madiran where it traditionally makes up 40 to 60 per cent of the blend – the wines require at least ten years before drinking. But nowadays (big-structured, black wines being fashionable) it is moving towards cult status, and often makes up the entire blend. It is the richer, bolder wines from Uruguay, however, that really take the spotlight these days: here Tannat's rough tannins are softened by New World heat and sunshine. It is also blended to good effect with Uruguayan Merlot.

White

Colombard

With its roots in the Cognac region, Colombard was historically used in the production of brandy, but is now more likely to crop up in the blend of a crisp, fresh *vin de pays* des Côtes de Gascogne. Here it makes a floral counterpart to the essentially neutral Ugni Blanc. It also features in simple, inexpensive quaffing whites from South Africa and California, which should definitely be drunk young.

Furmint

You won't find this grape outside Hungary, where it is the
mainstay of the great, sweet white wine Tokaji, thanks to its high
acidity and propensity to succumb to noble rot. Dry Furmint wines
do exist; they can be very good but are rare, and not cheap.

Grüner Veltliner

The wines of Austria's Wachau show Grüner Veltliner at its very
best. With its hallmark crisp, spicy, peppery character, Grüner
Veltliner makes a welcome change from overtly fruit-driven wines
so common nowadays – and, happily, is becoming slightly less of a
rarity. Watch out for some interesting sweet wines too.

Macabeo/Viura

Mainly grown in the arc stretching from the Languedoc to northern
Spain, Macabeo is widely used in white wines. As Viura, it is the
principal grape of white Rioja, making occasionally delicious, but
unusual, peachy, minerally wines. Its lightly floral character from
cooler climates is possibly the reason why it is an important grape
in the standard Cava blend.

Malvasia

Malvasia's main characteristics – a deep colour, high alcohol and
propensity to oxidation – don't tend to put it high on anybody's list.
However, in Italy, Malvasia (in many different forms) is widely
planted and commonly blended with dull and neutral Trebbiano;
for example, it lends fatness and fragrance to some of the best
Frascatis. Malvasia is also grown in Spain and Portugal and can also
crop up in California. Perhaps its best incarnation is in the sweet
wines of *vin santo* and in Malmsey the richest of madeiras.

Palomino

For its role in the production of sherry, Palomino is certainly worthy
of attention. Grown in the white *albariza* soils of Jerez, Palomino
grapes make a low-acid, slightly flabby wine which would be
nothing to write home about if it weren't for its propensity, once
fortified, to transform – with *flor* – into extraordinarily tangy and
elegant manzanilla and fino sherries. With oxidation as well, darker,
nuttier amontillado styles are produced.

Outside Spain, Palomino can be found in most New World areas,
particularly South Africa, where it has very lowly, still wine status.
Where it is fortified outside Spain, the absence of *flor* keeps the
wines well below par.

Roussanne

Roussanne is generally found with Marsanne in the aromatic white
wines of the northern Rhône. It is also one of the main grapes in the

curiosity-value, more southerly, white Châteauneuf-du-Pape (the Vieilles Vignes wine of Château de Beaucastel is Roussanne). Roussanne can also be used in the whites of the Languedoc. Following its red Rhône cousin Syrah (Shiraz), this grape is also making experimental appearances in cooler regions of Australia.

Trebbiano/Ugni Blanc
Ugni Blanc of south-western France originates in Italy as Trebbiano, where it has a multitude of strains, and provides a significant chunk of DOC white wines. Trebbiano/Ugni Blanc's main feature is, perversely, its almost total lack of character. Expect vapid neutrality and very little else from the quaffing whites it produces.

ALSO-RANS

The following grapes are either widely planted but of only average quality, or have potential but are encountered infrequently.

Red

Baga
A sturdy, thick-skinned variety which forms the backbone of Bairrada reds in northern Portugal. Most versions are rather hard and tannic, although modern methods of vinification can produce fruitier reds with delicious blackberry character and a hint of spice. Luis Pato is the acknowledged master of the variety.

Cinsault/Cinsaut
Another widespread but frequently dreary grape of southern France that's no longer worthy of total derision: as with Carignan, some upbeat new-wave growers are making great Cinsault from old vines. Cinsaut, is still widely planted in the Cape, but has little influence.

Montepulciano and Negroamaro
Two Italian black grapes. Montepulciano – not to be confused with the Tuscan town of the same name where Vino Nobile is produced – makes large amounts of easy-drinking, spicy, berryish wine plus the occasional silky stunner in central and south-east Italy. For some reason, a little has been planted in Marlborough, New Zealand. Negroamaro produces similarly friendly, burly wines in the south of Italy, especially Puglia. With a little care, some extraordinarily good southern Rhône-like wine can be made.

Periquita
This grape variety is the mainstay of central and southern Portuguese reds, particularly in the regions of Alentejo,

Estremadura and Ribatejo, and is underrated. Progressive winemakers are squeezing pleasant, cherryish flavour from it.

Petite Sirah/Durif
There is increasing doubt as to whether these two are actually the same variety, but the wines produced certainly have similarities, both being tannic and not particularly refined. The grape appears in California, Mexico, Australia and South America.

Petit Verdot
A spicy, tough grape which is occasionally found in small quantities in Bordeaux blends, and in California. Bordeaux winemakers use it 'like salt and pepper', as one described it to us, to add a little zest and character to a blend; a few Western Australian growers are now using it in the same way. In Spain Marqués de Griñón has a varietal version, while Viña Alicia's Verdot from Argentina is extremely impressive. Gaining in popularity.

White

Aligoté and Melon de Bourgogne
Aligoté, the second grape of Burgundy, is best known for its tart, white wine – the traditional choice to which you should add a splash of Dijon crème de cassis to make kir. Melon de Bourgogne is the grape of Muscadet and grown in the Pays Nantais, where it copes with the cold and can develop well with lees ageing. Made carelessly it can be execrable.

Müller-Thurgau, Silvaner and Welschriesling
A trio of everyday, reliably yielding Germanic grapes, generally used to make cheap, everyday whites from Germany, Eastern Europe and also England. Müller-Thurgau is occasionally capable of passable things in skilful hands (often outside its German home) and turns up in some reasonable blends in New Zealand. Silvaner does best producing crisp, racy Franken whites. Welschriesling (no relation to the noble Riesling) is grown widely in central Europe and Italy and is usually associated with cheap whites such as Laski Rizling, although it is responsible for some stunning sweet wines in Austria's Burgenland.

THE LOOK, SMELL AND TASTE OF WINE

What's the big deal about this precious fluid, given that if you leave grapes in a bin in reasonably warm conditions they will turn into wine of their own accord? There must be something that makes an Australian Chardonnay different from a white burgundy – so what is it? Throughout the A–Z of wine-producing countries we have tried to explain the differences that country, region and site can bring to bear on individual wines, and we have introduced you to some of the winemakers who help to shape them. However, there is more to wine than places and people, so here we look at some of the other factors that determine what ends up in your glass.

APPEARANCE

'Good legs' is a classic comment which is made time after time about wine. It refers to the streaks of liquid seen on the side of a glass after swirling the wine around, described in a rare poetic moment by the Germans as 'cathedral windows'. These merely indicate that the wine has a high alcohol level.

Good colour is harder to fathom. If wine is bright, clear and does not show signs of premature ageing (brick-orange reds; dull yellow for whites) then that augurs well for the taste of the stuff. Clarity, just as with diamonds, is essential. No wine should ever be hazy. But good colour doesn't necessarily mean deep colour. A darker yellow, red or black is not always an indication of quality. Certain grapes have darker skins than others, for example, Syrah and Cabernet Sauvignon are naturally a much deeper purple-red colour than Pinot Noir. It is possible to increase the amount of colour in a wine by keeping the grape skins in contact with the juice for longer periods and by agitating the skins and juice, but since such procedures also extract other compounds such as tannin, the winemaker has to calculate the extent to which each is used

If young red wines show signs of browning, the chances are they have been poorly stored. Small, white tartrate crystals in white wines are harmless and indicate that the wine has not been over-filtered.

AROMA

Whether you're into one big 'sniff' or lots of little ones, it doesn't matter; stick your nose right in and go for it – you will come to no harm (unless you're sniffing Zinfandel or port, in which case, the alcohol might knock you sideways). And 'nosing' a wine is rather like foreplay, a necessary prelude to the main performance. If you've ever tried to smell fine wine with a heavy cold, you'll know that missing out on the aroma means you also miss out on a lot of the sensory thrill. Most of the wine's character that you will pick up on the palate is there to a greater or lesser extent in its perfume.

Certainly, oakiness, alcohol level and faults such as cork taint, or excessive use of sulphur, are all apparent, and some people even claim to be able to spot tannin and acidity in an aroma. As a wine opens out, either with time in the glass or with vigorous swirling of the liquid, the scent develops further. (The pros and cons of decanting, swirling and airing wine are discussed in *Serving wine*.) Give a fine wine's bouquet plenty of attention – it deserves it!

FLAVOUR

Swallow a wine straight away and you miss out on a multitude of flavours, undertones and textures. The alcohol will take effect, but that is about it. Instead, take a healthy slurp and swill the wine around in your mouth. Breathing in some air through your mouth while tasting can heighten the flavour of wine, but take care as it is easy to choke. Try to consider the flavours you are aware of – the level of acidity, the sweetness/dryness, any specific characteristics such as butter, fruit or toast. After you swallow or spit out the wine, assess the finish: how long the flavour stays in your mouth and whether it is, say, tannic, acidic or viscous.

The four main elements that affect the flavour of a wine are: which grape varieties were used, where and how they were grown, and how the wine was made – in short, variety, *terroir*, viticulture and vinification. (See below for a further explanation of *terroir*.) A fifth element is age. In mature wines, structural components – fruit, tannin, acidity, alcohol and oak – meld together and produce a range of different secondary characteristics. The wine is said to gain in complexity, losing its primary grape characteristics and taking on a whole load more.

Acidity

Acidity makes wine taste crisper and more refreshing; it also acts as a preservative. The great sweet Rieslings and Chenin Blancs rely on the high acidity levels of these grape varieties for their longevity, and to balance their sweetness. Contrary to popular belief, acidity does not necessarily soften with age. Taste certain red wines which are past their peak and one of the first things you will notice is the acidity.

Four factors are important in this respect: the grape variety itself; the time the grape is picked; its degree of shade or exposure to the sun; and the temperature of the region. Winemakers in warm areas where the grapes suffer from a lack of acidity have two options: to pick earlier, which could mean that the grape flavours are not fully developed – or to add acid (either tartaric or ascorbic), a procedure which is illegal in many European countries but is permitted in the New World. Winemakers in cool areas, on the other hand, have the opposite problem, and sometimes need to de-acidify by the addition of calcium carbonate. A further means of adjusting acidity is the use of malolactic fermentation (see *Glossary*), a bacterial conversion of malic acid – think of Granny Smith apples – to the softer lactic acid. Nearly all red wines go through the malolactic process, and its popularity for whites, particularly Chardonnay, is increasing. The skill is to add complexity without turning the wine into buttermilk.

Acidity in a wine also helps it partner food. Think of Italian red wines, they almost all have it in good quantity, and it makes them tangy and mouthwatering. The crispness lifts the wine flavours and helps distinguish them from those in the dish. In contrast, a plump, fat Chilean Merlot sits happily next to a meal but doesn't have quite the same tangy contrast.

Sugar/alcohol

Sweet wines are made in a number of ways. The yeasts that convert sugar to alcohol will only ferment up to a certain alcohol percentage, so if a wine reaches this level and still has some unconverted sugar, it will be sweet. Another method is to stop the fermentation process before all the sugar has been converted, either through the addition of spirit (as in port) or by chilling the must (see *Glossary*) and precipitating the yeasts out, a practice used in Germany. Method three is to concentrate the sugar in the grapes either by drying them in the sun (leaving them longer on the vine in the autumn for example), or through attack by a benevolent mould, *Botrytis cinerea*, which has the same dehydrating effect – especially on thin-skinned Sémillon and Riesling.

In winemaking sugar covers a multitude of sins. Liebfraumilch and Lambrusco are classic examples of wines whose blandness is often disguised behind a veil of sweetness, and numerous wines, especially those from hotter countries, are labelled 'dry' but still have residual sugar, making them seem rounder and fuller in flavour. Alcohol, deriving from the fermentation of sugar, also makes for weightier wines. The hotter the region, the riper and sweeter the grapes, the more alcoholic will be the wine: Zinfandel in California can reach as high as 16 or 17 per cent quite naturally, but in cooler Germany, wines achieve perfect balance at alcohol levels which can be as low as 7 per cent – although they usually have some unfermented sugar to balance the firm acidity. (Without the acidity to balance the sugar, as in Liebfraumilch and Lambrusco, they are flabby.)

493

Methods to increase sugar levels include: training the vine canopy so that the grapes are exposed to the sun; allowing the grapes to ripen longer; must concentration; and – the easy option – tipping sugar into the fermenter, a process called chaptalisation (see *Glossary*). This latter process is permitted in cool wine-growing regions, such as Germany, parts of France and other northern and eastern European wine regions, where there's sometimes not enough sun for the grapes to reach full ripeness, but not in most parts of the New World.

Yeasts

The job of converting sugar to alcohol is done by yeast. In traditional winemaking, wild yeasts native to the vineyard and winery are used to start the fermentation. Nowadays, the use of cultivated yeasts is widespread, since they are more reliable and efficient at fermentation and reduce the risk of spoilage. However, critics say that they introduce a uniformity of flavour and point the finger at 'flying' winemakers who use the same yeast strains the world over. Many of the most progressive wineries of the New World are switching back to wild yeasts, and there's no doubt, they do add interest to a wine, a kind of 'Burgundian' complexity. However, the funky, spicy, wild flavours they bring are not appropriate for every style.

After fermentation has finished, the wine may be left on the yeast lees – the words *sur lie* on a French wine label indicate a lengthier-than-usual period of lees ageing – in order to pick up something of their flavour. There is also a process called *bâtonnage* whereby the lees are stirred in order to impart more of their biscuity flavour.

Tannin

Tannin is the mouth-puckering quality found in some young wine, a bit like the taste of sucking on a wooden pencil. Sounds nasty? It can be if it is over-done or green and unripe, but tannins are essential to the structure of certain wines, and they diminish and soften with bottle age. Tannins are a group of complex organic chemicals found in the bark of some trees, and in some fruits. In wine, tannins derive from grape seeds, stems and skins, and also leach out of new barrels in which the wine is stored. Those from the seeds are not desirable, so care must be taken when pressing the grapes to avoid breaking the seeds and releasing their bitter character. Stems are more controversial; some winemakers ban them totally from the fermentation vats, some allow a few, while others positively encourage their addition.

Grape skins are the source of the majority of benevolent tannins. Extraction of these goes hand-in-hand with the extraction of colour, since that, too, is concentrated in the skins. The smaller the berries and the harder they are pressed, the greater the tannins will be. If a pressing is too aggressive, tannins will also be aggressive and bitter. If the grapes have been exposed to plenty of sun, the tannins will be riper and not as harsh as those in wines from cooler climates, which is why many New World wines often seem less tannic than their Old World counterparts. Ripeness is important, but get the fruit too ripe (we're talking California and Australia again) and winemakers often find they have to add powdered or liquid tannin to redress the balance. (See 'Other ingredients' below.)

Oak

Oak is the most apparent of the winemaker's additions to a wine. Just like salt in cooking, if the amount is right it will enhance the wine, but if it is overdone the wine will be spoilt. Wines can be fermented and aged in oak barrels, or simply aged after fermenting in stainless steel or concrete vats. The smaller the barrel, the greater the ratio of surface area to volume, and so the greater the oak influence. The fashionable format is the 225-litre *barrique*, but barrels can vary in size from less than 100 litres to tens of thousands of litres. One factor which is seldom considered is that winemakers who use a 10,000-litre tank make just one wine, while those who use several 225-litre *barriques* can make several wines, all of them different, which can then be blended in any number of ways for extra complexity.

The character that oak lends to a wine depends on where the wood came from, where and how the wood was dried, and who the cooper was. The char in the inside of the barrel is also significant, with heavily toasted barrels giving a much greater vanilla and spice character to the finished wine than lightly toasted ones. American oak, widely used in California, Australia and Rioja, has a warmer, fuller and stronger vanillin flavour than French oak. French oak tends to impart more subtle flavours – especially from the Allier, Vosges, Tronçais and Limousin forests.

There are cheaper methods to give wood influence to a wine. Barrel staves are sometimes suspended in fermentation or storage tanks to add an oaky character, while oak chips, which are cheaper still, are also used. Staves and chips can be made from French and American oak, with different levels of toasting, and cost far less than proper barrels. Chips, in particular, used to give a crude, sawdust flavour to many wines, but as the winemakers have become more skilful in using the chips or staves and the quality of the chips has improved, so the quality of the resulting wines has increased remarkably. However, neither chips nor staves can duplicate the process by which a wine in cask 'breathes' through the sides of the barrel, acquiring extra complexity as it does so.

Water

It is shocking but true that water is the major component in every bottle of wine – even one priced at £1,000. And the more water a vineyard receives, the more water, and therefore less flavour, there will be in the finished wine. Even the classic areas suffer from wet vintages when grapes suck in too much water and become relatively dilute. (The Bordelais have got clever these days and found themselves a 'reverse osmosis' machine that sucks the water back out again so their harvest isn't ruined. This might lead to a rather thick-textured wine but it certainly won't be watery.) At the opposite extreme, and despite the cliché that vines should struggle to produce fine wine, a badly drought-ridden vineyard has an adverse effect on the finished product, inhibiting ripeness and reducing the yield heavily. Some drought is acceptable, but in this case, a judicious amount of irrigation is a good thing.

Other 'ingredients'

Matter other than grapes (MOG), to use Australian parlance, normally refers to leaves, stems and the odd lizard (quickly fished out) finding their way into the winery receival hoppers. In fact, there's more than this. Matter other than grapes also includes such outsiders as acid, tannin, bentonite and sulphur, added to refresh flavours perceived missing from freshly picked fruit.

Acidity is usually added in tartaric, citric or ascorbic powder form to re-balance warm climate wines in which fruit often ripens to the point of over-fruity flabbiness (flabby as in vanilla or raspberry milkshake). Each of these acids is naturally present in the grape anyway, and, when added carefully, readily melds with the juice. Similarly, added **tannin** (used in a great many New World reds) is often extracted from pressed-out grape skins. **Bentonite** has a more medicinal function, and, thankfully, you won't necessarily taste it, you'll just miss what it removes. It's a clay which expands in water and has special absorptive powers; it takes out unwanted matter such as clumps of mould or rotten grape skins, which might come in with rained-on fruit. Purists (well, non-purists) argue that the bits and pieces of grape skin give fuller flavours and that bentonite strips out texture and makes a wine taste neutral. But the good thing about it is, once it's fallen out of suspension and taken all the gunk with it, it's gone: there's no trace left.

Sulphur is the MOG factor that makes us sneeze, wheeze or whatever – particularly if there's too much of it. Added at the crushing stage as metabisulphate, it acts as a cleansing agent, killing off bacteria and unwanted wild yeasts. It also prevents oxidation, and thus is an all-round assistant to a rapid, clean fermentation, letting the yeasts and grape juices do their job undisturbed. You might say it is the winemaker's ultimate control tool – but there are control-freak winemakers out there who use too much. Small amounts of sulphur are fine, as again, this is a natural by-product of winemaking. But adding sulphur right through fermentation leads not only to neutral ('reductive') flavours – too clean, too simple, and boring – but also to the occasional unpleasant whiff.

Next come the **fining agents**. All wines should be clear, and everyday wines will be filtered or centrifuged to clean them up: these are aggressive processes that strip out flavour, but at least the wine will be clean and stable. For very fine wines, winemakers just wait. Any bits of grape skin, dead yeasts, protein particles, etc., eventually fall out of vinous suspension in the vat or barrel. But not all of them have time. To hurry things along, fining agents such as isinglass, gelatin, casein (from milk) and egg white can be used to absorb and precipitate any unwanted oddments in suspension. None of these are substances we want to be tasting in our glass – wittingly or not. But a delicate egg-white addition – at as little as two parts per million – will have a far less flavour-stripping effect than pushing a fine wine through a centrifuge or narrow gauge filter, so this is an 'ingredient' we don't object to.

Terroir vs variety

Terroir and grape variety represent two different sides in a well-worn argument about the origin of a wine's character. *Terroir* is an ancient, quasi-mystical concept that defines wine as an expression of the soil, climate and cultural environment where it was grown. 'I do not make Pinot Noir, I make Volnay,' would be a typical remark from a Burgundian grower who is referring to the *terroir* of his vines. Until recently the attitude of a variety-driven New World winemaker would be that soil is just dirt. He or she would suggest that a competent winemaker should be able to produce decent wine no matter what grapes are brought to the winery, and where they are from. The two sides are coming closer together, however, with New World wineries increasingly bottling regional and single-vineyard wines. You'll even see Australians and Californians squabbling over specific vine plots, just as if they were *grands crus* in Burgundy. The Old World, on the other hand, is putting the accent on grape varieties as never before – witness the increasing number of single-varietal wines coming from the South of France.

THE LABEL

Information on all of the above is increasingly available on the wine label – especially (it's a New World trend) the one on the back of the bottle. Whether the wine contains four per cent Cabernet Sauvignon (usually detectable through its distinctive blackcurrant whiff, even in quantities this small); if the wine was barrel-aged; how much alcohol it contains; and what the winemaker was wearing when he made it (well, not quite). This isn't there merely to titillate the wine buffs (though it does that too), but to provide a useful clue as to how the wine will smell and taste. So now, more than ever before, you can gauge what you're getting before you open the bottle. We suggest you use this information wisely. Take the vintage date: even New World wines can fall victim to vintage variation – 1998's El Niño phenomenon, for example, had a beneficial effect in New Zealand but a disastrous, rainy one in California and Argentina. Taking a note of alcohol levels can make the difference between a sober supper and a sore head the next morning. More to the point, all this detail is a great help in matching a wine to an occasion – and making sure the lemon chicken isn't obliterated by a chunky Australian Shiraz.

STORING WINE

Setting up your own wine cellar at home can be straightforward. The basement of a house is ideal, provided it is not centrally heated or prone to flooding. The natural conditions of your average basement – a steady, fairly cool temperature (7–10°C/45–50°F), dampish environment, reasonable circulation of air and darkness – should keep your wine in pristine condition. Otherwise, look for a place where those conditions can be simulated: an old wardrobe, a disused fireplace, a cupboard under the stairs. Remember to store the bottles away from a radiator or boiler, which will heat up one corner of a room, and away from anything with a strong odour, such as paint or paraffin. And at all costs, avoid the attic – or cupboards under the eaves if you have a loft conversion. These heat up like nobody's business in the summer and are generally the wrong side of roof insulation to avoid cold in the winter. If you're really stuck for a cool space, a wine fridge is a good idea. Though not cheap, they maintain the ideal constant temperature, and store anything from 50 to 200 bottles.

Wine racks are useful but not essential. The boxes in which the wine was packed will do almost as well. The important thing is to store the bottles on their sides, so that the cork stays moist and makes an effective seal. If you are interested in keeping and collecting the labels on your bottles, spraying them with odourless hair spray should help preserve them. Be careful not to tear them when pulling bottles from metal wine racks.

Contrary to popular belief, age in wine is not necessarily a good thing, even in reds. One of our more depressing duties is to inform well-meaning readers that their treasured bottles of, say, 1977 Beaujolais Nouveau are not only worthless, but also cadaverously dreadful. The good thing about the wines made today is that many are deliciously fruity right from the word 'go', and that includes those from Bordeaux as much as those from Chile.

Even so, a constant diet of in-your-face fruit eventually palls, and having a small store of older wine offers more variety. With bottle age, a wine loses what is called its 'primary flavours' and develops 'secondary characteristics'. Translated into plain English, this means that the fresh fruit flavours give way to notes of dried fruit, with additional nuances which might be gamey, earthy, leathery, spicy or honeyed. The oak influence also becomes less pronounced, while tannins (in red wine) will bond together to form longer and heavier molecular chains which eventually precipitate out as sediment, leaving a softer, more mellow wine.

Tasting the difference between a young, mouth-puckering Bordeaux or burgundy, and a fascinatingly complex one 20 years older, proves it's worth the wait. Alternatively, here are a few suggestions for affordable candidates that'll benefit from ageing:

- Riesling from anywhere
- Australian Semillon and Shiraz
- southern French reds such as Coteaux de Languedoc and Costières de Nîmes
- Côtes du Rhône-Villages
- Douro reds
- Spanish Rioja
- sweet Loire Chenin Blanc.

Don't forget that vintage champagne has the quality to improve deliciously over 10 to 15 years, and the same applies to white Bordeaux from the top châteaux, which is horrendously unfashionable and relatively cheap. This is not an exhaustive list, nor is every example of the wines listed built for the long haul. However, a year or two extra in bottle should let you see what age can do to them, and then it is up to you to decide at what age you prefer each.

Good wine merchants are always willing to give advice on which wines will benefit from further ageing – the best offer storage space in which they'll keep them in perfect condition for you. If you take up any of the tempting *en primeur* offers, by which young wine is sold while still in barrel at the château or estate, then it's definitely best to leave cellaring to the merchants. Any appreciation in price will quickly be lost if your treasures have been poorly stored (they check up these days!), so if you're unsure about your cupboard under the stairs and might want to re-sell your wine, leave it to the professionals.

Once your wine's ready to drink, don't guzzle it all at once. Try one bottle out of the case every year so you can gauge exactly how you like your tannins – soft or al dente!

Learn from every mistake and don't get too precious about your wine. It is there to be drunk, not worshipped.

SERVING WINE

To decant or not to decant?

There are two reasons for decanting red wines, one of which – believe it or not – applies to white wines too. There's no need for alarm here. If your decanter (assuming you have one) is a forgotten relic lurking unused at the back of a cupboard, serving more as a nostalgic reminder of wedding days than as a useful tool for entertaining, then that's fine. If you don't have one, that's fine too. Most red wines are now soft and fruity enough to be drunk straight from the bottle, and even Bordeaux isn't quite as crusty as it once was. It is a good idea to decant mature red wine or port, however, if it has a notable sediment. As well as making a thoroughly unpleasant, woody mouthful, this can be tannic and often bitter-tasting and is better removed. The best way is to stand the bottle of wine you wish to drink upright for at least a couple of days before decanting in order that the deposit settles to the bottom of the bottle. Then uncork the wine, ensuring that the rim is clean, by wiping with a damp cloth, and pour slowly and steadily into the decanter. If you wish to emulate a seasoned sommelier, then hold the bottle close to a source of light or to a candle and watch for the sediment as you pour. When the first signs of it appear, stop decanting and throw away the dregs. *Voilà*! Remember though, that wine will not keep indefinitely in a decanter; most open bottles will become undrinkable within a day or so.

The second reason for decanting is to aerate the wine and release the aromas and flavours that have been locked into the bottle. As airy-fairy as this might sound, for young, tight French reds, Bordeaux and young burgundies, and tightly knit California Cabernets, it really does work. For whites, too, where there's a lot of packed-in complexity (as with those oak-aged or concentrated by *botrytis*), decanting allows the wine to breathe and its full characteristics to develop.

Remember four things. One: if you don't have a decanter, pour the wine into a jug and then back into the same bottle – that way you can still show the label off too. Two: allow the wine to recover; pouring can give it a shock, so let it settle for an hour or two after decanting. Three: this trick can also work for wines opened before they're quite ready to drink, by allowing the fruit to open out and cover tannins which are still young and bony. Four: for the vast majority of everyday-drinking wines, none of this is relevant.

Does wine need to breathe?

The more austere, top-quality reds and whites do need to breathe, and decanting (see above) is a good idea. As a beneficial half-measure (for wines just a little bit closed) just opening a bottle a couple of hours before serving can help. Despite the fact so little of its surface is in contact with the air, this does give a definite reaction. Swirling the wine in an appropriate glass once it is poured will also have the same positive effect. Don't forget, if the wine is too cold or too warm all this effort will be wasted – chilling will close up the aromas, and heating makes wines soupy and over-blown. Fortunately there's a wide temperature range in the middle that works just fine; no precision is necessary.

The glasses

Especially when a lot of thought (and budget) has gone into the choice of wine, it is a shame to skimp on the glassware, knowingly or not. This does not mean that glasses have to be expensive – although they certainly can be – but rather that you stick to the best shapes for drinking certain types of wine.

The most appropriate wine glasses are always made of clear glass (avoid the recycled green or blue ones) and should have a long stem and a large bowl which tapers towards the rim rather like a tulip head. In fact, the larger the better, as swirling the wine in the glass is part of the pleasure of discovering a wine's merits. Contrary to classic British traditions, flutes are really the only style of glass for champagne or sparkling wines, as the lack of surface area for the wine allows the bubbles to last longer. Traditional 'copita' shapes are best for sherry. Paris goblets are robust enough for your wilder parties – or outdoor use – but their thick glass does good wine no favours.

If you are a total wine fanatic, then you probably have already heard of Riedel glasses, the *sine qua non* of drinking vessels. At the top of the range, the fabulously expensive, hand-blown examples are the ultimate in sophistication. Happily for most of us, a more reasonably priced machine-made range, called Vinum, is also available. In both, the glasses have been developed in many sizes and shapes to suit particular types of wine and to direct the wine to exactly the right place on your palate (for example, the flared rim of a Riesling glass directs the wine to the sides of your tongue, where your tastebuds will best appreciate this grape's greatest asset – racy acidity). Mature clarets, delicate Loire Sauvignons, esoteric Tuscans and others, are all represented. There's even a new range (Vinum Extreme) for New World wines, developed with a kink round the middle for extra swirling capacity, so that every dense-packed layer is unpacked and released.

Remember, always clean your glasses properly. This is vital. Vigilance pays. If they won't go in the dishwasher, glasses should always be washed separately in piping hot water with a tiny drop of detergent, rinsed in cold water and cleaned with a linen tea towel or glass cloth specifically reserved for the purpose. Dirty glasses are a cardinal sin in wine terms and can ruin the aromas of a wine and therefore the pleasures of enjoying it.

Gizmos and gadgets

Much like any hobby, wine has its essential accoutrements for those in the know. There are avid collectors of corkscrews and wine paraphernalia the world over; the thousands of pages on the Internet devoted to this subject, let alone wine itself, must have opened up whole new avenues for enthusiasts.

The unbeatable must-haves for wine are a foil cutter and a reliable 'waiter's friend' lever corkscrew. Stoppers are fun to look at, but work best in a purely utilitarian role with sparkling wine; otherwise just replace the original cork. Anti-drip stoppers and collars are probably best left alone – better to perfect the natty little quarter twist of the bottle after pouring, which wine waiters do so well.

For picnics and alfresco summer dining, it is also a good idea to have a couple of padded cooling sleeves in the freezer. These are much quicker and less messy than an ice bucket and useful for all types of wines, including light reds.

If you want to drink only one glass of wine and save the rest of the bottle, the simplest way is to reinsert the cork and put the bottle in the fridge. This works for reds as well as whites, although you need to remember to take the reds out early enough so they can warm up ready for you to drink them. The wines may not be as fresh the day after, but they should still be drinkable (indeed, some young reds may even be better the next day). An alternative is the Vacuvin system, which pumps air out of the bottle through a special rubber stopper, creating a vacuum to preserve freshness. Critics feel it can also pump out flavour. A more reliable method is Wine Saver, a canister containing nitrogen which is squirted into a bottle, displacing the air.

FOOD AND WINE MATCHING

Most wines are reasonably satisfying with most food. But there are superlatives too, and so much decent wine is available nowadays that it is a crime not to experiment to your palate's content – either when entertaining at home or in a restaurant. One thing is certain though, decisions need to be made with confidence, and information about a wine is vital if you are not familiar with it. Good wine merchants and restaurant lists should provide details of the basic structure and taste you can expect and, increasingly, so should the labels themselves.

Broadly speaking – with simply too much vinous and culinary diversity in the world today to allow any – there are no rules. However, you do need to pay attention to the depth of flavours of a dish when considering a wine to go with it. This is the basic origin of the red wine with meat and white wine with fish and poultry routine, but such simplicity goes out of the window when you analyse cooking methods and sauces. Cooking? Think how different pork tastes, for example, when roast as Sunday lunch, when barbecued as chops, in a casserole, or served cold. Each version needs a totally different approach. Add sauces and the palette is broader still.

Acidity, tannin and sweetness are the three main areas to keep in mind – the rest will inevitably be a journey of discovery. Consider matching the acidity of a dish with a complementary wine (for example, citrus or fruit flavours with crisp white wines or light reds). Or ensure that tannin, that mouth-furring component of robust and full-flavoured red wines, is paired off only with rich and robust foods, usually red meats. Remember that sweet wines are for sweet food in the main – could it be easier? (Actually just to ruin the plot, sweet wines are also renowned partners for salty flavours, Sauternes and Roquefort cheese or ripe Alsace Gewurztraminer with smoked salmon, for example.)

Another good rule of thumb is to choose a wine with a cultural link with the dish you are preparing or choosing. Mediterranean cooking goes well with southern French, Italian and Spanish reds, for pasta and pizza stay in Italy, French regional food has traditional links with many wines, manzanilla sherry and tapas suit each other, and so on. Modern fusion or spicy food are somewhat tricksier, but often this is where you can safely start with New World wines.

There are food and wine matching bugbears, however, and here are some of them to watch out for:

Eggs A not too oaky Chardonnay is your best bet here, as eggs are mouth-coating and need something to cut through them without clashing. Reds are definitely out unless the dish itself involves red wine or a particularly strong cheese element.

Chocolate Again, because of its mouth-coating qualities, generally never to be mixed with light wine. Dessert Muscat wines, in all their guises, can accompany sweet chocolate dishes perfectly though, and with dark chocolate, so can some Cabernets (New World ripe, sweet ones and Malbecs).

Tomatoes Try matching the acidity of the tomato with Sauvignon Blanc or, if you must have a red, then try a crisp, young north-east Italian one, such as Valpolicella or a tomatoey red Xinomavro from northern Greece.

Fish Smoked salmon isn't difficult if you stick to a classic aperitif such as Chablis, other Chardonnays or champagne, but with oilier versions (mackerel, kippers) go for something lighter still, and more acidic, such as Sauvignon or Muscadet – at all costs, avoid reds.

Spinach and artichokes These make wine taste metallic (in a similar way to red wine and fish). See 'Tricks of the trade' below, for how to avoid this.

Chinese and Thai food Match the delicacy and vibrancy in the dish with the same in the wine. Crisp, aromatic whites are the best accompaniment – Riesling, Alsace Gewurztraminer or (especially when there's lemon grass in the dish) New Zealand Sauvignon Blanc. Light reds such as Pinot Noir are also a possibility.

Indian food Richly flavoured New World whites, such as Chardonnay, Semillon or Verdelho, are excellent, or mellow reds which have plenty of fruit and not overpowering tannins, such as Zinfandel, Shiraz or Merlot – again from the New World.

Puddings and cakes Match the weight of sweetness in the wine to that in the food, and use the acidity of a sweet Riesling or the tang of a *botrytis* wine to match a dessert (for example, a lemony one) with equal bite. Strawberries go with red wine, but little else does (though sweet, frothy Asti is a good partner too).

Tricks of the trade

Professional tactics used to combat clashes include adding a condiment of some kind – by doing this, you expand your wine choices. Salt makes tannic wines seem even more so, but grind or shake some black pepper on to your steak, for example, and the wine will seem smoother and fruitier right away. Add salt to a dish (instead) to balance a particularly crisp wine – such as a young Sauvignon. And add lemon juice to temper the metallic-ness of spinach (that, or soften it by stirring in cream). Coriander in a dish can lift the fruitiness of many a dull Soave, and rosemary or mint can ease the relationships between many a Cabernet and its platter (Pinot Noir too, for that matter).

To see things as good as they get, we suggest trying fresh-cooked prawns or langoustine with a buttery Chardonnay; goat's cheese with Sancerre; lamb and rosemary with top Bordeaux; Sauternes and Rocquefort cheese; fino sherry and sushi; port with Stilton. Plus, if ever you get the chance, champagne and oysters. But remember, if a different combination works for you, it works. Our palates are highly individual, and work in mysterious ways.

MAGAZINES AND BOOKS

If you fancy delving a little further into any of the subjects broached in *The Which? Wine Guide*, or if you'd like to keep up to date, over the year, with some of the more on-going issues we've mentioned, the following are magazines and books that might help.

MAGAZINES
Decanter

A monthly magazine; calls itself 'the world's best wine magazine' and isn't far off it. Monthly tasting panels review two major wine styles, and there are in-depth features covering news and views from the wine regions, plus winemaker interviews and wine recommendations. (To subscribe, call (01444) 475675)

Harpers

For those who are serious about wine (and know the basics already) *Harpers, The Wine and Spirit Weekly* is about the best read available at the moment. This weekly is first and foremost a trade publication, but for real 'news from the coalface' (i.e. straight from the vineyards), you won't do better. We particularly enjoy the occasional country supplements. (To subscribe, call 020–7575 5600)

The Wine Magazine

This stylishly presented Australian magazine is full of tempting photography (particularly good in the food section), with plenty of wine recommendations and reviews. Australia and New Zealand feature strongly (obviously), but the global outlook is good too. (To subscribe, email subsquery@acp.com.au)

Wine Magazine

A touch livelier than *Decanter*, with more of an introductory feel – a better read for the wine beginner. Covers similar ground: major wine reviews each month, interviews, get-to-know-the-region features, wine news and gossip in a chatty style. (To subscribe, call (01795) 414879)

Wine Spectator

For an all-American perspective this bi-monthly is about as glossy as they get. As well as wine reviews (complete with marks out of 100, if that's your thing) there's plenty on restaurants and food. Don't expect to learn about unusual bargain wines, this is all about the big money-spinning blue-chip boys. (To subscribe, call 001 212 684 4224)

BOOKS

The World Atlas of Wine by Hugh Johnson

Not only will the words help you work out a global wine perspective, the maps will help you visualise it all too.
(New edition, updated by Jancis Robinson, Mitchell Beazley, 2001)

The Oxford Companion to Wine by Jancis Robinson

For every wine term and wine region you've never understood, here is the book that explains it all fully. Alphabetically presented and meticulously detailed, once in your possession this is a reference source you'll never want to be without.
(2nd edition, Oxford University Press, 1999)

Hachette Wine Guide

Subtitled 'The French Wine Bible', this is an exhaustive volume detailing the best of France's producers: their wines, tasting notes, where to find them and how to contact them. Essential reference for anyone travelling the wine regions.
(English edition, Hachette UK, 2002)

Faber Books on Wine series

Covering every major wine region, each in a separate volume, written by acknowledged and esteemed experts. Some of these can be heavy going but they're well written and thoroughly researched, and if it's detail you're after you can't go wrong. We particularly recommend the following recent publications:

- *Barolo to Valpolicella* and *Brunello to Zibibbo* by Nicolas Belfrage MW If you want to make head or tail of the rat's nest that is Italy, these two volumes will do the trick (1999 and 2001).
- *The Wines of Britain and Ireland* by Stephen Skelton Award-winning and revelatory: more on English sparkling than you would ever have thought possible (2001).
- *The Wines of the South of France* by Rosemary George MW A breakdown of what's happening in France's most fashionable wine region (2001)
- *The Wines of California* by Stephen Brook We don't know of any better guide to the Golden State! (1999).

Languedoc-Roussillon by Paul Strang

Lovingly written and researched, this is a beautiful and unputdownable who's who (and why) of this up-and-coming region. (Mitchell Beazley, 2002)

The World Encyclopedia of Champagne & Sparkling Wine by Tom Stevenson

Nobody knows more about sparkling wine than Tom Stevenson and we highly recommend picking his brains. (Christie's, 1998)

Bordeaux, People, Power and Politics by Stephen Brook

A full explanation of the intrigues behind this pivotal wine region and why it wields the power it does – compelling reading. (Mitchell Beazley, 2001)

Crush by Max Allen

The best way to find out about Australia – its regions, its people and its wines. Max Allen is an effortless read! (Mitchell Beazley, 2000)

Vintage Wine by Michael Broadbent

If you're into your classics, here you can explore Bordeaux vintages (and others) from 1771 to the present day via Michael Broadbent's impeccable (and entertaining) tasting notes. Satisfying bedtime reading.
(Websters, 2002)

Real Wine by Patrick Matthews

The whys and wherefores of organic and biodynamic winemaking all explained – entertainingly, fascinatingly. (Mitchell Beazley, 2000)

Drink! – Never Mind the Peanuts
by Susy Atkins & Dave Broom

As amusing a beginner's guide as you could wish for!
(Mitchell Beazley, 2001)

WEB SITES

Compiled and reviewed by Tom Cannavan

A lot has changed in the web world of wine since I wrote the Websites section for the last edition of *The Which? Wine Guide*. Thankfully, most of the favourites I mentioned then are still around now, and many are bigger and better than ever. Some notable newcomers too have made an appearance, most newsworthy perhaps being the American wine guru Robert Parker, who has at long last established a web-based version of his influential newsletter *The Wine Advocate*.

Though a few of the more general areas of Parker's site are available free of charge, a subscription is required to access the juiciest content. This is a model that we will see more and more of, as professional-quality web publications look for an income other than advertising revenue. For some, like Parker, this is because they will not accept advertising, but others have been affected by a distinct downturn in advertising budgets globally, that has been keenly felt on the Internet. Favourite free sites from last year, such as *jancisrobinson.com* and *wine-searcher.com*, have switched to a subscription-basis in the last 12 months.

Another emerging trend has been for online retailers to pull back from investment in original editorial content. Sites such as *virginwines.com* once ploughed huge sums into creating their 'wine zone' magazine section, hoping they would become a 'destination site' for wine-savvy surfers, who might then go on to purchase wines from the Virgin site. This model has proved too expensive and ineffective however, and Virgin has all but abandoned new editorial. Other e-tailers that offered significant quality editorial content, such as *madaboutwine.com*, have similarly downgraded, or like *bringmywine.com* disappeared from view.

The story is far from being entirely doom and gloom. New, good-quality wine sites continue to emerge, and many of the old favourites are powering ahead with expanded features, re-designs and ever-deepening content. There is still a rich stream of wine entertainment, discussion, education and information to mine, and the vast bulk of it still offered free of charge. Our suggestion? Grab a glass and get surfing!

General information/online magazines

There are tasty pickings online for wine information and advice, from very specific sites celebrating a particular grape or region, to much more broadly based e-zines.

www.bath.ac.uk/~su3ws/wine-faq/

The design may be showing its age, and typing the address is a bit of a trial, but this simple, text-based resource of Frequently Asked Questions (and answers) is one of the oldest and most thorough wine resources on the web (note: the little '~' symbol can be found on the same key as '#').

www.champagnemagic.com

Single-minded site from enthusiast John Holland, with hundreds of links to champagne houses, feature articles, competitions and more – all centred on wine with holes in.

www.decanter.com

There have been many changes to this site and to its long-established print version, *Decanter* magazine, over the past year. *Decanter*'s publisher IPC was bought by the American giant Time Warner in 2001, and the web versions of several titles were immediately abandoned. Though decanter.com survived, its staffing was halved. The site still offers news and features including tasting notes, live 'chat' sessions with wine personalities and an archive of magazine articles. The good news is that the subscription Fine Wine Tracker service, which looked very over-priced last year at £160 per annum, is now offered free of charge. Use it to track auction prices on a portfolio of wines of your selection.

www.englishwine.com

There's not really a lot to this site, set up by Stephen Skelton, but it does have a very useful list of links to English wine producers and

other English wine sites, including the excellent hobby site of
academic, Oliver Richardson.

www.jancisrobinson.com

The doyenne of British wine writing puts a surprising amount of
personal time and effort into her site, something of a passion as
well as a creative outlet for her prodigious wine knowledge and
experience. Though a lot of content is available free, a subscription
area branded as Purple Pages has now been introduced, costing £39
per annum. For that you get exclusive, detailed tasting notes
unavailable on the main site, a first look at tips and observations
two weeks before they appear on the main site, and the chance to
put your questions directly to Jancis. In her introduction she even
promises 'scurrilous stuff I might not dare put on the open-access
section'.

www.harpers-wine.com

Harpers Wine & Spirits Weekly is the subscription-only journal of the
UK wine trade, and it has been pumping some effort into its online
version over the past year. An archive of news and feature articles is
available free of charge, as is a very useful and comprehensive set of
'wine reports' giving all sorts of useful statistics, information and
maps for every major wine-producing country. Subscription to the
weekly print magazine (£115 per annum) buys access to extended
features including directories of wine businesses in the UK and
abroad. You can have web-only access to this area too, but the fee
is £100.

www.investdrinks.org

This is the wine writer Jim Budd's crusade against wine-related
investment scams and rip-offs. It names names and issues sound
advice for those thinking of putting cash into fine wine.

www.thewinedoctor.com

Wine-loving medic Chris Kissack started his site as a low-key
hobby, but this has been continually updated and expanded with
feature articles, wine tips, educational material and restaurant
reviews. The most original feature is the 'wine saga', a series of
investigations into the wines of a particular region, or a single
grape variety.

www.vine2wine.com

A huge resource with hundreds of reviews for wine-related sites.
Sites are categorised and rated from one to three stars, and the
directory is updated regularly.

www.wineanorak.com

Jamie Goode moonlights in wine writing with his well-established, British-based e-zine. The "blog" - a sort of online diary of random wine thoughts, musings and experiences – is diverting enough, but there are plenty of more profound features, wine tips and editorial pertinent to the UK consumer. It can be a touch long-winded, with some of the content living up to the anorak billing.

www.winedine.co.uk

A 2001 makeover for this long-established site has dramatically improved its browser appeal and functionality. Author, Tony le Ray Cook, offers a hedonist's diary of fine food, wine and 'lifestyle' features that is a bit of a mish-mash, but worth checking out.

www.winelabels.org

Peter May once appeared on *BBC Food & Drink* chastising restaurants for bottled water rip-offs. A man of strong passions, he indulges himself here in a quirky and fun site that celebrates the odd, unusual and downright weird in wines and wine labelling. From Cat's Pee on a Gooseberry Bush, to Santa's Reserve, marvel at the tackier side of wine marketing.

www.wineontheweb.co.uk

The main thing going for this rather patchy site is a series of Radio Postcard audio reports on wine-related topics; ideal for visually impaired surfers.

www.winespectator.com

This is the sprawling online edition of the top US wine magazine, that some will find too US-centred (for example, 'Federal Judge Overturns Texas' Wine-Shipping Laws'). Once past its slightly bloated front screen there's a wealth of information on wine and 'gracious living' here, including travelogues, tasting reports and online discussion. Extended features, such as accessing all 100,000 wine reviews instead of a small sample, requires a paid subscription ($49.95 per annum).

www.wrathofgrapes.com

The site of a bunch of Dublin-based enthusiasts, with lots of tasting notes but also good information on wine-tasting techniques, feature articles and a huge collection of humorous and thought-provoking wine-related quotations.

Tasting notes/wine recommendations

Most of the sites listed above feature tasting notes and recommendations, but some sites are dedicated to the task of tasting, grading and cataloguing wines. We list these below.

www.andys-scribblings.co.uk

The eponymous Andy Barrow is an ex-manager of an Unwins shop, who began his weekly email newsletter in 2000 'to put my wine knowledge to some proper use'. It features a wide selection of tasting notes and suggestions for wines, beers and other drinks to be found on the UK high street. Subscribe to get the latest edition in your mailbox, or read the online archives.

www.erobertparker.com

Robert Parker is the world's most prominent wine critic, and his bi-monthly newsletter, *The Wine Advocate*, is hugely influential. Erobertparker presents a database of 50,000 of the great man's tasting notes, with powerful and efficient search facilities and new notes being added continually. The print edition requires a separate subscription, but retains the crucial advantage of notes appearing two months before making it on to the web. A free trial subscription is available.

www.finewinediary.com

The Edinburgh- and Oxford-based Bailey brothers have amassed a formidable collection of tasting notes, almost exclusively on fine wines. Scores are awarded for current drinking quality and development potential in this huge, searchable archive. A re-design during 2002 has added to the site's usability.

www.superplonk.com

Malcolm Gluck's site is a fund of snappy (some would say too snappy) assessments of low- and medium-priced wines available on the high street and in cyberspace. It boasts of being the largest collection of 'everyday' wine reviews on the web, and has some neat ways to search and browse the collection. Recently a discussion board has been added, as has a steady stream of editorial from Mr Gluck. Access to most areas of the site requires registration.

www.tastings.com

Professional US site claiming 40,000 wine notes in its database. All notes are dated and come with a score out of 100.

Wine talk

The opportunity to interact with others is one of the joys of the web as a medium, so here are two of the best sites for online wine discussion.

www.ukwineforum.com
Many forums are severely under-used, but the friendly, civilised and lively group that constitutes the UK Wine Forum makes it the number-one spot for online discussion of wine from a distinctly British angle. There's also a community tasting notes archive on thousands of wines, a 'who's who' of members and even a dedicated area for planning 'offline' get-togethers.

www.wldg.com
Huge US-centred discussion group with international participation, but some may find it too biased to a North American viewpoint.

Wineries

Almost every wine producer in the world, large or small, New World or Old, has a website. Some try harder than others of course, but from the tens of thousands out there, here are just a few suggestions.

www.haut-brion.com
This venerable estate leads the way with videos, webcams, a discussion forum and a wonderful pictorial almanac of a year in the vineyard.

www.moet.com
If you have a fast Internet connection, this ultra-stylish, high-tech site presents a gorgeous multimedia introduction to how champagne is made.

www.robertmondavi.com
This site has been put together very well and offers features on winemaking, tasting and food and wine, as well as product information.

www.thevintageportsite.com
The Symington family (Dow's, Graham's, Warre's) offers excellent information on port history, styles, storage and serving, as well as vintages back to 1900.

More than the hard sell

Some e-commerce wine sites have spent considerable time and money developing editorial content with regional guides, wine courses, quizzes and more.

www.bbr.co.uk
This esteemed St James's retailer blazes the trail with online resources including feature articles, quizzes and a wine FAQ (frequently asked questions). There's even a fun, arcade-style wine knowledge game.

www.virginwines.com
The 'Wine Zone' is no longer being developed, but there's still an archive of good stuff.

www.winevault.co.uk
This small Australian specialist has extensive information, quizzes and articles, as well as a section on wine and health penned by Philip Norrie, an Australian GP and winemaker.

And finally . . .

www.wine-pages.com
My own site. Established in 1995, it is updated daily and includes a six-part wine appreciation course, tricky quizzes to test your knowledge, guides to the world's wine regions, 8,000 tasting notes, wine recommendations, BYO directory, free competitions and more.

Tom Cannavan is publisher of wine-pages.com and author of *The Good Web Guide to Wine*.

GLOSSARY

almacenista (Spain) a small-scale sherry stockholder

Amarone (Italy) dry PASSITO wine from Valpolicella

amontillado (Spain) an aged FINO sherry on which yeast FLOR has stopped growing but which is matured further without *flor* to develop delicate, nutty flavours; commercial 'medium amontillados' are not made in this way, but are blended, sweetened sherries

appellation contrôlée (AC) (France) the best-quality category of French wine, with regulations defining the precise vineyard area according to soil, grape varieties, yields, alcohol level, and maybe vineyard and cellar practices

aromatic wines usually refers to wines made from highly perfumed grapes, for example, Gewürztraminer, Muscat and Pinot Gris

aromatics the perfumes released by AROMATIC WINES

Ausbruch (Austria) dessert wine, between BEERENAUSLESE and TROCKENBEERENAUSLESE, from nobly rotten grapes

Auslese (Germany, Austria) usually sweet wine from selected ripe grapes, possibly with noble rot (*see* BOTRYTIS)

barrique 225-litre barrel, of French or American oak, in which both red and white wines are matured and white wines sometimes fermented. Normally replaced every 2–3 years, as new *barriques* have a more pronounced effect on taste

bâtonnage (France) the operation of stirring the LEES

Beerenauslese (BA) (Germany, Austria) wine from specially selected ripe berries, probably with noble rot

biodynamics (Burgundy, and elsewhere) an extreme form of organic viticulture, based on the teachings of Rudolf Steiner, which takes into account the influence of the cosmos on a vine

blanc de blancs white wine or champagne made from white grapes only

blanc de noirs white wine or champagne made from red grapes vinified without skin contact (the juice of most red grapes is colourless; all the colouring matter is in the skins)

bodega (Spain) cellar, winery

Botrytis cinerea a form of bunch rot that shrivels grapes and concentrates their sugars ('noble rot')

boutique wines small-production wines, made with the utmost care; frequently expensive

brut (Champagne) dry or dryish (up to 15g sugar/litre)

Bual (Madeira) sweetest style of madeira after Malmsey; must now legally be made from 85% Bual/Boal grapes

bunch rot rotting of the grape bunches, generally caused by fungi and bacteria, and brought about by rain; can happen anywhere

canopy management training and pruning a vine in such a way as to optimise the exposure of the grapes to the sun and air

carbonic maceration fermentation of whole bunches of grapes in a vat filled with carbon dioxide to give fruity wines with low tannin

Cava (Spain) champagne-method sparkling wines; now a DO in its own right

chaptalisation the addition of sugar to the MUST to increase the final alcohol content of the wine

classico (Italy) heartland of a DOC zone, producing its best wines, e.g. Soave *clos* (France) vineyard site that was walled in the past, and may still be walled

Colheita (Portugal) vintage (table wine); single-vintage TAWNY PORT

cream (Spain) sweet sherry

crianza (Spain) basic wood-aged wine, with a minimum of six months' oak-cask ageing and one year's bottle- or tank-ageing; can only be released after two full calendar years

cru (France) literally 'growth', meaning either a distinguished single property (as in Bordeaux) or a distinguished vineyard area (as in Beaujolais or Burgundy)

Cru Bourgeois (Bordeaux) classification system of the Médoc just below classed growth (CRU CLASSÉ) status. In descending order: Cru Bourgeois Exceptionnel, Cru Bourgeois Supérior, Cru Bourgeois

cru classé (Bordeaux) 'classed growth', indicating a wine from the Médoc's primary classification system, divided into five strata (*premiers*, *deuxièmes*, *troisièmes*, *quatrièmes* and *cinquièmes crus classés*); or from the classification systems of the Graves, Sauternes or St-Emilion. (See also GRAND CRU CLASSÉ.)

crusted/crusting (Portugal) a blend of port from different years for short-term cellaring; needs decanting

cuve (France) vat or tank

cuve close a method of making sparkling wines by carrying out the second fermentation inside a sealed tank rather than in bottle. Also known as the 'tank method' and 'Charmat method'

cuvée (France) term applied to a batch of wine, usually of superior quality but with no precise legal definition

demi-sec (Champagne, Loire) sweet (up to 50g sugar/litre)

denominação de origem controlada (DOC) (Portugal) the Portuguese equivalent to France's AC category

denominación de origen (DO) (Spain) wines of controlled origin, grape varieties and style

denominación de origen calificada (DOCa) (Spain) as DO, but entails stricter controls including bottling at source; so far, only Rioja has been given a DOCa status

denominazione di origine controllata (DOC) (Italy) wine of controlled origin, grape varieties and style

denominazione di origine controllata e garantita (DOCG) (Italy) wine from an area with stricter controls than DOC

domaine (Burgundy) estate, meaning the totality of vineyard holdings belonging to a grower or NÉGOCIANT

doux (Champagne, Loire) sweet to very sweet (over 50g sugar/litre)

Eiswein (Germany) wine made from frozen grapes

en primeur (Bordeaux) agreeing to buy in advance of a wine's being released for sale

entry-level wine cheapest wine made by any one producer (the starting point in the range)

Erstes Gewächs (Germany) 'first growths', regions' own system of classification of vineyards

extra-brut (Champagne) absolutely dry (no added sugar)

extra-dry (Champagne) off-dry (12–20g sugar/litre)

extract the solids in a wine: sugars, acids, minerals, glycerol, proteins from grape skin particles, etc. Modern winemaking often squeezes the most out of the grape, resulting in 'high-extract' wines

fino (Spain) pale, dry sherry matured under FLOR

flor (Spain, Jura) the layer of yeast growing on wine or sherry in a part-empty butt

frizzante (Italy) lightly sparkling

garrafeira (Portugal) better-than-average table wine given longer-than-average ageing; a producer's selection of his best wine; a COLHEITA port given bottle as well as cask age

'garage' style wines wines made on a small scale; the original garage wines were made by winemakers who had nothing but a garage to work in. (See also BOUTIQUE WINES.)

grand cru (Alsace) classified vineyard site

grand cru (Burgundy) finest category of named vineyard site

grand cru classé (Bordeaux) 'fine classed growth'; in St-Emilion indicates wine from the second level of the classification system

grand vin (Bordeaux) 'fine wine': the top wine of a Bordeaux château, blended from selected CUVÉES only, as opposed to the 'second wine', which is blended from less successful *cuvées* and perhaps the wine of younger vines, and which is generally sold at a lower price; in other regions the term is used more loosely

gran reserva (Spain) wine aged for a minimum of two years in oak cask and two years in bottle; can only be released after five full calendar years

'green wines' wines made from organic, biodynamic or holistically managed vineyards. (See also LUTTE RAISONÉE.)

Halbtrocken (Germany) semi-dry

hang-time the length of time the grapes are on the vine, from formation to harvest time

indicação de proveniência regulamentada (IPR) (Portugal) similar to France's VDQS status

indicazione geografica tipica (IGT) (Italy) wine of controlled origin, grape varieties and production methods, with less stringent regulations than DOC. Now covers many SUPER-TUSCANS

Kabinett (Germany, Austria) first category of PRÄDIKAT wine, light and delicate in style

late-bottled vintage (LBV) (Portugal) a medium-quality red port of a single year

late harvest sweet wine made from grapes picked in an over-mature or maybe BOTRYTISED condition

lees dregs or sediment that settles at the bottom of a container

lutte raisonée (France) a balanced approach to vine growing which respects the environment. A long way along the road to organic viticulture

maceration process of leaving grapes to 'stew' on their skins before, during and after fermentation

Malmsey (Madeira) the most sweet and raisiny of madeiras; now must legally be made from 85% Malvasia grapes

malolactic fermentation a secondary, non-alcoholic 'fermentation' that converts malic acid into lactic acid. The process is accomplished by bacteria rather than yeast

manzanilla (Spain) salty FINO from Sanlúcar de Barrameda

manzanilla pasada (Spain) aged MANZANILLA

méthode ancestrale (France) very traditional method of making sparkling wine, whereby part-fermented MUST finishes its first/only fermentation in bottle. Also called *méthode rurale*

méthode cap classique (MCC) (South Africa) champagne-method sparkling wines

méthode dioise same as MÉTHODE ANCESTRALE, but sparkling wine is separated from yeast and transferred to new bottles following fermentation. Especially used for the sweet wine Clairette de Die, France

méthode gaillacoise (South-western France) same as MÉTHODE ANCESTRALE, but from Gaillac

méthode rurale (Rhône) same as MÉTHODE ANCESTRALE

méthode traditionnelle (France) the Champagne method of producing sparkling wines

micro-cuvée wine of which only small amounts are made

mis en bouteille par (France) 'bottled by'

mis-en-cave (France) literally, 'put in cellar'. Refers to the place the wine was aged, or cellared, usually in barrel

moelleux (France) medium-sweet to sweet

monopole vineyard wholly owned by one grower, usually in Burgundy

mousse (France) term used to describe the effervescence in sparkling wine

mousseux (France) sparkling

mouthfeel the texture of the wine, the way it feels in the mouth; for example, a Chilean Merlot might feel velvety, a Gewürztraminer oily or fat

must a mixture of grape juice, stem fragments, grape skins, seeds and pulp prior to fermentation

MW Master of Wine (UK qualification)

négociant (France) wholesale merchant and wine trader

noble rot *see* BOTRYTIS

non vintage (NV) a wine or champagne made from a blend of wines of different years

nouveau (France) new wine which in Beaujolais is sold from the third Thursday in November after the harvest. Other areas may be earlier

oloroso (Spain) sherry aged oxidatively rather than under FLOR

organic wine wine produced according to eco-friendly principles in both the vineyard and the winery, and which has received accreditation from one of a number of official bodies

palo cortado (Spain) light and delicate style of OLOROSO

passerillage (France) the process of leaving grapes to dry and dehydrate on the vine with the eventual aim of producing a dessert wine from them

passito (Italy) dried or semi-dried grapes or wine made from them

petits châteaux (Bordeaux) properties modest in reputation and price, but which can provide some of the best wine value in the region

phylloxera aphid which kills vines by attacking their roots. Phylloxera devastated Europe's vineyards in the second half of the nineteenth century, since when vines have had to be grafted on to disease-resistant rootstock

pipe (Portugal) a port cask containing between 534 litres (shipping pipe) and 630 litres (lodge pipe)

Prädikat (Germany, Austria) a category of wine with a 'special attribute' based on natural sugar levels in MUST, such as KABINETT, SPÄTLESE, AUSLESE, BEERENAUSLESE, TROCKENBEERENAUSLESE or EISWEIN

premier cru (Burgundy) second highest category of named vineyard site. If no vineyard name is specified, wine made from a number of different *premier cru* sites

premier grand cru classé (Bordeaux) 'first fine classed growth', indicating a wine from the top level of the St-Emilion classification system

Prosecco (Veneto, Italy) refers both to the grape and to the wine (usually sparkling), characterised by fresh fruit flavours with a faintly bitter twist

Qualitätswein bestimmter Anbaugebiete (QbA) (Germany) quality wine from a specific region

Qualitätswein mit Prädikat (QmP) (Germany) quality wine with a 'special attribute' (*see* PRÄDIKAT)

quinta (Portugal) farm, estate. In the port context, any style may be branded with a quinta name, but *single quinta* port generally refers to a single-farm port from a lesser year

Recioto (Italy) sweet PASSITO wine from the Veneto

récolte (France) harvest

reserva (Portugal) better-than-average wine; slightly higher (0.5%) in alcohol than legal minimum; at least one year old

reserva (Spain) wine aged for a minimum of one year in oak cask and one year in bottle; can only be released after three full calendar years

riserva (Italy) wines aged for longer than normal. If DOC wines are *riserva*, then a minimum (but variable) ageing period is laid down. Usually the best wines are held back for *riserva*

Schilfwein (Austria) sweet wine made from grapes dried on racks of lakeside reeds which become shrivelled and concentrated before being crushed, the equivalent of France's VIN DE PAILLE

sec (Champagne, Loire) medium-dry (17g–35g of sugar per litre of wine); (other wines) dry

secco (Italy) dry

seco (Portugal, Spain) dry

second wine (Bordeaux) *see* GRAND VIN

Sekt (Germany, Austria) sparkling wine

sélection des grains nobles (Alsace) wine made from *botrytis*-affected grapes (*see* BOTRYTIS)

semi-seco (Spain) medium dry

Sercial (Madeira) the driest madeira, though cheap examples are rarely fully dry; must now legally be made from 85% Sercial grapes

sin crianza (Spain) without wood-ageing

solera (Portugal, Spain) ageing system which, by fractional blending, produces a consistent and uniform end product

sous-marque (France) a wine sold or labelled under a secondary, possibly fictional, name

Spätlese (Germany, Austria) wine from late-picked grapes, possibly with noble rot (see BOTRYTIS)

special reserve (Madeira) madeira with a minimum age of ten years

spumante (Italy) sparkling

sulfites (US) sulphur dioxide, present in all wines (including organic wines), used as a preservative and disinfectant

supérieur (France) higher alcohol content than usual

superiore (Italy) wine with higher alcohol, and sometimes more age

Super-Tuscan (Italy) usually non-DOC wine of high quality from Tuscany. Most now fall under IGT category

sur lie (Loire) this should refer to a wine (generally Muscadet) bottled directly from its LEES, without having been racked or filtered. It may contain some CO_2

Süssreserve (Germany) unfermented grape juice

Tafelwein (Germany) table wine

tank method *see* CUVE CLOSE

tawny port (Portugal) basic light port. True wood-aged tawny ports are either marketed as COLHEITAS or as 'ports with an indication of age'

terroir (France) term encompasses a number of factors, including the soil, climate, aspect, altitude and gradient of a vineyard, all of which can affect the way a vine grows and therefore the taste of the ultimate wine

Trocken (Germany) dry

Trockenbeerenauslese (TBA) (Germany, Austria) very sweet wine from grapes affected by noble rot (see BOTRYTIS)

varietal a wine based on a single grape variety

VDQS (France) (Vin Délimité de Qualité Supérieure) covers the very much smaller category, below APPELLATION CONTRÔLÉE, with very similar regulations

vecchio (Italy) old

velho (Portugal) old

vendange tardive (Alsace) 'late harvest', meaning wine made from especially ripe grapes

Verband Deutscher Prädikatsweingüter e.V. (VDP) (Germany) group of estates whose members have agreed to a set of regulations

verde (Portugal) 'green', meaning young

Verdelho (Madeira) medium-dry madeira; must now be made from 85% Verdelho grapes

viejo (muy) (Spain) old (very)

vigneron (France) wine grower

viña (Spain) vineyard

vin de paille (France) sweet wine made from grapes which have

519

been allowed to dry out (traditionally on straw (*paille*))

vin de pays (France) literally translates as country wine, and describes wine that is better than basic VIN DE TABLE, with some regional characteristics. Usually *vins de pays* are determined by administrative geography, with more flexible regulations than for APPELLATION CONTRÔLÉE

vin de table (France) the most basic category of French wine, with no provenance other than country of origin given on the label

vin doux naturel (France) sweet wine made by adding spirit partway through the fermentation process before all the grape sugar has been converted to alcohol

vinho de mesa (Portugal) table wine

vinho regional (VR) (Portugal) equivalent to VIN DE PAYS

Vinho Verde (Portugal) literally, green wine (after the greenness of youth); can be white or red

vino da tavola (VdT) (Italy) table wine: wine that is neither DOCG, DOC, nor fortified, nor sparkling, nor low in alcohol. Many SUPER-TUSCANS used to come under this category

vino de la tierra (Spain) country wine

vino de mesa (Spain) table wine

vin santo (Italy) type of PASSITO wine from Trentino, Tuscany and Umbria

vintage champagne champagne made from a blend of grapes from a single year, sold after at least three years' ageing

vintage character (Portugal) medium- to premium-quality ruby port

vintage madeira (Madeira) the finest madeira from one specific year

vintage port (Portugal) very fine port, bottled young and requiring long cellaring (8 to 40 years); needs decanting

Vitis vinifera the species of the *Vitis* genus in which virtually all of the major wine grape varieties are found

VQPRD (Italy) 'quality wine produced in a specified region'; EU term indicating AC, DOC, DOCG, DO, DOCa and other similarly controlled quality categories

WSET (Wine and Spirit Education Trust) (UK) training courses, resulting in wine qualifications

INDEX OF MERCHANTS

A & A Wines	424	Colombier Vins Fins	433
A & B Vintners	424	Connolly's Wine Merchants	433
Adnams Wine Merchants	312	The Co-op	434
Amey's Wines	424	Corkscrew Wines	333
John Armit Wines	313	Corney & Barrow	334
Arriba Kettle & Co	425	Croque-en-Bouche	335
Asda Stores	315		
The Australian Wine Club	316	Davy & Co	434
Averys of Bristol	317	deFINE Food & Wine	435
		Direct Wine Shipments	337
Bacchus Fine Wines	318	Domaine Direct	338
Ballantynes of Cowbridge	319	Drinks Etc	435
Balls Brothers	320		
Barrels & Bottles	321	Eckington Wines	436
Bat & Bottle	322	Edencroft Fine Wines	436
Bennetts Fine Wines	323	Ben Ellis Wines	436
Benson Fine Wines	425	English Wine Centre	437
Bergerac Wine Cellar	425	European Wine Growers	
Berkmann Wine Cellars/		Associates	339
Le Nez Rouge	324	Evington's Wine Merchants	437
Berry Bros & Rudd	325		
Bibendum Fine Wine	326	Falcon Vintners	438
Bloomsbury Wine & Spirit Co	426	Farr Vintners	340
Booths Supermarkets	327	Ferrers le Mesurier and Son	438
Booths of Stockport	426	Fine and Rare Wines	341
Bordeaux Index	426	Le Fleming Wines	439
The Bottleneck	427	For the Love of Wine	
Bottoms Up		*see I Love Wine*	
see Thresher Wine Shops		Forth Wines	439
Budgens	427	Fortnum & Mason	342
The Burgundy Shuttle	428	Four Walls Wine Company	439
The Butlers Wine Cellar	329	John Frazier	440
Anthony Byrne Fine Wines	428	Friarwood	440
D Byrne & Co	330		
		Garrards Wine & Spirit	
Cairns & Hickey Wines	428	Merchants	441
Cape Province Wines	429	Gauntley's of Nottingham	343
Ceci Paolo	429	J A Glass	441
Cellar 28	429	Gloag Taylor Wines	441
The Cellar D'Or	430	Goedhuis & Co	442
Chandos Deli	430	Gordon & MacPhail	442
Andrew Chapman Fine Wines	331	The Grape Shop	443
Charterhouse Wine Co	431	Grapeland	443
Châteaux Wines	431	Great Gaddesden Wines	443
Brian Coad Fine Wines	432	Great Northern Wine	
Cochonnet Wines	432	Company	344
Cockburns	332	Great Western Wine	
		Company	345

Alexander Hadleigh Wine Merchants	346
H & H Bancroft	444
The Halifax Wine Company	444
Hall Batson & Co	445
Handford-Holland Park	347
Roger Harris Wines	445
Harrods	446
Richard Harvey Wines	446
Haslemere Cellar	447
Haynes Hanson & Clark	348
Charles Hennings (Vintners)	447
Hicks & Don	448
High Breck Vintners	448
George Hill	448
Hopton Wines	449
Hoults Wine Merchants	349
House of Townend	449
Ian G Howe	450
I Love Wine	450
Inspired Wines	450
Irma Fingal-Rock	350
Irvine Robertson Wines	451
ItsWine	451
Jeroboams	351
S H Jones	352
Justerini & Brooks	353
Richard Kihl	452
Laithwaites	355
Lay & Wheeler	356
Laymont & Shaw	452
Laytons see Jeroboams	
Lea & Sandeman	358
Liberty Wines	452
O W Loeb	359
The London Wine Company	453
madaboutwine	453
Majestic Wine Warehouses	360
Marks & Spencer	454
Martinez Fine Wine	361
Mayfair Cellars	363
F & E May	454
Mills Whitcombe	455
Mitchell & Son	364
The Moffat Wine Shop	455
Montrachet Fine Wines	365
Moreno Wine Merchants	366
Morris & Verdin	455
Morrison Supermarkets	367
James Nicholson Wine Merchant	367
Nickolls & Perks	369
Nicolas UK	456
Noble Rot Wine Warehouses	370
The Nobody Inn	371
Oddbins	372
Parfrements	456
Partridges	374
Penistone Court Wine Cellars	457
Peter Graham Wines	375
Philglas & Swiggot	376
Christopher Piper Wines	457
Terry Platt Wine Merchants	458
Playford Ros	458
Le Pont de la Tour	377
Portland Wine Company	378
Quellyn Roberts	458
R S Wines	459
Arthur Rackham Emporia	379
Raeburn Fine Wines	380
Reid Wines	459
La Réserve	381
Richards & Richards Fine Wines	460
Howard Ripley	382
Roberson	383
Safeway Stores	384
Sainsbury's Supermarkets	386
Savage Selection	460
Sebastopol Wines	461
Seckford Wines	461
Selfridges	387
Edward Sheldon	461
Slaughden Wines see Richard Kihl	
Somerfield Stores	388
Sommelier Wine Company	389
Spar UK	462
Springfield Wines	462

Frank Stainton Wines	462
John Stephenson & Sons (Nelson)	463
Stevens Garnier Wine Merchants	463
Stratford's Wine Agencies	464
Sunday Times Wine Club *see Laithwaites*	
Swig	390
T & W Wines	391
Tanners Wines	392
Tesco	393
Thos Peatling Fine Wines	395
Thresher Wine Shops	396
Trout Wines	464
Turville Valley Wines	464
Uncorked	397
Unwins	398
Valvona & Crolla	399
Helen Verdcourt Wines	400
Victor Hugo Wines	401
Victoria Wine *see Thresher Wine Shops*	
La Vigneronne	402
Villeneuve Wines	404
Vin du Van Wine Merchants	405
Vinceremos Wines & Spirits	406
Vine Trail	465
El Vino	407
Vino Vino	408
Vintage Roots	409
Virgin Wines	410

Waitrose	411
Waterloo Wine Company	465
Weavers of Nottingham	412
Wessex Wines	465
Whitebridge Wines	466
Wimbledon Wine Cellar	466
Windermere Wine Stores	467
Wine and Beer Company *see The London Wine Company*	
The Wine Bureau	467
Wine Cellar	468
Wine Rack *see Thresher Wine Shops*	
Wine Raks (Scotland)	413
The Wine Shop	468
The Wine Society	414
The Wine Treasury	468
The Winery	416
Wines of Interest	417
Wines of Westhorpe	469
Woffenden Wines	469
The Wright Wine Company	418
Wrightson & Co Wine Merchants	419
Peter Wylie Fine Wines	420
Yapp Brothers	421
Noel Young Wines	422
Young's Wine Direct	470

INDEX

A Mano Promessa 218
Abadia Retuerta 272
Abbotts 150
Abouriou grape 177
Abruzzo 216–17
Abymes 146
Accademia dei Racemi
  219
Achs, Paul 62
acidity 492–3, 496
Acininobili 210
Aconcagua 75–6
Adams, Tim 50
Adelaide Hills 44, 45, 46,
  48, 50, 52, 53, 54, 56
Adelsheim 301
African Terroir 258
Agapito Rico, Bodegas
  279
AGE 268
age 499–500
Aghiorghitiko grape 8,
  195–6, 197
Aglianico del Vulture
  218
Aglianico grape 23, 202,
  218, 219
La Agricola 37
Ahr 192
Ajaccio 145
Alary, Daniel & Denis
  171
Albana di Romagna 216
Albariño grape 265, 273,
  274
Albet i Noya 276
Albillo grape 272
alcohol level 9, 286, 494
Alenquer 237, 239
Alentejo 237, 240
Alexander Valley 291

Alicante Bouschet grape
  237, 239, 241
Aligoté grape 128, 131,
  283, 490
Alion 273
Alkoomi 50
Allegrini 209
Allende 268
Almaviva 76
Aloxe–Corton 119, 129
Alpha Domus 229
Alquier, Jean-Michel 150
Alsace 87–94
  appellations and
    quality levels 89
  producers 91–3
  red wines 91
  sparkling wine 91
  styles 89
  vintages 93–4
  white wines 90–1
Alta Vista 37
Altare 206
Alter Ego de Palmer 107
Altesino 212
Altesse/Roussette grape
  146
Alvarinho grape 238
Amarone wines 209,
  210, 211
Amberley 50
Amigne grape 283
Amiot, Guy, & Fils 129
Amiral de Beychevelle
  104
Amity 301
amontillado 280
Angas Brut 46, 57
Angeli, Marc 158
Angélus 104

Angerville, Marquis d'
  120
Anjou Blanc 158
Anjou-Saumur 157–60
Anselmi 209
Antinori 213, 217
Antiyal 76
appearance of wine 491
Apremont 146
Aquitania/Paul Bruno 76
Aragón 277–8
Aragonês (Tempranillo)
  grape 240
Araldica/Alasia 206
Arbois 145
d'Arenberg 45, 47, 50
Argentina 8, 33–40
  producers 37–40
  red wines 34–5
  regions 36–7
  vintages 40
  white wines 35–6
Arghyros 196
Argiolas 220
Arinto grape 238
Arizona 305
d'Arlay, Château 146
l'Arlot, Domaine de 120,
  128
Armand, Comte 120
Arneis grape 202, 205,
  207
Arnoux, Robert 12
aroma 491–2
Arrufiac grape 177, 178
Artadi 268
Assyrtiko grape 8, 195,
  197
Asti 205–6
Ata Rangi 229
Atlas Peak 291

Atlas Vineyards 223
Au Bon Climat 293
Auffray, Ancien
  Domaine 128
Aupilhac, Domaine d'
  150
Ausbruch 60–1, 62, 64
Auslese 183
Ausone 99, 104
Australia 24, 40–58
  producers 50–7
  red wines 43–4
  regions 47–50
  sparkling wines 45–6
  'sticky' (dessert)
    wines 46–7
  vintages 57–8
  white wines 44–5
Austria 58–60
  dry white wines 60
  producers 61–5
  red wines 59
  regions 61
  sparkling wines 61
  sweet white wines
    60–1
  vintages 65
Auxerrois grape 91, 93,
  128
Auxey-Duresses 128
Aveleda, Quinta da 239
L'Avenir 258
Avignonesi 213
Axelle de Valandraud
  109

Babich 229
Bablut, Domaine de 158
Bacchus grape 83, 84
Baco Noir grape 68, 69
Baden-Württemberg
  186
Badia a Coltibuono 213
Baga grape 235, 237, 489
Bahans-Haut-Brion 100,
  106
Bairrada 238, 239, 241
Bairrada 242
Balbi, Bodegas 37
Balbo, Susanna 37
Bandol 162, 163
Banfi 213

Bannockburn 50
Banyuls 150, 153
Barbadillo 281
Barbaresco 207
Barbera grape 35, 51,
  205, 206, 207, 293,
  298, 486
Barolo 206, 207
Barón de Ley 268
Baron Villeneuve de
  Cantemerle 104
Baron'Arques 151
Barossa Valley 43, 44,
  46, 48, 50, 53, 54, 55,
  56, 57
Barral, Léon, Domaine
  151
Barry, Jim 50
Barsac 111, 112
de Bartoli, Marco 220
Baruel, Mas 151
Basedow 50
Basque Country 273
Bassermann-Jordan 191
Bastor-Lamontagne 112
Bâtard-Chevalier 104
Bâtard-Montrachet 129,
  131
Baumard, Domaine de
  158
Baume, Domaine de la
  151
Les Baux de Provence
  162
Béarn 177
Bearsted 85
Beátes, Domaine des
  163
Beaucastel, Château de
  171
Beaujolais 124–5
Beaujolais-Villages 124
Beaulieu Vineyard 293
Beaumes-de-Venise 170
Beaune 120, 129
Beaux Frères 301
Beblenheim 91
Beck, Graham 258
Becker, J B 190
Beerenauslese 60, 183
Beldi grape 283
Belgrave 103

Bellet 162
Bellingham 258
Bellondrade y Lurton
  274
Bendigo 43, 49
de Berbec, Château 112
Bergdolt 191
Bergerac 177
Beringer 293
Beronia 268
Berrod, Domaine 124
Berthoumieu, Domaine
  178–9
Bests 51
Bethel Heights 301
Beychevelle 104
Beyer 92
Beyerskloof 260
Bianchi 37
Bianco di Custoza 208
Bianco Gentile grape
  144
Biancolella 218
Bical grape 238
Bienvenues-Bâtard 131
Bierzo 273–4
Bigi 217
Billecart-Salmon 138
Bío-Bío 76
Biondi-Santi 213
Bize, Simon 120
Black Sereskia grape
  222
Blackwood Valley 50
Blanc de Blancs 137,
  139, 142
Blanc de Noirs 138, 139
Blanck, Paul, et fils 92
Blanquette de Limoux
  149
Blaufränkisch grape 58,
  59, 62, 63, 64, 198
Blaye 99
Blue Mountain
  Vineyard 70
Boavista, Quinta do 239
Boeger 293
Boekenhoutskloof 258
Boillot, Jean-Marc 129
Boisset 120
Bolgheri de Sassicaia
  212

Bolivia 65–6
Bollinger 139
Bon Gran, Domaine de la 132
Bon Pasteur 98
Bonarda grape 8, 33, 35
Bonhomme, André 133
Bonneau du Martray 129
Bonnes Mares 121, 123
Bonnezeaux 155, 158, 159
Bonny Doon 293
books and magazines about wine 505–8
Bordeaux 94–100
  classification 96–7
  dry white wines 109–11
  producers 103–11, 112–13
  red Bordeaux 97–100, 103–9
  regions 97–100
  second wines 100
  sweet white wines 111–14
  vintages 100–3, 110–11, 113–14
Bordeaux Rosé 114
Bordeaux Supérieur 100
De Bortoli 51
Bosca, Luigi 37
Boschendal 258
Bosquet des Papes 171
Bott-Geyl 92
Bouchard Finlayson 258
Bourboulenc grape 21, 22, 149, 171
Bourdy, Jean 146
Bourg 99
Bourgeois, Henri 157
Bourgogne Blanc 128, 129, 130, 131
Bourgogne Côte Chalonnaise 131
Bourgogne Grand Ordinaire 118
Bourgogne Passetoutgrains 118
Bourgogne Rouge 118
Bourgueil 158

Bouscaut 100
Bouvet-Ladubay 158
Bouvier grape 61
Bouzeron 131
Braida/Giacomo Bologna 206
Braunstein 62
Brazil 66
Breaky Bottom 85
breathe, allowing wines to 501
Breuer 190
Bright Brothers 239
Britain, buying wines in 25–30
British Columbia 70
BRL Hardy 51
Brocard, Jean-Marc 128
Brokenwood 51
Brouilly 124
Brown Brothers 45, 51
Bruguière, Mas 151
Brumont, Alain 178–9
Bründlmayer 62
Brunello di Montalcino 211, 212, 214, 215
brut 138
Bual grape 249
Bucelas 238
Bugey 145, 146
Buhl, Reichsrat von 191
Buitenverwachting 259
Bulgaria 66–7
Bunan, Domaines 163
Burge, Grant 51
Burgenland 60, 61, 62, 63, 64, 65
Burgund Mare grape 250
Burgundy 115–34
  biodynamic viticulture 118–19
  hierarchy 118
  producers 120–3, 128, 129–301, 132–3
  red wines 118–26
  sparkling wine 134–5
  vintages 125–6, 133–4
  white wines 126–34
Bürklin-Wolf 192
Burmester 245
Bussola, Tommaso 209

Ca' del Bosco 206
Ca' dei Frati 209
Cabardès 149
Cabernet d'Anjou 158
Cabernet Franc grape 43, 44, 69, 70, 71, 75, 99, 104, 155, 158, 209, 215, 227, 254, 287, 479
Cabernet Sauvignon grape 473–4
  Argentina 34, 35, 37, 38, 39
  Australia 43–4, 46, 48, 49, 50, 52, 53, 54, 55, 56, 57
  Austria 59, 62, 64
  Bolivia 66
  Bulgaria 66
  California 286–7, 291, 295, 297, 298
  Canada 69, 70, 71, 77
  Chile 73–4, 76, 77, 78, 79
  China 81
  Cyprus 82
  England 86
  France 97, 99, 106, 151, 152, 162, 164
  Hungary 198
  Italy 212, 213, 215, 219
  Lebanon 221
  Mexico 222
  Moldova 222
  Morocco 223
  New Zealand 227
  Portugal 240, 241
  Slovakia 251
  South Africa 254, 259, 261, 262, 263
  Spain 267, 272, 273, 275, 276, 277
  Tunisia 283
  Uruguay 307
  Washington State 303, 304
Cabernet Sauvignon grape Italy 23, 206
Cabriz, Quinta de 239
Cáceres, Marqués de 268
Cadaval, Casa 239

Cadillac 112
Cafayate 36
Cahors 22, 177, 179, 180
Cailleau, Pascal 158
Les Cailloux 171
Cain 293
Cairanne 170, 171, 172
Cakebread 293
Calabria 218
Calatayud 277
Cálem 245
Calera 293
California 284–300
  producers 293–9
  red wines 286–9
  regions 291–3
  sparkling wines
    290–1
  vintages 299–300
  white wines 289–4
Caliterra 77
Calon-Ségur 98
Camel Valley 85
Campania 218, 219
Campbells 47, 51
Campo de Borja 265,
  277
Campo Viejo 268
Canada 67–72
  producers 70–2
  red wines 69
  regions 70
  white wines 69–70
Canaiola grape 211
Canale, Humberto 38
Canard-Duchêne 139
Candido 218
Canepa 77
Cannonau di Sardegna
  219
Cannonau grape 219,
  220
Canon-Fronsac 99
Cantemerle 98, 104
Canterbury 229, 230
Cantina Sociale Santadi
  220
Cantina Sociale
  Settesoli 220
Cape Mentelle 51
Capezzana 213
Capo de Borja 265

Caprai, Arnaldo 217
Carema 205
Carignan/Cariñena
  grape 20, 21, 22, 78,
  79, 82, 144, 147,
  148–9, 151, 153, 154,
  219, 220, 275, 277, 486
Carignanissime 151
Carignano del Sulcis
  219
Carillon, Louis 129
Carmen, Viña 77
Carmenère grape 73,
  74, 77, 79, 80, 206
Carmignano 212
Carmo, Quinto do 239
Carneiro, Quinto do
  239
Carneros Valley 292
Carruades de Lafite-
  Rothschild 106
Cartuxa, Herdade de
  239
Carvalhais, Quinta dos
  238
Casa de Saima 239
Casablanca Valley 76
Casablanca, Viña 77
Cassis 162, 163
Castano, Bodegas 279
Castel di Paolis 217
Castellare 213
Castello di Brolio 213
Castello di Fonterutoli
  213
Castello dei Rampolla
  214
Castilla y Léon 273–4
Castilla-La Mancha
  278–9
Castillo de Monjardín
  271
Catalonia 275–7
Catena 38
Cauhapé, Domaine 179
Causses-Marine,
  Domaine des 179
Cava 275, 276, 277
Cave de Chusclan 172
Cave de Tain-
  l'Hermitage 167
Cave Estezargues 172

Cave Spring Cellars 70
Caves Aliança 239
Caymus 294
Cayron, Domaine du
  172
Cayuse Winery 303
de Cazenove 139
Cazes Frères 151
Cèdre, Château du 179
Celliers d'Anguera 276
Celliers de Capçanes
  276
Celliers de Meknès 223
Central Coast,
  California 292
Central Otago 226, 227,
  229
Central Valley, Chile 76
Cepparello 214
Cérons 111
César grape 118
Cesconi 209
Chablis 127–8, 128
La Chablisienne 128
Chacolí de Bizcaia 273
Chacolí de Getaria 273
Chalone Wine Group
  294
Chambers 47, 51
Chambolle-Musigny
  115, 119, 120, 122, 123
Champagne 135–40
  champagne method
    137
  grape varieties 137
  organic production
    135–6
  producers 138–42
  styles 137–8
  vintages 142–4
Chancellor 230
Chandon de Briailles
  120, 21
Chandon, Domaine
  (Australia) 46, 51–2
Chandon, Domaine
  (California) 294
Chanrion, Nicole 124
Chapel Down 83, 86
Chapel Hill 44, 52
La Chapelle Haut-Brion
  107

Chapoutier 167–8
chaptalisation 494
Chardonnay grape
    476–7
    Argentina 34, 35, 38,
        39
    Australia 42, 44, 47,
        48, 49, 50, 51, 52,
        53, 54, 55, 56
    Austria 60, 61, 62, 63,
        64, 65
    Bolivia 66
    Bulgaria 66
    California 289, 291,
        292, 293, 294, 295,
        296, 297, 298
    Canada 69, 70, 71, 72
    Chile 75, 77, 78, 79, 80
    China 81
    England 84, 85, 86
    France 126–7, 137,
        145, 146, 152
    Germany 185
    Greece 195
    Hungary 198
    Israel 200
    Italy 205, 206, 207,
        210, 211, 213, 214,
        217, 220
    Lebanon 221
    Long Island 305
    Mexico 222
    Moldova 222
    New York State 305
    New Zealand 224,
        226, 228, 229, 230,
        232, 233, 234
    Oregon 302
    Portugal 239, 240, 241
    Slovenia 251
    South Africa 255, 257,
        258, 259, 260, 261,
        262, 263
    Spain 265, 271, 272,
        276, 277, 278
    Uruguay 307
    Washington State
        303
Charmes 130
Charmes, Château des
    70
Chassagne Morgeot 129

Chassagne-Montrachet
    120, 122, 129, 130
Chasse-Spleen 104
Chasselas grape 146,
    283
Chateau Ste Michelle
    303–4
Château-Chalon 146
Châteauneuf-du-Pape
    20, 165, 170, 171, 172,
    173, 174
Châtillon-en-Dios 174
Chave, Gérard 168
Chemins de Bassac 151
Chénas 124
Chenin Blanc grape 36,
    45, 50, 71, 152, 155,
    156, 157–8, 159, 226,
    231, 254, 259, 263,
    290, 294
Cheval Blanc 99, 104,
    482–3
Chevalier, Domaine de
    104, 110
Chevalier-Montrachet
    Les Demoiselles 130
Chianti 202, 211–12,
    214, 215
Chianti Classico 212,
    213, 214, 215, 216
Chignin-Bergeron 146
Chile 72–80
    producers 76–80
    red wines 73–5
    regions 75–6
    vintages 80
    white wines 75
China 81
Chinon 158, 159
Chiroubles 124
Chivite, Julian 272
Chorey-lès-Beaune 120,
    123
Chrysoroyiatissa
    Monastery 82
Churchill 245
Chusclan 170
Cinsault/Cinsaut grape
    20, 21, 144, 148, 254,
    489
CIRA 151
Cirò 218

Cismeira, Quinta da
    239–40
Clair, Bruno 121
Clairet 114
Clairette de Die 174
Clairette grape 149, 152,
    162, 163, 171, 174
La Clape 21, 22, 147, 153
Clape, Auguste 168
Clare Valley 43, 44, 45,
    48, 50, 55
claret see Bordeaux
Clerico, Domenico 206
Climens 112
Cline Cellars 294
Clinet 96, 98, 104
Les Clos 128
Clos de l'Arlot 120
Clos Bagatelle 151
Clos de Bèze 121, 122
Clos de Blanchais 157
Clos du Cadaret 179
Clos Centeilles 151
Clos des Ducs 120
Clos des Epeneaux 120
Clos des Forêts-St-
    Georges 120
Clos Fourtet 99
Clos Lapeyre 179
Clos Malverne 259
Clos du Marquis 100,
    106
Clos du Mesnil 140
Clos Mogador 276
Clos du Mont Olivet
    172
Clos des Mouches 121
Clos des Papes 172
Clos Pegase 294
Clos de la Roche 119,
    121
Clos St Thomas 221
Clos St-Denis 121
Clos Sainte Magdeleine
    163
Clos St-Georges 112
Clos Triguedina 180
Clos des Ursules 122
Clos du Val 294
Clos Vougeot 121, 122
Clos d'Yvigne 180
Cloudy Bay 228, 230

Clovallon, Domaine de 151–2
Clusel-Roch 168
co-pigmentation 286
Coche-Dury, Jean-François 129–30
Cockburn 245
Coda di Volpe 218
Codorníu 276
Coldstream Hills 52
Colheita 242–3, 244
Colin-Deléger, Michel 130
Colli Orientali del Friuli 208
Collio 208, 210, 211
Collioure 150, 153
Colombard grape 177, 178, 487–8
Colombo 168
Colomé, Bodegas 38
Colorado 306
colour in a wine 491
Columbia River Valley 302
Columbia Winery 304
Commandaria 82
Comtesse de Lalande 98
Con Class 274
Conca de Barberà 276
La Concepción 66
Concha y Toro 77
Condado de Huelva 282
Condrieu 167, 168, 169
Cono Sur 77
La Conseillante 98
Constantia 255–6
Conterno, Aldo 206
Conterno, Giacomo 206
Contino 268
Coonawarra 43, 45, 48, 53
Copertino 218
Corbières 22, 149, 154
Cordier 133
cork taint 492
corkscrews 502
Cornalin grape 283
Cornas 166, 168, 170
Corsica 144–5

Cortes de Cima 240
Cortese grape 202, 205
Corton 119, 120, 123
Corton-Charlemagne 129, 130
Corvina grape 33, 37, 209
Cos d'Estournel 96, 98, 105
Costanti 214
Costers del Segre 276, 277
Costers del Siurana 276
Costières de Nîmes 22, 147, 149, 153
Cotat Frères 157
Côte de Baleau 103
Côte de Beaune 119–20, 121, 128
Côte de Brouilly 124
Côte Chalonnaise 124, 131
Côte de Nuits 119, 123, 128
Côte de Nuits-Villages 119
Côte d'Or 115, 119–26, 128–31
Côtes du Rhône 165–6, 168, 169, 170, 171, 174
Côtes du Rhône-Villages 165, 170, 172, 173
Côte Rôtie 166, 168, 169
Coteaux d'Aix 162, 163
Coteaux de l'Aubance 158, 160
Coteaux du Chery 169
Coteaux du Languedoc 21, 147, 149, 153
Coteaux du Layon 155, 158
Coteaux de la Loire 160
Coteaux de Pierrevert 162
Coteaux Varois 162, 163
Côtes de Blaye 99
Côtes de Bourg 99
Côtes de Castillon 99
Côtes de Duras 177, 179
Côtes du Forez 157
Côtes de Francs 99

Côtes du Frontonnais 177
Côtes de Gascogne 180
Côtes de Grand Lieu 160
Côtes du Jura 145
Côtes du Lubéron 162, 171
Côtes du Marmandais 177, 180
Côtes de Provence 162
Côtes du Roussillon 149, 150, 151
Côtes de St Mont 178, 180
Côtes du Ventoux 171, 173
Côtto, Quinta do 240
Coudert, Fernand 124
Coufran 98
Couhins-Lurton 110
Coulée de Serrant 159
Couly-Dutheil 159
Courbu grape 177, 178
Couroulu, Domaine 172
Coursodon, Pierre 168
Courtade, Domaine de la 163
Cousiño Macul 77
Coutet 112
Cowra 47
Craggy Range 230
Crasto, Quinta do 240, 245
Crawford, Kim 230
Creisses, Domaine des 152
Crémant d'Alsace 89, 91, 92
Crémant de Bourgogne 134–5
Crémant de Die 174
Crémant de Limoux 149
crianza 266
Croatia 81
Croft 245
La Croix 95
La Croix Canon 99
Crozes-Hermitage 166, 168, 169
crus bourgeois 96, 98
crus classés 96

crusted/crusting port 244
Cuilleron, Yves 168
Cullens 52
Curson, Château de 168
Cuvaison 294
CVNE (Compañia Vinícola del Norte de España) 269
Cyprus 81–2
Czech Republic 82–3

Dagueneau, Didier 157
Dal Forno, Romano 209
Dallas Conte 77
Dalwhinnie 52
La Dame de Montrose 107
Dão 237, 238, 242
Darviot-Perrin, Didier 130
Daumas Gassac, Mas de 152
Dauvissat, René & Vincent/Dauvissat-Camus 128
De Bortoli 51
De Toren 259
De Trafford 259
De Wetshof 259
decanting 500–1
Deinhard 187
Deiss 92
Delaforce 245
Delaire 259
Delamotte 139
Delas 168
Delegat's 230
Delheim 259
Delille 304
demi-sec 138
Denbies 86
denominação de origem controlada (DOC) 236
denominacion de origen calificada (DOC) 266
denominacion de origen (DO) 266
denominazione di origine controllata (DOC) 203

denominazione di origine controllata e garantita (DOCG) 203
Descendientes de J Palacios 274
Deutscher Landwein 182
Deutscher Tafelwein 182
Deutz 139
Devil's Lair 52
Diamond Creek 294
Diamond Mountain 291
Diel, Schlossgut 189
diet wines 11
Diez-Merito 281
Doisy-Daëne 112
Doisy-Védrines 112
Dolcetto grape 51, 205, 207, 486
Domaine Boyar 66, 67
Domecq 281
Domergue, Daniel 151
Dominus 294
Dönnhoff 189
Dopff au Moulin 92
Dornfelder grape 85, 86, 87, 186, 192
Douro 237
Dow 245
Drappier 139
Droin, Jean-Paul 128
Drouhin, Domaine 301
Drouhin, Joseph 121, 130
Druet, Pierre-Jacques 159
Dry Creek 291, 294
dry oloroso 280
Dry River 230
Drylands Estate 233
Duboeuf, Georges 124
Duca di Salaparuta 220
Duckhorn 294
Ducru Beaucaillou 96, 105
Dudet, Marc 125
Dujac, Domaine 121
Dumazet, Pierre 168
Durand-Perron 146
Durif grape 49, 51
Durup, Jean 128
Duval-Leroy 139

East Gippsland 49
Echeverria 78
Echézeaux 120
L'Ecole 41, 304
Edelzwicker 91
Eden Valley 45, 48, 52, 54, 55
Edna Valley 292
Edwards, Luis Felipé 78
l'Eglise-Clinet 96, 105
Ehrenfelser grape 68
Eiswein 61, 64, 183, 188
El Coto 268
Elderton 47
Elgin 257
Elk Cove 301
Ellis, Neil 259
Emilia-Romagna 211
Enate 278
Encruzado grape 238
Engel, René 121
England 83–7
    producers 85–7
    red wines 85
    sparkling wines 85
    vintages 87
    white wines 84–5
Entre-Deux-Mers 109
Erath Vineyards 301
Ermitage de Pic St-Loup 152
Errázuriz 78
Erstes Gewächs 183
Esk Valley 230
Esmonin, Michel, et Fille 121
Esporão, Herdade do 240
Est!Est!!Est!!! di Montefiascone 217
Estoublan, Château d' 163
Estremadura 237
Etchart 38
Etko 82
L'Etoile 146
l'Evangile 105
extra-dry (champagne) 138
Eymael, Robert 187
Eyrie 301
Eyssards, Château des 179

Fabre Montmayou/Domaine Vistalba 38
Fair Valley 252
Fairview 259
Faiveley 121
Falanghina grape 23, 218
Falesco 217
Falset 275, 276
Far Niente 295
de Fargues 112
Fariña, Bodegas 274
Faugères 22, 147, 149
Faustino Martínez 269
Favorita grape 205
Federspiel 61
Feiler-Artinger 62
Felluga, Livio 209
Felluga, Roberto 209
Felsina 214
Felton Road 230
Fer grape 177
Fern Hill 47
Fernão Pires grape 238
Ferreira 240, 246
Fesles, Château de 159
Feteasca Neagra grape 250
Fetzer 295
Feudi di San Gregorio 218
Feuillatte, Nicolas 139
Fèvre, William 128
Fiano d'Avellino 218, 219
Fiano grape 23
Les Fiefs de Lagrange 100, 106
de Fieuzal 105, 110
Figeac 99, 105
Fikardos 82
Filliatreau, Domaine 159
Finca El Retiro 38
Finca la Anita 38
Fincha Flichman 38
Fines Roches, Château des 172
fino 280
Firesteed 302
Fitou 149
Fiuza 240

Fixin 119
Flagstone 260
flavour 492
Fleurie 124
flor 280
Flora Springs 295
foil cutters 502
Fonseca 246
Fonseca, José Maria da 240
Font Caude 152
Fontanafredda 206
Fontenil 99, 103
Fontodi 214
food and wine matching 503–5
Forastera 218
Fortant de France 152
Les Forts de Latour 106
Fourn, Domaine de 152
Fox Creek 52
France 87–180
  see also individual regions and appellations
Franciacorta 206
Franken 187
Frankland Estate 52
Frankland River 43, 50
Frankovka grape 82, 83, 251
Franschhoek 256
Frascati 217
Freie Weingärtner Wachau 62
Freixenet 276
Frescobaldi 214
Friedrich-Wilhelm-Gymnasium 187
Friuli Isonzo 208
Friuli-Venezia-Giulia 208–11
Frog's Leap 295
Fromm 230
Fronsac 99, 104
Frontignan *see* Muscat
Fronton 22
Fuissé, Château de 132
Fumé Blanc 290
Furmint grape 64, 198, 488
Fürst, Rudolf 187

La Gaffelière 99
Gaglioppo grape 218
Gagnard, Jean-Noël 130
Gaia 196
Gaillac 22, 178, 179
Gaivosa, Quinta da 240
Gaja 207, 214
Galicia 273
Galil Mountain 200
Gallo, E & J 295
Gamay Fréaux grape 222
Gamay grape 87, 118, 146, 283, 486–7
Gamza grape 67
Gardet 139
Garganega grape 202, 208
Garrut grape 275
Gattinara 205
Gauby, Domaine 152
Gavi 205
Geantet-Pansiot 121
Geelong 44, 49, 50
Genevrières 130
Gentilini 196
Geographe 50
Georgia 180
Gerin, Jean-Michel 169
Germany 180–93
  Classic and Selection wines 181
  producers 186–92
  red wines 185–6
  regions 186–92
  sparkling wines 186
  vintages 192–3
  white wines 184–5
  wine classification system 182–4
Gerovassilou 196
Gevrey-Chambertin 119, 120, 121, 123
Gewürztraminer grape 53, 55, 62, 71, 75, 77, 90, 92, 93, 185, 192, 197, 198, 200, 208, 226, 231, 263, 278, 483
Ghemme 205
Giacosa, Bruno 207
Giesen 230

Gigondas 170, 172, 173, 174
Gilette 112
Gillmore 78
Gimblett Gravels 228–9
Gimonnet, Pierre 139
Gini 210
Girardin, Vincent 130
Gisborne 228
Givry 124, 131
glasses 501–2
Glen Carlou 260
Gobelsburg, Schloss 62
Godello grape 273
Goisot, Jean-Hughes 128
Goldwater Pioneering 231
González Byass 281
Gosset 140
Goulburn Valley 45, 49, 54
Goutorbe, Henri 140
Gouveio grape 238
Graciano grape 267
Graham 246
Graillot, Alain 169
gran reservas 267
Grand Tinel, Domaine du 172
Grand-Puy-Lacoste 98
grands crus 89, 118, 127
Grange des Pères, Domaine de la 152
Grangehurst 260
Grangeneuve de Figeac 105
grape skins 491, 495
grape varieties 473–90
Grassa, Domaines 179
Gratien & Meyer 159
Gratien, Alfred 140
Grauburgunder/Rüland er grape 60, 63, 185, 186
Graves 99–100, 109
Gravner, Josko 210
Great Western/The Grampians 46, 49
Greco di Tufo 23, 218, 219
Greece 8, 23, 194–7

producers 196–7
red wines 195–6
white wines 195
Grenache/Garnacha grape 20, 22, 35, 44, 54, 55, 56, 62, 82, 148, 149, 150, 151, 152, 170, 171, 172, 267, 289, 479–80
Grèves 122
Grgich Hills 295
Griffith 45, 48, 50
Grillet, Château 167
Griñón, Marqués de 269
Gripa, Bernard 169
Grivot, Jean 121
Grolleau grape 158
Groot Constantia 260
Gros, Anne 121
Gros Manseng grape 177, 178
Gros Nore 163
Gros Plant grape 160
Gros Plant du Pays Nantais 160
Gross 62
Grosset 52
Grove Mill 231
Gruaud-Larose 96, 98, 105
Grüner Veltliner grape 58, 60, 61, 62, 63, 64, 65, 83, 251, 488
Guelbenzu 272
Guffens-Heynen 132
Guigal 169
Guillemot-Michel 132
Guiraud 112
Gunderloch 191

Haag, Fritz 188
Haart, Reinhold 188
Haas, Franz 210
Hacienda Monasterio 272
Halbtrocken 183
Hamilton Russell 260
Hanzell 295
Harlan Estate 295
Hárslevelű grape 198
Hartenberg 260

Harveys 281
Haut-Bages-Avérous 107
Haut-Bailly 99
Haut-Brion 96, 99, 105, 110
Haut-Médoc 97, 104
Hautes-Côtes de Beaune 120
Hautes-Côtes de Nuits 119
Hawke's Bay 227, 228–9, 230, 233, 234
Heathcote 43, 49
Hedges 304
Heger, Dr 186
Heidsieck, Charles 140
Heinrich, Gernot 62
Henriot 140
Henry Estate 302
Henry of Pelham 71
Henschke 45, 48, 52
Les Héritiers de Comte Lafon 133
Hermitage 166, 167, 168, 169
L'Hermitage de Chasse-Spleen 104
Herrick, James 152
Hess Collection 295
Hessische Bergstrasse 192
Heyl zu Herrnsheim 191
Heymann-Löwenstein 188
Hidalgo 281
Hidden Spring 86
Hilltops 48
Hirsch 62
Hirtzberger, Franz 62
Hogue Cellars 304
Hortus, Domaine de l' 153
Hospices de Beaune 121–2
Hospitalet, Domaine de l' 153
Houghton 45, 51, 52–3
Howard Park 53
Howell Mountain 291
Huber, Bernard 186

Huet 159
Hugel 92
Huia 231
Humagne grape 283
Hungary 197–9
Hunter Valley 43, 44, 47, 51, 53, 54
Hunter's 228, 231

Icewine 67–8, 69–70, 71
Idaho 305
Igler 62
Ijalba, Viña 269
Inama 210
India 199
indicação de proveniência regulamentada (IPR) 236
indicazione geograficha tipica (IGT) 203
Inniskillin 71
l'Interdit de Valandraud 109
Irouléguy 177
Irsay Oliver grape 82, 83, 198
Isabel Estate 231
Isole e Olena 214
Israel 23, 200–1
Italy 23, 201–20
    producers 206–8, 209–11, 212–16, 217, 218–20
    regions 205–20
    vintages 203–4
    wine classification system 203

J P Vinhos 241
Jaboulet Aîné, Paul 167, 169
Jackson Estate 231
Jackson-Triggs 71
Jacquart 140
Jacquère grape 146
Jacques, Château des 125
Jacquesson 140
Jadot, Louis 122, 130
Jaen grape 235, 237
Jamek 63
Jamet 169

Janasse, Domaine de la 172
Janin, Paul 125
Janodet, Jacky 125
Jasmin 169
Jasper Hill 53
Jermann, Silvio 210
Jobard, François 130
Joguet, Charles 159
Johannisberger, Schloss 190
Jolivet, Pascal 157
Joly, Nicolas 159
Jordan (South Africa) 260
Jordan (California) 295
JosMeyer 92
Jougla, Domaine des 153
jug wine 292
Juillot, Michel 124
Juliénas 124
Juliusspital 187
Jullien, Mas 153
Jumilla 265, 279
Jura 145–6
Jurançon 22, 178, 179
Jurançon Sec 178
Juris 63
Juvé y Camps 276

Kabinett 183, 187
Kanonkop 260
Kanu 260
Karlsmühle 188
Karthäuserhof 188
Katnook Estate 53
Kefraya, Chateau 221
Keller, Franz 191
Kendall-Jackson 296
Keo 82
Kerner grape 68, 84
Kesseler, August 190
Kesselstatt, Reichsgraf von 188
King Estate 302
Kistler 296
Klein Constantia 261
Knoll 63
Koehler-Ruprecht 192
Koehly, Charles et fils 92

Kopke 246
Kracher, Alois 63
Kreydenweiss, Marc 92
Krug 140
Krutzler 63
Ksara, Chateau 221
Ktima Alpha 197
Ktima Katsaros 197
Ktima Voyatzis 197
Kuehn, Peter Jacob 190
Kuentz-Bas 92
Kumeu River 231
Künstler 190
KWV International 261
Kyr-Yianni 196

Labet Père et Fils 146
Lackner-Tinnacher 63
Ladoix 120
de Ladoucette 157
Lafarge, Michel 122
Lafaurie-Peyraguey 112
Lafite 98
Lafite-Rothschild 106
Lafleur 98, 106
Lafon, Comtes 122, 130
Lafon Rochet 106
Lagar de Fornelos 274
Lageder 210
Lagoalva, Quinta do 241
Lagorthi grape 195
Lagrange 106
Lagrein grape 208, 210
Lake County 292
Lambrusco 211, 493
Lamouroux, Château 108
Lamy-Monnot, Hubert 130
Landmark 296
Lanessan 98
Lang, Helmut 63
Langhe 205
Langhorne Creek 48
Langlois-Château 159
Languedoc-Roussillon 21, 146–54
    AC wines 148–50
    producers 150–4
    vins de pays 150–4
    vintages 154

Langwerth von Simmern 190
Laniote 99
Lanson 140
Laona 82
Lapostelle, Casa 77
Large, André 125
Larose, Viña de/Las Casas del Toqui 78
Laski Rizling 83
late-bottled vintage (LBV) 242, 244
Latour 98, 106
Latour, Louis 130
Laudan 170
Laurent, Dominique 122, 173
Laurent-Perrier 141
Laville-Haut-Brion 110
Lawson's Dry Hills 231
Lazaridis, Constantin 196
Lazio 216–17
Lebanon 23, 200, 221
Leeuwin Estate 53
Leflaive, Domaine 131
'legs' 491
Lehmann, Peter 53
Leitz, Joseph 190
Lemberger grape 186
Len de l'El grape 177, 178
Lenswood 53
León, Jean 276
Leonetti 304
Léoville-Barton 97, 106
Léoville-Las-Cases 97, 106
Leroy, Domaine 122
Leyda 76
Libournais 98–9
Librandi 218
Liebfraumilch 493
Ligré, Château de 159
Limarí Valley 76
Limnio grape 8, 196
Limoux 22, 149
Lindemans see Southcorp
Lingenfelder 192
Liqueur Muscat 51, 54
Lirac 170, 172, 173

La Livinière 22, 149, 153
Lladoner Pelut grape 21
Loel 82
Loewen, Carl 188
Loire 155–62
    producers 157, 158–9
    vintages 161–2
    see also individual areas
Lombardy 205–7
Long Island 305
Longridge 261
Loosen, Dr 188
López de Heredia 269
Lorentz, Gustave 92
Los Llanos 279
Loupiac 112
Loureira grape 238
La Louvière 110
Lower Austria 61
Lower Great Southern Region 43, 50, 52
Luce 214
Lugana 206, 209
Lumières, Cave de 172
Lungarotti 217
Lupicaia 216
Lurton, Bodegas 39
Lurton, Hermanos 274
Lussac 99
Lustau 281
Lynch-Bages 98, 106

Macabeo grape 275, 488
Maccabéo grape 149
Le Macchiole 214
McCrea 304
Macedon 49
McLaren Vale 43, 44, 48, 50, 51, 54, 55
Macle, Jean 146
Mâcon Blanc 132
Mâcon-Clessé see Viré-Clessé
Mâcon-Pierreclos 132
Mâcon-Villages 131, 132
Mâcon-Viré see Viré-Clessé
Mâconnais 132
Maculan 210
McWilliams 53
madeira 248–50

Madeleine Angevine grape 84, 86, 87
Madiran 22, 177, 179
Maias, Quinta das 241
Maladière, Domaine de la 128
Málaga 282
Malagousia grape 195
Malandes, Domaines des 129
Malat 63
Malbec grape 480
    Argentina 34–5, 36, 37, 38, 39, 40
    Australia 43
    Chile 75, 77
    France 177
    New Zealand 227
Malepère 149
Malivoire Wine Company 71
Mallia 82
malmsey 250
malolactic fermentation 493
Malvasia grape 217, 220, 238, 250, 267, 488
Mandurah 50
Manjimup 43
Mann, Albert 92
manzanilla 280
Marcassin 296
Marches 216
Marechal Foch grape 69, 71
Maremma 202–3, 212
Margaret River 43, 44, 45, 49–50, 51, 52, 53
Margaux 97, 107, 108, 110
Marimar Torres 296
Marlborough 225, 227, 230, 231
Marsala 219, 220
Marsannay 119, 121
Marsanne grape 45, 49, 54, 56, 149, 154, 162, 163, 167, 168, 169, 301, 483–4
Martinborough see Wairarapa

Martinborough Vineyard 231
Martínez Bujanda 269
Maryland 306
Marynissen 71
Marzieno 216
Mascarello, Giuseppe 207
Masi 210
Masía Barril 276
Massaya 221
Masseria Monaci 218
Masseto 212
Masson-Blondelet 157
Mastroberardino 219
Matakana 228
Mataro (Mourvèdre) grape 44, 56
Mateus Rosé 238
Matrassa grape 180
Matua Valley 231
Maury 150
Mauzac grape 149, 178
Mavro grape 82
Mavrodaphne grape 196
Mavrud grape 67
Mazuelo grape 267
Médoc 97–8, 103
Meerlust 261
La Méjanelle 149
Mellot, Alphonse 157
Melník grape 67
Melon de Bourgogne grape 160, 490
Melton, Charles 46, 53
Mencia grape 273, 274
Mendocino County 292
Mendoza 36
Menetou-Salon 156, 157
Méo-Camuzet 122
Mercurey 121, 124, 131
Merino, Miguel 269
Meritage grape 71, 287
Merlot grape 474
    Argentina 34, 35, 38, 39, 40
    Australia 43, 44, 46, 50, 52
    Austria 59, 64
    Bolivia 66
    Bulgaria 66, 67

California 287, 297
Canada 69, 71
Chile 74, 76, 77, 78, 79, 80
England 86
France 98, 104, 107, 108, 164
Greece 196, 197
Hungary 198
Israel 200
Italy 23, 202, 210, 212, 213, 219
Long Island 305
Moldova 222
New Zealand 227, 230, 232
Portugal 240
South Africa 254, 256, 258, 261, 262, 263, 264
Spain 271
Uruguay 307
Washington State 303, 304
Merwah grape 221
méthode cap classique 255
méthode traditionnelle 255
Meursault 115, 129, 130, 131
Meursault-Perrières 129
Mexico 222
Mezzogiorno 23, 203
Michael, Peter 296
Michigan 305
Michel, Louis 128
Michelot, Alain 122
micro-négociants 117
micro-oxygenation 22
Mildara-Beringer Blass 54
Millton Vineyard 231
Minervois 22, 149, 151
Mission Hill Family Estate 71
La Mission-Haut-Brion 99, 107
Missouri 306
Mitchelton 54
Mittelrhein 192
Moët et Chandon 66, 141

Moldova 222
La Monacesca 217
Monastrell grape 275, 279
Monbazillac 112, 178, 180
Mönchhof 187
Mondavi, Robert 296
Mondeuse grape 146
Monica grape 219
Monin, Eugène 146
mono-cru 138
Montagny 131
Montana 231
Monte Vertine 214
Montecillo 269
Montepulciano d'Abruzzo 216, 217
Montepulciano grape 489
Monterey 292
Montes 78
Montevetrano 219
MontGras 78
Monthelie 120, 122
Montilla-Moriles 282
de Montille 122
Montlouis 158
Montpeyroux 149
Le Montrachet 129, 130
Montrose 98, 107
Montsant 275
Moravia 83
Mordorée, Domaine de la 172
Morellino di Scansano 212, 213
Morey, Bernard 122
Morey-St-Denis 119, 121
Morgon 124
Mornington Peninsula 44, 49, 55
Morocco 23, 223
Morris 54
Mortet, Denis 123
Morties, Domaine de 153
Morton Estate 232
Moscatel de Set£bal 238, 241
Moscato d'Asti 206

Moscato di Pantelleria 220

Moscophilero grape 8, 195

Mosel-Saar-Ruwer 187–9

Moser, Lenz 63

La Motte 261

Mouchão, Herdade de 241

Moulin des Costes 163

Moulin Pey Labrie 99

Moulin-à-Vent 124

Moulis 108

Mount Barker 50

Mount Benson 49

Mount Difficulty 232

Mount Horrocks 47, 54

Mount Langi Ghiran 54

Mount Veeder 291

Mountadam 54

Mourges du Gres, Château 153

Mourvèdre grape 20, 21, 22, 33, 51, 82, 147, 148, 151, 152, 154, 162, 163, 170, 173, 289, 294, 487

Mouton-Rothschild 98, 107

Mtsvane grape 180

Mudgee 55

Muga 47, 269

Mulderbosch 261

Müller-Catoir 192

Müller-Scharzhof, Egon 188

Müller-Thurgau grape 83, 85, 184–5, 208, 226–7, 490

Mumm 141

Mumm Cuvée Napa 296

Murana, Salvatore 220

Muré 92

Murray River 49

Murrieta, Marqués de 269

Murrumbidgee Irrigation Area 48

Musar, Château 221

Muscadelle grape 180

Muscadet 160

Muscat de Beaumes de Venise 171

Muscat de Rivesaltes 151

Muscat du Cap Corse 145

Muscat grape 46, 47, 51, 90, 92, 278, 290, 484

Musigny 119

Musigny Blanc 128

Nahe 189

Napa Valley 287, 291, 294, 295

Navajas, Bodegas 270

Navarra 271–2

Navarro Correas 39

Nebbiolo grape 35, 37, 44, 51, 205, 206, 207, 222, 262, 480–1

Nederburg 261

négociants 117–18

Negrette grape 177

Negroamaro grape 218, 489–90

Nekowitsch, Gerhard 63

Nelson 225, 229

Nepenthe 44, 54

Nero d'Avola grape 23, 202, 219, 220

Neuburger grape 61, 83

Neudorf 232

Neusiedlersee 60, 61, 62, 63, 64

New Mexico 306

New South Wales 46, 47–8

New York State 305

New Zealand 223–35
    producers 229–34
    red wines 227
    regions 228–9
    sparkling wine 228
    Sustainable Wine Growing New Zealand (SWNZ) initiative 224–5
    vintages 234–5
    white wines 225–7

Newton 297

Ngatarawa 232

Niagara 70, 71

Niebaum-Coppola 297

Nielluccio grape 144

Niepoort 238, 241, 246

Nieto y Senetiner 39

Nigl 63

Nobilo 232

non-vintage champagne 138

Noon 54

North Island, New Zealand 228–9

Northland 228

Norton 39

Noval, Quinta do 246

de Nozet, Château 157

Nuits-St-Georges 120, 121, 122, 128

Nuragus 219

Nyetimber 86

oak 182, 495–6

oak chips 496

Obeideh grape 221

Oberto 207

Ochoa 272

Oenoforos 197

Offley-Forrester 246

Ogereau, Domaine 160

Ogier, Michel 169

Okanagan Valley 70

Olifantsrivier 256

Olympus 82

Omar Khayyam 199

Ontario 70, 71, 72

Opitz, Willi 63–4

Opthalmo grape 82

Optima grape 83

Opus One 297

Orange 46, 48, 55

Orange River 256

Oratorie St-Martin, Domaine de l' 172

Oregon 300–2

Orlando 54–5

Ornellaia 212, 215

Orvieto 217

Osborne 281

Ostertag 92

Overgaauw 262

Paarl 256, 263
Pacherenc du Vic Bilh 178, 179
Padthaway 48
Pago de Carraovejas 273
Les Pagodes de Cos 105
Paillard, Bruno 141
Palacio 270
Palacio de la Vega 272
Palacios, Alvaro 277
Palette 162, 164
Palliser Estate 232
Palmela 237
Palmer 107
palo cortado 280
Palomino grape 280, 488–9
Pancas, Quinta de 241
Pannier 141
Pantelleria 219
Papaioannou 197
Pape-Clément 96, 100, 107, 110
Parellada grape 275
Parrina 212
Parxet 277
Pasanau, Bodegas 277
Paternina, Federico 270
Pato, Luis 241
Patrimonio 145
Pauillac 97, 98, 106, 107, 108
Paulinshof 188
Pavelot, Jean-Marc 123
Pavie 107–8
Pavie Macquin 107
Pavillon Blanc de Château Margaux 110
Pavillon Rouge de Margaux 107
Pays Nantais 160
Pazo de Barrantes 274
Pazo de Señorans 274
Pech Redon, Château 153
Pécharmant 177
Pedro Ximénez grape 281, 282
Pedroncelli 297
Pegasus Bay 232

Pégaü, Domaine du 173
Pelaquie, Luc 173
Pellé, Henry 157
Pellegrino 220
Pemberton 43, 50
Penedès 275, 276
Penfolds 47, 55
Periquita grape 235, 237, 240, 490
Pernand-Vergelesses 119–20, 128
Pernot, Paul 131
Perret, André 169
Perrier, Joseph 141
Perrier-Joüet 141
Pesquera 272, 273
Pessac-Léognan 99, 105, 106, 107, 108, 109
Petaluma 48, 55
Le Petit Cheval 104
Petite Arvine grape 283
Petite Sirah/Durif grape 297
Petite Verdot grape 262
Petit Manseng grape 152, 177, 178
Petit Verdot grape 37, 43, 77, 287–8, 490
Petite Sirah/Durif grape 71, 75, 222, 289, 490
Pétrus 98, 108
Peyre Rose, Domaine de 153
Pfalz 191–2
Phelps, Joseph 297
Pibarnon, Château de 163
Pic St-Loup 21, 147, 149, 151, 152, 153, 154
Piccinini, Domaine 153
Pichler, FX 64
Pichon Longueville/Pichon Baron 98, 108
Pichon-Longueville-Lalande 108
Picpoul de Pinet 21, 22
Piedmont 203–4, 205–7
Pierce's disease 284–5
Pieropan 210
Piesporter 188
Pignier 146

Le Pin 96, 98, 108
Pingus 272
Pinot Blanc/Pinot Bianco grape 37, 64, 69, 70, 83, 90–1, 92, 93, 191, 208, 283, 302, 484
Pinot Gris/Pinot Grigio grape 36, 45, 51, 54, 55, 64, 65, 69, 70, 83, 92, 198, 202, 208, 210, 224, 226, 228, 290, 300, 301, 302, 484–5
Pinot Meunier grape 51, 86, 137, 487
Pinot Noir grape 474–5
   Australia 44, 48, 49, 51, 52, 53, 54, 55, 56
   Austria 59, 61, 62, 63
   California 288, 291, 292, 293, 294, 295, 296, 297, 298, 299
   Canada 69, 70, 71
   Chile 74, 78, 80
   Czech Republic 83
   England 85, 86, 87
   France 91, 92, 93, 118, 137, 139, 145, 146, 151
   Germany 185, 186, 187, 190, 192
   Michigan 305
   Moldova 222
   New Zealand 224, 227, 228, 229, 230, 232
   Oregon 300, 301, 302
   Portugal 239
   Romania 250
   Slovakia 251
   South Africa 254, 257, 258, 260
   Spain 278
   Switzerland 282
Pinotage grape 227, 230, 253–4, 259, 260, 262, 263, 487
pioneer winemakers 19–20
Piper-Heidsieck 141
Pipers Brook 44, 45, 46, 49, 55

Piquepoul grape 21, 22, 147, 149
Pirineos, Bodegas 278
Pivot, Jean-Charles 125
Plaimont, Producteurs 179
Plaisir de Merle 262
Planeta 219, 220
Plavac Mali grape 81
Pöckl 64
Poggio Scalette 215
Poggio di Sotto 215
Poggiopiano 215
Pojer e Sandri 210
Pol Roger 141
Poliziano 215
Polz 64
Pomerol 97, 98, 105, 106, 108, 109
Pomino 212
Pommard 119, 120
Pommery 142
Ponzi 302
port 242–8
    port houses 245–7
    styles 243–5
    vintages 247–8
Porta, Viña 78
Portugal 245–50
    madeira 248–50
    port 242–8
    producers 238–42
    red wines 237
    rosé 238
    white wines 237–8
    wine classification 236
Poruzot 130
Potel, Nicolas 123
Pouilly-Fuissé 132
Pouilly-Fumé 156, 157
Pouilly-Loché 132
Pouilly-Vinzelles 132
Poujeaux 108
Poulsard grape 145
Prager 64
premiers crus 118, 119
prestige cuvée/de luxe cuvée 138
Les Preuses 128
Le Prieuré de St-Jean de Bébian 153

Prieuré Lichine 104
Primitivo grape 23, 33, 37, 202, 218, 219, 482
Primo Palatum 179
Priorato 275, 276, 277
Prosecco 208
Provence 162–4
Prüm, JJ 188
Prunotto 207
Puffeney, Jacques 146
Puglia 218
Puligny Les Referts 129
Puligny-Montrachet 115, 129, 130, 131
Le Pupille 215
Pyrenees 49, 52, 56

Quady 297
Quail's Gate 71
Qualitätswein bestimmter Anbaugebiete (QbA) 182
Qualitätswein mit Prädikat (QmP) 183
Quarts de Chaume 158
Quebreda de Macul, Viña 78
Queensland 46, 48
Quénard, André et Michel 146
Quénard, Raymond 146
Querciabella 215
Quilceda Creek 304
Quincy 157
Quintarelli 210
Quintessence 179
Qupé 297

Rabiega, Domaine 163
Rabigato grape 238
Raïmat 277
Ramonet 131
Ramos, João Portugal 241
Ramos-Pinto 241, 246
Rapel 76
Raspail-Ay 173
Rasteau 170, 171
Rauzan-Ségla 108
Raveneau, Jean-Marie 128
Ravenswood 297

Rayas, Château 173
Rebholz 192
Rebula grape 251
Recioto wines 209, 210, 211
Rectorie, Domaine de la 153
Red Mountain 302
Refosco grape 35, 208, 209
Regaleali 219, 220
Régnié 124
Reichensteiner grape 84
La Remejeaune 173
Remelluri 270
Renaissance 297
Renaudin, R 142
reservas 266, 267
Réserve de la Comtesse 108
La Réserve de Léoville-Barton 106
Retsina 195, 196
Reuilly 157
Reverdy, Pascal et Nicolas 157
Reyes Teòfilo, Bodegas 273
Rheingau 189–90
Rheinhessen 190–1
Rhône 164–76
    northern Rhône 166–70
    producers 167–70, 171–4
    red wines 166, 170–1
    rosé 171
    southern Rhône 170–4
    vintages 174–6
    white wines 167–70, 171
Rhône Rangers 289
Rías Baixas 273
Ribatejo 237
Ribeauvillé 93
Ribera del Duero 272–3
Richebourg 119, 121
Richou 160
Richter, Max Ferd. 188
Ridge 297
Ridge View 86

Riecine 215
Rieflé 93
Riesling grape 477–8
  Argentina 36
  Australia 45, 47, 48, 50, 51, 52–3, 54, 55, 57
  Austria 60, 61, 62, 63, 64, 65
  California 290, 293, 297
  Canada 69, 72
  Chile 75
  Czech Republic 83
  England 86
  France 90, 92, 93, 152
  Germany 11, 184, 187, 188, 189, 190, 191, 192
  Greece 195
  Idaho 305
  Israel 200
  Italy 208, 211
  Michigan 305
  Moldova 222
  New York State 305
  New Zealand 226, 229, 230, 231, 232, 233, 234
  Oregon 301, 302
  South Africa 255, 257, 259
  Washington State 304
Rieussec 113
Rimbert, Domaine 154
Rio Negro 37
Rioja 265–6, 267–71
La Rioja Alta 270
La Rioja (Argentina) 36–7
La Riojana 39
Riojanos, Bodegas 270
Ripaille, Château de 146
ripasso 209, 210
Rippon Vineyard 232
Riscal, Marqués de 270, 274
Rivaner grape see Müller-Thurgau
Riverina 48
Riverland 53

Rivesaltes 150
Rkatsiteli grape 180
Roaix 170
Robe 49
Robertson 256–7
Robin, Gilles 169
Robola grape 195
Roc de Cambes 99
Rocailles, Domaine de 146
Rocca, Bruno 207
Rochegaude 170
Roches Neuves, Domaine des 160
Rockford 55
Roda, Bodegas 270
Roditis grape 195
Roederer, Louis 142
Roederer Estate 297
Roero 205
Rolet Père et Fils 146
Rolle grape 152, 162, 163
Rolly-Gassmann 93
Romanée-Conti, Domaine de la 123
Romania 250
Rondinaia 216
Rondo grape 85
La Roque, Château 154
Roques, Quinta dos 238, 241
Ros, Elian da 180
Rosa, Quinta de la 238, 242, 246
Rosa, Viña La 78
Rosanna grape 275
Roscetto grape 217
rosé champagne 138
Rosé d'Anjou 158
Rosemount 47–8, 55
Rosso Conero 216
Rosso del Conte 220
Rosso di Montalcino 211, 212
Roulot, Domaine 131
Roumier, Georges et fils, Domaine 123
Roussane grape 146, 151, 152, 167, 171, 301, 489
Rousseau, Armand 123

Rousset-les-Vignes 170
Roussillon see Languedoc-Roussillon
Routas, Château 163
Royal Oporto Wine Company 246
ruby port 243
Rueda 274
Rufina 212
Ruinart 142
Rully 124, 130, 131
Russian River Valley 291
Rust-en-Vrede 262
Rustenberg 262
Rutherglen 46, 47, 49, 51

Saale-Unstrut 192
Saarstein, Schloss 189
Sablet 170
Sachsen 192
Sacred Hill 232
Saes, Quinta de 242
Sagrantino di Montefalco 216, 217
Sagrantino grape 8
Sainte-Anne, Domaine 173
Sainte-Cosme, Domaine 173
Saint-Didier, Cave 173
Saint-Gayan, Domaine 173
St-Amour 124
St-Aubin 120, 127, 130
St-Bris-le-Vineux 128
St-Chinian 22, 147, 149, 151, 153
St Clair 233
St-Emilion 98–9, 103, 104, 105, 107, 108, 109
St-Estèphe 97, 98, 105, 106, 107
St-Gervais 170, 173
St Hallett 55–6
St-Joseph 166, 168, 169
St-Julien 97–8, 104, 105, 106
St Laurent grape 59, 83, 251

St-Maurice 170
St-Nicolas de Bourgueil 158
St-Pantaléon-des-Vignes 170
St-Péray 167
St-Romain 129
Saintsbury 297
St-Véran 132
Ste-Croix du Mont 112
Salentin 39
Salice Salentino 218, 219
Salomon/Undhof Estate 64
Salon 142
Salta 36
San Felice 215
San Joaquin Valley 292
San Leonardo 210
San Pedro 79
San Rafael 36
Sancerre 156, 157
Sandeman 246
Sanford 298
Le Sang des Cailloux 173
Sangiovese di Romagna 216
Sangiovese grape 35, 44, 75, 78, 200, 202, 211, 214, 215, 216, 289, 298, 301, 481
Santa Barbara County 292, 297
Santa Carolina, Viña 79
Santa Cruz 292
Santa Duc, Domaine 174
Santa Inés 79
Santa Maria Valley 292
Santa Rita, Viña 79
Santa Ynez Valley 292
Santenay 120, 122, 128, 130
Santorini 195
São João, Caves 242
Saperavi grape 180, 222
Sardinia 219–20
Sarget de Gruaud-Larose 100, 105
Sassicaia 215
Sauer, Horst 187

Saumur 158, 159, 160
Saumur-Champigny 158, 159, 160
Saussignac 112
Sauternes 111, 112
Sauveroy, Domaine 158
Sauvignon Blanc grape 478–9
    Argentina 34, 36, 38, 39, 45
    Australia 47, 48, 50, 51, 52, 53, 55, 56
    Austria 58, 60, 61, 63, 64
    California 289–90, 292, 293, 294, 297, 298
    Canada 69
    Chile 75, 78, 80
    France 109, 110, 151, 162, 163
    Greece 195, 197
    Hungary 198
    Israel 200
    Italy 202, 208, 215
    Moldova 222
    New Zealand 224, 225, 230, 231, 232, 233, 234
    Slovenia 251
    South Africa 254–5, 255, 257, 259, 260, 261, 262, 263
    Spain 274
    Washington State
Sauzet, Etienne 131
Savagnin grape 70, 146
Savennières 156, 158
Savigny-lès-Beaune 119, 120, 121, 123
Savoie 145, 146
Scala Dei 277
Scavino, Paolo 207
Scheurebe grape 185, 192
Schilfwein 60, 63, 64
Schiopetto, Mario 210
Schlumberger 64, 93
Schoffit 93
Schönborn, Schloss 190
Schönleber, Emrich 189
Schramsberg 298

Schrock, Heidi 64
Schubert, von 189
Schug 298
Sciacarello grape 144
Screaming Eagle 298
screw-capped wines 10, 225
Le Second Vin de Mouton-Rothschild 107
sediment 500
Seghesio 298
Ségonzac 99
Séguret 170
Sekt 61, 62, 64, 186
Selaks 233
sélection de grains nobles 89, 92
Sella & Mosca 220
Sélosse, Jacques 142
Selvapiana 215
semi-crianza style 267
Sémillon grape 485
    Argentina 36, 38
    Australia 42, 44–5, 46, 47, 48, 50, 51, 53, 54, 55
    Chile 75, 77, 78
    France 109, 110, 162, 179
    New Zealand 226, 232
    Oregon 301
    South Africa 255, 256, 258, 263
    Washington State 304
Seña 79
Seppelt 46
Sercial grape 249
Seresin 233
Servadou grape 177
serving wine 500–3
Settesoli 219
Set£bal 238, 240
Seyssel 146
Seyval Blanc grape 85, 87
Shafer 298
Sharpham 86
Shaw and Smith 56
Shawsgate 86
sherry 279–81

producers 281–2
styles 280–1
Shiraz grape *see*
Syrah/Shiraz
Sicily 219–20
Sierra Foothills 292–3
Sigalas 197
Sileni 233
Silice de Quincy 157
Silvaner grape 185, 191,
490
Simi 298
Simone, Château 162,
163–4
Simonsig 262
sin crianza 266, 267
single quinta port 242,
244
Sinskey 298
Skouros 197
Slovakia 251
Slovenia 251
Smaragd 61
Smith Woodhouse 247
Smith-Haut-Lafitte 96,
99, 108, 110
Soave 208, 210, 211
Sobon Estate 298
Sociando-Mallet 98
Sogrape 242
Sokol Blosser 302
Solaia 213
Solis, Felix 279
Somontano 23, 277
Sonnhof Jurtschitsch 64
Sonoma Coast 291
Sonoma County 291–2
Sonoma–Cutrer 298
Sonop 258
de Sours, Château 114
South Africa 252–64
producers 258–64
red wines 253–4
regions 255–8
sparkling wine 255
vintages 264
white wines 254–5
South Australia 48–9
South Island, New
Zealand 229
south-western France
22, 176–80

Southcorp 52, 56
Spain 23, 264–82
fortified wines 282
producers 268–70,
271–3, 274, 276–7,
278, 279
regions 267–79
sherry 279–81
vintages 270–1
wine classification
266
Spanna 205
Spätburgunder *see*
Pinot Noir
Spätlese 183
Spice Route 262
La Spinetta 207
Springfield Estate 262
Spyropoulos 197
Squinzano 218
Staatliche
Weinbaudomäne,
Niederhausen-
Schlossböckelheim
189
Stag's Leap Wine
Cellars 298
Steenberg 262
Steinfeder 61
Stellenbosch 257, 259,
260, 261, 262, 263, 264
Stellenzicht 262
Sterling Vineyards 299
Stonecroft 233
Stonyridge 233
stoppers 502
storing wine 498–500
Strofilia 46, 197
Styria 60, 61, 62, 63, 64
Suduiraut 113
sugar 493–4
sulphur compounds
497
Sumac Ridge 71
Super-Tuscans 212, 213,
214, 215, 216
sur lie 160
süssreserve 182
Swan Valley 49, 52
Swartland/Tulbagh/Mal
mesbury 257
Switzerland 282–3

Sylvaner grape 48, 93,
187
Syrah/Shiraz grape
475–6
Argentina 34, 35, 37,
38, 39, 40
Australia 20, 42, 43,
46, 48, 49, 50, 51,
52, 53, 54, 55, 56, 57
Austria 62
Bulgaria 67
California 288, 292,
293, 294, 297, 298
Canada 69, 71
Chile 75, 76, 78, 79
France 20, 21, 22, 148,
150, 151, 152, 153,
162, 163, 164, 166,
170
Greece 196
Italy 212, 214, 217,
220
Morocco 223
New Zealand 227,
232, 233
Oregon 301
Portugal 241
South Africa 254, 258,
259, 260, 261, 262,
263, 264
Spain 275, 276
Tunisia 283
Uruguay 307
Washington State
302, 303, 304

La Tâche 123
Tafelwein 182
Tahbilk, Chateau 56
Taittinger 142
Talmard, Domaine 133
Taltarni 56
Tannat grape 8, 22, 38,
39, 177, 306, 307
tannin 494–5
Tapada do Chaves 242
Tarapac 79
Tardieu Laurent 174
Tarragona 23
Tarrawarra 56
Tasmania 44, 46, 49, 55
Tassinaia 216

Tatachilla 56
Taurasi 218, 219
Taurino 219
tawny port 243, 244
Taylor, Fladgate &
    Yeatman 247
Te Mata 233
Tedeschi, Fratelli 211
Tement 64
Tempier, Domaine 164
Tempranillo grape 8,
    35, 37, 38, 54, 222,
    267, 271, 274, 276, 481
Tenuta dell'Ornellaia
    212
Tenuta del Terriccio 216
    Tenuta Capichera
    220
Tenuta de Trinoro 216
Teroldego Rotaliano
    208
TerraMater 79
Terrazas 39
Terre di Franciacorta
    206
Terre di Ginestra 219,
    220
Terredora 219
Terret grape 21
terroir 42, 497–8
Le Tertre-Rôteboeuf
    108
Texas 306
T'Gallant 45
Thandi 252, 272
Thanisch, Dr H/Erben
    Thanisch 189
Thebes 197
Thelema 263
Thévenet, Jean 132
Thieuley, Château 114
Thirty Bench Wines 72
Thivin, Château 125
Thomas, Charles,
    Domaine 116, 123
Three Choirs 87
Tiefenbrunner 211
Tignanello 213
Tinhof 64
Tinta Negra Mole grape
    249
Tinto Fino grape 272

Tinto Roriz grape 237,
    239, 242
Tinto de Toro grape 274
Tiollier, Philippe &
    François 146
Tirecul La Gravière,
    Château 180
Tissot, André et Mireille
    146
Tohu 233
Tokaji 198
Tokay 198–9
Tokay-Pinot Gris grape
    90, 92, 93
Tollot-Beaut 123
Torbreck 56
Torcolato 210
Torgiano 216
Toro 23, 274
Torres 277
Torres, Miguel 79
Torrontés grape 34, 36,
    39
La Tour Carnet 104
Tour des Gendres,
    Château 180
La Tour Figeac 104
Touraine 157–60
Les Tourelles de
    Longueville 108
Touriga Nacional grape
    33, 235, 237, 240, 241,
    242, 481–2
Tours, Château des 125
Tracy, Château de 157
Traminer grape 64, 83
Trapiche 39
Trebbiano grape 216,
    217, 489
Trentino-Alto Adige
    208–11
Tréssot grape 118
Trévallon, Domaine de
    164
Tribut, Laurent 128
Triebaumer, Ernst 64
Triennes, Domaine de
    164
Trimbach 93
Trincadeira grape 240
Trinity Hill 233
Triomphe grape 85, 87

Trocken 183, 184
Trockenbeerenauslese 60,
    183
Trotanoy 109
Trousseau grape 145
Trulli 219
Tselepos 197
Tua Rita 216
Tukulu 252
Tumbarumba 48
Tunisia 23, 283
Tupungato 36, 39
Turckheim 93
Turkey 283–4
Tuscany 203–4, 211–16
Tyrrells 56

Ugni Blanc grape 144,
    163, 178, 489
Uiterwyk 263
Umani Ronchi 217
Umathum 64–5
Umbria 216–7
Unison 233
United States of
    America 284–306
    see also individual
    states
Uruguay 306–7
Utiel-Requena 278

Vacheron 157
Vacqueyras 170, 172,
    174
Vacuvin system 503
Val Brun, Domaine du
    160
Val d'Orbieu 154
Valandraud 109
Valdeorras 273
Valdepeñas 278–9
Valdespino 281
Valdivieso 79–80
Valencia 278
Valentini 217
Valley Vineyards 87
Valpolicella 208–9, 210
Valréas 170
Vancouver Island 70
Varichon et Clerc 146
Los Vascos 80
Vatan 157